FREE APPROPRIATE PUBLIC EDUCATION

THE LAW AND CHILDREN WITH DISABILITIES

6th EDITION

H. Rutherford Turnbull III
Ann P. Turnbull
University of Kansas

with

Matt Stowe and Brennan L. Wilcox
University of Kansas

LOVE PUBLISHING COMPANY®
Denver • London • Sydney

Dedication

To our family—J. T., Amy, Kate, and H.F.P.—who daily make
advocacy on behalf of students with disabilities a joyful battle.
And to Paul Marchand and Bobby Silverstein,
advocates, colleagues, and friends.

Published by Love Publishing Company
Denver, Colorado 80222

Sixth Edition

Library of Congress Catalog Card Number 99-75490

Copyright © 2000, 1998, 1993, 1990, 1986, 1978 by Love Publishing Company
Printed in the U.S.A.
ISBN 0-89108-275-1

Contents

Preface   vii
Acknowledgments   x

Part 1   Introduction to the Law   1

1 Introduction to the American Legal System   3

Federalism   3
Lawmakers: Who Makes the Law?   4
Case Law and the Courts   6
Brown v. Board of Education   7
Role of Law   12
Cases   13

2 Federal Policy and Disability   15

The History of Federal Legislation   15
School Practices   17
Reasons for the Practices   19
Reasons for the Change in Practice   20
The ADA Community Integration Decision   23
Federal Responses to Disability Discrimination: Entitlements   31
Federal Responses to Disability Discrimination:
    Antidiscrimination Laws   40
The Principle of Dual Accommodations   52
Other Core Concepts in Disability Law   52
Conclusion   59
Notes   59
References   60
Cases   60

Part 2   The Six Major Principles   61

3 Zero Reject   63

Individuals with Disabilities Education Act   63
Effects of the Zero-Reject Rule   121
Conclusion   131
Reference   132
Cases   132
Hearing Officer Decisions   134

4 Testing, Classification, and Placement   135

Pre-IDEA Criticisms of Testing   136
Pre-IDEA Court-Ordered Remedies   137
Why Evaluation Is Required   138
Individuals with Disabilities Education Act (IDEA)   138
Major Legal Restraints on Consequences of Classifications   149
Section 504   151
Case Law   152
Observations About Classification   160
Effects of the Nondiscriminatory Evaluation Rule   168
Conclusion   171
References   171
Cases   172

5 Appropriate Education   173

Statutory Definition of Appropriate Education   173
The Rowley Decision: IDEA and the Process Definition   174
Individualized Education—The I-Plans   175
Other Statutory Provisions for Appropriate Education   204
Related Services   204
Appropriate Education, the Supreme Court, and the Benefit Standard   216
Judicial Reliance on Expert Judgment; Deference to Professionals   219
Remedies for Denial of a Free Appropriate Education   220
Interests of Children with Disabilities and Functions of Government   237
Conclusion   239
References   240
Cases   240

6 Least Restrictive Appropriate Educational Placement   243

Constitutional Foundations   243
Individuals with Disabilities Education Act   245
LRE as a Rebuttable Presumption; Its Value Base   257
The Judicial Interpretation   259
Conclusion   273
Notes   276
Reference   277
Cases   277

7 Procedural Due Process   279

Individuals with Disabilities Education Act   279
Case Law   290
Conclusion   300
Cases   301

8 Parent Participation and Shared Decision-Making   305

Individuals with Disabilities Education Act   306
Related Services and Benefits to Parents   312
Part C   313
Parent Responsibilities   314
Significance of ADA and IDEA for Families   314
Case Law on Parent Participation   317
Conclusion   318
Reference   320
Cases   320

Part 3   Enforcing The Law   321

9 Compliance Through the Courts   323

Compliance: Pre-IDEA Techniques   323
Damages and Educational Malpractice   327
Individuals with Disabilities Education Act   341
Damages Under IDEA and Other Federal Statutes   343
Coupled Claims Under IDEA, Section 504, ADA, and Section 1983   348
Sovereign Immunity   360
Attorney Fees   363
Cases   368

10 Enforcement of the Six Principles and Systems-Change for School Reform   373

Putting Money Where the Students Are   374
Systemic Improvement, Systems-Change, and School Reform   382
Conclusion   385
Reference   387

Appendix A   Brown v. Board of Education   389
Appendix B   Southeastern Community College v. Davis   393
Appendix C   Board v. Rowley   403
Glossary   417
Table of Cases   423
Table of Hearing Officer Decisions   434
Case Index   435
Hearing Officer Decisions Index   440
Name Index   441
Subject Index   441

Preface

We wrote the first edition of this book during the Christmas season of 1977. At that time we both were on the faculty at the University of North Carolina at Chapel Hill. Our dining room table was awash with cut-and-pasted sections of what then was referred to as PL 94–142, the Education for All Handicapped Students Act.

At that very same time our son, J. T., was in his second year of education under that law—an education he would not have had but for the federal law and its impact on North Carolina law. He not only was a young boy with disabilities (mental retardation and autism) but also was one of the first "class" of students to benefit from IDEA.

As we were writing that first edition, we kept J.T.'s collection of education rights firmly in mind and tried to understand the law as it would apply to him. That guidepost proved valuable, for it helped us analyze the law according to the ways in which schools were required to deal with J. T.: enroll him (the zero reject principle), determine what he needs (the nondiscriminatory evaluation principle), provide it to him (the individualized appropriate education principle), do so in the most typical setting (the least restrictive environment principle), hold schools accountable for what they do (the procedural due process principle), and let us have a say in what happens to him in school (the parent participation principle).

Throughout that Christmas we had a sense that J. T. was our best teacher, and that insight has been confirmed many times since then. Even so, we sometimes wish our "lessons" were not so hard. Of course, it is not just J. T.'s disabilities that create hard lessons. The world in which he has to live—the world of schools and other service-delivery agencies—teaches its own lessons, lessons about discrimination, inadequacy of the quality of services, and segregation into a "disabled only" world.

Hence, two other principles reflected in this book and in the 1997 amendments to IDEA reflect J. T.'s life. One is the principle of dual accommodations, and the other is the principle of "capacity building." J. T. has to learn how to fit into the world. To that end his capacities have to be developed and he has to be educated. At the same time the world (and its schools) have to learn how to accommodate to his disabilities. Their capacities to teach, use knowledge, implement rights, and collaborate across professions and with parents must be developed.

Time has passed between the writing of that first edition and the writing of this, the sixth. Now it is fall of 1999, and Congress has reauthorized IDEA and the Department of Education has recently issued regulations. It is closer to the truth to say that Congress has just created a nearly new and substantially different world in which students with disabilities will be educated. What J. T. experienced in school is now a far cry from what students with disabilities first entering early intervention just after their birth, or first entering schools at age 3 or perhaps as late as age 6, will experience if IDEA is implemented as it should be.

What is the difference between J. T.'s experience and the one that today's students will experience? How is IDEA so different?

As this edition shows, IDEA is not nearly as concerned about whether students have access to schools. That was the big problem when J. T. started school. In 1999, IDEA is concerned about providing them with an education that leads to their full participation in society. Now it is an outcome-oriented, result-focused law, and the outcomes and results are those that nondisabled citizens have taken for granted: independence and chosen interdependence, productivity at a workplace and contribution outside of it, and integration into a setting and inclusion in the hearts and minds of fellow citizens.

In part through his schools, but mainly through his network of informal support from family and friends (including friends who are professionals in the disability field), J. T. now works in a regular job for a regular wage and with nondisabled people. He is buying his own house, where he lives with young men and women who do not have disabilities.

That kind of outcome, that kind of result, is what the 1997 amendments to IDEA seek. They want full citizenship, full participation, for students with disabilities, in an inclusive society.

That vision, that result, would not have been achieved for many people like J. T., and that kind of law would not have been crafted for them without the fierce advocacy of many people whom we have been privileged to know and work with over the past 22 years. In the early mornings and late evenings of our work, we tender silent and sometimes not so silent gratitude to them. They may be nameless here, but they know, directly, how much they have meant to J. T. and us. They are creative, dogged, principled, and reliable allies.

None of what IDEA now expects and requires would have been possible without the research, demonstration, model programs, and personnel preparation activities of so many of our colleagues in institutions of higher education.

- Those who demonstrated that even individuals who have the most severe limitations nevertheless can learn are responsible for IDEA's zero reject rule.
- Those who understood that a full picture of a student cannot be obtained only in clinical settings are responsible for IDEA's nondiscriminatory evaluation rule.
- Those who demonstrated how to individualize and make effective teaching techniques are to be applauded for helping put teeth into the appropriate education principle.

- Those who have poked into the corners of human behavior assiduously and sought more humane ways to respond to its challenges are responsible for IDEA's emphasis on functional assessment and positive behavioral supports.
- Those who have helped others understand that behavior is a form of communication contributed to the IDEA rule against cessation of services for students suspended or expelled from school.
- Those who have insisted that ideology will and must guide practice have made it a rule of law that inclusion is the presumptively correct environment.
- Those who railed against schools' inflexibility and showed how schools can become effective can take a bow as system-change seeks its way into IDEA and the education-culture.

Because of the advocates and the researchers, we can say that IDEA is the fruitful product of ideology, vision, power, and knowledge. We are grateful to all who improved it so much in the reauthorization years of 1995 through 1997.

J. T.'s sisters, Amy Turnbull and Kate Turnbull, and J. T.'s beloved grandfather, H. F. Patterson, themselves have been instrumental in our lives and in J. T.'s, beyond the ability of words to describe. Their individual and collective compassion, courage, commitment, and competence on behalf of so many people who are disadvantaged in so many ways have sustained and comforted us on innumerable occasions. A perfectly fine result of the reauthorized IDEA will be if some students and educators in the mainstream of schools and community life will learn, as our family members have, that people with disabilities have many positive contributions to make to the world, and then act on that knowledge.

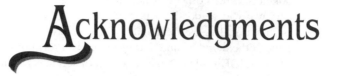Acknowledgments

No book ever is written or produced, published, and marketed without significant contributions from our close-at-hand colleagues. That is especially so in this edition.

Our colleagues at the Beach Center on Families and Disability, Matt Stowe and Brennan L. Wilcox, were most helpful in analyzing the statutes, regulations, and cases; they drafted some parts of some chapters, helped in the seemingly endless task of rewriting and polishing, tracked down a large number of references, and did all that with good cheer.

Lois Weldon was so swift and accurate in preparing the manuscript that each chapter's production seemed flawless once the text was in her hands. Her willingness to keep at the job of producing the manuscript so it would not just meet but beat deadlines is remarkable. Yes, she learned it from a great teacher, her mother and our colleague, Opal Folks, but she demonstrated it to an extent we have seen rarely in others before.

Stan and Tom Love at Love Publishing Company continue to be unflappable, flexible, convivial, and—in their quiet ways—brilliant and insightful publishers and distributors. The book's market success—indeed even the fact that it was the first special education law book ever published—is attributable to Stan.

When all is said and done, IDEA/1997—the invigorated, outcome/result-focused law—owes so much to so many. So does this edition of our book.

At the bedrock of our gratitude, and indeed as the icon for IDEA/1997, is a young man who has survived and prevailed in spite of his disabilities and because of his innate goodness: J. T. Would that every parent of a student with a disability be able to say that when the child is 32 years old! And would that every teacher in every school in the United States be able to point to a host of students who, though they may have a disability, are full citizens because of their own attributes and because of how their schools, the law, and their fellow citizens have responded to the perfectly natural human condition of disability!

Rud and Ann Turnbull
Lawrence, Kansas
November, 1999

Part 1

Introduction to the Law

1
Introduction to the American Legal System

Federalism ⌒

The law serves many purposes. Among them are ordering the public affairs of individuals and their governments and resolving disputes between them. These seemingly simple purposes are accomplished through an intricate network. To explain the workings of that network, we will use some familiar images.

Parallel Governments

Public law can be represented by three parallel ladders. Each has descending rungs of authority affecting the relationships between individuals and their governments and between various levels of government. At the top of the federal ladder is the United States Constitution. In the middle are laws enacted by Congress pursuant to constitutional authority. On the bottom are regulations federal agencies issue pursuant to congressional authority. Next to this ladder stands one representing the state governments. It has similar rungs of parallel authority: state constitutions, state statutes, and state agency regulations. Finally, next to the state ladder is the local ladder with its three rungs: the charters of local governments, local ordinances, and local regulations.

The image of three parallel governments depicts the sharing of power and responsibility between these governments. It also depicts that the highest source of law in each "ladder" is a fundamental document: the federal Constitution, the state constitution, and the local charter. Federal, state, and local statutes are next in line, followed by federal, state, and local agency regulations. Figure 1.1 depicts this concept.

This system of parallel governments (federal, state, and local) is known as the *federal system.* As a form of government, it is known as *federalism.*

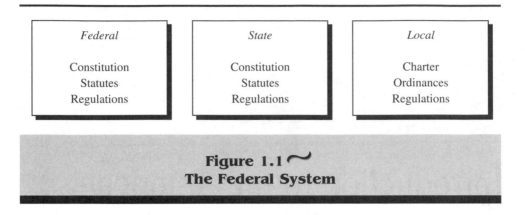

Figure 1.1 ⌐
The Federal System

Principles of Federalism

Two major principles are involved in the form of government known as federalism.

1. The federal, state, and local governments share responsibility and power. As pointed out later in this chapter, those governments share the responsibility for and power over the education of children with disabilities. Traditionally, local and state school boards (or other similar governing bodies) had the greatest responsibility and power. Recently, however, responsibility and power have shifted to the federal government. (Chapters 2 and 3 discuss the shifting of responsibility and power.)
2. Federal constitutional and statutory law have supremacy. Early in the history of this country, the Supreme Court, in *Marbury v. Madison* (1803), made it clear that the Constitution of the United States and laws passed by Congress to implement the Constitution are the supreme law of the land. This means that state and local school boards must comply with federal law if, among other things, they receive federal funds (as they do) or if their laws are in conflict with federal constitutional law or federal statutes. Clearly, the supremacy doctrine has permitted the federal role in the education of children with disabilities.

Lawmakers: Who Makes the Law? ⌐

Each source of law has a lawmaker—a group of persons who make the law. For the federal Constitution and its amendments the initial lawmakers were the delegates to the constitutional convention and, subsequently, the legislatures of the various states that acted to ratify constitutional amendments (other than the first ten, the Bill of Rights, which were drafted by delegates themselves). The delegates were representatives of the franchised citizens of the states. Thus, the source of the federal Constitution was the citizenry of the United States. This is generally true, too, with respect to the constitutions of states and charters of local governments. This form of direct democracy—delegates enact a constitution—still holds true: Congress may propose an amendment to the federal constitution, but the states, through their legislatures, have to ratify the amendment before it becomes effective.

Legislation

In the case of statutory law, the lawmakers are elected representatives serving in Congress or in state legislatures. Consistent with the concepts of federalism and the supremacy of the federal constitution, Congress and the legislatures may not enact laws that violate the federal Constitution, nor may state legislatures enact laws that violate the state Constitution. All federal and state laws are subject to *testing* to determine if they are *constitutional* under the federal Constitution and the applicable state constitution.

Also, the fundamental law of each state is its constitution, and no state law or state agency regulation has the effect of law unless authority for it can be found in the state constitution.

There are, then, lawmakers for each of government's laws, fundamental laws that have greater authority than any other. And each of the three governments has its hierarchies.

Regulations to Implement Legislation

As a rule, any law enacted by Congress or a state legislature will be general in its terms. No legislature can anticipate precisely all of the situations to which its statutes apply. At the most, statutes give general direction. General direction, however, is not always sufficient to inform the individuals or governments affected by the statutes about exactly how the statutes apply to them. Accordingly, executive agencies issue regulations to implement the statutes. Thus, though statutes are enacted by legislatures whose members are elected by the franchised citizens, regulations are made by regulatory agencies whose staffs are not elected but, rather, are appointed or approved by the legislatures or by the chief of that government's executive branch. Agency regulations must be based on authority the legislatures give to them. The regulators act simultaneously as executives, persons who execute or carry out the legislature's statutes, and legislators—in the limited sense that they write regulations designed to carry out legislation.

This complex system for enacting and carrying out laws exists in the area of education for children with disabilities. The system can be outlined as follows:

1. Constitutional law
    Federal Constitution (especially Fifth and Fourteenth Amendments)
    State constitution (especially provisions about education)
    Local charter (especially provisions creating schools or school boards)
2. Legislature (legislative body)
    Congress (e.g., the Individuals with Disabilities Education Act)
    State (e.g., equal educational opportunities legislation)
    Local (e.g., school board policies establishing programs for children)

3. Regulations (executive agency)
     Federal (Special Education Programs, Office of Special Education and
       Rehabilitative Services)
     State (e.g., Kansas State Board of Education)
     Local (e.g., director of pupil services or coordinator of special education).

Case Law and the Courts ⌒

One important type of law and lawmaker have not yet been identified: case law (judicial decisions) and the courts. When the delegates to federal and state constitutional conventions wrote those constitutions, they created three branches of government: legislative, executive, and judicial. Whereas the function of the legislature is to make law and the function of the executive is to carry it out, the function of the judiciary is to resolve disputes between citizens or between a citizen and his or her government. Courts do this by applying law to a given set of facts and interpreting the meaning of the law in that factual context. Courts' unique function is to say what the Constitution or a federal statute or regulation means in a given case, to issue a decision setting forth the facts that underlie their interpretation, and to enter an order commanding the parties in the case (or other courts, if the case is on appeal) to take certain action.

How are the courts organized? For cases involving federal law, the United States courts are organized in a hierarchy: trial courts, courts of appeals, and the Supreme Court (the court of last resort). State systems also consist of trial courts, courts of appeal, and a court of last resort. Why a case may be tried in one court, appealed or reviewed by another, and finally disposed of by yet another is a matter of great complexity. We do not need to enter that thicket. A brief discussion of court jurisdictions will serve our purpose.

The terms used to describe trial and appellate courts vary from state to state and sometimes differ from the terms that describe the U.S. courts. This creates difficulty from time to time in understanding precisely which court is deciding a case. For example, trial courts in the United States are called *district courts,* but trial courts in the state system are called *circuit courts, district courts,* or even *supreme courts.* Likewise, the U.S. appellate courts are called *circuit courts* or *circuit courts of appeals,* with the country divided into eleven circuits (regions) over which the appeals courts have jurisdiction. In some states the appeals courts consist of intermediate courts of appeals, together with courts of final appeals. And states use different terms to describe the intermediate courts and courts of final appeals.

The U.S. Supreme Court is the court of last resort for all cases, whether from the state court system or from the federal courts, and its decisions are binding throughout the United States. The U.S. circuit courts of appeals have appellate power over cases decided in the trial courts in their circuits. Their decisions are binding throughout the circuit but may be only persuasive, not binding, in other circuits and in all district courts. The U.S. district courts are the trial courts in their respective districts; their decisions are generally binding in the district only (not

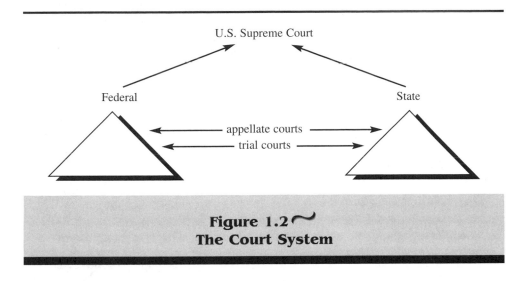

Figure 1.2
The Court System

throughout the appellate circuit in which they are located) and may be only persuasive, but not binding, on circuit courts and other district courts.

Paralleling the U.S. court system are the state court systems. Each state has a
court of final appeals or last resort, whose decisions are binding throughout the state.
The diagram in Figure 1.2 illustrates the relationships between the courts in a federal system.

Note that decisions may be appealed to the U.S. Supreme Court from the U.S.
circuit courts of appeals and from the courts of final appeals (or last resort) of the
states. Again, as to when a case may be taken to the U.S. Supreme Court is a matter
of great complexity. Several special education cases have gone to the U.S. Supreme
Court from the U.S. circuit courts of appeals. The most important education case
(arguably, one of the most important cases involving any issue ever) decided by the
U.S. Supreme Court was the first school race-desegregation case, *Brown v. Board of
Education* (1954).

Brown v. Board of Education

In the field of education law, the diagram in Figure 1.3 is well reflected by the original school desegregation case, *Brown v. Board of Education* (1954). *Brown* was not
one case but, rather, four that were consolidated and heard as one by the U.S.
Supreme Court. Three of the cases were on appeal from federal courts; one was on
appeal from a state appellate court after having been heard first in a state trial court.
Thus, *Brown* is illustrated by Figure 1.3. *Brown* was a landmark because it had an
impact on so many aspects of educational law and procedure, as the following
excerpts from the Supreme Court's decision demonstrate.

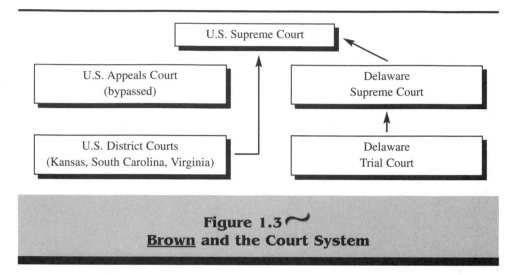

Figure 1.3
<u>Brown</u> and the Court System

In each of the cases, minors of the Negro race, through their legal representatives, seek the aid of the courts in obtaining admission to the public schools of their community on a nonsegregated basis. In each instance, they had been denied admission to schools attended by white children under laws requiring or permitting segregation according to race. This segregation was alleged to deprive the plaintiffs of the equal protection of the laws under the Fourteenth Amendment. . . .

In the first cases in this Court construing the Fourteenth Amendment, decided shortly after its adoption, the Court interpreted it as proscribing all state-imposed discriminations against the Negro race. The doctrine of "separate but equal" did not make its appearance in this Court until 1896 in the case of *Plessy v. Ferguson,* . . . involving not education but transportation.... In more recent cases, all on the graduate school level, inequality was found in that specific benefits enjoyed by white students were denied to Negro students of the same educational qualifications.... Here,...there are findings below that the Negro and white schools involved have been equalized, or are being equalized, with respect to buildings, curricula, qualifications and salaries of teachers, and other "tangible" factors. Our decision, therefore, cannot turn on merely a comparison of these tangible factors in the Negro and white schools involved in each of the cases. We must look instead to the effect of segregation itself on public education.

In approaching this problem, we...must consider public education in the light of its full development and its present place in American life throughout the Nation. Only in this way can it be determined if segregation in public schools deprives these plaintiffs of the equal protection of the laws.

Today, education is perhaps the most important function of state and local governments. Compulsory school attendance laws and the great expenditures for education both demonstrate our recognition of the importance of education to our democratic society. It is required in the performance of our most basic public responsibilities, even service in the armed forces. It is the very foundation of good citizenship. Today it is a principal instrument in awakening the child to cultural values, in preparing him for later professional training, and in helping him to adjust normally to his environment. In these days, it is doubtful that any child may reasonably be expected to succeed in life if he is denied the opportunity of an education. Such an opportunity, where the state has undertaken to provide it, is a right which must be made available to all in equal terms.

We come then to the question presented: Does segregation of children in public schools solely on the basis of race, even though the physical facilities and other "tangible" factors may be equal, deprive the children of the minority group of equal education opportunities? We believe that it does.

. . . To separate (Negro students) from others of similar age and qualifications solely because of their race generates a feeling of inferiority as to their status in the community that may affect their hearts and minds in a way unlikely ever to be undone. The effect of this separation on their educational opportunities was well stated by a finding in the Kansas case by a court which nevertheless felt compelled to rule against the Negro plaintiffs:

"Segregation of white and colored children in public schools has a detrimental effect upon the colored children. The impact is greater when it has the sanction of the law; for the policy of separating the races is usually interpreted as denoting the inferiority of the Negro group. A sense of inferiority affects the motivation of a child to learn. Segregation with the sanction of the law, therefore, has a tendency to [retard] the educational and mental development of Negro children and to deprive them of some of the benefits they would receive in a racial[ly] integrated school system."

. . . We conclude that in the field of public education the doctrine of "separate but equal" has no place. Separate educational facilities are inherently unequal. Therefore, we hold that the plaintiffs and others similarly situated for whom the actions have been brought are, by reason of the segregation complained of, deprived of the equal protection of the laws guaranteed by the Fourteenth Amendment.

Undoubtedly, *Brown* was the most significant education-law decision ever written by the Supreme Court—or any other court, for that matter. This is so for many reasons:

1. *Brown* illustrates the principle that the federal Constitution, as interpreted by the U.S. Supreme Court, is the supreme law of the land, is binding on all federal, state, and local governments, and is the precedent that all federal and state courts must follow in subsequent similar cases.
2. *Brown* is a nearly perfect example of one of the major lessons of this book: All educational issues (such as the educational rights of students with disabilities) are essentially political policy and social issues cast in the guise of constitutional litigation (Should those students be educated and, if so, how, with whom, and by whom?) and, because they are presented in the garments of the law, they ultimately are resolved by the courts.
3. *Brown* also demonstrates that the truly difficult educational issues are fought on various civil rights battlefields. Just as *Brown* was the first successful case on the battlefield of racial desegregation of schools, so it was the seed that gave birth to other civil rights battles and to successful challenges to governmental discrimination against certain persons because of their unalterable personal characteristics (such as race, sex, and disability). *Brown* gave rise to the right to education for children with disabilities and to other rights for people with disabilities. The point—so obvious, yet so important—is that

judicial resolution of educational issues on constitutional grounds becomes a precedent for judicial resolution of other civil rights issues on similar constitutional grounds. (Chapter 3 will illustrate this point in great detail.)

4. *Brown* gave immense comfort and support to civil rights activists, legitimizing their legal arguments and furnishing them with a powerful tool for persuading legislatures, particularly Congress, to enact entitlements and antidiscrimination laws. Case law frequently underpins legislation, and federal cases and legislation frequently precede state case law and legislation. Nowhere has this been more true than in establishing the rights of children with disabilities to an education.

5. *Brown* demonstrates that, although the U.S. Constitution never once refers to a public education, the principles of equal protection and due process under the Fifth and Fourteenth Amendments have a significant effect on public education. Nowhere is this fact clearer than in the disability right-to-education cases. This is significant because, as noted, the federal Constitution does not guarantee the right to an education. State constitutions do guarantee it. But if a state denies (as many had) an education to some students, usually those with disabilities, but provides it to others, the state violates the equal-protection doctrine of the federal Constitution and, depending on the provisions of the state constitution, its own constitution as well (see Chapter 2). The essential point of *Brown,* however, is that the states were violating the equal-protection clause of the federal Constitution. Chapter 3 discusses this point in detail.

6. *Brown* illustrates one kind of lawsuit—the civil action—that is typical of litigation between citizens and their governments. This type of suit is brought by a citizen who alleges that a government or a governmental official denied him or her rights or benefits to which the person is entitled under the law (constitution, statutes, or regulations). In this case, the plaintiff, Brown, sued the defendant, the Topeka Board of Education. In two of the consolidated cases, other citizens sued governmental officials who represented school agencies. A civil action is typical of the right-to-education cases. Criminal actions—in which the state prosecutes a person accused of a crime—are alien to educational law.

7. *Brown* is almost ideal for teaching someone how to read a case and how cases are decided, particularly in the right-to-education area. If *disabled* or *students with disabilities* is substituted for *Negro* and *nondisabled* is substituted for *white* wherever those words appear in *Brown,* we can understand why *Brown* is important to the education of students with disabilities and how the Fourteenth Amendment became the constitutional basis for the rights of students with disabilities to be educated.

    a. What are the *controlling* (or *dispositive*) facts of the case? In the language of the 1950s, Negro students are denied admission to schools attended by whites under laws requiring or permitting segregation according to race, and racial segregation in public education is inherently damaging to the educational opportunities of Negro children.

  b. What are the *allegations?* The facts constitute a denial of equal protection of law as guaranteed by the Fourteenth Amendment because segregated public schools are not and cannot be made equal.
  c. What are the *issues of law* the Court must resolve? The Court must determine whether the doctrine of separate-but-equal education and whether segregation, under that doctrine, violates the equal protection clause.
  d. What is the Court's *holding* (answer to the issue)? Segregation solely on the basis of race in the public schools violates equal protection and denies minority (Negro) children an equal educational opportunity.
  e. What is the Court's *reasoning?* Equal educational opportunities are denied when, in light of (1) the importance of education, (2) the stigmatizing effects of racial segregation, and (3) the detrimental consequences of racial segregation on the education of those against whom segregation is practiced, a state segregates by race.
  f. What is the Court's *order?* The cases are to be argued again before the Court, and the argument should focus on the nature of the remedy the Court should order.
  g. What is the *principle* of the case? State action in segregating the races in public education violates equal protection, and, by extension, any state-required or state-sanctioned segregation solely because of a person's unalterable characteristic (race or disability) is usually unconstitutional.
  h. What is the *public policy* in the case? State-created stigma or badges of inferiority based on race (or other characteristics, such as disabilities) are constitutionally intolerable because they mean that the state acts invidiously (i.e., discriminatorily, by denying equal opportunities) with respect to persons who have certain traits, such as disability. In brief, invidious (discriminatory) action is unconstitutional.
  i. Whose *interests* are at issue? The interests or claims of Blacks to an equal educational opportunity are at issue.
  j. Finally, what *functions* of government are at issue? At issue are the functions of education—namely, cultural assimilation, preparation for participation in the political process, and training so that economic opportunities might become available. Given the interests, the functions could not be parceled out or denied solely according to race.

Brown is worth an extended discussion here because it speaks directly to public schools, special education, and children with disabilities. The *Brown* plaintiffs and children with disabilities had undeniable similarities.

- Both proved they had been denied equal educational opportunities.
- Both alleged an unconstitutional denial and based their arguments on equal protection principles.
- Both challenged separateness in education.
- Both found comfort in the holding of *Brown* and the right-to- education cases concerning denials of equality.

- Both were strengthened by the reasoning that relies on concepts of stigma and detrimental educational consequences.
- Both successfully advanced a public policy against invidious state action.
- Both had similar interests in obtaining an education.
- Both laid claim to the functions of the schools to meaningfully educate all students.

Brown fundamentally changed the federal system. As precedent for other federal school desegregation cases and as the legal foundation for federal education and other civil rights legislation, *Brown* heralded the massive entry of the federal government into public education. Thus, it made significant inroads into an area that had been reserved almost wholly by state and local governments as their province. Over the long run, its effect has been to shift the balance of the federal system heavily toward the side of the federal government. Right-to-education cases and legislation also had the effect of diminishing the areas of state and local autonomy in education. Until recently, it was questionable whether there was any such thing as a "purely local" concern in education. Are all educational concerns truly national, requiring national leadership in the form of case-law precedents and legislation enacted at the federal level? This surely was the conclusion that had been reached in the right-to-education movement. This also was the conclusion that prevailed during the 41 years between the *Brown* decision in 1954 and recent Supreme Court decisions (see Chapter 3).

Role of Law ∼

The role of law in our society clearly is twofold.

1. The law seeks to regulate the affairs of individuals in relation to each other. The Individuals with Disabilities Education Act (IDEA) does this by enabling parents, school personnel, and children with disabilities to have certain regularized relationships with each other. It does this by setting forth certain rules these people must follow. In this way, the IDEA regulates the relationships of individuals to each other.
2. The law seeks to regulate the affairs of an individual in relation to his or her government. IDEA does this in the same way that it regulates the affairs of individuals in relation to each other. The parents and children have a specified relationship to the state education agency (SEA) and local education agency (LEA). These are agencies of the government of the state in which the parents and children live. Thus, IDEA regulates the relationship of the citizens (parents and children) to their government.

Beginning in Chapter 3 and continuing throughout the book, IDEA, its specific provisions, and the courts' interpretations will be described in detail. Having described the American legal system, its structure, and its roles in this chapter, we will describe next how that system directly affects citizens with disabilities, especially students.

Cases 〜

Brown v. Board of Education, 347 U.S. 483 (1954).
Marbury v. Madison, 5 U.S. 137 (1803).

2
Federal Policy and Disability

The History of Federal Legislation

More than *Brown* and a revolution in constitutional law had to happen to establish the educational rights of children with disabilities. To be sure, the cases were indispensable (as Chapter 3 will demonstrate). Nonetheless, a slowly evolving federal role that turned into a massive involvement in the education of those children was an equally indispensable ingredient.

The earliest federal role—creating, between the 1820s and 1870s, special schools for those who were mentally ill, blind, and deaf—paralleled a similar movement at the state level, in which state schools were established as early as 1823. No further significant federal activity occurred until World Wars I and II spurred Congress to authorize vocational rehabilitation programs and aid for disabled veterans and, in time, other persons with disabilities. Application of the Social Security Act to blind, disabled, aged, and dependent persons, especially the grant of benefits under the Act's Medicare and Medicaid programs, the payment of Supplementary Security Income, and a host of social service programs all evidence the federal government's concerns.

Congress first addressed the education of children with disabilities in 1966, when it amended the Elementary and Secondary Education Act of 1965 (PL 89–750) to establish a program of federal grants to the states that would assist them in initiating, expanding, and improving programs and projects for the education of children with disabilities. In 1970 Congress repealed the 1966 law but established a grant program that had a similar purpose (PL 91–230). Both the 1966 and 1970 laws tried to stimulate the states to develop special education resources and personnel.

By 1974 Congress had become dissatisfied with the states' progress and was confronted with the courts' decisions in two pioneering special education cases: *Pennsylvania Ass'n for Retarded Citizens (PARC) v. Pennsylvania* (1972) and *Mills v. D.C. Bd. of Educ.* (1972). As Chapter 3 makes clear, those cases ruled that children with disabilities must be given access to public education.

Accordingly, in 1974 Congress substantially increased federal aid to the states for special education and required them to adopt a goal of providing "full educational opportunities to all children with disabilities" (PL 93–380). In enacting PL 93–380 in 1974, Congress had at least four outcomes in mind.

1. It wanted to enforce the Fourteenth Amendment and the equal protection guarantees on behalf of students with disabilities. In this respect, it responded to the *PARC* and *Mills* cases.
2. It wanted to help the states carry out their own self-imposed duties, reflected in their constitutions and statutes, to provide an education to all students, including especially students with disabilities. In this respect, it expected that the states would comply not just with the federal guarantee of equal protection but also with their own state laws.
3. It wanted to overcome the practices of total and functional exclusion. In this respect, too, it wanted to secure the legal rights of students with disabilities, ensuring the benefits of an education.
4. It wanted to initiate a "system change" process, reforming the school systems so they would accommodate students with disabilities.

Having recognized that PL 93–380 was but a first step, Congress in 1975 enacted PL 94–142, the Education for All Handicapped Children Act. This law had the same four purposes as its predecessor, but it strengthened them substantially. For one thing, it created an "in-put" into the education of students with disabilities, represented by the four principles of zero reject (Chapter 3), nondiscriminatory evaluation (Chapter 4), appropriate education (Chapter 5), and least restrictive environment (Chapter 6). For another, it created two accountability techniques, procedural due process (Chapter 7) and parent participation (Chapter 8).

Although the 1975 law was the most significant amendment of the Education of the Handicapped Act (EHA) up to that time, it has not been the only amendment. Congress amended the EHA in 1978 by PL 95–561, in 1983 by PL 98–199, in 1986 by PL 99–372, in 1986 by PL 99–457, in 1990 by PL 101–476, and most recently, in 1997, by PL 105–17.

Of all the federal special education laws Congress has enacted, the two most significant are the 1975 law, PL 94–142, and the 1997 law, PL 105–17. The first of these, PL 94–142, laid the foundation for the federal approach, establishing the six principles of the law and using federal funds to assist and induce states to change their state and local schools so students with disabilities would have an equal opportunity to be educated.

The second law, PL 105–17, went far beyond the refinements that other amendments made in the fundamental federal-state scheme. While the 1997 amendments retained the basic six principles and strengthened them, they also declared that the federal presence in special education had new purposes, required state and local education agencies to implement reforms in schools, and targeted federal research, training, and other funds so those dollars would have a greater impact on schools and their abilities to assure the students' rights. (This chapter and those that follow discuss these matters in greater detail.)

Congress had an effect upon special education in other ways as well. The Elementary and Secondary Education Act itself was the springboard for the EHA. The Vocational Education Amendments of 1968, the Economic Opportunities Act of 1972 (Head Start), the Rehabilitation Act of 1973, the Higher Education Amendments of 1972, and the Developmental Disabilities Assistance and Bill of Rights Act of 1974 not only contributed to the political feasibility of PL 94–142 but also underscored the federal concern for people with disabilities.

School Practices ⌐

Why were federal education laws needed? On what basis were they justified? To answer those questions, one need only know the history of discrimination in education that state and local education agencies perpetrated.

As a general rule, the nation's public schools were ingenious and successful in denying educational opportunities, equal or otherwise, to children with disabilities. Their success was evidenced by data showing how many children were excluded. In 1974, when it enacted PL 94–142, Congress found that approximately half of the nation's 8 million children with disabilities were not receiving an appropriate education and about 1 million were receiving no education at all. The multitude of exclusionary practices that the courts found in violation of educational rights of individuals with disabilities also was proof of the problem. Among these practices, two dominated: exclusion and classification.[1]

Exclusion

Exclusion occurs when children are denied education. Total or pure exclusion involves a school's refusing to admit a child to any education whatsoever. Another type of exclusion—called functional exclusion—occurs when programs are inadequate or unresponsive to students' needs, as when Spanish-speaking children are given an English curriculum and no special provision is made to accommodate the fact that they do not understand English or when children are placed in classes but are given little or no beneficial education. Practices such as these constitute functional exclusion. Although the child has access to a program, the program is of such a nature that the child cannot substantially benefit from it and, therefore, receives few or none of the intended benefits of education.

Exclusion took many different forms. The schools excluded school-aged children with disabilities individually and as a class. They admitted some but not all of the students with the same disability. They inadequately funded tuition-subsidy programs that would have enabled families to purchase appropriate education from alternative sources (such as private schools) when appropriate education was not available in the public schools. When appropriate programs were not available, the schools placed pupils with disabilities in special education programs that were inappropriate for them. When faced with a shortage of special education programs, schools created waiting lists for admission to the few available programs, thereby excluding many eligible pupils.

Also, the schools created different admission policies for children with disabilities. They placed pupils with disabilities in situations with virtually no programs of instruction available. They excluded children with mental retardation on the spurious grounds that these children created behavioral or disciplinary problems. Finally, they limited the number of students who could be enrolled in special education programs by using incidence projections that bore little relation to the actual number of children in the school district or by restricting state-level funding for hiring special education teachers.

Classification

When children are misplaced or wrongly tracked, classification is at issue. Misclassification denies children the right to an equal educational opportunity because it results in their being denied schooling that will benefit them. Past challenges to school placement criteria often were accusations of racial discrimination as much as they were complaints about denial of education. The objection was that the tests used to classify children were biased toward knowledge of English and familiarity with White middle-class culture.

Accordingly, test scores resulted in minority children being placed in special education programs in far greater numbers than were other children. The result was a dual system of education based on race or cultural background.

Other Practices

A host of other practices, not easily categorized, also denied education to students with disabilities. State and local appropriations for special education were shamefully sparse. Institutionalized children often were denied even the barest programs of care and habilitation. The responsibility of state and local governments was fragmented, and competitive bureaucratic structures within the school or institutional agencies rarely undertook any cooperative efforts. The result was that meager resources (money and personnel) were diluted, gaps existed in service, services often overlapped, and accountability was nearly impossible.

Also contributing to exclusion were architectural barriers, the lack of adaptive materials and materials for children with vision, speech, and hearing impairments, and the inability or unwillingness of school personnel to teach some children. Teachers often were uncertified to teach children with disabilities, or were the least skilled teachers in a school system. They frequently were required to use the oldest, least adequate facilities, located far from the classrooms of students without disabilities.

The separateness and devaluation were underscored by separate financing, administration, and organization of special education services.

Once a child was placed in a special education program, the placement often became permanent. For the child it was a terminal assignment, and reconsideration or reevaluation was out of the ordinary. The assignment usually was carried out without parental participation and without opportunities for due process. Frequently, schools failed to identify the children with disabilities in their districts; child census procedures were rare, and the school's target population was not known, planned for, or served.

Early intervention programs were the exception, not the rule. Placement in private programs was encouraged because it relieved the school of any responsibility for serving children whose families were able or desperate enough to pay for private school opportunities. Local noncompliance with state law requiring education of children with disabilities was rarely punished. Preschool, elementary, and secondary school programs—when they existed at all—were unequally available. Finally, the schools' longstanding discouragement of pupils ("don't call us; we'll call you") made many parents weary of trying to rectify wrongs, kept them ignorant of their children's rights, and reinforced the unbalanced power relationships between the powerful schools and the less powerful parents.

These practices had been the rule more often than the exception. Court decisions amply documented these practices. And Congress itself filed a broad-based indictment of the public schools based on the findings of many of these practices.

Reasons for the Practices ⌒

Schools followed these practices for many reasons. Not only was the cost of educating or training a child with a disability normally higher than the cost of educating a child without a disability, but manpower, money, and political clout for children with disabilities also were limited when compared with the same resources for children without disabilities. Many educators had not considered pupils with disabilities, particularly those with mental retardation, to be educable in the traditional sense. The time-honored "reading-writing-arithmetic" philosophy has been a reason for exclusion. The fact that special education had been separated from the mainstream of education and that both special educators and educators in programs for students without disabilities have desired this separation also tended to diminish educational opportunities for individuals with disabilities.

Special education had served as an important escape hatch, permitting schools to classify as disabled those children they considered undesirable: those who were from racial minorities, were disruptive, or were just different. Behind this practice (indeed, underlying all of the discrimination) was the widely held attitude that governmental benefits, including education, should be parceled out to the most meritorious—a belief that equates merit with average intelligence or nondisabling conditions and asserts that the less able are less worthy.

Reasons for the Change in Practice ◠

No change in such entrenched practices and ideologies comes about easily, and certainly no change is attributable to any one factor. Indeed, many factors converged during the late 1960s and early 1970s to produce the fundamental reform movement known as the right-to-education revolution.

Ideologies

The concept that "less able" necessarily meant less worthy was jettisoned for an assertion that less able does not mean less worthy. This change occurred because, as Chapter 3 will show, there was a convergence of legal doctrine (equal protection), political doctrine (egalitarianism), and human service doctrine (normalization) that justified, indeed required, a taproot-deep reform of how people with disabilities should be regarded. The theories of social Darwinism—that survival of the fittest is normal and should be accepted and even advanced through means such as segregation, compulsory sterilization, and even euthanasia—became anathema to a citizenry recently made aware of the horrific extent to which Nazi Germany carried them.

Language

Language and terms about people with disabilities—a reflection of how people regard each other—were amended. The term *handicapped* fell into disfavor and disuse. It signified a person with a cap in hand, begging for public or private charity and privileges. That image—of a person with a disability as a supplicant for alms—called forth a singular policy response: privileges, but no rights.

In the place of *handicapped,* law and policy used new wording: "person/citizen with a disability." This language represented two changes.

1. The person comes first, and the attribute comes second; this "person-first" approach emphasized the common humanness of people with a disability and people who do not have disabilities.
2. As a result of establishing the humanness of the person, law and policy were called on to produce rights, not mere privileges. Thus, the person-first approach linked with a rights approach.

Science

The ideological and symbolic (language) reforms were accompanied by practical, reform-making factors. Through carefully controlled experiments, scientists began to prove that people with significant mental retardation could acquire the ability to speak and understand. This breakthrough may seem unremarkable now, but during the 1950s and 1960s it was a provocative finding. It meant, quite simply, that those who previously were regarded as unable to learn (because they could not learn to speak or respond to language) actually were able to learn. From this body of science came, in time, the concept of educability: All people can learn, and no one is ineducable.

Working nearly side by side with the language-acquisition scientists were scientists whose studies in human behavior led them to believe that mental retardation is a combination of impaired intellectual functioning and impaired ability to adapt one's behavior to the demands of one's environment. This concept—that mental retardation necessarily implicates adaptive (or nonadaptive) behavior—reinforced the arguments in favor of educability. If those who have a great deal of cognitive limitation can learn to respond to and use language, and if their behaviors can be shaped to be more adaptive, it follows that these people should not be written off as ineducable but, instead, should be given opportunities to learn and should be included in school.

Technology

Accompanying these scientific breakthroughs were developments in technology. Increasingly, educators (whether they be language specialists, behaviorists, or others) were learning how to teach. The "human technology" of a skillful cadre of professionals became more and more common. Simultaneously, new "hard" technologies, such as adaptive equipment and, in time, computer-based hardware, were put to use to help students learn.

Family Leadership

Articulate, powerful, and strategically placed families led the rights revolution. The parent movement was typified by formation of The ARC (previously called the Association for Retarded Citizens of the United States and, before that, the National Association for Retarded Children/Citizens) in the 1950s and its increasing clout on the federal and state scenes in the 1960s. President John F. Kennedy and his family were leaders—especially his mother, Rose Fitzpatrick Kennedy, whose willingness to discuss her daughter Rosemary's mental retardation on national television marked a bold "coming out." He established the President's Committee on Mental Retardation, commissioning a national white paper on rights of people with mental disabilities, and proposed and secured the enactment of early laws providing community-based mental health and mental retardation services.

Senator Hubert Humphrey (Democrat of Minnesota) and Representative James Foggarty (Democrat of Rhode Island) were early leaders in Congress. They later were joined by Senator Lowell Weicker (Republican of Connecticut), the father of a son with mental retardation, and Representative Tom Harkin (Democrat of Iowa), whose brother was profoundly deaf from birth.

Funding

Money seemed to be available to launch all sorts of "wars"—not just in Vietnam but also on poverty and on disability. Amendments to the Social Security Act authorized federal funds to improve state institutions where people with mental disabilities were housed. Other laws created community-based programs. Launching of the space vehicle Sputnik by the Soviet Union in the late 1950s pitted the United States against that country in a race for space and technological superiority. To win that race, Congress authorized federal grants to the states so science, math, and related areas would become a centerpiece of America's schools.

Vietnam

Ironically, the Vietnam conflict played its part. As the number of wounded veterans mounted and as the antiwar sentiment increasingly gripped the country, a new constituency—the veterans and youth in the civil rights movement—galvanized. When people with disabilities and their advocates needed help, the disabled Vietnam veterans and the civil rights advocates were there to help.

Institutions and Right to Treatment

Finally, the disability-rights movement itself was spurred by the horrible conditions in the states' mental retardation institutions (the so-called state schools) and psychiatric hospitals. The Pennhurst State School and Hospital in Pennsylvania (*Halderman v. Pennhurst*, 1981) and the Partlow State School and Hospital in Alabama (*Wyatt v. Stickney*, 1974) were the objects of the law-reform litigation that came to be known as "right to treatment."

In both institutions, the conditions in which "residents" were kept were wholly unacceptable to disability advocates and, ultimately, to the federal courts that tried these cases. Warehousing best described the best of the conditions; abuse and maltreatment best described the worst of the conditions.

When disability rights advocates focused on these two institutions, they developed a three-pronged strategy for deinstitutionalization.

1. To reform the conditions within the institutions (*Wyatt*). Ratcheting up the standards of care, the number and qualifications of the staff, and the physical facilities were important elements of institutional reform.
2. Simultaneously, to prevent further admissions to the institutions, especially admissions of children (*J.R. v. Parham*, 1979). This strategy sought to keep people out of the institutions and to create community-based services for them, including special education services.
3. Institutional discharge. This strategy aimed at forcing state governments to set deadlines for the certain closure of institutions and the simultaneous transfer of the residents to home- or community-based programs that were more appropriate (in the sense that they would be more habilitative) and less restrictive (in the sense that they would be in the community and less limiting of a person's freedom).

Over a long time—the twenty-plus years between the decisions in the early deinstitutionalization cases and the late 1990s—new legal rights for people with disabilities were fashioned from well-established constitutional precedents. In Chapter 3 we will explore those rights in detail.

In fairly short order Congress began to enact laws to carry out those rights. These laws included the Developmental Disabilities Bill of Rights and Assistance Act and the Social Security Act, especially Title XIX, Medicaid. Likewise, state laws (the so-called patients rights laws) were enacted to implement the newly established constitutional rights. Whether the source of these rights were judicial (in the right-to-treatment cases) or statutory, their effects were widespread and deep, especially among state and local education agencies.

As children were turned away from institutions increasingly and as the children who already were in them were discharged, the education agencies faced the challenge of educating these children. This challenge took at least two forms.

1. The agencies had to accept the children into the school system.
2. The schools had to educate the children appropriately and in the least restrictive, most typical settings and programs.

Those two commands derived from at least three sources:

1. State law (the state constitution or the state education laws, which usually commanded the education agencies to accept children with disabilities)
2. The federal special education laws
3. State or federal court decisions.

Thus, the right-to-treatment/deinstitutionalization movement interacted with the right-to-education movement in two ways. First, it created a challenge—to accept the students and educate them; and, second, it required Congress and the states to activate existing right-to-education laws or to create education rights for children with disabilities who were not beneficiaries of the existing laws already.

In summary, just as many factors had justified (or attempted to justify) discrimination in education against students with disabilities, so, too, many, more recent factors successfully justified or compelled their education. These factors converged to create two kinds of rights for children with disabilities: (a) rights to entitlements (such as education), and (b) rights not to be discriminated against solely because of their disabilities.

The fight against segregation and for integration via deinstitutionalization continued for many years after the *Wyatt* (1972) and *Parham* (1979) decisions. Indeed, the *Wyatt* litigation is ongoing in 1999 and *Parham* echoes in the 1999 decision of the United States Supreme Court in *Olmstead v. L.C.* (1999). There, the question (in the Court's language) was "whether the proscription of discrimination based on disability may require placement of persons with mental disabilities in community settings rather than in institutions."

The ADA Community Integration Decision

Restating the Issues

The issue raised in *L.C.* can be stated in at least two different ways:

1. The case can be analyzed as raising a right to community-based treatment: May individuals with disabilities use the ADA to compel states to provide

them with community-based treatment so their segregation in institutions is eliminated? In this analysis, the case involved the deinstitutionalization issue: placement outside of institutions. (As related to special education, the case involves the claim of students with disabilities, under ADA, to be included in general education when there is no justifiable educational reason for them to be excluded therefrom.)

2. A more comprehensive, historically valid, and contemporaneously focused analysis of the case is equally defensible. Comprehensively stated, the case involved segregation—the sometimes unjustified state-compelled, state-endorsed isolation of a discrete class of citizens from others, without justification. This much is clear from the Court's characterization of segregation through institutionalization: That kind of treatment "perpetuates unwarranted assumptions that persons so isolated are incapable or unworthy of participation in community life." The stereotypical assumptions—and the stigma (negative connotations) that underlies them—are precisely what ADA attempts to overturn: A person is protected under ADA on the basis (among others) that people "regard" the person as having a disability, as being less capable and, therefore, less worthy. When a person is denied community placement when the person could participate in the community, it is entirely defensible to ascribe that denial to prejudice and prejudice alone. (As we make clear in this and later chapters, segregation of students with disabilities has occurred through the use of special education, and, far too often, that segregation existed—and still exists—because of prejudice, not because of the needs of the students with disabilities.)

Historically, the case was a throw-back to the school desegregation case, *Brown v. Board* (1954): Just what limits exist on the ability of a state to discriminate, without justification, based on trait? Just as race and sex are traits that have been the basis for disparate treatment, so too has disability. To have segregated black students because—and only because—they are black is reprehensible and unconstitutional. To continue to segregate persons with disabilities because—and only because—they have disabilities is, by analogy to the unchosen trait, equally opprobrious. (We discuss *Brown's* significance for special education in this Chapter and in Chapter 3.)

Contemporaneously, the case relates to the conflict between state compulsion (segregation), individual choice (to not be in an institution), individual and public interests in securing the medical or other interventions that may benefit an individual who experiences mental disabilities, the extent of federal court oversight of state policy judgments and fiscal decisions, and the deference to which professionals are entitled in making decisions about the community or institutional placement of any given individual. We discuss each of these aspects in the following paragraphs.

The Court's Holding

With these formulations of the issue in *L.C.*, the question, now, is this: What did the Court decide? What is its holding in the case? The answer to that is both straight-forward and not.

In a nutshell, the Court held that placement of persons with mental disabilities in community settings rather than in institutions is in order when the state's treatment professionals have determined that community placement is appropriate for the person, the affected individual does not oppose transfer from institutional care to a less restrictive setting, and the placement can be reasonably accommodated, taking into account the resources available to the state and the needs of others with mental disabilities.

Affirming the Integration Principle

What is to be made of this holding? To begin with, it affirms the community-integration principle that ADA announced, as long as the community placement is not counter-indicated for the particular individual. Stated from a different perspective, it condemns segregation that cannot be justified for that individual.

Determining ADA's Beneficiaries

Just who is the individual who is "qualified" for ADA's benefits? Whom does the decision benefit? An individual is qualified if the person is able to handle or benefit from community placement. As the Court said, "Nothing in the ADA or its implementing regulations condones termination of institutional settings for persons unable to handle or benefit from community placements."

Some people with mental disabilities, the Court acknowledged, are able to handle or benefit, and others are not. For the former, ADA is a great shield against discrimination based on stereotypes and stigma, and against confinement that severely diminishes their everyday life activities. ADA's purpose, the Court is saying, is to protect those persons against stigma/stereotyped discrimination and unjustified denial of a normalized life (the normalization principle—see Chapter 3).

Those who are unable to handle or benefit from community placement are not discriminated against when they are confined to institutions: They do not qualify for ADA's protection and, thus, their confinement cannot be discriminatory (in the sense that they are singled out for disparate negative treatment when others like them receive non-negative treatment). (As we point out in Chapters 3 and 6 particularly, disability is a distinction that can make a difference in how schools decide to segregate students because of contagious diseases, how they discipline them, and how they exclude them from regular education.)

Justifying a Range of Services: Continuums and Arrays

It is notable that the Court expressed the judgment that a state is justified in providing "a range of facilities for the care and treatment of persons with diverse mental disabilities." Underlying the Court's language seem to be two concerns—altruism and dumping—as well as becoming trapped in the continuum.

Altruism: A Double-Edged Instinct

For one thing, the Court seems to be worried that some people will be discharged from institutions to the community and thereby be made worse off. ADA's mission, the Court said, is not to drive the state to move institutionalized people into an inappropriate setting, such as a homeless shelter. That sense of altruism—of protection and concern for persons with mental disabilities—is to be both commended and condemned. It is commendable because it expresses a very human feeling of concern for people with disabilities: They are especially worthy of our protection and beneficence. But it is condemnable because (as we show elsewhere in this book, especially in Chapter 4) altruism has been perverted and, in its perverted form, has justified second-class citizenship for people with disabilities and laws that require such degraded status.

Dumping and Community Aesthetics

For another, the Court is concerned about "dumping"—depopulation of institutions that results in former residents (patients) being released to the community where they find few, if any, supports. There, they could end up in inappropriate (non-treatment-providing) places such as shelters, and despoil the aesthetics of the community (present an offensive presence to the "rest of us" who live in the community). It is curious that the Court interprets ADA as prohibiting discrimination based on stereotype and stigma and, at the same time (in the "range" and "homeless shelter" language) seems to give vent to some stigma, some distaste for the presence of persons with disabilities in the community. (As we point out in Chapter 4, the reasons for segregation of students and others with disabilities sometimes reflects a visceral rejection—one is tempted to say, repulsion—of them.)

Becoming Trapped in the Range/Continuum

The Court's language about a "range" of facilities is also notable. Whatever characteristics people with mental disabilities have in common with each other, they clearly are just as different from each other as they may be from people with other disabilities or from people who have no disabilities at all. The population of "persons with mental disabilities" is not homogenous; they are as much heterogeneous as homogeneous. One person's treatment needs are that person's alone.

True, others may need similar treatment and may receive similar treatment regimens, but treatment, such as educational services, should be determined individually. For that reason, the Court asserts that some people with mental disabilities can indeed prosper in the community (they can handle and benefit from community placement). Others might not. A proper response, says the Court, is for the state to provide a range of facilities.

This approach—a range of facilities—mirrors other disability policy: IDEA provides for a "continuum" of special education placements (see Chapter 6); and federal funding of medical services (through Title XIX of the Social Security Act—the Medicaid provisions) is available for both institutional and community services. ADA does not compel, and the Court does not seem to believe in, a single-shot, one-way only, approach to service provision. Ranges, continua, arrays of service—these, the Court says, are defensible policy choices and do not necessarily reflect any animus, any discrimination, toward persons with mental disabilities. Of course, the problem is that the outside range—such as institutionalization—is an escape hatch, an outlet, for communities, professionals, and even families that want to exclude persons with disabilities (see Chapter 6).

Individualized Decision Making

Another important facet of the Court's decision relates to the decision-making process. The decision requires individualized decision making. The State's focus must be on the individual. The first issue for the State and that individual is whether the individual can handle or benefit from community placement. (As we point out below, the second issue for that individual is whether the individual opposes community placement.) Due process requires individualized decision making, and so do ADA and IDEA (see Chapters 3 through 8).

Judicial Deference to Professional Judgment

This case also illustrates that any decision about an individual is entitled to deference when that decision is made by professionals employed by the state. The Court's decision defers to the judgments of the state's own treatment professionals. As we point out elsewhere in this book, judicial deference to professional judgments is a standard legal convention—an ordinary way of courts making decisions on matters in which they lack sufficient expertise. (See particularly Chapter 3, relating not only to contagious diseases but also to student discipline; see Chapter 4, related to evaluations of students to determine whether they have disabilities; see Chapter 5, related to the types of educational programs that states are required to provide to students with disabilities; and see Chapter 6, related to inclusion of students in general education.)

The problem with the Court's decision concerning deference to professional judgment is not that the Court restated that doctrine. Rather, it is that the Court stated that the deference should be to the state's own professionals. Does this mean that only those professionals will be entitled to deference by a court when a person with a disability challenges a placement decision? Perhaps, unless state law or regulations provide otherwise. (As we point out in Chapter 4, students with disabilities are not required to rely solely on the judgment of school officials.)

Does this deference rule suggest that state professionals are entitled to make a placement decision utterly unfettered by any considerations other than what is beneficial for the person with a disability? Must they consider only the person's qualifications for community placement? That is to be hoped for but not expected. After all, as the Court points out, and as we discuss below, the state, and thus its professionals, also are entitled to bear in mind various cost considerations related to the immediately affected person and to other persons as well.

The potential for conflict of interests is great, arguably too great, when state public and fiscal policy is linked so inextricably with individualized decision-making processes. Deference, yes—that is solid law; conflict of interests, no—that is not tolerable when the issue is the mental health and liberty of a person with a disability. (As we discuss in Chapter 7, students with disabilities have significant due process rights—rights to challenge school officials' decisions and to have their challenges heard by impartial hearing officers or judges.)

Acknowledging Individual Consent and Capacity

Another notable aspect of the court's decision is that it underscores the role that individual consent plays: A state may not place any person (capable of giving effective consent and qualified for such placement) outside of an institution and into a community setting if the individual objects to the community placement. This part of the Court's decision is to be applauded for this single reason: It states that individuals with disabilities have a right, if they have the mental capacity, to say what happens to them at the hands of the state.

For so many people with disabilities for so many years, the exercise of their right to consent had been curtailed. That is to say, the exercise of a fundamental constitutional right of autonomy had been limited, without justification. (As we show in Chapter 5, related to transition from school to adulthood, and in Chapters 7 and 8, students and their families have powerful rights to consent and to participate with educators in decisions affecting education services.)

But this aspect of the Court's decision has a downside: If a person with mental capacity to consent refuses to consent to community placement, the individual can effectively veto a state's decision to place the person out of the institution. Then the state's only alternatives are to continue to allow the person to stay in the institution or to discharge the person from any state care whatsoever, effectively terminating all services to the person. At least for some period of time, the state's decision to discharge the person from any state care may settle the matter of placement (community or institutional), but it leaves the person at the mercy of the state. After all, if the state does decide to discharge the person from any care whatsoever, it effectively denies the person the benefits of state care and leaves the person potentially worse off than if the person had consented to community placement and that state had retained the person in the institution. (IDEA differs from ADA in an important respect: It assures every student with a disability of the right to go to school—see Chapter 3. It is universal in its coverage. ADA is not, for it protects only "qualified" individuals.)

State Defenses: Fundamental Alterations

A fifth important aspect of the decision relates to the Court's interpretation of ADA. The decision requires community placement, if individually warranted (according to professional judgment) and if consented to by the individual, as long as the placement does not create a fundamental alteration of the state's service system. The phrase "fundamental alteration of the state's service system" bears close examination.

Under ADA, a state may defend itself from a claim of illegal discrimination if it can show that the remedy the plaintiff (person with a disability) seeks will, if granted by a court, cause a fundamental alteration of the state's services and programs. As the Court put it, the state's responsibility, once it provides community-based treatment to persons with disabilities who qualify for that treatment (that is, for whom there is no treatment justification for keeping them in an institution), is not boundless.

Thus, the Court interpreted the "fundamental alteration" defense as allowing a state to show that, in allocating available resources, relief (placement in the community) for a plaintiff (person with a disability) would be "inequitable, given the responsibility the State has undertaken for the care and treatment of a large and diverse population of persons with mental disabilities." Thus, the state (and a court) must take into account "the resources available to the State and the needs of others with mental disabilities."

This defense articulates a classic "competing equities" dilemma. Who should be burdened in order to benefit another? What group of persons should have to bear a cost that is necessary to incur in order to advantage another group of people? This is precisely the kind of issue that IDEA raises, as we will make clear when we discuss the education of students with contagious diseases and of students whose behavior impedes the education of other students (Chapter 3), and of students with disabilities whose inclusion into general education might disadvantage other students (Chapter 6).

Two Federal Constitutional Principles

Underlying the Court's language and its approach are two principles of the United States Constitution. The first is the principle of federalism. The second is the principle of separation of powers.

The Principle of Federalism

The principle of federalism deals with the assignment of rights and duties between the federal government on the one hand and state governments on the other. It essentially allocates the functions of governments—that is to say, the rights that citizens have to receive benefits from governments and the duties that governments have to citizens—between the federal and the state governments.

In regard to institutional or community placement, the fundamental alterations defense and the competing equities dilemma warrant a few more comments. First, the Court clearly understands that a state decision about the nature of services (community or institutional) is a state decision, not one to be made by a federal court (much less the Supreme Court) but, rather, to be made by the appropriate state legislative and executive authorities. Here, the principle of federalism (a balance of power between federal and state governments) comes into play and requires the Court to defer to state decision-making.

The Principle of Separation of Powers

The second principle is that of separation of powers. This principle assigns powers to each of the three branches of the federal government: the legislative branch (which enacts laws and appropriates money), the executive branch (which carries out laws), and the judicial branch (which interprets laws). In *L.C.*, the Court makes clear the role of a court—any court—as interpreting law, not "making" law, not becoming a legislative-type body.

That role—of making law that courts then must later interpret—is for the legislative and executive authorities. Here, the principle of separation of powers (between legislative, executive, and judicial functions) comes into play. The decision whether to provide for any service—whether community or institutional—is not a judicial one to make.

Moreover, the amount of fiscal support—appropriations—that a state may decide to provide is also a legislative and executive function. And exactly how that funding should be allocated across all persons who can benefit from the funded program is equally a matter for state legislative and executive decision making.

That is to say, just how much money should be spent on community placement and on institutional placement, and exactly who benefits from the available funds, especially when the funding is not sufficient to benefit all who might benefit from it, is a matter for the state to decide. As long as it acts with an even hand, treating all possible beneficiaries comparably (without favor), the state may successfully defend against an ADA-based lawsuit that it discriminates by not providing community placement for some while it provides for such placement for others. The state's defense is especially strong (even-handed) if it can show, said the Court, that it has a comprehensive, effective working plan for placing qualified persons with mental disabilities in less restrictive settings (the community) and a waiting list (for community placements) that has moved at a reasonable pace not controlled by the state's endeavors to keep its institutions fully populated.

The qualifications—"comprehensive," "effective," "working plan," "reasonable pace," "not controlled by the state's endeavors to keep its institutions fully populated"—will be the basis for future litigation. As the precise meaning of these terms is developed by courts, the underlying principles of federalism and separation of powers will continue to come into play and will shape what courts believe the Supreme Court meant by these terms. It also bears noting that, as we point out in later chapters, issues around federalism (state and local control of education) and separation of powers (the role of courts in interpreting and enforcing statutes) permeate IDEA and its interpretation and implementation.

Remission to Majoritarian Decision-Making

The effect of the Court's decision to give a middle-of-the road, balanced interpretation to the ADA integration principle and to explicate, for the first time, the dimensions of the "substantial alterations" defense is to put the policy issue—which persons with mental disabilities should be served in communities or institutions, and in what priority order—squarely into the state policy-making process. It places, in the first place, the choices about serving people with mental disabilities in the hands of the state's legislative and executive leadershsip.

The effect of that remission to the state policy-making process, in the second place, is to remit the decision to the majoritarian decision-making process of the state's electorate: The voters, the constituents, who elect state legislators and state executive officers ultimately have the responsibility, through their exercise of their right of the franchise, to determine who shall be served and where.

The Court's approach is utterly consistent with the principles of federalism and separation of powers; and it is utterly democratic: Those who vote should, through their representatives, determine state policy. However much one may have hoped that the Court would have supported the integration policy far more vigorously, one also must admit that the Court's position—its interpretation of ADA and the underlying justifications for that interpretation—is defensible.

Summing Up

For now, it seems clear that the movement away from the institutional model—whether called (as it was early on) deinstitutionalization or (as it is now known) inclusion (the opposite of segregation)—is advanced, but cautiously, by the *L.C.* decision.

The ADA prescription for integration and proscription against segregation stands. Those who benefit from ADA are those who can show that institutional placement is unjustified; they alone are "qualified." And even then, their claim to community placement depends on state professionals' decisions and on state policy, as mitigated by the claims (competing equities) of others who also are qualified.

Federal Responses to Disability Discrimination: Entitlements ⌐

To carry out the right to education and right to treatment (also called the right to habilitation), advocates sought, and Congress provided, a series of entitlements for people with disabilities. The term entitlement refers to a benefit that a person can receive if the person qualifies by meeting certain standards of eligibility.

Individuals with Disabilities Education Act (20 U.S.C., Ch. 33, §§ 1400–1491 (1997))[2]

IDEA is an excellent example of an entitlement program. Under it, a student is entitled to federally assisted special education if (a) the student has a disability and (b) the student needs special education because of the disability [20 U.S.C. Sec. 1401(3) (1997)]. Before describing exactly who those students are, how their disabilities are determined, and what services they are entitled to receive, we will explain IDEA's purposes and how it assists the states in educating students with disabilities.

Original Purposes

When it was first enacted in 1975 as PL 94–142, IDEA's purposes were to

1. assure that all students with disabilities have a right to a free appropriate public education,
2. protect the rights of the students and their parents in securing such an education,
3. assist state and local education agencies to provide for the education of those students, and

4. assess and assure the effectiveness of state and local efforts to educate those students.

In declaring these four fundamental purposes [20 U.S.C. Sec. 1400(d) (1975)], Congress also recognized a broader, more overarching purpose, which was to enforce the equal protection clause of the federal constitution [20 U.S.C. Sec. 1400(c)(6) (1975)]. The equal protection clause provides that no state (and no local government) may deny anyone the equal protection of the laws; because state and local law and practice had been to exclude and misclassify students with disabilities, the schools were violating the equal protection clause, treating students with disabilities differently than students without disabilities (as Chapter 3 points out in detail).

Current Purposes

In enacting PL 105–17 in 1997, Congress

1. recited the original purposes and thus the historical justification for a continued federal presence in special education,
2. noted the success that state and local education agencies have had in carrying out the 1975 law (as it had been amended over the twenty years since its enactment),
3. identified barriers to effective special education—namely, the low expectations that education agencies have had regarding the capacities of students with disabilities and the agencies' "insufficient focus on applying replicable research on proven methods of teaching and learning for children with disabilities" [20 U.S.C. Sec. 1400(c)(4)], and
4. proposed specific solutions to the attitudinal and capacity barriers—namely [20 U.S.C. Sec. 1400(c)(5)]:
   a. Have high expectations for the students.
   b. Ensure their access to the general curriculum to the maximum extent possible.
   c. Strengthen parents' roles and ensure that families will have meaningful opportunities to participate in their children's education at school and home.
   d. Coordinate IDEA with other local education agency, state, and federal school improvement efforts so students with disabilities will benefit from broad-based school reform.
   e. Redefine special education to be a service for students rather than a place to which they are sent.
   f. Support high-quality, intensive professional development for all school personnel.
   g. Provide an incentive for whole-school approaches and prereferral intervention to reduce the need to label students as having a disability in order to address their learning needs.
   h. Focus resources on teaching and learning while reducing paperwork and requirements that do not assist in improving educational results.

Capacity-Building for Schools and Students

One of the pervasive themes of IDEA is effective education for improved student results. Congress noted not only that schools have low expectations and do not sufficiently use state-of-art research in their teaching but also that IDEA's promise has not been fulfilled for too many students with disabilities: Too many of them cannot pass their courses and their school dropout rates are excessive (Committee Report, p. 85).

Accordingly, IDEA now has a double-barreled focus: It seeks to improve schools' capacities and also to boost student results by giving students rights to an education that improve their own capacities (Committee Report, p. 85). This dual focus—school capacity building and student capacity building, also known as system-reform and human investment, respectively—is purposeful in a highly specific way.

The results or outcomes for students should be that they will have "productive independent adult lives, including employment" (Committee Report, p. 85). As this chapter points out below and as other chapters (especially Chapters 5 and 6) show, this result or outcome is entirely consistent with other federal law, especially the Americans with Disabilities Act and the Rehabilitation Act.

In brief, IDEA promotes outcome-based education, links student outcomes to school reform, and reasserts that free appropriate public education (FAPE) is constitutionally based.

Minority Students

In IDEA, Congress also addressed at great length another longstanding serious problem: the overrepresentation of minority students in special education. Among these minority students are those of African-American and Hispanic/Latino origin; but the population also includes Asian-American and American Indian students [20 U.S.C. 1400(c)(7)].

Congress then cited the shortage of minority special educators; acknowledged that poverty, minority status, and disability are linked; and noted that the limited-English population is the fastest growing minority population in the United States and that services to students in that population often do not respond primarily to the pupils' academic needs, in part because many of those pupils are classified incorrectly into special education [20 U.S.C. Sec. 1400(c)(7) (1997)].

Another pervasive theme of IDEA, then, is the federal effort to assure that when minority students are classified into special education, they are identified accurately as having a disability, they are not placed into special education in large part because they have not received adequate instruction or are limited in their ability to use English (and not because that lack of ability is attributable to a disability), and that they are provided an appropriate education by a well trained cadre of minority and non-minority educators who will work in collaboration with the students' parents.

What is the significance of these changes? As the House Committee on Education and The Workforce noted in its report on H.R. 5 (the bill that would later become PL 105–17 (The 1997 IDEA Amendments)), "…the critical issue now is to place greater emphasis on improving student performance and ensuring that children with disabilities receive a quality public education. Educational achievement for children with disabilities, while improving, is still less than satisfactory" [Committee Report, pp. 83–84]. To carry out this general purpose, then, Congress added to IDEA provisions that

1. place the emphasis on what is best educationally for children with disabilities rather than on paperwork for paperwork's sake,
2. give professionals, especially teachers, more influence and flexibility and school administrators and policymakers lower costs in the delivery of education to children with disabilities,
3. enhance the input of parents of children with disabilities in the decision making that affects their child's education,
4. make schools safer, and
5. consolidate and target discretionary programs to strengthen the capacity of America's schools to effectively serve children, including infants and toddlers, with disabilities.

IDEA's Beneficiaries

Having described IDEA's purposes and its basic approaches, we now identify the students who are beneficiaries of the law, those who are entitled to federally assisted special education.

As noted earlier in this section, a student is eligible for special education if (a) the student has a disability and (b) the student, because of the disability, needs special education and related services. Note the two-part standard for eligibility. First is the categorical element: The student must have a disability. Second is a functional element: The disability must cause the student to experience certain special needs.

Under IDEA [20 U.S.C. § 1401 (3)(A)(i)], the disability categories are governed by a student's age. For children aged 6 through 21, each inclusive, the categories are the following:

1. Mental retardation
2. Hearing impairments, including deafness
3. Speech or language impairments
4. Visual impairments, including blindness
5. Serious emotional disturbance (also referred to as "emotional disturbance," in IDEA to remove the pejorative connotation attached to the term "serious," but otherwise not to affect the definition [Committee Report, pp. 86–87])
6. Orthopedic impairments
7. Autism
8. Traumatic brain injury
9. Other health impairments
10. Specific learning disabilities.

For children aged 3 to 9, each inclusive, these categories apply, but each state or local education agency, in its own discretion, may include children who

1. are experiencing developmental delays as defined by the state and as measured by appropriate diagnostic instruments and procedures, in one or more of the following areas: physical development, cognitive development, communication development, social or emotional development, or adaptive development [20 U.S.C. § 1401(3)(B)]; and
2. because of these delays, need special education and related services [20 U.S.C. § 1401 (3)(B)(ii)].

A few words of explanation about the categories and about the state-local option to serve children ages 3 through 9 who are experiencing developmental delays are in order. With respect to the categories, IDEA now allows a state to "count" students by the traditional categories, but it also allows states to use "non-categorical" approaches to identifying the students. Why?

One reason is that a specific disability category for determining whether a student is eligible for special education frequently caused schools to develop a program for students and to place them into special education to a greater extent that the students actually needed (Committee Report, p. 86). Classification by category, then, caused overrepresentation of many students in special education or limited their opportunities for an appropriate education.

Another reason is that states have moved away from the categorical approach to identifying which children are eligible for special education and from educating them, once they qualify, in a categorical way. For those states, eligibility depends more on the functional definition: Does the child need special education? Also in those states, special education services are delivered to heterogeneously grouped students: Students with one type of disability will receive their education with students who may have other types of disability or none at all.

With respect to the state-local option to serve students ages 3 through 9 who are experiencing "developmental delays," Congress pointed out that in the early years of a child's life, determining precisely the nature of the child's disability can be difficult. Using "developmental delay" now can allow special education to be tailored to the child's needs; it also prevents a state or local agency from locking a child into a disability category that may be inappropriate or incorrect; and it may reduce the possibility that, later in the child's life, an agency would refer the child to special education (Committee Report, p. 86). Thus, the state-local option is targeted on (a) providing services when and how they are needed, thereby mitigating the effect of disability, and (b) on preventing subsequent special education placement.

Just as IDEA defines the eligible students, so it also defines the services to which they are entitled.

1. Special education means specially designed instruction, at no cost to the student's parents, to meet the student's unique needs, and includes

   a. instruction conducted in the classroom, home, hospitals and institutions, and other settings, and

   b. instruction in physical education [20 U.S.C. § 1401 (25)].

2. Related services are those the student needs to benefit from special education (see Chapters 3 and 5 for further definitions) [20 U.S.C. § 1401 (22)].

3. Supplementary aids and services are those the student needs to be educated with nondisabled students (see Chapter 6 for further definition) [20 U.S.C. § 1401 (29)].

4. Transition services are those the student needs to make the move from school to the adult world successfully (see Chapter 5 for further definition) [20 U.S.C. Sec. 1401 (30)].

Just how do these students get the federal entitlement and these many services? Unlike, say, Social Security payments that go directly to the individual beneficiary, federal special education money is authorized by IDEA, appropriated annually by Congress as part of the budget of the U.S. Department of Education, and then allocated by that Department to each state.

To secure the federal funding, a state must submit an application to the Department. The state education agency (SEA) files the application, indicating how the state and each of its local education agencies (LEAs) will comply with the conditions and provisions set out in IDEA. (For more on the conditions, see Chapters 3 through 8.) No SEA or LEA may receive any federal funds under IDEA unless it can demonstrate that it will comply with IDEA's conditions and provisions.

What are those conditions, and what do they mean for the student? Basically, IDEA consists of six principles, each of which is the topic of later chapters.

1. *Zero reject* (Chapter 3): Each school-aged person ("student") with a disability has a right to be educated and included in a system of free appropriate public education (FAPE). That is a positive way of characterizing this principle. A negative way of characterizing it is to say that it is a rule against the exclusion of any student with a disability from FAPE.

2. *Nondiscriminatory evaluation* (Chapter 4): Each student with a disability must be evaluated fairly, so that socioeconomic, language, or other factors are discounted and do not bias the student's evaluation and so that special and general education will be able to remedy the student's impairments and build on the student's strengths.

3. *Appropriate education* (Chapter 5): Each student is entitled to a beneficial education. The essence of this principle is that education must have a positive outcome for the student.

4. *Least restrictive environment* (Chapter 6): Each student must be educated, to the maximum extent appropriate (beneficial) for the student, in the school environment that is most typical. This principle presumes that education will occur in "inclusive" settings.

5. *Procedural due process* (Chapter 7): Each student's family (or other guardians) and the student have a right to challenge the school's decisions and

hold the school accountable for complying with all of the other five principles of IDEA. It is a rule of "fairness" and is expressed as a set of "procedural safeguards."

6. *Parent and student participation* (Chapter 8): Because education is more effective when the parents and students participate with the educators in designing and delivering special education, parents and students have specific rights to participate in the decision-making process regarding special education.

Developmental Disabilities Assistance and Bill of Rights Act (42 U.S.C. §§ 6000–6083 (1996))

As important as IDEA is, other federal laws also relate to people with disabilities. One of these is the Developmental Disabilities Assistance and Bill of Rights Act (DD Act). This law, like IDEA, provides federal funds to each state (if the state agrees to comply with its conditions) so the state may carry out some important planning and advocacy activities for people with a "developmental disability." That term, which uses a noncategorical (i.e., functional) approach to defining the Act's beneficiaries, means a severe, chronic disability of an individual 5 years of age or older that

1. is attributable to a mental or physical impairment or a combination of mental or physical impairments [42 U.S.C. § 6001(8)(A) (1996)];
2. is manifested before the person attains age 22 [42 U.S.C. § 6001(8)(B)];
3. is likely to continue indefinitely [42 U.S.C. § 6001 (8)(C)];
4. results in substantial limitation in three or more of the following areas of major life activity [42 U.S.C. § 6001(8)(D)(i)–(iv)]:
   a. self-care
   b. receptive and expressive language
   c. learning
   d. mobility
   e. self-direction
   f. capacity for independent living
   g. economic self-sufficiency
5. reflects the person's need for a combination and sequence of special, interdisciplinary, or generic care, treatment, or other services that are of lifelong or extended duration and are individually planned and coordinated [42 U.S.C. 6001 (8)(E)].

The Act's ultimate purpose is to help people with such a disability attain three outcomes:

1. independence (the extent to which the person exerts control and choice over his or her own life);
2. productivity (income-producing work or work that contributes to a household or community); and

3. integration (using the same community resources that are used by and available to other people, participating in the same community activities in which nondisabled people participate and having regular contact with nondisabled people, and residing in homes or homelike settings in proximity to community resources and having regular contact with nondisabled citizens in their communities) [42 U.S.C. §§ 6000(b), 6021].

To help achieve these outcomes, the Act provides money to the states so that the states, their local agencies, and public or private nonprofit agencies may

1. provide comprehensive services;
2. plan those services;
3. establish model programs;
4. operate university-affiliated programs of interdisciplinary training and service provision; and
5. operate statewide systems of protection and advocacy for people with developmental disabilities and those with mental illness [42 U.S.C. § 6000(b)].

Like IDEA, the DD Act

1. uses both categorical and functional approaches to defining its eligible beneficiaries;
2. authorizes federal funding of activities carried out at the state and local levels;
3. conditions a state's receipt of federal funds on certain undertakings by the state; and
4. specifies certain outcomes (independence, productivity, and inclusion—IPI).

Rehabilitation Act (29 U.S.C., Ch. 16, §§ 706(8) and 794–794b)

As noted earlier, U.S. participation in international conflict—World War I, World War II, and the Vietnam War—were the causes for the enactment and later amendment of the Rehabilitation Act. Originally directed at the vocational rehabilitation of wounded and disabled veterans, the Rehabilitation Act now is a double-barreled source of benefits for people with disabilities.

1. The basic state grant program—whereby a state agrees to certain conditions in order to get federal funds to operate its vocational rehabilitation system—benefits working-age people (including young adults who still may be in school) by providing a wide range of services so they can be trained to work, get jobs, and advance in their jobs.
2. The supported employment program benefits people (including young adults) who have severe disabilities and need ongoing assistance in learning and performing their jobs.

A person with a disability is supported in employment by a job coach, a specially trained co-worker who teaches the client the job and assists him or her in doing it. One way to think about job coaching is to regard it as a different form of job sharing, in which the job is shared by the worker with a disability and the coach. The coach is paid either by the state vocational rehabilitation agency or by the employer of the person with a disability. The person with a disability must be paid at least the minimum wage, work at least 20 hours a week, and be integrated at the job with people who do not have a disability.

Like IDEA, the Rehabilitation Act's programs:

1. authorize federal funding of state and local activities;
2. condition the funding on the state and local agencies' compliance with certain conditions, and
3. seek specified outcomes (employment in integrated settings) [29 U.S.C. § 794 (1996)].

Unlike IDEA, however, the Rehabilitation Act (like the DD Act) uses a functional approach to defining its eligible beneficiaries; the extent of the person's disability and its effect on the person's work capacity, not the type of disability, is controlling.

Social Security Act

Under the Social Security Act, people with disabilities may be eligible to receive a range of benefits.

1. Supplemental Security Income (SSI) is available if
   a. a child (birth to age 18) has a medically determinable physical or mental impairment that limits the child's functioning to a marked and severe degree; and
   b. the child's family meets certain income-eligibility standards (must be "poor" under the federal definition) [42 U.S.C. § 1381–1383f (1997)].
2. Social Security Disability Insurance (SSDI) is available if an adult has a disabling condition and meets income-eligibility standards (is low-income), and does not include a means-test such as that of SSI [42 U.S.C. § 401, 420–425 (1997)].
3. Medicaid, a program that reimburses for certain medical and behavioral-care costs, is available to (among others) families who are low-income and have children with severe disabilities [42 U.S.C. §1396 et. seq. (1997)].

The SSI and SSDI programs are personal entitlements; that is, the child-family-person applies to the local Social Security Administration office and, if eligible, receives benefits from that office. The Medicaid program, however, is administered jointly by the Social Security Administration and the state (usually through its public health or welfare agency). Accordingly, the funds are conditioned on the Social Security Administration's approval of a state plan for determining who is eligible and what benefits, including home- and community-based services, they will fund jointly.

Federal Responses to Disability Discrimination: Antidiscrimination Laws ⌒

When a person with a disability has an entitlement, the person is eligible to receive services funded under the entitlement program. The services certainly can help to mitigate the effect of the disability; they augment inherent capacities, restore lost ones, or create new ones. To that end, they are indeed necessary. But they alone are not sufficient to ameliorate the impact of the disability.

Entitlement programs do not, for example, prohibit public and private agencies from discriminating against the person on the basis of the person's disability. A person may receive education, rehabilitation, or other services, but these services may not create opportunities or access for the person to use the skills he or she has acquired through those services. Prejudice against people with disabilities—even against those whose capacities are demonstrable—still may foreclose opportunities for the person to show that, although the person has a disability, the person is nonetheless able. "Disabled, yes; unable, no" is a concept that always will be thwarted by prejudice and discrimination on the basis of disability.

To combat this prejudice and discrimination, Congress has enacted two civil rights laws prohibiting discrimination based solely on a person's disability. These laws—Section 504 and the Americans with Disabilities Act—rest on the precedents that prohibit discrimination on the basis of race or sex.

Section 504 (29 U.S.C. § 794 (1996))

In 1973, Congress amended the Rehabilitation Act and, in Section 504 of the Amendments, prohibited disability discrimination. Section 504 provides that no otherwise qualified individual with a disability shall, solely by reason of his or her disability, be excluded from the participation in, be denied the benefits of, or be subjected to discrimination under any program or activity receiving federal financial assistance [29 USC § 794 (1996)].

For the purposes of education and special education, the term individual with a disability is one who

1. has a physical or mental impairment which substantially limits one or more of the person's major life activities [29 U.S.C. § 706(8)(A)(i)];705(20)(B)(i)]
2. has a record of such an impairment [29 U.S.C. § 706(8)(B)(ii)];705(20)(B)(ii)]; or
3. is regarded as having such an impairment [29 U.S.C. § 706(8)(B)(iii)].705(20)(B)(iii)].

The regulations implementing § 504 (30 Code of Federal Regulations, Part 104) further define these terms.

1. "Physical or mental impairment" means (a) any physiological disorder or condition, cosmetic disfigurement, or anatomical loss affecting one or more of the following body systems: neurological; musculoskeletal; special sense organs; respiratory, including speech organs; cardiovascular; reproductive, digestive, genitourinary; hemic and lymphatic; skin; and endocrine; or (b) any mental or psychological disorder, such as mental retardation, organic brain syndrome, emotional or mental illness, and specific learning disabilities.
2. "Major life activities" means functions such as caring for oneself, performing manual tasks, walking, seeing, hearing, speaking, breathing, learning, and working.
3. "Has a record of such an impairment" means having a history of, or having been misclassified as having, a mental or physical impairment that substantially limits one or more major life activities.

With respect to public preschool, elementary, secondary, or adult educational services, a "qualified" person is

1. of an age during which nondisabled people are provided such services;
2. of an age during which it is mandatory under state law to provide services to people with disabilities; and
3. one to whom a state must provide special education under IDEA.

Thus, if a student has a disability, has a history (record) of a disability, or is regarded as having a disability and is of school age, the student—even though not a beneficiary of IDEA—still may not be discriminated against in education solely because he or she has a disability.

After all, a student can be "qualified" under Section 504—that is, be protected by it against discrimination in school—and still not be a beneficiary of IDEA. For example, a student who has HIV may not need any special education. Yes, the person has a disability; indeed, under IDEA, a person with HIV is categorized under "other health impairments."

Simply having HIV, however, does not necessarily mean that the person also needs special education. The HIV condition may not have impaired the student's ability to participate in the general or regular education programs; the person may not be experiencing any negative effects of the HIV and thus not need special education (specially designed instruction to meet the student's unique needs).

Nonetheless, and simply because the student has HIV, he or she may experience discrimination, such as total exclusion from school or exclusion from the opportunities to participate in the curriculum or in extracurricular activities. Such a student experiences discrimination just as surely as if the HIV had impaired his or her ability to function. There is, then, every reason to protect the student against education discrimination: The discrimination itself closes access to opportunities to be educated.

Like IDEA, Section 504 uses a functional definition to describe students who are protected under it (beneficiaries of the law). Students must have a significant impairment in their ability to learn. Also like IDEA, Section 504 uses a categorical definition, listing under "physical" and "mental" impairments the conditions or disorders that constitute such an impairment.

Unlike IDEA, however, Section 504 applies not just to schools that receive federal funds but also to a wide range of other recipients (e.g., employers, institutions of higher education, and health care providers). Because it covers employment and because schools are employers who receive federal financial assistance (e.g., IDEA funds), Section 504 applies to schools not only as providers of services but also as employers.

The U.S. Supreme Court's very first Section 504 decision, *Southeastern Community College v. Davis* (1979) defined the term *otherwise qualified.* In that case, a licensed practical nurse, Frances Davis, sought admission to the registered-nurse program at the Southeastern Community College in North Carolina. Upon learning that Ms. Davis was partially deaf, used a hearing aid, read lips but required the speaker to address her directly, and had a degenerative condition that ultimately would cause her to be profoundly deaf, the college refused to admit her to its program.

Davis sued the college, claiming that she had been denied the opportunity to participate in its curriculum solely because of her disability and that the college, a recipient of federal financial assistance, therefore was in violation of Section 504 and should be required to modify its curriculum so she could take classroom and clinical training there and, upon completing her training and taking her degree, ultimately be licensed as a nurse.

The issue between Davis and the college was whether Davis was an "otherwise qualified" person with a disability. The college did not deny that it refused to admit her because of her hearing impairment; indeed, it was clear about its refusal to admit her, claiming that she was not qualified to participate in its curriculum and that, to accommodate her, it would have to make substantial adjustments in its curriculum. Moreover, the college said, these adjustments not only would affect its curriculum's integrity but also may place Davis's patients in some danger; there was no assurance that, upon leaving the college, she would be able to work with physicians or patients and thus be able to keep from harming patients in her care.

The Supreme Court held that Davis is not an "otherwise qualified" person and that the college did not discriminate against her in violation of Section 504. Finding that Davis's participation in the nursing program would be limited to taking only classroom-based training and that she would have to be excluded from clinical training where she might endanger patients, the Court determined that a "fundamental alteration" in the college's program would be required if it were obliged to admit Davis and grant her a degree on the basis of classroom-based training only.

This type of fundamental alteration is more than Section 504's "reasonable accommodations" rule requires. Under Section 504, a federal-aid recipient must make only "reasonable accommodations" to a person with a disability; if, after making those accommodations, the person still cannot participate in the recipient's program, the recipient may exclude the person without violating Section 504.

In Davis's case, the accommodation she needed—a quantum change in the college's curriculum that still would not enable Davis to serve as a nurse in "all customary ways"—was far more than a "reasonable one"; it was one that not only would require the college to effect "substantial modifications" in its curriculum but also would not ultimately safeguard patients from being cared for by a deaf nurse.

As the Court made clear, an "otherwise qualified" person is one who, with reasonable accommodations, can participate "in spite of" a disability. In Davis's case, she could not participate, even with unreasonable accommodations, because of her disability. She was, therefore, not "otherwise qualified."

Davis is significant because, as is typically the case involving a conflict of rights, it recognizes the need to balance the rights of a person with a disability (Frances Davis) against the rights of other people—namely, the patients who would be cared for by a nurse who may not be able to hear adequately and the institutions of higher education, which have a claim to control their curriculum and make independent judgments concerning the suitability of a person for the curriculum. As Chapters 4, 6, and 7 point out, balancing the interest of people with disabilities against the interests of others is a matter that arises under both Section 504 and IDEA.

School Bd. of Nassau County v. Arline (1987) also shed light on this balancing issue. In that case, a teacher infected with tuberculosis, whom the Court found to be a "person with a disability" under Section 504, was dismissed from her job because she allegedly posed a risk of infecting others. After finding that she was a "person with a disability," the Court developed a four-part standard for balancing the rights of the individual against the risk of exposing others to the disease in order to determine whether the plaintiff was an "otherwise qualified individual" under Section 504: Evaluate (1) the nature of the risk, (2) the duration of the risk, (3) the severity of the risk, and (4) the probability of transmitting the disease to others. (We discuss *Arline* at length in Chapter 3).

Americans with Disabilities Act (42 U.S.C., Ch. 126, §§12101–12213 (1996))

Because Section 504 covers only recipients of federal financial assistance, it necessarily is limited in scope. Yes, it protects otherwise qualified individuals in those programs, but what if an individual seeks employment from a company that does not receive any federal funds? Or wants to participate in state and local government programs that are not federally aided? Or wants to have access to telecommunications systems, such as closed captioning for people with hearing impairments? In none of those domains of life would the person receive any protection from Section 504.

To close the very large gap between Section 504 coverage and the legitimate desires of people with disabilities to have access to all of the domains of life that people without disabilities take for granted, Congress enacted in 1990 the most sweeping of disability-discrimination prohibitions, ADA.

ADA recognizes that discrimination occurs in many ways, for many reasons, and in almost all sectors of society and that the proper goals of the nation for individuals with disabilities are to assure equality of opportunity, full participation, independent living, and economic self-sufficiency.

General Coverage

Consistent with its goals, the ADA extends its civil rights/nondiscrimination protection to the following sectors of American life: employment in the private sector; privately owned public accommodations (for example, theaters, hotels, restaurants, shopping centers, and grocery stores); services provided by state and local governments, including public and private transportation services; and telecommunications services (for people with hearing or visual impairments) [42 U.S.C. § 12101 (1996)].

Clearly, ADA anticipates certain outcomes for people with disabilities. These are that they will enjoy equal opportunity to participate fully in the life of the community and will have equal opportunity to live independently and to achieve economic self-sufficiency. Accordingly, ADA now prohibits discrimination in the domains of life in which those opportunities exist, thus opening up the possibility that students (as students) and individuals with disabilities (as citizens, not just as students) will have access to the community, despite their disabilities and the community's barriers. Just as IDEA's zero-reject rule (see Chapter 3) is a rule of inclusion and against exclusion, so, too, is the ADA a rule of inclusion and against exclusion.

Protected Individuals

Those who are entitled to ADA's benefits are "individuals with disabilities" as the term is defined under Section 504 of the Rehabilitation Act: a person who has, has a history of having, or is regarded as having an impairment that significantly limits one or more of life's major functions [42 U.S.C. § 12102 (2)]. Generally speaking, a student who is entitled to the benefits of IDEA will be covered under ADA as one who has a disability. But there may be more people covered by ADA than by IDEA; a person may have a history or be regarded as having a disability but still not need special education and thus not be covered by IDEA.

Employment Discrimination

With respect to employment, the ADA prohibits discrimination against a person with a disability who is "otherwise qualified" to perform the essential functions of the employment position, with or without reasonable accommodation [42 U.S.C. § 12111(8)].

The United States Supreme Court interpreted the ADA employment-discrimination provisions in three very recent cases. In *Murphy v. United Parcel Service, Inc.* (1999), *Sutton v. United Air Lines, Inc.* (1999), and *Albertsons, Inc. v. Kirkingburg* (1999), the common issue was whether an individual whose disability was corrected is entitled to the ADA's protection. In *Murphy*, the individual was a truck driver whose blood pressure had been controlled by medication; in *Sutton*, the individuals were airline pilots whose vision had been corrected by eyeglasses; and in *Albertsons*, the individual was a truck driver with impaired vision in one eye who had received a "vision waiver" from the Federal Highway Administration (FHWA) program as a result of his excellent driving record. In each case, however, the employer dismissed the employee(s) to assure the safety of other individuals.

Faced with a conflict between the assertion of individual rights (to nondiscrimination) and an antidiscrimination statute on the one hand and an employer-liability and public safety concerns on the other, the Court held, in each case, that the determination of whether a person has a disability and is protected by ADA on that account should be made with reference to measures (such as eyeglasses, contact lenses, or medication) that mitigate the individual's impairment. So, if an individual uses any form of measure that reduces the impact of the impairment and renders the person not significantly limited in one or more of life's major functions (here, employment), the individual is not "disabled" under ADA.

The Court's decisions require an individualized inquiry, narrow the category of protected persons with a disability, tend to curb "disability spread" (the seemingly unlimited definition of disability and its extension to people who, by some accounts, do not have, or do not seem to have, a disability), and tend to tip the scales toward public safety and insulate employers from liability to various claims of discrimination based on disability.

But they also create an ironic result: A person is too disabled to work but not disabled enough to sue because he or she has been discharged from work because of the disability.

Finally, it is worth noting that these decisions and ADA as a whole relate to special education and students with disabilities in some rather direct ways. First, they reduce the number of students who can sue under ADA for educational discrimination. As we pointed out, some students with disabilities may be entitled to ADA protection but IDEA benefits. Among that class of students, some may have disabilities (for example, attention deficit/hyperactivity deficit or mental illness) that are mitigated by, for example, medication; they now are barred from claiming that the schools discriminate against them on account of their disabilities.

Second, the cases may create a disincentive to students' use of assistive devices. These devices (as we point out in Chapter 3) are available to students with disabilities, but, if a student were to use one, the student would not be entitled to ADA protection—a consequence that may persuade the student to forego the use of the device in order to retain various antidiscrimination rights. When the student has a choice of an assistive device that will marginally improve the student's functioning (for example, an enlarged keyboard and monitor on a computer), the student may well choose not to use the device. When, however, the student clearly needs the device in order to function (for example, a wheelchair), the chilling effect of these decisions will almost certainly be minimal.

Likewise, the Court's interpretation of ADA very well may affect its, and other courts', interpretations of Section 504. This is so because the language of ADA and of Section 504 are identical: A person is entitled to ADA and 504 protection because he or she has a disability that results in a substantial (now, not mitigated) impairment in one or more of life's major activities (such as education).

For students who do not receive IDEA benefits but who nonetheless have disabilities, the analogous interpretation—ADA and Section 504 read alike and therefore must be interpreted alike—is ominous, for such students will be barred from protection under Section 504. Given that some students have disabilities (for example, sensory disabilities) that are not so limiting as to qualify the student for IDEA benefits, and given also that those students sometimes are classified as having a disability under Section 504 and therefore are entitled to some accommodations in their education, these three cases may disqualify these students from Section 504 protection. If that result obtains, the number of students whom a school must accommodate because of disability will drop. That could be good news for schools that claim they are already overburdened with disability-accommodation demands, but it surely will not be good news for the students themselves.

What is not disturbed by these three cases is the clear implications of ADA for special education and students' curriculum. As you will learn in Chapter 4, IDEA anticipates an outcome of employment during, and especially after, the student exits from school. That outcome cannot be achieved in many cases as long as there are barriers to employment. These barriers are the targets of ADA's employment provisions, which make them illegal.

Accordingly, the role of special education is now clear. It is to prepare individuals with disabilities to take advantage of the new opportunities available in employment.

Public Services and State/Local Governments

State and local governments provide many opportunities for employment and participation in a community. These governments operate many programs, such as recreational activities, libraries, health services, social services, and so on. Although Section 504 of the Rehabilitation Act prohibited these governments from discriminating against otherwise qualified persons with disabilities if the governments received federal financial assistance, many functions of state and local government were not federally supported and thus still could discriminate against people with disabilities. These functions—employment and services including transportation, as well as facilities—now may not do so [42 U.S.C. § 12132].

Two recent decisions by the United States Supreme Court clarify exactly what the public services provisions mean. In *Pennsylvania Department of Corrections v. Yeskey* (1998), the Court held that state prison systems are subject to the ADA. The question in that case was whether an inmate who had hypertension is—for that reason alone—barred from participating in a "boot-camp" program that, if completed successfully, would lead to early release from prison. The Court had no difficulty in deciding that ADA's language is clear and unmistakable: ADA covers states and state agencies (such as prison systems), and the categorical prohibition of the inmate, because of disability alone, violates ADA.

In 1999, the issue before the Court (in the *L.C.* case) was whether the ADA compels states to provide community-based placements (in lieu of institutional-based placements) for individuals who can be served as effectively in the community as in an institution.

As previously discussed, the Court answered this question with a qualified "yes." The consequence of this change in law is to ensure that people with disabilities will have access to those functions and be able to participate in the community as service users. The role of special education is to prepare them to participate and take advantage of these functions.

Public Accommodations and Services Operated by Private Entities

The ADA also bans discrimination in public accommodations such as restaurants, hotels, theaters, doctors' offices, pharmacies, retail stores, museums, libraries, parks, recreational programs and facilities, private schools, and day-care centers [42 U.S.C. § 12182]. Private clubs and religious organizations are exempt from that ban [42 U.S.C. § 12187].

In *Bragdon v. Abbott* (1998), the issue before the United States Supreme Court was whether a person who has HIV (but whose disability has not yet progressed to the so-called symptomatic phase) is protected by ADA. There, a dentist, upon learning that a patient had nonsymptomatic HIV, refused to provide services in his office; instead, the dentist had offered to provide services but only in a hospital operating theatre, claiming that to provide the services in his office would subject him to risk of infection.

The Court held, simply, that the patient is entitled to ADA's protection, but it refused to decide (and remanded the case to the lower courts to decide) whether the dentist's refusal was justified under ADA's provision that allows a provider (a public accommodation) to protect himself against the risk of infection. Just as in the case of employment and state/local government functions, the ADA removes barriers to community participation and anticipates that the role of special education is to prepare students with disabilities to take advantage of the opportunities for participation.

Transportation

As a general rule, ADA bans discrimination in public and private transportation on the basis of disability [42 U.S.C. § 12141–12150, 12184]. It creates separate rules for complying with this ban for various types of transportation systems ("demand-responsive systems," "designated public transportation," and "fixed-route systems"). It has special rules for public bus systems, public rail systems, and privately operated bus and van companies [42 U.S.C. §§ 12142, 12162] . It permits paratransit systems to operate as a complement to fixed-route systems [42 U.S.C. § 12143]. It bans new construction that is not handicap-accessible and requires alterations to be handicap-accessible [42 U.S.C. § 12183].

The implications for special education are, simply put, that one role of special education is to provide instruction to students with disabilities—no matter the nature or extent of disability—on the use of public transportation systems. There is no reason to prohibit discrimination in the systems if, at the same time, students are not taught how to use them.

Telecommunications

The ADA requires all telecommunications services to offer relay services for hearing-impaired and speech-impaired individuals, as well as the closed-captioning of public service announcements. Thus, companies offering telephone service to the general public must offer telephone relay services to individuals who use telecommunications devices for the deaf (TDDs) or similar devices.

Here again, the role of special education seems clear. It is to provide instruction on the use of telecommunications systems to all students, especially those with hearing or speech impairments.

Enforcement and Remedies

The ADA creates separate enforcement procedures and remedies for each of the major areas in which it prohibits discrimination [42 U.S.C. §§ 12117, 12133, 12188, 12205, 12212, 12213].

- In employment, an individual may file a complaint with the U.S. Equal Employment Opportunity Commission and take appeals from it to court. If the individual wins the complaint, the remedies include back pay and court orders to stop discrimination [42 U.S.C. § 12117].
- In public services (state and local government operations), an individual may file a complaint with federal agencies that the U.S. Attorney General will designate or bring private lawsuits to recover actual damages and obtain court orders to prohibit further discrimination [42 U.S.C. § 12133].
- In public accommodations, an individual may seek a court order to prohibit discrimination but may not obtain money damages; the individual also may file a complaint with the Attorney General, who then may file a lawsuit to stop discrimination and also to obtain money damages and penalties [42 U.S.C. § 12188].
- In transportation, individuals may file complaints with the U.S. Department of Transportation or bring private lawsuits to prohibit discrimination. In telecommunications, the individual may file complaints with the U.S. Federal Communications Commission to prohibit discrimination.

ADA and IDEA are similar in their approaches to remedies. Both require a complainant to use administrative, quasi-judicial remedies, and both open the federal courts' doors to complainants (see Chapter 10).

Attorneys' Fees

Any individual who prevails in any complaint or lawsuit against an entity covered by ADA may recover the attorneys' fees incurred in connection with the complaint and lawsuit [42 U.S.C. § 12205]. This is the same rule adopted by IDEA (under the Handicapped Children's Protection Act, discussed in Chapter 10).

Alternative Dispute Resolution

ADA encourages, but does not require the use of, alternative means of resolving disputes, including settlement negotiations, conciliation, facilitation, mediation, fact-finding, minitrial, and arbitration [42 U.S.C. § 12212]. As Chapter 9 points out, IDEA also encourages alternative dispute resolution.

Exemptions

The insurance industry is exempt from ADA's provisions.

State Immunity

One of the most hotly contested issues before the United States Supreme Court during the last five years of the millenium has been the issue of federalism. As we pointed out earlier in this chapter when we discussed the Court's 1999 decision in *Olmstead v. L.C.*, a majority of the Court (five of the current Justices) are exceedingly keen to assert the federalism principle and thereby to curb what they see to be an unwarranted (and, to them, undesirable) expansion of federal control over the lives of citizens of the states.

The federalism issue comes into play in disability policy in several important cases. In Chapter 9, we discuss the Court's interpretation of the Developmental Disabilities Assistance and Bill of Rights Act in *Pennhurst State School and Hospital v. Halderman* (1984). But, more to the point here, the federalism issues come into play with respect to ADA.

ADA makes it clear that no state is immune, under the Eleventh Amendment to the federal Constitution, from any lawsuits filed under ADA. The question arises as to whether this provision means that a person with a disability may sue a state, under ADA, in either federal or state court.

That is not a frivolous question for several reasons. First, the Court explicitly has left that issue unresolved. It took that position in *Pennsylvania Department of Corrections v. Yeskey* (1998). There, the issue was whether ADA protected a person with a disability who is imprisoned in a state facility. Stated alternatively, the issue was whether ADA applied to the state prison system.

The Court had no difficulty saying that ADA does apply to the state prison system: Title II of ADA plainly says that the ADA protects people from discrimination in any service, program, or activity of a public entity, and the operation of a state prison system is such a service, program, or activity. Thus, ADA, Title II, applies to the prison system.

What is remarkable about the *Yeskey* decision, however, is what the Court said at the very end of its short decision: The Court does not address the issue of whether ADA is a constitutional exercise of Congress' power under either the Commerce Clause or under the Fourteenth Amendment. By not addressing that issue, the Court left the issue wide open for later decision.

In 1999, the Court revisited the issue of state sovereign immunity in three cases. These three—*Alden v. Maine*, *College Savings Bank v. Florida Prepaid Postsecondary Education Expense Board*, and *Florida Prepaid Postsecondary Education*

Expense Board v. College Savings Bank—raised the issue of whether Congress (in two different statutes) abrogated (overturned) a state's sovereign immunity and allowed a citizen to sue, under the federal statutes, a state in its own courts. Stated alternatively, under what conditions may Congress authorize a citizen to sue a state for a violation of a federal law and to bring the suit in a state court?

The issue had been hinted at by the Court's earlier decision, in *Seminole Tribe of Florida v. Florida* (1996). There, the Court held that Congress may not authorize a citizen to sue a state, in federal court, unless Congress has authority to abrogate the state's sovereign immunity from suit or unless the state consents to the suit. In that case, the Court found that Congress did not sufficiently abrogate the state's sovereign immunity and the state did not consent to be sued in federal court.

The question left unanswered by the case was what the Court would do when confronted with a case where Congress authorizes a citizen to sue a state in state court for a violation of a federal law. That was, however, precisely the issue raised in the three cases the Court decided in 1999: the *Alden* case and the two *College Savings Bank* cases (In Chapter 9, we discuss the ability of a citizen to sue a state official in federal or state court—that is, a suit against an individual, not against the state itself).

In those three cases, the Court held that the federal statutes in question did not give a citizen the right to sue a state in its own court for a violation of a federal statute. Before Congress may set aside a state's immunity from a lawsuit for a violation of a federal law, either of two conditions must exist. First, Congress must explicitly abrogate the state's sovereign immunity and must have authority to do so; or, second, the state itself must consent to be sued.

Notice the language of the first condition: Congress must explicitly abrogate the state's immunity and have authority to do so. The "authority to do so" was the dispositive factor in the Maine and Florida cases. Both dealt with business matters: the *Alden* case, with the right of an employee of the state to sue for a violation of the federal Fair Labor Standards Act, and the *College Savings Bank* cases, with the right of the state or a private business to sue each other under the Trademark Remedy Clarification Act or under the Patent and Plant Variety Protection Remedy Clarification Act.

In decisions that undoubtedly will be regarded as redefining the nature of federalism, the Court held that Congress simply lacked authority to provide, under any of the three statutes, that a state may be sued, in its own courts, for a violation of these business-related statutes.

When, then, may Congress abrogate a state's sovereign immunity and allow a citizen to sue a state, in its own courts, for a violation of a federal statute or a violation of the federal Constitution? Here, the Court gave an answer: First, the state is not immune and Congress can abrogate its sovereign immunity in order to enforce the Fourteenth Amendment of the federal Constitution; or, second, the state is not immune when it explicitly agrees to be sued in its own courts for a violation of a federal law or the violation of the federal Constitution.

Does ADA meet either or both of these standards? (Remember, this is the issue that the Court in *Yeskey* refused to address.) It seems so. First, ADA explicitly provides that it abrogates state immunity [42 U.S.C. § 12202]. Second, ADA also explicitly provides that it is enacted to enforce the Fourteenth Amendment [42 U.S.C. § 12101(b)]; and indeed Congress recited, in its findings of fact, that ADA is necessary to overcome the discrimination that the Court has found to be unconstitutional in race discrimination cases [42 U.S.C. § 12101(a)].

Despite these two clear provisions, however, the three 1999 decisions, coupled with the Court's refusal to deal with ADA's constitutionality in *Yeskey* (1998), make it uncertain that the Court will hold that ADA abrogates state immunity. If the Court holds that ADA does abrogate state immunity, states will be subject to suit for violations (as in *Yeskey*); if not, they will escape being sued (see Chapter 9 for further discussion of liability for violations of ADA).

In light of the three 1999 cases (the *Alden* and the two *College Savings Bank* cases), a similar issue arises with respect to IDEA. May a state be sued in either a federal or a state court for an IDEA violation? It seems so. First, IDEA abrogates state immunity [20 U.S.C. § 1403]. Second, IDEA is enacted to enforce the rights of students—historically, their rights under the Fourteenth Amendment to equal educational opportunities [20 U.S.C. § 1400(d)(ll)(B)]. Third, the states receive federal funds and thereby consent—if not explicitly, at least constructively—to IDEA's conditions, which include the condition [20 U.S.C. § 1403] that they surrender their immunity (see 20 U.S.C. § 1412 related to the conditions that IDEA imposes on the states in order to receive the federal funds).

Unfortunately, IDEA does not contain explicit language that the states consent to be sued—there is no such language as, "As a condition of receiving funds under IDEA, each state explicitly and thereby consents to be sued and to waive its sovereign immunity." Nonetheless, the fact that the states accept the federal funds and have complied with IDEA's conditions seems to be strong evidence that they do in fact waive their immunity; they "constructively" waive it.

Given the *Seminole* case (1996) and the three 1999 cases, it seems clear that ADA and IDEA both are bound to be challenged as unconstitutional. But it also seems, given that each law has an abrogation provisions and that each is enacted to enforce the Fourteenth Amendment, that they can, and should, survive that kind of challenge.

The Dream

Senator Tom Harkin of Iowa was the principal ADA sponsor in the 101st Congress, and its chief manager. What he said on the Senate floor on the date the Senate enacted ADA is worth restating here:

> Across our Nation mothers are giving birth to infants with disabilities. So I want to dedicate the Americans with Disabilities Act to these, the next generation of children and their parents. With the passage of ADA, we as a society make a pledge that every child with a disability will have the opportunity to maximize his or her potential to live proud, productive, and prosperous lives in the mainstream of our society. We love you all and welcome you into the world. We look forward to becoming your friends, our neighbors, and your co-workers. We say, whatever you decide as your goal, go for it. The doors are open and the barriers are coming down.

The Principle of Dual Accommodations ⌒

As noted early in the discussion on IDEA and the antidiscrimination laws, entitlement and antidiscrimination statutes have different but complementary purposes. Together, they create the principle of dual accommodations.

The entitlement programs create benefits for people with disabilities. These benefits are essentially in-puts to the person; they help the person respond to disability challenges inherent in the person. Thus, special education under IDEA and vocational rehabilitation under the Rehabilitation Act are techniques for blunting the effect of the disability: They are "counter-impairment" interventions. When delivered effectively, they increase the likelihood that the person will be able to accommodate to the demands a nondisabled world imposes, such as the demands to be able to learn, work, be mobile, communicate, and so on.

By contrast, the antidiscrimination laws require the nondisabled world to accommodate to the person who has a disability. Section 504 requires recipients of federal financial assistance not to discriminate and instead to make reasonable accommodations. The Americans with Disabilities Act imposes the same obligations on a much larger group of covered entities. Together, Section 504 and ADA not only create access but also require a different kind of access, one based on reasonable accommodation. With access and accommodations, the person with a disability is much more likely to be able to participate in the nondisabled world.

Together, the entitlement laws (accommodations of the person to the non-disability world) and the anti-discrimination laws (accommodations of that world to the person) create an interlocking, two-part accommodation: The person accommodates to the world, and the world accommodates to the person. This is the dual (two-part) accommodation.

Another way of viewing the principle of dual accommodations is to think in terms of civil rights. Indeed, civil rights is a core concept in disability law and policy. The very phrase "civil rights" encompasses a variety of approaches: nondiscrimination and antidiscrimination (as assured by Sec. 504 and ADA); equal treatment, equal opportunity, and accommodations to secure equal treatment and equal opportunities (again, as assured by IDEA, Sec. 504, and ADA); and even-handed treatment of similarly situated individuals (as we explain further in Chapter 3).

Other Core Concepts in Disability Law ⌒

Although the principle of dual accommodations and the concept of civil rights comprise the centerpiece of disability policy, it is by no means the only one. Other core concepts derive from or interact with IDEA, Section 504, and ADA. (Silverstein, 1998; Braddock, 1998; Levy & Rubenstein, 1996).

Several of these core concepts are closely related to the concept of civil rights. Consider that civil rights means equality before the law; the very concept of civil rights extends to people with disabilities the same rights, privileges, and immunities that are available to people who do not have disabilities. Equality is manifest in public policy in several ways.

Disabled But Not Unable

One basis for the concept of civil rights relates directly to the ways in which policy affects people with disabilities. As just noted, the purpose of IDEA and the Rehabilitation Act is to help blunt the effect of disability and create new capacities. Both are "pathology"-focused and "strength"-focused. That is to say, they target the disability, and in that respect they look at the "pathology" or "disabled" aspects of the person. At the same time, they build on the person's strengths. So one of the basic concepts of disability law is a combined pathology and strengths approach. The governing phrase is "disabled, yes; unable, no." That phrase recognizes that, although the person has an impairment, the person also has inherent strengths.

Developmental Model

In a very real way, the strengths approach adopts the developmental approach to people with disabilities. This model recognizes that all people with disabilities, no matter the nature or extent of their disabilities, have inherent capacities, including the ability to learn and be educated. IDEA reflects the developmental model, too, through its principles of zero reject and appropriate education: No child may be excluded from education, and all must be provided with a beneficial education. The consequence of zero reject and appropriate education, and of the developmental model, is reflected in the principles of IPI.

Independence, Productivity, and Inclusion—"IPI"

Not surprisingly, IDEA, the Developmental Disabilities Act, Section 504, and the Americans with Disabilities Act are consistent. IDEA seeks beneficial education and useful outcomes (see Chapter 5). The DD Act declares that the purpose of the law is to equalize the opportunities of people with disabilities to enjoy independence, productivity, and inclusion.

Building on Section 504, ADA declares that the nation's proper goals are to assure equal opportunity, full participation, independent living, and economic self-sufficiency. To these ends, and as will be pointed out in detail in Chapters 5 and 6, IDEA gives a student a right to an individualized transition plan that promotes the student's transition from school to the adult world and to the opportunities that adults without disabilities take for granted.

The core concept of independence refers to the extent to which individuals with disabilities exercise consent, control, or choice over their own lives. It also refers to the extent to which they are able to do various activities without assistance or with assistance that they control and direct. Under IDEA, for example, the student with a disability has a right to be involved in planning for transition from school to various post-school activities (see Chapters 5 and 6), and the Rehabilitation Act authorizes vocational rehabilitation services for the student, beginning as early as age 16.

Empowerment

Closely related to the concept of independence is that of empowerment. That term refers to the participation, choice, and control by families or persons with disabilities in decisions related to the services and supports they will receive from public agencies. Another way of saying this is that empowerment relates to the family's or person's participation in setting service delivery priorities and in planning, developing, implementing, and evaluating the services that a public agency delivers. Thus, IDEA provides a student's family and the student (at age 16) with various rights of participation in education decision-making (see Chapters 7 and 8).

Empowerment is not an easy concept to understand. It has several dimensions worth mentioning here, albeit briefly. When a person is empowered, the person is (a) motivated to get what he or she wants and (b) has the skills and knowledge to act on the motivation and get what he or she wants (Turnbull & Turnbull, 1997). Clearly, one dimension of empowerment, motivation, is largely psychological (Turnbull & Turnbull, 1997):

1. self-efficacy: believing in our own capacities;
2. perceived control: believing that we can apply our capabilities to affect what happens to us;
3. hope: believing we will get what we want and need;
4. energy: lighting the fire and keeping it burning; and
5. persistence: putting forth a sustained effort.

The other part of empowerment—skill and knowledge—has to do with what we do, not what we feel:

1. information: being knowledgeable and in the know;
2. problem solving: knowing how to bust the barriers that stand in the way of our getting what we want;
3. coping skills: knowing how to handle what happens to us; and
4. communication skills: being on the sending and receiving ends of expressed needs and wants (our own and others').

If special education is effective, it will develop both of these capacities by providing an appropriate education (Chapter 5) in the least restrictive environment and settings (Chapter 6).

Privacy and Confidentiality

One of the most prized rights of Americans is the right to privacy, as assured by the First and Fourteenth Amendments to the federal Constitution (the right to liberty has been interpreted by the United States Supreme Court to mean a right to privacy). IDEA carries forth this right by providing that the student's records are subject to certain confidentiality rules (see Chapter 7).

Consent, Choice, and Client Participation

A hallmark of constitutional government in the United States is that government exists by and with the consent of the governed. IDEA recognizes that special education, as a service of the government, should be consistent with the principle of government by consent, and it therefore provides for the consent of parents for evaluation and placement, their and the student's participation in evaluations and in the development of the student's educational program through the right to an IEP, and the family's right to be involved in the development of early education programs for the child through individualized family service plan (IFSP) (described in Chapters 3 and 5).

Liberty

The concept of liberty relates to one's right to be free from physical restraint or other types of confinement. Of course, the state always may confine people who are dangerous to others. That is one of the purposes of and functions served by the criminal law (imprisonment following conviction) or by the civil commitment law (confinement in a state hospital because of dangerousness to self or others).

In IDEA, however, the concept of liberty emerges in a rather interesting way. Some students display behaviors that may impede their learning or that of others; their behaviors also may cause injury to themselves or to others. As we point out in Chapter 3, IDEA has special provisions related to these students—provisions that deal with school discipline and school interventions (see the sections of Chapter 3 related to discipline and to positive behavioral supports and interventions). These IDEA provisions basically address the issue of liberty—the right of the student to remain physically unconfined and to benefit from education.

Protection from Harm

Another right of people with disabilities is to be protected against harm while they are in state custody. For example, a student with a disability has the right to be free of harm imposed by school staff and even other students while in school. This right exists under both IDEA and other federal laws (as we point out in Chapter 9).

Individualized and Appropriate Services

To assure ADA and DD Act outcomes, federal law requires individualized benefits. Under IDEA, the individualization rule is reflected in various student-centered plans and programs; likewise, Rehabilitation Act services also must be individualized (see Chapters 3 through 6). Moreover, the due process principle requires that government make individual determinations when allocating benefits and burdens. This constitutional principle avoids the "meat-ax" approach of treating all students with disabilities exactly alike (see Chapter 7).

Capacity-Based Services

One of the consequences of regarding individuals with disabilities and their families as having strengths ("disabled but not unable"—see above) is that services should enhance the capacities of the person and family, not merely address their needs (sometimes called "deficits"). Thus, for example, IDEA provides for an individually tailored program for infants and their families (Part C, early intervention, infants and toddlers, ages birth to 3) and for students (ages 3 through 21). The program is called the Individualized Family Services Plan (IFSP) for infants and toddlers, and the Individualized Education Program (IEP) for students (3–21). In each case, the services are based, in part, on what the infant-toddler and family, or the student, can do, not just on what they need (see Chapter 5).

Priority based on Severity

Until it was amended in 1997, IDEA provided that the federal funds authorized to implement it were to be spent according to a priority: first, on those students not in school and, second, on those in school who have the highest need (or greatest degree of disability). The 1997 amendments eliminated the requirement because, by 1997 (in contrast to 1975, when IDEA was first enacted) there were no students not in public school and because by 1997 the schools had developed a rather impressive ability to serve students who had great educational needs. Nonetheless, the priority based on capacity criterion still is part of federal law. For example, the Rehabilitation Act authorizes supported employment services for individuals who have the greatest needs (supported employment means working for at least the minimum wage for at least 20 hours a week, with support, with or among individuals who do not have a disability).

Productivity

Madeleine Will, Assistant Secretary of Education from 1983 through 1989, often has said that the implied promise of special education is a job. Granting that her statement is accurate (and no responsible people dispute it), IDEA clearly seeks to build the capacities of people with disabilities so they can take their place in the workforce of America. It does this not only by the general principles of appropriate education and least restrictive placement but also by providing for the education of youth up to age 21 (see Chapter 3) and by providing for the employment of people with disabilities in special education programs (see Chapter 5).

Inclusion

A hallmark of the civil rights principle is equality before the law. As we point out in Chapters 3 and 6, and as we noted earlier in this chapter, segregation on account of disability has a long and horrific history. Whatever altruistic and habilitative purposes the state institutions originally served or were meant to serve, that purpose soon was perverted as the institutions became nothing more than warehouses— places where people with disabilities were kept out of sight and often out of mind (Blatt, 1966, 1970, 1973, 1976).

A cardinal purpose of IDEA as enacted in 1975 and as strengthened in 1997 is to assure that students with disabilities do not experience unwarranted segregation in school (see Chapter 6). A stated purpose of ADA is to assure that students have access to the community—that is to say, a right against segregation and a right to integration and inclusion in society.

As we pointed out earlier in this chapter, the United States Supreme Court, in the *L.C.* case, interpreted the ADA to advance the principle of inclusion. It also allowed the state to raise a defense of "fundamental alterations." Thus, the ADA provides a qualified right to inclusion in community-based settings, where the other option is placement in institutional settings.

Family Integrity and Unity

Family integrity and unity refers to preserving and strengthening the family as the core unit of society, maintaining it intact, assuring the services the family needs and making sure that the services respond to the needs of the family as a whole (not just the needs of the student with a disability), coordinating services on the family's behalf, and responding to the family in ways that are culturally appropriate to the family.

Many federal laws seek to keep families together, recognizing that the family is the most important and the basic structure of civilization. In IDEA, the effort to maintain the family's participation in the student's education is the sixth major principle: parent participation. And the principle of the least restrictive alternative also is relevant to this effort in that it seeks to have children with disabilities educated in the community and thereby in settings where they can continue to live with their families. Moreover, IDEA's provision for home-based education as an alternative in the continuum of services explicitly recognizes the desirability of having children educated in the care of their families so that families may stay unified and not have to place the child into an institution.

Service Coordination and Collaboration

Because a student with a disability can benefit not only from educational but also from other services (such as health, mental health, social service, and advocacy services), a core concept is service coordination (across providers) and collaboration (among providers and between providers and the family and student). IDEA advances this core concept by requiring a statewide system of education and a statewide system of early intervention; and by requiring (especially in early intervention (ages birth to 3) and in transition (ages 16 through 21)) that the schools and other providers will coordinate their activities (see Chapter 5). In addition, IDEA requires schools to collaborate with parents and students (see Chapter 8).

Cultural Responsiveness

As we note in Chapter 4, a disproportionately large number of students in special education are from culturally, ethnically, and linguistically minority backgrounds. For this reason, and also to assure that services to these students and their families are effective, a core concept in disability policy, and in IDEA itself, is that services should be provided by culturally appropriate means, including in the dominant language of the student's family. In Chapter 4, we will describe how cultural, ethnic, and linguistic differences are required to be accommodated so a student is classified into special education on account of educational need, not cultural, ethnic, or linguistic traits.

Accountability

The Constitution provides for procedural safeguards, and the IDEA simply describes those safeguards as applicable to the education of children with disabilities (see Chapter 7). Moreover, the 1986 amendment of IDEA, granting the prevailing party in a due process hearing or appeal from such a hearing the right to recover attorneys' fees, is a more recent statement of the concept of accountability and due process.

Prevention and Amelioration

A large number of disabilities, and many of the conditions that aggravate a disability, are caused by social or environmental conditions. Only a few disabilities are organic and caused by biological or inherent conditions in a person. Because of this, many federal laws seek to prevent, cure (absolutely reverse), or ameliorate (reduce the effects of) a disability.

Clearly, IDEA is consistent with those laws. By its principle of zero reject, it seeks to open the doors of education and its ameliorating effects to all children. By its principles of appropriate education and the least restrictive environment, it seeks to provide educational benefit in the community instead of deprivation—absolute or relative, it does not matter—by institutional placement. By its principle of parent participation, and especially through the IFSP for children from birth through age 2 and the provision of some related services for families, it seeks to ensure that families themselves receive some benefits from the child's education and that their circumstances, which sometimes can add to the child's disability, receive some attention, too.

Advocacy and Advocates

Accountability and due process will not be obtained unless parents and students with disabilities have advocates. IDEA's procedural safeguards (e.g., the right to a surrogate parent, the right of natural and surrogate parents to consent to certain procedures such as evaluation and placement and to have a due process hearing if they and the schools disagree about the child's right to a free appropriate public education, and the right to recover counsel fees if prevailing in due process hearing or appeal [see Chapter 7] are explicit recognitions that advocacy and advocates are essential to enforcement of the child's educational rights.

Normalization

The doctrines of normalization, social role valorization, integration, mainstreaming, and the least restrictive alternative are reflections of the constitutional doctrine of equal protection (see Chapter 6), altruism (an effort to bring persons with disabilities into a more "normal" way of life, where they can be more valued as contributing citizens), and deinstitutionalization (an effort to provide community-based, integrated education instead of programs in segregated institutional settings). The fourth major principle of IDEA—education in the least restrictive environment—sets forth the presumption that children with disabilities will be educated to the maximum extent appropriate with children who do not have disabilities.

Conclusion ~

The major concepts of federal law and service delivery are based on entitlements to services and rights against discrimination, and they seek consistent outcomes.

It now is appropriate to describe the constitutional foundations for IDEA and then, in detail, each of IDEA's six principles. These are, after all, the legal techniques that assure that the students, and their schools, are moving toward the national outcomes and putting these concepts into place.

Notes ~

1. The early documentation of discrimination in education on the basis of disability is set out best in "The Exclusion of Children with Special Needs," in *Children Out of School in America: A Report of the Children's Defense Fund, Washington Research Project, Inc.* (Washington, DC: Children's Defense Fund, 1974).

   An early criticism of special education policy and practices is found in Milofsky, "Why Special Education Isn't Special," 44 *Harvard Education Review*, 437 (1974).

   The earliest cases striking down discrimination through pure and functional exclusion, discrimination in classification, and discrimination through other school policies and practices are *PARC v. Commonwealth, Mills v. D.C. Board of Education, Wolf v. Legislature of Utah, Maryland Association for Retarded Children (MARC) v. Maryland, North Carolina Association for Retarded Children v. North Carolina, Tidewater Ass'n. for Autistic Children v. Tidewater Bd. of Ed., LeBanks v. Spears, David P. v. State Dept. of Ed., Larry P. v. Riles, Hobson v. Hansen, Guadalupe Org., Inc. v. Tempe Elem. School Dist., Diana v. State Bd. of Ed., Hernandez v. Porter, Mattie T. v. Holladay,* and *Lau v. Nichols.*

   Of all of these cases, two—*PARC* and *Mills*—were particularly heavily cited in, and centrally influenced, the Congressional history accompanying PL 94–142, the Education for All Handicapped Children Act (now, Individuals with Disabilities Education Act).

   For excellent early summaries of the legislative history of PL 94–142, see LaVor, "Federal Legislation for Exceptional Persons: A History," in F. Weintraub, and A. Abeson (Eds.), *Public Policy and the Education of Exceptional Children* (Reston, VA: Council for Exceptional Children, 1976); E. Boggs, "Federal Legislation Affecting the Mentally Retarded," in J. Wortis (Ed.), *Mental Retardation,* Vol. 3, (New York: Grune & Stratton, 1971); and S. Herr, "The Right to a Free Appropriate Public Education," in M. Kindred, J. Cohen, D. Penrod, and T. Shaffer, (Eds.), *The Mentally Retarded Citizen and the Law* (New York: Free Press, 1976). For a recent history of the perspective of the "insiders" behind PL 94–142, see H. R. Turnbull, and A. P. Turnbull, "The Synchrony of Stakeholders: Lessons from the Disability Rights Movement," in S. Kagan, and N. Cohen (Eds.), *Reinventing Early Care and Education* (San Francisco: Jossey-Bass, 1996).

2. References to sections of IDEA that are cited in the text in brackets [ ] are references to the Act itself, as passed by Congress, or its regulations. If the reference is to the current law, PL 105–17 (1997), the reference does not contain a date. If it is to a previous version of IDEA, it does contain a date. The Act has been codified at 20 United States Code, Sections 1400–1487. The Department of Education has issued regulations implementing the Act, codified in 34 Code of Federal Regulations, Parts 300 and 303.

The Rehabilitation Act, of which Section 504 is part, is codified at 29 United States Code, beginning at Section 706. Section 504 is codified at 29 U.S.C., Section 794. The Department of Health and Human Services has issued regulations implementing Section 504, which are codified at 30 Code of Federal Regulations, Part 104, and are cited in the text as, e.g., § 104.2.

References ~

Blatt, Burton. (1966). *Christmas in Purgatory: A Photographic Essay on Mental Retardation.* Boston: Allyn & Bacon.

Blatt, Burton. (1970). *Exodus from Pandemonium: Human Abuse and a Reformation of Public Policy.* Boston: Allyn & Bacon.

Braddock, David, et al. *The State of the States in Developmental Disabilities.* Washington, DC: American Association on Mental Retardation, 1998.

Committee Report, House of Representatives Committee on Education and The Workforce, on H.R. 5 (IDEA Amendments of 1997) (Passed as PL 105-17). H. R. Rep. No. 95, 105th Cong., 1st Sess. (1997).

Levy, Robert M., and Rubenstein, Leonard S. *The Rights of People With Mental Disabilities: The Authoritative ACLU Guide to the Rights of People with Mental Illness and Mental Retardation.* Carbondale and Edwardsville: Southern Illinois University Press, 1996.

Silverstein, Robert. *Our Nation's Emerging Disability Policy.* In press, 1998.

Turnbull, A. P., and Turnbull, H. R. (1997). *Families, Professionals, and Exceptionality: A Special Partnership.* Columbus: Merrill/Prentice Hall.

Cases ~

Albertsons, Inc. v. Kirkingburg, No. 98–591 (U.S. Supreme Court, June 22, 1999), 143 F.3d 1228 (9th Cir. 1998).

Alden v. Maine, No. 98-436 (U.S. Supreme Court, June 23, 1999), 715 A.2d 172 (Me. 1998).

Bragdon v. Abbott, 118 S.Ct. 2196, 524 U.S. 624 (1998).

College Savings Bank v. Florida Prepaid Postsecondary Education Expense Board, No. 98–149 (U.S. Supreme Court, June 23, 1999), 131 F.3d 353 (3d Cir. 1997).

Florida Prepaid Postsecondary Education Expense Board v. College Savings Bank, No. 98–531 (U.S. Supreme Court, June 23, 1999), 148 F.3d 1343 (Fed. Cir. 1998).

Mills v. D.C. Bd. of Educ., 348 F. Supp. 866 (D.D.C. 1972), contempt proceedings, EHLR 551:643 (D.C. 1980).

Murphy v. United Parcel Service, Inc., No. 97–1992 (U.S. Supreme Court, June 22, 1999), 141 F.3d 1185 (10th Cir. 1998).

Olmstead v. L.C., No. 98–536 (U.S. Supreme Court, June 22, 1999), 138 F.3d 893 (11th Cir. 1998).

Parham v. J.R., 442 U.S. 584 (1979).

Pennhurst State School and Hospital v. Halderman, 465 U.S. 89 (1984).

Pennsylvania Ass'n for Retarded Children (PARC) v. Pennsylvania, 334 F. Supp. 1257 (E.D.Pa 1971); 343 F. Supp 279 (E.D.Pa 1972).

Pennsylvania Department of Corrections v. Yeskey, 524 U.S. 206, 118 S.Ct. 1952 (1998).

School Bd. of Nassau County v. Arline, 480 U.S. 273, 107 S.Ct. 1123 (1987).

Seminole Tribe of Florida v. Florida, 517 U.S. 44 (1996).

Southeastern Community College v. Davis, 442 U.S. 397 (1979).

Sutton v. United Air Lines, Inc., No. 97–1943 (U.S. Supreme Court, June 22, 1999), 130 F.3d 893 (10th Cir. 1997).

Wyatt v. Stickney, 325 F. Supp. 781 (M.D. Ala. 1971), 344 F. Supp. 373 (M.D. Ala. 1972). This case has a long history and is ongoing. The most recent filing in the case is *Wyatt by & Through Rawlins v. Rogers*, U.S. Dist. LEXIS 7429 (M.D. Ala. 1998).

Part 2

The Six
Major Principles

3
Zero Reject

Nothing is clearer in IDEA than Congress's intent to include all children with disabilities in school and to require all state agencies to follow a policy of zero reject. Finding (as the *PARC* and *Mills* courts did) that both total and functional exclusion existed [20 U.S.C. §§ 1400 (c)(2)(B) and (C)] and concluding that it was in the national interest to provide programs to meet the needs of children with disabilities and thereby assure them equal protection of the law [20 U.S.C. § 1400 (c)(6)], Congress declared that IDEA's purpose is to ensure that all children with disabilities receive a free appropriate public education [20 U.S.C. § 1400 (d)(1)(A)].

Individuals with
Disabilities Education Act

Ages Covered

IDEA requires states to provide full educational opportunities to all children with disabilities between the ages of 3 and 21 [20 U.S.C. § 1412 (a)(1)(A)]. This general rule has a longstanding exception: States need not obey it if a state law, practice, or court order is inconsistent with these requirements [20 U.S.C. § 1412 (a)(1)(B)(i)] respecting the provision of public education to children aged 3 to 5 and 18 through 21. In a very real sense, the exception pays deference to the tradition of state and local autonomy over education. This provision recognizes that the states themselves should have some autonomy in educating their own citizens.

The 1997 amendments to IDEA added another exception to IDEA's eligibility rules: Students between the ages of 18 and 21 who are incarcerated in adult prisons are not entitled to services in prison if their disability was not identified or if they did not have an IEP before they were incarcerated [20 U.S.C. § 1412(a)(1)(B)(ii)].

Despite the state-local autonomy principle, courts have consistently held that IDEA, coupled with state law and Section 504, entitles students with disabilities to remain in school beyond the age at which nondisabled students' right to education expires (*Evans v. Tuttle* (Indiana Sup. Ct., 1993; *Helms v. Indep. School Dist. No. 3 of Broken Arrow* (1985)).

Early Intervention: "Zero to Three"

A different example of state autonomy exists under IDEA. A state may (or may not) choose to provide federally assisted services to infants and toddlers and their families. If it chooses to do so, it may receive federal funds under IDEA's early intervention provisions.

In 1986, Congress, through PL 99–457, extended IDEA benefits to infants and toddlers, from birth to age 3. It did this by enacting what currently is known as "Part C" of IDEA [20 U.S.C. §§ 1431-1445], formerly known as Part H. As members of Congress made clear when they were enacting Part C, the legislation is a "pro-family" bill. The focus of Part C is on the infant and toddler with a disability and his or her family [20 U.S.C. § 1431]. This is very different from Part B [20 U.S.C. §§ 1411–1419], which provides for the free appropriate public education of children (3–21) with disabilities and focuses primarily on providing services to the student and only minimally on serving a student's parent(s).

Moreover, Part C is motivated by concerns that are broader than those that persuaded Congress to enact Part B. As pointed out in Chapter 2, Congress intended, when it enacted IDEA in 1975, to accomplish four purposes:

1. Assure that all students with disabilities have a right to a free appropriate public education.
2. Protect the rights of the students and their parents in securing such an education.
3. Assist state and local education agencies to provide for the education of all such students.
4. Assess and assure the effectiveness of state and local efforts to educate those students.

By the time Congress enacted Part C, however, it had become far more sophisticated in declaring its reasons and purposes. For one thing, it is perfectly clear from the legislative history of Part C that Congress has been convinced that early intervention services are cost-effective. Similar evidence simply was not available when Congress enacted Part B in 1975.

In addition, Part C sets five goals that are different and more comprehensive than Part B, as follows:

1. Develop the capacities of infants and toddlers and minimize their potential for developmental delays.
2. Reduce the costs of special education.
3. Minimize the likelihood that people with disabilities will be institutionalized.
4. Enhance families' capacities for working with their children.
5. Enhance the capacities of state and local agencies and service providers to identify, evaluate, and meet the needs of historically underrepresented populations [20 U.S.C. § 1431 (a)].

Part C provides separate funding for the education of infants and toddlers (ages zero to 3). Infants and toddlers who qualify for the services must need early intervention because they either (a) experience developmental delays or (b) have diagnosed physical or mental conditions that carry a high probability of causing developmental delays [20 U.S.C. § 1432 (5)]. In addition, each state and local education agency has the option of serving infants and toddlers who are "at-risk" of experiencing substantial developmental delays if they do not receive early intervention.

Developmental delays must be in the following areas of development: cognitive, physical, language and speech, psychosocial, or self-help. The states may otherwise define "developmental delay" but must include delays in the enumerated areas of development [20 U.S.C. § 1432(3)]. To contrast the broad eligibility provisions of Part C (zero to 3) with Part B (ages 3 through 21) is important. Under Part B, only children and youth beyond age 9 who actually have disabilities that cause a need for special education are entitled to the benefits of the law. Part B does not include the 3- to 9-year-olds who are "at-risk" students [20 U.S.C. § 1401(3)(B)].

Under Part C, early intervention services are those that:

— are designed to meet the infant's needs in any one or more of certain areas of development (physical, cognitive, communication/language and speech, social and emotional, and adaptive/self-help);
— comply with state standards;
— include at least 14 different types of intervention, provided by qualified personnel;
— are designed to meet the family's needs related to enhancing the child's development in the stated areas, selected in collaboration with the parents;
— are provided under public supervision by qualified personnel;
— are provided in conformity with an individualized family service plan (IFSP);
— are free unless the state establishes a sliding-fee scale of payment [20 U.S.C. § 1432(4)]. (Part C allows the state and local agencies to establish a system of payments for early intervention services, including a sliding-fee schedule. Certain services must be free; these include child-find, evaluation and assessment, case management, and certain administrative and coordinative functions. If state law provides for free early intervention services, however, state law prevails and a state may not use the federal law as permission to charge fees);
— are provided, to the maximum extent appropriate, in natural environments, including the home, and in community settings in which children without disabilities participate.

The 14 different types of intervention are:

1. Family training, counseling, and home visits
2. Special instruction
3. Speech-language pathology and audiology

4. Occupational therapy
5. Physical therapy
6. Psychological services
7. Service coordination services
8. Medical services for diagnostic and evaluation purposes
9. Early identification, screening, and assessment services
10. Health services necessary to help the infant or toddler to benefit from the other intervention services
11. Social work services
12. Vision services
13. Assistive technology devices and assistive technology services
14. Transportation and related costs that are necessary for the infant, toddler, or infant or toddler's family to receive another service [20 U.S.C. § 1432 (4)(E)].

Professionals implementing Part C have new or expanded roles and responsibilities with respect to families. They are expected to consult and train parents, participate in family assessment and IFSP development, provide case management and service coordination, provide psychological and social work services, and offer special instruction to the child and related information to the parents. This list of services is not exhaustive; other services, such as respite and additional family-support services, may be provided.

Part C expands not only the services professionals must offer but also who may offer them. The personnel authorized to provide these services include those who have qualified as special educators, speech-language pathologists, audiologists, occupational therapists, physicians, physical therapists, psychologists, social workers, nurses, nutritionists, family therapists, and orientation and mobility specialists [20 U.S.C. § 1432 (4)(F)].

Transition and Aging Out of School

Just as Congress recognized the importance of early intervention, so it has recognized the importance of another stage in a student's life: "transition" or "aging out." This is the stage in which the student, usually in the late-teen years, begins to plan for graduation or other departure from school (dropping out, even).

Beginning in 1983, again in 1986, and most recently in the 1997 amendments to IDEA, Congress expressed its concerns that far too many students were exiting special education and entering the adult world without the competence to be employed or otherwise live as nondisabled peers ordinarily live. As we will explain in Chapter 5, the transition provisions are extensive. The point to emphasize here, however, is that they, like the early intervention provisions, are explicitly outcome-oriented and result-focused.

Having recognized before the 1997 amendments that students were leaving special education unprepared to lead productive lives as independent citizens in the mainstream, and having recognized in the 1997 amendments that special education can and must do a better job of providing effective services that lead to the students taking their place as productive citizens, Congress now requires state and local education agencies to carry out specific duties when a student attains the age of 14 (again, see Chapter 5).

The decision of Congress to emphasize transition is consistent with its decision in 1986 to amend the Rehabilitation Act to create a supported-employment program for people with severe disabilities (see Chapter 2 for a discussion of the Act). Supported employment substantially changes the notion of vocational rehabilitation services. Traditionally, vocational rehabilitation services were targeted to individuals with mild to moderate disabilities who, with short-term interventions (evaluation and training), could return to work and not require much, if any, further vocational rehabilitation service. The supported employment program, in contrast, focuses vocational rehabilitation services on people with severe disabilities, who, with continuous vocational rehabilitation services (as contrasted with short-term services), can work in competitive employment with support from a job coach. By combining IDEA's focus on transition with the Rehabilitation Act's focus on supported employment, Congress attempted to ensure that special education would have lasting benefits for all students, especially those with severe disabilities.

Comprehensive Coverage

IDEA applies to public elementary and secondary LEAs and IEUs (intermediate educational units) [20 U.S.C. § 1412 (a)(11)], private schools [20 U.S.C. § 1412 (a)(10)], publicly operated residential facilities that provide elementary or secondary education [20 U.S.C. § 1412 (a)(11)], and charter schools [20 U.S.C. § 1413 (a)(5)]. By providing for such comprehensive coverage, Congress obviously intended to prevent "service gaps" or "cracks," reaching all children without regard to the nature of the educational system by which they are or should be served. In addition, students with disabilities are citizens of a state that receives IDEA funding, so these students should benefit from the law and federal aid wherever they are served or live within the state. Otherwise they are not treated as full citizens of the state.

Private School Placement

Several factors make private school placement problematic under IDEA. One relates to the choices that LEAs make. The other relates to choices that parents make.

With respect to the choices that LEAs make, it is well to bear in mind that historically, and even in the late 1990s, some LEAs have not been or are not now always able or willing to provide an appropriate education to every child. Instead, they usually contract with private schools to educate children whom the LEAs do not want to serve. These children become the beneficiaries of the contract between the LEA and the private school; accordingly, they are entitled to the full benefits of IDEA. Thus, if an LEA places a child in a private school as its way of discharging its IDEA duties to that child, the child's IDEA rights follow him or her to the private placement. Otherwise the LEA could divest itself of its duties to the child by making a private school placement. The child is a citizen of the state and is entitled to benefit from IDEA in the same manner as any other citizen of the state.

With respect to the choices that parents make, it is well to bear in mind that some parents simply do not want their children to be educated in public schools. Some of those parents are willing to absorb the entire cost of private education. Most, however, seek to shift the cost to the LEA that their child would attend if not enrolled in private school.

Thus, students who are enrolled in private schools are in one of two categories: those placed in private schools by public agencies and those enrolled in private schools by their parents. With this background, it is now appropriate to discuss the two types of placements.

Placement by public agencies Specific requirements apply to children placed in private schools by public agencies. These children must (a) be provided with special education and related services (b) in conformance with their individualized education program (c) at no cost to their parents [20 U.S.C. §§ 1412 (a)(10)(B)(i) and 34 C.F.R. § 300.401(a)]. Moreover, when the agency makes such a placement or referral, the state must have determined previously that the private school or facility meets the state standards and that the child retains all rights under IDEA [20 U.S.C. § 1412 (a)(10)(B)(ii) and 34 C.F.R. §§ 300.401(b), (c)].

Placement by parents ("elective") Within the general category of placements by parents are two types: "elective" and "nonelective". The term *elective placement* describes a placement that parents make on their own and solely because they prefer their child to be educated in a private school. The parents act under no compulsion to make an elective placement; they freely elect it. This type of placement advances the longstanding legal principle that parents have the right and duty to rear their children as they want to rear them, just as long as they educate them and thereby do not violate the state's truancy and child neglect laws.

The general rule regarding elective private school placement by parents is that, to the extent consistent with the number and location of children in the state who are enrolled by their parents in private elementary and secondary schools, provision will be made for their participation in the state program by furnishing them special education and related services [20 U.S.C. § 1412 (a)(10)(A)]. In providing these services, the LEA is required to provide an amount of funds from its IDEA subgrant (from the state) that is of the same proportion as the number of private school children with disabilities in its jurisdiction is to the total number of children with disabilities in its jurisdiction [20 U.S.C. § 1412 (a)(10)(A)(i)(I); 34 C.F.R. §§ 300.452, 300.453]. This provision has the purpose of limiting a state's and an LEA's financial exposure to private school placements that could absorb (and in the past did absorb) a great deal of a state's and an LEA's special education funds (because private schools traditionally are more expensive than public schools).

An advantage of the elective placement is that it advances parental choice. A disadvantage is that the parents surrender IDEA rights. This is so because no private school child who was electively enrolled has an individual right to receive some or all of the special education and related services that the child would receive if enrolled in a public school [20 U.S.C. § 1412 (a)(10)(A); 34 C.F.R. § 300.454 (a)]. Instead, each LEA must consult with representatives of private school children with disabilities in light of available funding (under the proportionate expenditure rule), the number of private school children with disabilities, the needs of private school children with disabilities, and their location to decide: (a) which children will receive services; (b) what services will be provided; (c) how and where the services will be provided; and (d) how the services provided will be evaluated [34 C.F.R. § 300.454 (b)]. Despite the consultation requirement, the LEA ultimately makes the final determinations on these issues [34 C.F.R. § 300.454 (b)(4)].

For each of these children who is provided services, the state education agency is responsible for ensuring, as part of its oversight duties, that a "services plan" has been completed [34 C.F.R. § 300.452 (b)]. It is, however, up to the student's LEA to develop, review, and revise these plans and ensure that representatives of the private school are involved in the planning process [34 C.F.R. § 300.454 (c)]. This services plan is much like an IEP for a child in a public school and must meet many of the same requirements [34 C.F.R. § 300.455 (b)].

Due process procedures that would be available to a family whose child is enrolled in public school do not apply for these children, though they may file a complaint to the SEA (under 34 C.F.R. §§ 300.660 - 300.662) that the SEA and the LEA have failed to comply with the requirements for providing services to electively placed students [34 C.F.R. §§ 300.457 (a), (c)]. It is important to note that, even in the case of children electively placed, all "child find" requirements still must be met (and due process rights under IDEA, for the purposes of child find and student evaluation, are retained by these children) [34 C.F.R. §§ 300.451, 300.457 (b)]. Furthermore, expenditures for child find activities may not be considered in the determination of whether the LEA has met the proportional spending requirements of 34 C.F.R. § 300.453 [34 C.F.R. § 300.453 (c)].

Placement by parents ("nonelective") Sometimes parents remove their children with disabilities from public school and place them in private schools because they believe that their children are not receiving an appropriate education in the public school. These are called "nonelective placements" because the parents do not freely choose the private placement; they must make the placement because the LEA does not provide FAPE to their children. These cases are treated somewhat different from cases in which the decision by the parents is discretionary and is not clearly a decision made to meet the child's educational needs.

If the parents of a child with a disability, who previously received special education and related services in a public school, enroll the child in a private school without consent of or referral from the LEA or SEA, a court or hearing officer may require the agency to reimburse the parents for the cost of that enrollment upon finding that the agency had not made a free appropriate public education available to the child in a timely manner and that the private placement is appropriate [20 U.S.C. § 1412 (a)(10)(C); 34 C.F.R. § 300.403 (c)]. The parents, however, also must have first attempted in good faith to work out any disagreements they have with the public agency and must have met other requirements, including proper written notice to the LEA [20 U.S.C. §§ 1412 (a)(10)(C)(iii), (iv) and 34 U.S.C. §§ 300.403 (d), (e)].

Religious Schools and the Establishment Clause

What if a parent places a child in a private religious (parochial) school and wants the student's LEA to pay for that placement? Does the LEA have to do so, and, if it does, does its payment violate the federal constitutional prohibition against church-state relationships?

The establishment clause of the First Amendment to the federal Constitution forbids state-established or state-sponsored religion. The leading case is *Lemon v. Kurtzman* (1973). There, the Supreme Court held that a federal or state government does not violate the establishment clause if its programs (1) have a secular purpose, (2) do not have the primary effect of advancing religion, and (3) do not create excessive entanglement between church and state. At the same time, IDEA provides for private-school placements and for students' participation in private schools in special education and related services. Several cases have dealt with the issue of whether a state or a local education agency may spend federal (IDEA) or state funds to pay for special education services provided on the grounds of religious schools or by faculty at those schools.

Is the establishment clause violated when a student claims the benefit of IDEA for related services provided at or by religious schools? The short answer is no. The U.S. Supreme Court has held that the establishment clause does not forbid a student from receiving, at public expense, related services while enrolled in a parochial school. The Court reasoned that the service itself is "neutral"; that is, it is part of a government program (IDEA) that is not skewed toward or supportive of religion (*Zobrest v. Catalina Foothills School Dist.*, 1993).

In the *Zobrest* case, a district court and the circuit court of appeals held that the establishment clause is violated when a deaf student receives publicly paid day-long interpreter help and the parochial school that he attends inextricably intertwines its secular education and religious training. Both courts reasoned that, for federal aid (IDEA) to be available to the student at a parochial or other religious school, the aid must have a clearly secular purpose, one that is separable from the school's religious mission.

The Supreme Court disagreed. It ruled that students who are placed in parochial schools (even if placed by their parents) may receive special education or related services provided to them there by the parochial school and at public expense.

The legal test under the *Lemon* decision for determining whether IDEA funds violate the establishment clause is one of "skewing" or "entanglement." Does the service or the public program tilt (skew) the public funding toward the religion? Stated alternatively, is the service or public program so entangled and intertwined with the religious mission of the school that the service or public program advances or furthers the school's religious mission?

In *Zobrest*, the use of federal funds to pay for an interpreter for a deaf student does not entangle the government in the religious mission of the school; it does not skew, tilt, or favor the school's religion. The interpreter does not advance the school's religious mission deliberately, nor does the student's placement there, with a publicly paid interpreter, mean that the federal aid is assisting the school as it carries out its mission of religiously based education.

In *Agostini v. Felton* (1997), the Supreme Court reiterated the *Zobrest* criteria, allowing teachers whose salary is a federal-state package to teach at parochial schools when (a) the federal aid is allocated on the basis of neutral, secular criteria; (b) the criteria neither favor nor disfavor religion; and (c) the aid is made available to both religious and secular programs on a nondiscriminatory basis. The Court held that such aid does not result in governmental indoctrination of students or teachers into any religion; it does not define its recipients by reference to religion; and it does not create an excessive entanglement of government with a church.

The *Zobrest* case involved only one student and one school. What if a state legislature enacts a law that benefits many students and many schools and does so solely to accommodate their religion and to fund their special education in religious schools? That was the issue in *Bd. of Educ. of Kiryas Joel Village School Dist. v. Grumet* (1994). There, the state legislature redrew school district lines to create a school district that was exactly contiguous with the boundaries of a separate religious community of Hasidic Jews. Under this redistricting, public money (including IDEA funds) would fund a district that was to educate only the children of that religious community.

Consistent with the *Zobrest* decision, the New York State Court of Appeals held that state law created a distinct school district solely to accommodate a separatist, exclusionary religious community, had the inevitable effect of advancing a religious belief, and was deliberately and unconstitutionally skewed toward that belief. The U.S. Supreme Court agreed.

What is the upshot of the *Zobrest*, *Agostini*, and *Grumet* cases? Predictably (in an area of law as complex as the establishment clause and in a statute so expensive to the state to carry out as IDEA), there are several distinguishable lines of cases.

One line holds that various types of instructional and related services may be provided to students in parochial schools without violating the establishment clause. The schools do not violate the establishment clause when they use IDEA money to provide the following services in parochial schools:

1. Transportation between parochial and public schools (where the student receives services in both settings) (*Felter v. Cape Girardeau School Dist.*, 1993).
2. Remedial classes delivered in a mobile unit located on the grounds of a parochial school involving only secular subjects (*Walker v. San Francisco Unified School Dist.*, 1995).
3. A consulting teacher and teaching aide to a student enrolled in a parochial school (*Russman v. Sobol*, 1996).
4. Occupational therapy for a student enrolled in a parochial school (*Natchez-Adams School Dist. v. Searing*, 1996).

These services are essentially neutral and do not entangle the public and IDEA money with a religion. They are indeed just the kind of services that were at issue in *Zobrest* and that the Supreme Court held to be religiously neutral. By contrast, they are quite unlike—in degree and purpose—the entanglement that was so evident in *Grumet*.

The second line of cases involves the withdrawal of services from children in parochial schools (as differentiated from the furnishing of services to them). For example, the court in *Natchez-Adams* held that an LEA could not coerce parents into enrolling their child in public school by offering related services at the public school but retracting those services if the student attends a private school. That "take-it-or-leave-it" approach limits the child's education and impinges on the parents' right to practice their own religion freely.

A third line of cases involves a financial inducement for public school (LEA) placement. The court in *K.R. v. Anderson Community School Corp.* (1996) held that a student enrolled in a parochial school is not entitled to receive the services of a full-time instructional aide. In that case, an Indiana school district offered not only transportation, occupational therapy, and speech therapy to the student but also an instructional aide—but only if the student were to remain in the public school. When the student's parents enrolled her in a parochial school, the school district withdrew the offer of the instructional aide but continued to provide transportation, occupational therapy, and speech therapy.

The issue was whether the school district had to provide the instructional aide in the private school. The court said no, because (a) the district already was providing so much to benefit the student, and (b) regulations implementing IDEA's private-placement provisions [34 C.F.R. §§ 300.451-300.452] allowed the school district a great deal of discretion in providing private school-based services. Indeed, those regulations require only that the district provide comparable service to private-school students; they do not have to provide identical services. The district accordingly is entitled to exercise its discretion regarding whether to provide the instructional aide, and it may take into account the costs of doing so.

The *Anderson* case is not so much an "establishment" case as a "school discretion/cost consideration" case. Although it did involve services in a parochial school, it also involved a costly service that seemed unnecessary for the student to receive an educational benefit. In this respect it was unlike the *Zobrest* line of cases, in all of which the service was necessary to enable the student to benefit. Thus, that one specific service need not be provided, as the comparability test, coupled with cost considerations, forgives the school from providing it. Indeed, it seems that, if the school had provided the service, even this court would have held, consistent with *Zobrest*, that the services did not violate the establishment clause. After all, it did not find that the other services (transportation, occupational therapy, and speech therapy) violated that clause. The new regulations address this issue in 34 C.F.R. § 300.453(d), which states that the SEA/LEA is not prohibited from providing services to private school children with disabilities in excess of those otherwise required.

A fourth line of cases, expressed by the court in *Cefalu v. East Baton Rouge Parish School Bd.* (1997), involves the application of a three-part test to determine whether the LEA must provide services to a unilaterally placed student at a private sectarian school. The court held that, first, the student must prove a genuine need for onsite services based on more than merely convenience; second, the burden shifts to the LEA to provide the service unless it can prove a "justifiable reason—either economic or noneconomic"—for refusing to do so. The burden of proof then shifts back to the student to prove that the district's reason for denying the service is arbitrary, irrational, or contrary to IDEA.

As reathorized in 1997, IDEA does nothing to change the line of cases involving church-state entanglement. Indeed, IDEA now provides for a "bypass provision" to allow federal funds to be used for parochial-school education. That provision [20 U.S.C. Secs. 1412(a)(10) and 1412(f)] allows the U.S. Secretary of Education to make arrangements to provide services to students in private schools if a state law prohibits the state itself from providing for those students to receive special education in certain kinds of schools (essentially, in parochial schools). This provision acknowledges that states may have enacted laws, based on state constitutional provisions assuring separation of church and state or on other grounds, that prohibit them from directing any state money to the education of students in private schools. Those laws would deny IDEA benefits to private school students with disabilities. Accordingly, IDEA contains this important by-pass provision.

As evidenced by *Zobrest* and *Agostini*, the Supreme Court is increasingly tolerant of federal-state programs being delivered on parochial school premises. The post-*Zobrest* cases (reviewed above) certainly are in good standing after *Agostini*, so it seems safe to assume that students with disabilities will continue to receive the benefits of IDEA despite their enrollment in parochial schools.

Charter Schools

Many state legislatures have enacted laws providing for the creation of charter schools. Although the state statutory schemes may vary, basically these provisions allow qualified individuals or groups who meet criteria developed by the SEA to establish public education programs ("charter schools") that are independent from other school district programs. The 1997 IDEA amendments require LEAs to serve children with disabilities in charter schools in the same manner that they serve children in other schools. Furthermore, LEAs must provide funds to charter schools in the same manner that they provide monies to other schools [20 U.S.C. § 1413(a)(5)].

Direct Services by SEA

As stated previously, the purpose of the zero-reject principle is to include every child in the educational process and ensure each student a free appropriate education. When the LEA fails to do its job, however, the SEA must remedy the problem. Section 1413 (h) of IDEA provides that an SEA must use the federal funds otherwise available to an LEA to provide services directly to children with disabilities whenever it determines that an LEA is unable or unwilling to do so, is unwilling or unable to be consolidated with another LEA, or has students who can be served best in a state or regional center. The purpose of the direct services provision is to ensure that all eligible students in a state receive a free appropriate public education; it is another one of the "gap-closing" provisions of the law.

Although use of the direct services provision preceded the Supreme Court in *Honig v. Doe* (1988), the Court left standing the court of appeals' decision that ordered the SEA (California) to provide services directly to two students who had been suspended illegally from an LEA (San Francisco).

A similar result—court-ordered direct services—was reached in *Doe v. Rockingham County School Bd.* (1987), when an LEA suspended a student who received (a) no hearing on his suspension and (b) no services for the 29 days of the suspension. The irreparable detriment that the student experienced during the 29 days and the LEA's refusal to make a hearing available were decisive facts, justifying direct services by an SEA. Similarly, when an LEA has failed to comply with a decision by a hearing officer (see Chapter 8 for a discussion of hearing officers and due process protections) for 18 months and the SEA's withholding of funds from the LEA had not produced LEA compliance with the decision for still another 18 months, an SEA may be compelled to provide services directly (*Wilson v. McDonald*, 1987).

These cases suggest that advocates will succeed in obtaining direct services if there is a long period of interrupted education, bad faith on the LEA's part (refusal to convene a hearing), or illegal action (suspending in violation of the IDEA).

Single-Agency Responsibility

Congress sought to make the zero-reject principle effective by providing for one, and only one, point of responsibility and accountability. IDEA requires a single state agency, the SEA, to be responsible for assuring that the requirements of IDEA are carried out. In addition, all special education programs within the state, including programs administered by another state or local agency (such as social welfare, mental health, mental retardation, human resources, public health, corrections, or juvenile services), are under the general supervision of the SEA, must be monitored by the SEA, and must meet the SEA's educational standards [20 U.S.C. § 1412 (a)(11)(A)].

To ensure that all children are provided a free appropriate public education, the SEA must develop interagency agreements or mechanisms for interagency coordination with other human services agencies [20 U.S.C. § 1412 (a)(12)]. These interagency agreements or mechanisms must contain provisions that address the financial responsibilities each agency has for providing education or related services.

To buttress the single-agency device for zero reject, the SEA also may reallocate funds to other LEA programs in the state that are not adequately providing an appropriate education to students in those districts [20 U.S.C. § 1411 (g)(4)] and require LEAs to consolidate their services [20 U.S.C. § 1413 (e)(1)]. There is no doubt that these provisions were designed to close the service gaps and prevent the buck-passing and responsibility-shuffling that resulted in some children being excluded from educational programs in the past.

Cost Shifting

As states attempted to implement IDEA with limited federal and state dollars (IDEA never has been funded by Congress at the full limit it authorizes—see Chapter 10 for a description of the authorization of federal funds), they found that they were facing huge expenses. States and LEAs increased their own appropriations, but funds still were not sufficient, particularly for students with severe disabilities. A major funding stream, however, existed outside of IDEA: the Medicaid program of the Social Security Act. This program provides federal funds to pay for some of the medical or medically related expenses of people with severe disabilities, who usually are required to be poor to qualify for the medical assistance funds.

To tap into the Medicaid funding stream, some states created programs that combined the special education personnel and funds under IDEA with the medical personnel and funds under the Medicaid program. By taking this approach, they could ensure enough funds in the aggregate to pay for the education and related services (such as physical therapy, occupational therapy, medical evaluations) required to provide an appropriate education to students with severe disabilities. In short, by using more than just IDEA funds, they sought to prevent either total exclusion or functional exclusion, either of which violates the zero-reject principle.

The federal agency that administers Medicaid—the Health Care Financing Agency, Department of Health and Human Services—challenged this approach and refused to reimburse Massachusetts for Medicaid dollars that it had spent for meeting the education costs of students with severe disabilities who lived in a Medicaid-approved facility. Massachusetts sued the federal government for reimbursement, and the Supreme Court, in *Bowen v. Massachusetts* (1988), approved use of the Medicaid funds for students' education.

Shortly after that decision, Congress enacted the Medicare Catastrophic Coverage Act of 1988. This law [42 U.S.C. § 1396b(c)] prohibits Medicaid agencies from refusing to pay for medical services that are (a) covered under a state's Medicaid or Medicare plans, (b) provided to children with disabilities, and (c) included in the students' individualized education programs (IEPs and IFSPs are discussed in Chapter 6). Typically, the reimbursable services include speech pathology and audiology, psychological services, physical and occupational therapy, medical counseling, and services for diagnostic and evaluation purposes.

The effect of the *Bowen* case and the Medicaid Catastrophic Coverage Act is that a new funding stream for related services exists for states that decide to combine educational programs (funded under the IDEA) with medical programs (funded under the Social Security Act's Medicaid program). This relieves the pressure on the state's educational dollars but increases the pressure on its health-care dollars. In the case of students who have medical complications or are primarily in health-care delivery systems (such as those in congregate-care facilities), the prospects are that they will receive jointly operated and jointly financed services. This could have the ultimate effect of ensuring no violation of the zero-reject rule through their total or functional exclusion from special education.

The 1997 amendments to IDEA further clarify the issue of the financial responsibility for public agency services. The amendments mandate that public agencies (including state Medicaid agencies), through interagency agreements, assume financial responsibility for services to children with disabilities before LEAs or SEAs must assume these obligations. Essentially, the interagency agreements must provide that the other public agencies are the first payors and the SEA is the payor of last resort.

Furthermore, the amendments declare that public agencies that are legally obligated under state or federal law to provide or pay for educational or related services to children with disabilities must fulfill these obligations and responsibilities [20 U.S.C. § 1412 (a)(12)(A)(i) and (B)(i)]. If public agencies fail to fulfill their responsibilities, the IDEA authorizes LEAs or SEAs to claim reimbursement for services from the public agencies that fail to provide or pay for special education or related services [20 U.S.C. § 1412 (a)(12)(B)(ii)].

Free Education; Use of Private Insurance

Schools traditionally excluded students with disabilities when they charged them fees for special services—that is, for services that were based on disability only and therefore were not provided to nondisabled students. The fees often were very high because (a) the services were expensive, or (b) the LEA wanted to discourage the students' enrollment. Under IDEA, however, if an LEA charges any fees to all students, it may charge students with disabilities as well; uniformly assessed fees are permissible. But expenses for transportation may not be billed.

In addition, parents who have insurance policies that reimburse for medically related services may not be required to make a claim on their insurers if the services are provided to comply with IDEA and utilization of such insurance benefits would require them to incur a financial loss (*Seals v. Loftis*, 1985; *Raymond S. v. Ramirez*, 1995).

States may not charge for the living expenses of students whom they place in public or private residential programs to comply with IDEA as well (*Parks v. Pavkovic*, 1985; *Jenkins v. Florida*, 1991). IDEA, however, does not relieve an insurer or similar third party from an otherwise valid obligation to provide or pay for services rendered to a student with a disability [34 C.F.R. § 300.301 (b)]. Accordingly, a parent may, at his or her option, offer to have an insurer pay for services that an LEA otherwise must provide.

Child Census

Another gap-closing provision is the child-census requirement. Each SEA and LEA must conduct an annual program to identify, locate, and evaluate all children with disabilities residing in their respective jurisdictions, regardless of the severity of their disabilities [20 U.S.C. § 1412 (a)(3)]. Congress recognized that a zero-reject policy would be meaningless without a child identification program. It also realized that identification of those children was a necessary prerequisite to planning, programming, and appropriating money for them to attend school.

The purposes of the child census are to ensure that no children are denied a free appropriate education because they have not been located, to ensure cooperation between the education agencies and others (such as health, mental health, developmental disabilities, social services, corrections, and even private agencies), and to enable the SEA and LEA to appropriate funds, plan and deliver programs, and be held accountable to all children with disabilities. As pointed out in Chapter 2, an SEA may conduct a "noncategorical" child census, counting the students without labeling them with or putting them into one of IDEA's 10 disability categories.

Architectural Barriers

Physical barriers can cause some students with disabilities to be excluded from school. Therefore, Congress authorized the Secretary of Education to make grants and to enter into cooperative arrangements with SEAs to remove architectural barriers [20 U.S.C. § 1404].

Comprehensive System of Personnel Development

IDEA also requires SEAs and LEAs to offer personnel development programs [20 U.S.C. §§ 1412 (a)(14), 1413 (a)(3), and 1435 (a)(8)] to ensure a sufficient number of adequately trained teachers and related-services personnel to educate all students appropriately and to ensure that general education faculty members in the schools are trained to accommodate students with disabilities in their programs (in the least restrictive environment). IDEA sets out general personnel standards that the states must follow but allows them the flexibility to develop specific standards with regard to certification, licensing, and registration of personnel [20 U.S.C. §§ 1412(a)(15) (A) and (B)(i), (ii)].

In particular, SEAs and LEAs may continue to use paraprofessionals and assistants who are "appropriately trained and supervised in accordance with state law, regulations, or written policy" to assist in providing special education and related services [20 U.S.C. § 1412 (a)(15)(B)(iii)]. SEAs also may require LEAs to make ongoing good-faith efforts to satisfy personnel needs [20 U.S.C. § 1412(a)(15)(C)].

IDEA's requirements regarding staff qualifications and training are important. Without a sufficient number of adequately trained personnel, the zero-reject principle (as well as principles relating to appropriate education and least restrictive environments) could not be implemented.

State Custody Generally

Children in the care and custody of the state itself often fall through the gaps of the service-provider system, yet they, too, are entitled to IDEA benefits if they have disabilities. Thus, in *Petties v. District of Columbia* (1995), a federal court held that IDEA applies to the District of Columbia and all of its agencies. These agencies include not only the Board of Education but also the Department of Health and Human Services (DHHS), which must pay for the special education placement of students who (a) need full-time residential placements in the District of Columbia Public Schools (DCPS), (b) have already been placed in a private special education school funded by the DCPS and who enter the DHHS system as the result of abuse, neglect, or delinquency proceedings, and (c) are placed by judges of the Superior Court of the District of Columbia or by the DHHS on its own initiative in cases involving child abuse, neglect, or delinquency.

Similarly, in *David B. v. Patla* (1996), the court rejected the contention of the Illinois Department of Child Family Services (DCFS) that it no longer was required to comply with Section 504 (of the Rehabilitation Act—antidiscrimination) by providing special education services to juveniles with disabilities. DCFS argued that recent changes in state law, which no longer allowed delinquents to be committed to DCFS custody, rendered the juveniles no longer "otherwise qualified" to receive DCFS services. The court disagreed, finding that the changes in state law did not relieve DCFS of its duty to provide services to juveniles already in its custody.

Juvenile Offenders

Incarcerated juveniles who qualify for special education can be especially vulnerable to policies that result in denial of a free appropriate education. This is so because they tend to be difficult to serve. They not only have disabilities but also are lawbreakers and are locked up in penal facilities. But IDEA applies to them, just as it does to other youth with disabilities. The growing trend of trying juveniles as adults is likely to further complicate the provision of special education and related services to juveniles with disabilities who are convicted as adults and incarcerated in adult correctional facilities.

The 1997 amendments to IDEA addressed the issue of providing special education to juveniles incarcerated in adult prisons. One provision excludes them entirely from IDEA benefits; another excludes them only partially.

The new provisions state that IDEA does not apply at all to students ages 18–21 who are incarcerated in adult correctional facilities and who, before they were incarcerated, were not identified as being classified under IDEA as a child with a disability or did not have an IEP [20 U.S.C. § 1412 (a)(1)(B)(ii)]. This new provision wholly prevents juveniles who are imprisoned in adult correctional facilities from attempting to alter the conditions of their confinement by claiming they are eligible for special education (unless state law provides for services in this instance where IDEA does not).

But juveniles who have IEPs (and thus already have been identified as needing special education or related services) and are incarcerated in adult correctional facilities continue to have a right to a free appropriate public education. Their right, however, is limited in several ways.

1. They are not required to participate in general and statewide assessment programs.
2. Juveniles who will become ineligible for special education during their incarceration because of their age (also known as "aging out" of eligibility for services) are not entitled to receive transition planning or transition services.
3. Juveniles are not entitled to be served in the least restrictive environment; their program and/or placements may be modified if the state can demonstrate a "bona fide security or compelling penalogical interest that cannot otherwise be accommodated" [20 U.S.C. § 1414 (d)(6)].

4. Governors may assign to any other agency (most likely the state department of corrections) the duty to comply with IDEA with regard to students with disabilities who are convicted as adults and incarcerated in adult prisons [20 U.S.C. § 1412 (a)(11)(C)].

The 1997 amendments to IDEA leave intact earlier case law holding that IDEA applies to incarcerated juveniles with disabilities. For example, as early as 1981, *Green v. Johnson* held that inmates in prison who are not yet 22 years of age have a right to special education under IDEA. The New Hampshire Supreme Court held in *Ashland School Dist. v. New Hampshire Div. for Children, Youth and Families* (1996) that an LEA could not evade its responsibilities to pay for and participate in the implementation of a juvenile's special education needs while he was held in a state youth facility.

Likewise, in *New Hampshire Dept. of Educ. v. City of Manchester* (1996), the state incarcerated for manslaughter a 20-year-old student with emotional and learning disabilities. While he was housed in a maximum security unit, the state correctional facility failed to provide him with the 5.25 hours of daily instruction that was specified in his IEP. The court ordered the facility to develop a practice that would balance the state's interest in enforcing prison sentences and maintaining secure prisons against the student's right to a free appropriate education.

In *Alexander S. v. Boyd* (1995), incarcerated juveniles challenged substandard care and living conditions in a state facility, alleging that the state failed to comply with its obligation to provide special education to its residents. The court held that each such student has a right to the IEP developed at the student's previous placement. The court also ordered the state to develop and implement a new IEP for students who are transferred subsequently to a long-term correctional facility.

Clearly, IDEA benefits incarcerated juvenile offenders. But may these student offenders also claim that the denial of educational opportunities in the facilities violates their Section 504 or ADA rights to be free of discrimination? The court in *Alexander v. Boyd* said "yes." That decision has become the law of the land: in 1998, the United States Supreme Court held that ADA applies to individuals with disabilities who are incarcerated in state prisons (*Pennsylvania Dept. of Corrections v. Yeskey*, 1998).

Discipline and Expulsion

In the beginning and throughout its more than 20-year history, one of the most pressing questions—if not *the* most pressing question—regarding IDEA has been whether school districts may expel children with disabilities. Does IDEA prevent schools from doing so because expulsion would exclude them totally from special education? Prior to the 1997 amendments, the courts spoke with a nearly unanimous voice: IDEA prevents an LEA from expelling a student if the behavior that triggered the student's expulsion is causally related to or a manifestation of his or her disability (the causal relationship or manifestation standard).

Despite these cases, many school officials and their professional organizations took the position that they had the duty to provide a safe learning environment for other students and a safe teaching environment for their faculty and staff, and that this duty should enable them to exclude students with disabilities (and students without disabilities) who endanger other students. The issue of school safety—made all the more visible and intolerable by the violent behavior of some students—caused Congress to amend IDEA in 1997 to clarify the rules regarding expulsion, manifestation, and the cessation of services. In many respects, the amendments codify earlier court decisions. Some provisions, however, are entirely new, and their implementation and interpretation will present challenges to all who are involved in expulsion decisions: school administrators, general and special educators, hearing officers, parents, students, and the courts. Before considering the IDEA provisions, we would do well to review the courts' decisions, for the Act itself relies on them.

Supreme Court's Honig Decision

In 1988, the Supreme Court decided the most important expulsion case to date, *Honig v. Doe.* (The 1997 amendments codify *Honig,* as this section will show.) *Honig* involved two students with emotional disabilities who were expelled by the San Francisco Unified School District for violent and disruptive behavior. The first student's IEP identified him as a "socially and physically awkward 17-year-old who experienced considerable difficulty controlling his impulses and anger." He always had been the target of harassment by other students and suffered much humiliation throughout his school years. In response to this taunting, he choked a fellow student and kicked out a school window. The LEA suspended him for 5 days and referred the matter to the appropriate committee recommending expulsion. At the end of the suspension, the LEA notified the student's mother that it was commencing expulsion proceedings and that the student could not return to school until a resolution was reached.

The second student displayed many of the same problems. His records indicated that he had difficulty controlling verbal and physical outbursts and exhibited "a severe disturbance in relationships with peers and adults." The LEA's decision to expel him resulted when he continued to engage in disruptive behavior—stealing, extorting money from fellow students, and making sexual comments to female classmates.

The Supreme Court determined that both students' behavior was causally connected to—a manifestation of—their disabilities. Therefore, the students' expulsion would violate IDEA's cardinal rule, zero reject.

Honig is significant for many reasons. First, it enforced IDEA's stay-put provisions, which at that time prohibited an LEA from moving a student from his or her current placement while a dispute was pending before a hearing officer or a court concerning the student's rights under IDEA. The Court said that IDEA is clear and unequivocal in its language that the student must stay put. These provisions prohibit an LEA from excluding children with disabilities unilaterally from the classroom or appropriate programs because of dangerous or disruptive conduct that grows out of their disabilities, at least while the dispute between the school and students is being adjudicated. Moreover, the Court found that Congress intended to prevent school authorities from making unilateral changes of placement. Of course, if parents and school authorities agree on a change while a dispute is being contested, the student's placement may be changed.

Second, *Honig* established that schools may suspend students with disabilities for up to 10 days before triggering IDEA's procedural safeguards. That is to say, an LEA may suspend a student for a maximum of 10 days without being prevented from doing so by a parent's filing of a request for a due-process hearing. The 10-day suspension is an absolute right of an LEA.

In addition to the 10-day right, the Supreme Court approved an avenue of relief for schools involving students who, they believe, are truly dangerous and likely to harm themselves or others. The Court noted that school authorities could file a lawsuit for "appropriate" relief under IDEA—namely, a preliminary injunction against the student being included in school if the parents and the school authorities cannot agree on an interim placement.

Third, the Court made it clear that IDEA creates a presumption in favor of the student's present placement but stated that this presumption could be overcome if the student's present placement and behavior were substantially likely to result in injury to self or others. (See *Township High School Dist. Bd. of Educ. v. Kurtz-Imig*, 1989; *Texas City Indep. School Dist. v. Jorstad*, 1990; *Borgna v. Binghampton City School Dist.*, 1991; *Prince William County School Bd. v. Wills*, 1989; and *Stafford County School Bd. v. Farley*, 1990).

The significance of this part of the Court's decision lies not just in the fact that the Court allows educators to balance the rights of students with disabilities to an education against the rights of other students and of faculty to receive an education and to teach, but also in the fact that the Court uses the approach of a rebuttable presumption as a means for interpreting IDEA and balancing the competing interests of students and faculty. As you will learn later in this chapter (relating to discipline) and in Chapter 6 (relating to education in the "least restrictive environment"), IDEA creates certain presumptions to benefit students with disabilities.

A presumption (at law) is a preference in favor of a certain result. For example, a person is presumed to be innocent until proven guilty; and, for a long time (but not nowadays), a mother was presumed to be the more appropriate parent of a child whose parents are separating or divorcing each other. Thus, the function of a presumption is to guide a decision-maker (here, a court or an LEA) into one direction.

Sometimes, that direction is not appropriate for the facts of the case or matter at hand; in that circumstance, the presumption is set aside—it is rebutted—and a different result is allowable. For example, the facts may prove that a person committed a crime; there, the presumption of innocence is overcome, or rebutted. Likewise, the presumption in IDEA that a student should remain in his or her present educational program can be overcome if remaining there is harmful to the student or others. That is precisely what the Court in *Honig* ruled: IDEA creates a rebuttable presumption in favor of the student remaining in his or her present program, but that presumption can be overcome if it would result in harm to others or the student.

Fourth and finally, the *Honig* decision is significant because, as will be obvious from the discussions that follow, the Supreme Court's decision carries over into the 1997 amendments to IDEA in several significant ways.

Before discussing the impact of *Honig*, however, it is important to note that the Supreme Court previously had decided an equally important case and that case, *Goss v. Lopez* (1975), interfaces with the *Honig* decision and the 1997 amendments to IDEA related to discipline.

Like *Honig*, *Goss* involved discipline of students by school officials. The issue in *Goss* was whether a student who is subjected to discipline has a right to challenge the school's decision to impose discipline on him. Fundamentally, the Court held that the student has a right, under the due process clause of the 14th amendment, to due process and that the right includes notice of the offense (charge), an opportunity to present evidence, and an opportunity to appeal an adverse decision.

In *Goss*, the Court allowed states to tailor their specific due process procedures to accommodate two kinds of discipline. If the discipline is for a short period (10 days or less), the school may give the student notice and hold the "evidentiary hearing" (on whether the student committed the offense) all at one time. If the discipline is for a longer period (more than 10 days), the school must give the student and his parents notice and must hold a more formal evidentiary hearing, one in which the student's parents may attend, the student may be represented by counsel, and the student may testify (or not) and ask for other evidence to be considered.

The impact of *Goss* on students with disabilities is relatively clear-cut. A school may not discipline a student with a disability unless it (1) offers the student an evidentiary hearing (that is, a hearing on the facts to determine whether the student committed the offense with which he is charged) and (2) determines, as a result of the hearing, that the student did indeed commit the offense. If the school determines that the student committed the offense, the school must proceed in conformance with *Honig* and IDEA.

Given that *Goss* requires an evidentiary hearing, the question now arises: How will an LEA conform to *Goss* and also meet its duties under *Honig* and IDEA? The answer depends on state law, but it is certainly permissible for a state to provide that the *Goss* evidentiary hearing may be held at the same time as, or before, the *Honig*-IDEA hearing. To have said that much, however, is to ask: what is the *Honig* rule as adopted by IDEA? The answer lies in the following sections.

Discipline and the Honig Manifestation Principle

One of the crucial holdings in *Honig* is that an LEA may not expel a student if the behavior that triggered the discipline was a manifestation of the student's disability. This rule survives in the 1997 amendments.

Basic rule The basic rule in IDEA is that a student whose behavior is a manifestation of disability may be disciplined, but significant limitations are placed on the discipline procedures that an LEA must follow and on the type of discipline an LEA may impose. Likewise, the obverse of the basic rule is that a student whose behavior is not a manifestation of disability may be disciplined just as any nondisabled student may be disciplined [20 U.S.C. § 1415 (k)(5)(A)]. Certain limitations, however, are placed on the LEA's power to discipline such a student.

First, the LEA may not completely terminate the student's right to FAPE; there may be no cessation of services [20 U.S.C. § 1412 (a)(1)(A)]. Second, if the LEA initiates disciplinary procedures, it must ensure that the student's special education and disciplinary records are transmitted to the person who is responsible for the discipline of nondisabled students [20 U.S.C. § 1415 (k)(5)(B)]. Thus, certain substantive limitations (no cessation of services) and procedural limitations (transmission of records) do not apply to nondisabled students (unless state or local law so provides).

The manifestation rule has two interesting and important effects. On the one hand, it prevents the student from being subjected to certain types of discipline because of a disability. In this respect, it is a form of accommodation to the disability and is consistent with the underlying federal policies of zero reject and reasonable accommodations.

On the other hand, the manifestation rule treats students with disabilities almost as though they were students without disabilities in this respect: As a general rule, if the behavior is not a manifestation of disability, the student may be dealt with as though the student did not have a disability. This rule has one important exception: There may be no cessation of services to the student with a disability. The equal protection doctrine, requiring equal treatment of equally situated individuals— which undergirds IDEA, and which disability advocates have relied on in creating rights to education and other benefits—thus applies to students with disabilities whose behavior is not a manifestation, but with the important protection of no cessation of education.

Before discussing the discipline issues in detail, it is important to note that matters involving discipline fundamentally are zero-reject issues, that matters involving "positive behavioral intervention" fundamentally are appropriate education matters (see Chapter 5), and that the two are interrelated. The U.S. Department of Education has made that connection explicit in its letter of September 19, 1997 to Chief State School Officers.

There, the Department addressed the question whether IDEA requires schools to consider a student's behavior as part of the process they follow in developing a student's IEP. It answered the question in the affirmative: yes. If a student's behavior impedes the learning of that student or of other students, Section 1414 (d)(3)(B) requires the student's IEP team to consider, when appropriate, "strategies, including positive behavioral interventions, strategies, and supports to address that behavior." This is now included in the regulations at 34 C.F.R. § 300.346(a)(2)(i). Thus, if a student is subjected to discipline because the student has engaged in "impeding" behavior that violates state or local school codes, the student's IEP team must consider those kinds of strategies.

The Department, however, went beyond the actual language of the IDEA and added the following important advice: Schools "should take prompt steps to address misconduct when it first appears" because those steps may "eliminate the need to take more drastic measures" (such as disciplinary measures). The IEP process is the appropriate one for taking these steps (see Chapter 5 for a full description of the IEP process). The Department advised that when a student engages in misconduct, the school "could" conduct a functional behavioral assessment and determine whether the student's current program is appropriate and whether the student could benefit from more specialized instruction or related services (such as counseling, psychological services, or social work services). Furthermore, if an IEP team is proactively addressing a student's behavior through a positive behavioral intervention and support plan (or other appropriate strategy) in the IEP, that plan will constitute the behavioral intervention plan that must be reviewed as required by the discipline provisions [see Fed. Reg. 12,620 (1999)]. Thus, proactive measures to address misconduct are strongly encouraged.

In addition, the school could consider training teachers in the "effective use of conflict management and/or behavior management strategies"—both of which "could be extremely effective." Thus, inservice training of all staff members who work with the student and, when appropriate, other students, "also can be essential in ensuring the successful implementation" of the positive behavioral interventions.

Although any further discussion of the IEP and appropriate education, including positive behavior supports, is premature, in this chapter, it is important to bear in mind that discipline and positive behavioral support are linked in IDEA. Indeed, as the Department indicates, positive behavior support could be exactly the intervention that would make discipline unnecessary because it would ensure that the student would behave in ways that do not violate school codes.

Manifestation determination team The first critical issue in discipline matters is whether the behavior is a manifestation of disability. IDEA requires a "manifestation determination review" in all cases where disciplinary action amounting to a change of placement is contemplated (34 C.F.R. § 300.523(a)). The student's IEP team (which includes the parents) must make all manifestation determinations, but the team may be augmented by "other qualified personnel" [20 U.S.C. § 1415 (k)((4)(B); 34 C.F.R. § 300.523(b)].

It is difficult to anticipate the effect of the parents' participation on the team or in any other group that makes decisions about the student's right to FAPE (parents have an absolute right to be a member of such a group—20 U.S.C. § 1414 (f)). Some parents may well disagree with the LEA's representatives on the team concerning manifestation (is there a manifestation or not?) and discipline measures (is the discipline justified?). Others may concur with the professionals' judgments. And, of course, the "other qualified personnel"—undefined by IDEA—may or may not be LEA representatives who would be inclined to concur with the judgments of the LEA representatives on the team. In any case, if the parents disagree with a manifestation determination or placement decision, they may request a due process hearing, and the SEA/LEA in those cases will arrange for an expedited hearing to address the matter (34 C.F.R. § 300.525).

Manifestation decision-making process and standards When making a manifestation determination, the IEP team (as augmented) must consider, in terms of the student's behavior, all information relevant to the connection between the student's disability and behavior, including evaluation and diagnostic results, information supplied by the parents, observations of the student, and the student's present IEP and placement [20 U.S.C. § 1415 (k)(4)(C)(i); 34 C.F.R. § 300.523(c)]. Besides the preexisting records (evaluation results and IEP), the team must consider new evidence—namely, information supplied by the parents and observations of the student. IDEA does not specify what information the parents may furnish, but it certainly allows them to bring in exculpatory information (evidence that the behavior is a manifestation and that proposed discipline does not meet IDEA's standards).

Moreover, "observation" evidence is not limited to observations by LEA representatives. It is conceivable that the parents will ask their own experts to observe the student or to file reports based on previous observations. In that event, it seems that IDEA requires the team to take those reports into account as it makes its decision.

After considering these matters, the team may find no manifestation and may discipline the student as though the student had no disability:

1. if the student's IEP and placement were appropriate and if the LEA provided special education, related services, supplementary aids and services, and behavior intervention strategies consistent with the IEP and placement [20 U.S.C. § 1415 (k)(4)(C)(ii)(I)];
2. if the disability did not impair the student's ability to understand the impact and consequences of the behavior [20 U.S.C. § 1415 (k)(4)(C)(ii)(II)]; and
3. if the disability did not impair the student's ability to control the behavior [20 U.S.C. § 1415 (k)(4)(C)(ii)(III)].

These three determinations have a crucial role: to guide the LEA about what action it may, or may not, take with respect to the student. In this matter—action relevant to the student—IDEA creates a general rule and an exception to the general rule.

The general rule is this: If the team determines that any one (or more) of these circumstances is present, then the team will have determined that there is a manifestation—the student's behavior is causally related to, is a manifestation of, the student's disability. Note that, to find that there is no manifestation, the team must find all three: that the IEP and placement were appropriate, the student did understand the impact and consequences of his behavior, and that the student could control his behavior.

The consequence of this finding (manifestation exists) is that the team may not impose a sanction that constitutes a change of placement (defined in 34 C.F.R. § 300.519 as either a removal of more than 10 consecutive days or a short-term removal that is part of a pattern). The exception to the general rule, however, is this: If the student's offense involves weapons, drugs, or dangerousness, the child may be suspended and placed in an interim alternative educational setting (IAES) for a period of 45 days or less. IDEA, then, requires the team to make a finding of fact concerning each of these three determinations. Unless it does so, it will not be able to justify any sanction that would constitute a change of placement. Thus, the role of these three determinations is to guide the LEA about the action it may—or may not—take with respect to the student.

Of course, a student may appeal the team's findings of fact and the imposition of a sanction based on the team's findings. If the student's appeal is successful, the sanction will have to be modified to fit the new facts (as determined on appeal).

The first standard—whether the student's IEP and placement were appropriate and whether the LEA discharged its service-provision obligations under the IEP and placement—allows the student to shift the blame for his or her behavior to the LEA. If the student can prove that his or her IEP was not appropriate, in that it did not provide for interventions to address the behavior for which he or she was disciplined, or if the student can show that, although the IEP and placement were appropriate, the LEA did not follow through and provide the services called for, the student should not be held liable for the misbehavior. In a word, this is a "school incapacity" defense: The school did not discharge its duties to the student and may not hold the student liable for behavior that the school should have targeted for remediation.

The House Committee has clarified this standard, as follows:

> This standard recognizes that where there is a relationship between a child's behavior and the failure to provide or implement an IEP or placement, the IEP team must conclude that the behavior was a manifestation of the child's disability. Similarly, where the IEP team determines that an appropriate placement and IEP were provided, the IEP team must then determine that the remaining two standards have been satisfied. This section is not intended to require an IEP team to find that a child's behavior was a manifestation of a child's disability based on a technical violation of the IEP or placement requirements that are unrelated to the educational/behavior needs of the child. (Committee Report, pp. 110–111)

The second standard—the student's disability impaired his or her ability to understand the impact and consequences of the behavior—allows a student to assert that the disability was related to his or her cognitive functioning and was so great that it effectively impeded the student's ability to understand what he or she was doing and how and why it was wrong. This is a "mental incapacity" defense.

The third standard—the student's disability impaired his or her ability to control the behavior — allows the student to assert that, despite knowing or not knowing the behavior was wrong, the disability was so great that it prevented the student from controlling himself or herself. This is a "behavioral incapacity" defense.

Stay-Put Rule Retained as General Rule; Allowable Discipline

Stay-put general rule The 1997 amendments also codify the Supreme Court's holding in *Honig* on the stay-put rule. The general rule is that, while a parent and LEA are engaged in a hearing before a due-process hearing officer or a court (or in any appeal from these decision-makers), the student must "stay put" in his or her then-current placement or, if the student is seeking admission to special education for the first time, the student must be placed in the public school program until all of the due-process and court proceedings have been completed [20 U.S.C. § 1415 (j); 34 C.F.R. § 300.514]. The LEA and the parents, however, may agree to a different placement during the "pendency" of the hearings and thereby waive the stay-put rule. (Note: The stay-put rule has exceptions for cases involving weapons, drugs, or injuriousness, as discussed below).

Short-term discipline (10 days or fewer) The 1997 amendments, however, bow to school-safety concerns and codify *Honig*'s short-term 10-day suspension right by allowing school personnel to remove the child from the current placement to an "appropriate interim alternative educational setting, another setting, or suspension, for not more than 10 schools days (to the extent that such alternatives would be applied to children without disabilities)" [20 U.S.C. § 1415 (k)(1)(A)]. Note that an LEA has three choices for the 10-day maximum discipline:

1. "an appropriate alternative interim educational setting" (IAES);
2. "another setting"—which apparently also must be appropriate but which is not an interim alternative educational setting (IAES) (it is not clear what that would be, but homebound or other more restrictive settings may be permitted);
3. "suspension"—apparently either from school altogether or by way of an "in-school" suspension, with the student allowed to have some, partial participation in school activities (e.g., not permitted to attend school except to take mandatory examinations).

This IDEA section [20 U.S.C. § 1415 (k)(1)(A)] uses the language "change in placement" in a general sense to mean any removal, whereas the regulations have defined "change of placement" more narrowly [34 C.F.R. § 300.519]. What the regulations make clear is that short-term removals (10 or fewer consecutive days) are allowed. Indeed, school officials have the authority to initiate any number of these short-term removals, as long as the series of removals do not constitute a pattern [34 C.F.R. §§ 300.519 (b) and 300.520 (a)(1)].

The only limitation on this authority is that FAPE services must be provided to IDEA-qualified children after the 10th cumulative day of removal during the same school year and both a functional behavioral assessment (FBA) and behavioral intervention plan (BIP) must be developed, even though "change of placement" (as defined in 34 C.F.R. § 300.519) has not occurred [34 C.F.R. § 300.520 (a)(1)(ii)]. School personnel, in consultation with the child's special education teacher, are responsible for determining what services will be provided in these cases [34 C.F.R. § 300.121 (d)(3)(i)].

It is important to note that on the first removal beyond 10 cumulative days, the IEP team is required to meet to develop the functional behavioral assessment (FBA) and behavioral intervention plan (BIP) or to review the BIP if one already exists, but that in the case of further removals (that still do not constitute a change of placement), the IEP team members need only review the BIP and need not meet unless one team member requests it [34 C.F.R. §§ 300.520 (b) & (c)].

Stay-Put Applies Note, too, that the "stay-put" rule still applies in some cases of short-term removal: If a student is subjected to any removal, and if the student's parents challenge a school's decision to impose the removal on the basis that it constitutes a wrongful change of placement, the student will remain in the current placement until the issue is resolved (in a due process hearing or otherwise)(with previously noted exceptions for weapons, drugs, or dangerousness). Stay-put, however, is limited to cases involving change of placement. Because short-term removals that cumulate to less than 10 school days do not amount to a change of placement, they will not be eligible for stay-put. Nevertheless, those cases of short-term removal in which a child will have been removed for more than 10 days in the same school year might be shown to be a change of placement because the removals create a pattern, and therefore would be eligible for stay-put. In effect, the child would have to be given temporary stay-put eligibility while a determination is made of whether the removals constitute a pattern.

Other Key Issues

The regulations and a September 1997 letter from U.S. Department of Education Assistant Secretary Heumann to Chief State School Officers clarified certain issues regarding short-term discipline.

1. What is the proper way to count the "10 days" for which a school may unilaterally remove a student? The school may remove a child for up to 10 cumulative days in any given school year before IDEA protections take hold. This is an important limitation because it prevents schools from "tacking" one short-term suspension onto another and all the time saying that each suspension is a different one that is not subject to the 10-day rule. For example, if a school has suspended a student for 8 days and then, a week or so later, has suspended the same student for 5 days, the school might argue that there are two different suspensions, each for fewer than 10 days, and that the two do not add up to or constitute a total of 13 days. That is a position that some schools had taken before the 1997 amendments.

That argument is no longer inviolate. Instead, the student may assert that there have been 13 days of suspension and that the school has engaged in a pattern of short-term suspensions (we discuss this issue of "patterns" below) that constitute a change of placement. Moreover, for purposes of providing a free, appropriate public education (FAPE), services must be provided to the child for each day past the 10th cumulative day of removal in the same year. Thus, using the case above as an example, the child must receive FAPE services on the 11th, 12th, and 13th days of removal.

2. Does the student have a right to free appropriate public education (FAPE) during removal prior to the 11th cumulative day of removal in the same school year? No, there is no right to services. On the other hand, the school may, in its discretion, provide services during that short-term removal.

Moreover, if the school does not contemplate any further removal of the student from school or the student's present educational placement, the school is not required to take any other actions during the short-term removal period. The Department of Education does urge the schools, however, to review as soon as possible the circumstances that led to the student's removal and to consider whether the student was being provided services in accordance with the IEP and whether (a) the student's behavior could be addressed through minor classroom or program adjustments or (b) whether the IEP team should be reconvened to address possible changes to the IEP.

3. Does a "manifestation determination" have to be made before a student may be removed from the current educational placement for a period of 10 or fewer days during a given school year? No, IDEA does not require a manifestation determination to be made before the school removes the student for the short-term period of 10 days or less during a given school year (unless the removal is part of a pattern of removals that constitute a change of placement).

If, however, the school contemplates any action that constitutes a change of placement under 34 C.F.R. §§ 300.519, 300.520(a)(2), or 300.521, a manifestation determination is required. In these instances, the parent(s) of the child must be given proper notice not later than the date on which the decision is made to change the child's placement [34 C.F.R. § 300.523 (a)(1)], and the manifestation determination itself must take place as soon as possible but no later than 10 days after the school decides to change the student's placement [34 C.F.R. § 300.523 (a)(2)].

4. Must the school conduct a functional behavioral assessment of the student before removing him or her from school for 10 cumulative days or less in a given school year? No, IDEA does not require a functional behavioral assessment before the short-term removal, provided that the school does not contemplate any change of placement.

If, however, the school does contemplate a disciplinary-based change of placement or the institution of any sanction that will result in removal of more than 10 cumulative days in a given school year, the student's IEP team must conduct a functional behavioral assessment (FBA) and develop a behavioral intervention plan (BIP) or must review the BIP if one has been created already.

Note, finally, limitations of authority of the LEA (school personnel) in disciplining a student with a disability:

1. School personnel have the authority to implement short-term removals (as long as they do not establish a pattern). [34 C.F.R. § 300.520]
2. School personnel have the authority to implement changes of placement to an interim alternative educational setting (IAES) for up to 45 days in cases of weapons or drugs. [34 C.F.R. § 300.520]
3. If maintaining the current placement of a child is substantially likely to result in injury to the child or to others (the so-called "dangerousness" provision), school personnel may remove the child and have an expedited hearing, at which the hearing officer may remove the child to an IAES for up to 45 days. [34 C.F.R. § 300.521]
4. School personnel otherwise have no authority to discipline a child through change of placement if the behavior in question is a manifestation of the child's disability. [34 C.F.R. § 300.520]
5. School personnel have authority to discipline a child with a disability in the same manner they would discipline a child without a disability if the behavior

in question is not a manifestation of the child's disability. [34 C.F.R. § 300.524] (Note: FAPE still must be provided as described in 34 C.F.R. § 300.121 (d)).

6. Each option is limited by another IDEA rule: An LEA may not resort to any form of discipline of a student with a disability unless it also may apply the same discipline to students who do not have disabilities.

Two Exceptions to Stay-Put Rule

IDEA creates two exceptions to the stay-put rule, acknowledging thereby that school safety and student rights must balance each other. Whether the balance will tip toward the LEA or toward the students will depend in large part on the gravity of students' behavior, their success in raising a defense to a discipline charge, the membership and attitudes of the decision-making bodies (the IEP team or the due-process hearing officer), and hearing officers' and courts' interpretations of the law. In the balance that Congress sought, the scales may tip toward the LEA or even the students (though this is not likely, given the nation's concern for school safety and the well-publicized view that there has been an increase in the number of juvenile offenders and the seriousness of their offenses).

Weapons and drugs   One exception relates to weapons and drugs.

1. The student's IEP team may place a student into an interim alternative educational setting (IAES) for up to 45 days if the student carries or possesses a weapon to or at school, on school premises, or to or at a school function [20 U.S.C. § 1415 (k)(1)(A)(ii)(I)]. Though this language in the statute had previously excluded the words "or possesses," the Department of Education had taken a position in the regulations that "carries" meant "carries or possesses." Congress amended IDEA in 1999 to clarify that in either case ("carrying" or "possessing" a weapon), the school should have removal power [Education Flexibility Partnership Act of 1999, PL 106–125].

"Weapon" is defined the same way it is defined in the federal criminal code's definition of "dangerous weapon"—namely:

> a weapon, device, instrument, material, or substance, animate or inanimate, that is used for, or is readily capable of, causing death or serious bodily injury, except that such term does not include a pocket knife with a blade of less than 2 1/2 inches in length. [20 U.S.C. § 1415 (k)(10)(D); 18 U.S.C. § 930 (g)(2)]

2. The student's IEP team may place a student into an IAES for up to 45 days if the student knowingly possesses or uses illegal drugs or sells or solicits the sale of a controlled substance while at school or a school function [20 U.S.C. § 1415 (k)(1)(A)(ii)(II)].

IDEA defines "controlled substances" as those that are regulated by the Federal Controlled Substances Act [21 U.S.C. § 812 (c)]. Illegal drugs also are considered to be controlled substances. IDEA does not, however, allow an LEA to discipline a student if the student legally possesses or uses drugs under the supervision of a licensed health-care professional or under any other federal law [20 U.S.C. §§ 1415 (k)(10)(A) & (B)]. Among the drugs included in the federal definition of illegal drugs/controlled substances are amphetamines, anabolic steroids, heroin, marijuana, mescaline, methadone, opium, peyote, and phenobarbital [21 U.S.C. § 812 (c)].

Note that an LEA has limitations on the ability to impose these punishments and to rely on the weapons-drugs exception to the stay-put rule:

1. Each of these disciplinary measures is time-limited: The LEA may not impose the discipline for more than 45 days.
2. Both approaches must be available for use with nondisabled students.
3. Each exception requires that the LEA use an "appropriate" IAES (see below under "Standards" for the IAES).

Note, too, that the school itself, through the student's IEP team, may take this action. It does not have to seek authority from a due process hearing officer or court.

Injurious behavior The second exception to the stay-put rule involves "injurious" behavior. IDEA provides that a school may avoid the stay-put rule if the student's current placement is substantially likely to result in injury to the student or to others (34 C.F.R. §§ 300.514; 300.521). (Throughout portions of this chapter, we refer to this as the "dangerousness" exception.) This is a codification of the *Honig* rule, called the "safety valve," that allowed an LEA to seek a court order to remove a student who is dangerous to others from the student's current placement.

Under IDEA, to remove a student because of dangerousness, the LEA now must seek permission from a due-process hearing officer (or a judge—we describe this option in further detail below). Unlike the weapons or drugs matters, where the LEA may act on its own, the LEA must seek a hearing officer's approval in cases of "dangerousness." Under present law [20 U.S.C. § 1415 (k)(2); 34 C.F.R. § 300.521], the hearing officer must conduct an expedited hearing and may remove the student because of dangerousness, for up to 45 days in an IAES, only on four conditions:

1. The LEA must demonstrate by substantial evidence that maintaining the student's current placement is substantially likely to result in injury to the student or others (i.e., other students or staff) [20 U.S.C. § 1415 (k)(2)(A)]. The term "substantial evidence" means "beyond a preponderance of the evidence" [20 U.S.C. § 1415 (k)(10)(C)]. This is a higher standard of proof than applies in an ordinary civil case, in which the standard is only a preponderance of the evidence (which roughly means "more than 50% of the evidence," in lay terms) but is a lower standard than "clear and convincing evidence," which is required in certain other cases.
2. The hearing officer must consider the appropriateness of the student's current placement [20 U.S.C. § 1415(k)(2)(B)].
3. The hearing officer must consider whether the LEA has made reasonable efforts to minimize the risk of harm in the student's current placement, including efforts by the use of supplementary aids and services [20 U.S.C. § 1415 (k)(2)(C)].

4. The hearing officer must determine that the proposed IAES allows the student to continue to participate in the general curriculum and to receive those services and modifications that will enable the student to meet IEP goals, including services and modifications that address the sanctioned behavior and ensure that it does not recur [20 U.S.C. § 1415 (k)(2)(D)]. The IAES is proposed by school personnel in consultation with the child's special education teacher (not by the IEP team), but this proposal is reviewed and a determination of placement is made by the due process hearing officer [34 C.F.R. § 300.521(d)]. Note that the LEA has the burden of proof and that the standard or degree of proof ("substantial evidence") is relatively high.

The Committee Report clarifies that these standards must be met before the hearing officer may place a student into an IAES on the basis of dangerousness:

> The bill requires the impartial hearing officer to consider the appropriateness of the child's placement and efforts by the school district to minimize the risk of harm in the child's current placement, including through use of supplementary aids and services. If the school district has failed to provide the child an appropriate placement or to make reasonable efforts to minimize the risk of harm, the appropriate response by an impartial hearing officer is to deny the school district's request to move the child to an alternative setting and to require the district to provide an appropriate placement and make reasonable efforts to minimize the risk of harm. Thus, it will not be permissible to move a child when the child's behavior can be addressed in the current placement. (Committee Report, p. 109)

These four conditions, creating defenses for the student and limiting the ability of the hearing officer to order placement in an IAES, should have the effect of requiring an LEA to anticipate whether a student's behavior is apt to make the student subject to discipline and then to act on that anticipation. If an LEA can reasonably predict that a student's behavior is likely to cause a need for discipline, then, if it ever wants to discipline the student for that behavior, it must be proactive and seek to modify or extinguish the behavior through a professionally defensible IEP and the provision of related services and supplementary aids and services. Even then, the LEA carries a heavy burden of proof, for it must satisfy the hearing officer that a "substantial" risk of injury is present (this must be shown by substantial evidence (beyond a preponderance)) and that the proposed IAES will be beneficial in correcting the punishable behavior.

The "dangerousness" provision (substantial likelihood of injury to self or others) allows a school to seek the approval of a due process hearing officer to remove an allegedly dangerous student. That provision, however, does not prevent a school from also seeking a court order allowing it to remove the student. That right—to seek court approval (injunctive relief)—was established under the *Honig* decision and is not repealed by the 1997 amendment. Thus, a school now has two forums in which it may seek authority for an immediate or expedited removal of the so-called "dangerous" student: (a) the expedited due process hearing under the 1997 amendments and (b) the *Honig*-created court hearing (see U.S. Department of Education letter, Assistant Secretary Heumann to Chief State School Officers, September 19, 1997).

It is not clear under the U.S. Department of Education advisory or IDEA whether a court is bound by the same standards that apply to the hearing officer in the expedited hearing. Logically, IDEA should apply to both the court and the hearing officer. Otherwise the student may receive different treatment depending on the forum in which the school elects to proceed. That would be inconsistent with the attempt of Congress in the 1997 amendments to create special protections for the student in the due process hearing. If the student's rights in the due process hearing do not apply in the court hearing, the schools will almost always seek relief in court, where the student would have fewer rights.

Pre/Post "Change of Placement" Requirements

Not later than the date on which the LEA decides to discipline the student by means of a change of placement (i.e., for weapons or drug violations [34 C.F.R. § 300.520 (a)(2)], dangerousness [34 C.F.R. § 300.521], or other violations of LEA policy if the removal meets the definition of "change of placement" under 34 C.F.R. § 300.519), the LEA must notify the student's parents of its decision and of the student's and parents' rights to procedural safeguards [20 U.S.C. § 1415 (k)(4)(A)(i); 34 C.F.R. § 300.523 (a)(1)]. The notice gives the parents a timely opportunity to challenge the proposed imposition of discipline.

In addition, no later than 10 school days after making the decision, the student's IEP team and any other qualified personnel must review the relationship between the student's disability and the student's behavior and determine whether the student's behavior was a manifestation of his or her disability (the manifestation determination) [20 U.S.C. § 1415 (k)(4)(A)(ii); 34 C.F.R. § 300.523 (a)(2)]. This is a requirement of timeliness in making the manifestation determination. The LEA may not drag its feet when it wants to discipline a student; too much is at stake for the student.

If the LEA has not already conducted a functional behavioral assessment (FBA) and implemented a behavioral intervention plan (BIP), the IEP team must meet to develop an "assessment plan" within 10 business days of the removal [20 U.S.C. § 1415 (k)(1)(B)(i); 34 C.F.R. § 300.520 (b)(1)(i)]. As soon as practicable after developing this plan and completing the assessments it requires, the LEA shall convene another IEP meeting to develop and implement appropriate behavioral interventions to address the behavior (the behavioral intervention plan) [34 C.F.R. § 300.520 (b)(2)].

If the LEA has already developed a behavioral intervention plan (BIP) and put it into the student's IEP, the team must meet to review the plan and modify it, as necessary, to address the behavior for which the student was disciplined [20 U.S.C. § 1415 (k)(1)(B)(ii); 34 C.F.R. § 300.520 (b)(1)(ii)]. This requirement commands the LEA to be proactive, either starting or reviewing (and probably modifying) an IEP that has a goal of extinguishing the student's punishable behavior.

Note that in the case of a student whose behavior impedes his or her learning or that of others (even where there is a change of placement), the IEP team must consider the use of positive behavioral interventions and support in order to address the behavior [20 U.S.C. § 1414 (d)(3)(B)(i)]. If a student engages in behavior subject to disciplinary action, it well may be appropriate in every such case to put positive behavioral supports into place. Moreover, if the IEP team is proactively addressing the student's behavior through a positive behavioral intervention and support plan (or other appropriate strategy) in the IEP, that plan will constitute the behavioral intervention plan that must be reviewed as required by the discipline provisions [see 64 Fed. Rg. 12,620 (1999)].

Appeals

As noted, the student who is involved in disciplinary proceedings is often subject to decision-making (i.e., manifestation determinations and placement decisions) by the IEP team, which includes the student's parents and any other appropriate individuals. If a parent disagrees with the IEP team's manifestation or placement decisions, the parent may appeal and may request a hearing on either or both of these two matters [20 U.S.C. § 1415 (k)(6)(A)(i)]. In these cases, the SEA or LEA must arrange for an expedited hearing if the parents request it [20 U.S.C. § 1415 (k)(6)(A)(ii); see also 34 C.F.R. § 300.525(a)], and the hearing must be conducted before an impartial hearing officer [20 U.S.C. § 1415 (f)(3); 34 C.F.R. § 300.508].

In reviewing a manifestation determination, the hearing officer must determine whether the LEA has demonstrated that the student's behavior was not a manifestation of his or her disability [20 U.S.C. § 1415 (k)(6)(B)(i); 34 C.F.R. § 300.525 (b)(1)]. In so doing, the hearing officer must follow the same procedures that the IEP team (as augmented) must follow [20 U.S.C. §§ 1415 (k)(4)(C)(i) & (k)(6)(B)]. Thus, the hearing officer will consider evaluation and diagnostic reports, observations of the student, and the student's IEP and placement. In addition, the hearing officer must apply the same standards that the IEP team must apply [20 U.S.C. § 1415 (k)(4)(C)(ii)]. The hearing officer may therefore determine that there was no manifestation if the student's IEP and placement were appropriate, the student's disability did not impair his or her ability to understand that the behavior was wrong, and the student's disability did not impair his or her ability to control the behavior.

After 45 days of IAES placement due to a weapon or drug removal, the LEA may seek to lengthen or renew the IAES placement through a hearing. In review of such requests, the due process hearing officer applies the same standards as when making a placement decision based on injurious behavior [20 U.S.C. § 1415 (k)(6)(B)(ii); 34 C.F.R. § 300.525 (b)(2)]. A court would also (it is assumed) apply the same standard if (a) it were reviewing an appeal of an IAES decision by a due process hearing officer for injurious behavior or (b) it were hearing a petition by the school for an IAES placement because of injurious behavior. In these cases, the reviewer (hearing officer or court) may uphold the placement in IAES if it:

1. determines that the public agency has demonstrated by substantial evidence that maintaining the current placement (prior to IAES placement) of such child is substantially likely to result in injury to the child or to others;

2. considers the appropriateness of the child's current placement (prior to IAES placement);
3. considers whether the public agency has made reasonable efforts to minimize the risk of harm in the child's current (prior to IAES) placement, including the use of supplementary aids and services; and
4. determines that the interim alternative educational setting (a) enables the child to continue to participate in the general curriculum, although in another setting, and to continue to receive the services and modifications, including those described in the child's current IEP, that will enable the child to meet the goals set out in that IEP and (b) includes services and modifications designed to address the behavior that led to the removal so it does not recur. [20 U.S.C. § 1415 (k)(2); 34 C.F.R. § 300.521].

Discipline Overview

If *Goss* requirements (for an evidentiary hearing on the factual issues of whether the student committed an offense) have been satisfied, the following IDEA provisions come into effect. This overview and the following "Decision Tree" (see Figure 3.1 pages 100–101) assume *Goss* has been satisfied.

Limitations of the Authority of School Personnel

- School personnel may order any removal of a child with a disability from the child's current placement (to the extent a removal would be applied to children without disabilities), as long as the removal does not constitute a "change of placement" as defined in 34 C.F.R. § 300.519. [34 C.F.R. § 300.520]
- School personnel may order the "change of placement" of a child with a disability to an appropriate interim alternative educational setting (IAES) for the same amount of time that a child without a disability would be removed, but for not more than 45 days, if
  - the child carries or possesses a weapon to or at school or to or at a school function, or
  - the child knowingly possesses or uses illegal drugs or sells or solicits the sale of a controlled substance while at school or a school function. [34 C.F.R. § 300.520]
- If school personnel believe that a child with a disability poses a substantial threat of injury to himself/herself or to others, they may remove the child and initiate an expedited due process hearing. A due process hearing officer (or court) may order a change of placement of the child to an appropriate IAES for not more than 45 days if the hearing officer (or court)
  - determines that the public agency has demonstrated by substantial evidence that maintaining the current placement of the child is substantially likely to result in injury to the child or to others,

— considers the appropriateness of the current placement and whether the agency has made reasonable efforts to minimize risk of harm in the current placement, and

— determines that the IAES proposed by school personnel (in consultation with the child's special education teacher) will enable the child to continue to progress in general curriculum and IEP goals, and will address the behavior in question to prevent its recurrence. [34 C.F.R. § 300.521]

Four Key Discipline Questions

1. Is the student a "child with a disability" under IDEA?

   - See 20 U.S.C. §§ 1401(3)(A) and (B); 1401 (26)

     — A "child with a disability" is a child with mental retardation, hearing impairments (including deafness), speech or language impairments, visual impairments (including blindness), emotional disturbance, orthopedic impairments, autism, traumatic brain injury, other health impairments, or specific learning disabilities (see 34 C.F.R. § 300.7 for further definition of these categories)

     — who, by reason thereof, needs special education and related services.

   - If an LEA knows or should know that a child is a "child with a disability," it must treat the child as such for purposes of IDEA compliance (see 34 C.F.R. § 300.527).

2. Is the disciplinary action a removal?

   - The discipline is a removal unless the student is afforded the opportunity to:

     — continue to progress appropriately in the general curriculum,

     — continue to receive the services specified on his or her IEP, and

     — continue to participate with nondisabled children to the extent they would have in their current placement.

   - Every "portion of a school day" (every hour!) counts toward the 10-day limits regarding both FAPE and change of placement.

   - Bus suspensions also count toward those limits if transportation is included in the student's IEP and the local education agency does not otherwise provide transportation. [34 C.F.R. § 300.520; 64 Fed. Reg. 12,619]

3. Is the removal a "change of placement?"

   - 34 C.F.R. § 300.519 defines a "change of placement" in the disciplinary context. A removal is a "change of placement" if:

     — a child is removed for more than 10 consecutive school days, *or*

     — a child is subjected to a series of removals that constitute a pattern

       • because they cumulate to more than 10 school days in a school year, *and*

       • because of factors such as the length of the removal, the total amount of time the child is removed, and the proximity of the removals to one another.

- A "change of placement" triggers the following requirements:
  — Manifestation determination
    - This review must be carried out "immediately, if possible, but in no case later than 10 school days after" the decision to remove the child [34 C.F.R. § 300.523].
    - If the behavior *is not* a manifestation of the child's disability, the child may be disciplined in the same manner as a child without a disability, except the requirements concerning FAPE, FBA/BIP, and other due process provisions will still apply.
    - If the behavior *is* a manifestation of the child's disability, change of placement may not be used to discipline the child (with exceptions for weapons, drugs, injury to self or others, or when parents consent to the change of placement).
  — FAPE (Free Appropriate Public Education)
    - Services must be provided in accordance with 34 C.F.R. § 300.121 (d)—generally speaking, they must allow the child to progress appropriately in the general curriculum and to progress appropriately toward their IEP goals.
  — Functional Behavioral Assessment (FBA) and Behavioral Intervention Plan (BIP)
    - If there is a change of placement, the IEP team must meet (not later than 10 business days after commencing the removal) to develop an assessment plan.
    - "As soon as practicable" after developing this plan and completing the assessments required by the plan, the IEP team must meet to develop appropriate behavioral interventions to address the behavior and shall implement those interventions.
    - If the child already had a behavioral intervention plan, the IEP team must meet to review the plan and its implementation and to modify the plan and its implementation as necessary. [34 C.F.R. § 300.520]
  — Other due process requirements
    - Parental notice [34 C.F.R. § 300.523 (a)(1)]
      — of parents' procedural safeguards, and of the removal decision
      — must be given by the date of the removal decision.
    - Mediation [34 C.F.R. § 300.506]
      — available to parents at no cost, with a list of mediators maintained by the LEA/SEA.
    - Due process hearing [34 C.F.R. § 300.507]
      — available to parents for review of LEA decisions.
    - "Stay-put" [34 C.F.R. § 300.514]
      — If parents object to the school's decision, the child remains in the current placement until an expedited hearing can occur.

— Exceptions for weapons, drugs, substantial risk of injury, or pending expedited hearings on these three issues.

4. Even if a change of placement has not occurred, will the child have been removed for more than 10 cumulative days in the same school year?

- If so, the following rules apply:
- — FAPE
    - Services must be provided in accordance with 34 C.F.R. § 300.121 (d).
- — Due process, mediation, and stay-put apply.
    - Parental notice does not apply in the same sense as it would for change of placement (except that procedural safeguards notice is required if an IEP meeting is to be held or a parent requests due process). [34 C.F.R. § 300.504]
- — FBA (Functional Behavioral Assessment) and BIP (Behavioral Intervention Plan) required.

More on Manifestation Determinations

- The IEP team and other qualified personnel may determine that the behavior of the child was not a manifestation of the child's disability only if:
- — they first consider, in terms of the behavior in question, all relevant information, including evaluation and diagnostic results (this may include information supplied by the parents of the child), observations of the child, and the child's IEP and placement,
- — and then determine that:
    - in relationship to the relevant behavior, the IEP and placement were appropriate and the special education services, supplementary aids and services, and behavior intervention strategies were provided consistent with the child's IEP and placement,
    - the child's disability did not impair the ability of the child to understand the impact and consequences of the behavior in question, and
    - the child's disability did not impair the ability of the child to control the behavior in question. [34 C.F.R. § 300.523]
- If the behavior *is* a manifestation of the child's disability:
- — Change of placement may not be used to discipline the child, with the aforementioned exceptions (weapons, drugs, substantial likelihood of injury).
- — If any deficiencies in the IEP or placement have been identified as a result of the manifestation determination, "immediate steps" must be taken to remedy those deficiencies [34 C.F.R. § 300.523 (f)]. Because the behavioral intervention plan (BIP) is part of the IEP, it should be modified as necessary to address the behavior.

More on FAPE—Who decides what services will be provided?

- For short-term removals that *do not* constitute a change of placement, school personnel, in consultation with the child's special education teacher decide what services will be provided [34 C.F.R. § 300.121 (d)(3)(i)].
- For long- or short-term removals that *do* constitute a change of placement, the IEP team determines the services to be provided, as well as the place in which they will be provided [34 C.F.R. § 300.121 (d)(3)(ii)].
- For weapon or drug removals to an interim alternative educational setting (IAES), these decisions are made by the IEP team [34 C.F.R. § 300.522 (a)].
- For removal to an IAES for "substantial risk of injury to self or others," placement and services are proposed by school personnel in consultation with the child's special education teacher, and reviewed and determined by the due process hearing officer [34 C.F.R. § 300.521 (d)].

More on FBA's and BIP's—Four Key Scenarios

- Removal for fewer than 10 cumulative days, with no change of placement
  - No FBA/BIP required, no FAPE required
- First removal beyond 10 cumulative days
  - IEP team is required to meet to develop the FBA, and to develop and implement the BIP. If the BIP has been done already, the IEP team must meet to review and modify the BIP as necessary.
- Subsequent removals that do not constitute a change of placement
  - IEP team is required to review the BIP, but need not meet. If any team member believes a modification is necessary, the team is required to meet.
- Changes of placement
  - IEP team is always required to meet to develop and implement the FBA and BIP, or to review and modify the BIP as necessary if one is already in place.

Precedents on Discipline and Manifestation

Although the process for making a manifestation determination is standardized and requires the LEA to conduct a complete review of the student, the disability, and the behavior, the results will not be uniform by any means. This is so for at least two reasons:

1. The manifestation determinations preceding the 1997 amendments have depended in part on the nondiscriminatory evaluations, which have been and still will be as highly variable as the students and their conduct.
2. The students' behavior, whether it clearly is or is not a manifestation, seem to govern the results.

That is to say (and assuming the past is precedent for the future), the more dangerous the behavior, the less likely it is that manifestation will be found. This well may

Following is a basic "decision tree" and summary of key issues for determining the responsibilities of school personnel and limitations of their authority under IDEA in disciplining children with disabilities.

I. **Summary of basic key questions regarding disciplinary removal of a child with a disability**: Is the disciplinary intervention a removal? If so, does the removal constitute a change of placement? Even if not a change of placement, will the child have been removed for more than 10 cumulative days within the same school year? What duties or limitations of authority are involved with each of these circumstances?

II. **Decision tree for removal:** When does removal constitute a change of placement? What are the limitations of school personnel authority with regard to removal?
   A. Removal for *more than 10 consecutive days:*
      1. When is this allowed? Only in the following instances:
         a. Weapon or drug violations in accordance with 34 C.F.R. § 300.520(a)(2), OR
         b. Maintaining current placement is substantially likely to result in injury to the child or others (34 C.F.R. § 300.521), OR
         c. Parents of the child with a disability do not object, OR
         d. The behavior is not a manifestation of the disability (as decided in a manifestation determination meeting in accordance with 34 C.F.R. § 300.523) and the child is being disciplined in the same manner as a child without a disability.
      2. In all cases of removal for more than 10 consecutive days, a change of placement has occurred (34 C.F.R. § 300.519).
   B. Removal for *10 consecutive days or less:*
      1. When is this allowed? This is allowed when the student commits "any violation of school rules" and if nondisabled students are subject to the same discipline (34 C.F.R. § 300.520(a)(1)(i))
      2. May more than one such removal be imposed during a school year? Yes, but only for "separate incidents of misconduct (as long as those removals do not constitute a change of placement under § 300.519(b))" (34 C.F.R. § 300.520(a)(1)).
      3. Do removals of 10 consecutive days or less constitute a pattern?
         a. This decision is made by school personnel, subject to due process rights of parent(s).
         b. A series of removals "constitute a pattern because they cumulate to more than 10 school days in a school year, and because of factors such as the length of each removal, the total amount of time the child is removed, and the proximity of the removals to one another" (34 C.F.R. § 300.519(b)).
         c. Where a pattern exists, a change of placement has occurred.
      4. Where removals do *not* constitute a pattern, no change of placement has occurred.
         a. BUT will the child have been removed for more than 10 *cumulative* days in the same school year?
            (1) If so, the LEA must (a) perform a functional behavioral assessment and implement a behavioral intervention plan (or review that plan, if one already exists), and (b) provide services (adequate to ensure FAPE) in accordance with 34 C.F.R. § 300.121. In this case, *school personnel, in consultation with the child's special education teacher, determine what services will be provided.* 34 C.F.R. § 300.121 (d)(3)(i).
            (2) If not, no behavioral assessment/plan development/review is required, and no services are required.

III. **FAPE and service provision requirements**: *Any removal for more than 10 cumulative days in the same school year* triggers two key requirements:
   A. The IEP team is required to *perform a functional behavioral assessment and implement a behavioral intervention plan* (or review that plan, if one already exists).
      1. An LEA must conduct a functional behavioral assessment and implement a behavioral intervention plan either before or not later than 10 business days after either first removing the child for more than 10 school days in a school year or after commencing a removal that constitutes a change of placement. That is to say that *any* time a change of placement occurs, even after the FBA and BIP have been done, the IEP team must meet to review the BIP. Also, the IEP team is required to meet upon the *first* removal of a child for more than 10 school days in a school year, regardless of whether the FBA and BIP have been completed previously. The IEP team, however, is *not* required to meet when the FBA and BIP have been already done and another short-term removal is imposed that is not a change of placement but is subsequent to the first removal beyond 10 days within the same school year. In this case, the IEP team members must review the plan

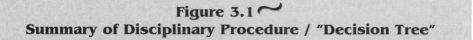

Figure 3.1 ∿
Summary of Disciplinary Procedure / "Decision Tree"

individually. A meeting must be held in these cases only if any member of the IEP team believes that a modification is necessary.

2. An FBA plan is required within 10 business days of the proposed removal, and the BIP is required to be prepared in a second, separate meeting as soon as practicable after the FBA plan meeting. "As soon as practicable," however, may be right away after the FBA meeting. Therefore, in effect, an IEP team might not be required to call separate meetings on separate days but could do the FBA and the BIP in separate, consecutive meetings on the same day (but only if practicable to do so).

B. The *LEA must provide services* to the child in accordance with 34 C.F.R. § 300.121(d)(3).

IV. **Change of placement** (34 C.F.R. § 300.519):

A. School personnel have no authority to unilaterally institute a removal that constitutes a change of placement, *except* that if a "substantial likelihood of injury", weapons, or drugs is at issue, the child can be removed immediately, subject to later review, to protect the safety of others in the current placement setting (the same is true for violations of the school's code of conduct, if the behavior is determined not to be a manifestation). Also, the school can remove a child and discipline him or her just as it would a child without a disability if the child's behavior was not a manifestation of his or her disability.

1. In cases of weapons or drug violations (34 C.F.R. § 300.520(a)(2)), removal can be ordered unilaterally by school personnel (and implemented by the IEP team, who determines the IAES), subject only to due process rights of the parent(s) (but parents have no rights to use the 34 C.F.R. § 300.514 "stay-put" rule in these instances).

2. Similarly, a school can hold an expedited due process hearing and the hearing officer can institute a removal to an IAES under 34 C.F.R. § 300.521 if school personnel believe that maintaining current placement is substantially likely to result in injury to the child or others. ("Stay put" does not apply here, either).

B. When change of placement occurs, additional requirements are triggered (see 64 Fed. Reg. p. 12,626), including:

1. A *manifestation determination* must be done (34 C.F.R. §§ 300.523 and 300.524).

    a. There is a general rule that children with disabilities may not be disciplined through a change of placement for behavior that is a manifestation of their disability (this arises out of Section 504 of the Rehabilitation Act). Exceptions to that general rule are the 45-day alternative placements described in § 300.520(a)(2) for weapons or drug violations and in § 300.521 for "substantial likelihood of injury." Parental consent to a change of placement is also an exception. When the child falls under one of these exceptions but the behavior is a manifestation of the child's disability, the child *may* be returned to class after the IEP team makes adjustments to the plan (but this is not required) (See 64 Fed.Reg. p. 12,625 – 12,626).

    b. If it is determined that the behavior was not a manifestation of the child's disability, the child may be disciplined in the same manner as a child without a disability would be disciplined—with the exception that FAPE services must be provided, and of course the work on the functional behavioral assessment/behavioral intervention plan must be done.

2. *FAPE services must be provided,* and the IEP team is required to perform a functional behavioral assessment and implement a behavioral intervention plan (or review that plan if one already exists). The FBA is a form of nondiscriminatory evaluation, and the BIP that derives from the FBA should be included in the IEP. The *IEP team (which always includes the parent(s)) determines what FAPE services will be provided* (34 C.F.R. § 300.121(d)(3)(ii)). This is true for all changes of placement *except* those involving *removal under 34 C.F.R. § 300.521* for "substantial likelihood of injury," *in which case FAPE services (IAES) determinations are made by school personnel in consultation with the child's special education teacher, and are reviewed by the hearing officer* (34 C.F.R. § 300.521(d)).

3. School personnel must provide *notice to parent(s)* (34 C.F.R. § 300.503) (prior to removal).

4. The LEA/SEA must provide *mediation* procedures through which parents may seek to resolve any dispute (34 C.F.R. § 300.506).

5. Parents are provided *due process* hearing and appeal rights under 34 C.F.R. §§ 300.507 – 300.513.

6. Removal is subject to the right of parent(s) to invoke the *"stay-put" rule* (pendency provisions—34 C.F.R. § 300.514)(except in the cases of removal for 34 C.F.R. § 300.520(a)(2) weapon or drug violations, 34 C.F.R. § 300.521 removals for substantial likelihood of injury, or during pending expedited hearings on these issues under 34 C.F.R. § 300.526 (c)).

Figure 3.1
(continued)

be result-oriented decision-making, but it also evinces a concern for school safety, a not inconsequential concern in the late 20th century.

The case law on manifestation, though it predates the 1997 amendments to IDEA, therefore is instructive in that it demonstrates the criteria that LEAs and hearing officers use in determining whether students' disruptive or dangerous behavior is causally related to a disability. These standards likely will be incorporated, in whole or in part, into hearing officers' and courts' interpretation of the 1997 amendments. For that reason, a review of them is warranted.

Manifestation and nondangerous conduct Some challenging but relatively nondangerous behavior, such as verbal assaults, shouting expletives, excessive talking, threatening teachers, and being generally disruptive, has been found to arise out of a student's disability, as the following decisions (by due process hearing officers, not courts) show.

In *Thomas v. Davidson Academy* (1994), a student who had been diagnosed with a serious autoimmune disease and who, therefore, was susceptible to life-threatening bleeding, cut herself with an Exacto knife in art class, whereupon she shouted expletives in the classroom and the nurse's office. The school wanted to expel her for this conduct, but the educators conducting the manifestation-determination meeting concluded that the behavior was causally related to her disability, as this type of behavior could be expected from this student under these circumstances.

Likewise, educators in *Oakland Unified Sch. District* (1993) determined that excessive talking by a student with mental retardation who functions at a 5-year age level was causally related to his disability. The district's own recent assessments and evaluations already had concluded that the student engaged in excessive talking because of his disability.

In Re J.W. (1995) presented the situation of a student who received services under Section 504 for a language impairment. The student participated in detonating an explosive device in the school bathroom. The school expelled the student, determining that the behavior was not related to his disability. Some time later the district received a letter from a psychiatrist who was treating the student and who had diagnosed him as having "major depressive illness" and unspecified "post-traumatic stress disorder." This psychiatrist urged the district to reconsider its decision to expel the student.

The district eventually conducted its own evaluation of the student and found that the student's involvement in the detonation clearly was a manifestation of his emotional disability, and that the student may have engaged in this behavior to "escape from the perceived pressures of school." The hearing officer ordered the LEA to expunge the record of the expulsion from the student's record because the LEA district either knew or should have known that the student may have severe emotional disturbance and should have reinstated the student when it learned of the depressive illness.

In *Bay County School Dist.* (1995), a student with severe emotional disturbance suffering from post-traumatic stress disorder engaged in striking students and staff members, making continuous verbal assaults, and throwing objects. The manifestation-determination team concluded that the behavior arose out of the student's disability, as this was precisely the type of behavior that she was expected to display.

By contrast, in *Walpole Public School* (1995), a hearing officer upheld an LEA's decision to expel a student with physical disabilities for excessive unexcused absences. The LEA made numerous accommodations for the student, relocating classes, providing elevator access, furnishing specialized transportation and parking, and allowing him to arrive later to school. The student presented no evidence that his disability was causing his absences, and thus the manifestation-determination team found no relationship between the student's disability and his behavior.

Manifestation and sexual misconduct Students who have threatened other students through sexual misconduct have had difficulty convincing hearing officers that this behavior is related to their disabilities. One such case involved a sexual assault upon a female student on the school bus (*C.A. v. Christina School Dist.*, 1993). Another involved a student diagnosed with attention deficit/hyperactivity disorder who exposed himself to a female student in art class (*Academy School Dist. #20*, 1994). In *Academy*, the student's behavior was found to be planned, part of a pattern of behavior, and not an uncontrollable outburst resulting from impulsivity. Yet another case involving sexual harassment of a female student (*Limestone County School Dist.*, 1997) also resulted in a finding that the behavior was not a manifestation of the child's disability.

Manifestation and alcohol and drugs Although the 1997 amendments, by allowing for an appropriate IAES for up to 45 days, make clear the zero tolerance for students who have illegal drugs at school or a school function, they still require a "manifestation determination." Accordingly, the precedents involving those kinds of violations are apt to influence the new (1997) manifestation determinations.

When an LEA has found a student possessing alcohol or drugs at school, the manifestation-determination team usually has determined that the behavior and the disability have no correlation, and hearing officers generally have sustained the "no-manifestation" finding. In *Snowline Joint Unified Sch. Dist.* (1994), the manifestation-determination team determined that a student with a speech and language impairment and learning disabilities who was ruled truant from school and who used alcohol could be expelled for this behavior. The manifestation-determination team decided that the student understood the consequences of his actions and, thus, his misbehavior was not causally related to his disability.

Furthermore, the LEA, in *Modesto City School* (1995), expelled a student with a visual-motor-integration learning disability who was caught selling marijuana at school. The manifestation-determination team stated that the student possessed no other disabilities and that low self-esteem is an insufficient basis on which to create a causal connection between the misbehavior and the student's disability.

Since the 1997 Amendments, there does not seem to have been an increase in findings that alcohol or drug violations are a manifestation of a child's disability. In 1999, in the *Lakeland Sch. Corp.* case, a child was accused of alcohol consumption on school grounds and was suspended. The manifestation determination hearing resulted in a finding that the behavior was not a manifestation of the child's disability.

Manifestation and weapons As in the case of drugs, the 1997 amendments adopt zero tolerance for students who possess weapons at school. Like the drug violators, a weapons violator may be punished by being removed to an appropriate IAES for up to 45 days. And, as in the alcohol and drug violations, the precedents (predating the 1997 amendments) may affect how those amendments are interpreted.

As a general rule, due process hearing officers and courts have been reluctant to determine that weapons possession is causally related to a disability. In nearly every case, a student who has a weapon has been unsuccessful in arguing that there is a "manifestation" of behavior based on the disability. For example, two LEAs expelled students with learning disabilities who were in possession of a gun at school. Both LEAs determined that this behavior did not relate to either student's disability (*Bryan County School Dist.*, 1993; *Philadelphia School Dist.*, 1994). This also was the finding in a more recent case of a child with ADHD who carried a firearm to school, in which it was found that because the student considered the consequences of his actions on several occasions that day, the behavior could not be considered a manifestation of the child's ADHD (*Oconee County School System*, 1997).

Similarly, a school district treated a can of mace as a dangerous weapon and expelled a student with a learning disability for his involvement in a group attack in which students took turns spraying another student with mace (*Kershaw County School Dist.*, 1993). The school district determined that the behavior was not causally related to the student's disability because he possessed the intent and cognitive abilities to appreciate his actions and the situation.

In addition, the LEA, in *Beaumont Indep. School Dist.* (1994), determined, based on a psychiatric evaluation, that a student's possession of two razor blades at school did not arise out of his disability. The psychiatrist had concluded that the student was experiencing an identity crisis and attempting to resolve his problems by acting out. The doctor explained that the student's behavior took the form of oppositional defiant disorder and recommended that the LEA place the student in a highly structured, small classroom. The doctor also determined that the LEA should expect the student to adhere to the school's disciplinary code as he could understand and follow it. The manifestation-determination team concurred that the student's misbehavior bore no relationship to his disability, and the hearing officer agreed.

Congress, public safety concerns, and the Supreme Court These decisions, the 1997 amendments of IDEA, and other recent activities of Congress show that educators and policy-makers alike are interested in sending a zero-tolerance message regarding the possession of dangerous weapons. These concerns about safety—safety of students, faculty, and other staff, and safety that promotes a learning environment and that is consistent with student discipline and good order—was reflected in Congress's enactment, in 1994, of the Gun-Free Schools Act [20 U.S.C. §§ 8921-8923 (1994)].

The Act required state and local education agencies that receive any federal funds—that is to say, all such agencies in the United States—to have in effect a state law requiring LEAs to expel from school for a full year any student who has brought a weapon to school. To make the Gun Free Schools Act consistent with IDEA and its provisions for interim alternative placements for weapons-carrying special education students, the Act provided that the state law shall allow the LEA's chief administrative officer (superintendent of schools) to modify the expulsion on a case-by-case basis.

In enacting the Act, Congress relied on its power under the Interstate Commerce Clause of the Constitution [Art. 1, § 8]. For at least the past 50 years this power had been unlimited. The Supreme Court had permitted whatever regulation of commerce (that is, America's business) Congress wanted to exercise. Inasmuch as weapons ostensibly are manufactured and distributed through interstate commerce channels, it seemed nearly beyond argument that Congress could regulate state and local school systems' response to students who carry weapons.

To the surprise of nearly every Supreme Court watcher, the Court invalidated the Gun-Free Schools Act, holding in *United States v. Lopez* (1995) that Congress had exceeded its authority under the Commerce Clause, there being no finding by Congress that weapons were trafficked in interstate channels and there being, as well, a serious matter of federalism. State and local education agencies, not the federal government, should have the autonomy to regulate student behavior.

The Supreme Court reached a similar result in *Printz v. United States* (1997). That case involved a provision of the "Brady Bill"—the federal handgun statute—that required local law enforcement officers to carry out background checks on people who want to purchase handguns. The Court held that provision (and a related one involving "Brady Forms" that gun-sellers were required to complete) is unconstitutional under two theories.

1. The doctrine of state sovereignty prevents Congress from imposing a federal obligation on states, without the states' consent.
2. The Commerce Clause did not justify the Brady Bill provisions, there being no authority in the Commerce Clause for Congress to override the principle of state sovereignty and the constitutional scheme of "dual sovereignty," under which the federal and state governments share duties and responsibilities.

School safety is not the concern of only the U.S. Congress. Indeed, state legislatures and state and local school boards have expressed their own concerns with school safety, creating, by law or regulation, provisions for the expulsion, or at least the suspension and reassignment, of weapons-carrying students, those with and those without disabilities alike.

In 1997, Congress continued this policy trend by codifying an important exception to the IDEA's stay-put rule for cases involving weapons. Clearly, Congress wanted to ensure that, in the case of weapons-carrying students, they would be segregated sufficiently from, and thereby prevented from harming, other students or staff. Thus, the public safety concerns outweighed the student's stay-put interests. At the same time, the student's education cannot be terminated completely. Special education services cannot be stopped.

Summary of precedents The manifestation cases teach some clear lessons.

1. As a general rule, if students engage in behavior that, according to their nondiscriminatory evaluations, they are likely to engage in, the manifestation-determination team undoubtedly will oppose expulsion.
2. If students undergo additional expert evaluations and assessments subsequent to the punishable behavior, the manifestation-determination team educators are inclined to accept those professionals' findings.
3. Manifestation-determination teams and LEAs generally will expel and find no manifestation when students' behavior can result in significant harm to other students and teachers, possibly subjecting the school to liability. Thus, students who bring weapons, drugs, or alcohol to school or threaten other students through sexual misconduct can expect to be punished severely for that behavior.
4. The current concerns about school safety dictate that LEAs deal with dangerous children swiftly and harshly.

Standards That the IAES Must Meet

When change of placement occurs (except for 34 C.F.R. § 300.521 "dangerous child" removals), the student's IEP team has the responsibility for determining what disciplinary action should be taken and what an "appropriate" IAES is. The IAES must meet certain standards, including IDEA's requirements that schools provide a free appropriate public education, and the team may place the student only in one that does so. The IAES option always has existed under the IDEA, but the 1997 amendments now require the IAES to meet specific standards.

The IAES must be "appropriate" in the sense that it must comply with statutory standards [20 U.S.C. § 1415 (k)(3)]. The IEP team or a hearing officer must assure that the IAES meets each of the following three standards:

1. The IAES must enable the student to continue to participate in the general curriculum, although in a different setting.
2. The IAES must enable the student to receive the services and modifications, including the ones described in the student's current IEP, that will enable the student to meet the IEP goals.
3. The IAES must include services and modifications designed to address the behavior for which the student was disciplined, so the behavior does not recur.

Because an LEA may have difficulty developing an IAES that meets these three standards, a student may challenge any IAES proposed by the IEP team or the hearing officer on the ground that the IAES does not meet these standards. If the student files that challenge and prevails, the IAES may not be used and the student must remain in the student's then-current placement.

Placement Following Interim Alternative Education Settings

If the LEA places the student in an IAES for a weapons or drug violation or because of dangerousness, and if the LEA then proposes to change the student's placement after the interim placement expires but the parents challenge this proposed change in placement, the general rule is that, during the pendency of the hearing on the parents' challenge, the student remains in the placement that existed before the IAES. This rule, however, will not apply, and an exception to it exists, if the LEA maintains that it is dangerous for the student to return to the "old" or original placement and if it also requests an expedited hearing.

To determine whether the student will return to the original placement or will remain in another setting (the IAES) for up to 45 additional days, the hearing officer must make the same four findings of fact that are required when placing a student initially in an IAES for dangerousness, and decide on an appropriate placement [20 U.S.C. §§ 1415 (k)(7)(B) and (C); 34 C.F.R. § 300.526] (see above under "Dangerous Behavior").

No Cessation of Services

Before the 1997 amendments, there had been a great deal of dispute and a split in the cases regarding the cessation of services when the manifestation determination team found no causal relationship between the student's misbehavior and disability. See *Virginia Dept. of Educ. v. Riley* (*Riley III*, 1997), *Morgan v. Chris L.* (1997), *Lunceford v. District of Columbia Bd. of Ed.* (1984), *Kaelin v. Grubbs* (1982), and *S-1 v. Turlington* (1981). The debate had focused upon whether it was permissible for LEAs to stop providing special education and related services to students with disabilities who had been suspended or expelled, as they do when they suspend or expel students who do not have disabilities.

In 1997, Congress settled this conflict by requiring SEAs and LEAs to provide a free appropriate public education to all children with disabilities, including those who have been suspended or expelled from school [20 U.S.C. § 1412 (a)(1)(A)]. The 1997 amendments forbid the SEAs and, through them, the LEAs from discontinuing the education of these students altogether. By adding these provisions to the IDEA, Congress acknowledged that students with disabilities would suffer inordinately if they were to be excluded permanently from schools, and that, ultimately, the costs of their exclusion to society in general would be too great.

Preemptive Strike

Another controversial issue that surfaced before the 1997 amendments involved whether a student who had not been classified already as having a disability may launch a preemptive strike against an LEA expulsion, assert that he or she has an as-yet undetected disability, and thereby invoke the stay-put provision to prevent expulsion. In 1992 the Ninth Circuit rejected the notion that IDEA applies only to children already identified as having a disability, holding in *Hacienda La Puente Unified School Dist. v. Honig* (1992) that the stay-put provision must be applied to all students, regardless of whether an LEA had determined previously that the student has a disability. Other courts followed this decision (see *M.P. by D.P. v. Grossmont Union High School Dist.*, 1994; *Steldt v. School Bd. of the Riverdale School Dist.*, 1995; and *J.B. v. Indep. School Dist.*, 1995).

Just a year before Congress amended IDEA (in 1997), *Rodiriecus L. v. Waukegan School Dist. #60* (1996) limited the scope of *Hacienda* and cases consistent with it. In *Rodiriecus L.*, the court held that, for a student who presently does not qualify for special education to invoke the stay-put provision, the student must be known or reasonably should be known to the LEA to have a disability. The student may not base this showing on the opinion of only one expert and must demonstrate that school officials knew or should have known of the student's genuine disability. The court emphasized that IDEA is not designed to act as a shield to protect a disruptive child from routine and appropriate school discipline.

When Congress amended the IDEA in 1997, it settled the question of whether students who have not been identified as having a disability are entitled to IDEA's procedural safeguards. The 1997 amendments provide that, to gain the protections of IDEA's safeguards, a student who previously was not entitled to the protections of IDEA may become entitled to special education and related services and to the procedural safeguards if the LEA had knowledge that the student had a disability before the misconduct occurred [20 U.S.C. § 1415 (k)(8)(A)]. The LEA is deemed to have known that the student had a disability if

1. the parent expressed concern in writing to the LEA that the student is in need of services [20 U.S.C. § 1415 (k)(8)(B)(i)];
2. the student's behavior or performance has demonstrated that he or she needs those services [20 U.S.C. § 1415 (k)(8)(B)(ii)];
3. the parent has requested a nondiscriminatory evaluation [20 U.S.C. § 1415 (k)(8)(B)(iii)]; or
4. the student's teacher or other school personnel expressed their concern regarding the student's behavior or performance to the LEA's special education director or other personnel [20 U.S.C. § 1415 (k)(8)(B)(iv)].

A public agency would not be deemed to have knowledge under these provisions, however, if the agency did both of the following: (1) either conducted a proper evaluation and determined the child was not a child with a disability, or determined that an evaluation was not necessary, and (2) provided proper notice of its determination to the child's parents [34 C.F.R. § 300.527(c)].

If the LEA is not charged with knowledge that the student has a disability, it may subject the student to the same discipline as any other student without a disability who engages in comparable behavior [20 U.S.C. § 1415 (k)(8)(C)(i)]. These provisions tell parents that, however adverse they may be to a special education placement, they may want to request one, or at least a nondiscriminatory evaluation. These provisions also create a disincentive to educators who want to keep students out of special education for any of various reasons: high cost, and great protections, especially for students who are rule-breakers. Finally, the provisions allow a hearing officer to make an independent judgment: Did the student's behavior or performance demonstrate to a reasonable and disinterested professional that the student needs and should have qualified for special education?

If the LEA determines subsequently that the student is in need of special education and related services, it must provide those services in accordance with IDEA. Also, the student must remain in the educational placement determined by the school authorities pending the evaluation [20 U.S.C. § 1415 (k)(8)(C)(ii)]. If the student is evaluated during the time he or she is subjected to disciplinary measures, the LEA must expedite the evaluation [20 U.S.C. § 615 (k)(8)(C)(ii)].

Reporting Criminal Behavior; Documentation and Transfer of Records

The LEA may report to the appropriate authorities any crime a student commits. IDEA does not prevent those authorities from exercising any of their duties to enforce state or federal criminal law. If it files a report, the LEA must provide copies of the student's special education and disciplinary records to the authorities with which it filed the report [20 U.S.C. § 1415 (k)(9); 34 C.F.R. § 300.529].

The state may require an LEA to include in the student's file a statement of any current or previous disciplinary action taken against the student. This information may be transmitted to the same extent as such information is transmitted for students without disabilities. The Family Educational Rights and Privacy Act (FERPA) applies in this regard (see Chapter 8 for further discussion of FERPA) [34 C.F.R. § 300.529 (b)(2)].

The statement may include a description of the student's behavior that required disciplinary action, a description of the disciplinary action taken, and any other information relevant to the safety of the child and others [20 U.S.C. § 1413(j); 34 C.F.R. § 300.576]. The transmittal provision allows the decision-maker to take into account exculpatory or mitigating evidence, such as the student's disability; and it also allows the decision-maker to tailor the punishment to fit the offense, taking into account the student's disability and the safety of the student and others. This is another "balancing" provision: Rights of the student and others are balanced against each other, with evidence as the basis for striking the balance in the case of each student.

If the state adopts a disclosure policy and the student transfers from one school to another, the student's records must include a copy of the student's original IEP and a statement of current or previous disciplinary action taken against the student [20 U.S.C. § 1413 (j); 34 C.F.R. § 300.576]. This provision allows a "sending" LEA to put a "receiving" LEA on notice that the student has a disability, what the sending LEA proposed by way of an appropriate education in the least restrictive setting, and that there may be safety issues for the receiving LEA to consider.

IDEA requires SEAs to compile data on the suspension and expulsion of students with disabilities to determine if significant discrepancies are present in the rates of suspensions and expulsions among LEAs within the state, and to determine if students with disabilities are being suspended or expelled at greater rates than students without disabilities [20 U.S.C. § 1412 (a)(22)(A)]. If an SEA finds that discrepancies are present, the SEA should, if appropriate, revise (or require the LEAs to revise) the policies, procedures, and practices related to the development and implementation of IEPs, the use of behavioral interventions, and procedural safeguards, to ensure that the policies, procedures, and practices comply with the IDEA [20 U.S.C. § 1412 (a)(22)(B)].

Educability

Are any children totally ineducable and therefore not entitled to IDEA's protection because, by definition, they inherently lack the ability to learn? Until 1988, the courts followed the finding in *PARC v.* Commonwealth (1971, 1972) that all—repeat: all—children are capable of learning. In that year, however, *Levine v. New Jersey* (1980) put up the question for debate.

State Law Basis for Exclusion

In *Levine v. New Jersey*, the parents of children with severe mental retardation unsuccessfully challenged New Jersey's practice of billing them for the residential care the state provided to their children. The parents claimed that IDEA and its "free" education provision exempts them from having to pay for special education. The New Jersey Supreme Court, however, held that the state's constitution, mandating for a free public education, does not apply to children who are so severely mentally impaired that they are unable to absorb or benefit from education. The court also found that the residential care those children require for day-to-day well-being does not qualify as education.

The court based its interpretation on a finding that the "thorough and efficient" education clause of the state constitution was intended to provide children with an education that will prepare them to function politically, economically, and socially in a democratic society. Because those children never will be able to meet the so-called franchise test, they are not entitled to an education under the state constitution and, accordingly, their parents must pay the state for their care.

Although the *Levine* case is based on a state constitution, it is important because the court's interpretation of education casts doubt on the purposes of special education, which are not necessarily to train all students to the level that they will be capable enough to vote. More than that, the case suggests that some children do not qualify for special education under state law, and possibly under IDEA itself, because they never will be competent to vote.

If a state were to decline to accept IDEA funds and then try to exclude certain students because they cannot learn, the students' rights to an education would depend on state constitution and statutes, the Americans with Disabilities Act, Section 504, and the federal constitution's equal protection clause. Fortunately, the issues raised by *Levine* have been dormant, in large part because all states accept IDEA funds and because of an "educability" decision under IDEA, the *Timothy W.* case.

Timothy W. Case: IDEA Interpreted

A 1988 decision by a federal district (trial) court in New Hampshire, in *Timothy W. v. Rochester School Dist.* (1988), seemed to follow the reasoning in *Levine*. In *Timothy W.*, the student, denied admission to school because of his disability, was a 13-year-old who was blind and deaf, had cerebral palsy, was spastic and subject to frequent convulsions, lacked carotid tissue, was profoundly retarded, had no communication skills, operated "at the brainstem level," and had acquired reflex behavior (some ability to respond to external stimuli—light and noise), but had made no developmental progress in about a year. Moreover, Timothy seemed to be regressing, had not achieved a level of response to stimuli beyond his original baseline (first measured response), engaged in only passive and nonvolitional activities, and had to have his hands and feet manipulated completely to move them. For all of these reasons, he was found to be "not capable of benefiting from special education" at the present.

Given these facts, the legal issue was whether Timothy is entitled to IDEA's benefits and rights. The trial court engaged in curious reasoning to reach the result that he is not, disregarding IDEA's clear coverage of "all" students and interpreting the U.S. Supreme Court's decision in *Bd. of Educ. v. Rowley* (1982) in such a way that the school was entitled to exclude Timothy from school.

In *Rowley*, the Supreme Court said that IDEA's purpose is to help schools provide a benefit to the student. It logically followed (according to the trial court in *Timothy W.*) that a child who cannot "benefit" from special education, because he does not have learning capacity, is not entitled to receive IDEA benefits and rights. Surely, said the trial court, Congress would not legislate futility. In the rare cases in which a child is not able to benefit, IDEA allows an LEA to exclude those children. But the court did require that Timothy be subjected to "continuous, but periodic evaluations, intended to identify any development which illustrates a capability to benefit from special education."

In holding that Timothy is ineducable, the trial court attacked the underlying premise of *PARC* and IDEA itself. *PARC* held that all children are educable and that, therefore, there is no reason to exclude any of them from an educational system. IDEA was based on *PARC* (as shown in Chapter 2). If, however, some children do not seem to be educable, said the trial court in *Timothy W.*, there is no reason to include them in an educational system. The system would be asked to do that which it cannot do (by definition, the children are not able to benefit from the system's efforts), and no purpose would be served by including them in the system. Indeed, their inclusion would cause an unjustifiable expense to the educational system. Public policy would justify their exclusion from that system, then, on two grounds:

1. The system cannot benefit them; and
2. The expenditure of funds cannot be defended.

The court of appeals, however, reversed the trial court in *Timothy W.*, holding that IDEA was enacted to ensure that all children with disabilities are provided an appropriate public education. Indeed, "not only are severely handicapped children not excluded from the Act, but the most severely handicapped are actually given priority under the Act" (as it provided at that time; the priority for serving those with the greatest needs does not exist in the 1997 version). Moreover, the court of appeals said, IDEA has no prerequisite that the student be able to benefit from education. Instead, IDEA speaks about the state's responsibility to the child. As the court stated:

> The language of the Act in its entirety makes clear that a "zero-reject" policy is at the core of the Act, and that no child, regardless of the severity of his or her handicap, is to ever again be subjected to the deplorable state of affairs which existed at the time of the Act's passage, in which millions of handicapped children received inadequate education or none at all. In summary, the Act mandates an appropriate public education for all handicapped children, regardless of the level of achievement that such children might attain.

The appeals court cited Congressional history to support its contention that the Act is intended to benefit all children with disabilities, "without exception," and that an "educational benefit was neither guaranteed nor required as a prerequisite for a child to receive such an education." The court also noted that Congress had amended the Act four times since it was enacted in 1975 and that Congress not only had reaffirmed repeatedly the Act's original intent—to educate all children—but it also had expanded the provisions covering students with the most severe disabilities.

Next, the court noted that Congress relied on the *PARC* and *Mills* cases when enacting the Act; both cases establish a zero-reject principle. Moreover, "the courts have continued to embrace the principle that all handicapped children are entitled to a public education, and have consistently interpreted the Act as embodying this principle." And the court observed that courts have construed "education" in a very broad way, so that the trial court's conclusion that

> education must be measured by the acquirement of traditional "cognitive skills" has no basis whatsoever in the 14 years of case law since the passage of the Act. All other courts have consistently held that education under the Act encompasses a wide spectrum of training, and that for the severely handicapped it may include the most elemental of life skills.

In further disagreement with the trial court, the appeals court said that *Rowley* focused on the level of services and the quality of programs that a state must provide, not the criteria for access to those programs. The Supreme Court's use of benefit in *Rowley* was a "substantive limitation placed on the state's choice of an educational program; it was not a license for the state to exclude certain handicapped children." Instead, the Supreme Court acknowledged explicitly in *Rowley* that Congress intended to ensure public education to all children with disabilities without regard to the level of achievement they might attain; IDEA's intent was to open the doors but not to guarantee any particular level of education once they are open.

Finally, the court of appeals may have established a duty of schools to use state-of-the-art procedures for educating children with severe disabilities:

> The law explicitly recognizes that education for the severely handicapped is to be broadly defined, to include not only traditional academic skills, but also basic

functional life skills, and that educational methodologies in these areas are not static, but are constantly evolving and improving. It is the school district's responsibility to avail itself of these new approaches in providing an education program geared to each child's individual needs. The only question for the school district to determine, in conjunction with the child's parents, is what constitutes an appropriate individualized education program (IEP) for the handicapped child.

The problems with concluding that some children are not educable are manifold.

1. No conclusive research data, to date, justify the conclusion that some children are not educable. Indeed, there is strong debate on both sides of the educability issue. A conclusion that some children are not educable, then, seems scientifically debatable.
2. Where does one draw the line? Once a child is found not educable, the tendency may be to open up the class of ineducable children so as to include some children who are simply difficult or expensive to educate but who can be educated or benefit from training.
3. Special education and related professions would be relieved of the pressure to find ways to educate children with more profound disabilities, stifling the development of new knowledge that could benefit them.

Note that the debates about educability and expulsion are related. Both debates seek to define who should be classified as having a disability for the purpose of special education. If a school may expel a special education student because the disability did not cause the student's behavior, it would hope to be relieved completely of any duty to that student. Indeed, until the 1997 amendments reversed the *Riley* decision (discussed earlier in this section), that may have been the result. In a very real sense—in the sense of being entitled to special education—the student would not have been "disabled." Likewise, if a school may find as a matter of fact that a certain student is ineducable, it too may argue that it no longer is responsible for the student because IDEA is intended to benefit only those who are capable of learning.

Again, students who are incapable of learning would not be "disabled" in the sense of being entitled to special education. Clearly, some educators and school systems have been attempting to limit the meaning of disabled by excluding students who violate certain rules and students who allegedly are ineducable. Fortunately, these educators and school systems have been unsuccessful, and the 1997 amendments make it clear that they will continue to be unsuccessful: "All" means "all."

Contagious Disease

One other line of cases, like those involving expulsion and educability, has tested the outer limits of the zero-reject rule. These are cases involving the education of students with contagious diseases. Of the several such diseases (e.g., tuberculosis and varieties of herpes), the issues are drawn most sharply when a student has AIDS.

Section 504 and the Arline Decision

The Supreme Court, in *School Bd. of Nassau County v. Arline* (1987), involving a teacher who had tuberculosis, laid the foundation for interpreting IDEA as it applies to students with contagious diseases. In that case, Jean Arline had experienced TB some 15-plus years before the disease recurred. When it returned, she suffered several relapses. After the third, her LEA employer discharged her from all of her duties.

Claiming that Section 504 of the Rehabilitation Act protects her from discharge because of her disease, Arline sued to recover her job and damages. Her suit raised a critical question: Is a person with TB entitled to the protection of Section 504? Alternatively and more broadly stated, the issue was whether a person with a contagious disease, such as AIDS, is "otherwise qualified" to participate in various activities—in Arline's case, to be a teacher. In the case of students with AIDS, the analogous issue is whether they are entitled, under Section 504 or IDEA, to be enrolled in school.

The Supreme Court held that Section 504 protects Arline and others with contagious diseases against discrimination based on their disabilities. In her case, Arline met all three criteria for protection under Section 504: She had a disability, had a record of one, and was regarded as having one. Moreover, her medical condition significantly affected her ability to work as a teacher (though, perhaps, not to work in other capacities in an LEA, where the risk of infection was not so great).

Having found Arline to be a person with a disability, the Court then addressed the issue of whether she is "otherwise qualified" for employment. If she is, she may not be discriminated against because of her disability. To determine whether Arline, or another with contagious diseases, is "otherwise qualified," the Court laid down four tests or standards to be applied in the context of employment of a person with a disability:

1. What is the nature of the risk—i.e., how is the disease transmitted?
2. What is the duration of the risk—i.e., how long is the carrier infectious?
3. What is the severity of the risk—i.e., what is the potential harm to third persons of becoming infected?
4. What is the probability of transmitting the disease to others—i.e., what is the likelihood that the person will infect others and cause them various degrees of harm?

In all cases, the answers to these issues must be determined on an individual basis and by appropriately qualified professionals (physicians or other public health officials). Individualized decision-making, coupled with judicial or LEA deference to professional judgment, is the proper way to protect people with disabilities against "deprivations based on prejudice, stereotypes, or unfounded fear, while giving appropriate weight to such legitimate concerns...as avoiding exposing others to significant health and safety risks."

In Arline's case, the Court found that she was a person with a disability. It sent the case back to the lower courts to determine whether she is "otherwise qualified" and what accommodations, if any, could be made, consistent with Section 504's requirements of "reasonable accommodations," to continue Arline as an employee (though perhaps not as a teacher).

Arline and HIV/AIDS

The disability community, school authorities, and other public authorities looked to *Arline* to settle, once and for all, whether a person with AIDS is protected under Section 504 and therefore entitled to protection against discrimination and to reasonable accommodations in employment and education. The Court, however, dropped a significant footnote in *Arline,* stating that its decision does not deal explicitly with the issue of AIDS. Notwithstanding this disclaimer, lower courts and school authorities justifiably continued to rely on *Arline* to clarify AIDS-related issues.

Applying the Supreme Court's four-part test to students with HIV or AIDS is not difficult. Issues about the nature, duration, severity, and probability of risk can be applied to students as easily as to employees because the state of knowledge about the disease is well developed and individualized determinations by qualified professionals already underlie IDEA's command to conduct nondiscriminatory evaluations of each student.

The nature and effects of AIDS AIDS is caused by a retrovirus called the human immunodeficiency virus (HIV). Physicians use three categories to classify the nature and effect of HIV infection.

1. An infected person is diagnosed as having full-blown AIDS if he or she manifests one of the "opportunistic infections" listed by the National Centers for Disease Control and Prevention. These infections signal that the retrovirus has seriously damaged the person's immunological capability.
2. Another person may manifest lesser symptoms collectively, referred to as AIDS-related complex (ARC), ranging from swollen lymph nodes and simple fever or lethargy to more serious neurological disorders.
3. Still another person, typical of the vast majority of people who have been infected with the virus, is asymptomatic. In such a person, the virus cannot be routinely isolated, but prevailing medical opinion is that these "seropositive" people have been infected with the virus at one time, are presumed to have the virus dormant in their systems, and certainly are presumed to be able to transmit the virus to others.

The modes of transmission are limited to sexual intimacy involving the exchange of bodily fluids, transmission of blood via needles shared by intravenous drug users, or transmission of blood that is contaminated (as by way of blood infusions). The overwhelming evidence is that the AIDS virus is not transmitted by casual contacts.

The first issue: Section 504, ADA, and AIDS Section 504 defines a disabled person as one having a mental or physical disability that substantially limits one or more of the person's major life activities, has a record of that impairment, or is regarded as having that impairment. Clearly, Section 504 covers people with full-blown AIDS and ARC, but whether those who are seropositive also are covered was relatively unclear until recently. Many lower courts had concluded that people who test seropositive, and thus carry the disease, are covered by Section 504. The same result seems to have been applied in the few cases involving students with AIDS and IDEA (*Martinez v. School Bd. of Hillsborough County*, 1988).

In 1998, the U.S. Supreme Court clarified this issue in *Bragdon v. Abbott*, finding that HIV infection is a "disability" under the ADA, even if the infection has not yet progressed to the so-called symptomatic phase. In that case, the plaintiff (who was infected with HIV) brought action under the ADA against a dentist who refused to treat her in his office, which would have required the plaintiff to incur extra hospital operating room expenses.

ADA shares essentially the same definition of "disability" as that of Section 504 (one prong of which is actually having a physical or mental impairment that substantially limits one or more major life activities), and indeed the Court construed ADA to give at least as much protection as that of 504. In this case, the plaintiff's ability to reproduce and to bear children was substantially limited, and the Court declared that this qualified as a "major life activity." Further, it stated that "major life activity," for the purpose of this definition of disability, was not limited only to "public, economic, or daily" activities. Because of the interrelation of 504 and ADA, one may assume that in any 504 case regarding HIV infection, this case will apply.

The second issue: May an AIDS-affected person be excluded? In 1987, the New Jersey Supreme Court in *Bd. of Educ. of City of Plainfield v. Cooperman* (1987) approved regulations of the state commissioners of education and health that set forth the procedures through which children with AIDS may be placed in or out of general or special education programs (but not excluded wholly from some school services—typically, homebound or hospital-based special education). The state's regulations provide that, as a general rule, students with full-blown AIDS, ARC, or seropositive diagnoses will be admitted into regular school. Three exceptions are: children who are not toilet-trained, those who are unable to control their drooling, and those who are unusually physically aggressive toward other students. For them, other placements and programs must be developed.

A panel of medical experts must review all decisions in which an LEA decides to place a child on the basis of AIDS. The LEA bears the burden of proving that the child fits into one of the exceptions. And a full hearing must be held before the LEA and medical panel, with a right to appeal to the state commissioner of education.

The New Jersey Supreme Court approved the following principles:

1. The presumption is in favor of inclusion and against exclusion (zero-reject principle).
2. Medical judgment is controlling as long as it is reasonable.
3. Individualized determinations must be made and may be appealed through a fair-hearing process.

See *Dist. 27 Community School Bd. v. Bd. of Educ. of New York City* (1986) and *Parents v. Coker* (1987) for cases following these principles and procedures.

The rights of a child with AIDS to special education under IDEA, however, do not arise automatically upon the finding that the child has AIDS (*Dist. 27 Community School Bd. v. Bd. of Educ. of New York City*, 1986; *Doe v. Belleville Public Schools Dist. No. 118*, 1987). The child must qualify as "other health impaired" because of limited strength, vitality, or alertness that is caused by chronic or acute health problems and that adversely affects the student's educational performance [34 C.F.R. § 300.7 (c)(9)].

Furthermore, even if the child qualifies as "other health impaired," unless the student requires special education (or a related service if that service is considered special education under state standards) as a result of the disability, the child does not meet the standards for being classified as a "child with a disability" and is not entitled to IDEA rights [34 C.F.R. § 300.7(a)].

The third issue: Where must a student with AIDS be educated? Once a student meets the definition of a "child with a disability", the issue shifts from whether the child qualifies under IDEA to what services the child is entitled to under IDEA. *Thomas v. Atascadero Unified School Dist.* (1986) prohibited an LEA from excluding a student with AIDS who bit a classmate. The case did not determine that the student is disabled under IDEA but, rather, that he is disabled under Section 504. Because no evidence showed that he posed a significant risk of harm to his kindergarten classmates or teachers and because the LEA failed to meet its burden to show that he is not otherwise qualified to attend a regular-school kindergarten class, the court ordered that he be retained in that class.

Although the decision did not involve an interpretation of IDEA, it applies to IDEA. This is because the regulations and burden of proof under Section 504 are substantially the same as under IDEA. Thus, placement in the general class, in the absence of proof of dangerousness, is presumed to be correct.

Students who qualify for special education because they have a disability in addition to HIV and AIDS still are required to be educated in the least restrictive environment. In *Martinez v. School Bd. of Hillsborough County* (1988), the student, who was diagnosed as "trainable mentally handicapped" (TMH), began her fight to be educated in the regular TMH room although she was incontinent and sucked her thumb continually.

The Eleventh Circuit held that this student, like any other who is eligible for IDEA protection, has a right to be educated in the least restrictive environment. Certain precautionary measures must be taken, and instruction must be provided so the student will learn to use the toilet and refrain from sucking her thumb. The LEA must educate the student in the regular TMH classroom behind a glass barrier until she has acquired these desirable behaviors.

In addition, if a question arises as to the advisability of the student's being in the classroom on a certain day, the school nurse should be consulted for an evaluation of the student or any other student to prevent infections. The court concluded that the appropriate placement for the student, then, was the regular TMH classroom.

Conclusion and Rationale

The AIDS cases to date demonstrate clearly that determinations regarding students with HIV and AIDS must be individualized (not a "meat-ax" approach that covers all students or persons affected by an AIDS condition); there must be a public-health basis for exclusion (a close connection between the child's condition and behavior, on the one hand, and, on the other, the safety of students and teachers); the exclusion must rest on defensible and reasonable medical testimony; and the decision must be appealable through the fair-hearing process ("due process hearing"—see Chapter 7). The reasons for these results are the following:

1. People with AIDS are considered to have a disability under Section 504 and may be considered eligible for IDEA benefits if the disability causes them to need special education.
2. The zero-reject principle and the equal protection doctrine prohibit discrimination and exclusion, as long as the person is found to have a disability under Section 504 or IDEA.
3. The doctrine of the least restrictive alternative/environment (see Chapter 6) creates a presumption that students with AIDS should be educated in general programs. Although the presumption may be overcome in the event of dangerousness to others, the LEA has the burden of proof in seeking to overcome the presumption.
4. The due-process clause of the Fourteenth Amendment (see Chapter 7) requires not only individualized determinations but also opportunities for the student to protest any planned exclusion; and the regulations implementing Section 504, as well as IDEA and its regulations, codify the principle of due process and procedural protection.
5. The public's fear—"fear itself"—does not justify exclusion of the student any more than fear justified an exclusionary zoning ordinance that prohibited group homes for people with mental retardation (*Cleburne v. Cleburne Living Center, Inc.*, 1985) or permitted a person who is not dangerous to himself or others to be incarcerated involuntarily in a mental hospital (*O'Connor v. Donaldson*, 1975).
6. Education is an especially valuable public service, and access to it should not be denied except for the most serious of reasons (*Brown v. Board of Education*, 1954, and *Plyler v. Doe*, 1982).
7. Exclusion, coupled with identification of the student as having an AIDS condition, creates a special stigma and, in the words of the Supreme Court in *Plyler v. Doe* (1982), can cause "lifetime hardships on a discrete class of children not accountable for their disabling status."
8. Homebound or hospital-based special education is an appropriate alternative to total exclusion for the student whose dangerousness has been proved and for whom the presumption of inclusion in general education programs has been overcome.

Participation in Sports

One avenue to inclusion for students with disabilities is through participation in sports. Unfortunately, these students face certain roadblocks to their participation. Sometimes these barriers are products of a student's own disability, and sometimes they derive from eligibility rules.

Restrictions Based on Extent of Disability

The cases reach contradictory results in deciding whether children with disabilities are entitled to the protection of Section 504 when seeking to engage in contact sports. Factual differences explain the results in these cases. Where students win court decisions requiring LEAs to allow them to compete, the evidence is persuasive that the contact sports pose no unusual risk of injury and the student and his parents are willing to assume a risk of injury (*Grube v. Bethlehem Area School Dist.*, 1982; and *Pace v. Dryden Central School Dist.*, 1991). These cases adopt a risk-benefit approach so that, if the risk is high, the student may be excluded without being discriminated against under Section 504. He or she is not "otherwise qualified" (because risk is so high) and "no reasonable accommodations" can be made in a contact sport.

Restrictions Based on Age

Because students with disabilities are entitled to services under IDEA through age 21, many of them are enrolled in school past their 18th birthday. Some state interscholastic athletic associations, however, limit eligibility for participation in sports to students 18 years of age and younger. Students who turn 19 before September 1 of the current academic year often are denied participation in sports. Many advocates of children with disabilities regard this as an exclusionary practice—denying students with disabilities full participation in the high school setting—and have claimed that Section 504 prohibits interscholastic athletic associations from enforcing the "age-18" rule (or similar age-limit rules).

The Sixth and the Eighth Circuits have decided this issue in favor of the state athletic associations. In *Sandison v. Michigan High School Athletic Ass'n Inc.* (1995), the court struck down the students' Section 504 and ADA claims, holding that, to prevail under Section 504, there must be proof that (a) the student is a disabled person under the Act; (b) the student is "otherwise qualified" for participation in the program; (c) the student is being excluded from participation in, being denied benefits of, or being subjected to discrimination under the program solely by reason of the disability; and (d) the relevant program or activity is receiving federal financial assistance.

The court found that the students failed to meet two of the four required elements.

1. The plaintiffs did not meet the "solely by reason of disability" requirement. The only reason plaintiffs cannot meet the age requirement is their date of birth, and their age alone, not their disabilities, is the basis of their disqualification and ineligibility.

2. The plaintiffs are not "otherwise qualified" to participate in the program even with reasonable accommodations.

An accommodation is deemed unreasonable if it imposes undue financial and administrative burdens on the LEA or requires a fundamental alteration in the nature of the program. Asking the athletic association to waive the age requirement is not a reasonable accommodation, because waiving the age requirement fundamentally alters the sports program and creates an undue burden on the athletic association to determine if the students' participation creates an unfair competitive advantage to the student's school.

The court also concluded that the students were not discriminated against under ADA. Title III of ADA (42 U.S.C. §§ 12181-12189) prohibits discrimination on the basis of a disability in public accommodations operated by private entities. Because public school grounds and public parks holding interscholastic sporting events are operated by public entities (LEAs), they cannot by definition constitute privately operated business under Title III. Thus, they are exempt from ADA, Title III.

Next the court evaluated the students' claims under ADA, Title II, which prohibits any state or local government from excluding any qualified individual with a disability from participation in or the benefits of the services, programs, or activities of a public entity (42 U.S.C. § 12132). Were the students "otherwise qualified?" No. The students were excluded not because of their disabilities but, instead, as a result of their age. Other cases reaching the same result include *Pottgen v. Missouri High School Activities Ass'n.* (1994) and *Rhodes v. Ohio School Athletic Ass'n.* (1996).

Children's Residence

Some parents of children with disabilities have shopped for appropriate programs and, in the process, raised questions about the child's legal residence and the identity of the school district responsible for the child's education. As a rule, the courts have not been sympathetic to these parents.

A good illustration is *Connelly v. Gibbs* (1983), in which the court found that, when the parents and child have their principal residence in one school district and a secondary residence in another, the second district is not required to educate the child. The plaintiffs were unable to show any reason, other than education of their child with a disability, for establishing a second residence. Similarly, if parents send their child out of state to be educated without consulting the LEA, the parents will bear the cost for their child's education (*Wise v. Ohio Dept. of Educ.*, 1996).

Likewise, in *Fairfield Bd. of Educ. v. Connecticut State Dept. of Educ.* (1983), a Connecticut LEA was found not liable for the costs of placing a child with a disability at a residential center in Connecticut. The child's natural parents, who had moved to Vermont, had transferred guardianship to another couple in Connecticut to maintain the child's placement in that state. The transfer of guardianship was a "sham" not binding on the Connecticut LEA. Its sole purpose was to retain the Connecticut placement.

A student, however, does have bona fide residence in a state and school district when (a) the student's parents, who live outside of the United States and are not citizens, have transferred the student's guardianship to relatives who are residents of the state and who are citizens, (b) if the student herself is a citizen of the United States, and (c) guardianship was established legally, in good faith, and not just to obtain special education in a certain state or school district (*Sonya C. v. Arizona School for Blind and Deaf*, 1990).

Residency is properly determined by state law, which almost uniformly links the child's residence to the parents' residence. In *Catlin v. Sobol* (1996), the parents, who were located in one school district in New York, sent their child to live in a different school district with another couple, whom the child came to know as his parents. The LEA of his natural parents' residence paid for his education until his parents moved to Massachusetts, at which time it refused to continue to pay. The other New York LEA also refused to pay for the child's education, contending that the child now was a resident of Massachusetts and that state law excused it from paying for the child's education.

The court determined that a state statute is neither arbitrary nor unreasonable in creating a presumption that, in the absence of parental abandonment, children reside with their parents. Despite the natural parents' intention that their son reside in New York for many reasons other than his educational needs, a state is not required to inquire into the intentions of every parent who wants to educate his or her child in another state. Thus, the state statute does not violate the substantive due-process rule, as it is rationally related to the legitimate state interest of determining to whom it will provide a free education, and, accordingly, the New York LEAs are not obliged to educate the student. Nor does the statute violate the equal-protection doctrine, as it is rationally related to the legitimate state interests of protecting and preserving the right of the state's own residents to attend its schools free of charge and of maintaining local control over education.

Finally, the court determined that IDEA and the Rehabilitation Act (not just the state statute) both presume that a child resides with his or her parents and that the parents' resident school district is required to fund the child's education, wherever the child lives. Section 1412 (a)(11) of IDEA requires state education agencies to oversee the education of all children with disabilities within the state, even when that education is being administered by another state or local agency. Accordingly, the school district in which the student's parents reside is required to provide the child with a free appropriate education.

Effects of the Zero-Reject Rule

Having reviewed developments that led to adoption of the zero-reject rule by the courts and later by Congress, and having examined provisions of the IDEA and their interpretation by the courts, we now will discuss briefly the major effects of the zero-reject principle.

New Definitions for Equality

Students with disabilities owe an enormous debt to the civil rights movement. Without doubt, the Supreme Court's decision in *Brown* (the 1954 school desegregation case) is the most important case ever decided by any court insofar as the education of students with disabilities is concerned. At the very least, it established the doctrine of equal educational opportunity, attacked the dual system of education and law that had relegated African-Americans, students with disabilities, and other minority children to second-class status, and laid a foundation in the Constitution's Fourteenth Amendment (the equal protection clause) for *PARC*, *Mills*, and the other early special education cases.

The early cases and the IDEA began to fulfill the promise of the *Brown* case— that no schools or other government agencies may lawfully condone the second-class citizenship of any child. Extension of the civil rights movement from one discrete minority (African-Americans) to another (children and adults with disabilities) was the fulfillment of the Supreme Court's principle of equality under the eyes of the law.

Right-to-education cases following *Brown* deliberately and creatively expanded *Brown's* equal opportunities doctrine by establishing that the exclusion of children with disabilities from any opportunities to learn—much less from any reasonably beneficial opportunities—is unconstitutional under the equal protection clause. More than that, those cases, together with IDEA and other laws, established a new equal access (or equal opportunity) doctrine. They articulated the proposition that children with disabilities require access to the same or different types of resources as their nondisabled peers for the same, not necessarily different, purposes.

This notion of equality is different from the customary one. The usual meaning of equality (per *Brown*) is equal access to the same resources for the same purposes. The new meaning, in disabilities law, is access to the same resources (general education) or different resources (special education) for the same, not always different, purposes and outcomes. For an important reason, equality means something different for children with disabilities than it does for children without disabilities: The child's disability is a distinction that usually justifies a different approach.

This is illustrated best by examining the cases of three children with different disabilities. One child is mobility-impaired; his spina bifida condition has crippled his legs. He seeks to follow a college-preparatory curriculum in his local high school. For purposes of that curriculum only, to admit him into classrooms with students who do not have disabilities and to make no adjustments in his education is entirely consistent with the doctrine of equal opportunity. In most classrooms (a biology or chemistry lab or a physical education class may require physical, not academic, adjustments), equal opportunity for him consists of being treated exactly equally.

A second child has a hearing impairment but is not so disabled that she needs an interpreter. She uses a hearing aid. She is placed in the front of the room. The teacher distributes outlines of the course, writes frequently on the chalkboard, and faces the class directly, thereby enabling the child to be instructed both verbally and with written materials. To provide equal educational opportunity, some accommodations are required for this child. Equal opportunity for this student consists of equal treatment plus accommodations.

A third child has cerebral palsy and mental retardation, with speech and mobility impairments. Clearly, neither "exactly equal" nor "equal-plus" treatment will provide the child an opportunity to benefit from instruction. Here, special and different accommodations are required—typically, education by (among others) specially trained teachers, a curriculum that differs from, but is based on, that offered to children without disabilities, and perhaps extra services (the related services of IDEA). For this student, equal opportunity consists of *different (but favorable) treatment.*

Thus, one important effect of the early zero-reject rule is to *redefine the doctrine of equal educational opportunity* as it applies to children with disabilities and to establish different meanings of *equality* as it applies to people with and without disabilities. These fundamental redefinitions—based on the fact of the disability, which is the distinction that makes a difference— remain apparent in IDEA and various other laws.

IDEA makes it clear (through the principles of appropriate education and least restrictive environments (see Chapters 5 and 6) and through the transition provisions) that employment, full participation in community life, and integration into the general curriculum are high national priorities for students with disabilities. Likewise, the 1988 Technology-Related Assistance for Individuals with Disabilities Act funds statewide assistive technology programs to increase the independence, productivity, and integration of individuals with disabilities.

The 1986 amendments of the Rehabilitation Act created the supported employment initiative. The 1986 and 1990 amendments to the Developmental Disabilities Assistance and Bill of Rights Act clarified that the purpose of the law is to help individuals with disabilities become independent, productive, and integrated into society. Finally, the 1990 Americans with Disabilities Act (ADA) prohibited discrimination solely on the basis of disability in state and local government services, transportation, privately owned public accommodations, communications, and employment.

These laws reflect a major change in the concept of equality. When IDEA was first enacted in 1975, the equal-access doctrine required that students with disabilities have equal access to different resources (special education, primarily) but for different purposes (traditional outcomes generally included placement in group homes or sheltered workshops). The original doctrine assumed that, as a rule, individuals with disabilities would not be able to do what people without disabilities can do, even with support. Thus, although they should have equal access to the different resources of special education (to take into account their needs), they should have them in order to produce different results—that is, a life different from that of individuals without disabilities.

Today the equal-access doctrine means something radically different. It means that, as a general rule, individuals with disabilities should have equal access to the same resources for the same results. This doctrine assumes that individuals with disabilities will have the same or somewhat different kind of life as individuals without disabilities, depending on the extent of their disabilities, the extent to which society accommodates to their disabilities, their choices, and the availability of support to meet their needs. The key, of course, is the assumption of "sameness." No longer are "different" resources and outcomes the assumption; now "same" is assumed.

The doctrine thus assumes that equal access to the same resources—that is, access to general education services and to other public and private services and networks—will occur, with support. It also assumes that access to different resources—that is, special education, vocational rehabilitation, assistive technology, and special support systems—will occur, but for the purpose of enabling those with disabilities to have access to the "nondisabled" or "generic" world, as well as to a world that is primarily disability-oriented.

Thus, federal law no longer assumes a limited life for individuals with disabilities, lived separate and apart from people without disabilities. Instead, it assumes that individuals with disabilities will have opportunities to live in the "regular" world and be educated in regular programs, work in regular jobs, live in regular housing, and otherwise be more like than different from people without disabilities.

Change of Locus of Control of Education

By attacking school conduct that went to the very heart of education—exclusion from educational opportunity and improper educational assessment and placement—the early cases (*PARC* and *Mills*) and, later, the Congress in IDEA and the courts that interpreted IDEA have brought the conduct of schools—traditionally a matter of state and local control—under significant federal oversight. Frequently that oversight has been by federal judges, supervising the actions of state and local elected or appointed officials.

For example, *Brown* established federal control over where general education students were to be educated; Black and White students were to be educated together, because school segregation was unconstitutional under the equal-protection doctrine. But *PARC*, *Mills*, and the other early right-to-education cases established federal control over which students are to be educated ("All children can learn...all children shall be educated") and the terms under which they are to be educated (the new equal access doctrine). IDEA also affects what the students will be taught and where they will be taught; it affects the nature of the curriculum (appropriate education, Chapter 5) and the place it is delivered (LRE, Chapter 6).

Like *Brown*, the special education cases and IDEA together have had an enormous impact on state and local education budgets. They caused state and local legislators and school administrators to redirect the flow of funds within education so as to benefit students with disabilities. They also caused those same officials to seek new money for the education of students with disabilities.

In large part because of the large fiscal impact of IDEA on state and local budgets, and also in part because school reform efforts, initiated by the states and the federal government during the late 1980s and carried on throughout the 1990s, involve students with disabilities as well as those without disabilities, IDEA (in its 1997 version) allows state and local education agencies some flexibility in how they use the federal and state funds (see Chapter 10). This flexibility may mitigate, to some extent, the federal impact on education, but by no means does it signal a reversal of the *Brown*-originated, IDEA-solidified federal presence in education.

Law-and-Order Issues

As noted earlier in this chapter, the most controversial issue involving the zero-reject principle—and, arguably the most controversial issue involving all of IDEA—has been that of school discipline. The public's legitimate desire for safety in school—a desire shared by those involved in special education—has come into conflict with IDEA's policy to provide federal funds so that all (repeat: all) students with disabilities, whether they are or are not lawbreakers, shall receive an appropriate education.

In reconciling this conflict, the Supreme Court's decision in the 1988 case of *Honig v. Doe* created the "causal connection" or "manifestation" doctrine, enforced IDEA's "stay-put" rule, but created a "safety valve" (access to courts for an order allowing the schools to remove a dangerous student) so that a hard-and-fast rule of "all" would not collide with a valid need for school safety.

The 1997 amendments continue to balance the zero-reject principle with school-safety concerns. The House Committee with jurisdiction over IDEA noted that balance in its explanation of the "discipline" provisions:

> The Committee recognizes that school safety is important to educators and parents. There has been considerable debate and concern about both if and how those few children with disabilities who affect the school safety of peers, teachers, and themselves may be disciplined when they engage in behaviors that jeopardize such safety. In addition, the Committee is aware of the perception of a lack of parity when making decisions about disciplining children with and without disabilities who violate the same school rule or code of conduct.
>
> By adding a new section 615(k) to IDEA, the Committee has attempted to strike a careful balance between the LEA's duty to ensure that school environments are safe and conducive to learning for all children, including children with disabilities, and the LEA's continuing obligation to ensure that children with disabilities receive a free appropriate public education (FAPE). Thus, drawing on testimony, experience, and common sense, the Committee has placed specific and comprehensive guidelines on the matter of disciplining children with disabilities in this section.
>
> It is the Committee's intent that this set of practical and balanced guidelines reinforce and clarify the understanding of Federal policy on this matter, which is currently found in the statute, case law, regulations, and informal policy guidance. By placing all pertinent guidance in one place, the Committee anticipates that educators will have a better understanding of their areas of discretion in disciplining children with disabilities and that parents will have a better understanding of the protections available to their children with disabilities. (Committee Report, p. 108)

At the same time, IDEA's 1997 amendments resolve the difficult task of educating individuals with disabilities who, convicted as adults and imprisoned in adult correctional facilities, have, or may have, disabilities and thus a claim to special education. Again, there is a delicate balance between extending to these individuals, many of whom are from minority populations, the full rights of IDEA and at the same time assuring that the punitive and corrective/rehabilitative aspects of conviction and imprisonment can be carried out. IDEA seeks to find that balance, as the Committee made clear in its report:

> The bill provides that a State may also opt not to serve individuals who, in the educational placement prior to their incarceration in adult correctional facilities, were not actually identified as being a child with a disability under section 602 (3) or did not have an individualized education program under this part. The Committee means to set the point in time when it is determined whether a child has been identified or had an IEP. This makes clear that services need not be provided to all children who were at one time determined to be eligible under this part.
>
> The Committee does not intend to permit the exclusion from services under part B of children who had been identified as children with disabilities and had an IEP, but who had left school prior to their incarceration. In other words, if a child had an IEP in his or her last educational placement, the child has an IEP for purposes of this provision. The Committee added language to make clear that children with disabilities aged 18 through 21, who did not have an IEP in their last educational placement but who had actually been identified, should not be excluded from services. (Committee Report, p. 91)

Functional Assessments and Positive Behavioral Supports

Beginning in the mid-1980s and continuing to the time the 1997 amendments were enacted, professionals in the various disciplines relating to individuals with disabilities, and family members, too, have been greatly divided over another critical issue: Is it ever appropriate, as a matter of effective intervention, good law, and consensus-based ethics, to use aversive interventions to change the behavior of students with disabilities? Those interventions—sometimes called "negative" consequences or "punishments"—have included the use of electric shock, noxious substances, and extensive bodily restraints.

Even as the 1997 amendments were being debated and enacted, those who believe the students' rights to an education and to treatment justify, even demand, the use of aversive interventions, were locked in combat with those who believe that there is a better way—one that is more humane and also just as effective in overcoming the challenging behaviors that impede students' learning and disrupt the lives of others.

IDEA's 1997 amendments do not settle the matter entirely. Nevertheless, by requiring a state to have a policy regarding functional assessments and positive behavioral supports, and by requiring the decision-makers (in a "manifestation" determination and via other required findings) to consider whether functional assessment and positive behavioral supports should be used or have been used effectively

[20 U.S.C. §§ 1415 (k)(4) and 1414 (d)(3)(B)(i); 34 C.F.R. § 300.346 (a)(2)(i)], IDEA now goes a long way to settling the issue.

Even though IDEA does not absolutely prohibit state and local education agencies from using aversive or negative interventions, it does create a strong presumption in favor of functional assessment and positive behavioral supports, which are, needless to say, non-aversive and non-negative. In fact, consideration of positive behavioral support strategies is required in developing IEPs for children with impeding behavior [34 C.F.R. § 300.346 (a)(2)(i)]. Given IDEA's provisions and the state-of-art in functional assessments and positive behavioral supports, professionals will be hard-pressed to justify any other behavioral interventions.

A consequence of the zero-reject rule, then, is to merge research on behavior and interventions with the law and public policy, and to create, through that merger, a humane and effective environment—the school—applying state of the art. After all, one of the barriers to effective special education has been the schools' failure to replicate research on effective learning [20 U.S.C. § 1400 (c)(4)]; and one of the solutions to that problem is, at last, a legal presumption in favor of functional assessment and positive behavioral support—a thoroughly researched and effective intervention.

Expanded Practices and Individualization

The cases and IDEA have pushed hard at the limits of public education systems. They have demonstrated the plasticity of the system, that seemingly intransigent systems can change (albeit slowly; never underestimate the power of inertia), and that a (sometimes fragile) consensus exists about the inherent rightness of special education. The early cases, coupled with IDEA, thus have had the effect of both commanding and enabling change, and of requiring and facilitating expansion of the educational system so it can provide equal educational opportunities to children with disabilities.

One of the most significant changes in school practices has been in the methods of instruction. The zero-reject principle has individualized educational services for children with disabilities. More than that, it has caused educators to extend the practice of individualization to children who are gifted and talented (and enact special education laws that grant to those children substantially the same rights as are granted to children with disabilities). It also has caused educators and policy-makers to be particularly aware of the deficits in educating at-risk students (children who are not classified formally as having disabilities under IDEA but who still require special attention). The megapolitics of the zero-reject doctrine, then, have been to extend to others the benefits (individualized education) that children with disabilities have as a matter of right. (The "incidental benefit" rule, discussed in Chapter 6, underscores this conclusion.)

The Impetus Toward Integration

On still another level, the cases and IDEA have begun to integrate children with disabilities into the mainstream of life in the United States. The courts and the Congress both asserted the value of inclusion in requiring that, to the maximum extent appropriate, children with and without disabilities be educated together (see Chapter 6 for a detailed discussion of this principle).

The integration-inclusion principle also has had an important effect on state mental retardation centers, psychiatric hospitals for children, and schools for deaf or blind children. The children in those institutions have been given an opportunity to be deinstitutionalized. They have been given a right to education in the public school system. The result is that, in many cases, they have not been placed in the institutions to begin with, have been discharged from institutions, or have been kept in the institutions but given more adequate and effective educational services there or in cooperating local school districts.

The integration-inclusion principle in education was developing at the same time that the institutions (psychiatric hospitals and mental retardation facilities) were admitting fewer children. This reduction had at least several related and important causes. First, state legislatures were tightening up the procedures by which people could be committed to the state institutions. They were requiring much more due process, and thereby discouraging commitment. Similarly, legislatures were enacting stricter criteria for commitment, requiring that the usual standard of "dangerousness" be met more clearly and indisputably.

Second, the U.S. Supreme Court ruled in *Addington v. Texas* (1979) and in *Parham v. J.R.* (1979), respectively, that states must prove dangerousness by fairly strict procedures, and that states must provide for neutral review of admission decisions when children are candidates for institutionalization. Both cases had the effect of putting real clamps on institutionalization.

Third, the states (with federal assistance under the home-and-community-based authority in Title XIX, the Medicaid program of the Social Security Act) were developing more community-based treatment programs for children and using institutional placements less and less.

The cumulative effect of these three developments was to accelerate the impetus for integration. In conjunction with IDEA provisions for zero-reject and least-restrictive placement, these developments changed the character of the public schools significantly.

New Norms and Pluralism

The norms of schools themselves have changed in important ways. The norm now is not nearly as "nondisabled." The presence of children with disabilities in school has changed the composition of the schools. In a real sense, their presence has augmented the schools' cultural diversity and pluralism.

This enrichment undoubtedly will have important effects on the lives of adults. A result of the integration impetus is greater diversity in society. And professionals who once regarded some children as unworthy of an education or unable to benefit from training now are engaged in educating and training those same children. Not only have systems changed, but so, too, have people.

Lifetime Service

The court cases and IDEA also have forced health, mental health, social services/ welfare, and educational systems to begin serious efforts, separately or cooperatively and jointly, to provide community-based services. These include child-find, educational placement, cost-sharing, facility-sharing, and family support services. These efforts represent the first long-range efforts, on a large scale, to secure community integration and at-home placement of children with disabilities. They also represent the beginnings of a lifetime service system for people with disabilities.

Given the early childhood initiative, the requirement for related services, and the "transition" or "aging-out" initiative, IDEA set into motion a link between schools and other agencies in which the schools are the primary service providers and other agencies are secondary providers during the school years of persons with disabilities. Upon the person's exit from school, the latter take over the principal-provider role. Accordingly, the change wrought in schools also effected a change in adult service systems (regulated by Section 504 and ADA, just as the schools are).

"Defective" Newborns

At the same time that *Brown* and the zero-reject rule were being applied to students with disabilities, an awareness developed in the public, and especially among the professionals dealing with people with disabilities that gross discrimination was being practiced against newborns who have birth defects. Withholding medically appropriate treatment from "defective" newborns has been the center of a major policy and legal debate.

The policy issue is whether families, physicians, and the public should condone the withholding of treatment (or engaging in other practices that jeopardize the child's life). The legal issues, on the other hand, center on newborns' constitutional rights to be treated in the same way as nondisabled newborns are treated (equal protection in medical care), the enforcement of state and federal child abuse and neglect laws, and the tolerable zones of privacy that families and physicians may establish to fend off external review of their treatment/nontreatment decisions.

In a very real sense, the constitutional doctrines of *Brown* and the special education cases are applicable by analogy to the *Baby Doe* cases (so-called because of the name given to unidentified newborns in lawsuits involving their treatment). If equality before the law means anything, it means that these newborns are entitled to appropriate medical treatment. And if that treatment is given and is lifesaving, the medical and other interventions must be forthcoming: A society that compels a life to be saved is one that also must compel services to the person. Thus, special education is involved in the *Baby Doe* cases in two ways—first, by extension of the equal-protection doctrine; and second, by providing early intervention and education.

Cost-Effective Education

People have always argued—and probably always will—that spending public money to fund the education of students with disabilities is not a wise expenditure.

Nonetheless, early intervention for infants and toddlers with disabilities or at risk of having disabilities is clearly cost-effective. That is an undergirding premise of Part C (zero to 3). Moreover, it has become clear that special education at the elementary, middle school, and secondary levels is cost-effective. It reduces the number of persons classified as having disabilities, prevents or reduces grade retention, enables some people with disabilities to acquire skills that make them less dependent on others, and allows many to become wage earners.

The fiscal contribution of zero reject and the equality doctrine is important not only for persons with disabilities but also for the larger public. More than that, the naysayers of equality have been answered with doctrine and dollars. The response is, indeed, powerful.

In its 1997 version, IDEA recognizes that special education has been effective, though not as effective as it could have been [20 U.S.C. §§ 1400 (c)(3) & (4)]. To have improved the educational results for students with disabilities is itself a cost-effective accomplishment. Yet, the 1997 amendments also recognize that state and local education agencies have been limited in what they may do with federal funds; accordingly (as Chapter 10 points out in detail), IDEA creates new flexibility for those agencies, in the hope that general and special education will, together, become more effective [20 U.S.C. § 1400 (c)(5)].

IDEA's 1997 amendments also clarify that, when a student is eligible for federal or state benefits (in addition to special education), the agencies that provide those benefits must put up their funds first and in advance of the state and local education agencies. Only after the "payors of first resort" have done so and the student has exhausted his or her claim to those benefits may a state or local education agency be required to contribute to the student's education.

These provisions have a significant cost-effectiveness aspect. They marshal the entire range of federal-state funds for which the student is eligible, thereby assuring access to a wider and deeper pool of money for the student's education. That in itself is cost-effective for the student.

More than that, they shift some of the costs of the student's education from the state and local education agencies to other agencies, thereby relieving the education agencies' budgets of the cost of educating that student (and others similarly eligible for other funding sources) and simultaneously enlarging the agencies' ability to serve other students. In short, cost-spreading and cost-sharing are strategies for cost-effective special education.

Private Schools, Parent Choice, and Church-State Separation

Two themes underlie IDEA's provisions and the Supreme Court's decisions about the education of students with disabilities in private schools. One theme is pro-family: The family should have the opportunity, even a right, to choose where to educate its child, and if that choice is in favor of a private school, the choice should not be discouraged or made punitive by denying the student access to special education.

Accordingly, IDEA provides for a student in a private school, enrolled there by the parents, to benefit from IDEA.

IDEA also recognizes that charter schools are new and, in some parts of the country, popular alternatives to the longstanding, traditional public schools. IDEA extends to the charter schools the same duties that the usual public schools have, recognizing that parents who enroll their children in charter schools should not lose the right to benefits of IDEA as a consequence of that choice.

A second theme, originating in the constitution's requirement of separation between church and state, is more ephemeral and nebulous, but nonetheless very real. It is, in a word, that moral education is a valid dimension of public education and public policy. The Supreme Court's decisions (*Zobrest*, *Grumet*, and *Agostini*) can be read fairly as acknowledging that, though there must be a wall between church and state and that entanglement of those two entities of American life should be minimized, schools themselves are in the business of providing a moral basis for a student's life; indeed, that is an express purpose of religion-based schools, and it arguably is a purpose of many private, non-religion-based schools, too.

By extending IDEA's benefits to students enrolled in private, religion-based schools, Congress not only codified the Supreme Court's *Zobrest* decision (Committee Report, p. 93), but it also anticipated the *Agostini* decision. More fundamentally, it declared that, like the Court, it will support some enmeshment of church and state so moral education may be made available to those who seek it. Note, however, that children who are placed in private schools by their parents have no individual right to receive some or all of the special education and related services that the child would receive if enrolled in a public school [20 U.S.C. § 1412 (a)(10)(A); 34 C.F.R. § 300.454 (a)].

Hiring People with Disabilities

For a child's education to be meaningful after he or she leaves school, SEAs and LEAs must make positive efforts to hire and promote qualified persons with disabilities in programs receiving IDEA funds [20 U.S.C. § 1405]. All of the education and training the schools provide to students is meaningless unless the students have a realistic opportunity to make use of it later. Zero reject in special education should not be an empty promise. And, of course, economic benefits will accrue to the public if individuals with disabilities are hired. The employment provisions in 1405 of IDEA (Section 606 of the Act but 1405 in the U.S. Code) dovetail with Section 504 of the Rehabilitation Act and the Americans with Disabilities Act to prohibit discrimination in employment and to require reasonable accommodations in the employment, in the school system, of people with disabilities.

Conclusion ⌒

When Congress first enacted IDEA in 1975, it intended the law to benefit all students with disabilities. Despite some slight modifications in the extent of students' rights, the 1997 amendments adhere to the original intent.

"All" means "all," and "zero reject" means "zero." More than just benefiting all students with disabilities, IDEA benefits all students, including those without disabilities. Its impact on schools extends to other domains of society as well: IDEA has justified Congress in declaring that disability is a "natural part of the human experience," leading us all to accommodate, even to welcome, those who so many had rejected. Today, it is correct to declare that, in part because of the zero-reject principle, "disabled" does not mean unworthy.

Reference ∾

Committee Report, House of Representatives Committee on Education and The Workforce, on H.R. 5 (IDEA Amendments of 1997)(Passed as PL 105–17). H.R. Rep. No. 95, 105th Cong., 1st Sess. (1997).

Cases ∾

Addington v. Texas, 441 U.S. 418 (1979).

Agostini v. Felton, 138 L.Ed.2d 391 (U.S. 1997).

Alexander S. v. Boyd, 876 F. Supp. 773 (D.S.C. 1995).

Ashland Sch. Dist. v. New Hampshire Div. for Children, Youth & Families, 681 A.2d 71 (N.H. 1996).

Bd. of Educ. of City of Plainfield v. Cooperman, 523 A.2d 655 (N.J. 1987).

Bd. of Educ. of Kiryas Joel Village School Dist. v. Grumet, 618 N.E.2d 94 (N.Y. 1993), aff'd, 512 U.S. 687 (1994).

Bd. of Educ. v. Rowley, 458 U.S. 176 (1982).

Borgna v. Binghampton City School Dist., 18 IDELR 121 (N.D.N.Y. 1991).

Bowen v. Massachusetts, 487 U.S. 879 (1988).

Bragdon v. Abbott, 118 S.Ct. 2196, 524 U.S. 624 (1998).

Brown v. Board of Education, 347 U.S. 483 (1954).

C.A. v. Christina Sch. Dist., 20 IDELR 967 (D. Del. 1993).

Catlin v. Sobol, 881 F. Supp. 789 (N.D.N.Y. 1995), rev'd, 93 F.3d 1112 (2nd Cir. 1996).

Cefalu v. East Baton Rouge Parish Sch. Bd., 907 F. Supp. 966 (M.D.La. 1995); vacated 103 F.3d 393 (5th Cir. 1997).

Cleburne v. Cleburne Living Center, Inc., 473 U.S. 432 (1985).

Connelly v. Gibbs, 445 N.E.2d 477 (Ill. App.Ct. 1983).

David B. v. Patla, 24 IDELR 952 (N.D.Ill. 1996).

Dist. 27 Community School Bd. v. Bd. of Educ. of New York City, 502 N.Y.S.2d 325 (Sup. Ct. NY 1986).

Doe v. Belleville Public Schools Dist. No. 118, 672 F. Supp. 342 (S.D. Ill. 1987).

Doe v. Rockingham County School Bd., 658 F. Supp. 403 (W.D.Va. 1987).

Evans v. Tuttle, 613 N.E.2d 854 (Ind. Ct. App. 1993).

Fairfield Bd. of Educ. v. Connecticut State Dept. of Educ., 466 A.2d 343 (Super. Ct. 1983), aff'd, 503 A.2d 1147 (1986).

Felter v. Cape Girardeau School Dist., 830 F. Supp. 1279 (E.D.Mo. 1993).

Goodall v. Stafford County School Bd., 930 F.2d 363 (4th Cir. 1991), cert. denied, 502 U.S. 864 (1991), appeal granted, 60 F.3d 168 (4th Cir. 1995); cert. denied, 133 L.Ed2d 661 (U.S. 1996).

Goss v. Lopez, 419 U.S. 565 (1975).

Green v. Johnson, 513 F. Supp. 965 (D.Mass. 1981).

Grube v. Bethlehem Area School Dist., 550 F. Supp. 418 (E.D.Pa. 1982).

Hacienda La Puente Unified School Dist. v. Honig, 976 F.2d 487 (9th Cir. 1992).

Helms v. Indep. School Dist. No. 3 of Broken Arrow, 750 F.2d 820 (10th Cir. 1984), cert. denied, 471 U.S. 1018 (1985).

Honig v. Doe, 484 U.S. 305 (1988).

J.B. v. Indep. School Dist., 21 IDELR 1157 (D.Minn. 1995).

Jenkins v. Florida, 931 F.2d 1469 (11th Cir. 1991).

K.R. v. Anderson Community Sch. Corp., 81 F.3d 673 (7th Cir. 1996), vacated, 138 L.Ed.2d 1007 (U.S. 1997).

Kaelin v. Grubbs, 682 F.2d 595 (6th Cir. 1982).

Lemon v. Kurtzman, 411 U.S. 192 (1973).

Levine v. New Jersey, 522 EHLR 163 (N.J.Sup. Ct. 1980).

Lunceford v. District of Columbia Bd. of Ed., 745 F.2d 1577 (D.C. Cir. 1984).

M.P. by D.P. v. Grossmont Union High School Dist., 858 F. Supp. 1044 (S.D.Cal. 1994).

Martinez v. School Bd. of Hillsborough County, 675 F. Supp. 1574 (M.D.Fla. 1987), vacated, 861 F.2d 1502 (11th Cir. 1988).

Mills v. District of Columbia Bd. of Ed., 348 F. Supp. 866 (D.D.C. 1972); contempt proceedings, EHLR 551:643 (D.D.C. 1980).

Morgan v. Chris L., No. 94-6561, 1997 U.S. App. Lexis 1041 (6th Cir. 1997), cert. denied, 138 L.Ed.2d 207 (U.S. 1997).

Natchez-Adams School Dist. v. Searing, 918 F. Supp. 1028 (S.D.Miss. 1996).

New Hampshire Dept. of Educ. v. City of Manchester, 23 IDELR 1057 (D.N.H. 1996).

O'Connor v. Donaldson, 422 U.S. 563 (1975).

Pace v. Dryden Central School Dist., 574 N.Y.S.2d 142 (Sup. Ct. 1991).

Parents v. Coker, 676 F. Supp. 1072 (E.D. Okla. 1987).

Parham v. J.R., 442 U.S. 584 (1979).

Parks v. Pavkovic, 753 F.2d 1397 (7th Cir. 1985).

Pennsylvania Ass'n for Retarded Children (PARC) v. Pennsylvania, 334 F. Supp. 1257 (E.D. Pa. 1971); 343 F. Supp. 279 (E.D. Pa. 1972).

Pennsylvania Dept. of Corrections v. Yeskey, 524 U.S. 206 (1998).

Petties v. District of Columbia, 897 F. Supp. 626 (D.D.C. 1995).

Plyler v. Doe, 457 U.S. 202 (1982).

Pottgen v. Missouri State High School Activities Ass'n., 40 F.3d 926 (8th Cir. 1994).

Prince William County School Bd. v. Wills, 16 EHLR 1109 (1989).

Printz v. United States, 138 L.Ed.2d 914 (U.S. 1997).

Raymond S. v. Ramirez, 918 F.Supp. 1280 (N.D. Iowa 1995).

Rhodes v. Ohio High School Athletic Ass'n., 939 F. Supp. 584 (N.D.Ohio 1996).

Rodiriecus L. v. Waukegan School Dist. #60, 90 F.3d 249 (7th Cir. 1996).

Russman v. Sobol, 85 F.3d 1050 (2nd Cir. 1996), vacated, 138 L.Ed.2d 1008 (U.S. 1997).

S-1 v. Turlington, 635 F.2d 342 (5th Cir. 1981); cert. denied, 454 U.S. 1030 (1981).

Sandison v. Michigan High School Athletic Ass'n Inc., 863 F. Supp. 483 (E.D.Mich. 1994), rev'd in part, appeal dismissed in part, 64 F.3d 1026 (6th Cir. 1995).

School Bd. of Nassau County v. Arline, 480 U.S. 273 (1987).

Seals v. Loftis, 614 F. Supp. 302 (E.D.Tenn. 1985).

Sonya C. v. Arizona School for Deaf and Blind, 743 F. Supp. 700 (D.Ariz. 1990).

Stafford County School Bd. v. Farley, 16 EHLR 1119 (Va. Cir. Ct. 1990).

Steldt v. School Bd. of the Riverdale School Dist., 885 F. Supp. 1192 (W.D.Wis. 1995).

Texas City Indep.School Dist. v. Jorstad, 752 F. Supp. 231 (S.D.Tex. 1990).

Thomas v. Davidson Academy, 846 F. Supp. 611 (M.D. Tenn. 1994).

Thomas v. Atascadero Unified School Dist., 662 F. Supp. 376 (C.D.Cal. 1986).

Timothy W. v. Rochester School Dist., 559 EHLR 480 (D.N.H. 1988), 875 F.2d 954 (1st Cir. 1989), cert. denied, 493 U.S. 983 (1989).

Township High School Dist. Bd. of Educ. v. Kurtz-Imig, 16 EHLR 17 (N.D.Ill. 1989).

United States v. Lopez, 514 U.S. 549 (1995).

Virginia Dept. of Educ. v. Riley, 23 F.3d 80 (4th Cir. 1994), appeal, 86 F.3d 1337 (4th Cir. 1996), on reh'g, 106 F.3d 559 (4th Cir. 1997).

Walker v. San Francisco Unified School Dist., 46 F.3d 1449 (9th Cir. 1995).

Wilson v. McDonald, EHLR 558: 364 (E.D.Ky. 1987).

Wise v. Ohio Dept. of Educ., 80 F.3d 177 (6th Cir. 1996).

Zobrest v. Catalina Foothills School Dist., 963 F.2d 1190 (9th Cir. 1992), rev'd, 509 U.S. 1 (1993).

Hearing Officer Decisions ∼

Academy School Dist., No. 20, 21 IDELR 965 (1994).

Bay County School Dist., 20 IDELR 920 (1995).

Beaumont Indep. School Dist., 21 IDELR 261 (1994).

Bryan County School Dist., 20 IDELR 930 (1993).

In re J.W., 23 IDELR 459 (1995).

Kershaw School Dist., 20 IDELR 445 (1993).

Lakeland Sch. Corp., 29 IDELR 1133 (1999).

Limestone County (AL) Sch. Dist., 27 IDELR 231 (1997).

Modesto City School, 21 IDELR 685 (1995).

Oakland Unified School Dist., 20 IDELR 1338 (1993).

Oconee County Sch. Sys., 27 IDELR 629 (1997).

Philadelphia School Dist., 21 IDELR 318 (1994).

Snowline Joint Unified School Dist., 21 IDELR 491 (1994).

Walpole Public School, 22 IDELR 1075 (1995).

Testing, Classification, and Placement

The purpose of the zero-reject principle is to assure that each student with a disability has access to education. It is a door-opener, a rule against exclusion, and a rule in favor of participation. The zero-reject principle, however, does not assure that, once the student is admitted to the school system, the student will benefit from it. Much more is required than simply opening the doors. That "more" begins with an evaluation of the student's strengths and needs.

Once an evaluation has been conducted, the schools are in a position to provide an appropriate education, one that benefits the student. In evaluating the student, the key is to do so in a way that accurately identifies the student's abilities (strengths) and disabilities (needs). For many years, however, education evaluation relied extensively—some would say exclusively—on tests of intellectual ability. Although these tests had many strengths, they also had at least two shortcomings:

1. They focused solely on the student's cognitive, but not other, characteristics.
2. They arguably discriminated against certain students—namely, those who were from minority populations or who had physical or sensory disabilities that prevented them from demonstrating, through the tests, their strengths and needs.

Given these two shortcomings, IDEA requires nondiscriminatory evaluation of each student. Before describing IDEA's provisions and the ways in which the courts have interpreted them, we will explore the fundamental criticism of the schools' traditional evaluations: the various IQ tests.

Pre-IDEA Criticisms of Testing 〜

Most of the criticism has been directed at IQ tests and their use. These tests supposedly are objective and allegedly do not depend on irrelevant variables such as teacher prejudice or social class. Nevertheless, they have been subject to criticism, particularly when test results have been the primary bases for assigning a disproportionate number of minority pupils—African-American or those who are non-English speaking—to special education programs for students (*Larry P. v. Riles,* 1972, 1974, 1979, 1984; *Mattie T. v. Holladay,* 1979; *Hobsen v. Hansen,* 1967; *Guadalupe Org. Inc., v. Tempe,* 1979; *Diana v. State Bd. of Ed.,* 1973; *LeBanks v. Spears,* 1976). Those assignments threaten to reestablish racially dual systems of education.

One basis for criticizing the tests has been that they have been used to determine the intelligence of children who are unfamiliar with the English language or with the White middle-class culture that underlies the test questions. In short, it has been argued that tests based on a White middle-class socioeconomic group should not be used with persons who are not of that group because the tests put the latter at an initial disadvantage and could lead to their being classified mistakenly as having a disability. This is especially true when the tests are not administered in the child's native language (e.g., Spanish) or when they do not also measure adaptive behavior, a child's ability to cope and get along in his or her own cultural environment.

Misclassification resulting from inappropriate testing can impose on students the stigma of disability. Misclassification tells a child that he or she is deficient, and the injury to the child's self-esteem is incalculable. It can isolate students from normal school experiences and cause them to be rejected by students and adults alike. It can create stereotypical expectations of behavior and can lead to a self-fulfilling prophecy—all to the student's irreparable harm.

Often a disability label is permanent and cannot be escaped, outgrown, or rebutted. Similarly, assignment to a special education program can become permanent, despite an original intention to make it temporary. Moreover, the label can limit (or increase) the resources available to the student, because public and private agencies tend to serve only persons identified as belonging within their categorical clientele. Misclassified students might be placed in special education programs whether they do or do not need it, or they might be placed in inappropriate special education programs or be institutionalized inappropriately. Being placed in a special education program does not necessarily ensure that the student will receive training that will be effective in overcoming the disadvantages of being classified as disabled.

Although testing alone is not sufficient for developing an accurate picture of a student's abilities and disabilities, it often has been treated as if it were. In some cases, a single test has been used as the sole criterion for classification and placement. When not supplemented by other evaluation techniques (e.g., medical information, parent conferences), such testing results are particularly subject to misinterpretation.

All of these criticisms were leveled in the years before IDEA was first enacted in 1975 as PL 94–142. Sadly, the problem of classification continues in the late 1990s. Indeed, in its reauthorization of IDEA in 1997, Congress [20 U.S.C. § 1401(c)(7) through (10)] went to great lengths to point out that

1. U.S. society is increasingly diverse,
2. its racial profile is changing rapidly,
3. minority students are an ever larger percentage of public school students,
4. there is a need to bring more minority individuals into the professions that serve students with disabilities,
5. the limited-English population in the United States is the fastest growing population,
6. greater efforts are needed to prevent problems associated with mislabeling and high dropout rates among minority students with disabilities, and
7. minority and underserved people are socially disadvantaged because of the lack of opportunities in training and educational programs.

For all of these reasons, and also because of the lingering criticisms of the tests that schools use, nondiscriminatory evaluation is a core principle of IDEA. Indeed, those criticisms are one of the major reasons, if not the sole reason, why IDEA insists on nondiscriminatory evaluation. Likewise, the early remedies have found their way into IDEA.

Pre-IDEA Court-Ordered Remedies ~

Given the early criticisms, it is not surprising that pre-IDEA judicial responses were massive (*Larry P. v. Riles,* 1972, 1974, 1979, 1984; *Diana v. State Bd. of Ed.,* 1973; *Guadalupe Org., Inc., v. Tempe,* 1979; *Lau v. Nichols,* 1973; *LeBanks v. Spears,* 1976). Accepting the argument that intelligence tests bear little relationship to the intelligence they are supposed to measure in the event of language or cultural unfamiliarity, some courts held early that IQ tests could not be used to place children in ability tracks. They forbade schools to use biased (invalidated) tests that do not account properly for the cultural background and experiences of the children being tested. They enjoined school authorities from placing minority students in classes for students classified as educable mentally retarded on the basis of IQ tests if using the tests brought about racial imbalance in the composition of these classes. They also ordered the dismantling of EMR classes in which Hispanic/Latino students were overrepresented.

Additionally, they imposed on the schools the burden of proving that a test is a valid measure of intelligence and does not discriminate because of race or culture if the test was the primary basis for classifications that resulted in racial imbalance. In addition, they ordered that pupils be tested or retested in their primary language or be given bilingual instruction.

By ordering these remedies, the courts made it clear that they presumed that statistical imbalance (racial imbalance) would not have occurred without some sort of testing discrimination based on race. Moreover, the courts ordered that factors such as socioeconomic background, social adaptation, and adaptive ability be considered in making an evaluation for appropriate placement.

The early decisions on testing took the fundamental position that the use of the IQ test alone was found to violate substantive due process, because the basis for the school's action—the IQ score—was not reasonably related to the purpose for which it was used—namely, to determine a pupil's ability and what would constitute an "appropriate" education for him or her. As is true with respect to the zero-reject principle, so, too, with the principle of nondiscriminatory evaluation ("NDE"): The early cases influenced IDEA significantly as it was enacted originally in 1975. That original version remains intact in 1997, with improvements. Before discussing the NDE principle, however, reviewing why evaluation is important will be useful.

Why Evaluation Is Required ⌒

Evaluation, classification, and placement in special education programs must be continued, for several reasons.

1. The schools must be able to identify and evaluate students and determine who among them have disabilities (and of what kind and degree) in order to (a) plan, program, and appropriate funds for them, (b) provide appropriate services for them, (c) comply with federal and state laws requiring that students be counted and served, (d) evaluate their own efforts to educate children, and (e) serve their bureaucratic interests in maintaining and expanding their own services.
2. Classification can assist in measuring the results of special education efforts.
3. Classification can create educational opportunity for students regarded as having a disability, supply a common denominator to create and stimulate activities of volunteer or professional interest groups, assist in enacting legislation to aid individuals in a specific category, provide structure for governmental programs, and serve as a basis for financial appropriation decisions.
4. Classification is useful for determining disability incidence and prevalence data, which are helpful in planning how many professionals will be needed for a wide variety of services.
5. Some of the reasons students perform poorly on standardized tests—such as slow work habits, emotional insecurity, low motivation, lack of interest, and culturally related conditions—also account for their below-average performance in school. Thus, testing can provide an early warning of probable or possible future problems.

Individuals with Disabilities Education Act (IDEA) ⌒

For all of these reasons, procedures should be established to protect students from improper evaluation, misclassification, and inappropriate placement, and to ensure that evaluation and classification, when necessary, accurately describe students' strengths and disabilities and becomes a useful device for appropriately educating them. Thus, IDEA addresses both the techniques for classification and the action founded on the classification, requiring both procedural safeguards and substantive protection.

Child Find

Of course, schools need to know what students they must serve. Thus, states have an affirmative duty to ensure that all children with disabilities are identified, located, and evaluated [20 U.S.C. 1412(a)(3)(A)]. The exact procedures and policies that must be followed in meeting these "child find" obligations is left up to the individual states. Generally, the procedures require evaluation whenever the school officials have or should have knowledge or reasonable suspicion that the child might have a disability (*Hoffman v. East Troy Comm. Sch. Dist.,* 1999).

Parental requests for assessment are almost always sufficient to meet this reasonable-knowledge standard. School districts in some states must attempt to assist the student through regular education before referring him or her to special education for assessment, unless sufficient evidence suggests that an immediate referral is necessary (*San Jose U.S.D.,* 1998). Having identified students who have or may have a disability, the schools then must undertake a comprehensive evaluation of these students.

Nondiscriminatory Evaluation Procedures

Generally speaking, IDEA requires a multidisciplinary, multifaceted, nonbiased evaluation of a child before classifying and providing special education to that child. The requirement of fair evaluation as a prerequisite to classification also is a requirement of individualization. Due process mandates nothing less. If a student is not assessed individually when the result of that assessment could be a benefit (e.g., special education if needed) or a special burden (e.g., assignment to special education if the child does not have a disability), the student's constitutional rights to due process—enjoyment of life, liberty, and property—may be violated. In this regard, the law has erected substantive protection.

These safeguards also reflect sound professional practice, assuring that service providers will deal appropriately with students they are trained to serve. This result inures to the benefit of the student and the professional alike.

Evaluation Team

IDEA specifies the membership of the team that is to carry out the nondiscriminatory evaluation. This team is the same team that develops the student's individualized education program (IEP) (see Chapter 5), assuring a link between the evaluation, program, and placement. The evaluation team must consist of [20 U.S.C. § 1414(d)(1)(B)]

1. the student's parents;

2. at least one general education teacher of the student (if the student is or may be participating in the general education environment);
3. at least one special education teacher or (where appropriate) a provider of special education to the student;
4. a representative of the school district who is qualified to provide or supervise specially designed instruction to meet the unique needs of students with disabilities and is knowledgeable about general curriculum and the availability of local educational resources;
5. an individual who can interpret the instructional implications of evaluation results (who may be a member of the team already); and
6. at the parents' or school's discretion, other individuals who have knowledge or special expertise (including related services personnel), and the student (when appropriate).

Standards and Procedures

For IDEA to simply designate the membership on the evaluation team is not sufficient. To respond to the risks that a student may be misclassified or not evaluated properly, IDEA specifies the standards the evaluation team must adhere to and the procedures it must follow.

Standards relating to the student; cultural bias

The team must assess the student in all areas of suspected disability and ensure that

1. tests and other evaluation materials are selected and administered so as not to be discriminatory on a racial or cultural basis [20 U.S.C. § 1414 (b)(3)(A)(i)] and
2. tests and other materials are provided and administered in the student's native language or other mode of communication unless it is not feasible to do so [20 U.S.C. § 1414 (b)(3)(A)(ii)].
3. tests and other materials that are selected and administered to children with limited English proficiency measure the extent to which the child has a disability and needs special education, rather than measuring the child's English language skills [34 C.F.R. 300.532(a)(2)].

Standards relating to the tests' validity and administration

The team must ensure that all standardized tests [20 U.S.C. § 1414 (b)(3)(B)]

1. have been validated for the specific purpose for which they are used;
2. are administered by trained and knowledgeable personnel; and
3. are administered in accordance with any instructions from the test's producers.

Standards relating to the evaluation process

The team must

1. use a variety of assessment tools and strategies to gather relevant functional and developmental information to determine whether the student has a disability

and the content of the student's IEP, including information provided by the parent and information that enables the student to participate in the general curriculum or, for preschoolers, appropriate activities [20 U.S.C. § 1414 (b)(2)(A) and 34 C.F.R. 300.532(b)];

2. not use any single procedure as the sole criterion to determine whether the student has a disability or, if so, the student's appropriate education [20 U.S.C. § 1414 (b)(2)(B)];

3. use technically sound instruments to assess the student across four domains, determining the relative contribution of cognitive, behavioral, physical, and developmental factors [20 U.S.C. § 1414 (b)(2)(C)];

4. use evaluation methods that are sufficiently comprehensive to identify all of the child's special education and related service needs, whether or not linked to one of the disability categories in which the child has been classified [34 C.F.R. 300.532(h)];

5. use assessment tools and strategies that assist the team directly in determining that the student's educational needs are satisfied [20 U.S.C. § 1414 (b)(3)(D)];

6. provide a description of the extent, if any, to which an assessment is not conducted under standard conditions [34 C.F.R. 300.532(c)(2)];

7. review existing evaluation data, including current classroom-based assessments and observations and teacher and related services providers' observations [20 U.S.C. § 1414 (c)(1)(A)]; and

8. in reviewing existing data, identify what additional data they need to determine these matters [20 U.S.C. § 1414 (c)(1)(B)]:

   a. Does the student have a particular category of disability, and does the student continue to have that disability?

   b. What are the student's present levels of performance and educational needs?

   c. Does the student need (or continue to need) special education and related services?

   d. What, if any, additions or modifications to the student's special education and related services are needed to enable the student to meet the measurable annual goals of his or her IEP and to participate as appropriate in the general curriculum?

Exclusion of Certain Students

To ensure that students, especially minority students, are not classified into special education unless they truly have a disability, IDEA creates an exclusionary rule that the evaluation team must follow. Thus, the evaluation team may not conclude that a student has a disability and is eligible for special education if the "determinant factor" for the team's eligibility determination is the student's lack of instruction in reading or math or the student's limited English proficiency [20 U.S.C. § 1414 (b)(5)].

This section does not prevent the evaluation team from making students eligible for special education even though the students may have experienced no or poor instruction in reading or math or have limited English proficiency. It does, however, prevent the team from making either of those two shortcomings the "determinant factor"—the one factor on which the team's decision turns, the so-called dispositive factor.

The House Committee explained that this provision "will lead to fewer children being improperly included in special education where their actual difficulties stem from another cause and that this [provision] will lead schools to focus greater attention on these subjects in the early grades" (Committee Report, p. 99).

Parent Participation

Because IDEA always has been concerned about protecting the rights of students and their parents, it has abided by yet another major principle: parent participation (see Chapter 8 for a detailed discussion of this principle). Nowhere is parent participation more important than in the critical issues of identifying whether a student has a disability and, if so, what the student needs in general and special education, including what individualized program and placement are appropriate. The link between evaluation, program, and placement is explicit in IDEA [20 U.S.C. § 1414]; and the participation of the student's parents in decisions that affect each element of that link is therefore essential.

Accordingly, IDEA provides that a student's parents will be members of the evaluation and IEP teams [20 U.S.C. § 1414 (d)(1)(B)], and it specifies that the parents

1. must be a member of the evaluation team (indeed, the evaluation team also is the team that develops the student's individualized program) and must be afforded an opportunity to participate in any group meeting where decisions may be made with respect to the identification, evaluation, placement, or provision of FAPE to the child [34 C.F.R. 300.501];
2. must be given a copy of the evaluation report and documentation concerning their child's eligibility (or lack of eligibility) for special education;
3. may submit to the team and require it to consider evaluations and information that they (the parents) initiate or provide;
4. have a right to be notified that the team has determined it does not need any part of the team that determines eligibility and what, if any, additional data are needed for purposes of deciding whether their child is or remains eligible for special education (still has a disability); [34 C.F.R. 300.533(a)(1) and 300.534(a) (1)]; and
5. have a right to request an assessment to determine whether their child continues to be eligible for special education (the team does not have to conduct the assessment unless the parents request one).

The parents have extensive consent rights [20 U.S.C. § 1414 (c)(3)].

1. Parents may give or withhold consent to the initial evaluation, all reevaluations, and any exit evaluation.
2. If the parents do give their consent, their consent is good for that evaluation only and not for any other evaluations or for the student's placement into or out of special education [20 U.S.C. § 1414 (a)(1)(C)].

3. If the school has taken reasonable measures to secure the parents' consent and if the parents have failed to respond to the schools' request for consent, the school then may evaluate the student (initial or reevaluation) [20 U.S.C. § 1414 (a)(1)(C) and (c)(3)].

4. If the parents refuse to give consent, the school may go to mediation or a due-process hearing to try to get permission from an impartial individual to evaluate the student (except to the extent inconsistent with state law relating to parental consent) [20 U.S.C. § 1414 (a)(1)(C)(ii)].

Reevaluation

Although an LEA may initially evaluate a student as having a disability and then provide an individualized education program and least restrictive placement for the student on the basis of the initial evaluation, IDEA recognizes that reevaluation is desirable. Students' disabilities are not constant. They change over time, especially as a student develops and if special and general education interventions prove effective in ameliorating the effect of the disability.

Moreover, the change in the student's disability (it may become more or less severe) may be accompanied by changes in the student's life that affect how the student learns. Often, the student's home and family life impacts the student's learning capacities, especially as significant life changes occur. These may be divorce, death, marriage, moves out of or into the family, the birth of siblings, and other events.

Accordingly, IDEA provides for reevaluation of the student under three circumstances [20 U.S.C. § 1414 (a)(2)(A)]:

1. A reevaluation must be done at least every 3 years; the 3-year evaluation is mandatory.

2. A reevaluation must be conducted if "conditions warrant" it more often than every 3 years; for example, a dramatic improvement or deterioration in the student's disability condition would warrant a reevaluation.

3. A reevaluation must be conducted if the student's parents or a teacher requests it, because they may have or need new information about the student to make the student's special education more effective.

IDEA requires that LEAs obtain parental consent prior to conducting reevaluations of students with disabilities. LEAs are exempt from this requirement only if they can demonstrate that reasonable measures were taken to obtain parental consent and the parent did not respond [20 U.S.C. § 1414 (c)(3)].

Whenever it conducts a reevaluation, the evaluation team must comply with all of the standards and procedures governing the initial evaluation. These standards and procedures also apply to the "exit evaluation"—the one conducted for the purpose of determining whether the student should be removed from special education and placed into general education entirely [20 U.S.C. § 1414 (c)(5)].

When doing a reevaluation, the team (including the parents and other qualified personnel as appropriate) also must [20 U.S.C. § 1414 (c)]

1. review existing evaluation data, including current classroom-based assessments and observations and teacher and related service providers' observations, and
2. identify what additional data they need to determine four facts, namely:

    a. Does the student have a particular category of disability, and does the student continue to have that disability?
    b. What are the student's present levels of performance and educational needs?
    c. Does the student need (or continue to need) special education and related services?
    d. What, if any, additions or modifications to the student's special education and related services are needed to enable the student to meet the measurable annual goals of his or her IEP and to participate as appropriate in the general curriculum?

When conducting a reevaluation, the evaluation team has two sources of data. *First,* it has and must consider all of the data from the preceding evaluation. *Second,* it must administer tests and other evaluation materials as may be needed to determine whether the student still has a disability and, if so, what the student's educational needs are [20 U.S.C. § 1414 (a)(2) and (c)(1) and (2)].

If the evaluation team determines that it does not need any new data to complete its duties, it must [20 U.S.C. § 1414 (c)(4)]

1. notify the parents that they do not need additional data to determine whether the student remains eligible for special education and let the parents know why they reached that conclusion and that the parents may appeal it via mediation or due process; and
2. administer or have administered by the local agency all tests and other evaluation materials that are needed to produce the required data, but if the team determines that it does not need additional data, it must so notify the student's parents, say why it reached that conclusion, and not collect additional data unless the parents request it to do so.

This is a significant provision in that it relieves the team, the student, and the parent from having to undergo a complete reevaluation; there may well be no need to retest the student, and retesting would not be productive, and may in fact be counterproductive, for the student if existing data are sufficient for the team to accomplish its duties. Moreover, it is cost-conscious not to retest unnecessarily; resources should be spent only on necessary evaluation and services.

Note, however, that the parent may require the team to conduct any assessment that it has proposed to omit; the parents essentially may veto the "no new tests/assessments" decision [20 U.S.C. § 1414 (c)(4)(b)].

Moreover, parents have the right to obtain independent evaluations and to submit them to the team as additional "information" for the team to consider [20 U.S.C. §§ 1414 (b)(2), (c)(1), and 1415 (b)(1)]. According to IDEA's regulations, parents have a right to charge the cost of independent evaluation to LEAs under certain circumstances—namely, if the LEA's evaluation was inappropriate or the LEA was under an order by a due-process hearing officer or court to pay for an independent evaluation. [34 C.F.R. § 300.502].

No Placement Without Evaluation

IDEA commands that no placement shall be made until the child is evaluated according to the nondiscriminatory evaluation requirements [20 U.S.C. § 1414(a)(1)]. This general rule—that no program or placement in special education shall be made until evaluation occurs according to the nondiscriminatory evaluation requirements—also is the command of *Honig v. Doe* (1988) (the "stay-put" case involving expulsion—see Chapter 3).

Exceptions to Rule

As Chapter 7 (due process) points out, a change of the child's placement in the sense of movement from one school to another does not trigger the nondiscriminatory evaluation requirement. Only a change of program triggers the requirement, which can occur simultaneously with a change of placement.

By the same token, it is well settled that the administration of standardized tests to an entire group of students does not constitute an individualized assessment that must comply with the nondiscriminatory evaluation requirements. That was the explicit holding in *Rettig v. Kent City School District* (1980), ruling that IDEA does not require the school district to obtain parental consent for testing a student with standardized tests when the test results are not used for evaluation, an appropriate education, or placement, but only to comply with funding legislation. Thus, a school may administer the Iowa or California achievement tests, state-required minimum-competency tests, or state- or district-wide assessments to a student with a disability and not have to comply with the nondiscriminatory evaluation requirements, because those tests are not administered for the purpose of evaluating or reevaluating the child for special education services.

Part C—Infants and Toddlers

IDEA provides that a state's system of early intervention must include a component for a timely, comprehensive, multidisciplinary evaluation of the functioning of each infant or toddler and a family-directed identification of the needs of each such family. Both the evaluation of the infant/toddler and identification of family needs must assist appropriately in the infant's/toddler's development [20 U.S.C. § 1435 (a)(3)].

The remainder of the nondiscriminatory evaluation safeguards for an infant/toddler and the family are set out in the regulations implementing Part C. In a nutshell, these regulations require that tests be given by appropriately qualified personnel who are entitled to apply informal clinical opinion to reach an evaluation result, in the parent's native language or other mode of communication, that they not be racially or culturally discriminatory, that no single procedure be used, and that qualified personnel administer the tests [34 C.F.R. 303.323]. Evaluation is for the purpose of determining a child's eligibility for Part C and identifying the child's needs, the family's strengths and needs, and the services necessary to meet the child's and family's needs [34 C.F.R. 303.322].

The purpose of the family assessment is to determine the family's strengths and needs related to enhancing the child's development. The family assessment must be voluntary on the family's part, and it must be based on information the family provides through a personal interview and incorporate the family's description of its strengths and needs with respect to enhancing the child's development [34 C.F.R. 303.322(d)].

As a general rule, child and family evaluations and assessments must be completed within 45 days after the state lead agency (the agency designated by a Governor to oversee Part C; it can be the SEA) is notified of the family's application for service [34 C.F.R. 303.322(e)].

Learning Disability Narrowly Defined

Congress carefully defined "children with specific learning disabilities" so that children who do not satisfy the definition will not be classified as having a disability [20 U.S.C. § 1401 (26)]. IDEA defines "specific learning disability" by way of inclusionary and exclusionary criteria.

The inclusionary criteria [20 U.S.C. § 1401 (26)(A) and (B)] provide that

1. a specific language disability is a disorder in one or more of the basic psychological processes involved in understanding or using written or spoken language;
2. the disorder may manifest itself in imperfect ability to listen, think, speak, read, write, spell, or do mathematical calculations;
3. those disorders may include perceptual disabilities, brain injury, minimal brain dysfunction, dyslexia, and developmental aphasia.

IDEA also defines specific learning disability by way of exclusionary criteria [20 U.S.C. § 1401(26)(C)], provided that the term does not include a learning problem that is primarily the result of

— visual, hearing, or motor disabilities,
— mental retardation,
— emotional disturbance, or
— environmental, cultural, or economic disadvantage.

The U.S. Department of Education has adopted regulations that specifically regulate the procedure for evaluating students to determine if they have a learning disability.

1. The general requirements of nondiscriminatory evaluation must be followed [34 C.F.R. §§ 300.530-300.536]. These are the same requirements that apply to all children who are thought to have a disability. If the child is thought to have a specific learning disability, additional evaluations must be made. [34 C.F.R. § 300.540-300.543].

2. The evaluation team must consist of the child's regular education teacher, or a regular education teacher if the child is not then in regular education, or an early education specialist if the child is younger than school age. In addition to one of those people, the evaluation team must include at least one person who is qualified to conduct an individual diagnostic examination (school psychologist, speech/language pathologist, or remedial reading teacher) [34 C.F.R. § 300.540].

3. The regulations allow the evaluation team to determine that the child has a specific learning disability if:

   a. The child does not achieve commensurate with his or her age and ability levels in one or more of the areas listed when provided with learning experiences appropriate for the child's age and ability levels [34 C.F.R. § 300.541(a)(1)]; and

   b. The team finds that a child has a severe discrepancy between achievement and intellectual ability in one or more of the following areas:

      i. oral expression,
      ii. listening comprehension,
      iii. written expression,
      iv. basic reading skill,
      v. reading comprehension,
      vi. mathematics calculation, or
      vii. mathematic reasoning [34 C.F.R. § 300.541(a)(2)].

4. The team may not identify a child as having a specific learning disability if the severe discrepancy between ability and achievement is primarily the result of

   a. a visual, hearing, or motor disability,
   b. mental retardation,
   c. emotional disturbance, or
   d. environmental, cultural, or economic disadvantage [34 C.F.R. § 300.541(b)].

The purposes of the general and special evaluations in the area of specific learning disability are several.

1. They seek to reduce the number of children classified as having a learning disability. They do this by erecting additional procedural hurdles to that classification.

2. By seeking to limit the number of children so classified, they seek to hold down the costs of special education. Congress and the states realize that a large number of children could be classified as having learning disabilities. After all, a large number of children simply do not perform well but do not have other obvious disabilities—and they are candidates for classification as having a learning disability. If all students were classified as having that disability, the costs of educating them appropriately would be enormous.

3. The general and additional evaluation requirements recognize that a stigma is attached to having any disability. Accordingly, they seek to disallow that classification to prevent the child from being stigmatized. Yet the general and special evaluation requirements for learning disabilities convey a strange message: that to have the stigma of sensory, physical, mental, or emotional disability is worse than to have the stigma of learning disability. This message is inherent in the definition of learning disability.

Significance of IDEA Amendments

The 1997 amendments are significant because, at the very least, they

1. increase parent participation rights substantially,
2. create a team that includes the parents and even the student, and also a host of other individuals who are responsible for not just evaluation but also for program delivery and monitoring, and for placement decisions,
3. thereby link the evaluation to the IEP and program,
4. emphasize that evaluation also must take into account the student's participation in the general curriculum (a pro-LRE provision),
5. require classroom-based data to be generated and considered, and thus target not only the student's behavior but also the staff's capacity to deliver effective general and special education services,
6. focus equally on four domains of the student—cognitive, behavioral, physical, and developmental—thereby providing data that can be used to develop effective interventions (including those that prevent suspension and expulsion) and that incidentally assess the effectiveness of the services the student receives, and
7. require the team to use "tools and strategies" that indicate whether the school is meeting the student's educational needs, thereby adding yet another accountability provision in favor of the student and linking evaluation and intervention to general school-improvement initiatives.

Another way to appreciate their significance is to regard them as requiring holistic and fair evaluations. They are holistic because they require the evaluation team to

1. assess the student's strengths and needs in four domains: cognitive, behavioral, physical, and developmental,
2. link all assessments to the student's IEP and especially to participation in the curriculum,
3. decide what the student needs to be able to meet annual goals (including participation in the general curriculum),
4. determine how to increase the teachers' capacity to deliver an appropriate education, and
5. identify the tools and strategies the team will use to decide whether the school and its teachers are meeting the student's educational needs.

And they are fair because the team

1. now consists of special educators and other specialists as well as the student's parents and regular educators,
2. must use bias-free assessment instruments and procedures,
3. must gather and take into account parent and teacher observations.

Major Legal Restraints on Consequences of Classifications ~

It is not legally sufficient that the procedures for classification be regulated. The use that one makes of the procedures is an important concern as well. The procedures may be entirely acceptable, but invidious classification and treatment of people still could occur unless their uses were scrutinized. Thus, IDEA creates other protections.

Standards

A student may not be classified under IDEA unless he or she has one or more of the disabilities listed in the statute (see Chapter 3) and "by reason thereof require(s) special education and related services" [20 U.S.C. § 1401 (3)(A)]. Similarly, a student does not qualify for a related service unless it is "required to assist the student to benefit from special education" [20 U.S.C. § 1401 (22)]. In both cases, classification (as disabled or as qualifying for related services) has a "but-for" functional element; the causal relationship between the service, the classification, and the student's functioning (needs) must exist. Thus, IDEA insists that the techniques and effects of evaluation be connected.

Procedures and Notice

Due-process safeguards also tend to minimize the risk of error. Thus, under IDEA the student's parents are entitled to notice of the action the school proposes to take, a hearing before an impartial trier of fact and law, an opportunity to present and rebut evidence, and the right to appeal from the initial decision (see Chapter 7).

The student's parents also are entitled to notice if the IEP team finds that it does not require additional data to determine whether the student remains eligible for special education. The team must give the parents an explanation for its conclusion, and the parents may appeal it via mediation or due process. In such cases, the school may not collect additional data regarding the student unless the parents request it to do so [20 U.S.C. § 1414 (c)(4)].

Access to Records

A third technique is to grant affected persons or their representatives access to the professional records concerning them or service systems that may be brought to bear on them. Thus, IDEA allows a student's parents to see the school records or records of the school system special education programs [20 U.S.C. § 1415 (b)(1)] (see also Chapter 8.)

Some states also have enacted statutes that allow people with disabilities or their representatives access to social work, health, or mental health records. People with disabilities or their representatives normally can access court and quasi-judicial proceedings or records (such as the impartial hearing guaranteed under IDEA).

Substitute Consent

Courts even have been able to address one of the most debilitating aspects of classification as mentally disabled—the loss of legal capacity to act on one's own behalf. As a general rule of law, a person may not legally consent or withhold consent to educational, health, or mental health services if he or she is not mentally competent (unable to engage in a rational process of decision-making); mental capacity is an indispensable element of consent.

Moreover, children generally are presumed to be incompetent, because of their age, to act for themselves, especially in regard to special education services. And some children with disabilities have no parents alive or available and are wards of the state. Those children usually are subject to judicial proceedings that result in the appointment of a legal guardian, who has power to consent to services on their behalf. In addition, IDEA requires states to continue to rely on parental consent for an adult child who has not been adjudicated as incompetent but who may be so (see Chapter 7).

Participatory Decision-Making

IDEA provides for the participation of persons with disabilities or their representatives with professionals in planning the goals and methods of professional services (see Chapter 8).

Advocacy

To challenge the discriminatory effect or intent of classification, the student may need an advocate. Thus, IDEA requires state education agencies to appoint surrogate parents for children who have no parents or are wards of the state. The Developmental Disabilities and Bill of Rights Act of 1975 also has established a protection and advocacy (P&A) system to enable people with developmental disabilities or mental illness to challenge unwarranted classification. Under this law, states that receive federal funds for use in serving people with disabilities must create a system to advocate for them against state and local governmental agencies.

Federally financed P&A offices have been involved extensively in special education lawsuits involving retarded children's classification and education. Another federal effort to provide advocates for people with disabilities has been by way of funding the Legal Services Corporation, which in turn allocates its money for local legal services for citizens with disabilities and other disadvantages.

Eligibility for Benefits

IDEA has created eligibility standards (e.g., if a student has a disability, he or she becomes entitled to special education), and accompanying funding streams (federal special education funds may be spent principally on special education students or for administrative costs associated with their education). IDEA also selects certain kinds of students for special benefits and thereby denies others those same benefits, especially those with limited English proficiency but no disability.

Least Restrictive Alternative

In its many responses to classification, IDEA takes the position that the schools are the victimizers and the student is the victim. The issue is how to govern the schools, recognizing that they become involved in classification because they offer services (education) or exclude some students from those services.

A major principle of constitutional law—the doctrine of the least restrictive (least drastic) alternative—has become a useful device for curbing governments (see Chapter 6). The doctrine forbids a government from acting in a way that restricts a person's liberty any more than necessary to accomplish its legitimate purposes. If a government has a defensible reason for restricting someone and may accomplish that restriction in either of two ways—one that infringes individual liberty to a greater extent and another to a lesser extent—it must choose the lesser of the two ways.

For example, sometimes (although rarely) it is legitimate to place students for an entire school day in separate, segregated special education programs. But that placement may not be done until the student has been given a nondiscriminatory evaluation that, among other things, justifies that placement and describes why a less restrictive, more typical placement is unwarranted. (See Chapter 6 for a full discussion of the LRE rule.)

Prohibiting Discrimination

Another legal response to classification is to prohibit governmental agencies or recipients of governmental aid and the private sector from discriminating against otherwise qualified people solely because of their disabilities [Section 504 and ADA]. Thus, for a school system to exclude children with disabilities solely because they are disabled is a violation of law (see Chapters 2 and 3).

Accounting and Sanctions

Congress provided that SEAs and LEAs must report and account for the receipt and expenditure of IDEA money by filing annual reports with the Secretary of Education [20 U.S.C. §§ 1411 (f)(5), 1418]. IDEA authorizes the Secretary of Education to withhold federal funds, in whole or in part, from any SEA that is found to be in violation of provisions of the IDEA [20 U.S.C. § 1416].

Section 504 ∿

Like the IDEA regulations, the regulations of Section 504 acknowledge that failure to provide students with an appropriate education can result from misclassification. Accordingly, Section 104.35(a) requires an evaluation of any person who needs or is believed to need special education or related services because of a disability. The evaluation must be completed before a school takes any action (including denial or placement) with respect to initial placement in a general or special education program or any subsequent significant change in placement. But a full reevaluation is not obligatory every time a lesser adjustment in the child's placement is made.

Section 104.35(b) and (c) sets out procedures to ensure that children are not misclassified, unnecessarily labeled as disabled, or placed incorrectly because of inappropriate selection, administration, or interpretation of evaluation materials. Section 104.35(b) requires schools to establish standards and procedures for evaluation and placement to ensure that tests and other evaluation materials are validated for the specific purpose for which they are used and are administered by trained personnel in conformance with the instructions of their producer. Tests and other evaluation materials are to include those tailored to assess specific areas of educational need and not merely those designed to provide a single general intelligence quotient.

In addition, tests are to be selected and administered to students with impaired sensory, manual, or speaking skills so that the test results accurately reflect the student's aptitude or achievement level—or whatever other factor the test purports to measure—rather than the student's impaired skills, except when those skills are the factors the test seeks to measure. Section 104.35(b) drives home the point that tests should not be misinterpreted, that undue reliance on general intelligence tests is undesirable, and that tests should be administered in such a way that their results will not be distorted because of the student's disability.

Section 104.35(c) requires schools, when evaluating and placing students, to draw upon information from a variety of sources, including aptitude and achievement tests, teacher recommendations, physical conditions, social or cultural background, and adaptive behavior. Schools must establish procedures to ensure that information obtained from all such sources is documented and considered carefully, and the placement decision is to be made by a group of people including those who are knowledgeable about the child. The meaning of the evaluation data and the placement options must be made clear to all concerned, and placement decisions are to conform with the doctrine of least restrictive (most integrated) setting.

Section 104.35(d) requires periodic (though not necessarily annual) reevaluation. It makes clear that reevaluation procedures consistent with the IDEA (which allows reevaluation at 3-year intervals unless more frequent reevaluations are requested) are a means of meeting the reevaluation requirement.

Section 104.36 requires schools to provide for due process in evaluation procedures. This includes notice, right of access to records, impartial hearing, right to counsel, and appeal procedures. Chapter 7 focuses on due process in detail.

Case Law ⌇

As noted in the early part of this chapter, a vital and hotly debated issue is whether standardized intelligence tests discriminate against students from economically deprived or racial minority backgrounds by placing them in classes for children with mental retardation or learning disabilities. The early decisions in *Larry P. v. Riles* (1972, 1974, 1979, 1984) seemed to signal the death knell of these tests. But a later case, *PASE v. Hannon* (1980), validates use of the tests when evaluation is accomplished by additional means and seems to mute the tune that *Larry P.* sang.

Larry P.

Larry P. v. Riles (1972, 1974, 1979, 1984) held that schools no longer may use standardized IQ tests for the purpose of identifying and placing African-American children into segregated special education classes for students classified as educable mentally retarded. The district court ruled that schools using such tests violate Title VI of the Civil Rights Act of 1964, Section 504 of the Rehabilitation Act of 1973, IDEA, and the equal protection clause of the Fourteenth Amendment to the federal Constitution.

The violation occurs because (a) the tests are racially and culturally biased and have a discriminatory impact on African-American children, (b) the tests have not been validated for the purpose of essentially permanent placements into "educationally dead-end, isolated, and stigmatizing classes for students regarded as educable mentally retarded," (c) the tests are evidence of the schools' discriminatory intentions (in violation of equal protection), and (d) the tests cannot be justified under the "compelling interest" standard applicable to racial discrimination cases.

The district court found that the Stanford-Binet, Wechsler, and Leiter IQ tests discriminate against African-Americans on several grounds:

1. They measure achievement, not ability.
2. They rest on the "plausible but unproven assumption that intelligence is distributed in the population in accordance with a normal statistical curve" and thus are "artificial tools to rank individuals according to certain skills, not to diagnose a medical condition (the presence of retardation)."
3. They "necessarily" lead to placement of more African-Americans than Whites into classes for students with mild or moderate mental retardation.

The court rejected two explanations for the disproportionate enrollment: the genetic argument ("natural selection has resulted in persons having a 'gene pool' that dooms them as a group to less intelligence") and the socioeconomic argument (poverty and inferior home and neighborhood environments explain why more African-Americans than Whites have mental retardation). Instead, it explained the difference in IQ test scores by the cultural bias argument, that IQ tests measure intelligence as manifested by White, middle-class children and therefore are racially and culturally biased against African-Americans.

The district court crafted a comprehensive remedy that

1. enjoined the state from using any standardized IQ tests for identifying children or placing them into classes for students with mild mental retardation without

prior court approval, which would be granted only if the defendants, by statistical evidence, can show that the tests are not racially or culturally discriminatory, will not be administered in a discriminatory manner, and have been validated for the determination of mild mental retardation or placement into those classes;

2. required the state superintendent and board to compile statistics enabling them to monitor and eliminate disproportionate placement of African-Americans into classes and required local school boards to prepare and adopt plans to correct the imbalance; and

3. required the state superintendent and board to direct each local school to reevaluate on a nondiscriminatory basis every African-American student already identified as having mild mental retardation.

On appeal, the Ninth Circuit Court of Appeals affirmed the district court's conclusions and remedies. Specifically, it

1. rejected the state's argument that tests that are valid predictors of future performance can be used even if they have a discriminatory impact;

2. found that the state could not sustain the burden of showing that the tests predict specifically that African-American elementary-school children who score in the IQ of 70 or below have mental retardation and are incapable of learning in the general school curriculum;

3. found that the state did not use other measures or criteria—such as the child's educational history, adaptive behavior, social and cultural background, or health history—for determining special education placement;

4. noted that improper placement in those classes has a demonstrable and negative impact, putting children into dead-end classes that do not teach academic skills but do stigmatize them, and that no nondiscriminatory factors, only the tests, are the cause of the adverse impact; and

5. upheld the district court's remedy of suspending use of the tests and requiring school districts with disproportionate racial balance in special education to devise 3-year remedial plans and to report racial disparities to the district court.

Larry P. was, as much as anything, a race discrimination case that put the court in the unenviable position of choosing among three possible explanations for the overrepresentation of minority children in special education:

1. the tests and their invalidity,

2. the "gene pool" argument that minority children are inherently less intelligent than nonminority children, and

3. the socioeconomic explanation of low performance on standardized tests.

Given that the court in *Larry P.* found minority overrepresentation in special education, the tests were the most likely candidates for the court's remedy. The court could hold them invalid and impose a remedy (no more testing, under most conditions), but it would have been at a loss to impose a remedy that would speak to the politically charged gene pool or socioeconomic arguments.

PASE

In *PASE,* the court did not face these choices as dramatically as in *Larry P.* and took care to consider the tests' validity. Far more than *Larry P., PASE* is a special education decision that, in light of IDEA requirements for multifaceted, multidisciplinary evaluation, commands special educators' adherence.

PASE upheld the same tests that *Larry P.* had held unlawful as racially discriminatory. Although *PASE* found that some items in the tests were discriminatory, it upheld the tests as generally nondiscriminatory. More important, it found that the tests were not the sole basis for classification and that the school district therefore was complying with IDEA, which requires multifaceted testing. The minimal discrimination in tests and the adherence to classification safeguards were the decisive factors in this carefully reasoned opinion. To understand that *PASE* is an exceptionally appealing case, at least as it compares with *Larry P.,* we will examine the court's reasoning.

Gene-Pool Argument

With respect to the gene-pool argument, the court recognized that since "the early days of standard intelligence tests, around the time of World War I, [African-Americans] as a group score about one standard deviation—15 points—lower than Whites" on the tests. There is, however, "considerable disagreement" about the causes of that result. Noting that the genetic view never did take account of the fact that many Blacks scored above the White mean, that northern [African-Americans] scored higher on the average than southern [African-Americans]," that African-Americans who moved north often experienced an increase in their IQ scores, and that African-American infants adopted by White families tended to achieve IQ scores in later years that correlated "highly" with the scores of the natural children of the adoptive parents, the court

1. concluded that IQ tests measure something that is changeable rather than fixed for all time, something that can be increased and improved;
2. noted that the parties to the case—the students and the school officials—agreed on that much;
3. stated that no evidence supports a hypothesis that African-Americans have less innate mental capacity than Whites; and
4. rejected the gene-pool argument as an explanation for the disproportionate representation of African-Americans in special education.

Racial/Cultural Bias Arguments

The court also rejected the argument that the disproportion is caused by African-Americans' use of nonstandard English:

> The evidence does not establish how the use of nonstandard English would interfere with performance on the Wechsler and Stanford-Binet tests.... What is unclear is how the use of such nonstandard English would handicap a child either in understanding the test items or in responding to them.

Moreover, a child's response in nonstandard English should not affect a child's score on the (test) item, because the test manuals specifically instruct the examiners to disregard the form of the answer as long as the substance is correct.

In addition, the plaintiffs made no effort to show that any of the 96 words challenged as racially biased are unique to the culture of Whites but not African-Americans. The vocabulary words are of "ordinary, common usage." Accordingly, the court also discounted the argument that the tests are "Anglocentric" rather than "Afrocentric" and therefore necessarily biased against African-Americans. African-Americans' lack of exposure to White culture and the fact of a separate coexisting African-American culture, said the court, "has not been connected to the specific issue in this case," which was "whether the three tests—WISC-R, WISC (Wechsler), and Stanford-Binet—are culturally biased against African-American children, so that it is unfair to use these tests in the determination of whether an African-American child is mental retardated."

In determining that the tests are culturally neutral, the court examined carefully all items of the three tests, particularly the ones the plaintiffs alleged were culturally biased. It found—after 35 pages of its opinion—that only eight items on the WISC-R and WISC are "either racially biased or so subject to suspicion of bias that they should not be used," and only one item on the Stanford-Binet falls into the same category.

As to the WISC-R and WISC, the suspect items are:

1. What is the color of rubies?
2. What does C.O.D. mean?
3. Why is it better to pay bills by check than by cash?
4. What would you do if you were sent to buy a loaf of bread and the grocer said that he did not have any more?
5. What does a stomach do?
6. Why is it generally better to give money to an organized charity than to a street beggar?
7. What are you supposed to do if you find someone's wallet or pocketbook in a store?
8. What is the thing to do if a boy (girl) much smaller than yourself starts to fight with you?

On the Stanford-Binet, the only item that the court found to be biased or racially suspect was on the "aesthetic comparison" test. In it, 4½-year-old children are asked to identify which of two similarly colored persons is "prettier."

Having found that only nine of 488 items on the three tests are racially biased or racially suspect, the court turned its attention to interpretation of the tests. It found that the importance of an individual item is lessened by the fact that "the child continues with the sub-test (in which the item appears) until he has a certain number of consecutive misses."

In addition, as far as some items of the tests are concerned, they occur at a level of difficulty that children in their early school years (when special education placement generally is made) are not expected to reach the item or answer it correctly. The tests thus are not interpreted in a way that indicates racial bias but, rather, in a way that reflects racially free educational assessment. In the Stanford-Binet, the consequences of racial bias are "negligible" because only one item of 104 is biased or racially suspect.

Moreover, the IQ score is "not the sole determinant" of whether a child is classified as having mental retardation; "clinical judgment plays a large role in the interpretation of IQ test results." Indeed, "the examiner who knows the milieu of the child can correct for cultural bias by asking the questions in a sensitive and intelligent way."

Finally, "the likelihood of an African-American child being placed in an EMH (educably mentally handicapped) class without at least one African-American professional having participated in the evaluation is very slight." The court thus concluded that "the possibility of the few biased items on these tests causing an EMH placement that would not otherwise occur is practically nonexistent."

Socioeconomic Argument

The court addressed the socioeconomic explanation for special education placement by acknowledging that, "[E]arly intellectual stimulation is essential. . . . Lack of opportunity for cognitive development is . . . often due to factors associated with economic poverty in the home." Moreover, it was "uncontradicted that most of the children in the EMH classes do in fact come from the poverty pockets" of Chicago. "This tends to suggest that what is involved is not simply race but something associated with poverty."

Assessment Process

The court then addressed the assessment process, finding that it involves several levels of investigation (IQ testing, observation in the classroom, screening conferences by educators, individualized examinations by professionals, multidisciplinary staff conferences, and a potential veto of special education placement by the psychologist who evaluated the child). In that process, the court observed, any "hypnotic effect" of an IQ score is substantially mitigated. Indeed, later reevaluation of the children involved in the case indicated that they did not have mental retardation and had normal intelligence but "suffer from learning disabilities which make it difficult for them to perform well in certain kinds of learning situations."

Comparison with *Larry P.*

Finally, the court addressed *Larry P.,* noting that, while the court there devoted its lengthy and scholarly opinion "largely" to the question of legal consequences resulting from a finding of racial bias in the tests, it engaged in "relatively little analysis of the threshold question of whether test bias in fact exists" and even noted that the cultural bias of the tests "is hardly disputed."

Indeed, the *Larry P.* court made reference to specific test items on only one page and, then, with respect to only one item. Its inferences of bias from the one item, in a case that "hardly disputed" the cultural bias of the tests, were unpersuasive, lacking a more detailed examination of the test items.

Ability Grouping

Although the first school classification case, *Hobson v. Hansen* (1969), successfully challenged ability grouping and the disproportionate effect it has on racial minorities, so another, more recent case charged unsuccessfully that ability grouping is illegal because of its effects on minorities. In *Georgia State Conference of Branches of NAACP v. Georgia* (1985), the NAACP challenged the use of ability or achievement grouping on the basis that the disproportionate racial impact of those tests violates the equal-protection clause of the Fourteenth Amendment, Title VI of the Civil Rights Act (prohibiting discrimination on the basis of race), Section 504 (prohibiting discrimination on the basis of disability), and IDEA.

The federal court of appeals found that ability or achievement grouping violates none of those laws. The court ruled that ability or achievement grouping is a sound education practice that provides the benefit of significant educational and academic progress. It also noted that the plaintiff had failed to show the existence of equally beneficial education practices that would result in less racial disproportionality.

Larry P., PASE, and Ability Grouping Cases—Effects

Fundamentally, *Larry P.* and *PASE* were school desegregation cases that took the form of a challenge to special educational practices. *Georgia NAACP* was a school desegregation case that took the form of a challenge to a general education practice that had special education impacts.

On their surface, *Larry P.* and *PASE* clearly sought to prevent the schools from classifying students as having a disability and providing them with special education. Both cases challenged the use of IQ tests, which are the integral—some would argue, the principal—means for classifying students as having a disability. If the tests could be held invalid because they discriminate against minority students and if their use were prohibited because of their invalidity, a major tool for classification would be outlawed.

One result of prohibiting use of IQ tests would be that schools would have to find other means for classifying students as having a disability. But another, and probably more fundamental, result would occur: Classification of minority students into special education would be more difficult because the primary means for classification would be illegal. In turn, the number of minority students placed into special education would decrease. Finally, the number of minority students retained in general education would increase, so the schools—that is, the general education programs—would be more racially integrated.

Thus, *Larry P.* and *PASE* clearly were cases that sought racial desegregation of the schools; this was their basic purpose. Their secondary purpose was to reduce the number of minority students who would be placed into special education and thereby acquire the stigma of being "disabled." Likewise, the *Georgia NAACP* case sought to prevent the use of tracking systems that had racially disproportionate results: more minority students than Whites being placed into lower or "special" tracks, as a proportion of their representation in the school population as a whole.

Whatever one might think of the results of the cases—and it seems clear that the court's reasoning and use of evidence in *Larry P.* is not as persuasive as in *PASE*—several policy issues clearly are being fought out and resolved:

1. The issue of means of classification is being challenged. In *Larry P.* and *PASE,* the means were the IQ tests; in *Georgia NAACP,* the means were ability or achievement tracking systems.
2. The means are challenged to prevent minorities from being classified as having a disability and having to bear a double stigma of racial minority and disability. (This observation assumes that, for some, the racial minority stigma is a reality. It does not condone that result: Race should not be stigmatizing. But it accepts as a fact that, for some people, both African-American and White, it may be. It also accepts as a fact that disability is stigmatizing. Again, it does not condone that fact.)
3. The challenge seeks not simply to affect special education. At its heart, it seeks to retard the resegregation of general education. It acknowledges that school desegregation by race is an elusive goal. It admits that the goal is imperfectly realized. And, to more fully realize the goal, it attacks the means by which segregation by race, allegedly under the guise of classification by disability, occurs.
4. The challenge is less than fully successful. Although *Larry P.* outlawed the use of IQ tests, *PASE* did not, and *Georgia NAACP* sustained the use of ability or achievement grouping. Do the results make good law? In *PASE* and *Georgia NAACP,* the results seem defensible on the basis of the legal analysis. In *Larry P.,* the results are defensible but not as carefully reasoned. Do the results make good social policy? That is a question that the reader must answer.

In thinking about these cases, it is important to remember the findings of Congress in the 1997 IDEA Amendments. Among these findings are the facts that a greater percentage of the student population in the future will consist of minorities, that minority students are disproportionately underserved, and that, therefore, a greater emphasis is needed on serving minority students and minority personnel development [20 U.S.C. §§ 1400 ©(7), (8), (9), (10)].

5. The issue of educational policy is only the surface issue. These cases—and IDEA—essentially are issues of social policy. The underlying issue is this: What is the role of a government agency (the schools) and of the law in addressing the segregation of people by race and disability? Posed another way, the issue is this: What kind of society shall the schools and the law seek? Shall it be one that is more integrated than segregated? And posed still another way, the issue is this: How shall "we" (whether we are African-American or White, nondisabled or disabled) be with "them?" How shall people be with others, or shall they have the liberty not to be in the presence (and in the schools) with others who are different?

Observations About Classification ⌒

As the early cases on nondiscriminatory evaluation recognized, and as Congress acknowledged in IDEA, classification of a person as having a disability can have important educational and adult-life consequences. At the worst, it can relegate the person to second-class citizenship and, as such, subject the individual to a dual system of law. That dual system allows those without disabilities to treat those with disabilities as less worthy because of their disabilities. To show how a dual system occurs by discussing the "classification system" and its consequences at law may be helpful.

"Dominance Theory"

Special education, you will recall, is not a new invention. It originated, according to Sarason and Doris (1975), as a response to the inability of the schools to accommodate the wave of immigration that began in the middle of the 19th century. As Irish, Italian, German, Russian, and other immigrants came to the United States, they were classified as "special" and segregated in their education from well-established Americans. (The fact that this classification had religious undertones and was done on the basis of native language, country of origin, or ethnicity should not pass unnoticed.)

For Sarason and Doris, classification of the new immigrants was a prelude to classification of other students who are different, in a different time. The separation of African-Americans and Hispanics/Latinos from other students during the remainder of the 19th century and into the 20th century has its origin in the mid-19th century. Yet its reasons are the same, according to Sarason and Doris: Classification occurs to (a) preserve the social status quo and prevent disruption of the social structure, (b) put distance between people so those who are different (read: subject to a negative stigma) are not in the presence of others, and (c) altruistically justify some ameliorative (read: special education) interventions.

"Transactional" Aspects and Social Construct

Sarason and Doris direct their attention to a single disability—mental retardation—arguing that classification of a person as having mental retardation reflects social policy—that the disability itself is a social invention. To make this point, they argue that disability—unlike genetic make-up—is not a characteristic necessarily inherent in a person. Rather, disability is a consequence of how a person functions within a social context. It is a transactional phenomenon—something that results from the way a person relates to and transacts social relations with others. If the person functions differently from others, the person is said to have a disability. And thus the person is said to be at fault; the disability is part and parcel of the person (it is inherent in the person).

That being the case, special interventions—special education, for example—are warranted. The disability reflects a "broken" aspect of the person, and the person must be "repaired" or "fixed." Similarly, separation of those who are "different" or "broken" from those who are not "different" becomes justifiable. Those with disabilities need certain interventions that the others do not. The "abnormal" and the "normal" are not just different but should be maintained as different. The consequence of this "pathology focus," Sarason and Doris show, is that special education is justified. The person with a disability is provided something that is intended to change the person.

What that focus fails to acknowledge, however, is that changing the person is only one part of the solution to the "misfit" of the person in society—only one way of accommodating to the fact of difference. The other part of the solution, of course, is to change the society itself. Accommodation, after all, should be a two-way street (see Chapter 2).

Given that mutual accommodations must be made and that IDEA, Section 504, and ADA attempt to ensure those accommodations, the issue remains: How shall the law respond to the fact of classification? To answer that question, we will make additional observations about classification and then document the law's response.

Perceptions and Dominance Through Bias Classification

Consider the person who has a disability, has a history of a disability, or is regarded as having a disability. The characteristic of the person on which intervention usually has been and still is predicated is "disability," not "person." The person is seen to be qualitatively different from other people in this important and debilitating sense: The person is "deviant."

For example, the newborn with an observable anomaly has been called a "defective child." Because the defect is seen to inhere *in* the child rather than in the society into which the child is born, the defect, and indeed the child, must be "treated" in the sense of being subjected to diagnosis, prescription, regimen, and "cure." The treatment is rendered by many "helping" professionals, not just physicians (Gleidmann and Roth, 1980).

The person then can be regarded as "perpetual patient" for whom a cure never can be found. Those so classified are defined by what they are not, instead of what they are or may become. Regarded as "sick" (i.e., disabled) and not responsible for their own condition, they are obliged to play the role of an obedient patient. In this role they learn to be helpless and inferior, to accept professionals' control over their lives. Infrequent rebellion against professional dominance itself is treated as a symptom of sickness, and the person's parents or family also become "patients" (Turnbull and Turnbull, 1985).

Obedience of the person and family to professional dominance reinforces the original perception that the person is incapable and possibly incurable. "Treatment" of this sort essentially reflects the prevailing social mores. Classifying a person as having a disability enables "us" to use a convenient concept—one ostensibly rooted in science—to do unto others what we would abhor having done to us, all in the name of altruism. Seeing persons with disabilities incorrectly as sick and not responsible for their condition, "we" easily can conclude, as "the law" traditionally did, that they are not responsible (competent) and must be dealt with in unusual ways (Morse, 1978).

Thus, able-bodied and mentally competent people—those who fit a norm—come to regard the incapacity of the person with a disability as a kind of failure of the person. Given that the person is a failure, the professions and society as a whole have a reduced duty, if any, to act on the person's behalf. "We" are off the hook for any responsibility to "them." "We" have, ultimately, no responsibility for their exclusion from the normal patterns of life and, with relatively clean conscience and legal impunity, we can assign them to lower echelons of life, to second-class citizenship at law.

Who Classifies

Every society needs professionals who will bring their expertise to bear on difficult situations and resolve those difficulties through the use of special training, talents, and status.

Physicians

Physicians' curative abilities (to prevent a disability, to intervene early so as to minimize its effects, and to be a sustaining force throughout a person's life) make them important resources for saying who has a disability. They do this through developmental testing of newborns, infants, children, and youth. Once they diagnose or classify, the physicians intervene. Little wonder it is that physicians have become agents for deciding what to do about disabilities.

Educators

Another of society's classifiers are educators. Arguably, schools label more children as having a disability than does any other governmental or social entity (Sorgen, 1976. This classification has massive consequences—both positive and negative—for the children, as noted above.

Other Professionals and Agencies

Physicians and educators are not the only professional sorters. Any profession having contact, however tangential, with people classifies. Social workers, psychologists, and rehabilitation specialists classify. Institutions of higher education, particularly vocational, technical, and community colleges, do their own classification. Law enforcement and criminal justice agencies classify. Courts accept classification arguments to assess whether and, if so, to what extent persons are criminally or civilly liable for their actions or failures to act. The armed forces classify.

Professional Organizations

Professional organizations classify. The American Association on Mental Retardation classifies by changing its concept and definition of mental retardation, as it has done several times. The American Psychiatric Association classifies when it changes the standards and definitions in its *Diagnostic and Statistical Manual.* Societies classify learning disabilities by defining a specific learning disability to exclude some types of children.

Families

Families classify. It is not so much that families say their child, brother or sister, or relative has a disability; others do that for them. It is more that they classify by determining how they will react to what others say. The decision to keep a child in their own home or to secure placement in an institution, or to try an inclusive education instead of a more separate one, is in the first (and sometimes the last) place a family decision. Among other things, it reflects a decision to classify a person more or less into or out of a disabled status.

Everyone

Everyone classifies. We all make choices to associate or not to associate with certain other people. Human beings are discriminating in the neutral sense of the word. We make discriminations about ourselves and others. We also are discriminating in a different sense. We discriminate for invidious as well as altruistic purposes. Some of us let defective newborns die because their existence horrifies us, but we say we do it because we are concerned about the quality of their and others' lives. Classification is not inherently wrong, merely natural.

How We Classify

By Resorting to Science

The concept of science has some magical quality. Call something scientific and it becomes less assailable. The presumption is that science and its products are researched, reliable, validated, evaluated, and unbiased. But what we do—our policies—are not always based on good science, on defensible science. It is little wonder, then, that our policies are not always good.

The fallibility of the medical model is well known (Blatt and Kaplan, 1979). After all, science taught that people with mental retardation were a menace, so the eugenics movement spawned legalized compulsory institutionalization and sterilization (Wald, 1976). Science teaches that intelligence can be measured, so classification as having a cognitive impairment, with consequent categorization into special education, receives the blessings of the law. It is no great matter that some bases for scientific "facts" are open to doubt as long as they are not clearly erroneous. Yet, decisions by physicians, other service providers, and families, made on the basis of relatively acceptable assessment techniques, still can be highly debatable.

The case of Phillip Becker (*In re Phillip B.,* 1979) proves the point. There was no doubt that he was a young boy with Down syndrome and a heart defect that could be corrected surgically, with little risk to his life, as a means of prolonging his life substantially. Yet his family decided to refuse to authorize the surgery and, up to a point, so did the courts of California, because of debatable medical decision-making (namely, a person with Down syndrome should not have an operation to prolong and improve his quality of life solely because he has mental retardation). Thus, we classify by using relatively fallible or infallible science or by acting in someone's interests on the basis of what that science tells us.

By Social Vulnerability

Classification is affected by other scientific means, and by nonscientific means as well. Educators, for example, too often identify students as having disabilities if they make life difficult for the educators. Boys seem to be more subject to special education classification than girls are, aggressive students more than acquiescent ones, racial and ethnic minority students more than White students (Mercer, 1996). The "science" of these classifications is highly doubtful. Instead, some students' differential vulnerability to special education classification seems to be a factor in cultural, social, or economic differentness.

By Legal Proceedings

Likewise, classification as having a disability occurs in a host of legal proceedings, often without a sufficient "scientific" basis. For example, if persons are aggressive, unable to care for themselves, or, because of mental disability, are "in need of treatment," family members, mental health, public health, or social services agencies may choose to intervene by (a) asking a court to commit them involuntarily, (b) adjudicate them to be incompetent so third-party consent to treatment or placement can be obtained, (c) secure temporary social service custody for treatment of neglect or abuse, or (d) obtain criminal prosecution for alleged violation of a crime.

Any of those four responses is legally sanctioned and may be effective as a way of intervening appropriately. So, too, is doing nothing; inaction is a form of action. Whatever the choice—whether to intervene and, if so, how—classification results. In Alan Stone's typology (Stone, 1976), the classified person becomes mad, sad, or bad—mad if committed involuntarily, sad if referred to special education, social services, mental retardation, or developmental disabilities agencies, or bad if convicted of a crime. The classifier, of course, is good.

By Reason of Serendipity

There is, moreover, no clear reason why a particular intervention prevails. So much depends on serendipity. Is the school's staff overloaded with students who have disabilities? Is the state psychiatric hospital full? Does a developmental center or community-based service have enough beds? What agency does the person's family have the most contact with? Are private or third-party funds available to pay for services? Is the person an "interesting case" for the professional staff? How effectively does a lawyer represent the parties? Have political or social influences been brought to bear on the agencies or courts? Have community resources been tried unsuccessfully?

These are some of the factors—all of them far removed from the allegedly precise scientific basis for classification that is supposed to be obtained in special education or mental health intervention, for example—that affect whether a person is classified and, if so, how, why, and with what effect.

Why We Classify

Classification may be impossible to avoid. We are, after all, discriminating, choosy, selective, and exclusive in almost every facet of our lives, whether the issue is so trivial as the choice of food at a carry-out restaurant or so momentous as the choice of a partner for life. In addition to our natural restrictions (age, gender, race, and ability), we restrict ourselves voluntarily, such as by the jobs we choose. And in most cases the law recognizes our rights to be selective in the important matters of speech, religion, and personhood, as well as in less significant matters such as the types of clothes we wear ("symbolic speech").

Yet our natural instincts and legal rights to be selective, to classify ourselves and others, are not unbridled. Our rights of free speech do not extend to some aspects of pornography. Some consensual conduct is regulated and, of course, so is nonconsensual conduct (crimes against persons or property).

One reason for regulation is that the effects of absolute liberty for anyone are unacceptable to someone. Thus, the possession of pornography may be protected but its sale or distribution may not be. The reasons for governmental classification must be examined; the due process and equal protection clauses of the federal Constitution forbid invidious, irrational, indefensible classifications (such as those made on the basis of race or, in some instances, disability). To inquire into why people classify others as having a disability, therefore, is legally relevant.

Altruism

Sometimes classification is done for the most altruistic of purposes. When someone is classified as having a disability, it enables him or her to be the recipient of services that the classifier (schools), and sometimes the classified, thinks will be helpful (special education). Classification also may prevent the person from being subject to disadvantaging conditions. Some think segregation of students by disability will protect them from nondisabled students and the ordinary conditions of schools.

Classification that is motivated by social beneficence, however, has negative results. Lionel Trilling (1980) made the point that people who are the objects of our pity become the objects of our coercion. Kai Erickson (1966) highlighted the paradox that deviance—differentness on account of disability—is nourished by the agencies that were designed to inhibit it, in proportion to society's ability to control it. Thus, the conditions of education, including special education, have been disadvantageous to children in some instances.

Sarason and Doris (1975) cast doubt on the motives and efficacy of special education systems. Blatt (1979) documented the horrible conditions to which people with disabilities were subjected in institutions originally predicated on a medical model. And Gleidman and Roth (1980) produced strong evidence of the shortcomings of the medical model in a host of "helping" professions.

Negative Reactions

We also classify for reasons having to do with our instinctive negative reaction to disabilities. After all, the grossly macrocephalic child may not be easily or immediately lovable to some people. Fecal smearers can be unpleasant to live or work with. Some children are aggressive, and some are slow to show affection. Many aspects of disabilities, such as severe self-injurious behavior, are not only especially intractable but also deeply disturbing to families and caregivers alike. Thus, when the decision is made to place a child in special education, to institutionalize a child or, more seriously, to withhold medical treatment of a "defective" newborn, it seems inevitable that, for some people, the instincts for being with pleasant, attractive, able, and promising people, are at work.

By the same token, one's ability to "succeed" with a person who has a disability—if we are a physician, to "cure," or an educator, to "teach"—is threatened by some people with disabilities. Surely the emotional reactions of parents are not the only ones operating in a classification decision. Physicians know firsthand the terribly difficult task of telling parents that their child has a disability. To place a child in an institution—to put him or her out of sight and sometimes out of mind—is partly a human condition. And the human condition is an imperfect one.

Riddance Motive

We also classify because some of us at times actively and admittedly wish to rid ourselves of the person who has a disability. The decision to abort a "defective" fetus, while protected constitutionally, may reflect the mother's wish to avoid life with a child with a disability. Decisions to withhold life-sustaining medical treatment or to institutionalize a child may reflect similar reactions of parents not to be disabled themselves by reason of having a child with a disability.

Parents are not alone in their reaction to disabilities. Educators who refer a child to a special education program, community agency social workers who counsel for institutionalization, and institutional psychologists who recommend deinstitutionalization—all may be motivated by a desire to rid themselves of a "problem" person.

Agency Self-Interest

Another motive that explains classification is related more to agency interests than to personal interests. Educators and others test and thereby engage in classification decisions to absolve themselves of moral responsibility for decisions about what happens to people with disabilities, taking refuge in science. By resorting to science, they also gain credibility with parents.

Finally, agencies serve school interests in categorization and program efficiency. A well-organized school system has to have students so programs can be planned, financed, operated, and perpetuated. By the same token, social services, health, and mental health agencies sometimes classify a person as having a disability, or as having a certain degree of disability, for self-serving purposes. They may want to include or exclude a person from a service category because it will increase their head count (number of people served) and thereby their budget or constituency base, or decease it and thereby enable them to serve someone else. Resource allocation is a powerful motive.

Deference to Professionals

As Chapters 5 and 6 indicate, Congress (in the IDEA) and the courts (in appropriate education and least restrictive cases) rely heavily on professionals to say who has a disability and needs special education. By turning to the professionals to help determine who is disabled enough to be treated differently, Congress and the courts can avoid coming to grips directly with the social, political, and moral dilemmas posed by the disability. Thus, decisions about institutionalization are characterized as "medical" just as other types of decisions are called "educational." The consequence is that the true nature of the decisions—what shall be done about disabilities, people with disabilities, and schools—is answered by letting professionals decide.[31]

Classification, Professionals, and Policy Consequences

By the fiction that people with disabilities really are different and should be treated differently, largely by professionals, the law has avoided the ultimate questions: Who should decide who should care for them, where, how, at whose expense, and why? Even more fundamentally, who is different enough to be treated differently? And who has the sagacity to tell us the answer? These are the issues of classification.[32]

The answer to these questions has been: the professionals. Once policy-makers know that professionals can give the answers, they tend to seek answers to other questions from them. (Is this psychological examination valid for the purpose it is used? Is the student's program appropriate?) Thus, our responsibility (or lack of it) for "other" people, for people with disabilities, is made manifest to us: Do as the professionals say.

By avoiding some of the hard policy questions and by allowing people to be classified and sorted, the law can do an injustice not only to them but to itself. It condones a double standard, a dual system (see Chapter 6). But when courts and legislatures insist on substantive and procedural changes in dealing with people who have disabilities, the law reshapes not only itself but, it is hoped, our culture itself. That is the ultimate purpose of IDEA's nondiscriminatory evaluation rules.

Effects of the Nondiscriminatory Evaluation Rule ~

The requirements for nondiscriminatory evaluation have had multiple benefits and drawbacks. They also have raised several important concerns.

Standard Intelligence Tests

First, the requirements for nondiscriminatory evaluation, as interpreted by the courts, clearly have both outlawed and legitimized standard intelligence tests and their use in classifying students. The *Larry P.* and *PASE* cases cannot be read consistently with each other insofar as intelligence tests are concerned. On the whole, *PASE* is the better decision because it is better reasoned and because it interprets and legitimatizes IDEA and the standardized tests. The tests are here to stay, and so are the IDEA safeguards.

Additional Measures for Classification

The IDEA limitation that other measures for classification also must be used is an important one and reflects another significant contribution of the requirements for nondiscriminatory evaluation. The requirements for multifaceted and multidisciplinary evaluation have created more equitable and more elaborate procedures for classification. In a sense, they have recognized that intelligence testing has a hypnotic effect, and they have tried to mitigate that effect by requiring that other procedures be brought to bear in classification.

Investments in Time

Of course, in creating these more equitable and elaborate procedures, the IDEA requirements have caused educators and their colleagues to spend a great deal more time in evaluation and classification. The benefit of this new investment is a more thorough, comprehensive picture of the student and, as a consequence, a greater ability to identify a student's strengths and build on them, and a greater ability to identify a student's weaknesses and remedy them.

Careful Documentation

A fourth effect of the nondiscriminatory evaluation requirements is that educators, their colleagues, and parents have documented more carefully the child's abilities and disabilities and have related those to educational decisions. The benefits of careful documentation are to establish more data-based and objective foundations, created by all affected persons, for educational decisions. Although subjective evaluation still is valid because IDEA recognizes the legitimate role of clinical experience, this type of evaluation is less likely to prevail, especially as it is made by a single person.

Who Has a Disability and
the Prevalence and Incidence of Disabilities

The new requirements clearly have impacted policy-makers' concerns about who has a disability, how to define a disability, and the prevalence of disability. For example, Congress in 1984 required the Secretary of Education to review and evaluate the term "behaviorally disordered" and to submit a report of that review and evaluation within 6 months after the effective date of the amendment (PL 98–199). The report recommended against any change.

Another example of policy-makers' and educators' concerns involves the classification of students as having a learning disability. On the one hand, the category has been extraordinarily useful. It is an accurate way to classify a child who has problems with academics. In addition, it is a relatively stigma-free classification. The rapid and large growth of the category, however, has posed some problems. Educators and policy-makers are worried about overclassification—placing too many children into that category because of its relatively low stigma and relatively high acceptability. They also are concerned about the increased cost of educating so many children who arguably may not have a true disability or who have a marginal disability.

In addition, the definition of mental retardation has posed similar problems. In 1973, the American Association on Mental Retardation (AAMR), the nation's oldest and largest professional organization concerned exclusively with mental retardation, reduced the IQ cutoff for classification as having mental retardation from 85 to 70. In 1983, the AAMR defined *mild mental retardation* as having a cutoff at IQ 70 but being particularly subject to the evaluators' clinical judgment and experience. Indeed, even then the AAMR recognized a "zone of uncertainty" of between IQ 62 and 78. The 1992 definition by the AAMR does not alter the IQ ranges (70–75 or lower) but does focus much more on adaptive behavior and situational capacity.

Will nondiscriminatory evaluations of a person thought to have mental retardation now evaluate the levels of needs that the person may have, as AAMR recommends? Or will the traditional approach, which excludes that kind of analysis of situational capacity (levels of need across several domains of life), still be used? That is hard to say, given that professionals in the definition and classification issues in mental retardation still have not reached consensus on the meaning (definition) of the term. The 1997 amendments to IDEA, however, make clear that the AAMR's 1992 approach is correct: The student's evaluation must be connected to the student's program, placement, curriculum, services, and supports.

Sharing Techniques and Resources

It is important for special education to share its techniques with general education. Individualization and the related-service provisions are powerful tools for helping a child. Sharing techniques, however, is not the same as sharing funds, personnel, and other resources. As IDEA's definition of disability was expanded to include new categories such as autism, traumatic brain injury, and attention deficit/hyperactivity disorder, new claims were made on federal, state, and local resources, particularly on funds and personnel.

Every new claim was accompanied by at least two responses.

1. The special education profession and the parents of children in special education sought to increase appropriations for special education. This has been problematic given the success, or lack thereof, of any education program in commanding new resources, and the current fiscal conditions of federal, state, and local governments.
2. Disincentives for special education placement, with incentives for retaining a student in general education, were developed. Among the disincentives were state-required preassessments, screenings, prereferrals, and other procedural barriers to a full-blown evaluation. These were designed to retain the student in regular education by assuring that his or her teachers are using appropriate and effective teaching techniques, providing consultation and other additional resources for the teachers, and, in those beefed-up ways, preventing special education placements.

Not surprisingly, those ways also used some special educators and, certainly, special education techniques (evaluation and individualized intervention). The 1997 amendments to the IDEA strengthen the evaluation, making it more robust, as a way of limiting overclassification. They also allow special education funds to benefit nondisabled students (the "incidental benefit" rule). They give LEAs flexibility in using IDEA funds to prevent placement into special education (see Chapter 10). And they provide SEAs and LEAs with incentives to undertake school reform that can lead to fewer special education placements and a more unified system of education (the heterogeneous school).

Dual Diagnosis

A subtle issue in classification is that of double diagnosis. Some people with mental retardation or autism display symptoms of emotional disturbance. And some people whose behavior can be characterized as a mental illness have other disabilities as well. How should the person be classified—as having mental retardation, mental illness, autism, or how? May a person be classified as having more than one of those disabilities? Both mental retardation and mental illness? The same choice of classification applies to mental retardation and learning disabilities, and to learning disabilities and emotional disturbance.

The choice of diagnosis is important. It may determine whether the person receives one or more labels, whether he or she receives one type of special education service or another, whether confinement in a mental retardation center or a psychiatric hospital could occur, whether the person will be placed in one type of community-based residential or service system or another, and so on.

Many times, regulations or operating procedures of service agencies require them to classify a person as having a single disability. As a result, they report a single diagnosis even though a double diagnosis would be professionally feasible. The regulations or agency procedures may be valid in the sense that they seek to channel into the agency's service streams only those who can benefit from the services provided or who can be served effectively by agency personnel. But they also may have untoward consequences. They may prevent a person from obtaining services for a coexisting disability and, in the long run, make intervention less than maximally useful. Agency regulations or procedures also may have the consequence of locking a person into the primary system and preventing him or her from transferring out of it and into another (or into none) when the system has outlived its usefulness or has become dysfunctional and harmful to the person.

The choice of diagnosis, therefore, is critical, especially when a dual diagnosis may be a choice. Special attention to the classifier's motivation and to the effect of classification is warranted in these difficult cases. Because professionals cannot help but take into account parental or family wishes (e.g., the learning disabilities classification seems to be far less stigmatizing to families and client than the mental retardation classification), the motives of parents and family also are of concern.

Conclusion

The problems of classification are, at their root, philosophical, political, and programmatic. The challenges of evaluation are more scientific, more in the domains of various professionals and families. The bad news is that IDEA cannot solve the classification problems; it can only contribute to their solution by insisting on fair, robust, and program/placement-linked evaluation. That contribution goes a long way toward solving the challenges of evaluation, and the 1997 amendments' contribution to fairness in evaluation and to appropriateness of program and placement cannot be overstated.

References

Blatt, B. and Kaplan, F., (1966). *Christmas in Purgatory.* Boston: Allyn and Bacon.

Blatt, B., (1973). *Souls in Extremis.* Boston: Allyn and Bacon.

Blatt, B., McNally, and Ozolins, (1979). *The Family Papers.* Boston: Longman Press.

Committee Report, House of Representatives Committee on Education and The Workforce, on H.R. 5 (IDEA Amendments of 1997) (Passed as P.L. 105-17). H.R. Rep. No. 95, 105th Congress, 1st Session (1997).

Erickson, K., (1966). *Wayward Puritans: A Study in the Sociology of Deviance.* New York: John Wiley and Sons.

Gleidman, J. and Roth, W., (1980). *The Unexpected Minority: Disabled Children in America.* New York: Harcourt Brace Jovanovich.

Mercer, J., (1987). *Labeling the Mentally Retarded* (Berkeley: University of California Press, 1973); Office of Civil Rights, U.S. Department of Education.

Morse, S., "Crazy Behavior," *Southern California Law Review,* 51(1978):528.

Sarason, S. and Doris, J., (1975). *Educational Handicap, Public Policy, and Social History: A Broadened Perspective on Mental Retardation* (New York: Free Press, 1979). See also N. Hobbs (Ed.), *Issues in the Classification of Children* (2 vols.). San Francisco: Jossey-Bass.

Sorgen, M., (1976). "The Classification Process and Its Consequences," in *The Mentally Retarded Citizen and the Law,* edited by Kindred et al. New York: Free Press.

Stone, A., (1976). *Mental Health and Law: A System in Transition.* Washington, DC: National Institute of Mental Health.

Trilling, L., quoted in Rothman, (1980). Convenience and Conscience: The Asylum and Its Alternatives in *Progressive America.* Boston: Little, Brown.

Turnbull, H. R. and Turnbull, A., (1985). *Parents Speak Out: Then and Now.* Columbus, OH: Charles E. Merrill.

Wald, P., (1976). "Basic Personal and Civil Rights," in *The Mentally Retarded Citizen and the Law,* edited by M. Kindred et al. New York: Free Press.

Cases ᕔ

Diana v. State Bd. of Ed., No. C-70-37 (N.D. Cal. 1973).

Georgia State Conference of Branches of NAACP v. Georgia, 775 F.2d 1403 (11th Cir. 1985).

Guadalupe Org., Inc. v. Tempe Elementary Sch. Dist. No. 3, 587 F. 2d 535 (10th Cir. 1979).

Hobson v. Hansen, 269 F. Supp. 401 (D.D. C 1967), cert. dismissed, 393 U.S. 801 (1968), aff'd in part, rev'd in part sub nom., Smuck v. Hobson, 408 F.2d 175 (D.D.C. 1969).

Hoffman v. East Troy Community Sch. Dist. 26 IDELR 1074 (E.D. Wisc. 1999).

Honig v. Doe, 484 U.S. 305 (1988).

In re Phillip B., 156 Cal. Reptr. 48 (1979).

Larry P. v. Riles, 343 F. Supp. 1306 (N.D. Cal. 1972), 502 F. 2d 963 (9th Cir. 1974), No. C-71-2270 RF P (N.D. Cal., October 16, 1979), 793 F.2d. 969 (9th Cir. 1984).

Lau v. Nichols, 483 F. 2d 791 (9th Cir. 1973).

LeBanks v. Spears, 417 F. Supp. 169 (E.D. La. 1976).

Mattie T. v. Holiday, 522 F. Supp. 72 (N.D. Miss. 1979).

PASE v. Hannon, 506 F.Supp. 831 (N.D. Ill. 1980).

Rettig v. Kent City School Dist., 94 F.R.D. 12 (N.D. Ohio 1980).

San Jose Unified School Dist., 29 IDELR 813 (Cal. 1998).

5
Appropriate Education

When the federal courts decided *PARC* and *Mills* in 1972, they held that a student is entitled to individually tailored special education The purpose of their decisions was simple: to assure that the schools provide some educational benefit to the student— a goal best accomplished by individualizing the student's education. A few years later, Congress incorporated into IDEA the concept of appropriateness, achieved through individualized education and benefit into IDEA.

This chapter is directed to various aspects of an appropriate education including: (1) IDEA's definition of an appropriate education; (2) the "process definition" of an appropriate education; (3) the different types of individualized plans for implementing an appropriate education; (4) other statutory provisions for assuring an appropriate education; (5) related services; (6) the Supreme Court's "benefit" definition of an appropriate education; (7) issues related to judicial reliance on expert judgment; (8) remedies for denial of an appropriate education; and (9) government functions relating to children with disabilities and how these functions affect a student's right to and receipt of an appropriate education.

Statutory Definition of Appropriate Education ~

Under IDEA and its regulations, an "appropriate education" is defined by two concepts: standards and individualization [20 U.S.C. § 14021401 (8) and 34 C.F.R. § 300.8].300.13]. First, under the "standards" criterion an appropriate education is one that consists of special education and related services that

1. are provided at public expense, under public direction and supervision, and without charge,
2. meet the standards of the state education agency, and

3. include appropriate preschool, elementary school, and secondary school education.

Second, under the "individualized" criterion, each student must have an individualized education program (IEP) tailored to fit his or her educational needs and each infant/toddler and family must have an individualized family service plan (IFSP) tailored to fit their needs.

The three "standards" criteria and the one "individualized" criterion are not especially clear if read in isolation from their history and from the rest of IDEA. When, however, they are read against the holdings in *PARC* and *Mills* and in light of Congress' finding that many students were functionally excluded (enrolled but not benefiting), the criteria take on a more concrete meaning. The U.S. Supreme Court explained these concepts in its first special education decision, *Board of Education v. Rowley* (1982).

The Rowley Decision:
IDEA and the Process Definition ⁓

In *Rowley*, the Court had to decide whether IDEA requires an LEA to provide an interpreter for a student with a hearing impairment. The Court answered "no." Amy Rowley did not have a right to an interpreter because she already was benefiting from her education: She was progressing from grade to grade without interpreter services. That fact alone, however, did not make all the difference. IDEA's overall scheme, together with IDEA's congressional history, were just as important in reaching this conclusion. What is that overall scheme? What is the legislative history?

The two statutory definitions of "appropriate education"—the "standards" criterion and the "individualized" criterion—are best understood together and in the overall context of IDEA and its approach to special education. IDEA's approach is highly procedural and defines appropriate education by a process.

As the Court noted in *Rowley*, IDEA "imposes extensive procedural requirements upon States receiving federal funds under its provisions." The Court stated that Congress clearly intended to require the states "to adopt procedures which would result in individualized consideration of and instruction for each child." Among these procedures are those related to "individualized consideration"— namely, nondiscriminatory evaluation—and to "individualized instruction"— namely, the IEP. Likewise, the Court identified procedural requirements, especially (a) notification of the student's parents whenever an LEA proposes or refuses to change the student's identification, evaluation, educational placement, or the provision of a free appropriate public education to the student, and (b) an opportunity to protest the decision (the procedural due process safeguards—see Chapter 7).

Therefore, an appropriate education—under IDEA as interpreted by *Rowley* and as restated in the 1997 amendments [20 U.S.C. §§ 1401 (8) and 1414 (d)]—is one that conforms to IDEA's process. For example, assume that school personnel are concerned about what kind of education and placement are appropriate for a 9-year-old child who has a disability. How do they answer this question? They do it by

— making a nondiscriminatory evaluation,

— developing an individualized education program,

— attempting to place the child in the least restrictive appropriate program,

— seeing that the parents have access to the child's school records throughout this process, and

— convening a due process hearing if the parents wish to protest the placement or any other action related to the child's right to a free appropriate education.

IDEA's technique for defining "appropriate," then, is to require that a process be followed, in the belief that a fair process will produce an acceptable result.

Individualized Education—The I-Plans

Process alone is a necessary but not a sufficient means for assuring an appropriate education. As IDEA itself and the Court in *Rowley* make clear, the linchpin of a student's education is the "individualized" plan. There are two of these, each covering a different period of the student's life. The individualized family services plan (IFSP) in Part C covers infant-toddler programs (so-called "zero to three"). For students in Part B early intervention programs (ages 3 through 5) and Part B's subsequent special education programs (ages 6 through 21), the plan is called the individualized education program (IEP).

Part C and the Individualized Family Service Plan (IFSP)

Membership on IFSP Team

Family members play a variety of roles in enhancing the child's development [34 C.F.R. § 303.334, Note 2]. This note emphasizes the importance of the child's parents in determining the child's needs and enhancing the child's developmental progress. Throughout the process of developing and implementing IFSPs, agencies have to recognize these roles as well as the needs of the family (See 34 C.F.R. § 303.344).

Participants in the initial and each annual IFSP meeting thereafter must include:

1. the child's parent or parents,
2. other family members as requested by the parent(s) if it is feasible to include them,
3. an advocate or a person outside the family, if the parent requests that the person participate,
4. the service coordinator,
5. a person or persons directly involved in conducting the child and family evaluations and assessments, and

6. as appropriate, persons who will provide services to the child or family. [34 C.F.R. § 303.343]

If a required person is not available to attend the meeting, other means for securing that person's participation must be used, such as telephone conference calls, attendance by a knowledgeable representative, or making pertinent records available at the meeting [34 C.F.R. § 303.343(a)(2)].

Components of the IFSP

Part C [20 U.S.C. § 1436] is specific about the IFSP. It must:

1. be based on a multidisciplinary assessment of the unique strengths and needs of the infant or toddler and identify the appropriate services to meet those needs [20 U.S.C. § 1436 (a)(1)];
2. include a family-directed assessment of the resources, priorities, and concerns of the family and identify the supports and services necessary to enhance the family's capacity to meet the developmental needs of the infant or toddler [20 U.S.C. § 1436 (a)(2)]; and
3. be developed in writing by a multidisciplinary team that includes the infant's or toddler's parents [20 U.S.C. § 1436 (a)(3)].

In addition, the IFSP must include:

1. a statement of the child's present levels of physical, cognitive, communication, social or emotional, and adaptive development, based upon objective criteria [20 U.S.C. § 1436 (d)(1)];
2. a statement of the family's resources, priorities, and concerns relative to enhancing the development of the family's infant or toddler [20 U.S.C. § 1436 (d)(2)];
3. a statement of the major outcomes expected to be achieved for the infant or toddler and the family, and the criteria, procedures, and timelines used to determine the extent to which progress toward achieving the outcomes is being made and whether modifications or revisions of the outcomes or services are necessary [20 U.S.C. § 1436 (d)(3)];
4. a statement of specific early intervention services necessary to meet the unique needs of the infant or toddler and the family, including the frequency, intensity, and method of delivering services [20 U.S.C. § 1436 (d)(4)];
5. a statement of the natural environments in which early intervention services shall be provided appropriately, including justification of the extent, if any, to which services will not be provided in a natural environment [20 U.S.C. § 1436 (d)(5)];
6. the projected dates for initiation of services and the anticipated duration of services [20 U.S.C. § 1436 (d)(6)];
7. identification of the service coordinator who will be responsible for implementing the plan and coordinating with other agencies and persons [20 U.S.C. § 1436 (d)(7)]; and

8. the steps to be taken to support the toddler's transition to preschool or other appropriate services [20 U.S.C. § 1436 (d)(8)].

This last provision, regarding transition, is especially important. IDEA requires each state, as a condition of receiving Part C funds, to file an application that must contain a description of policies and procedures to be used:

1. to assure transition from infant/toddler programs to preschool or other appropriate services. This must include a description of:
   a. how the families will be included in transition plans; and
   b. how the state's lead agency (the agency the Governor designates to direct the Part C program) will:
      (1) notify LEAs about the eligibility of infants/toddlers for preschool services;
      (2) for a child who is eligible for preschool, convene a conference between the parents, Part C providers, and the LEA to discuss the services the child needs in preschool; and
      (3) for a child who is not eligible for preschool, make reasonable efforts to convene a conference of parents, Part C providers, and providers of other appropriate services to discuss the services the child needs [20 U.S.C. § 1437 (a)(8)(A)];
2. to review the child's options for services during the period from the child's third birthday through the remainder of the current school year [20 U.S.C. § 1437 (a)(8)(B)]; and
3. to establish a transition plan [20 U.S.C. § 1437 (a)(8)(C)].

In addition, Part B (ages 3–5, 6–21) sets out three prerequisites to a state's receipt of Part B funds:

1. A state must have in place policies and procedures to assure that infants/toddlers in Part C programs who will participate in preschool programs funded under Part B will experience a smooth and effective transition;
2. A state must assure that, by the child's third birthday, the child will have an IEP or an IFSP, and that those individualized plans are being implemented implemented; and
3. The child's LEA will participate with the child's early intervention provider or other agency designated by the state's Part C lead agency in transition planning conferences arranged by the lead agency. [20 U.S.C. § 1412 (a)(9)].

Timing

The initial meeting for developing the IFSP must be held within 45 days after the child or family is referred to the state's lead agency [34 C.F.R. § 303.342 (a)]. The IFSP must be developed within a reasonable period after assessment is completed [20 U.S.C. § 1436 (c)].

The IFSP must be evaluated once a year, but the family must be provided a review (not an evaluation of the IFSP but, rather, a review of it) at 6-month intervals, or more often if the infant/toddler or family needs such a review. Thereafter, periodic review is available in two ways:

1. by a meeting or other agreeable means every 6 months to review the child's progress and provide appropriate revision [20 U.S.C. § 1436 (b); 34 C.F.R. § 303.342 (b)(1)], or
2. by the aforementioned annual meeting to review its appropriateness [20 U.S.C. § 1436 (b); 34 C.F.R. § 303.342 (c)].

The meetings must be at times and places convenient to the family and must be scheduled so the family can plan to attend. Also, the meetings must be conducted in the family's native language or other mode of communication [34 C.F.R. § 303.342 (d)(1)].

Special rules apply to providing services before the evaluation and assessment of the child and family are completed, and services may begin prior to evaluation and assessment if the parents agree [20 U.S.C. § 1436 (c)]. An interim IFSP names the service coordinator and demonstrates that the child and family need the services immediately, and the evaluation and assessment must be completed within the allotted 45-day period [34 C.F.R. § 303.345].

Accountability; Potential Impact of IFSP

Every agency or person having a direct role in providing early intervention services is responsible for making a good-faith effort to assist the child in achieving his or her IFSP outcomes. No agency or person, however, may be held accountable if the child does not achieve the growth projected by the IFSP [34 C.F.R. § 303.346].

Clearly, the IFSP and Part C generally have potential for strengthening families by helping them

1. develop great expectations for their infant/toddler and themselves,
2. see the positive contributions the infant/toddler can make to the family, its friends, and society,
3. make choices about how they want to be involved in their infant's/toddler's life,
4. create relationships with professionals and with others who are not in the business of providing disability services,
5. learn what their infant's/toddler's strengths and needs are,
6. learn what new strengths can be developed,
7. determine how the family can cope with difficulties and learn new coping skills,
8. improve or develop new techniques for communicating within the family and with professionals,
9. see the possibilities for the integration and independence of the infant/toddler and, indeed, of the whole family,
10. secure and coordinate services from a variety of disciplines, service providers, and funding streams,

11. learn how to take charge of their situation and become their own case manager if they wish to do so, and
12. be launched successfully as families affected by a disability.

Moreover, the IFSP recognizes that families play a crucial role in the infant's/toddler's development and always will play an important role in child development. The IFSP extends the notion of "parent participation" to that of "family participation," subject to the final decision by the parent(s). It recognizes that families are systems and that no one member of the family (the infant/toddler) can be helped unless all members of the family are strengthened and the whole family comes from a position of strength (Turnbull & Turnbull, 1997).

Part B and the Individualized Education Program (IEP)

The second "I" plan is the IEP. IDEA and good practice dictate that, for a student's education to be appropriate, it must be individually tailored to fit that student. The policy of providing an appropriate education is achieved principally by the IEP [20 U.S.C. §§ 1401 (8), (11), and 1414 (d); Appendix A to 34 C.F.R. § 300, Notice of Interpretation].

Membership on the IEP Team

An IEP is a written statement for each student developed by a team whose membership is the same as that of the evaluation team [20 U.S.C. § 1414 (d)(1)(B)]. It consists of:

1. the student's parents;
2. at least one regular education teacher of the student, if the student is or may be participating in the regular education environment;
3. at least one special education teacher or (where appropriate) a provider of special education to the student;
4. a representative of the local agency who is qualified to provide or supervise specially designed instruction to meet the unique needs of students with disabilities and is knowledgeable about general curriculum and the availability of local agency resources;
5. an individual who can interpret the instructional implications of evaluation results (who may be a member of the team already);
6. at the parents' or agency's discretion, other individuals who have knowledge or special expertise (including related services personnel, if appropriate); and
7. the student (when appropriate).

Regular Educator's Role

The 1997 amendments [20 U.S.C. § 1414 (d)(3)(C)] require a regular education teacher to be a member of the IEP team and specify the teacher's duties, which are, to the extent appropriate for the teacher and the student, to assist in

1. developing the IEP and

2. determining in particular
   a. what, if any, appropriate positive behavioral interventions and strategies should be provided to the student, and
   b. what, if any, supplementary aids and services for the student, program modifications, and support for school personnel are appropriate.

To the extent appropriate, the general education teacher also must participate in reviewing and revising the student's IEP. The general education teacher's role also relates to the discipline and expulsion issues (see Chapter 3).

Parent Participation

Because parent participation in the student's education, and particularly in developing the IEP, is a high priority under IDEA, the LEA must take specified steps to ensure that one or both of the student's parents are members of any group (including the IEP team) that makes decisions on the educational placement of their child [20 U.S.C. § 1414 (f)]. These steps include advance notice of the meeting, mutually convenient scheduling of the meeting, and arranging for interpreters for deaf or non-English-speaking parents. If the parent(s) cannot attend the meeting, they still may participate through individual or conference telephone calls.

The agency may have an IEP meeting without parent participation only when it can document that it attempted unsuccessfully to have the parents participate. The documentation should include detailed records of telephone calls, copies of letters to and from the parents, and the results of visits to the parents' homes or places of work. Also, the agency must give the parents a copy of the IEP if they ask for it [34 C.F.R. § 300.345 (d), (f)].

The requirement that parents must be members of the IEP team assures that they will participate in placement decisions. Most of those decisions will be made by the IEP team, but when a placement is not made by the team, the parents still must be "involved in the group making the decision" (Committee Report, p. 103).

Significance of Membership Requirements

What is significant about the membership of the IEP team? In a nutshell, the answer is: consistency of evaluation and programmatic intervention across all aspects of the student's life. *First,* the student's parents are members of the team. Their ability to inform their child's educators thus increases, as does their ability to hold the team's professional members accountable for developing and implementing an individualized program.

More than this, the parents' participation may ensure that the parents will help the schools carry out the student's IEP when the student is at home or in the community. A disability, after all, is not a 6-hour condition but, rather, is a 24-hour one. Carrying out the student's IEP in school, in the home, and in the community helps the student to develop skills in all the environments in which they are needed. Parent participation advances the principle of generalization of skills across environments.

Second, it is significant that the team consists of the individuals—professionals and parents alike—who were members of the nondiscriminatory evaluation team. The linkage between evaluation and program, and between program and placement, is strengthened when the evaluators also are the developers and implementers of the student's IEP. This is true especially when related services personnel are team members; they should be on the team when the student's parents or school personnel request that the team discuss a certain related service [Committee Report, p. 103; 34 C.F.R. § 300.344 (a)(6); 64 Fed. Reg. 12,585 - 12,586].

Among the team members may be a school nurse, whose presence is desirable whenever the team has to make decisions about how to safely address a student's educationally related health needs [Committee Report, p. 103; 34 C.F.R. § 300.344 (a)(6); 64 Fed. Reg. 12,585 - 12,586]. A stable team membership assures consistency in evaluation findings and recommendations, on the one hand, and in the student's program and placement, on the other.

Third, it is significant that the team includes a regular educator. That person's presence on the team assures that the regular educators will participate in the student's IEP development, be more able and willing to carry it out, suggest what school personnel need by way of supplementary aids and services to accommodate the student in the general curriculum, and assist in developing and carrying out behavioral interventions. The Committee Report acknowledges that the requirement that the general educator must participate on the IEP team may "create an obligation that the teacher participate in all aspects of the IEP team's work," but the Report says that is not the intended outcome; it is intended only that the teacher participate to the extent appropriate, and that the IEP designate what kind of supports all school personnel, including the regular education personnel, will need to support the student in the general curriculum (Committee Report, p. 103). (See also 34 C.F.R. § 300.344 (a)(2); 64 Fed. Reg. 12,472, 12,583 12,584.)

Components of an IEP

Having specified the membership on the IEP team, IDEA also specifies what each student's IEP must contain. The IEP must include:

1. a statement of the student's present levels of educational performance, including how the student's disability affects the child's involvement and progress in the general curriculum [20 U.S.C. § 1414 (d)(1)(A)(i)(I); 34 C.F.R. § 300.347 (a)(1)];
2. a statement of measurable annual goals, including benchmarks or short-term objectives, related to (a) meeting the student's needs that result from his or her disability to enable the student to be involved in and progress in the general curriculum, and (b) meeting the student's other educational needs that result from the disability [20 U.S.C. § 1414 (d)(1)(A)(ii)].(d)(1)(A)(ii); 34 C.F.R. § 300.347 (a)(2)];
3. a statement of (a) the specific special education and related services and (b) supplementary aids and services to be provided to, or on behalf of, the student

and the program modifications or supports for school personnel that will be provided for the child [20 U.S.C. § 1414 (d)(1)(A)(iii); 34 C.F.R. § 300.347 (a)(3)]. The Committee Report (p. 101) notes that although it is quite acceptable for the IEP team to discuss teaching and related services methodologies and approaches, the team is not expected to write them into the student's IEP (though it may do so). Moreover, a change in particular methods or approaches does not necessitate an additional IEP team meeting.meeting (See also 64 Fed. Reg. 12,593);

4. an explanation of the extent, if any, to which the child will not participate with nondisabled children in general education and other general curriculum activities [20 U.S.C. § 1414 (d)(1)(A)(iv); 34 C.F.R. § 300.347 (a)(4)];

5. a statement of any individual modifications in the administration of state and districtwide assessments of student achievement or, if the IEP team determines that the student will not participate in a particular assessment or part of an assessment, a statement of why the assessment is not appropriate for the student and how the student will be assessed [20 U.S.C. § 1414 (d)(1)(A)(v); 34 C.F.R. § 300.347 (a)(5)]. The Committee Report acknowledges that excluding students with disabilities from statewide or districtwide assessments "severely limits and in some cases prevents children with disabilities, through no fault of their own, from continuing on to postsecondary education" (Committee Report, p. 101). Accordingly, IDEA requires the IEP to propose modifications in assessment procedures and standards and, if those still are not sufficient to allow the student to participate in the assessments, the nature of alternative assessments to be made available to the student;

6. the projected dates for beginning the listed services and modifications and the anticipated frequency, location, and duration of those services and modifications [20 U.S.C. § 1414 (d)(1)(A)(vi); 34 C.F.R. § 300.347 (a)(6)]. Because the location of special education and related services "influences decisions about the nature and amount of these services and when they should be provided to a particular child" (Committee Report, p. 101), the IEP must specify the services' location, thus requiring team members to consider the extent to which the location affects (negatively or positively) the student's participation in the general curriculum. The term "location" in this context generally refers to the type of environment that is appropriate for provision of a service (64 Fed. Reg. 12,594);

7. Transition planning consists of

   (a) beginning at age 14 and annually thereafter, a statement of the student's transition service needs, according to the student's IEP, focusing on the student's course of study (such as participation in advanced-placement courses or a vocational education program), [20 U.S.C. § 1414 (d)(1)(A)(vii)(I); 34 C.F.R. § 300.347 (b)(1)];

   (b) at age 16 (or earlier, if the IEP team so determines), a statement of needed transition services for the student, including, where appropriate, a statement of interagency responsibilities or any needed linkages [20 U.S.C. § 1414(d)(1)(A)(vii)(II)]; 34 C.F.R. § 300.347 (b)(2)]; and

(c) beginning at least one year before the student reaches the age of majority, a statement that the student has been informed of those rights under the IDEA, if any, that will transfer to the student upon reaching the age of majority [20 U.S.C. § 1414 (d)(1)(A)(vii)(III); 34 C.F.R. § 300.347 (c)];

8. a statement of

(a) how the student's progress toward the annual goals will be measured, and

(b) how the child's parents will be informed regularly (at least as often as parents are informed of their nondisabled children's progress) of their child's progress toward the annual goals and the extent to which that progress is sufficient to enable the student to achieve the goals by the end of the year [20 U.S.C. § 1414 (d)(1)(A)(viii); 34 C.F.R. § 300.347 (a)(7)]. The Committee Report (p. 102) endorses the use, as appropriate, of an IEP report card, a general education report card, or both, to provide parents with information and feedback on their child's progress.

The Committee Report (p. 100) notes that specific day-to-day adjustments in instructional methods normally would not require IEP team action, but the team must reconvene to address any changes that educators or others contemplate in the student's measurable annual goals, benchmarks, or short-term objectives, or in any of the services, program modifications, or other content of the IEP. The Committee Report (p. 100) also regards the statement of measurable annual goals, benchmarks, and short-term objectives to be "crucial" in at least these respects:

1. The statement will help the student's parents and teachers determine if the goals can reasonably be met during the year.
2. It will allow parents to monitor their child's progress.
3. It will specify how students may participate in the general education curriculum, but the Committee Report states that:

   this language should not be construed to be a basis for excluding a child with a disability who is unable to learn at the same level or rate as nondisabled children in an inclusive classroom or program. It is intended to require that the student's annual IEP goals should focus on how the student's disability-related needs can be addressed so the student can participate, at the individually appropriate level, in the general education curriculum that is offered to all students. (Committee Report, p. 100)

To assure that the team develops an IEP that contains these required elements and also to assure that the team addresses matters that sometimes might be overlooked, IDEA requires the team to separately consider additional matters—student strengths and other "special factors" (described below).

Student strengths When developing the IEP, the team must consider the student's strengths, the parents' concerns, and the results of all evaluations [20 U.S.C. § 1414 (d)(3)(A); 34 C.F.R. § 300.346 (a)(1)]. This requirement is notable because it changes the focus of special education. For many years, special education has been both applauded and criticized for concentrating so much on a student's disability and related needs. The "fix-it" approach has been useful in that it has had the purpose, and often the effect, of ameliorating the effects of a disability. It also has been limiting, however, in that it often has overlooked a student's natural strengths and has sent a message of a pathological nature, emphasizing only that the student is "broken" and has to be "fixed"—a message that can be discouraging as well as inaccurate.

Special factors The IEP team must consider other special factors:

1. For a student whose behavior impedes his or her or others' learning, the IEP team shall consider appropriate strategies, including positive behavioral interventions, strategies, and supports, to address that behavior [20 U.S.C. § 1414 (d)(3)(B)(i); 34 C.F.R. § 300.346 (a)(2)(i)];
2. For a student with limited English proficiency, the team shall consider the student's language needs [20 U.S.C. § 1414 (d)(3)(B)(ii); 34 C.F.R. § 300.346 (a)(2)(ii)];
3. For a student who is blind or visually impaired, the team shall provide for the use of braille or other appropriate reading and writing media [20 U.S.C. § 1414 (d)(3)(B)(iii); 34 C.F.R. § 300.346 (a)(2)(iii)];
4. The IEP team must consider the communication needs of any child, and for a student who is deaf or hard of hearing, the team shall consider the student's language and communication needs, opportunities for direct communications with peers and professionals in the student's language and communication mode, academic level, and full range of needs [20 U.S.C. § 1414 (d)(3)(B)(iv); 34 C.F.R. § 300.346 (a)(2)(iv)]; and
5. For all students, the team must consider whether assistive technology devices and services are appropriate [20 U.S.C. § 1414 (d)(3)(B)(v); 34 C.F.R. § 300.346 (a)(2)(v)].

The IEP team must consider these five special factors as appropriate for the individual student. Some students may need interventions to address their behavior, and indeed they also may need assistance with learning English, using braille, communicating with peers and others who have hearing impairments or are deaf, or acquiring or using assistive technology. Other students may need only one of these five types of assistance. Whatever the student's special education and related services needs are, the IEP team, because it is required to consider these five factors, is more likely to address them by taking the mandatory, broad-based view that these five factors command.

Specific Provisions Concerning Impeding Behavior: Positive Behavioral Interventions and Supports (PBIS)

Defining PBIS The term "positive behavioral interventions and supports" (PBIS) describes an approach to a student's behavior that broadens an intervention related to behavior from a traditional behavior management approach designed to reduce inappropriate behavior (Turnbull, Turnbull, Wilcox, Sailor, and Wickham, 1999). Instead, positive behavioral interventions and supports involve four interrelated components: systems change activities, environmental alterations activities, skill instruction activities, and behavioral consequence activities. Positive behavioral interventions and supports bring these four activities to bear with respect to the student's behaviors. Set out below is a definition of each of these components as developed by a multi-university consortium that provides technical assistance related to PBIS.*

1. *Systems change.* A student's behavior is affected by the philosophies, policies, procedures, practices, personnel, organization, and funding of education agencies (general and special education programs) and other human service agencies involved in the student's education. To develop or implement a student's positive behavioral interventions and supports plan, it usually is necessary to engage in a process of systems-change, namely, the process of changing the agencies' philosophies, policies, procedures, practices, personnel, organization, and funding. Also, many students with impeding behavior can benefit substantially from service integration in which the services of a broad constellation of agencies are provided in a unified and responsive manner. That is another reason why systems change is part of positive behavioral interventions and supports.

2. *Environmental alterations.* A student's behavior is also affected by the environments in which the student receives general and special education and related services. To develop or implement a student's positive behavioral interventions and supports plan, those environments usually have to be altered by

   a. making different life arrangements for the student, including building on the student's strengths and preferences, visually depicting for the IEP team the student's preferred daily and weekly activities, identifying priorities for change in those activities and collaborating with various professionals and family members and friends to implement those priorities, networking with individuals in the student's school or with local education or other agencies in the community that are able to connect the student with activities the student prefers, facilitating the development of friendships between the student and peers (with and without disabilities), and promoting the student's health and wellness;

   b. increasing the quality of the student's physical environment, such as by enhancing the predictability of events, modifying the student's schedule, and minimizing noise and other environmental irritants;

   c. making personal accommodations for the student, such as by providing the student an increased range of choices and accommodating for atypical neurophysiological and other physiological conditions; and

   d. making instructional accommodations for the student, such as by interspersing easy tasks when the student is working on more difficult ones,

*For further information, please contact the authors, Rud Turnbull or Ann Turnbull, at the Beach Center on Families and Disability, 3111 Haworth Hall, University of Kansas, Lawrence, Kansas 66045.

modifying the curriculum, offering choices in tasks and methods, increasing access to engaging activities, and decreasing the number of instructions given to the student.

Often, environmental factors influence a student's behaviors negatively and should be taken into account in the functional behavioral assessment that undergirds the student's positive behavioral interventions and supports plan, and the plan itself should address life arrangements, quality of physical environment, personal accommodations, and instructional accommodations.

3. *Skill instruction.* A student's behaviors can become more appropriate if the student receives appropriate skill-building instruction. In addition, a student's behaviors can become more appropriate if individuals involved with the student (such as family members, educators, related service providers, local education agency administrators, and peers with and without disabilities) also receive instruction in how to interact with the student.

    a. The student and others should receive appropriate academic, independent living skill, or other instruction designed to enhance the likelihood that the student will achieve the results of independence, productivity, and inclusion.

    b. Skill instruction consists of teaching the student alternative behaviors that produce the same consequences as the impeding behaviors (e.g., teaching the student to make requests using socially acceptable and desirable behavior, teaching the student to participate using alternative communication modes, or providing the student with physically stimulating activities.

    c. Skill instruction consists of teaching the student adaptive behaviors (e.g., choice-making, self-management, relaxation techniques, and general skill development) that reduce or ameliorate the impeding behaviors.

    d. Individuals involved with the student, including members of the student's IEP team and present or potential members of the student's social networks (including peers in general and special education), should receive instruction in communicating with the student, developing social relationships with the student, problem-solving with the student, preventing impeding behaviors, and developing appropriate responses to the student's impeding behaviors. The functional behavioral assessment that underlies the student's positive behavioral interventions and supports plan and the plan itself should address these factors.

4. *Behavioral consequences.* A student's impeding behaviors often can be eliminated or reduced if the student is able to acquire appropriate behaviors. Accordingly, the student should receive behavioral consequences so impeding behaviors are eliminated or minimized and appropriate behaviors are established and increased. The functional behavioral assessment that undergirds the student's positive behavioral interventions and supports plan and the plan itself should address these factors.

5. The characteristics of positive behavioral interventions and supports include the following, without limitation:

    a. Rather than viewing the student alone and the student's behavior as the problem to be addressed, positive behavioral interventions and supports view the systems and environments in which the student receives education or related services and the student's and others' skill deficiencies as interrelated aspects that influenced or potentially caused the impeding behaviors.

    b. Rather than attempting to remedy only the student and the behavior, positive behavioral interventions and supports attempt to make adjustments to and accommodations in the systems and environments and to intervene by promoting appropriate skills in the student and complementary skills of others in those systems and settings.

    c. Rather than simply attempting to extinguish the student's impeding behavior, positive behavioral interventions and supports create new contacts, experiences, relationships, and skills for the student.

    d. Rather than being a short-term intervention, positive behavioral interventions and supports acknowledges that significant investments of effort, over a long time, might be required to achieve systems change, make environmental alterations, develop and deliver skill instruction, and develop and deliver behavioral consequences.

    e. Rather than being implemented only by a behavioral specialist, often in atypical settings, positive behavioral interventions and supports are developed, implemented, and evaluated by a team of professionals, family members, the student, and members of the student's and family's social network through a person-centered planning process, in typical environments, including the general curriculum.

    f. Rather than being used by and within systems of service delivery that are relatively inflexible, positive behavioral interventions and supports are used by and in systems that are flexible and person-centered or that become so through their use of positive behavioral interventions and supports.

    g. Rather than being used as technologies that shape a student's behaviors according to criteria of acceptability determined solely by the professionals delivering services to the student, positive behavioral interventions and supports are techniques for

        i.   identifying the type of lifestyle that the student and, as appropriate, the student's family desire,

        ii. determining the social validity of the education and interventions that the student receives, and

        iii. assessing the quality of life that the student may attain through positive behavioral interventions and supports, so that the development and evaluation of any positive behavioral interventions and supports plan should take into account, as appropriate for the student and family, quality of life measures such as the student's inclusion into and progress through the general curriculum, employment or volunteer opportunities, inclusion into and acceptance by members of the student's and the family's community, independent living opportunities, social and friendship connections, and similar measures related to independence, productivity, and inclusion.

   h. Rather than being technologies that are so specialized that they can be designed and implemented effectively only by special educators or other highly trained personnel (such as school psychologists or school social workers) and then only in one of the non-general education environments included in the continuum of special education settings approved by IDEA, positive behavioral interventions and supports can and should be designed and implemented in the general curriculum and in all other educational settings and other life-settings of the student and by individuals who have received some (but not necessarily exhaustive, comprehensive, in-depth) training in their use and evaluation.

6. The purpose of a positive behavioral intervention and supports plan and its systematic implementation as part of the student's free appropriate public education is to develop and implement a set of procedures uniquely appropriate to the student so the student may achieve a life characterized by independence, productivity, and inclusion and to enhance the student's capacity for learning and socialization.

7. To this end, positive behavioral interventions and supports seek to understand why impeding behaviors occur and what, if any, function they have. Accordingly, positive behavioral interventions and supports use functional behavioral assessment procedures to define the conditions or factors that reliably predict when the behaviors occur, the events that maintain those behaviors, and strategies for replacing those behaviors with behaviors that advance the student's independence, productivity, and inclusion.

"Considering" PBIS   As mentioned above, 20 U.S.C. § 1414 (d)(3)(B) requires the student's IEP team to consider "special factors" when it develops the IEP. In the case of a child "whose behavior impedes his or her learning or that of others," this section states that the IEP team "shall . . . consider, when appropriate, strategies, including positive behavioral interventions, strategies, and supports to address that behavior."

IDEA creates a *rebuttable presumption* in favor of positive behavioral interventions and supports when a student's behavior impedes his or her learning or the learning of others. It does this by acknowledging these interventions and supports to be techniques that the IEP team members must consider in the case of impeding behavior.

Note that the word "consider" simply means that the team members must think about whether to use positive behavioral interventions and supports. They are not required to use positive behavioral interventions and supports, only to think about— to consider—whether to use them or other interventions or no interventions at all.

Defining "Impeding" The term "impeding behavior" means those behaviors of a student that impede the learning of that student or the learning of others, and includes without limitation behaviors that

1. are aggressive, self-injurious, or destructive of property, or are manifestations of depression, passivity, or social isolation, or are manifestations of obsessions, compulsions, stereotypies, or irresistible impulses, or are annoying, confrontational, defiant, taunting, or disruptive, and
2. could cause the student to be disciplined, including being suspended or expelled from school, pursuant to any applicable state or federal law or regulation, or could cause any consideration of a change of educational placement, and
3. are recurring and therefore require a systematic and frequent application of positive behavioral interventions and positive behavioral support.

IDEA and its regulations do not define "impeding behavior" (though the *Federal Register* has some brief commentary, explained below). The definition set out above (a) is based on research, (b) includes students who have been the most usual subjects of research—namely, those with "challenging behaviors" that derive from mental retardation or autism or a combination of those or other developmental disabilities, (c) includes students who have serious emotional disabilities, (d) includes students who have learning disabilities, attention-deficit/hyperactivity disability, or comparable impairments, and (e) includes students whose behaviors derive from one or more movement disorders.

Because this definition includes many types of behaviors, it is theoretical and pragmatic. It is theoretical in that it does not rest on any single theory or explanation of impeding behaviors. It is pragmatic in that it recognizes that many types of behaviors impede the learning of a student with a disability and of other students, too. Accordingly, it encompasses those behaviors.

Moreover, it encompasses the identified behaviors in part because IDEA 97 does not exclude them, in part because students with those behaviors have been subjected to discipline in school (and discipline triggers at least a functional behavioral assessment, 20 U.S.C. Sec. 1415(k)(1)), in part because the research into positive behavioral interventions and supports is beginning to address impeding behaviors in students who do not have developmental disabilities, and in part because students with impeding behaviors, whatever the etiology of those behaviors and however school systems may classify (label) those students, deserve the benefits of positive behavioral interventions and supports.

Two key possibilities arise because of a student's impeding behaviors. One relates to discipline, a matter covered by IDEA 97 (20 U.S.C. Sec. 1415 (k)(1)). If a student's behavior could result in discipline, the student has an interest in receiving an intervention to change the behavior.

The other relates to behavior that "could cause any consideration of a change of educational placement." Any change must be addressed through the IEP process and by the student's IEP team (20 U. S. C. 1414(d)) and could result in the student being placed in a more restrictive program, possibly to the detriment of the student's right to receive an appropriate education. Whatever the consequences of the behavior, the behavior impedes and should result in a plan for evaluation (functional behavioral assessment) and intervention (IEP-based positive behavioral interventions and supports.)

IDEA and its regulations also do not specify the level of impediment that triggers a functional behavioral assessment and a positive behavioral interventions and supports plan, so a state or local education agency may or may not set a level. The benefit of setting no level is that any impediment arguably should justify a functional behavioral assessment and positive intervention, because proactive intervention can prevent possible subsequent and sometimes less easily remediable behavior.

The consortium's approach, however, sets a level by requiring the behaviors to be "recurring," and therefore to "require a systematic and frequent application" of positive behavioral interventions and supports. The consortium recognizes that educators face various constraints when it comes to their use of positive behavioral interventions and supports. It also acknowledges that some students could benefit from positive behavioral interventions and supports even though their behaviors are not durable and chronic—that is, not a regular part of their behavioral repertoire. Setting a level requiring recurrence balances the present limitations of school systems and the claims of students with durable and chronic behaviors against the interests of students who have less durable and chronic behaviors by excluding the latter from the definition of students with impeding behaviors.

Of course, if a school decides to provide positive behavioral interventions and supports to students with nondurable, nonchronic impeding behaviors, that would be consistent with a schoolwide approach to improving all students' behaviors via the use of positive interventions and supports.

Department of Education Regulations and Commentary   The regulations implementing the IDEA ("impede") provisions are set out at 34 C.F.R. § 300.346 (a)(2)(i). They essentially repeat the statutory language. The Department's response to comments on the preliminary regulations is set out in the *Federal Register* and is somewhat helpful.

The Department notes that "school officials have powerful incentives to implement positive behavioral interventions, strategies, and supports whenever behavior interferes with the important teaching and learning activities of school" [64 Fed. Reg. 12,588]. This is an interesting statement.

1. It acknowledges that school officials are not required to implement PBIS; the fact that they have incentives is different from the fact that they may be (but are not) required to do so.
2. It makes clear that the term "positive" modifies all of the following words—namely, "behavioral interventions, strategies and supports" and that there is a single "PBIS package" consisting of interventions, strategies, and supports.
3. It uses the word "interferes" as a synonym for "impedes," so the dictionary definition of either word may be used to interpret IDEA.

4. It qualifies the statutory language (the student's learning or others' learning) with the term "important learning and teaching activities of the school," suggesting that, if a student's behavior does not impede/interfere with the important ones but only the unimportant ones, the student may not be a candidate for PBIS. Of course, to reach that conclusion, one must know what distinguishes the important from the unimportant learning and teaching activities.

5. It uses "learning and teaching" conjunctively, suggesting that a student may be a candidate for PBIS if his or her behavior impedes/interferes with not only others' learning but also with the faculty's teaching. This may open up PBIS for more students than if the only criterion for PBIS is "impede" the learning of the student or of other students.

With respect to a concern by some commentators that the IEP team should examine in- and out-of-school behavior to develop interventions to sustain learning, the Department declined to issue such a regulation, for fear of over-regulation. Instead, it said that it "might be helpful to all parties for the IEP to identify the circumstances or behaviors of others that may result in inappropriate behaviors by the child." This is at least an invitation to IEP team members to evaluate the impact of others' behavior on the student, including the behavior of other students and of faculty and the behavior of others outside the school (including parents).

Regarding "aversive behavioral management strategies" and whether the regulations prohibit these, the Department said that "the needs of the individual child are of paramount importance in determining the behavioral management strategies that are appropriate for inclusion in the child's IEP. In making these determinations, the primary focus must be on ensuring that the behavioral management strategies in the child's IEP reflect the Act's requirement for the use of positive behavioral interventions and strategies."

What is to be made of this language? *First,* that the regulations do not explicitly prohibit aversive strategies. *Second,* that the strategies must "reflect" IDEA. That is, they may not be inconsistent with IDEA. What, then, would make strategies inconsistent with IDEA? The answer is: those that do not reflect, or are inconsistent with, IDEA's "requirement for the use of positive behavioral interventions and strategies."

That sentence (concerning IDEA's "requirement") bears close reading. Here, the Department says that IDEA requires the use of positive interventions and strategies. That is not exactly the same as saying that IDEA prohibits non-positive or aversive ones, but it comes awfully close to saying that.

At the very least, the Department fortifies the presumption in favor of PBIS. At the next level, arguably it creates an irrebuttable presumption in favor of PBIS and against non-positive or aversive strategies, requiring LEAs to "use" only positive strategies and not to use non-positive or aversive ones.

Just how this language will be read is not certain. All that seems certain is that the language is grist for lawyers' and courts' mills; that one can expect the Department (OSEP and OCR) to issue opinions and advisories that do not back down from "require the use of positive behavioral interventions and strategies"; and that state and local education agencies, and others, who want students to benefit from PBIS and not be subjected to non-positive or aversive interventions, now may look to the Department for support for their opposition to non-positive or aversive interventions.

Linking PBIS to Nondiscriminatory Evaluation and the IEP Regarding the requirement that the IEP team consider PBIS, note the following:

1. The IEP team must take this action, but the membership on the IEP team is fundamentally the same as that of the team that completes the student's nondiscriminatory evaluation, the consequence being that the evaluation data are known to the IEP team and can be taken into account when the team decides whether to consider positive behavioral interventions and supports.
2. The team must consider positive behavioral interventions and supports "when appropriate"—namely, when the student's behavior impedes learning (that is, the student's progress toward IEP goals and objectives or others' learning).
3. The team must "consider" various "strategies, including positive behavioral interventions, strategies, and supports," thereby allowing it to "consider" using other strategies than, or in addition to, positive behavioral interventions and supports, or the use of no interventions at all.
4. The strategies (whatever they may be) must "address" the student's behavior; that is, they must be targeted at preventing, reducing, replacing, or otherwise appropriately addressing the behavior (or behaviors).

In addition, the new requirements related to positive behavioral support interventions, strategies, and supports are consistent with, and should be part of, the IEP for such students. The student's "behavioral intervention plan" (positive behavioral intervention and support plan) is part and parcel of the student's IDEA rights and should be part of the IEP, which itself is the linchpin to an appropriate education.

Private School Students and IEPs

If an SEA or an LEA places a student in a private program, he or she still is entitled to an IEP in the private school [20 U.S.C. § 1412 (a)(10)(B)(i); 34 C.F.R. §§ 300.341(a)(2), 300.348]. The SEA and the placing LEA must assume responsibility for implementing the student's IEP in a private or parochial school. This responsibility includes initiating a meeting to develop an IEP before the student is placed in the private or parochial school and ensuring that a representative of the school attends the meeting or participates through other methods, such as individual or conference telephone calls [34 C.F.R. § 300.348 (a)].

Meetings must be held to review or revise the IEP after a student is placed in a private or parochial program. A representative of the public agency must be involved in any decisions made at these meetings and must agree to proposed IEP changes [34 C.F.R. §§ 300.341]. Please recall that a more in-depth discussion of issues regarding placement in private schools can be found in Chapter 3.

Timing of IEPs

Each LEA must establish or revise, if appropriate, and have in effect an IEP for each student at the beginning of each school year [20 U.S.C. § 1414 (d)(2)(A); 34 C.F.R. § 300.342]. The LEA must review and revise the IEP at regular intervals, but not less than annually [20 U.S.C. § 1414 (d)(4)(A)(i); 34 C.F.R. § 300.343(c)(1)].

Review of IEPs

The purpose of the review is to determine whether the student's annual IEP goals are being achieved [20 U.S.C. § 1414 (d)(4)(A)(i)]. If they are not being achieved, a revision of the IEP is warranted, because the team must revise it to address [20 U.S.C. § 1414 (d)(4)(A)(ii)]:

1. any lack of expected progress by the student toward the annual goals, and in the general curriculum, where appropriate;
2. the results of any nondiscriminatory reevaluation;
3. information about the child provided to or by the parents;
4. the student's anticipated future needs; or
5. any other matters.

IEP conferences for a student who already is receiving special education and related services must be conducted early enough to ensure that the student's IEP is revised and in effect by the beginning of the next school year [20 U.S.C. § 1414 (d)(2)(A); 34 C.F.R. § 300.342]. To meet this provision, the LEA may conduct the meeting at the end of the prior school year or during the summer. If a student is not receiving special education, an IEP meeting must be held within 30 days of the determination that the student needs special education and related services [34 C.F.R. § 300.343 (b)(2)].

Related Services, Other Services Necessary for FAPE, and Supplementary Aids and Services

Recall that one of the mandatory elements of each student's IEP [20 U.S.C. § 1414 (d)(1)(A)(iii) is a statement of

1. the special education and related services and supplementary aids and services that will be provided to the student or on the student's behalf, and
2. the program modifications or supports for school personnel that will be provided for the student.

These components—related services, supplementary aids and services, and program modifications and personnel support—have three purposes. They are to benefit the student so that he or she may
— advance appropriately toward attaining the annual goals,
— be involved and progress in the general curriculum and to participate in extracurricular activities and other nonacademic activities, and
— be educated and participate with other children with disabilities and nondisabled children in those extracurricular and nonacademic activities.

Part B Related Services Under Part B of IDEA, the related services to which a student is entitled to accomplish these three results include the following [20 U.S.C. § 1401 (22); 34 C.F.R. § 300.24]:

- "Audiology" includes identifying children with hearing loss; determining the range, nature, and degree of hearing loss; providing habilitative activities; creating and administering programs for treatment and prevention of hearing loss; counseling and guidance of children, parents, and teachers regarding hearing loss; and determining a student's amplification needs [34 C.F.R. § 300.24 (b)(1).
- "Counseling services" includes rehabilitation counseling and services provided by qualified social workers, psychologists, guidance counselors, or other qualified personnel [34 C.F.R. § 300.24 (b)(2)].
- "Early identification and assessment of disabilities in children" means implementing a formal plan for identifying a disability as early as possible in a child's life [34 C.F.R. § 300.24 (b)(3)].
- "Medical services" are those provided by a licensed physician to determine a child's medically related disability that results in the child's need for special education and related services [34 C.F.R. § 300.24 (b)(4)].
- "Occupational therapy" means services provided by a qualified occupational therapist, and includes improving, developing, or restoring functions impaired or lost through illness, injury, or deprivation [34 C.F.R. § 300.24 (b)(5)].
- "Orientation and mobility services" means services provided to blind or visually impaired students by qualified personnel to enable attainment of systematic orientation to and safe movement in school, home, and community environments [34 C.F.R. § 300.24 (b)(6)].
- "Parent counseling and training" means assisting parents in understanding the special needs of their child, providing parents with information about child development, and helping parents acquire necessary skills that will allow them to support the implementation of their child's IEP (or IFSP for Part C—see below under Part C Early Intervention Services) [34 C.F.R. § 300.24 (b)(7)].
- "Physical therapy" refers to services provided by a qualified physical therapist (though the particular services of a physical therapist are not described in 34 C.F.R. § 300.24, a list of services is laid out in 34 C.F.R. § 303.12 (d)(9)—see below under Part C Early Intervention Services) [34 C.F.R. § 300.24 (b)(8)].
- "Psychological services" includes administering psychological and educational tests and other assessment procedures; interpreting assessment results; obtaining, integrating, and interpreting information about the child's behavior and conditions relating to learning; consulting with other staff members in planning school programs to meet the special needs of children as indicated by psychological tests, interviews, and behavioral evaluations; planning and managing a program of psychological services, including psychological counseling for children and parents; and assisting in developing positive behavioral intervention strategies [34 C.F.R. § 300.24 (b)(9)].

- "Recreation" includes assessing leisure function, therapeutic recreation services, recreation programs in schools and community agencies, and leisure education [34 C.F.R. § 300.24 (b)(10)].
- "Rehabilitation counseling services" means services provided by qualified personnel that focus specifically on career development, employment preparation, achieving independence, and integrating a student with a disability in the workplace and community. This term also includes vocational rehabilitation services provided under the Rehabilitation Act [34 C.F.R. § 300.24 (b)(11)].
- "School health services" refers to services provided by a qualified school nurse or other qualified person [34 C.F.R. § 300.24 (b)(12)].
- "Social work services in schools" includes preparing a social or developmental history on a child with a disability; group and individual counseling with the child and family; working with problems in a child's living situation (home, school, and community) that affect the child's adjustment in school; mobilizing school and community resources to enable the child to learn as effectively as possible in his or her educational program; and assisting in developing positive behavioral intervention strategies [34 C.F.R. § 300.24 (b)(13)].
- "Speech pathology" and "speech-language pathology" include identification, diagnosis, and appraisal of specific speech or language impairments; referral to or provision of speech and language, medical, or other services; and counseling and guidance of parents, children, and teachers regarding speech and language impairments [34 C.F.R. § 300.24 (b)(14)].
- "Transportation and related costs" covers travel to and from early intervention services, school, and between schools; travel in and around school buildings; and specialized equipment (such as special or adapted buses, lifts, and ramps), if required to provide special transportation for a child with a disability [34 C.F.R. § 300.24 (b)(15) and, for Part C, § 303.12 (d)(15)].

Part C Early Intervention Services Under Part C, many of the "early intervention services" to which the student is entitled are the same as or similar to the related services provided under Part B. There are a few differences, however, and a list of early intervention services has been included here to make comparison easier. The similarities and differences between the services provided under each Part are set out in the list of early intervention services available under Part C, below [34 C.F.R. § 303.12]:

- "Assistive technology device" means any item, piece of equipment, or product system, whether acquired commercially off the shelf, modified, or customized, that is used to increase, maintain, or improve a student's functional capacities [20 U.S.C. §§ 1401 (1) and (2); 34 C.F.R. § 303.12 (d)(1)] (see comment about assistive technology, below, under Other Services Necessary for FAPE).

- "Assistive technology service" means service that directly assists a child with a disability in the selection, acquisition, or use of an assistive technology device. These services include

  (1) the evaluation (including a functional evaluation of the child in the child's customary environment) of the child's needs,

  (2) purchasing, leasing, or otherwise providing for the acquisition of assistive technology devices by children with disabilities,

  (3) selecting, designing, fitting, customizing, adapting, applying, maintaining, repairing, or replacing assistive technology devices,

  (4) coordinating and using other therapies, interventions, or services with assistive technology devices, such as those associated with existing education and rehabilitation plans and programs,

  (5) training or technical assistance for a child with disabilities or, if appropriate, that child's family, and

  (6) training or technical assistance for professionals (including those providing early intervention services) or other individuals who provide services to or are otherwise substantially involved in the major life functions of individuals with disabilities (see comment about assistive technology, below, under Other Services Necessary for FAPE) [34 C.F.R. § 303.12 (d)(1)].

- "Audiology" includes identification of children with auditory impairment; determination of the range, nature, and degree of hearing loss and communication functions; referral for medical and other services necessary for habilitation or rehabilitation; provision of auditory training, aural rehabilitation, speech reading and listening device orientation and training, and other services; provision of services for preventing hearing loss; and determining the child's need for individual amplification, including selecting, fitting, and dispensing appropriate listening and vibrotactile devices, and evaluating their effectiveness [34 C.F.R. § 303.12 (d)(2)].

- "Family training, counseling, and home visits" refers to services provided, as appropriate, by social workers, psychologists, and other qualified personnel to assist the child's family to understand the child's special needs and to enhance the child's development [34 C.F.R. § 303.12 (d)(3)].

- "Health services" means services necessary to enable a child to benefit from the other early intervention services during the time the child is receiving the other early intervention services [34 C.F.R. §§ 303.12 (d)(4) and 303.13].

- "Medical services," allowed for diagnostic or evaluation purposes only, are services provided by a licensed physician to determine a child's developmental status and need for early intervention services [34 C.F.R. § 303.12 (d)(5)].

- "Nursing services" includes [34 C.F.R. § 303.12 (d)(6)]

  (i) the assessment of health status for the purpose of providing nursing care, including identification of patterns of human response to actual or potential health problems;

(ii) provision of nursing care to prevent health problems, restore or improve functioning, and promote optimal health and development; and

(iii) administration of medications, treatments, and regimens prescribed by a licensed physician.

- "Nutrition services" includes [34 C.F.R. § 303.12 (d)(7)]

    (i) conducting individual assessments in:
    - (a) nutritional history and dietary intake;
    - (b) anthropometric, biochemical, and clinical variables;
    - (c) feeding skills and feeding problems; and
    - (d) food habits and food preferences;

    (ii) developing and monitoring appropriate plans to address the nutritional needs of children;

    (iii) making referrals to appropriate community resources to carry out nutrition goals.

- "Occupational therapy" encompasses services to address the functional needs of a child related to adaptive development, adaptive behavior and play, and sensory, motor, and postural development. These services are designed to improve the child's functional ability to perform tasks in home, at school and in community settings, and include (1) identification, assessment, and intervention, (2) adaptation of the environment, and selection, design, and fabrication of assistive and orthotic devices to facilitate development and promote the acquisition of functional skills, and (3) prevention or minimization of the impact of initial or future impairment, delay in development, or loss of functional ability [34 C.F.R. § 303.12 (d)(8)].

- "Physical therapy" includes services to address the promotion of sensorimotor function by enhancing musculoskeletal status, neurobehavioral organization, perceptual and motor development, cardiopulmonary status, and effective environmental adaptation. These services include (1) screening, evaluation, and assessment of infants and toddlers to identify movement dysfunction, (2) obtaining, interpreting, and integrating information appropriate to program planning to prevent, alleviate, or compensate for movement dysfunction and related functional problems, and (3) providing individual and group services or treatment to prevent, alleviate, or compensate for movement dysfunction and related functional problems [34 C.F.R. § 303.12 (d)(9)].

- "Psychological services" are defined as they are in Part B, except these do not include assisting other staff members in developing school planning or assisting in the development of positive behavioral interventions [34 C.F.R. § 303.12 (d)(10)].

- "Service coordination services" means assistance and services provided by a service coordinator (case manager) to a child and the child's family [34 C.F.R. § 303.12 (d)(11)].

- "Social work services" includes (1) making home visits to evaluate a child's living conditions and patterns of parent-child interaction, (2) preparing a social or emotional developmental assessment of the child within the family context, (3) providing individual and family-group counseling with parents and other family members, and appropriate social skill-building activities with the child and parents, (4) working with those problems in a child's and family's living situation that affect the child's maximum utilization of early intervention services; and (5) identifying, mobilizing, and coordinating community resources and services to enable the child and family to receive maximum benefit from early intervention services [34 C.F.R. § 303.12 (d)(12)].

- "Special instruction" includes (1) the design of learning environments and activities that promote the child's acquisition of skills in a variety of developmental areas, including cognitive processes and social interaction, (2) curriculum planning, including the planned interaction of personnel, materials, and time and space, that leads to achieving the outcomes in the child's IFSP, (3) providing families with information, skills, and support related to enhancing the child's skill development, and (4) working with the child to enhance the child's development [34 C.F.R. § 303.12 (d)(13)].
- "Speech-language pathology" is defined in essentially the same manner as in Part B [34 C.F.R. § 303.12 (d)(14)].
- "Transportation and related costs" is defined in essentially the same manner as in Part B [34 C.F.R. § 303.12 (d)(15)].
- "Vision services" means (1) evaluation and assessment of visual functioning, including the diagnosis and appraisal of specific visual disorders, delays, and abilities, (2) referral for medical or other professional services necessary for the habilitation or rehabilitation of visual functioning disorders, or both, and (3) communication skills training, orientation and mobility training for all environments, visual training, independent living skills training, and additional training necessary to activate visual motor abilities [34 C.F.R. § 303.12 (d)(16)].

Other Services Necessary for FAPE   Other services are necessary to ensure that students receive a free and appropriate public education under Part B. These include the following:

- Assistive technology. Under IDEA, if a student with a disability needs technology-related assistance and the student's IEP calls for such assistance (either "devices" or "services" [note that these are defined in the same manner as they are in Part C]), the student may obtain them from the student's LEA or any existing statewide system for delivering assistive technology [34 C.F.R. § 300.308]. These services or devices may be included in the IEP as a part of the child's special education, as a related service, or as supplementary aids and services. Thus, assistive technology services or devices should be part of the student's educational program where appropriate, and, to be regarded as legally sufficient, a student's IEP should call for these services and devices.

  When developing an IEP, the IEP team is required to consider whether the student needs assistive technology [34 C.F.R. § 300.346 (a)(2)(v)]. Under the federal Technology-Related Assistance for Individuals with Disabilities Act of 1988 (PL 100–407), each state receives federal funds to enable it to create a statewide system for delivering assistive technology. This system can be accessed through a student's IEP and the related services of IDEA.

- Nonacademic services. Each public agency shall take steps to provide nonacademic and extracurricular services and activities in the manner necessary to afford children with disabilities an equal opportunity for participating in those services and activities. These may include counseling services, athletics, transportation, health services, recreation, special interest groups or clubs, referrals to agencies to provide relevant assistance, and employment-related activities [20 U.S.C. § 1412 (a)(1); 34 C.F.R. § 300.306].
- Physical education. These services must be available to every child who receives a FAPE. Further, each child with a disability must be allowed to participate in the regular physical education program unless the child is enrolled full-time at a separate facility, or the child needs specially designed physical education, and that is described in the IEP [20 U.S.C. §§ 1412 (a)(25) and (a)(5)(A); 34 C.F.R. § 300.307].
- Residential placement. If placement in a public or private residential program is necessary to ensure that FAPE is provided for the child, the program, including nonmedical care and room and board, must be at no cost to the child's parents [20 U.S.C. §§ 1412 (a)(1) and (a)(10)(B); 34 C.F.R. § 300.302].
- Proper functioning of hearing aids. Each public agency must ensure that the hearing aids worn in school by children with hearing impairments (including deafness) are functioning properly [20 U.S.C. § 1412 (a)(1); 34 C.F.R. § 300.303].
- Extended school year services (ESY). These are services that are provided to a child with a disability (1) beyond the normal school year of the public agency, (2) in accordance with the child's IEP, (3) at no cost to the child's parents, and (4) that meet standards set by the SEA. If ESY services are necessary to ensure FAPE, the LEA/SEA is required to provide them [20 U.S.C. § 1412 (a)(1); 34 C.F.R. § 300.309].

Supplementary Aids and Services "Supplementary aids and services" are those aids, services, and other supports provided in general education classes or other education-related settings so the student can be educated with nondisabled students to the maximum extent appropriate [20 U.S.C. § 1401 (29); 34 C.F.R. §§ 300.28, 300.550 - 300.556]. Note that the focus of these services is not on the provision of a free appropriate public education but, instead, on making accommodations to allow education to occur in the least restrictive environment. Undoubtedly, these often overlap the special education services that promote these separate but equally important goals.

Transition Services

An important component of each student's IEP is the individualized transition program. Section 20 U.S.C. § 1414 (d)(1)(A)(vii)(I) requires that a "statement of the transition service needs" of the student must be added to the student's IEP beginning at age 14, and must be updated annually. The statement must focus on the student's courses of study, such as an advanced-placement course or a vocational education program.

At age 16 (or younger, if the students' IEP team deems it appropriate), the student's IEP must include a "statement of needed transition services," including, when appropriate, a statement of interagency responsibilities or needed linkages [20 U.S.C. § 1414 (d)(1)(A)(vii)(II)].

Beginning at least one year before the student reaches the age of majority, the IEP also must include a statement that the student has been informed of what IDEA rights, if any, will transfer to the student upon reaching the age of majority [20 U.S.C. § 1414 (d)(1)(A)(vii)(III)]. In cases where the student has been found to be legally incompetent, however, the student's parents or guardian will continue to retain their rights under IDEA. Furthermore, if a student is not legally incompetent, but is determined to be unable to provide informed consent regarding his or her educational program, the SEA may appoint the student's parents or another appropriate person to represent the student's educational interests [20 U.S.C. § 1415 (m)].

By requiring that transition planning is to start at age 14 and that transition services are to begin at age 16 or younger, Congress recognized that transition is a process and that providing such services earlier than age 16, if necessary, is entirely consistent. [20 U.S.C. § 1414 (D)(1)(A)(vii); 34 C.F.R. § 300.347 (b)]. The services must be "needed," as determined in the context of "appropriate education." Thus, a transition service that is necessary to ensure an appropriate education must be provided [34 C.F.R § 300.347 (b)(2)].

20 U.S.C. § 1401 (30) defines "transition services." The term has several components.

1. It includes a "coordinated set of activities" for the student. This language means that the student must have more than one transition activity and that the activities must operate in sync with each other.
2. This set of activities "shall include instruction, related services, community experiences, the development of employment and other post-school adult living objectives, and, when appropriate, acquisition of daily living skills and functional vocational evaluation."
3. Moreover, this set of activities must be "designed within an outcome-oriented process." This language means that the activities must be rationally related to each other and to IDEA outcomes.
4. These activities must be based on the individual student's needs, taking into account the student's preferences and interests.
5. The transition plan also must "promote" movement from school to post-school activities, including postsecondary education, vocational training, integrated employment (including supported employment), continuing and adult education, adult services, independent living, or community participation. Note that the word "promote" implies the concept of "benefit." If the transition services

are not effective, in the sense of promoting movement to the specified outcomes, the services do not confer any benefit on the student. Thus, if a student's transition goals are not being met, the student likely can successfully claim a violation of the "benefit" test and a denial of appropriate education based on *Rowley*.

6. With respect to "transition" issues generally, 20 U.S.C. § 1436 (which provides for an individualized family service plan), § 1412 (a)(9) (which addresses the transition from Part C to preschool programs), § 1414 (d)(1)(A)(vii) (which relates to transition planning for adolescents), and § 1451 (b) (which relates to grants, contracts, and cooperative agreements awarded by the Department of Education and allows the Secretary to require recipients to address transition issues) acknowledge that transition planning is a generic skill that is appropriate at various life stages of the student and family.

7. Congress further required transition plans to include a statement of the interagency responsibilities or linkages (or both) that the student needs before he or she leaves school [20 U.S.C. § 1414 (d)(1)(A)(vii)(II)]. Accordingly, 20 U.S.C. § 1414 (d)(5) requires the local education agency to reconvene the IEP team when adult agencies do not carry out their agreement to provide transition services.

These transition provisions supply three directives for LEAs to follow. [20 U.S.C. § 1401 (30)]

1. LEAs must use specified means, including instruction and community experiences, to achieve the outcomes the transition provisions specify. Thus, the law sets out both the ends and the means.

2. LEAs are on notice that "acquisition of daily living skills and functional vocational evaluation" are appropriate in transition plans for some, but not all, students. Therefore, the law sets a general rule in favor of "employment or other post-school adult living objectives" for most students. Note that Congress put parentheses around "including supported employment," showing that it intended supported employment (work with a job coach) to be only one work-related outcome, but not the only one [20 U.S.C. § one.1401 (30)(A)]. Indeed, Congress intended regular employment to be preferred over supported employment.

3. LEAs should use community-referenced, community-based, and community-delivered instruction. This ensures that the student will learn the skills in the place the student will have to use them. As a result, it acknowledges the principles of generalization and durability (students learn best and retain information when they actually must use their skills in the settings where the skills are required) and skill development in the least restrictive setting of the community.

Some schools play the same role in the late 1990s as they did prior to the 1990 transition amendments by acting as "sending agencies": They prepare a student for the adult world. Today, however, the "receiving agencies"—those to which schools send students—are much different. Before the 1990 amendments, the receiving agencies too often were disability-provider agencies such as local mental health or mental retardation/developmental disability centers, independent living centers for people with physical disabilities, vocational rehabilitation agencies, group homes, or sheltered workshops.

After the 1990 amendments, the receiving agencies include not only these traditional agencies but also programs of postsecondary education, continuing and adult education, adult services, and integrated employment. Given these expected outcomes, schools as sending agencies must include nondisability "generic" agencies in transition planning. Because schools must associate with generic as well as specialized receiving agencies, the principle of the least restrictive environment affords an opportunity for more integration and greater power.

Section 1401(30)(B) also requires the IEP team to take into account the student's preferences with respect to post-school goals during the transition planning process. This is an explicit affirmation that student participation in the IEP process is appropriate when the transition process begins. It also is an implicit recognition that a student's curriculum should include decision-making and choice-making skills as part of the student's progress toward "independence," which is an outcome of special education.

The transition amendments represent a significant change in the IDEA. Until they were enacted, IDEA generally was process-oriented; it told the LEAs and SEAs what processes to follow to educate students with disabilities. Now IDEA is outcome-oriented as well, stating explicitly that outcome-oriented education shall be provided.

Accountability

The regulations indicate clearly that the IEP is not a legally binding contract and that no agency, teacher, or other person may be held accountable if the student does not achieve the projected progress based on the annual goals and objectives [34 C.F.R § 300.350 (b)]. This section, however, does not prevent parents from using due-process procedures (see Chapter 7) for problems related to the IEP, the agencies, or the teachers.

In a further effort to assure accountability and effective special education, the state plan must contain procedures for the SEA or other responsible public agencies to evaluate, at least annually, the effectiveness of LEA programs in meeting students' educational needs. The evaluation is to include an evaluation of IEPs [20 U.S.C. § 1412 (a)(4); 34 C.F.R. § 300.341].

Rationale for the IEP

The IEP is justified on many grounds:

1. The IEP is a method for connecting the LEA's duty of conducting a nondiscriminatory evaluation to the LEA's duty of providing an appropriate program, with related services, and placement in the least restrictive environment.

2. The IEP enables educators to better help the student develop his or her potential. Thus, it is one of the most important contributors to the student's success in school.

3. It enables the school and the parents to monitor the student's progress in school, measure development, identify areas of strength and need, build on strengths, and concentrate on remediating weaknesses.

4. It recognizes that each student is unique and should be treated in light of his or her own strengths and needs.

5. It is a safeguard and reassurance not only for the student but also for the parents, inasmuch as they are concerned legitimately about misclassification, inappropriate placements, and inadequate programs.

6. The requirement of parental involvement not only recognizes parents' legitimate concern to have their child protected against potential wrongs but also strengthens the student's educational program by linking the parents' views of the student's strengths and needs and their own needs to the school's duty and programs. Parents have a wealth of information about their child that can enhance his or her education and be carried over into the family's life if it is shared with school personnel and incorporated in the IEP. Quite simply, what happens to the student in school is relevant to his or her home life, and vice versa.

7. The IEP is a technique for sharing decisions and decision-making powers among school personnel and parents. It is another step along the line toward achieving participatory democracy in public education.

8. The IEP also is a powerful device for assuring accountability. It makes the schools accountable to the student for what they do by requiring an assessment of achievement, a statement of goals, services, timetables, procedures, and criteria for determining if the goals are being met. It makes schools accountable to the parent as a taxpayer and as a participant in developing the individualized program. Parent involvement in curriculum decisions also promotes accountability on the part of the parents. As an outgrowth of IEP development, parents may want to assume specific responsibility for teaching or reinforcing certain skills and concepts at home.

9. By securing parent participation, the IEP also helps forestall the possibility of a due-process protest and hearing under Section20 U.S.C. § 1415 (see Chapter 8). It is not a device of cooption, although some may see it that way. Rather, it is a positive force that assures parent/school decision-sharing, contributing to a collaborative relationship instead of an adversarial confrontation between parents and school personnel.

10. IEPs are necessary to accomplish the zero-reject principle because they assure that no student, once identified as having a disability, is overlooked. IEPs enable school authorities to plan and provide services for students. IEPs focus the capacity of a school system on the student. Like procedural due process, the IEP is student-centered, not system-centered.

11. Finally, individualization, which is the policy of the IFSPs, IEPs, and transition plans, is reflected in other federal laws affecting students or adults with

disabilities, such as the Rehabilitation Act [29 U.S.C. §§ 1400-1485, 1491] and the Developmental Disabilities Assistance and Bill of Rights Act [42 U.S.C. § 6000 et seq.].

Other Statutory Provisions for Appropriate Education ~

Although the "standards" and "individualized" criteria of IDEA, together with the process definition and outcome-oriented focus, constitute key elements of "appropriate education," they are not the only IDEA provisions that assure a student's appropriate education.

1. Procedures to assure nondiscriminatory evaluation serve as safeguards against inappropriate placement and inappropriate education [20 U.S.C. §§ 1412 (a)(6)(B), 1414].
2. The requirement of placement in the least restrictive environment also protects against inappropriate placement and unsuitable programs [20 U.S.C. § 1412 (a)(5)].
3. The right of parents to see and comment on LEA records enables them to hold the school accountable for providing an appropriate education to their child [20 U.S.C. §§ 1414 (b)(4)(B), 1415 (b)(1)].
4. The due-process procedures are yet another method for accountability and compliance with the requirements of appropriate education [20 U.S.C. § 1415].
5. IDEA requires state education agencies to develop and implement a "comprehensive system of personnel development." The CSPD is a means for (a) ensuring an adequate supply of qualified special and general educators and related services personnel to carry out a state's school improvement plan (see Chapter 10), and for (b) disseminating to school personnel "significant information derived from educational research, demonstration, and similar projects" [20 U.S.C. §§ 1412 (a)(14), 1413 (a)(3)]. The CSPD requirements are intended to improve the schools so they can meet their duty of providing each student an appropriate education.
6. IDEA requires each state to establish and maintain personnel standards, including certification and similar requirements, plans for upgrading personnel capacities, and plans for using appropriately trained and supervised paraprofessionals [20 U.S.C. § 1412 (a)(15)].
7. SEA evaluation of LEA compliance, particularly IEP compliance, also helps LEAs provide appropriate programs [20 U.S.C. § 1412 (a)(4)].

Related Services ~

In the *Rowley* case, the Court was compelled to decide whether Amy Rowley was entitled to interpreter services in order to receive an appropriate education. Those services are only one of the many services to which students are entitled in order to receive an appropriate education. IDEA clearly makes an appropriate education depend, in part, on the availability of related services [20 U.S.C. § 1401 (22)]. These include services that are relatively controversial.

"Medical Services" and Other Health Care Services

One issue the courts often address within the context of related services is whether a specific service is a related service that an LEA must provide or pay for or whether it is a medical service needed for purposes other than medical diagnosis and evaluation for special education placement and services. These cases involve catheterization, nursing services, and mental health services.

Catheterization

In *Irving Indep. School Dist. v. Tatro* (1984), the Supreme Court clarified the definition of a related service. *Tatro* involved the meaning of a related service as applied to clean intermittent catheterization (CIC). CIC is a procedure in which a catheter tube is inserted into the urethra and the bladder to drain urine from the kidneys. The Court held, in a unanimous opinion, that CIC is a related service that schools must provide.

The Court found as a matter of fact that CIC is a "simple procedure...that may be performed in a few minutes by a layperson with less than an hour's training." Indeed, the student herself soon would be able to perform the service, as her parents, baby-sitters, and teenage brother had been doing all along.

To conclude that CIC is a related service under IDEA, the Court had to determine:

1. whether CIC is a supportive service that enables students to benefit from special education; and
2. whether CIC is excluded from the supportive service definition because it is a "medical service" serving purposes other than diagnosis or evaluation.

The Court held that CIC is a supportive service because, without it, the student could not attend school and thereby benefit from special education. Relying on its earlier decision in *Rowley*, the Court stated that Congress' intent was to make public education available to students with disabilities and to make their access to school meaningful. A service that allows the student to "remain at school during the day is an important means of providing the child with the meaningful access to education that Congress envisioned." The Court was not about to allow any violation of the zero-reject principle by permitting schools to escape their obligation of providing such a beneficial service.

Next, the Court found that CIC is not a "medical service" needed for purposes other than diagnosis and evaluation. *First,* the Court deferred to the Department of Education regulations, which defined CIC to be a related, school health service, not a medical service. *Second,* the Court found that Congress plainly required schools to hire various specially trained personnel, such as school nurses. Because nurses long have been a part of educational systems and perform duties such as dispensing oral medication and administering emergency injections, which are difficult to distinguish from CIC, it follows that CIC is a service that school nurses (among others) are qualified to provide.

Tatro held that the term "medical services" refers only to services that must be performed by a physician, and not to school health services. This is the "bright-line" rule: The definition is the bright line that separates health care services that are provided as a related service (health services that are not provided by a physician or that are provided by a physician but are evaluative or diagnostic in nature), and those that do not qualify as a related service (medical services (physician-provided) that are not evaluative or diagnostic in nature). No other factors may be considered—only the precise language of the definition. This interpretation was reinforced in *Cedar Rapids Community School District v. Garret F.* (1999).

Full-time Nursing Services

In March 1999, the Supreme Court ruled in *Cedar Rapids Community School District v. Garret F.* that the "related services" provision of IDEA requires a public school district to provide nursing services to a child with a disability during school hours if those services are required to assist the student to benefit from special education. In that case, the student, Garret F., required nursing services that included urinary bladder catheterization, suctioning of tracheostomy, ventilator setting checks, ambubag administrations as a back-up to the ventilator, blood-pressure monitoring, observations to determine if he was in respiratory distress (autonomic hyperreflexia), and disimipation in the event of autonomic hyperreflexia. Because these services were necessary if Garret were to remain in school, the school district must fund these services, the Court held, to guarantee the meaningful access to education and integration that IDEA requires.

Until the *Garret F.* decision, not all medically associated services were so easily included as a related service. This was true particularly for services provided by full-time nurses or similar health-care providers and technicians. Not surprisingly, a number of cases focused on nursing services. The leading case prior to *Garret F.* was *Detsel v. Bd. of Educ. of the Auburn Enlarged City School Dist.* (1987), which involved a student who was oxygen-dependent, requiring constant supply of oxygen administered through a respirator. The respirator was operated by a nurse or other qualified professional who was required to be in attendance with the student and monitor the respirator on a constant basis.

The issue in *Detsel* was whether the LEA must pay for the nurse to constantly monitor and provide necessary respirator support and oxygen. The federal Court of Appeals held that the district does not have to provide the nurse and that the service is not a school-health or related service. The court examined the following factors, which focus on the nature of the service and its relationship to the child's education, to arrive at its decision:

1. The person who must provide the service must be professionally licensed, such as a registered nurse or a licensed practical nurse, and an aide for the principal professional usually is required.

2. Traditionally, a school nurse's duties have not included this service.
3. The procedure itself is complex, consisting of many separate but interrelated steps.
4. The expense of providing the service is great.
5. The service is life-sustaining, and the risk of a malfunction in the service—that the student would experience respiratory distress and, if not rescued, may die—is great.
6. Provision of the service is supervised and prescribed by a physician.
7. The student, although clearly benefiting from the service, is not using the service directly to benefit from special education.

Detsel had a prolonged impact. After the court's ruling, Congress amended the Medicaid law in 1986 to allow Medicaid funds to be used for health-related services of a student whose IEP calls for those services, as long as a state's Medicaid plan permits the funds to be used for those services and the child is eligible for Medicaid [PL 99–272, 42 U.S.C. § 1396n(g)]. (See Chapter 3 for a discussion of the Medicaid Catastrophic Coverage Act and its impact on special education funding.)

After Congress amended the Medicaid law, Detsel's parents sued to require the Department of Health and Human Services (HHS), which administers the Medicaid program, to provide a private-duty nurse to the student during her time in school. The HHS Secretary declined to authorize payment for the private-duty nurse. A federal appeals court ruled that the Secretary's regulations (prohibiting payment) were unreasonable because they contravened Congressional intent (*Detsel v. Sullivan*, 1990).

As a result of the court's decision, HHS in 1991 announced a new policy concerning private-duty nursing services. Consistent with the *Detsel* decision, the Health Care Financing Agency (HCFA, which administers Medicaid under the auspices of the HHS) began paying for private-duty nursing services (via the Medicaid program) for eligible recipients when those services were provided during the hours when a student is outside his or her home engaging in normal life activities such as attending school (*Pullen v. Cuomo*, 1991). Thus, a student whose IEP called for private-duty nursing services during school hours and who was entitled to Medicaid benefits now could charge the private-duty nursing costs to Medicaid for the time in school and receiving those services.

This result will encouraged schools to help students qualify for Medicaid services, write IEPs calling for private-duty nursing services, and charge the costs of those services to Medicaid. Simply because a student could obtain Medicaid-financed services, however, did not mean that schools were off the hook. Not all students qualified for Medicaid, and those who did not qualify continued to want the schools to provide health-related services.

Generally, LEAs remained unwilling to pay for full-time nursing services when a student did not qualify for Medicaid assistance, and some courts agreed with that position. For example, *Neely v. Rutherford County School* (1995) found that a student with congenital central hypoventilation syndrome was not entitled to receive full-time nursing services at the school's expense. The LEA offered to provide a nursing assistant but rejected the parents' wish for a registered nurse or respiratory assistant. The student required almost constant care because of the life-threatening nature of her disease, and the court therefore determined that the burden on the LEA of providing such services was too great.

The court held that in such a case, monitoring and suctioning the student's feeding tube was a medical service not provided for in the Act (see also *Bevin H. v. Wright*, 1987; *Granite School Dist. v. Shannon M.*, 1992; and *Fulginiti v. Roxbury Township Public Schools*, 1996). Moreover, because the care required for these students was varied, intensive, provided by a nurse under a physician's supervision and prescription, time-consuming, expensive, and, perhaps most important, involved life-threatening situations that required the constant vigilance of a professional, courts remained reluctant to require a full-time nurse as a related service (see *Granite School Dist. v. Shannon M.*, 1992).

The *Garret F.* Court, however, restated the *Tatro* "bright-line" standard and disagreed with the *Detsel/Neely* line of cases, stating that their decisions, relying on the nature and extent of services performed, hinged erroneously on dicta articulated in *Tatro. Garret F.* explicitly rejected the *Detsel* arguments regarding costs of providing such services as well. The Court made it clear that the "related services" provision was broad enough to encompass those services that would be required to assist a child with a disability to benefit from special education *without regard to cost.*

Applying *Tatro*'s two-prong test, the Supreme Court found that the services were supportive services that the student must be provided for him to benefit from special education, as he could not attend school without those services. Furthermore, the Court found that the services were not medical services for purposes beyond diagnosis and evaluation because such services can be administered by a nurse or layperson and are not required to be administered by a physician. This determination of who administers the service—namely, that the administrator is not a physician— is *Tatro*'s bright-line rule.

Mental Health Services

Although the *Tatro* and *Garret F.* decisions clarified the issues around related services that are targeted on students' physical health, they did not address—and thus left unresolved—the issues around related services and students' mental health.

The Basic Issue: When is the LEA Required to Pay? Fundamentally, the issue is whether an LEA is required to pay for services that are associated with a student's mental health needs. It is helpful to frame the issue by developing some factual scenarios.

Assume, for example, that an LEA has formally classified a student as one who has emotional disturbance (one of IDEA's disability categories—see 20 U.S.C. § 1401 (3)(A)(i)). Or assume that an LEA has classified a student as one who has other disabilities and who also has some mental health issues—the so-called "dual diagnosis" classification, in which a student is classified as having more than one disability.

Assume further that the LEA, the student's parents, or both, believe that the student could benefit educationally from receiving mental health services. Now assume that the LEA and the student's parents disagree about whether IDEA requires the LEA to pay for these services; both the LEA and the parents say they are not required to pay for them; there is a stand-off between these two potential sources of payment.

Assume still further that both the LEA and the parents seek to place the student into a residential facility and to charge the cost of the services that the facility provides to the facility and its funding source; and assume that one available facility is privately operated, in which case it wants to look to the LEA and the parents' private health insurance for payment, and that another available facility is publicly funded, in which case it wants to avoid its budget from becoming the sole, or even principal, source of funding. There is a stand-off between the three parties—the LEA, the parents, and the facility—with each attempting to shift the costs to one or both of the others.

The Courts' Response   How have the courts responded to this kind of conflict? The bottom line is that they have not responded with a single voice; there seem to be several "trends" and multiple factors for the courts to consider. Here, the law is by no means as well settled as it is in the conflict regarding health services that are both educationally beneficial and that address the student's physical health. In that area of the law, the *Tatro-Garret F.* bright-line test prevails. In the mental-health services area of the law, considerable confusion reigns. All courts, however, begin by looking to the language of IDEA and its regulations.

IDEA Language   Here, they find scant help. What is clear is that the costs of medical services that are for diagnostic and evaluation purposes only are IDEA-covered costs; an LEA must pay them [20 U.S.C. § 1401(22)]. This is the clear language of IDEA's definition of related services. Thus, if the mental health services are provided solely for the purposes of determining whether the student has a disability and, if so, what the educational implications of that finding are, the services are chargeable against the LEA.

Beyond that, the courts look to the definition of the "related services," turning to the IDEA regulations. They look principally at the regulations' definition of "psychological services." Under this definition, psychological services includes "planning and managing a program of psychological services, including psychological counseling for children and parents" [34 C.F.R. § 330.24(b)(9)].

There is a common assumption that "psychological counseling" includes one-on-one or group-therapy through traditional psychotherapeutic means—through traditional psychotherapy. A dictionary definition of psychotherapy is "treatment of mental or emotional disorders or of related bodily ills by psychological means" (*Merriam-Webster's Collegiate Dictionary*, 10th edition, 1996). Arguably, psychological services (the related services in question) include psychotherapy, and thus psychotherapy should be classified as a related services. Lay definitions, however, are both circular (as in "psychotherapy") and are not controlling when courts interpret IDEA.

Functional Analysis Failing to receive much, if any, guidance from the available definitions, the courts conduct a "functional analysis." They ask: Who does what to whom, under what circumstances, where, why (for what purposes and outcomes), and with what connections between the student's educational program as it would be in the absence of the convoluted issues about mental health services? Using this method of analysis, the cases tend to yield two results.

First Line of Cases: The "Service Benefit Standard"—LEA Pays The first result is that mental health services and psychotherapy or psychological counseling are related services because a student often cannot actualize his or her educational abilities—cannot effectively learn—without them. A student who has emotional challenges (without regard to whether the student is classified as having primarily an emotional disturbance or as having another disability with emotional/mental health needs associated with it) therefore needs mental health services to obtain an educational benefit; accordingly, the LEA is required to pay for the services.

This is a "service benefit" standard: The service confers a benefit that is primarily educational. The services, though they respond to the student's mental and emotional needs, allow the student to benefit academically. The ultimate benefit is educational, though the means may seem to be medical.

Two cases illustrating this approach are *Papacoda v. Connecticut* (1981) and *Vander Malle v. Ambach* (1987). In *Papacoda*, the court held that an LEA must pay tuition, board, and psychotherapy for a student's placement at a residential facility. The purpose of that placement is to provide educational services in a therapeutic environment. Further, because of the intimate relationship between the student's need for psychotherapy and his ability to learn, and in light of the federal regulations' definition of related services, psychotherapy is a related service.

The court in *Vander Malle* followed this line of reasoning as well. *Vander Malle* involved a student with schizophrenia who required a residential placement that provided treatment in an extremely structured environment, the use of antipsychotic medication, and a behavior reinforcement plan to educate the student. This program, designed by the psychiatric staff, enabled the student to gain control of his emotions and improve his interpersonal relationships so he could learn. The court held that states may not escape their responsibility to pay for such treatment solely because the treatment program addresses a student's psychological needs.

In addition, the court followed *Papacoda* and agreed that the regulations and the plain meaning of the statute require the conclusion that psychotherapy is a related service. The court held that the "service-benefit" standard involves evaluating two criteria: (1) whether the program is designed to improve the student's educational performance; and (2) whether the program is based on the student's classification as having a serious emotional disturbance (see also *Mrs. B. v. Milford Bd. of Educ.*, 1997).

Second Line of Cases: The "Ends/Goals and Means/Techniques" Analysis The second line of cases regards mental health services fundamentally as ends for relief of mental or emotional problems, in and of themselves; they also may be a means for assisting the student to benefit from special education, but that benefit is a byproduct, not their primary purpose.

Under this approach, some courts refuse to hold LEAs responsible for the financial burden of providing mental health services to a student. *Clovis Unified School Dist. v. California Office of Admin. Hearings* (1990) held that an LEA may not be charged with costs of placement and therapy at a psychiatric hospital. The court declared that the "service-benefit" standard for determining whether psychotherapy is a related service is overbroad and inordinately encompassing.

The court compared a student who needs psychotherapy to benefit educationally with a student who is visually impaired and needs surgery to see better and thus benefit educationally. Because the public school is not required to pay for the student's eye surgery, it should not be required to pay for the student's psychotherapy. An interpretation requiring such a result would tremendously strain the fiscal resources of the public school system. In addition, the court found that, because the facility does not operate a full-time school and because physicians, not educators, determined which services the student received, the treatment could not qualify as a related service to enable the student to meet his or her educational needs.

Basically, *Clovis* applied a "medical model" analysis to mental health services, regarding them essentially as medical and not educational, and thus as excluded from the meaning of related services. They are fundamentally medical because their basic purpose and effect is to address and benefit the student's mental health. The student's educational benefit is secondary to the overarching medical model.

Other courts agree with *Clovis* in its medical-purpose approach, and take into account the type of facility, nature of services provided, existence of an educational component in addition to a medical component, and discipline of the providers in determining whether mental health services are related services. *Burke County Bd. of Educ. v. Denton* (1990) held that a 24-hour, in-home behavior-management training program for the student and family was a medical service (see also *McKenzie v. Jefferson*, 1983; and *Darlene L. v. Illinois State Bd. of Educ.*, 1983). *Field v. Haddonfield Bd. of Educ.* (1991) held that drug treatment programs are essentially medical, not educational, interventions. The type of placement is not always decisive, though. *River Forest School Dist. #90 v. Laurel D.* (1996) held that a nontraditional academic environment does not, per se, create a medical placement and relieve the school of paying for it.

These two lines of cases require further analysis. Other factors may help explain the past results and, in light of *Tatro* and *Garret F.*, will guide LEAs, parents, and the other facilities and providers.

The "School Day" Test One such factor has to do with the portion of the day when the services are provided. In both *Tatro* and *Garret F.*, the services were provided during the school day. That tends to suggest that the services were more education-ally related than not: They were for the purpose of assisting the student to benefit from special education.

The "Place of Service" Test A second factor has to do with the place where the services are provided. Again, in both *Tatro* and *Garret F.*, the services were provided at the school itself. That, too, tends to suggest that the services were more educa-tionally related than not—they, too, were for the purposes of assisting the student to benefit from special education.

Tatro and *Garret F.* involved students who were receiving services in an LEA during school hours. What about students who are receiving services outside of an LEA and not only during school hours but also thereafter? After all, that was the fact situation in *Papacoda*, *Vander Malle*, and *Clovis*. What happens when the student is placed into a residential program? Who pays? The answer depends on two factors.

1. *LEA appropriate placement.* The first has to do with whether the LEA pro-vided a valid alternative setting (other than the residential placement) in which the student could benefit and progress because he or she received a free appro-priate public education there. If the LEA provides such a placement, it seems that the cost of the residential placement will not be charged against the LEA. After all, it fulfilled its duty to the student (the duty to provide benefit, under *Rowley*) and it did so in a setting that is the more typical, least restrictive one (see Chapter 6 for the requirements of least restrictive settings) (*Mrs. B. v. Mil-ford Bd. of Ed.*, 1997; *Walczak v. Florida Union Free School District*, 1998).

2. *Residential placement and educational program.* The second factor has to do with whether the residential setting itself has an educational component. If so, and if the student is participating "in school" or receiving any traditional edu-cational services (howsoever they may be linked to the mental health thera-peutic services), it seems that the cost of the residential placement will be charged against the LEA. After all, it is fulfilling its duty through the assis-tance of the residential facility. Here, if the SEA has accredited the residential facility as an educational institution, the LEA should pay. The function of the facility is education; that's why it is accredited, and that is the defining char-acteristic of the services it provides. (*Mrs. B. v. Milford Bd. of Ed.*, 1997; *Tay-lor v. Honig*, 1990).

In this line of analysis, two factors stand out. The first has to do with the stu-dent: Does the student benefit from, or can the student benefit from, the nonresi-dential services that the LEA offers. If so, the LEA is exonerated from the costs of the residential facility. Why should it carry those extraordinary costs when, for (usu-ally) fewer funds, it can provide a benefit in its other, community-based programs?

Here, three factors converge: (1) the student benefits (per *Rowley*); (2) the services are in the LEA's community-based programs (*Tatro*, *Garret F.*, and the IDEA requirements for "least restrictive environments"—see Chapter 6); and (3) the LEA can hold down its costs by providing community-based services, not residen-tial-based services.

The second has to do with the place. Does the residential facility seem to be more "educational" or "therapeutic?" If "educational," the LEA is charged with the cost of placement; if "therapeutic," the LEA escapes the cost of placement.

Distinguishing between "Educational" and "Therapeutic"   To have said this much begs the question: What is the difference between "educational" and "therapeutic?" Several criteria come into play. The first two have to do with standards and programs.

1. *The "Standards" Standard.* Here, one question, related to standards, is this: Is the facility accredited by the state as a school, or by the state or other accreditation or licensing bodies as a hospital (psychiatric hospital)? If as a school, the LEA is more apt to have to pay; if as a hospital, the LEA is less apt to have to pay.

2. *The "Student Standard."* The other question, related to programs, is this: Does the student receive traditional educational services during what normally would be school hours (say, 8 a.m. to 3 p.m.) and then receive other services, or does the student receive both educational and therapeutic services during the regular school day? If the answer to either question, or to both, is "yes," the facility probably will be regarded as "educational." In trying to answer the "student" standard, courts are justified in asking about the nature of the staff that provides services to the student. Does the staff consist primarily of educators and related services personnel (psychologists, school social workers, or others)? Or does it consist primarily of health care providers (physicians, especially psychiatrists, or nurses and other individuals licensed, trained, or paid/reimbursed for delivering health services)?

    The reason for both results (having to do with accreditation/licensure and with program) is that the function and purpose of the facility is more educational than therapeutic.

3. *Initiative for Placement.* A third criterion relates to the initiative for the placement. If the LEA places the student into the facility or recommends that the student be placed there, and if in its recommendation are found reasons related to the student's education (such as the continuation of the student's IEP), the placement seems to be more "educational" than "therapeutic." This is so simply because the LEA itself says so. It declares an educational purpose and assures an educational program. By contrast, if a parent initiates the placement and then seeks to charge the cost of it to the LEA, some courts may be disinclined to hold the LEA responsible for the costs and to regard the placement more as a therapeutic one—for the student or the parents, or both.

Nexus and Nature, Purpose and Place   In sum, it seems that courts will enter into a rather complex, fact-driven calculus: Is there a nexus—a solid connection— between the placement and the education that the student receives? Is the placement itself one that provides education as a principal or important function, or is it one that provides therapy that involves some, but not a dominant, educational component? Is the purpose for educational reasons, with therapeutic benefits secondary? Or is it one that addresses primarily the student's mental health needs, with educational benefits secondary? Finally, is the place itself—the facility—accredited by the state as a school, or is it accredited or licensed by the state or other entities as a hospital? And, without regard to the nature of the place itself, does the LEA provide an appropriate education on its own, or is it necessary for the student to be placed into a facility to receive an education?

IDEA's First/Last Pay Provisions

As pointed out in Chapter 3, IDEA clarifies some of the cost-shifting issues surrounding related services, especially the health-related services. In brief, it provides that the state's agencies that provide related or other services to individuals with disabilities must pay—before the SEA or an LEA pays—for services for which the individuals are eligible [20 U.S.C. § 1412 (a)(12)(A)(i)].

Summary of Medical and Other Health Care Services

1. If the service is provided by a doctor, it is a related medical service and may be provided for diagnostic and evaluation purposes only.
2. If the service is provided by anyone else, fits within the categorical definition of 20 U.S.C. § 1401 (22), and is necessary for the child to receive a benefit from special education, it is a related service.
3. If a student is enabled to attend a general school program, as a result of the service (*Tatro, Garret F.*), it is apt to be a related service.
4. If the service is a traditional function of a school nurse or a modest extension of the nurse's function (in *Tatro* and *Garret F.*, CIC is not unlike other school nurse functions, whereas in *Detsel* and *Bevin H.*, the service is far more like a hospital-based service), and it is furnished during school hours, it is apt to be a related service. If a court determines that the service is being provided for other than educational reasons, as in *Clovis* (the mental health medical-model case), courts are less likely to find that the service qualifies as a related service under IDEA.

Teacher Training

Another issue that has arisen in the context of related services is teacher training. In *Sioux Falls School Dist. v. Koupal* (1994), the parent submitted an attachment to the student's IEP titled, "Other Related Services," requiring the student's teachers to complete a 5-day training course in the TEACCH method, an educational modality for teaching students with autism. The court held that teacher training is not a related service that benefits the affected student directly and thus is not required to be part of a student's IEP as a related service.

Though teacher or other staff training is not a "related service" for the child, it may be required to ensure that related services (i.e., psychological or social work services) are properly provided. Moreover, IDEA provides for comprehensive systems for personnel development in 20 U.S.C. § 1412 (a)(14).

Air Conditioning

An unusual case related to these issues, *Espino v. Besteiro* (1983), held that a school district must provide an air-conditioned classroom for a student with multiple disabilities who was unable to regulate his body's temperature. The court determined that the LEA's attempt to place him in an air-conditioned Plexiglas™ cubicle restricted him from interacting with his peers.

Specially Trained Animals

Some unusual techniques enabling students with disabilities to benefit from school are developing in the area of specially trained animals. Individuals with cerebral palsy and other physical disabilities use animals such as a guide dog or a trained monkey in their everyday life. Recognizing that specially trained animals are helpful and that banning them in schools may impair students' abilities to obtain educational benefit, one court ruled that an LEA violates Section 504 if it prohibits a physically disabled student from bringing a service dog to school (*Sullivan v. Vallejo City Unified School Dist.*, 1990).

Governmental Problems Arising from the Related Services Requirements

Those who propose providing related services as a solution to total and functional exclusion must be cognizant of the barriers to these services. Besides the difficulties in interpreting which services shall be provided, the practicalities of actually providing these services is a problem in and of itself. Essentially, these problems are intergovernmental; they go to the heart of the functions of governmental agencies involved with children with disabilities.

One major problem is intergovernmental coordination. The immediate task has been to assure that the federal, state, and local agencies that can offer special education and related services will provide those services in the least restrictive setting. Because there are so many service providers and because they often are operated by separate federal agencies (each with its own state and local counterpart), it is important, though difficult, to coordinate these agencies' activities and thereby assure through a "memorandum of understanding" (MOU) that their collective resources can be brought to bear on the educational problems of students with disabilities.

But federal interagency MOUs are not always translated into action at the point where federal services are delivered, and state and local counterparts do not necessarily enter into interagency agreements or carry out these agreements. When these fairly typical bureaucratic problems are added to the interpretation problems, the results are either failure to deliver services or its opposite—duplication of services (with a resulting competition for funding and a waste of professional time and effort and increased cost of service).

Appropriate Education, the Supreme Court, and the Benefit Standard ⌒

Thus far, an appropriate education clearly includes compliance with state standards, a regular process, and an individualized plan plus related services. The question remains: What is the substantive standard for judging whether a student's education is in fact appropriate for him or her? The Supreme Court answered the question and defined appropriate education in its first special education case, *Bd. of Educ. v. Rowley* (1982). The *Rowley* decision has become the touchstone for all subsequent appropriate education cases.

In *Rowley*, a federal trial court and the Second Circuit Court of Appeals both held that a school district must provide a sign-language interpreter in the classroom as part of a deaf student's individualized education program. These courts found that, as a matter of law, education for a student with a disability must be comparable to that given to nondisabled students, not the best education available. Under the facts in this case, they found that comparability could be achieved only with the assistance of an interpreter for the student, Amy Rowley.

The court of appeals noted that the decision was restricted to the facts of the case, inasmuch as Amy's parents also were deaf and, without an interpreter, Amy heard only 59% of what transpired in the classroom. The Supreme Court reversed the court of appeals, holding that IDEA does not require the school to furnish Amy with an interpreter to comply with its duty to provide her with an appropriate education.

"Open Doors," Not Maximum Development

One reason for the Court's decision was IDEA's legislative history. Congress did not intend that schools try to develop students with disabilities to their maximum potential. Instead, IDEA's purpose was to open the schools' doors to them, granting them access to educational opportunities. Accordingly, Congressional intent is satisfied when the school provides the student with a reasonable opportunity to learn. Because Amy advanced easily from grade to grade without an interpreter's help, performed better than the average student, and maintained an extraordinary rapport with her teachers, there was evidence of the school's compliance with the "open doors" intent of Congress.

Rowley undoubtedly is quite limited by its facts as precedent for other cases. For example, because Amy was included in the general education program, the Court's emphasis on grade-to-grade promotion arguably does not apply to students with disabilities who cannot progress from grade to grade or whose progress cannot be measured by that standard, as noted below.

Appropriate Education: The Rowley Benefit Standard

A second reason for the Court's decision was that, although it was reluctant to impose too great a duty on schools, it also understood fully that "opening the doors" meant that the schools had to meet some kind of substantive standard and provide some level of benefit to each student. That is the ultimate meaning of individualized appropriate education with necessary related services. Accordingly, the LEA must develop an individualized education plan that is reasonably calculated to enable the student to benefit educationally from individualized instruction with related services. Therefore, a blanket policy applicable to all students is not individualized or calculated to benefit a particular student and is invalid under the *Rowley* benefit test (*Polk v. Central Susquehanna Intermediate Unit 16*, (1988)).

Educational Benefit, Not Maximum Development, and Not Regression

Rowley's first principle is that IDEA is designed to provide students with disabilities the same basic opportunities for education that nondisabled students enjoy. The dominant theme of IDEA is equal opportunity. What does equal opportunity mean, if not maximum development? It means that the LEA is not required to provide every service that the student requests, or even that the student be placed in the best program. Rather, it must provide a curriculum, related services, and placement such that the student will receive some educational benefit. Courts have interpreted this to mean that the LEA must provide more than a mere trivial or *de minimis* benefit to the student (*Polk v. Central Susquehanna Intermediate Unit 16*, 1988; *Hall v. Vance County Bd. of Educ.*, 1985).

But no court has established a bright-line rule indicating that the student must receive a certain quantum of benefit. The concept of an appropriate education and educational benefit for each student requires fact-specific analysis that takes into consideration (a) the student's present level of development or skill acquisition, and (b) the student's ability to progress beyond that level if provided with an effective program. Simply put, the questions are:

- What is the student's present skill?
- What is the student's capacity?

Students who make more than trivial progress toward their capabilities have received an appropriate education because they have benefited from their schooling.

State Law and Maximum Development; A Higher Standard

A state may set a higher standard than IDEA and require its school districts to provide more than just the "appropriate education" outlined under IDEA and *Rowley*. If a state legislature imposes such a duty, the courts must determine whether the LEA has met the stricter, more demanding standard (*Doe v. Bd. of Educ. of Tullahoma City School Dist.*, 1993; *Thomas v. Cincinnati Bd. of Educ.*, 1990; *David D. v. Dartmouth School Committee*, 1985). What factors do courts use to measure an educational benefit?

Grade-to-Grade Advancement

A footnote in *Rowley* explained that, if a student is being educated in a general education classroom, grade-to-grade advancement and passing marks are evidence that the student is receiving an educational benefit. The grade-to-grade advancement criterion does not apply in every case. If the student is not being educated in the general classroom or if grade-to-grade advancement is not a goal for the student, such a factor should not be considered.

Bd. of Educ. of East Windsor Regional School Dist. v. Diamond (1986) refused to apply *Rowley*'s grade-to-grade advancement standard to a student who had never attended general education classes, because to do so would be fundamentally unfair. Similarly, *Thornrock v. Boise Indep. School Dist.* (1988) held that grade-to-grade advancement of a student classified as "trainable mentally retarded" is not reliable evidence of whether the student is receiving an educational benefit. The court reasoned that the "benefit" must be measured by some means other than such advancement; otherwise the student will be deprived of the opportunities for placement in general education programs (see Chapter 6).

Holistic Education

The meaning of educational benefit is not limited to only the academic needs of a student. In *County of San Diego v. California Special Education Hearing Office* (1996), an LEA placed a student with severe emotional disabilities at an isolated campus for students with severe emotional disabilities. The student's IEP goals included: (1) decreased inappropriate behavior, such as lying, stealing, and truancy; (2) improved self-concept and social self-esteem; and (3) increased ability to handle academic work. The LEA subsequently transferred the student to a day treatment facility, where her behavior deteriorated and culminated in truancy and stealing.

The court determined that the LEA did not provide an educational benefit to the student because it failed to provide her with counseling that would enable her to meet her IEP goals. Social and emotional concerns are subsumed in the concept of an educational benefit and must be addressed by the LEA. Here, the LEA failed to provide necessary mental health services, although they obviously were needed if she were to attain her IEP goals.

The court in *Ft. Zumwalt School Dist. v. Missouri State Bd of Ed.* (1996) also emphasized the importance of a holistic approach. The court agreed with *Rowley* that grades, test scores, and advancement from grade to grade constitute important evidence for a court to consider in determining whether an LEA has provided an educational benefit to a student, but a student's emotional problems, such as low self-esteem and low frustration level, also must be addressed if that student is to receive a benefit. Arguably, academic and emotional needs are inexorably linked.

Related to this holistic approach is the notion that if a student has experienced emotional trauma at a particular school, then, despite the appropriateness of the student's IEP, he or she cannot receive an educational benefit at that placement. This was precisely the scenario in *Greenbush School Committee v. Mr. and Mrs. K.* (1996). In *Greenbush* the parents objected to the student's placement because they believed he had suffered harassment by his peers and school personnel while attending that school previously.

The court upheld the hearing officer's determination that the parents' hostility toward the school had a significantly negative impact on the student's ability to learn at the school. Furthermore, the court determined that the student had serious anxieties about returning to the school and could recall instances of abuse, such as being required to clean a urinal after another student had used it, and being carried out of class by a principal and teacher, who then threw him around and held him down on the floor.

The court held that, despite personnel changes at the school, the student suffered from a gripping fear that accompanied him throughout his school day and therefore prevented him from obtaining an educational benefit if he were to be required to attend that school (see also *Bd. of Educ. of Community Consolidated School Dist. No. 21 v. Illinois State Bd. of Educ.*, 1991).

Weighing Benefits

To determine "benefit" requires courts to consider and weigh the relative importance of the student's educational needs, the availability of appropriate programs, and the cost of available programs. Thus, the court in *P.F. ex rel. B.F. v. New Jersey Div. of Developmental Disabilities* (1995) held that an LEA's budgetary concerns do not warrant transferring a student to a less costly program if the transfer likely would result in the student's regression and loss of skills.

Angevine v. Jenkins (1990) also illustrates a balancing approach when an LEA proposes to change a student's placement. The appropriate education and educational benefit requirements are met when: (1) one placement has higher expectations for the student than another proposed placement (as reflected in its IEP goals and objectives and in the classroom placement and curriculum); (2) that program uses appropriate curricula to teach functional academics to a student with mental retardation; (3) the program has identified and is using appropriate instructional and behavioral strategies to maximize the student's learning; (4) the program has addressed the student's unique learning styles and has demonstrated progress in rate of learning; (5) the program has helped the student learn to pay attention and interact socially with staff and peers; and (6) the program has demonstrated all this when the alternative placement has failed to demonstrate progress.

Judicial Reliance on Expert Judgment; Deference to Professionals ⌒

Finally, *Rowley* stated that the courts should defer to the judgment of educators and other experts in matters related to a student's right to an appropriate education. Judicial deference to expert judgment comes into play only after a court determines that the process definition and benefit standard have been met. Thus, if a dispute arises between parents and the school district about the appropriateness of a student's education and if some proof exists that these two tests (process followed and benefit conferred) have been met, the courts will not substitute their judgments for that of experts concerning a school's choice of curriculum or teaching methodology.

For example, in *Rowley* the Court mentioned many times that the experts had determined that Amy Rowley did not need an interpreter, in large part because she was receiving an educational benefit from schooling without an interpreter; after all, benefit—progress progress from grade to grade—was clearly evident. Likewise, in *Lachman v. Illinois Bd. of Educ.* (1988), a court found that, if an LEA fulfills its procedural responsibilities in developing an IEP and experts differ on whether the student should be educated by one means or another (here, by one type of educational method for the deaf or another), the parents have no right to insist on the child's placement in a program that uses only cued-speech instruction.

It bears mentioning that the Supreme Court has announced the rule of judicial deference to expert judgment in numerous cases, including *Honig* and *Arline* (both of which are discussed in Chapter 3). As pointed out in Chapter 4, the rule allows the courts to make "correct" judgments on matters that are highly technical and on which experts may disagree; the courts lack capacity to make their own independent judgments and must rely on experts. The rule, however, also allows the courts to duck the hard issues of social policy—deferring to experts instead, as in *PASE v. Hannon* (see Chapter 4) and *Armstrong v. Kline* (discussed in this chapter under Extended School Year).

Remedies for Denial of a Free Appropriate Education ↝

Tuition Reimbursement

If an LEA fails to provide an educational benefit, and therefore an appropriate education, the student and his or her parents must have some method of recourse. Often, parents will disenroll their child from the public school placement and enroll him or her in a private school. If they do so, must the parents pay the full cost? The answer is, "It depends."

In *School Committee of the Town of Burlington v. Dept. of Educ. of Massachusetts* (1985), the Supreme Court held that IDEA requires LEAs to reimburse parents for their expenditures for private placement if the LEA does not provide the student an educational benefit but the private school placement does. Parents' ability to recover private school tuition from an LEA thus depends on two factors: (a) The LEA does not provide an appropriate education, but (b) the private school does. Without this remedy, parents would be paralyzed in seeking an appropriate education for their child.

IDEA Provisions

Following the *Burlington* decision, courts dealt with many different aspects of the right-to-tuition reimbursement. As they increasingly awarded reimbursement and simultaneously established limits on that right, it became more and more obvious that Congress would have to clarify the right, with respect to both its substantive and its procedural aspects. The 1997 amendments to IDEA do just that.

General Rule

The general rule is that an LEA is not obliged to pay for the cost of education, including special education and related services, for a student who is enrolled at a private school or facility. This rule, however, is subject to a major qualification: It applies only if the LEA has made a free appropriate public education available to the student and the parents nevertheless have elected to enroll their child in the private school or facility [20 U.S.C. § 1412 (a)(10)(C)(i)].

An LEA's defense against a tuition reimbursement claim, then, is that the LEA offered an appropriate education. This defense essentially codifies the cases that were decided before the 1997 amendments (as will be made clear by the discussion below).

Limitations

The 1997 amendments also codify the obverse of this rule and add a significant limitation to it. If the parents enroll their child in a private school or facility without the consent of or a referral to that school by the LEA, they may recover the cost of that enrollment if (a) the student previously had received special education and related services from the LEA and (b) a due-process hearing officer or court finds that the LEA did not make a free appropriate public education available to the student in a timely manner before the parents enrolled their child in the private program [20 U.S.C. § 1412 (a)(10)(C)(ii)].

This provision codifies the prior case law, which held that the parents may receive tuition reimbursement only if the LEA did not provide an appropriate education and the private school did. But it adds the limitation that the student must have been enrolled in the LEA and receiving special education and related services. This limitation prevents parents from avoiding the LEA's programs altogether and then seeking to charge private education to the LEA.

Amount of Reimbursement

As they followed the *Burlington* decision, courts had to decide not only whether to award tuition reimbursement but also how much reimbursement they must award. IDEA now guides the courts by detailing the procedures that parents must follow as they seek reimbursement and then by limiting the amount of reimbursement if parents do not follow these procedures. IDEA allows a hearing officer or a court to reduce or even to deny reimbursement in the three instances discussed next.

Lack of notice to LEA The first instance relates to parents and their duty to comply with "notice and cure" conditions. The parents, at the most recent IEP meeting they attended before removing their child from the LEA, must (a) inform the IEP team that they are rejecting the LEA's proposed placement and its proposed free appropriate public education, and (b) state their concerns and their intent to enroll their child in a private school at public expense [20 U.S.C. § 1412 (a)(10)(C)(iii)(I)(aa)].

This provision codifies early case law requiring parents to give notice, but it extends that case law by requiring them to state also why they reject the LEA's placement and program. More than that, it gives the LEA an opportunity to offer a placement and program that the parents may accept as appropriate. Thus, it secures notice for the LEA, it eliminates the element of surprise, and it encourages the LEA to respond to the parents' concerns.

If the parents have not attended a recent IEP meeting, they must, at least 10 business days (including holidays that occur on a business day) before removing their child from the LEA, give the LEA written notice that they intend to enroll their child in a private school and seek reimbursement, and what their concerns are about the LEA program and placement [20 U.S.C. § 1412 (a)(10)(C)(iii)(I)(bb)]. This requirement has the same purpose and effect as the IEP meeting requirement, but it applies to parents who did not attend their child's most recent IEP meeting.

Because the "notice" requirements imposed on parents may prove difficult for some parents or problematic for their child, IDEA creates four exceptions [20 U.S.C. § 1412 (a)(10)(C)(iv)]:

1. The parent is illiterate and cannot write in English.
2. Compliance with the notice requirement likely would result in physical or serious emotional harm to the child.
3. The LEA prevented the parent from providing the notice.
4. The parents themselves have not received the notice, pursuant to 20 U.S.C. § 1415, that the LEA must give them concerning their rights and responsibilities (including that they are responsible for providing the aforementioned notice to the LEA) (see Chapter 7 for a description of the LEA-required notices to parents).

If the parent is illiterate and cannot write in English, it is not clear yet whether a verbal notice will suffice. IDEA regulations do not clarify that point. The "likelihood-of-harm" rule essentially codifies prior case law. The other two exceptions recognize that LEAs sometimes do not comply with IDEA deliberately and thus can thwart parents' and students' rights—a point made by a tuition reimbursement case decided a year or so before the 1997 amendments were enacted.

Parental refusal of evaluation by LEA A major limitation on reimbursement relates to nondiscriminatory evaluation. In its effort to assure that the LEA may respond to parents' concerns and perhaps avoid the duty to reimburse for private education, IDEA entitles the LEA to notify the parents, in writing and at some time before the parents actually remove their child from the LEA, that the LEA wants to evaluate the child and why. If the parents refuse to make their child available for the LEA's evaluation, a hearing officer or court may reduce or deny reimbursement on that account [20 U.S.C. § 1412 (a)(10)(C)(iii)(II)].

Unreasonableness Another major limitation on reimbursement allows a court to reduce or deny reimbursement if it finds that the parents acted unreasonably [20 U.S.C. § 1412 (a)(10(C)(iii)(III)]. This is a curious provision in two respects.

1. It addresses only the power of a court to reduce or deny reimbursement; it does

not grant that authority to a hearing officer, although a hearing officer may reduce or deny reimbursement under the other LEA-safeguards.

2. It does not define "unreasonable," although it is safe to assume, based on prior case law, that parents will be found to act unreasonably if they are not straightforward and candid in their dealings with the LEA or if they enroll their child in an unnecessarily expensive, albeit appropriate, private program.

Having described the IDEA, it still is appropriate to describe the case law on tuition reimbursement, because some of it is codified into the 1997 amendments and thus will be precedent for interpreting them.

When Will a Court Award Tuition Reimbursement?

Process Definition/Procedural Violations

The process definition is a road map for schools to follow to ensure that each student receives a free appropriate education. If an LEA fails to comply with the process definition and especially IDEA's procedural rules and if, as a consequence, the student experiences some likelihood of harm or actual harm, the student's IEP is inappropriate and the parents are entitled to tuition reimbursement for any appropriate private placement, as the following cases (all involving tuition reimbursement claims) illustrate.

IDEA's provisions are not likely to change this rule. If anything, they codify it by making the LEA liable for tuition reimbursement if the LEA has not provided an appropriate education—that is, one that, pursuant to *Rowley*, complies with the process definition.

1. When an LEA fails to follow procedural safeguards in nondiscriminatory evaluation and fails to identify a student as having a severe emotional disability, the LEA must reimburse the parents for hospital costs incurred when the parents unilaterally place the student in a psychiatric hospital to avoid the student's expulsion from school (*Babb v. Knox County School System*, 1992).
2. An IEP that fails to identify a student's disability accurately and/or fails to respond to the student's specific disability (as determined by the nondiscriminatory evaluation) by providing appropriate services violates the process definition principle and thus fails to provide an education reasonably calculated to enable a child to obtain an educational benefit (*Russell v. Jefferson School Dist.*, 1985; *Bonadonna v. Cooperman*, 1985; *Metropolitan Nashville v. Guest*, 1995).
3. When a student moves from a state in which she received special education services, the new state of residence must inform the parents or guardian if it proposes to change the student's identification, evaluation, or placement in the present out-of-state residential placement (*Salley v. St. Tammany Parish Sch. Bd.*, 1995).
4. A student is entitled to have a complete IEP, not an interim IEP, when entering a school district for the first time, even if the development of a permanent

IEP requires the district to convene at an IEP team meeting during the summer (*Myles S. v. Montgomery County Bd. of Ed.*, 1993).

5. An LEA may not try to remove a student from a residential program and place the student in its program without assessing first whether it is capable of implementing the student's IEP (*Day v. Radnor Township School Dist.*, 1994).

6. In *Evans v. Bd. of Ed. of the Rhinebeck Central Sch. Dist.* (1996), the LEA violated a student's procedural rights in four ways.

   a. The parent requested a due process hearing on July 7, 1994, but the LEA did not schedule a hearing until September 21, 1994. IDEA's regulations state that the LEA "shall ensure that not later than 45 days after the receipt of a request for a hearing . . . a final decision is reached in the hearing."

   b. The LEA did not have an appropriate IEP for the student until January 19, 1995, a semester after he enrolled in the district.

   c. The IEP failed to include a statement of the student's present level of educational functioning and strategies to evaluate his progress, and it also contained broad goals and vague subjective methods for monitoring his progress, thus failing to establish his individual needs precisely.

   d. The LEA failed to prepare a written report or provide a basis for determining that the student has a learning disability.

7. In *Rose v. Chester County Intermediate Unit* (1996), the LEA violated the student's procedural rights by not granting a due-process hearing until 8 months after the parents had requested one and by failing to review the student's IEP within 6 months after he was due for a reevaluation.

8. In *Christen G. v. Lower Merion School Dist.* (1996), the court found that a procedural violation was sufficient to deny a student a free appropriate education when the LEA failed to make any formal offer of placement until 10 months after the LEA offered an inappropriate placement and 7 months after a hearing officer deemed the placement inappropriate.

9. In *Briere v. Fair Haven* (1996), the court determined that the LEA contravened IDEA by (a) failing to perform a supplemental evaluation after the parents informed the LEA of their intentions to place their child in a private placement; (b) failing to provide notice of, or an explanation for, its refusal to consider the request; (c) failing to draft a revised IEP after the private placement became effective; and (d) failing to include appropriate teachers in the IEP process. In addition, the court held that IDEA does not authorize transitional IEPs and that "[t]ransitional IEPs inhibit coordination and planning and violate the spirit of the statute."

10. The LEA's procedural failures clearly constitute denial of an appropriate education if the failures are so great that the student is functionally or actually excluded from an appropriate program, as demonstrated by *Bd. of Educ. of Cabell v. Dienelt* (1988). In *Dienelt*, the LEA (a) failed to conduct triennial reevaluations; (b) did not notify the student's parents of their rights; (c) failed to use an interdisciplinary team to evaluate the student; (d) failed to conduct proper evaluations (that is, those tailored to the student's disabilities); (e)

drafted an IEP before the student had been evaluated; and (f) failed to provide an appropriate curriculum. In that case, and probably because of the egregious noncompliance by the LEA with IDEA, the court also awarded damages to the parents for their lost wages when they were seeking to have the LEA comply with the IDEA.

11. In *McMillan v. Cheatham County Schools* (1997), the court found that the LEA committed procedural violations that resulted in a tuition reimbursement award by (a) failing to provide an official sufficiently knowledgeable of the proposed placement options at the team meeting; (b) failing to provide an official from the LEA's proposed placements at the team meeting, and thus not informing the parents accurately regarding available placements; and (c) failing to provide written notice to the parents of its reasons for refusing the placement sought by the parents, other placement options, and the factors considered in determining the student's placement.

In all of these cases, the procedural violation actually impaired the student's right to an appropriate education and left the parents with no choice but to enroll their child in a private school and seek tuition reimbursement.

The Harmless Error Rule

If the LEA commits a procedural violation but the violation does not result in denial of an appropriate education and the LEA confers a benefit, the LEA has not deprived the student of IDEA rights and the student's parents are not entitled to a reimbursement award; a procedural default does not always invalidate a student's IEP. IDEA's provisions are not likely to change this rule. In *Urban v. Jefferson County School Dist R-1* (1996), for example, the LEA provided an IEP that (a) lacked an explicit statement of transition services, (b) did not designate a specific outcome or goal for the student to meet upon turning 21 years of age, and (c) did not include a specific set of activities for the student to accomplish that goal.

The court ruled, however, that these deficiencies did not deprive the student of a free appropriate education, especially because the IEP provided for need-responsive services such as community awareness, daily living skills, and functional math for purchases. Further, the IEP emphasized the need for the student to transfer the skills learned in the educational setting to everyday life. Although the court ordered the LEA to rewrite the student's IEP, it concluded that, even in its deficient condition, the IEP was reasonably calculated to enable the student to receive an educational benefit.

Nor is the procedural defect fatal if (a) the process is only slightly flawed (in that the IEP does not contain all of the relevant information IDEA requires) and (b) the parents, as well as the school, are aware of the missing information (*Doe v. Defendant I*, 1990; and *Burke County Bd. of Educ. v. Denton*, 1990). Furthermore, if a student's parents interrupt or block the process or procedures from being carried out, they are not entitled later to claim that the process definition has not been satisfied (*Doe v. Defendant I*, 1990; *Burke County Bd. of Educ. v. Denton*, 1990).

The harmless error rule, then, does not stand for the proposition that any procedural error is excusable. It does mean that errors that result in little, if any, harm cannot support a claim for reimbursement.

To summarize, an LEA may violate the first prong of the *Rowley* standard— the process definition—and be required to reimburse tuition if it causes the student not to benefit because it:

1. fails to conduct a nondiscriminatory evaluation,
2. fails to classify the student's disability correctly and appropriately,
3. fails to respond to the student's disability appropriately,
4. offers only an interim IEP when the student enters the school district for the first time,
5. fails to provide a due-process hearing within the time provided for in the Act,
6. fails to provide an appropriate IEP with all of its required elements within the time provided for in the Act,
7. fails to make an appropriate offer of placement within the time provided for in the Act,
8. fails to inform parents of their rights under the Act,
9. fails to perform supplemental evaluations as directed by the Act,
10. fails to revise an IEP as directed by the Act,
11. fails to include the appropriate personnel in the IEP meeting,
12. provides only transitional IEPs, which are not warranted by the Act,
13. fails to conduct triennial reevaluations, and
14. fails to use an interdisciplinary team to evaluate the student.

Substantive Violations

To satisfy the second prong of the *Rowley* standard—the benefit test— the LEA must provide an IEP that is reasonably calculated to enable the student to obtain an educational benefit. Thus, the student's IEP must be devised to meet the unique needs of that student. Individualization is the key. The following cases illustrate LEA failures to comply with the second prong of the test and, thus, failures to provide an appropriate education. IDEA's provisions are not likely to change this rule and, indeed, they seem to codify it by insisting that an LEA must reimburse tuition and related expenses if the LEA has not provided the student with a free appropriate public education. After all, the substantive standard of "appropriate," established by the *Rowley* decision, is that the LEA's program and placement must actually benefit the student.

1. The Supreme Court in *Florence County Sch. Dist. Four v. Carter* (1993) approved private placement reimbursement for a student classified as having a learning disability who did not make educational progress in the public placement. The public school's IEP resulted in her achieving only 4 months of progress in a 9-month year, the student having received only three periods of resource classroom work per week. Its program also resulted in her regression and failed to ensure her passing from grade to grade (in compliance with the *Rowley* standard as appropriately

applied to this student, who has a learning disability and thus is capable of grade-to-grade advancement during the high school years).

The Court held that the parents may recover private tuition, even though the private school did not meet state accreditation standards, if (a) the public school placement is not appropriate; (b) the private school placement is appropriate in that it is reasonably calculated to provide an educational benefit to the student; and (c) the costs assessed by the private school are reasonable.

In this case, the Supreme Court reasoned that IDEA's state accreditation requirement cannot be applied to unilateral placements by parents because it would condition tuition reimbursement on state approval of the private school, thereby enabling the state to avoid its duty to provide a free appropriate education. By withholding its approval, the state would foreclose the student's placement and thereby relegate the student to only the inappropriate program in the public school. Moreover, the parental right of placement, established in the *Burlington* case, would be nullified if the parent could not make a private school placement. Finally, IDEA's requirement that a student's education be provided under public supervision and that the student's IEP be developed and annually reviewed by a local agency does not apply because it cannot feasibly be met in the case of a unilateral parental placement. For that reason, these requirements do not apply to such a placement.

2. *Capistrano Unified School Dist. v. Wartenberg* (1995) involved a student with a specific learning disability, attention deficit disorder, and a conduct disorder. His parents unilaterally placed him in a private facility and sought reimbursement. The student had a history of misbehavior and had been hospitalized in the past. The LEA's IEP first placed the student in 4 hours of special education and 1 hour of resource time, but he was unsuccessful in meeting that program's standards. The LEA then reduced his special education classes to 3 hours, but again he was unsuccessful in making any progress.

The court found that the LEA's placement lacked structure, individualized attention, and behavior management and failed to provide enough special education resource time to meet the student's IEP goals. The private placement, however, was adequate because the student received more individualized attention and a behavior management plan, both of which were necessary elements of an educational benefit.

3. When the LEA in *Union School Dist. v. Smith* (1994) offered to place a student with autism in a "communicatively handicapped class," supplemented by one-on-one behavior modification counseling, the parents placed their child in a private, nonaccredited placement and requested reimbursement. The court determined that the public program was inappropriate, as it did not address the student's need for a more restrictive and less stimulating environment. Experts testified that he required full-time, one-on-one instruction to benefit from group instruction. Furthermore, all of the witnesses testified that the student needed to acquire attending skills, which he had not yet attained, before he would be able to learn from language instruction, and therefore would not benefit from the LEA's placement.

4. In *Murphysboro Community Unit School Dist. v. Illinois* (1994) the LEA wanted to place a student with mental retardation and speech and language impairments and

possible autism in its "Choices" program, an education program designed to promote interaction between students with disabilities and students without disabilities, and to supplement that program with speech training and summer school. The LEA wanted to enroll the student in this program so she would develop good modeling habits. The parents thought their child's language skills were regressing and did not believe that behavior modeling should be a primary objective, considering her other needs.

The court determined that the LEA denied the student a free appropriate education because it failed to present an IEP with an appropriate placement and failed to offer any viable alternative. The court based its decision on the testimony of expert witnesses, who found the student's IEP and "Choices" program inadequate to meet the student's unique needs.

5. Like the parents in *Murphysboro*, the parents in *Still v. Debuono* (1996) had to fight for what they believed to be an appropriate program. Some experts believe that applied behavioral analysis (ABA) therapy is the leading educational modality for autistic children. ABA therapy seeks to break down activities into small, specific tasks and to reward accomplishments, resulting in the student's ability to separate information and associate instruction with a certain activity. Experts claim that ABA therapy is most effective if it is administered as early in the student's life as possible, thereby enabling him or her to adapt to more traditional learning styles later.

Still involved a student with autism who received early intervention services from the New York Department of Health, the state agency in charge of implementing early intervention services under IDEA. The student's language skills did not develop well, as he spoke slowly and had little language comprehension. His parents had him evaluated by doctors affiliated with the New York City Early Intervention Program, who diagnosed him as having a developmental delay and autism, qualifying him for early intervention services from the state. Although the student's doctor recommended that he receive ABA therapy, the Department refused to provide that therapy because it did not provide ABA therapy to any children under age 3. Instead, it offered an IFSP providing 5 hours a week of intervention services at a child development center.

The parents obtained ABA therapy services through a social worker specializing in ABA therapy, who in turn trained six college students to provide services to the child. The parents sought reimbursement for the ABA therapy obtained privately. The court determined that the state's program was inappropriate and inadequate because the child's early intervention program and IFSP were devoid of any substantive discussion of the child's autism and focused only on the state's inability to provide ABA instructors and the parents' use of noncertified instructors. The court emphasized that the state was allowing the availability of programs to dictate what was appropriate for the child instead of providing a program to fit the child's needs.

6. The court in *Russell v. Jefferson Sch. Dist.* (1985) held that if the student's physical or emotional health would be damaged by continuing in the present program or placement and the parent withdraws the student and enrolls him or her in a private program, the LEA must pay for the private program.

To summarize, an LEA may fail to offer an educational benefit if the student is regressing or not progressing, or if the student's IEP or IFSP inadequately addresses the student's individual needs. In those cases, appropriate private placement and tuition reimbursement are fully warranted, consistent with *Burlington*.

Other Aspects of Burlington and the Tuition Reimbursement Award

Several other aspects of the *Burlington* tuition-reimbursement rule concerning the award itself are worth noting.

1. If an LEA agrees to a private school placement and the placement has been made, it may not unilaterally refuse to pay tuition on the grounds that it now has an appropriate program (*Parks v. Pavkovic*, 1982; *Leo P. v. Board*, 1982; *Colin K. v. Schmidt*, 1983). As would be the case if the student were not in a private school but, instead, in a public one, the LEA may conduct the required nondiscriminatory evaluation, reconvene the IEP team, and propose a new program or placement. It also may go to a due-process hearing to try to get an order that its proposed program is appropriate, and thus to get relief from the private school tuition burden. But it may escape the tuition burden only if the LEA's program or placement is ordered to be appropriate, and until that order is entered and becomes final, it must continue to pay the tuition (*Bonadonna v. Cooperman*, 1985). IDEA's 1997 amendments entitle a hearing officer or court to reduce or deny tuition reimbursement if a parent refuses to comply with an LEA's request to evaluate the student. That provision codifies the essential holdings of these cases.

2. Tuition is not the only reimbursable expense. If a parent must spend funds to obtain related services so the student receives an educational benefit, the parent may recover those expenses (*Ojai Unified School Dist. v. Jackson*, 1993). IDEA explicitly provides that the parent may recover not only tuition but also related-service expenses.

3. If the LEA illegally suspends or expels a student and the parent incurs additional education expenses during the period of suspension or expulsion, the parent may recover those expenses (*Scituate School Committee v. Robert B.*, 1985).

4. Similarly, the parents' rights to reimbursement are available only if the parents notify the schools that they will seek private placement and tuition reimbursement (*Evans v. District No. 17*, 1988; *Garland Independent School District v. Wilks*, 1987; *Quackenbush v. Johnson City School District*, 1983). The parents also must file a due process hearing or a lawsuit seeking reimbursement of the tuition, and they should do so annually (for each school year). Otherwise, they waive their right to tuition reimbursement for the present school year and for future ones, too.

IDEA codifies the notice requirement and makes it apply to each school year through not only the notice requirement but also through the provision that the LEA must reimburse if it did not make an appropriate education available in a "timely" manner. The word "timely" can be interpreted to mean "annually," consistent with the LEA's duty to have an IEP in effect for the student at the beginning of each school year.

When Will a Court Deny Tuition Reimbursement?

Not Maximum Development

Simply, a court will deny reimbursement when the LEA's IEP and placement are appropriate. IDEA (both before and after the 1997 amendments) does not require public funding of a superior private program, only that an LEA offer an appropriate program (*Doe v. Bd. of Ed. of Tullahoma City Schools*, 1993). Also, even if a private school program is ideal for a student, tuition reimbursement is still unavailable when the LEA can provide a free appropriate education under *Rowley* (*Lenn v. Portland School Committee*, 1993).

The difficult aspect of the *Rowley* standard is knowing how much educational benefit is adequate. In *Petersen v. Hastings Public Schools* (1994), tuition reimbursement was denied because the level of educational benefit that the LEA provided was sufficient to support the LEA's defense that it offered an appropriate education to the student. There, the parents of three children with hearing impairments sued because the LEA chose to use a modified signing system that did not provide sign interpreters during nonacademic portions of the school day. The court, however, found that the LEA had conferred an educational benefit on each student, as each had progressed and continued to show academic and lingual improvement, both on standardized tests and in areas of word comprehension, language and communicative skills, reading, and math.

Substantial Compliance

As stated earlier, a student receives a free appropriate education if the IEP substantively addresses that student's needs. If a court believes that the LEA has provided services beyond IDEA's minimum standard, it will conclude that the LEA has complied with IDEA and accordingly will deny reimbursement. The 1997 amendments do not change this standard and codify the prior case law.

In *Mather v. Hartford School Dist.* (1996), the LEA placed a student with a learning disability in general education classes, supplemented by resource-room instruction one period per day, provided tutors to assist him during the summer months, and paid for a summer program at a residential school. The LEA also enrolled the student's resource-room teacher in workshops and a training program on teaching methods, observed the student in a residential setting, and invited teachers from the residential facility to participate in the IEP process. The parents unilaterally enrolled him in a residential school for students with learning disabilities and sought tuition reimbursement.

The court held that the LEA provided the student with an educational benefit, as his standardized test scores reflected progress, his levels of achievement were age-appropriate, and he showed increased involvement in school activities. The court noted that, although the student's grades remained poor, these, too, had increased before he transferred to the private school.

Role of LRE

The principles of appropriate education (AE) and least restrictive environment (LRE) complement one another and are inextricably connected (see Chapter 6). It is proper for a court to balance academic progress with a student's right to associate with nondisabled peers under the LRE doctrine and to refuse to award private placement reimbursement when the LEA program is less restrictive (provides more association with nondisabled students through the private placement) and still provides academic benefit (*Amann v. Stow School System*, 1992).

Similarly, in *Teague Indep. School Dist. v. Todd L.* (1993), the court denied tuition reimbursement and concluded that a student with severe emotional and behavioral disabilities should be placed in the LEA's program, not a psychiatric facility, because the LEA placement would yield an academic benefit for the student and because the student also would have the opportunity to associate with nondisabled peers and participate in the community more fully. The 1997 amendments do not change these decisions.

When, however, a student's disruptive and violent behavior persists in day school and in homebound placements even after the LEA has made efforts to support the student in those placements, the LEA may place the student in a residential program. Indeed, the LRE principle not only does not forbid that placement but actually requires it (*Johnson v. Westmoreland County School Bd.*, 1993). The 1997 amendments do not change this decision, although, as Chapter 6 points out, they do strengthen the LRE principle.

Other Than Educational Reasons

Often parents with children with severe emotional disorders seek a private placement when their child is presenting extremely challenging behaviors at home. Although sympathetic with the frustration these parents experience, the courts deny reimbursement if they believe a child is placed in a private facility for other than educational reasons. These cases, which are not disturbed or changed by the 1997 amendments, can be subdivided into two categories.

The "four-corners" cases comprise the first category. In these cases, the courts are not willing to examine the student's behavior outside the school setting; they look only to the "four corners" of the school environment. The following cases use this approach.

In *Hall v. Shawnee Mission School Dist.* (1994), the LEA placed a student with pervasive developmental disorder and attention deficit disorder in a "behavior disorder" classroom part-time and in a general fourth-grade classroom for the remainder of the day. The parents unilaterally placed him in a private facility and sought reimbursement. The student's teachers testified that he was being included gradually in the general program for more of the day, that he was a model student in the special education classroom, and that he was performing at grade level in all subjects except reading, where he was performing above grade level.

The student's parents testified that his behavior had deteriorated at home to a point at which they could tolerate it no longer. His private physician testified that the student was unmanageable at home and should be placed in a residential facility. Based on the teachers' testimony, the court determined that the LEA indeed did provide an educational benefit and that the residential placement was for other than educational reasons.

The case of *Rebecca S. v. Clarke County School Dist.* (1995) presented similar circumstances. There, a student with autism had made progress, performing independent tasks at school, learning to identify letters, and concentrating for longer periods of time. Despite the student's progress at school, her behavior at home had become increasingly destructive and violent toward her parents and siblings. Experts testified that she was functioning at a high level and did not need to be educated at a residential facility, as she already was enrolled in one of the nation's premier programs for teaching autistic children. The court was persuaded by the experts and the student's progress, denied reimbursement, and stated that *Rowley* does not require that the student make meaningful progress across all settings or be able to apply in the home all that she has learned at school.

Much like the "four-corners" cases, the second line of cases involves those in which the court denies reimbursement for a private facility because it believes that parents seek private placement only as a last resort and to obtain respite care from the duty of caring for their child. *Sanger v. Montgomery County Bd. of Ed.* (1996) involved a 17-year-old student with severe emotional disorders who suffered additional emotional trauma from having injured a baby in an automobile accident. Shortly thereafter, he attempted suicide. The student's physician recommended private placement after determining that the student refused to take his medication or commit to therapy on his own. His parents unilaterally withdrew him from his public placement and enrolled him in a private psychiatric facility, apparently as the last resort for treatment. The court denied reimbursement, stating that residential placement necessitated by emotional problems was separate from the learning process and not fundable under IDEA. The court stressed that his parents, not the LEA, are responsible to pay for his medical needs.

Similarly, in *Garcia v. California* (1996), the court denied tuition reimbursement when the parents of a student with a hearing impairment and learning disabilities unilaterally enrolled him in a private school after he had been involved in a fight on the playground. The court determined that the playground fight, not the LEA's inability to provide an appropriate education, prompted the parents' action. The court recognized that protection from danger could be required for a student to receive a free appropriate education but that IDEA provides no such remedy in the absence of proof that the risk is related to the student's disability.

Compensatory Education

Although *Burlington* held that parents and students are entitled to tuition reimbursement, it also stands for the analogous proposition that students are entitled to receive compensatory education if they are denied a free appropriate education. Compensatory education is an equitable remedy that entitles students to obtain services from the LEA beyond their 21st birthday. The 1997 amendments do not preclude the compensatory education remedy, and the cases on compensatory education remain as good law.

Compensatory education is awardable when the LEA denies a "basic floor of opportunity" under *Rowley*. Parents are not required to allege bad faith by the LEA, because under *Burlington*, tuition reimbursement cases do not require that kind of showing and because compensatory education is equivalent to tuition reimbursement (*McManus v. Wilmette School Dist.* 39 Bd. of Ed., 1992; *Harris v. D.C. Bd. of Ed.*, 1992).

The issues surrounding compensatory education are manifold. Because compensatory education is an equitable remedy, courts are free to exercise their discretion when awarding it. Thus, it is important to evaluate three aspects of the claim: (1) the legal standards that courts use to award compensatory education and to determine its duration; (2) facts that constitute a sufficient deprivation to warrant this award; and (3) defenses to a student's claim.

The Legal Standard

The Supreme Court has not articulated a legal standard for awarding compensatory education, and the IDEA regulations also are silent. Lower courts, however, evaluate a compensatory education claim on a case-by-case basis, examining the facts closely to determine whether the LEA's violation is so flagrant as to warrant such an award.

M. C. v. Central Regional School Dist. (1995) involved a 16-year-old student with severe mental retardation. Since 1987, the student's IEP had stressed personal and self-help goals, including toileting, eating, general communication, and community training skills. The student's progress plateaued in 1989 and thereafter regressed in all areas. In addition, the student's IEP failed to address the important goal of reducing his self-stimulatory behavior.

Finding that compensatory education is proper if (a) an LEA knows or should have known that a student's IEP is inappropriate or the student is not receiving more than a *de minimis* educational benefit, and (b) the LEA fails to correct the situation, the court awarded compensatory education based on a physician's testimony that the student's minimal progress resulted from a program that failed to address his needs and that the student would have progressed had the LEA placed him in a residential facility rather than a local day program.

Another standard—seemingly more stringent than inadequate IEP and *de minimis* benefit—is represented by *Mrs. C. v. Wheaton* (1990), which held that the appropriate standard for awarding compensatory education is a finding of such a "gross" deprivation of the student's procedural rights that it results in denial of a free appropriate education. The court held that the LEA grossly deprived a student of his rights by attempting to coerce him into terminating his right to further education and by engaging in undue delay in holding required hearings.

Facts Constituting Deprivation

Although many courts have awarded compensatory education, only the courts in the cases noted above have developed a legal standard for lower courts to follow: the inadequate IEP and *de minimis* benefit standard and the gross deprivation standard. To fully understand when a court may award compensatory education, then, we have to examine what constitutes a compensable deprivation of a free appropriate education.

In *Lester H. v. Gilhool* (1990) the court awarded compensatory education when (a) the LEA failed to admit for 30 months that the student's in-district placement was inappropriate, but (b) nevertheless refused to locate another placement for him despite the availability of at least six acceptable schools within the state. Similarly, the court in *Miener v. Missouri* (1986) awarded compensatory education against an LEA for denying educational services to a student with a severe emotional disorder who, as a result of that denial, spent 3 years in a mental health ward of a state hospital.

Likewise, the court awarded compensatory education to a 25-year-old adult with multiple disabilities in *Murphy v. Timberlane Regional Sch. Dist.* (1994) after determining that the LEA previously had denied the student a free appropriate education for a 2-year year period when it failed to provide an adequate IEP or initiate proceedings to resolve the inadequacy.

Thus, the length of time during which an LEA refuses to confer an educational benefit and the consequences of that denial are the controlling factors. Both must be "gross" or flagrant.

Defense

It also will be helpful to consider the cases in which courts have refused to award compensatory education. *Carlisle Area School Dist. v. Scott P.* (1995) denied a student compensatory education because he had progressed, albeit slowly, under the LEA's IEP. The court rejected the parents' assertion that their child did not progress at a sufficient rate. In addition, *Parents of Student W. v. Puyallup* (1994) refused to order compensatory education for a student even though the LEA had violated the IDEA by allowing the student to unilaterally disenroll himself from special education without consulting his parents. Upon realizing that the student qualified for special education, the LEA attempted to remedy the situation by offering tutoring services and an appropriate IEP, which the parents refused.

The court based its decision on both the parents' refusal of services and the fact that the student completed high school, graduating with his class without additional services. These cases stand for the proposition that student progress nullifies a claim for compensatory education. The progress is proof of benefit.

Finally, where an LEA takes reasonable steps to integrate a student, evaluate and pay for an independent evaluation, and provide some related services in the general education program (but not all the services the family wants), the district is not liable for providing compensatory education just because other related services were withheld (*Jeanette H. v. Pennsbury School District*, 1992; *Murphy v. Timberlane Regional Sch. Dist.*, 1994). Substantial compliance, together with benefit, is a defense to a compensatory education claim.

Parental Behavior: "Unclean Hands"

Puyallup raises the issue of parental vigilance. In *Pullayup,* the court admonished the parents for failing to pursue their child's rights and respond to his educational needs. As stated above, this was not the court's only reason for denying compensatory education, but it did play a role in its decision. The issue of parental vigilance also arose in *M.C. v. Central Regional Sch. Dist.* (1995). The court noted that a child's entitlement to special education does not depend on the vigilance of the parents, as they may be ill-equipped to handle the situation. The student's teachers, therapists, and administrators have the burden of determining whether the student is receiving a free appropriate education.

From these opposing views, it is not completely clear how proactive parents must be in asserting their child's right to a free appropriate education. As *Puyallup* shows, however, a court may not look favorably on parents who appear to have "unclean hands"—their obstinance or self-serving behavior being "unclean."

Parental Delay: Laches

As already shown, LEAs always can raise defenses on the merits of the claim (educational benefit and progress) and on the basis of process and procedures, including parents' unclean hands. Because compensatory education is an equitable remedy, however, it is subject to the claim of laches as well. Laches is an affirmative defense raised by the defendant that bars a claim for equitable relief where a party's delay in bringing suit was unreasonable and resulted in prejudice to the opposing party.

Courts generally have rejected the LEAs' defenses that parents are barred by laches; instead the courts have given latitude when LEAs have asserted a laches defense. Although the parents in *Murphy* waited 6 years to file their claim, the court rejected the LEA's laches defense, as the LEA presented no evidence that any key witness suffered from failed memory or was unavailable.

Summary: Quantitative and Qualitative Standards

Courts may determine the duration of a compensatory education award based on both a qualitative and a quantitative analysis. The court used a quantitative formula to determine duration in *M.C. v. Central Regional Sch. Dist.* (1995), holding that a student is entitled to compensatory education for a period of time equal to the period of deprivation minus the time required to rectify the situation. Other courts have awarded compensatory education based on both the length of the deprivation and the magnitude of that deprivation, which is a more qualitative measurement. Whatever the analysis, courts clearly have a great deal of discretion in determining the duration of compensatory education.

Although *M.C. v. Central Regional Sch. Dist.* held that bad faith by the LEA is not a prerequisite for an award of compensatory education, the LEA in each of the cases where the court awarded compensatory education acted flagrantly and therefore culpably. Each LEA displayed deliberate and egregious action, through either undue delay or failure to act. This type of reckless disregard of a student's rights to a free appropriate education caused significant negative consequences for the student.

Extended School Year Services (ESY)

Rowley's tenets that professionally developed, individualized education programs are deemed to be appropriate flies squarely in the face of legislative judgments, usually based on fiscal policy, that a school year should be limited to a fixed number of days a year. Although fiscally and politically defensible, the length-of-school-year decision does not satisfy *Rowley*'s demand for individualization of education, based on professional judgment.

Not surprisingly, inflexible school-year limits have been tested. They will be again, as the 1997 amendments do not preclude an ESY remedy (34 C.F.R. § 300.309 defines ESY services and explains that they are available as necessary to provide FAPE).

The seminal ESY case is *Armstrong v. Kline* (1979), which held that the state's refusal to pay for more than 180 days of schooling each year for students with severe or profound mental retardation and those with serious emotional disturbances violates their rights to an appropriate education under IDEA—an appropriate education being one that allows the children to become self-sufficient within the limits of their disabilities, not just one that allows them to share equally in programs provided to nondisabled students or to reach one of several other goals.

In *Geis v. Bd. of Ed. of Parsnippany-Troy Hills* (1985), the court noted that some children will regress significantly during breaks in their education and recoup their losses more slowly, and accordingly are denied an appropriate education unless they are given year-round education. Likewise, *Johnson v. Indep. Sch. Dist. #4* (1990) held that "under the Act itself, states must provide a continuous educational experience throughout the summer under the child's IEP if that is the appropriate educational experience for the handicapped child's situation."

A case of particularly egregious violations by the LEA is *Reusch v. Fountain* (1994). In *Reusch*, the LEA sent a letter to all parents of children with disabilities regarding the annual review of a student's IEP but failed to define the option of extended school-school-year services or describe students who may be eligible. As a result, many parents were uninformed about the availability of this option and many children were denied those services.

In an obvious attempt to disguise the students' right to ESY services, the LEA mentioned extended school-year services in a brochure that it sent to all parents of children in the district, but did so only in a section called "Summer Enrichment," for which the LEA charged a fee. The brochure described the LEA's eligibility standard and instructions for those who believe their children may qualify. The LEA mailed this brochure to parents in mid-May, after most of the students' annual reviews had been held. The following year, the LEA distributed a mailing that included only a section called "Procedural Safeguards—Parental Rights," explaining that parents will be notified if their child requires extended school-year services.

The court concluded that the appropriate standard of eligibility for ESY services is that "it must appear that an ESY is necessary to permit the child to benefit from his instruction." This standard is met when it is shown that the student will suffer a significant regression of skills or knowledge without a summer program, followed by an insufficient recoupment of already acquired skills during the next school year. The standard must be applied so as to give meaningful effect to a wide array of factors based on the entire evidence presented.

The court also cited numerous procedural violations by the LEA in failing to notify parents of their rights regarding ESY. It noted that under state law the schools must make reasonable efforts to keep the parents of students with disabilities informed and involved, by explaining the rights fully in the special education decision-making process of their child.

In summary, ESY, like compensatory education, is an equitable remedy, available in a court's discretion, for a violation of the right to an appropriate education. As a rule, the extent of the student's disability, as measured by regression and recoupment factors, sometimes exacerbated by LEA dissembling about student rights, are the bases for the award of ESY benefits.

Interests of Children with Disabilities and Functions of Government

Notwithstanding the progress made at federal, state, and local levels of government to overcome intergovernmental problems by adopting interagency agreements, fundamental problems remain. These problems stem from disagreements about the nature of public education for students with disabilities.

Traditional Roles of Education

Traditionally, public education has been mass education of the masses. The purpose and techniques of public education were remarkably stable until approximately 40 years ago. Ever since *Brown* (1954) ordered school desegregation by race, the schools have become the battleground for beginning and carrying forward substantial changes in American life: racial desegregation, extension of public services into historically private areas of family life (health and sex education, counseling, social services, and other activities that tend to supplement or even supplant, in the eyes of some, the family's role), integration of persons with disabilities into the mainstream of life, and individualized services for those who have disabilities (not the provision of mass-produced and mass-consumed services).

Education was nearly as inevitable as death and taxes. Second only to the tax collector, the school cast the largest net thrown by government. Thus, schools have been asked to bear the brunt of social reform. In making schools the focal point of social reform and new government services for children with disabilities, however, policymakers have undertaken to transform the school and change its function from one of education alone to one of education plus physical health, mental health, and social services. Can the schools carry this burden? Should they be asked to? If so, how can they be helped? If not, who should be active in this area? These are the questions that thoughtful observers raise.

New Functions of Education

Students with disabilities have a very real and defensible interest in obtaining an appropriate education and related services. The schools have an equally real and defensible interest and responsibility to satisfy those needs. In light of the present difficulties in providing related services, however, some people think it is only proper to ask whether schools alone should be required to meet every educational need of a student with a disability and, if so, how they best can carry out this responsibility and with what funds (federal, state, or local).

In this matter, the function of one agency of government (schools) is being balanced against the functions of other agencies (health, mental health, and social services) and against the interests of students with disabilities and the various agencies. It is increasingly clear that the decisions about governmental functions and whether the school alone should bear the brunt of efforts to educate (in its fullest sense, by providing related services) students with disabilities have not been addressed adequately in the context not only of students with disabilities but also of education as a whole.

The infants/toddlers law (PL 99–457), the Medicare amendments (PL 100–350), and the Technology-Related Assistance to Individuals with Disabilities Act of 1988 (PL 100–407) prove this point: Schools are asked to do more nontraditional functions. Fortunately, the 1997 amendments clarify the first/last payor issues; they do not, however, remove from the schools the ultimate responsibility for providing a free appropriate public education, in all of its fullness. Thus, the state must provide FAPE to all students, ages 3–21 (subject to a few exceptions, explained in Chapter 3).

The state must adopt a full educational opportunity goal applicable to all eligible students. It must conduct child-find activities, searching out all eligible students. It is responsible for the general supervision of all LEA activities and of all educational programs operated for eligible students by all other state agencies. It must have interagency agreements that cover all students.

The SEA itself is responsible for providing services directly to eligible students if LEAs do not do so. The state may not alter or reduce its medical or other assistance (under the Social Security Act) to eligible students. The school must provide funding for students in private schools [20 U.S.C. § 1412 (a)(10)].

Until the role issue is addressed adequately, perhaps through school reform and school-linked service integration, the present problems will continue and proposed solutions will fall short because they will not reach the underlying issue of how public agencies are to respond (or fail to respond) to the presence of persons with disabilities in society. This is an issue not only of behavior and function but of values and principles as well.

Values and Principles

The Supreme Court's *Tatro* and *Garret F.* decisions (concerning catheterization and nursing services) were decided correctly, and their principles are sound, both with regard to the behavior and functions of schools and with regard to values and principles of IDEA, ADA, and Section 504—namely, inclusion and dual accommodations. The same is true of the 12-month-school-year cases and *Rowley*. All of these cases seem to emphasize the need for integrating students into programs with their nondisabled peers.

Tatro required catheterization, and *Garret F.* required nursing services so the students could continue to be educated at school (instead of at home). The 12-month-school-year cases indicate that the extended school year is required so students who require extended services to prevent regression can continue to receive those services. And *Rowley* made much of the fact that the student was integrated with nondisabled students and passing from grade to grade.

Conclusion ~

In these and so many other cases, the principle that schools must provide certain services is associated with the value of integration. The cases thus require a new behavior of schools—appropriate education (the opposite of functional exclusion)—and a new function of schools—namely, taking on some of the responsibilities of other agencies. The value is integration. The objective is to advance integration and to prevent exclusion and segregation.

Just how far the courts will pursue these behavior-shaping and function-changing principles and values remains to be seen. The decisive tests in the past have been in *Detsel*, involving related services for technology-supported students, the mental-health service cases, and *Timothy W. v. Rochester,* involving the issue of educability. These cases pushed to, and arguably beyond, the then-existing outer limits of schools' capacities and functions and challenged traditional concepts about the fundamental roles of schools and the wisdom of requiring LEAs to do much for so few.

In these cases and in others where tradition, capacity, and roles were challenged so frontally, some courts decided that the integration principle should yield to practical considerations of cost, time, and professionalism, especially because the students could receive more effective individualized services in other service systems. The *Garret F.* decision, however, seems to have rejected the cost concerns and to have held IDEA's goals of inclusion to be of much greater importance. Apparently, the struggle for integration has gained new ground, and courts undoubtedly will go farther to promote that goal than they have in the past.

Nevertheless, there will continue to be cases of students for whom inclusion is impracticable (i.e., those who are removed from the general curriculum due to likelihood of injury to self or others under 34 C.F.R. § 300.521). In those cases, the student arguably would not be denied an appropriate education (because health, psychiatric, and educational services still would be provided by other agencies) but would receive them in a less integrated setting (e.g., in an interim alternative educational setting, or in a general or psychiatric hospital). Indeed, that result—exclusion from school-based services and inclusion in other service providers' systems for receipt of special education and related services—is a major issue of IDEA's requirements for student placement into the least restrictive environments (LRE). Therefore, it is timely to consider the LRE rules next, in Chapter 6.

References ~

Committee Report, House of Representatives Committee on Education and the Workforce, on H.R. 5 (IDEA Amendments of 1997)(Passed as PL 105-17). H.R. Rep. No. 95, 105th Cong., 1st Sess. (1997).

Turnbull, A. P., and Turnbull, H. R. (1997). *Families, professionals, and exceptionality: A special partnership.* Columbus, OH: Merrill/Prentice Hall.

Turnbull, A. P., Turnbull, H. R., Wilcox, B., Sailor, W., and Wickham, D. (1999). *Technical assistance guideline: Positive behavioral interventions and supports for students with disabilities who have impeding behaviors.* Lawrence: University of Kansas, Beach Center on Families and Disability.

Cases ~

Amann v. Stow School System, 982 F.2d 644 (1st Cir. 1992).

Angevine v. Jenkins, 752 F.Supp. 24 (D.D.C. 1990), rev'd sub nom., *Angevine v. Smith*, 959 F.2d 292 (D.C. Cir. 1992).

Armstrong v. Kline, 476 F. Supp. 583 (E.D. Pa. 1979), aff'd in part sub. nom, *Battle v. Commonwealth of Pennsylvania*, 629 F.2d 269 (3rd Cir. 1980), further proceedings, 513 F.Supp. 425 (E.D.Pa. 1980).

Babb v. Knox County School System, 965 F.2d 104 (6th Cir. 1992), cert. denied, 506 U.S. 941 (1992).

Bd. of Ed. of East Windsor Regional Sch. Dist. v. Diamond, 808 F.2d 987 (3rd Cir. 1986).

Bd. of Educ. of Cabell v. Dienelt, 843 F.2d 813 (4th Cir. 1988).

Bd. of Educ. v. Rowley, 458 U.S. 176 (1982).

Bd. of Educ. of Community Consolidated Sch. Dist. No. 21 v. Illinois State Board of Education, 938 F.2d 712 (7th Cir. 1991), cert. denied, 502 U.S. 1066 (1992).

Bevin H. v. Wright, 666 F. Supp. 71 (W.D.Pa 1987).

Bonadonna v. Cooperman, 619 F.Supp. 401 (D.N.J. 1985).

Briere v. Fair Haven, 948 F. Supp. 1242 (D.Vt. 1996).

Brown v. Board of Education, 347 U.S. 483 (1954).

Brown v. Wilson County School Board, 747 F. Supp. 436 (M.D. Tenn. 1990).

Burke County Bd. of Educ. v. Denton, 895 F.2d 973 (4th Cir. 1990).

Capistrano Unified Sch. Dist. v. Wartenberg, 59 F.3d 884 (9th Cir. 1995).

Carlisle Area Sch. Dist. v. Scott P., 62 F.3d 520 (3rd Cir. 1995), cert. denied, 116 S.Ct. 1419 (U.S. 1996).

Cedar Rapids Community Sch. Dist. v. Garrett F., 106 F.3d 822 (8th Cir. 1997).

Christen G. v. Lower Merion Sch. Dist., 919 F. Supp. 793 (E.D.Pa. 1996).

Clovis Unified School Dist. v. California Office of Admin. Hearings, 903 F.2d 635 (9th Cir. 1990).

Colin K. v. Schmidt, 715 F.2d 1 (1st Cir. 1983).

County of San Diego v. California Special Education Hearing Office, 93 F.3d 1458 (9th Cir. 1996).

Darlene L. v. Illinois State Bd. of Educ., 568 F. Supp. 1340 (N.D.Ill. 1983).

David D. v. Dartmouth School Committee, 615 F. Supp. 639 (D.Mass. 1984), aff'd, 775 F.2d 411 (1st Cir. 1985), cert. denied, 475 U.S. 1140 (1986).

Day v. Radnor Township School Dist., 20 IDELR 1237 (E.D. Pa. 1994).

Detsel v. Bd. of Educ. of the Auburn Enlarged City School Dist., 820 F.2d 587 (2nd Cir. 1987), cert. denied, 484 U.S. 981 (1987).

Detsel v. Sullivan, 895 F.2d 58 (2nd Cir. 1990).

Doe v. Bd. of Ed. of Tullahoma City Schools, IDELR 18/1089 (E.D.Tenn. 1992), aff'd, 9 F.3d 455 (6th Cir. 1993), cert. denied, 511 U.S. 1108 (1994).

Doe v. Defendant I, 898 F.2d 1186 (6th Cir. 1990).

Espino v. Besteiro, 520 F. Supp. 905 (S.D. Tex. 1981), rev'd, 708 F.2d 1002 (5th Cir. 1983).

Evans v. Bd. of Ed. of the Rhinebeck Central Sch. Dist., 930 F. Supp. 83 (S.D.N.Y. 1996).

Evans v. District No. 17, 841 F.2d. 824 (8th Cir. 1988).

Field v. Haddonfield Bd. of Educ., 769 F. Supp. 1313 (D.N.J. 1991).

Florence County Sch. Dist. Four v. Carter, 510 U.S. 7 (1993).

Ft. Zumwalt Sch. Dist. v. Missouri State Bd of Ed., 865 F. Supp. 604 (E.D. Mo. 1994), further proceedings, 923 F. Supp. 1216 (E.D.Mo. 1996), aff'd in part, rev'd in part sub nom., *Ft. Zumwalt Sch. Dist. v. Clynes*, Nos. 96-2503/2504, 1997 U.S. App. Lexis 17214 (8th Cir. 1997).

Fulginiti v. Roxbury Township Public Schools, 921 F. Supp. 1320 (D.N.J. 1996), aff'd, 166 F.3d 468 (3rd Cir. 1997).

Garcia v. California, 24 IDELR 547 (E.D.Cal. (1996).

Garland Independent School District v. Wilks, 657 F. Supp. 1163 (N.D. Tex. 1987).

Geis v. Bd. of Educ., 589 F. Supp. 269 (D.N.J. 1984), aff'd, 774 F.3d 575 (3rd Cir. 1985).

Granite Sch. Dist. v. Shannon M., 787 F. Supp. 1020 (D.Utah 1992).

Greenbush School Committee v. Mr. & Mrs. K., 25 IDELR 200 (D.Me. 1996).

Hall v. Shawnee Mission School Dist., 856 F. Supp. 1521 (D. Kan. 1994).

Hall v. Vance County Bd. of Ed., 774 F.2d 629 (4th Cir. 1985).

Harris v. D.C Bd. of Ed., IDELR 19/105 (D.D.C. 1992)

Irving Indep. School Dist. v. Tatro, 703 F.2d 823 (5th Cir. 1983), aff'd in part, rev'd in part, 468 U.S. 883 (1984).

Jeanette H. v. Pennsbury School District, No. 91-CV-3273, 1992 U.S. Dist. Lexis 7283 (E.D.Pa. 1992).

Jefferson County Bd. of Educ. v. Breen, 694 F. Supp. 1539 (N.D. Ala. 1987).

Johnson v. Westmoreland County School Bd., 19 IDELR 787 (E.D. Va. 1993).

Johnson v. Ind. Sch. Dist. No. 4, 921 F.2d 1022 (10th Cir. 1990), cert. denied, 500 U.S. 905 (1991).

Lachman v. Illinois State Bd. of Educ., 852 F.2d 290 (7th Cir. 1988), cert. denied, 488 U.S. 925 (1988).

Lenn v. Portland School Committee, 998 F.2d 1083 (1st Cir. 1993).

Leo P. v. Board of Education, EHLR 553:644 (N.D.Ill. 1982).

Lester H. v. Gilhool, 916 F.2d 865 (3d Cir. 1990), cert. denied, 499 U.S. 923 (1991).

M. C. v. Central Regional School Dist., 22 IDELR 1036 (D.N.J. 1995).

Mather v. Hartford School Dist., 928 F. Supp. 437 (D. Vt. 1996).

McKenzie v. Jefferson, 566 F. Supp. 404 (D.D.C. 1983).

McManus v. Wilmette School Dist. 39 Bd. of Ed., IDELR 19/485, 1992 U.S. Dist. Lexis 18167 (N.D. Ill. 1992).

McMillan v. Cheatham County Schools, 25 IDELR 398 (M.D.Tenn. 1997).

Metropolitan Nashville & Davidson County Sch. System v. Guest, 900 F. Supp. 905 (M.D.Tenn. 1995).

Miener v. Missouri, 498 F. Supp. 944 (E.D. Mo. 1980), aff'd in part, rev'd in part, 673 F.2d 969 (8th Cir. 1982), cert. denied, 459 U.S. 909, 916 (1982), on remand, *Miener v. Special School District*, 580 F. Supp. 562 (E.D. Mo. 1984), aff'd in part, rev'd in part, 800 F.2d 749 (8th Cir. 1986).

Mrs. B. v. Milford Bd. of Educ., 103 F.3d 1114 (2nd Cir. 1997).

Mrs. C. v. Wheaton, 916 F.2d 69 (2nd Cir. 1990).

Murphy v. Timberlane Regional Sch. Dist., 22 F.3d 1186 (1st Cir. 1994), cert. denied, 513 U.S. 987 (1994).

Murphysboro Community Unit School Dist. v. Illinois State Bd. of Educ., 41 F.3d 1162 (7th Cir. 1994).

Myles S. v. Montgomery County Bd. of Ed., 824 F. Supp. 1549 (M.D.Ala. 1993).

Neely v. Rutherford County School, 851 F. Supp. 888 (M.D. Tenn. 1995), rev'd, 68 F.3d 965 (6th Cir. 1995), cert. denied, 116 S.Ct. 1418 (U.S. 1996).

Ojai Unified Sch. Dist. v. Jackson, 4 F.3d 1467 (9th Cir. 1993), cert. denied, 513 U.S. 825 (1994).

P.F. ex rel. B.F. v. New Jersey Div. of Developmental Disabilities, 656 A.2d 1 (N.J. 1995).

Papacoda v. Connecticut, 528 F. Supp. 68 (D.Conn. 1981).

Parents of Student W. v. Puyallup, 31 F.3d 1489 (9th Cir. 1994).

Parks v. Pavkovic, 536 F. Supp. 296 (N.D. Ill. 1982), further proceedings, 557 F. Supp. 1280 (N.D. Ill. 1983), aff'd in part, rev'd in part, 753 F.2d 1397 (7th Cir. 1985), cert. denied, 473 U.S. 906 (1985).

Petersen v. Hastings Public Schools, 831 F. Supp. 742 (D.Neb. 1993), aff'd, 31 F.3d 705 (8th Cir. 1994).

Polk v. Central Sasquehanna Intermediate Unit 16, 853 F.2d 171 (3rd Cir. 1988), cert. denied, 488 U.S. 1030 (1989).

Pullen v. Cuomo, 18 IDELR 132 (N.D.N.Y. 1991)

Quackenbush v. Johnson City School District, 716 F.2d 141 (2nd Cir. 1983), cert denied, 465 U.S. 1071 (1984).

Rebecca S. v. Clarke County School Dist., 22 IDELR 884 (M.D. Ga. 1995).

Reusch v. Fountain, 872 F. Supp. 1421 (D.Md. 1994).

River Forest School Dist. #90 v. Laurel D., No. 95 C 5503, 1996 U.S. Dist. Lexis 4988 (N.D.Ill. 1996).

Rose v. Chester County Intermediate Unit, No. 95-239, 1996 U.S. Dist. Lexis 6105 (E.D.Pa. 1996), aff'd, 114 F.3d 1173 (3rd Cir. 1997).

Russell v. Jefferson Sch. Dist., 609 F. Supp. 605 (N.D.Cal. 1985).

Salley v. St. Tammany Parish Sch. Bd., 57 F.3d 458 (5th Cir. 1995).

Sanger v. Montgomery County Bd. of Ed., 916 F. Supp. 518 (D.Md. 1996).

School Committee of the Town of Burlington v. Dept. of Educ. of Massachusetts, 736 F.2d 773 (1st Cir. 1984), aff'd, 471 U.S. 359 (1985).

Scituate School Committee v. Robert B., 620 F. Supp. 1224 (D.R.I. 1985), aff'd 795 F.2d 77 (1st Cir. 1986).

Sioux Falls School Dist. v. Koupal, 526 N.W.2d 248 (S.D. 1994), cert. denied, 115 S.Ct. 2580 (U.S. 1995).

Still v. Debuono, 101 F.3d 888 (2nd Cir. 1996).

Sullivan v. Vallejo City Unified School Dist., 731 F. Supp. 947 (E.D.Cal. 1990).

Teague Indep. School Dist. v. Todd L., 999 F.2d 127 (5th Cir. 1993).

Thomas v. Cincinnati Bd. of Educ., 918 F.2d 618 (6th Cir. 1990).

Thornrock v. Boise Indep. School Dist., 767 P.2d 1241 (Idaho 1988), cert. denied, 490 U.S. 1068 (1989).

Union School Dist. v. Smith, 15 F.3d 1519 (9th Cir. 1994), cert. denied, 513 U.S. 965 (1994).

Urban v. Jefferson County School Dist R-1, 870 F. Supp. 1558 (D.Co. 1994), aff'd, 89 F.3d 720 (10th Cir. 1996).

Vander Malle v. Ambach, 673 F.2d 49 (2nd Cir. 1982), further proceedings, 667 F. Supp. 1015 (S.D.N.Y. 1987).

6

Least Restrictive Appropriate Educational Placement

No requirement of the right-to-education movement and IDEA was as likely at the outset to generate such controversy as the requirement that students with disabilities be educated in the least restrictive environment (LRE). Originally given the name "mainstreaming," this requirement had the potential for encountering the same levels of opposition, misunderstanding, and ill will as the earlier requirements for racial desegregation of the public schools. But this requirement also had the potential for improving the education of students with disabilities significantly, redressing some of the wrongs that schools had imposed on them and their families, and contributing to the education of all pupils, the training of all educators, and the enlightenment of the public at large.

The LRE requirement can be examined along several dimensions, paying attention to (1) the constitutional basis (foundations) for the requirement, (2) requirements of IDEA and other statutes, (3) the nature of the requirement as a rebuttable presumption and the public policy values the LRE requirement seeks to achieve, and (4) judicial interpretations of the LRE doctrine.

Constitutional Foundations

The LRE education of students with disabilities is derived from the constitutionally based legal doctrine of the least restrictive alternative. This doctrine states that even if the legislative purpose of a government action is legitimate (e.g., promoting public health, regulating commerce, or providing education), the purpose may not be pursued by means that broadly stifle personal liberties if it can be achieved by less oppressive or restrictive means. Thus, legislative and administrative action must take the form of the least drastic means for achieving a valid governmental purpose.[1] In

Chambers' memorable metaphor, the LRE doctrine forbids a state from using a bazooka to kill a fly on a citizen's back if a fly swatter would do as well.[2] LRE, then, is a constitutional principle that accommodates individual and state interests to each other. It enables government to act but does not permit it to take action that intrudes unjustifiably into a person's liberty.

The LRE principle generally has been applied in areas affecting state regulations of interstate commerce[3] and personal liberties.[4] The LRE doctrine also has been applied in cases involving persons with disabilities in public institutions. A long line of cases addresses this issue. In one notable case, *Wyatt v. Stickney* (1972), a federal court stated that residents of Partlow State School and Hospital, an Alabama state institution for persons with developmental disabilities, have a right to the least restrictive conditions necessary to achieve the purpose of habilitation. This phraseology is significant because it highlights the point that the primary purpose of commitment is treatment; elimination of infringement on rights (in this case, deprivation of liberty) is secondary.

In legal terminology this means that the LRE doctrine is a rebuttable presumption. That is to say, when it is not possible to grant liberty and at the same time provide effective treatment, the doctrine allows the state to deprive the citizen of his or her liberty but only to the extent necessary to provide the treatment. The presumption in favor of liberty thus is rebutted by the necessity for commitment, and treatment (intervention or education) is the trade-off for the loss of liberty. The same point applies to the principle of LRE in education. The right to placement in a general education environment is not an absolute right but, instead, is secondary to the primary purpose of an appropriate public education.

LRE's power is related to three other important constitutional principles: procedural due process, substantive due process, and equal protection.

Procedural Due Process

Procedural due process requires that a state must grant citizens access to procedures that allow them to challenge a government action before the government may infringe adversely upon their individual rights. The state must prove that the proposed action is warranted, and the individual is given the opportunity to point out less restrictive or less drastic means of accomplishing the state's goal.

In special-education matters, IDEA itself guarantees a hearing at which the student can try to show why the rebuttable presumption against placement in a special education program should be overcome. The hearing requires individualized decision-making and imposes an accountability device on government, all to the end of protecting the student's interest in receiving a free appropriate public education in the general education program.

Substantive Due Process

Substantive due process places an outer limit on what a state may do, independent of the level of procedural protections provided. It protects certain individual rights from government intrusion and requires that the government, when intruding on a citizen's rights, must use the least intrusive means to accomplish its goals. LRE is related to substantive due process in that it prohibits the state from using more restrictive means than are necessary to accomplish its purpose. LRE, then, acts as an outer limit on permissible government action. In special education affairs, LRE and substantive due process regard unwarranted, inappropriate special education classification and placement as too restrictive.

Equal Protection

The third and last principle, equal protection, requires that a state deal with similarly situated individuals in an even-handed manner. The equal protection doctrine places the burden of proof on the state to show a compelling, important, or rational reason for its unequal treatment of similarly situated individuals. The level of required justification depends in part on the nature of the rights being limited. The plaintiff who alleges a violation of equal protection is required to prove that the state's conduct is not rationally related to a legitimate government purpose.

Equal protection was the basis for the right-to-education cases that challenged exclusion of students with disabilities from public schools in the early 1970s. The courts' attitude toward educational segregation can be summarized in the following comment from *PARC*:

> [A]mong the alternative programs of education and training required by statute to be available, placement in a regular public school class is preferable to placement in...any other type of education and training.

In summary, the LRE doctrine is a constitutionally derived way of balancing the values surrounding provision of an appropriate education (the student's right to and need for an appropriate education) with the values associated with the individual's right to associate with nondisabled peers. It is supported by, and implemented through, the constitutional principles of procedural due process, substantive due process, and equal protection. As will be shown below, LRE has been a powerful doctrine for accommodating legitimate state interests (in educating all students, not just those with disabilities, appropriately) and individual interests (the interests of all students in receiving an appropriate education in settings that promote association between nondisabled and disabled students).

Individuals with Disabilities Education Act ⌢

Findings of Fact

It is not surprising that many of Congress' findings of fact in IDEA reflect the constitutional principle of LRE and are identical to the conclusions of the courts in pre-IDEA cases (see Chapters 2 and 3) and the reasons those courts required students with disabilities to be placed in the least restrictive school environments. In 1975, Congress found as a matter of fact that:

1. Students with disabilities had been educated inappropriately [20 U.S.C. § 1400 (c)(2)(B)(1997)];
2. Students with disabilities had been denied the opportunity "to go through the educational process with their peers" [20 U.S.C. § 1400 (c)(2)(C)];
3. Students had been having unsuccessful educational experiences because their disabilities had been undetected [20 U.S.C. § 1400 (c)(2)(D)];
4. Adequate services to students with disabilities within the schools had been lacking [20 U.S.C. § 1400 (c)(2)(E)].

Those findings of fact were the foundation for the 1975 law (PL 94–142). In 1997, they remained a basis for IDEA, but they are not the only ones. Indeed, the new findings of fact go much farther than the old ones in propelling students with disabilities into the center of American life; the "pro-inclusion" basis of IDEA centers on these findings, making them important to recite.

1. One of IDEA's purposes is to improve students' educational results so they can participate fully in American life [20 U.S.C. § 1400 (c)(1)]. The goal of "full participation" is linked to the principle of the least restrictive environment (LRE), because education in the LRE is a form of full participation in the life of the school and a technique for full participation in other domains of life.
2. A technique for improving educational results for students with disabilities is to ensure their access to the general curriculum to the maximum extent possible [20 U.S.C. § 1400 (c)(5)(A)].
3. Special education no longer should be a place to which students are sent but, instead, should be a service for the students, one requiring the coordination of educational and other services [20 U.S.C. § 1400 (c)(5)(C)].
4. Special education, related services, and other (supplementary) aids and services should be provided to students in the general classroom, whenever appropriate [20 U.S.C. § 1400 (c)(5)(D)].
5. Professionals should be able to provide services that assure the outcomes of productivity and independence [20 U.S.C. § 1400 (c)(5)(E)], and the purpose of IDEA is in fact to ensure that the students' education will prepare them for employment and independent living [20 U.S.C. § 1400 (d)(1)(A)].

Part B Requirements

Before setting out IDEA's many specific provisions that advance the LRE principle, it is important to state that LRE is, and always has been, a presumption that students with disabilities are to be educated in regular classes and other regular education activities (Committee Report, p. 100). Accordingly, once an LEA determines that a student is eligible for special education and related services, the LEA must strengthen the connections between them and the child's opportunity to benefit from the regular education curriculum (Committee Report, pp. 99–100).

Because the majority of students with disabilities are capable of participating in the general curriculum "to varying degrees and with some adaptations and modifications," the LEA must assure that the student's special education and related services "are in addition to and are affected by the general curriculum, not separate from it" (Committee Report, p. 100). Special education is, after all, a service, not a place to which students are sent [20 U.S.C. § 1400 (c)(5)(C)].

For these reasons, the "new focus" of IDEA is intended to be on the accommodations and adjustments necessary for the students to have access to the general curriculum and to special services that may be necessary for them to participate appropriately in specific areas of the general curriculum (academic, extracurricular, and other nonacademic activities) (Committee Report, p. 100).

As the following discussion points out, IDEA carries out this congressional intent by connecting a large number of discrete provisions to the general curriculum. It is fair to say—and to applaud the fact—that Congress has, at last, put a great deal of strength behind the LRE principle. No longer is there room for debate about the wisdom of the principle; there is room only for determining how to carry it out in the case of each student.

General Rule

Given these findings and LRE's constitutional basis, Congress properly requires SEAs [20 U.S.C. § 1412 (a)(5)] and LEAs [20 U.S.C. § 1413 (a)(1)] to follow a policy of least restrictive placement [34 C.F.R. § 300.550]. They must develop procedures to assure that, to the maximum extent appropriate, students (ages 3 through 21) with disabilities—including those educated in public agencies, private institutions, or other care facilities—will be educated with students who do not have a disability [34 C.F.R. §§ 300.550 and 300.552].

Further, special classes, separate schooling, or other removal of students with disabilities from the regular education environment may occur only when the nature or severity of a student's disability is such that education in regular classes with the use of supplementary aids and services cannot be achieved satisfactorily for that student [20 U.S.C. § 1412 (a)(5)and 34 C.F.R. 300.552]. A placement decision, accordingly, must focus on the severity of the student's disability and thus is linked inexorably to the concept of student-centered appropriate education, not system-centered, convenience-based placements.

Inclusion: Fully or Partially in Three Domains

Regular education is a broad classification, requiring integration/inclusion in at least three school environments:

1. The regular class (academic integration)
2. Extracurricular activities (school-sponsored clubs and sports)
3. "Other nonacademic activities" (such as recess, meal-times, transportation, dances, and the like) [20 U.S.C. § 1414 (d)(1)(A)(iii)].

Thus, a student's IEP must include an explanation of the extent, if any, to which the student will not participate, in the regular class and in extracurricular and other nonacademic activities, with students who do not have disabilities [20 U.S.C. § 1414 (d)(1)(A)(iv)]. This is a new and highly significant provision. It puts on the IEP team the burden of justifying why a student's program and placement will not be within each of the three dimensions of the regular education environment. As much as any other provision of IDEA, this one makes it clear that IDEA creates a presumption in favor of inclusion; there is no other explanation for putting the burden of proof on the IEP team for any separation from the regular education environment.

This provision is significant for yet another reason. It says that the IEP team must explain "the extent, if any," to which the student will be separated from the regular education environment. By requiring justification of the extent of separation, the provision allows for partial inclusion and partial separation from the regular education environment. No longer is LRE an "either/or" proposition; partial inclusion is contemplated, and indeed preferred, if total inclusion is not appropriate.

Also, by listing the three dimensions of the regular education environment, this provision instructs an IEP team to consider each of them and the extent to which a student must be removed from each to secure an appropriate education. So a "mix-and-match" approach now is codified: The IEP team may mix the student as is appropriate given the match between his needs and the dimension's capacity to respond to them. The student is "mixed" into the regular environment and "matched" to its three dimensions.

Finally, this provision essentially codifies the requirements of the IDEA regulations as they existed under the pre-1997 Act. Those regulations provided that students with disabilities must be given a chance to participate in nonacademic and extracurricular services and activities [34 C.F.R. §§ 300.553 and 300.306]. They are to have access to meals, recess periods, counseling services, athletics, transportation, health services, recreational activities, special-interest groups, clubs, referrals to agencies providing assistance to those with disabilities, and employment of students by the school or other employers. In giving personal, academic, or vocational counseling and placement services to students with disabilities, a school may not discriminate because of disability and must make sure that those students are not counseled toward more restrictive career objectives than nondisabled students who have similar interests and abilities.

NDE and IEP Provisions

As pointed out in detail in Chapters 4 and 5, each student has a right to a nondiscriminatory evaluation and an IEP. In creating those rights, IDEA linked them to the student's placement in the general education environment. Taken together, each of the NDE/IEP-linked rights confirm and strengthen the LRE presumption by commanding educators to (a) deliberately evaluate and plan for the student's participation and progress in the general curriculum, and (b) consider how the general curriculum itself can be modified to accommodate the student.

1. In conducting the evaluation, the NDE/IEP team must use assessment tools and strategies that determine the content of the student's IEP, including information related to enabling the student to be involved in and progress in the general curriculum (or, for preschool students, to participate in "appropriate activities") [20 U.S.C. § 1414 (b)(2)(A)]. This is a command to evaluate the student with a view toward placement in the general curriculum.

2. The "special rule" that excludes students from being classified into special education if the determinant factor for classification is the student's lack of instruction in math or English or the student's limited use of English will keep some students out of special education and require them to be retained in the general curriculum [20 U.S.C. § 1414 (b)(5)].

3. When conducting a reevaluation, the NDE/IEP team must determine whether the student needs additions or modifications to the existing IEP so the student may participate, as appropriate, in the general curriculum [20 U.S.C. § 1414 (c)(1)(B)(iv)]. This provision keeps continuous pressure on the team to evaluate not just what the student's strengths and needs are and how they relate to the general curriculum, but also to take into account what the general curriculum is and how it should be modified to accommodate the student.

4. The IEP itself must contain a statement of how the student's disability affects involvement and progress in the general curriculum (or, for preschoolers, in appropriate activities) [20 U.S.C. § 1414 (d)(1)(A)(i)(I)]. This provision places the disability into the context of the general curriculum and enables the NDE/IEP team to specify interventions for the student and modifications in the curriculum—a "dual accommodation" approach, changing both the student and the context in which the student is educated.

5. The IEP must contain annual goals, including short-term goals or benchmarks, related to meeting the student's needs and the disability's effect on the student's participation in the general curriculum [20 U.S.C. § 1414 (d)(1)(A)(ii)(I)]. This provision, like those in items 4, above, and 6, below, give a context for intervention—the context being the general curriculum. As the House Committee noted, this provision "should not be construed to be a basis for excluding a child with a disability who is unable to learn at the same level or rate as nondisabled children in an inclusive classroom or setting. It is intended to require that the IEP's annual goals focus on how the child's needs resulting from his or her disability can be addressed so the child can participate, at the individually appropriate level, in the general curriculum offered to all students" (Committee Report, p. 100).

6. The IEP must state what services the student will receive and what program modifications will be made so the student can be involved in and progress in the general curriculum, including extracurricular and other nonacademic activities [20 U.S.C. § 1414 (d)(1)(A)(iii)]. This is another contextual provision,

calling for the team to propose modifications in the general curriculum—a context—or system-centered focus, not a student-focused one. The context must change to fit the student; the education and interventions the student receives changes the student so he or she will fit the context better.

7. The IEP team must include a regular educator, as appropriate [20 U.S.C. § 1414 (d)(1)(B)(ii)], and that educator has specific duties related to the student's participation in the general curriculum [20 U.S.C. § 1414 (d)(1)(C)]. The purposes for including the regular educator are explained in detail in Chapter 5 and below: to assure that the context changes by having a context-leader (the regular educator) involved in the student's education.

8. The IEP team also must include an LEA representative who is knowledgeable about the general curriculum and LEA resources that advance IEP goals (including general-curriculum goals) [20 U.S.C. § 1414 (d)(1)(B)(iv)]. This provision assures that a person who is able to shape a school system's resources to fit the student's needs is involved on the team and in the student's education.

Assessments as an LRE Technique

IDEA focuses on the students' "full participation" and integration/inclusion rights in two other ways. These relate to the student's participation in statewide and districtwide assessments of all students. The presumption behind these provisions, as explained in Chapter 5, is that the student will participate in them and that excluding the student from such participation can severely limit the student's post-school activities (including those that are typical for nondisabled individuals, such as post-secondary education).

1. IDEA requires that each student's IEP contain a statement of what modifications in state or districtwide assessments will be made so the student can participate in those assessments and, if the IEP team determines that the student should be exempted from participation, an explanation of why the assessment is not appropriate and the alternative methods of assessment that will be used [20 U.S.C. § 1414 (d)(1)(A)(v)(I) and (II)].

2. IDEA also requires each student's IEP to contain a statement of when the services and modifications will begin, how often and where they will be delivered, and how long they will last [20 U.S.C. § 1414 (d)(1)(A)(vi)].

Transition and LRE

The student's rights to transition planning and transition services (explained in detail in Chapter 5) also advance the LRE principle. They do so by specifying that the outcomes of transition and the methods used to secure those outcomes are targeted on full participation in American life.

1. The outcomes of transition are those that many students without disabilities take for granted and will attain, including post-secondary education, vocational

training, integrated employment, and continuing and adult education; and the student's transition program should consist of a process that leads to these kinds of "full participation" outcomes [20 U.S.C. § 1401 (30)(A)].

2. The process by which transition services are provided includes inclusive methods such as community service and the development of employment and other post-school objectives [20 U.S.C. § 1401 (30)(C)].

Discipline and LRE

As pointed out in Chapter 3, students who are subject to discipline nevertheless retain important LRE rights (which are not always available to students in adult correction facilities). Even when a student is subject to discipline—and, some would say, especially because the student is subject to discipline—there are compelling reasons to continue to link that student's program and placement to the "full-participation" outcomes that underlie IDEA.

1. The students have a right to have a functional assessment created or reviewed (and, therefore, to have positive behavioral support intervention considered) if they are disciplined for weapons, drug violations, or exhibit behavior that is dangerous to themselves or others, and the intervention must address the behavior for which they are punished [20 U.S.C. § 1415 (k)(1)(B)]. Through this right, students may be able to acquire interventions that will prevent them from being disciplined and placed in a highly restrictive interim alternative educational setting (IAES).

2. Students who are placed in an IAES retain the right to continue to participate in the general curriculum [20 U.S.C. § 1415 (k)(3)(B)(i)].

3. Except in the case of weapons or drug violations, the usual stay-put rule is available to students, thereby retaining a placement that is presumptively less restrictive than the one to which they may be removed as part of a disciplinary sanction [20 U.S.C. § 1415 (j), and 1402 (k)(7)].

LRE and School Financing Mechanisms

Focusing on a student's rights is one thing, but if an entire school system is financed so it has no incentive to place students in the LRE, individual rights can be swallowed up by system-financing and system-organizational considerations. In the past, SEA and LEA financing and organizational practices often provided extra funds—a financial incentive—to programs that placed students into the less typical, more separate and specialized, more restrictive programs.

Recognizing the importance of overcoming the financial incentive for that kind of placement, IDEA provides that, to draw down federal funds under IDEA, a state must assure the U.S. Department of Education of two matters:

1. If the state uses a funding mechanism by which the state distributes state funds on the basis of the type of setting in which students are served, the mechanism does not result in placements that violate the LRE rule [20 U.S.C. § 1412 (a)(5)(B)(i)].

2. If the state does not have policies and procedures to comply with the funding-mechanism requirement, the state must assure that it will revise its present funding schemes so any such mechanism that it may adopt in the future will not result in placements that violate the LRE rule [20 U.S.C. § 1412 (a)(5)(B)(ii)].

Another provision also addresses the issues of money and funding: the "incidental benefit" provision [20 U.S.C. § 1413 (a)(4)(A)]. This rule allows an LEA to use IDEA funds for the costs of special education and related services and for the costs of supplementary aids and services that benefit a student with a disability even if the use of those funds also benefits nondisabled students. Indeed, these services can benefit nondisabled students, and the statute's previous restriction on their use (a "disabled-student only" benefit) now has been eliminated. Its elimination will let LEAs use IDEA money more flexibly and more deliberately to advance the LRE principle.

State Allotments and LRE

Another provision of IDEA related to funding mechanisms and inclusion of students in the general curriculum deals generally with federal aid to the states; it recognizes that some states have overidentified students as having a disability so they could draw down federal special education funds under IDEA (Committee Report, p. 89). Overidentification can occur at two separate times in a student's life:

1. When the student is evaluated initially to determine whether he or she has a disability that affects the student's participation in the general curriculum ("in/entry qualification");
2. When it may be appropriate for the student to exit special education altogether ("out/exit-qualification").

Accordingly, IDEA now authorizes the U.S. Department of Education to distribute IDEA funds to the states on the basis of the state's census and the state's poverty factor [20 U.S.C. § 1411(e)]. This new basis will supplement the original allocation formula, which now is based on the number of students the state qualifies for special education, only after the total federal appropriations under IDEA exceed $4.9 billion.

Thus, the traditional and longstanding head-count basis, which creates an incentive to classify students into special education and to retain them there so states can draw down federal funds, will be supplemented with a classification-neutral formula (census plus poverty) at a predetermined level (when the federal funds exceed $4.9 billion). Because the new formula contains no incentives for classification into or retention in special education, it may, in a mega-policy way, advance the LRE principle. This is so because states have been exploring alternatives for serving more students in the regular education classroom, and the new formula may spur the states to continue those explorations (Committee Report, p. 89).

As the House Committee noted, the change in funding formulas will enable states to undertake good practices for addressing the learning needs of more children in the regular classroom without unnecessary categorization or labeling, thereby risking the loss of federal funds. Changing the federal formula also may motivate states to change their own formulas for distributing state aid in ways that eliminate financial incentives for referring children to special education (Committee Report, pp. 89–90).

Other Statutory Techniques

Other provisions of IDEA that advance the "least restrictive environment" principle are:

1. Section 1471(a)(2)(B): provides special grants to state and local education agencies to help them with their integration efforts.
2. Section 1473: provides for special grants for inservice education of general educators so they might become more able to accommodate special education students in their programs.
3. Sections 1412 (a)(14), (15), and 1413 (a)(3): require SEAs to create comprehensive systems of personnel development (CSPD). Without properly trained professionals, education in the LRE would not be successful.
4. Section 1401 (22): clarifies that therapeutic recreation is a related service and thus emphasizes that students in special education will have opportunities to learn skills that help them participate in community park-and-recreation programs, which, under ADA, no longer may discriminate against otherwise qualified individuals with disabilities.
5. Section 1401(29): defines supplementary aids and services as "aids, services, and other supports" that are provided in general education classes. or other education-related settings to enable children with disabilities to be educated with nondisabled children to the maximum extent appropriate consistent with the LRE principle.
6. Regulation section 300.552(e) prevents a school district from removing a child with disabilities from the age-appropriate regular classroom solely because of needed modifications in the general curriculum.

Exception to the Rule

The IDEA contains one explicit exception to the mandate that students must be educated in the least restrictive environment. Juveniles who have been incarcerated as adults in adult prisons and who have IEPs are not entitled to placement in the least restrictive environment. The IDEA specifically grants to IEP teams for such incarcerated juveniles the authority to disregard the LRE mandate and the rules regarding IEP content, if the state demonstrates a "bona fide security or compelling penalogical interest that cannot otherwise be accommodated" [20 U.S.C. § 1414 (d)(6)(B)].

Juveniles who are incarcerated as adults also are not required to participate in general and statewide assessment programs [20 U.S.C. § 1414 (d)(6)(A)(i)].

Furthermore, incarcerated juveniles are not entitled to transition planning and services if they will be in prison past the age of eligibility for special education services [20 U.S.C. § 1414 (d)(6)(A)(ii)].

Part C Requirements

Part C regulations clearly create a strong preference for community-based services, to the extent appropriate for the child. The purpose of Part C is to enhance infants' and toddlers' development by maximizing their potential for independent living in society, minimizing their potential for a developmental delay, and assisting states to provide quality early intervention programs [20 U.S.C. § 1431(a)]. Accordingly, states must put into effect a statewide system of "appropriate early intervention services" [20 U.S.C. § 1434(a)(2)]. Under this system, early intervention services must be provided in "natural environments", including the home, in which infants and toddlers without disabilities normally or naturally would participate, to the maximum extent appropriate for infants and toddlers with disabilities [20 U.S.C. § 1431 (4)(G) and 1436(d)(5)].

The home is considered the primary natural environment for delivery of early intervention services, as the home is the usual environment in which infants and toddlers without disabilities are cared for and educated. Where group settings are utilized, the statute leaves no doubt about its preference for integration of infants and toddlers with disabilities in settings that include children without disabilities.

Part C's regulations, however, make it clear that separate environments, such as hospital settings, are permitted when infants and toddlers require extensive medical intervention [34 C.F.R. § 303.12(b)]. But this exception is narrow and depends on the necessity of medical services for the infant or toddler and the nature of the needed services ("extensive medical intervention").

The Department of Education acknowledges the narrowness of the exception and the strong integration presumption, urging providers to make efforts to provide services in "settings and facilities that do not remove the children from natural environments (e.g., the home, integrated child-care centers, or other community settings)" and recommending against isolating eligible children or families from settings or activities in which nondisabled infants and toddlers normally would participate.

Section 504 Requirements

Section 504 applies to students who (a) are entitled to Section 504 benefits (they have, are regarded as having, or have a record of a disability that significantly affects one or more of life's major activities, including their ability to learn), and (b) are not formally classified into special education and not entitled to IDEA benefits. Among the so-called "504 students" may be those with a contagious disease (see Chapter 3 on AIDS) or another impairment that does not interfere with their ability to learn (e.g., a student with attention deficit/hyperactivity disorder may not need special education but still is entitled to Section 504 benefits because he or she has a disability that may not require special education placement). For these students, Section 504 and ADA are protections against discrimination in education based solely on their disabilities.

The regulations of Section 504 [34 C.F.R. §§ 104-104.61] are substantially similar to those of the IDEA. Section 104.34 of the regulations requires that schools provide regular education to each qualified student with a disability, to the maximum extent appropriate to that student's needs. The school must place students with disabilities in the regular education environment operated by the school unless the school can demonstrate that a student's education in the general environment with the use of supplementary aids and services cannot be achieved satisfactorily. Although the student's needs determine what is a proper placement, the Department of Education's comments on § 104.34 make clear that if a student with a disability is so disruptive in a regular classroom that other students' education is significantly impaired or the student's needs cannot be met in that placement, the regular setting placement is not appropriate or required.

Students with disabilities also are to be provided with nonacademic services in as inclusive a setting as possible [34 C.F.R. § 104.34]. This requirement is especially important for students whose academic needs require them to be separated from general education programs during part of each day. In providing or arranging for the provision of extracurricular services and activities, including meals, recess periods, and nonacademic services and activities, a school must ensure that each student with a disability participates with nondisabled students to the maximum extent appropriate for the student in question [34 C.F.R. § 104.37 (a)(2)]. To the maximum extent appropriate, students in residential settings also are to be provided with opportunities to participate with other students.

If an LEA operates a separate facility for students with disabilities, the LEA must ensure that the facility and the services and activities it provides are comparable to its other facilities, services, and activities for nondisabled students [34 C.F.R. § 104.34]. This is not intended to encourage the creation and maintenance of such facilities. In fact, a separate facility violates Section 504 unless it is necessary for providing an appropriate education to specific students with disabilities.

Among the factors to be considered is the need to place a child as close to home as possible [34 C.F.R. § 104.34]. When proposing a placement, schools must take the proximity factor into account. The parents' right to challenge their child's placement extends not only to placement in special classes or a separate school but also to placement in a distant school and, in particular, a residential placement. If an equally appropriate educational program exists closer to home, the parent or guardian may raise this LRE issue through a procedural due process hearing.

An appendix to Section 504's regulations clarifies them and provides that LEAs must show that the needs of the individual student with a disability would, on balance, be furthered by placement outside the regular education environment. For many students with disabilities, the most normal setting feasible is that which combines the use of special and regular classes. Education of students with disabilities, including those in public and private institutions and other care facilities, in the most normal setting feasible means educating them with nondisabled persons "to the maximum extent appropriate." It also means educating them as close to home as possible.

ADA Requirements

The ADA also is dedicated to the integration principle; it sets the goals of equal opportunity, full participation, independent living, and economic self-sufficiency for individuals, including students, with disabilities [42 U.S.C. § 12101(b)]. In short, ADA advances the concept of least restriction and maximum inclusion, requiring accommodations and opportunities to live in an integrated society.

Rebuttable Presumption

The statute and regulations clearly create a strong presumption in favor of integration; integration of students with disabilities into the general curriculum should occur "to the maximum extent appropriate." From the legislative history and the courts' interpretation, "appropriate" clearly is to be defined in terms of what is appropriate for the student with a disability.

The legislative history of IDEA's 1997 amendments provides further evidence that the LRE rule is a rebuttable presumption. The House Committee Report points out that, although the Congress supports the LRE rule, it also supports the "long-standing policy of a continuum of alternative placements designed to meet the unique needs of each child with a disability" (Committee Report, p. 91). These placements include instruction in regular classes, special classes, special schools, home instruction, and instruction in hospitals and institutions (Committee Report, p. 91). For students in general classes, supplemental aids and services and resource room services or itinerant instruction also must be offered as the students need them (Committee Report, p. 91).

The concept of a "continuum of services" is, in many respects, an escape clause. It allows a student to escape the hard-and-fast interpretation of LRE that would place the student in regular classrooms, regular extracurricular activities, and regular "other nonacademic activities"—all without regard to the student's unique needs for appropriate (that is, beneficial) special education and related services.

As the continuum provisions suggest, LRE's presumption in favor of integration can be overcome (rebutted). Sections 300.550-556 of IDEA's regulations speak to one of the most potentially troublesome aspects of placement in the least restrictive environment: placing students with disabilities into general programs without regard for their individual needs. Section 300.552 makes clear that each student's educational placement must be determined at least annually and must be based on his or her individualized education program; unless the student's IEP requires special alternative arrangements, the student must receive an education in the same school, as well as the same age-appropriate regular classroom, that he or she would attend were it not for the disability.

In selecting the least restrictive environment, however, any potentially harmful effect on the student or on the quality of services received is to be taken into consideration [34 C.F.R. § 300.552]. This is a focus on the student's needs for an appropriate education; when those needs cannot be met in a regular education program, the student's placement there will be inappropriate and restrictive of his or her rights to an appropriate education.

Moreover, if the student disrupts nondisabled students in the regular classroom to the extent that their education is significantly impaired, the student's needs cannot be met in that classroom and placement there is inappropriate [34 C.F.R. § 300.550(b)(2)]. Recall that this also is the approach used in expulsion cases and those involving students with AIDS (see Chapter 3).

Finally, Section 300.551 puts pressure on public agencies to develop appropriate alternative placements by requiring that the placement options include instruction in regular classes, special classes, special schools, home instruction, and instruction in hospitals and institutions. This is a policy judgment favoring a continuum of services in which each placement represents increasing degrees of separation from the general education curriculum. The LRE doctrine permits this policy choice.

LRE as a Rebuttable Presumption; Its Value Base ∿

LRE is especially value-laden because it promotes three sets of public policy values:

1. The value of an appropriate education for students with disabilities. LRE promotes this value because it creates a strong impetus toward inclusion of special education students into general education programs where their education thereby can be enhanced.
2. The value of conservation of political and fiscal capital. Equal access for students with disabilities to regular education also decreases the likelihood that unequal services (special education) will be thought to be politically untenable and fiscally unfeasible. Duplication of resources, especially in times of economic retrenchment, can be neither politically astute nor economical.
3. The First Amendment's right of freedom of association. This refers to the right of those with disabilities to associate with nondisabled people. The right of association is more than a constitutional imperative; it also is a positive force in broadening individual and cultural dimensions of the citizenry and dispelling stigmatizing and discriminatory attitudes toward people with disabilities. As stigma is less attributable to disability and as *de jure* and *de facto* discrimination recede accordingly, persons with disability acquire greater opportunity to pursue the constitutional value of liberty and choice in association.

A synthesis of these values is illustrated in Table 6.1 by a matrix in which the three basic levels of the policy interact with the two major value assumptions concerning appropriate education and the right of association to produce six dimensions of the LRE policy.

LRE, then, is both a legal principle and an educational strategy that, in combination with each other, circularly produce social effects. The legal principle assures that a student with a disability receives an appropriate education, and thereby the right to associate with nondisabled students and other citizens. As an educational

---

Table 6.1 ⌢
Dimensions of the LRE Policy

	Value Assumptions	
Value Assumptions	A. That individuals and societies benefit when all are educated to our fullest potential	B. That individuals and society benefit when all its members are free to associate with each other
Produce:		
Legal Principles *and*	1. Right to Education	4. Right to Association
Educational Strategies	2. Appropriate Education	5. Integration
Resulting in:		
Social Effects	3. Enhanced Individual Potential	6. Decreased Stigma

---

strategy, LRE enhances individual potential through appropriate education. Education, in turn, is thought to mitigate the effects of disability by decreasing stigma and thereby increasing associational rights, individual opportunity, and individual potential to contribute to the general welfare of society.

These six dimensions provide a framework to organize stated goals of IDEA and the LRE principle. The following list summarizes the goals of IDEA and its LRE component:

1. Right to education: to provide education to all students with disabilities.
2. Appropriate education: to provide every student an education that is appropriate to that student's unique strengths and weaknesses.
3. Enhanced individual potential: to provide the opportunity for students with disabilities to develop to their potential.
4. Right of association: to provide education in an environment that promotes association with nondisabled peers.
5. Integration: to provide the opportunity for nondisabled peers to develop sensitivity to individual differences, and to prepare the student with a disability for integration into regular education and society in general.
6. Decreased stigma: to enhance the social status of the student with a disability.

Given this understanding of the goals of LRE, a question is how these goals are to be implemented and how the value conflicts embedded in the goals can be resolved in practice. To resolve these questions, we have to return to the legal concept of LRE as a rebuttable presumption and to translate that principle into an educational strategy.

The relative restrictiveness of an educational environment ideally should be judged only in light of the individual educational need (right to an appropriate education) of each student with a disability. In light of that need, the most "normal" environment—even after it has been modified consistent with IDEA, Section 504, and ADA—still may not always be the least restrictive of the student's right to an appropriate program of education. To determine the least restrictive environment for a given student, three decisions must be made.

1. The NDE/IEP team must choose the range of available programs or environments to satisfy the student's requirements for an appropriate education. Conceivably, this might include more than one possible environment.
2. Decision makers, such as the IEP committee, ideally must identify the specific programs or environment, from the range of satisfactory ones, that can contribute most substantially to the student's freedom to interact with students who are not disabled.
3. The NDE/IEP team must decide (a) how to develop an individualized program that helps the student fit into the program or environment, and (b) how to change the program or environment so the student, with the benefit of an LRE-focused NDE, IEP, and other IDEA entitlements, may accommodate the student.

To repeat a constant theme of Chapters 5 and 6, the principle of dual accommodation requires mutual change—by the student and by the environment. Thus, when making a placement decision, priority is given to providing an appropriate education in an accommodating environment that minimizes infringement on the liberty to associate with nondisabled peers.

This principle is illustrated in Figure 6.1 (shown on page 260). Circle A represents the set of all appropriate educational programs or environments available for a given student with a disability. Circle B represents the set of all environments that allow the same student to interact with nondisabled peers. In an ideal case, circles A and B overlay one another perfectly or nearly perfectly (1A). More likely, they will overlap marginally, providing decision-makers with relatively fewer choices for placement (1B). Or they may not meet at all, even with accommodations, forcing decision-makers to choose environments entirely on the basis of what is available within circle A (1C).

In actuality, the problem is much more complex because the interests and needs of others (e.g., students with and without disabilities) enter the decision process (1D). Moreover, the decision of Congress to have a continuum of services complicates the choice because the continuum allows placement in segregated or special programs and thus reduces the likelihood that appropriate programs always will be developed within more, rather than less, integrated environments.

The Judicial Interpretation ~

Having established that LRE is a rebuttable presumption with a three-part value base and interlocking goals and strategies, we now will explore how the courts have interpreted this complex principle. Although the U.S. Supreme Court has not ruled

A = All possible educational environments capable of providing an education for an individual disabled child

B = All possible environments capable of maximizing freedom to associate with nondisabled peers

C = Needs of other interested parties

IA = numerous choices available to satisfy both A and B (ideal case)

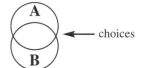
choices

IB = few choices available to A and B

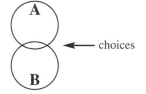
choices

IC = no available alternatives to satisfy needs of both A and

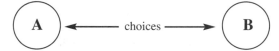
A ← choices → B

ID = complex decision process considering needs of A and B as well as other interested parties (C)

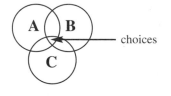
choices

Figure 6.1 〜
Choices for Maximizing LRE

directly on IDEA's LRE principle, other federal courts have. Indeed, the number of cases involving the interpretation and application of LRE principle is huge—and growing. Despite the absence of a definitive ruling by the nation's highest court, there are clear trends and a developing consensus regarding LRE's meaning.

The trend and consensus that had been developing in the courts, and culminating with the *Daniel R.R.* and *Holland* decisions (discussed fully below), now has been codified into IDEA, as this chapter will point out. Nonetheless, a review of the cases is useful, keeping in mind the statute's historical underpinnings. That is so because, despite IDEA's explicit provisions, controversy will remain: How should courts interpret them and apply them to a given student? The answers will come, in part, from the existing cases. Precedents are powerful. The answers also will come from the U.S. Department of Education's regulations.

First Wave: Either/or Choices

For the period between the enactment of IDEA in 1975 to the mid-1980s, the courts faced an unenviable task of interpreting and applying the LRE doctrine to a school system that had not yet developed a capacity, or arguably a willingness, to include students with disabilities in regular education programs.

In that (roughly) 10-year period, the courts were obliged to make a Hobbesian choice (one that would not be particularly good, no matter what the choice) between (a) ordering a school system to integrate a student with a disability into an unprepared and often resistant general education program, or (b) ordering the student to be placed into a special education program in which the professional staff generally was able and willing to provide an appropriate education—albeit one separate from the general education program in the school district.

Given this rather difficult choice—one that placed appropriateness above integration or another that placed integration above appropriateness—and also given that parents and professionals did not speak with a unanimous voice regarding integrated placements, the courts more often than not chose the placement that offered the more appropriate education. In making this choice, the courts seemed to say that the student's right to an appropriate education—which is a need-based right because it responds directly to the student's special education needs—is more important than the student's right to an LRE placement and interest in associating with nondisabled peers as a means for acquiring academic and other benefits.

In cases in which the student's need-based rights prevailed over the student's LRE rights, the right to an LRE placement was seen to be a means for securing an appropriate education. LRE itself was not regarded as an independent right but, rather, as an instrumental one, as an aide to the right to an appropriate education.

Moreover, in those same cases, the courts more often than not justified the separate non-LRE placement by taking into account the extent, not the nature of, the student's disability. It mattered a great deal whether the student experienced extensive impairments and had substantial education needs; it mattered very little whether the student was classified into any one of the special education categories (Turnbull et al., 1983).

For nearly 10 years, the schools' capacities, parents' attitudes, students' needs, and courts' interpretation of the LRE rule interacted to create a body of case law that favored overall the more separate and less typical placement. During this phase of law development, the courts essentially took what was offered to them: an arguably inappropriate but integrated program, or an arguably appropriate but separate program. Theirs was a relatively passive role in that they simply reacted to the programs the schools offered; they did not require the schools to take any action to make the general education program both appropriate and inclusive.

Moving Out of the First Wave

Not until 1983 did a federal court recognize that it had the power to use the LRE doctrine in a far more proactive, corrective way. In that year, however, the Sixth Circuit Court of Appeals, in *Roncker v. Walter* (1983), rejected the traditional "take it or leave it" attitude that had characterized the earlier choice between integration or appropriateness and converted the LRE doctrine into a proactive force for school reform.

In *Roncker,* the court was faced with a relatively clear-cut factual situation. The state of Ohio had operated a dual system of schools for many years. One system served only those students who were classified as having severe to profound disabilities; the other served students who were classified as having mild disabilities and those who had none. When a student classified as having "trainable mental retardation" sought to attend the "mild/nondisabled" system, the LEA rejected the student's application. The issue, then, was whether the court would simply acquiesce to the school district's "take it or leave it" approach, which was based on classification by extent of disability, or whether it would use the LRE doctrine as the rationale for ordering the "mild/nondisabled" system to change its ways. Following the trend of the cases to date, the trial court adhered to the "take it or leave it" approach.

Upon appeal, the Sixth Circuit reversed the trial court and ordered that the student be enrolled in the more integrated system. In reaching this result, the court established a new standard, or "test," for determining a student's placement. Sometimes called the "feasibility" test and sometimes called the "portability" test, the standard fundamentally requires the school system to take positive, affirmative steps to modify its general education curriculum so the student will be able to receive an appropriate education (one that complies with Rowley's "benefit" standard) in a more typical, more integrated setting.

Roncker and the "Feasibility-Portability" Test

The court of appeals observed a strong congressional preference for integration in IDEA's requirement that a student with a disability be educated with nondisabled students to the maximum extent appropriate. The first step in analyzing the inclusion doctrine, the court stated, is to determine whether the student's proposed placement is appropriate under IDEA. The next step is to consider whether the placement is in the least restrictive environment.

Acknowledging that these two different values (appropriate education and least restrictive environment/most typical placement) can be in conflict, the court noted that a placement that may be considered better for academic reasons may, however, fail to comply with the LRE rule. The perception that a segregated school system facility or institution is academically superior for a student with a disability, said the court, may reflect no more than a basic disagreement with the LRE concept. Such a disagreement is not, of course, a basis for not following IDEA's LRE mandate. Professional and parental disagreements with IDEA's mandates do not override congressional intent.

Furthermore, the court declared, when deciding whether a segregated facility is superior to a more inclusive environment, a court should determine whether the services that make the separate placement superior could be feasibly provided in an inclusive environment. If those services can be provided in a more inclusive setting, the placement in the segregated school is inappropriate under IDEA.

Framing the issue in this manner, the court said, accords the proper respect for the strong preference in favor of the LRE rule while still realizing the possibility that (a) some students with disabilities simply must be educated in segregated facilities either because the student will not benefit from mainstreaming or because any marginal benefits received from a more integrated placement are far outweighed by the benefits gained from services that could not feasibly be provided in the nonsegregated setting, or (b) the student is a disruptive force in the nonsegregated setting.

The court's use of the term "feasible" is, of course, the basis for the "feasibility" test: If it is possible (i.e., feasible) for the school to replicate the services that assure benefit (appropriate education) in the more integrated setting, the school system must do so. That is to say, it must "transport" the beneficial services from one setting to another; hence, the "portability" test.

Notice, however, that (a) the court recognized limits as to what is feasible, and (b) it did not require wholesale "portability." If the student would receive no or only little benefit from the more integrated system, or if the student's placement there would be disruptive to the education of other students (both those with and without disabilities), the more separate setting is still permissible. Despite its "safety valves" (no or little benefit, or disruptiveness), the "feasibility" and "portability" test put real force behind the LRE doctrine and established a much different mind-set for other courts to follow.

First, the test put pressure on the school system to make accommodations. In that respect, it turned the "take it or leave it" choice on its head in two respects:

1. By declaring that a court should use the LRE doctrine in a proactive, change-oriented way;
2. By compelling the schools to make accommodations that they previously had escaped having to make.

Congress' presumption in favor of integration must be honored; it cannot be honored if courts simply take what schools have decided to provide, and indeed it can be honored only with some judicial force behind the presumption, some power to make it come alive for students. *Roncker,* then, converted the LRE doctrine into a force for change.

Second, the test created a different mind-set in that it instructed other courts that they should be more forceful in attempting to reconcile the appropriate education doctrine with the LRE doctrine; they should refuse to simply "take it or leave it" (a posture in which they would not attempt to reconcile IDEA's two commands) and, instead, should seek ways to make IDEA's two commands mutually consistent. When Congress has created a presumption in favor of integration, the proper role of the courts is to enforce that presumption, even if doing so turns them into activist agents for change.

Roncker and Cost

Recognizing that "feasibility" and "portability" will impose a host of financial obligations on a school system, that school budgets have limits, and that other students have interests in having IDEA enforced on their behalf, the court also held that cost is a factor to consider because excessive spending on one student may deprive other students of services. Cost is no defense, however, if the school district has failed to use its funds to provide a proper continuum of alternative placements for students with disabilities. If a district does not provide a continuum-based alternative to an integrated appropriate program, it may not complain about the cost of modifying the integrated one.

The "cost-is-a-consideration" approach can be criticized on the basis that it permits a school district to raise a defense that the cost is too high to comply with the feasibility or portability test. Although it is true that cost is a defense, it also is true that the cost of complying with the feasibility or portability test should be amortized over a number of students and over a period of time.

Stated alternatively, a school district that raises a cost defense in a case involving one student may be able to show that, for this one student, costs of appropriate education in an LRE program are indeed high. The answer, however, is to think beyond that one student. The student seeking enrollment in a beneficial (appropriate) and integrated (LRE) program should answer the cost defense by saying that expenditures that benefit him or her now also will benefit other students later; the student "amortizes" costs over other benefited students and over time.

Other cases also discuss cost as a consideration in balancing the student's right to an appropriate education against the right to an integrated education. For example, in *A.W. v. Northwest R-1 School District* (1987), the Eighth Circuit Court of Appeals upheld a lower court decision to place a student with severe mental retardation into a segregated program. The district court concluded that no certified teacher was available for the student in an integrated program and that the addition of such a teacher was not an acceptable solution because of limited funds. The court stated that

> the funds available are limited so that placing a [certified] teacher [in the integrated setting] for the benefit of a few students at best, and possibly only one child [A.W.], would directly reduce the educational benefits provided to other handicapped students by increasing the number of students taught by a single teacher [in the segregated setting].

To educate that one child in an integrated setting creates a benefit for that child, but the benefit is "insufficient to justify a reduction in unquestionable benefits to other handicapped children which would result from an inequitable expenditure of the finite funds available." As in *Roncker,* the court considered the cost to the district and the benefit to the child (a cost-benefit approach) and reiterated that available financial resources must be distributed equitably among all students with disabilities.

The *Roncker* approach is valid for two reasons.

1. It forces courts to make a decision based on the student's rights to both an appropriate education and an inclusive environment for that education. It is a student-centered approach that focuses on individualized determinations, consistent with the IDEA's overall approach.
2. It forces the courts to look into what can be done to modify the otherwise inappropriate integrated setting. Thus, the LEA must show why an inclusive setting cannot be modified or accommodated to the student.

Under this approach, the schools bear the burden of proof that an inclusive setting (that is, the student's right to an integrated, least restrictive education) cannot possibly satisfy the "educational benefit" standard of *Rowley* (the student's right to an appropriate education). To put the burden on the school district to show why it cannot "feasibly" make the appropriate-education services "portable" is entirely consistent with LRE as a rebuttable presumption. IDEA presumes that the more integrated setting is the appropriate one. The schools must rebut that presumption by showing that, for a particular student, transporting the appropriate education services to the least restrictive setting is not feasible.

Second Wave: *Daniel R.R.*

Roncker marked the end of the first wave of "take it or leave it" cases, those that regarded the extent of a student's disability as dispositive of where the student would be educated. It also marked the transition from the first wave to the second wave of cases. With *Roncker* as a precedent, courts continued to put pressure on the schools to reconcile the appropriate education and LRE doctrines. In doing so, they began to view the LRE doctrine more expansively and require schools to make greater accommodations.

The most significant of these second-wave cases arose from the Fifth Circuit Court of Appeals. *Daniel R.R. v. State Bd. of Educ.* (1989) involved a 6-year-old boy with Down syndrome whom the LEA proposed to place in its segregated special education early childhood class. The parents requested that the LEA place their son in the segregated program for half of the day and an integrated pre-kindergarten general education class for the remainder of the day. The federal district court sided with the LEA, and the court of appeals affirmed that decision, agreeing that the LEA's refusal to remove the student from the special education academic program was not a violation of IDEA. The court of appeals rested its decision on the finding that the student could not receive an educational benefit in the general education program.

Despite the result in the *Daniel R.* case, the court of appeals actually opened up the avenue for that student and others to be included in general education. It did so in two different ways.

1. It observed and approved of the fact that, although the LEA had tried to accommodate the student in general education and had modified the curriculum "almost beyond recognition," and that the LEA did provide the student

with opportunities to eat lunch in the school cafeteria with nondisabled students on 3 days of the week (provided his mother was present to supervise him) and to have contact with nondisabled student during school recess.

2. It declined to follow the Roncker "feasibility" standard, finding that that standard "necessitates too intrusive an inquiry into the educational policy choices that Congress deliberately left to state and local school officials." Determining what is "feasible" is an administrative decision that "state and local officials are far better qualified to make than we (the court) are." But it also declined to follow the narrow "academic benefits" approach that the lower court used.

The problem with the lower court's standard—basically, whether the student can receive only an academic benefit—is twofold:

1. As a prerequisite to placement in a general education program, it requires a court to find that students with disabilities can "learn at approximately the same level as their nonhandicapped classmates."
2. The standard places "too much emphasis on the student's ability to achieve an education benefit."

The court of appeals noted that some students with disabilities may not be able to master as much of the general education curriculum as their nondisabled peers.

> This does not mean, however, that those [students with disabilities] are not receiving any benefit from general education. Nor does it mean that they are not receiving all of the benefit that their handicapping condition will permit. If the child's individual needs make mainstreaming appropriate, we cannot deny the child access to regular education simply because his educational achievement lags behind that of his classmates.

In short, placement in the least restrictive environment of general education is legally required for students with disabilities who can receive some, though not the full, benefit of such a placement. This result casts a somewhat different light on the LRE standard: Some, but not exactly equal, benefit justifies regular education placement.

Moreover, the court of appeals found that placement in the general education program "may have benefits in and of itself." The student may learn appropriate language and behavior from nondisabled peers; and the fact that the student may receive benefit from "nonacademic experiences in the regular education environment" must be taken into account when LEAs and parents make placement decisions.

To comply with the presumption in favor of a regular education placement, then, the court of appeals laid down a two-part test.

1. Can education in the general program be achieved satisfactorily with the use of supplemental aids and services? This first prong of the test requires a court to make four separate and sequential findings:

   a. Has the LEA taken steps to accommodate the student in general education? Has it provided supplementary aids and services? Has it attempted to modify the general education program? If the answers to these questions are "no," the LEA has violated IDEA. If the answers are "yes," the issue then is whether the LEA's efforts are "sufficient": Are they "mere token gestures?" If so, the LEA must do more, though it need not provide "every conceivable supplementary aid or service." The supplemental aids requirement has limits, as the LEA is not required to provide every possible service (see *Greer v. Rome City Sch. Dist.,* 1990; Harmon v. Mead School District No. 354, 1991). Nor does the LEA have to require regular educators to "devote all or most of their time" to the student with a disability. And it need not excuse the student from learning "any of the skills normally taught in regular education." Merely "sitting next to a nonhandicapped student" is not conferring a benefit to the student with a disability.

   b. Will the student receive an educational benefit from general education? To answer this, the court must pay "close attention" to the "nature and severity" of the student's disability and to the "curriculum and goals of the regular education class." If the LEA determines that:

   (1) the student will make significantly more progress in a self-contained special education environment; and

   (2) education in a regular classroom may cause the student to fall behind his or her peers with disabilities who are being educated in the self-contained environment, an LRE placement may not be appropriate because it actually may be detrimental to the student, depriving him or her of an appropriate education. But the court also must extend its inquiry beyond only the educational benefits of a placement.

   c. Accordingly, the next question is whether the student's "overall educational experience" in general education confers other than purely academic benefits. "(E)ven if the child cannot flourish academically," his or her benefit from "language models that his nonhandicapped peers provide him" may justify the regular education placement.

   d. Finally, what is the effect of the student's placement in the regular education environment and the education of other students? Behavior that disrupts the education of others may justify placement out of the general program. Also, if the student requires "so much" of the time of a teacher or an aide that the "rest of the class suffers," placement out of general education is justified.

2. If, after answering these questions, the court determines that education in the general education classroom or program cannot be achieved satisfactorily, it must determine whether the LEA has integrated the student into the general education program "to the maximum extent appropriate." The LEA must offer a "continuum of services" and "must take intermediate steps where appropriate," such as placing the student in regular education for some academic classes and in special education for others, enrolling the student in nonacademic (as distinguished from academic) regular education classes, or providing interaction with nondisabled peers during lunch or recess.

Daniel R. is a paradoxical case: It approved the special education placement of the student, but it set out a legal standard that accommodates a "mix-and-match" approach. Under that approach, an individualized decision must be made about how to increase both academic and nonacademic integration. The LEA must "mix" the academic and nonacademic opportunities in the general education program and "match" the student's abilities to those opportunities, all the while offering supplementary aids and services to promote integration.

In applying this two-part test, the burden of proving compliance with IDEA is placed on the school district no matter which party initiates the complaint [*Oberti v. Bd. of Educ. of the Borough of Clementon Sch. Dist.* 995 F.2d 1204 (3rd Cir. 1993)].

Not only is *Daniel R.* paradoxical, but it also is broadly visionary and highly prescriptive. Unlike *Roncker,* the broad vision of *Daniel R.* looks at both academic and nonacademic benefits. It thus acknowledges two "values" of integration: (a) the student's appropriate (academic) education (benefit), and (b) the student's opportunity to associate with and learn from nondisabled peers.

Unlike *Roncker, Daniel R.* set out highly specific inquiries that a court must make to determine whether a student's placement is consistent with the dual commands of IDEA that the student must receive an appropriate (beneficial) education and one that is delivered in the least restrictive, most typical setting possible, with the use of supplementary aids and services. Rather than relying on an arguably vague standard of "feasibility" or "portability" per the *Roncker* approach, the *Daniel R.* case provides courts and educators with highly individualized fact-finding guidelines.

Concluding the Second Wave: *Holland*

In 1992, yet another federal court of appeals set out specific criteria for determining whether a student's placement into general or special education is consistent with IDEA. In *Bd. of Educ. v. Holland* (1994), the Ninth Circuit Court of Appeals held that a 9-year old student with moderate mental retardation is entitled to be placed in all academic and nonacademic regular education programs. Several factors led the court to this result: The student consistently demonstrated good behavior and was not disruptive to other students in a regular classroom; she was popular and eager to learn; she learned by imitating and modeling her nondisabled peers; her IEP goals were consistent with the first-grade curriculum; and the cost of placing her in a regular classroom with supplemental aids was not excessive.

In consideration of these facts about this student and of IDEA's presumption in favor of general program placement, the court set out four tests for determining whether a placement is appropriate:

1. What are the educational benefits of a regular classroom placement, with supplementary aids and services, as compared to the educational benefits of a special education classroom? A court and LEA must determine whether the

student's disabilities are "so severe that he or she will receive little or no academic benefit" from regular class placement. Indeed, even if the special class placement is superior academically to the regular class placement, IDEA does not require the "best academic setting" for the student, only an appropriate one. Moreover, to ensure benefit in the regular class, the LEA must provide supplementary aids and services.

2. What are the nonacademic benefits to the student from "interaction" with nondisabled peers? A court and LEA must determine whether a student "may benefit from language and behavior models provided by nonhandicapped children." Likewise, improved self-esteem and increased motivation through general class placement must be taken into account. If nonacademic benefits flow from the regular class placement, it, not the special class placement, is appropriate and least restrictive.

3. What are the "possible negative effects" of regular class placement? If the student is disruptive to other students or "unreasonably" occupies the teacher's time "to the detriment of other students," the regular placement is not appropriate. A student who "merely requires more teacher attention than most students is not likely to be so disruptive as to significantly impair the education of other children." Moreover, the LEA must "keep in mind its obligation" to provide supplementary aids and services, minimizing the "burden on the teacher." The "disruptive" factor "weighs against" general education placement "only if, after taking all reasonable steps to reduce the burden to the teacher, the other children in the class will still be deprived of their share of the teacher's attention."

4. What are the costs involved in accommodating placement? This is a proper consideration, the LEA having to "balance" the needs of each student with a disability against the needs of the other students in the school district. If the cost of educating a student with a disability in a regular classroom is "so great that it would significantly impact upon the education of other children in the district, then education in the regular classroom is not appropriate."

Holland seems to summarize the factors that the *Roncker* and *Daniel R.* courts took into account: (1) academic benefit, (2) nonacademic benefit, (3) disruption, and (4) cost. More than that, it reaffirms the significant criterion of the *Daniel R.* case— namely, that the LRE principle presumes that academic and nonacademic benefits alike are available in the general education program and that both types of benefits must be made available to the student, consistent with the interests of other students to be free of disruption and to have access to a reasonable sum of money for their own educational benefit. To date, *Holland* stands as the most comprehensive statement of the ways in which the appropriate education and LRE principles can be made mutually consistent. It is not the only case, however, that raises significant integration/LRE issues.

Other Cases in Second Wave

Failure to plan for accommodations

Other courts have embraced inclusive education placements for students under IDEA, but under different facts and with different rationale. For example, in *Hendricks v. Gilhool* (1989), the court ruled that a separate placement violates the LRE rule when (a) the separate schools and programs are not comparable to those in the general education programs, (b) relocations of students with disabilities to accommodate an unexpected influx of nondisabled students were disruptive to the students' education, (c) restrictive special settings were the only ones offered to children with mild and moderate disabilities (but were legal when offered to students with severe disabilities), and (d) the LEA failed to create new classrooms to accommodate special education students.

The *Hendricks* court seemed most concerned that disparate and unfavorable treatment was the order of the day for children with disabilities. There is no reason to think that the principle of this case will be discarded under the 1997 amendments to IDEA, which (along with Section 504) requires physical accommodations; it remains good law.

The associational trump

In *Hulme v. Dellmuth* (1991), the LEA wanted to change the placement of a 14-year-old student with low-mild, high-moderate mental retardation and cerebral palsy from the school for orthopedically impaired students (where his parents wanted him to be retained) to a general-education high school. The student was not orthopedically impaired, and the district acknowledged that the special school was its most restrictive placement. His progress there had enabled him, in the judgment of the district's experts, to function in a school setting with nondisabled students, with age-appropriate peers, and with necessary support services (speech, occupational therapy, and transportation).

In agreeing with the school district and ordering the student's removal from the special school, the court placed a great deal of weight on the "associational rights" approach: "In a mainstream environment, [the student] will be able to interact with nondisabled peers and thus enhance his life support and social interaction skills." (See also *Liscio v. Woodland Hills Sch. Dist.,* 1989; *Gillette v. Fairland Bd. of Educ.,* 1989).

Likewise, *Chris D. v. Montgomery County Board of Education* (1990) used an "associational rights" approach, but with an unexpected, yet defensible result. There, the court held that a residential program is preferable to a homebound program for a student with severe emotional disabilities. The student required extensive positive behavioral support and training in adult and peer relationships. Without these services he was unable to obtain an educational benefit.

The court determined that homebound education was the most restrictive placement because it provided only an isolated, sterile environment that hindered the student's educational progress and provided no opportunity for the student to apply newly learned techniques so he could return to a general education environment. Therefore, the court determined that the residential placement offered the least restrictive environment.

As in *Chris D.,* it is in other cases: The LEA is not the party that favors a more restrictive placement; it is the parents. In *Wall v. Mattituck-Cutchogue Sch. Dist.* (1996), the federal district court approved the LEA's placement in regular education for science, English, art, music, library, physical education, and homeroom; and in a self-contained fifth-grade classroom for reading, social studies, spelling, and math. After the student experienced difficulty in English, the IEP team removed the student from only the regular education English placement.

Because the student was having difficulty socializing at school and was the subject of teasing and taunting, the parents unilaterally placed their child at a private school for children with learning disabilities and sued for reimbursement. The court denied reimbursement, holding that the student was receiving an educational benefit in the LEA; his test scores indicated that he was making progress and his abilities were within the range of the other students. Although the student had experienced some difficulty with another student, this alone is not sufficient to require a more restrictive placement. Furthermore, accommodating a parent's ideal educational program is beyond the scope of IDEA.

Because these cases all rest on the rights to association and because the 1997 amendments to IDEA place such an emphasis on the student's participation in not just academic but also extracurricular and other school activities, where the association between students with and without disabilities will occur, these cases will continue to be good law.

Neighborhood schools

IDEA's regulations state that "[t]he educational placement of each child with a disability [shall be] as close as possible to the child's home" [34 C.F.R. § 300.552(b)(3)]. Furthermore, regulation § 300.552(c) provides that "[u]nless the IEP of a child with a disability requires some other arrangement, the child [is to be] educated in the school that he or she would attend if nondisabled." Many parents who are unhappy with their child's non-local placement have argued that their child should be educated in his or her neighborhood school. They have met with little success. The federal circuit courts that have examined this issue agree that these regulations do not require a student with a disability to be educated in the neighborhood school. The leading early case is *Barnett v. Fairfax County School Bd.* (1991), and the most recent is *Murray v. Montrose County School Dist.* (1995).

Murray held that IDEA does not create a presumption that the least restrictive environment is in the student's neighborhood school with supplementary aids and services. The parents argued that § 1412 (a)(5) implicitly includes neighborhood schools and that "separate schooling" means non-neighborhood schools. The court disagreed: Although IDEA mandates that the student be educated in the least restrictive environment, it does not specify where such inclusion should take place.

Furthermore, IDEA's regulations provide that a student should be educated in the neighborhood school unless the student's IEP requires placement elsewhere. If placement elsewhere is required, the LEA must consider the proximity of a particular placement as only one factor (see also *Flour Bluff Indep. School Dist. v. Katherine M.* (1996)).

In making decisions in the neighborhood school cases, the courts balance several factors: the student's needs, the student's opportunities to benefit academically and by association with nondisabled peers, the LEA's right to make administrative and fiscal decisions that affect students' placements, the LEA's need to conserve fiscal resources by operating highly intensive (needs-responsive) programs where there is a critical mass of similarly needy (disabled) students, and the fact that LRE is a rebuttable presumption, not an iron-clad rule of conduct.

The 1997 amendments to IDEA should change, to a degree, the results in the neighborhood school cases. That is so because the amendments place a great deal more power behind the LRE principle and behind using every conceivable connection between the student and the school—nondiscriminatory evaluations, IEPs, specification of the location of services, participation in statewide and districtwide assessments, and so on—to advance the LRE principle for each student. As the amendments are implemented, LEAs may have to accommodate even more to students with disabilities in a location near their homes (they certainly should do so) and resort less and less to the centralized, non-neighborhood programs that the courts approved before 1997.

The harmful effects issue (competing equities)

As noted already, IDEA excuses LRE from being applied to a student who cannot be educated satisfactorily in general programs or schools, even with supplementary aids and services. This is the harmful effects standard. The harmful effect of integrating the student with a disability is a legitimate concern.

Likewise, the harmful effect of integration on nondisabled students is a legitimate concern. The comments of the U.S. Department of Education regarding Section 504 regulations state that schools may place the special education student outside of general education if placement in a general classroom would significantly impair the education of nondisabled children.

As Chapter 3 demonstrates, this balancing approach—benefit versus harm to self or others—is precisely the approach adopted in *Honig* and in the AIDS cases. Both of these harmful-effects criteria reflect a more general "competing equities" concern: To what extent should some students be disadvantaged to give advantage to others and thus accommodate the LRE rule? An SEA's or LEA's responsibilities extend to all students, not just one; if placing a student with a disability in a program with nondisabled children affects the education of the latter negatively, SEA or LEA responsibilities to those students are compromised.

The 1997 amendments related to discipline make clear that "harmful effects" and "competing equities" are major concerns (see Chapter 3). That is why the amendments address issues of weapons and drugs and why they also have a special provision regarding students whose behavior impedes their learning and that of other students. Building on *Honig* but refining it, the amendments strike a balance between the competing interests of all students (and staff)—a balance that some will quarrel with in its abstract form and many will litigate as it is applied. The last word about harmful effects and competing equities has not yet been written.

Prediction and placement

Most of the cases relying on the harmful effects exception have involved students whose education in less restrictive programs has been demonstrably unsatisfactory. Evidence of "no benefit" was so compelling as to require the students to be placed in a more restrictive (less integrated) program or school. The more normal placements or programs were more restrictive because they were less beneficial for these students.

These cases raise a disturbing question: Must students always be subjected to experiences (placements or programs) in which they predictably will not be educated satisfactorily before they can be placed in more restrictive programs? Or will educators, related services personnel, and parents be able to place a child in the less integrated placements or programs on the basis of reasonable, professionally defensible expectations and projections? In *DeWalt v. Burkholder* (1980), the clear answer is that professionally defensible predictions are permissible foundations for placements; the risk of unsatisfactory integration does not have to be undertaken.

Educability, expulsion, and cessation of services: not an LRE option

Unlike the harmful effects cases, which are statutorily grounded in appropriate education/LRE concepts, cases involving the attempted exclusion of allegedly ineducable students or students with contagious diseases and the attempted expulsion of students with disabilities because of disciplinary reasons rely on statutory zero-reject principles (see Chapter 3). These cases, however, are well positioned within the LRE ambit.

The most restrictive educational placement, after all, is outside any educational program: total exclusion of the purest kind. The most restrictive permissible placement is necessarily one within the continuum (i.e., within a free appropriate education, wherever furnished), not outside it. Exclusion and cessation of services are not options. They are, by definition, too restrictive. The 1997 amendments make that point entirely clear.

Conclusion 〰

Of all the IDEA issues, two have produced the greatest consternation among all persons interested in the education of students with disabilities. One, of course, is the matter of expulsion and cessation of services (see Chapter 3). The other is the matter of placement that is both beneficial (meets the "benefit" test of *Rowley*) and inclusive (meets the LRE requirements).

Neither of these issues has been resolved readily or quickly. Each required, and still requires, a considerable amount of litigation. Interestingly, each poses rather similar considerations, though they seemingly are unrelated to each other.

One common issue has to do with placement itself. When a student whose behavior violates school codes, is unlawful, or is harmful to self or others, is subjected to school-initiated discipline, the issue of suspension or expulsion necessarily involves placement. May the school place the student into a less typical, more restricted, or supervised program? May it even expel the student, thereby causing a total cessation of services? The answers (as Chapter 3 makes clear) depend on whether the behavior is a manifestation of the student's disability.

If the behavior is a manifestation of the disability, the student may be replaced but may not be subjected to a total cessation of services. If the behavior is not a manifestation, the law now is settled that, even though a student may be subjected to the same discipline as a student who does not have a disability, the student is entitled to continue to receive special education and related services. There is to be no cessation of services—not for the student covered by the manifestation rule and not for the student who is not covered by it. That result overrules the decision in the *Riley* case, but it continues to connect behavior and placement to the expulsion/discipline cases.

Moreover, behavior and placement are related in the LRE cases. This is so because the LRE rule allows a school to take into account, when it is making a placement decision, the student's behavior as a factor that impedes the education of either the student himself or herself, or the education of other students.

The student's attributes are related to placement in yet another way. Under the LRE rule, the student's ability to benefit from the services offered, even when the services are augmented by supplementary aids and services, is a determinant of placement. If the student is not able to benefit—academically or otherwise—from an augmented placement, the school may place the student into a program that is more intensive and usually less typical and more restrictive than is available to nondisabled peers or even to some peers with disabilities.

In still one other way the student's attributes are related to placement. For a student who arguably is "uneducable," the placement decision depends on the student's capacities to learn even the most rudimentary skills. The school may not exclude that student wholly from programs that it operates or pays for; instead, it must continue to provide some beneficial services. Thus, student attributes influence student placements and school decisions about the intensiveness and typicality of services.

The interstitial connections between the zero-reject rule, the appropriate education rule, and the LRE are but one aspect of the whole matter of student placement. They demonstrate how interrelated are matters of school obligations and student rights and needs. The 1997 amendments make that interrelatedness explicit by linking the nondiscriminatory evaluation to the IEP and by providing, in both the NDE and appropriate education principles, that evaluation and programming must advance the student's right to be in all three domains of the general curriculum, on a full-time or part-time basis (the "mix and match" and "full/partial" inclusion approaches).

Nowhere were these connections more litigated than in the situation where a student's needs—that is, the extent (but not the nature) of the student's disabilities—are such that the school's duty to provide an appropriate education apparently conflicts with its duty to do so in the least restrictive, most typical, most integrated program.

In meeting the challenge to comply simultaneously with two apparently different and arguably conflicting duties, courts developed increasingly greater willingness to require schools to develop a capacity to meet these two obligations at the same time. For nearly a decade after IDEA was enacted in 1975, courts took into account the extent of the student's disability and, if the extent were so great that the student would receive some benefit in a less typical, less integrated setting or program, they opted for that placement over one where, with accommodations, the student could benefit and would do so in an integrated setting. In this "take-it-or-leave-it" posture the extent of the student's disability was decisive and courts usually did not require schools to accommodate the student in a regular education program.

Beginning with the *Roncker* decision, the courts began to be more assertive and less compliant with LEA-proffered "either-or" choices. That is to say, they began to require the schools to specially justify a less typical, more restrictive placement. Thus, *Roncker* established the "feasibility" and "portability" standard and put pressure on the schools to adapt their general program to students with disabilities.

Thereafter, *Daniel R.* required schools to take into account the student's right to associate with nondisabled students, and it thus broadened the decision-making process to include more than academic factors. In its last iteration, the LRE rule, as interpreted in *Holland,* requires a four-part calculus: (1) academic benefit to the student, (2) nonacademic benefit to the student, (3) negative effects of the LRE placement on the student and other students and staff, and (4) cost of LRE placement.

In *Holland,* the first standard (academic benefit, in which the extent of the student's needs are considered) essentially adopts the type of analysis the courts used in the first decade after IDEA was enacted (the "needs over integration" approach). The second standard (nonacademic benefit) essentially uses the *Daniel R.* approach. The third standard (negative effects on student and others) takes into account the appropriate education claims not only of the particular student but of others as well, reflects *Roncker's* concerns, is grounded in the LRE exception that is part of IDEA and Section 504, and adopts the "balancing" approach that the expulsion, contagious disease, and tuition reimbursement cases use (see Chapter 3). The fourth and final standard (costs) picks up some of the *Roncker* approach (limitations to feasibility and portability) and constitutes still another form of balancing competing claims.

IDEA's 1997 amendments codify the *Daniel R.R.* and *Holland* decisions. They take into account that a student will participate in the academic, extracurricular, and other nonacademic programs, thereby picking up the first two parts of the *Holland* calculus. Through the discipline provisions, they also pick up the third part of the calculus. And, by removing a disincentive to more restrictive placements and by replacing the head-count formula for state allotments with one based on census and poverty, they also affect the final part of the calculus, although they do not prohibit LEAs from raising cost-based defenses and courts from responding to those defenses.

If the 1997 amendments have a solid bottom line, it is that "full participation"—"inclusion" and LRE policy—is stronger than ever.

Notes ⌐

1. For early cases establishing the right to the least restrictive environment or interventions, see *Shelton v. Tucker,* 364 (U.S. 479, 1960), *Covington v. Harris,* 419 F. 2d 617 (D.C. Cir., 1969), *Halderman v. Pennhurst State School and Hosp.,* 446 F. Supp. 1295 (E.D. Pa., 1977), *Jackson v. Indiana,* 406 (U.S. 715, 1972), *Lessard v. Schmidt,* 349 F. Supp. 1078 (E.D. Wis., 1972), *Wyatt v. Stickney,* 344 F. Supp. 373, 387, 396 (M.D. Ala., 1972), *New York ARC v. Rockefeller,* 357 F. Supp. 752 (E.D.N.Y., 1973), *Welsch v. Likens,* 373 F. Supp. 487 (D. Minn., 1974), *Dixon v. Weinberger,* 405 F. Supp. 974 (D.D.C., 1975), *O'Connor v. Donaldson,* 422 (U. S. 563, 1975), *Lake v. Cameron,* 364 F. 2d 657 (D.C. Cir., 1966), and *Youngberg v. Romeo,* 457 (U.S. 307, 1982).

   These cases involved civil commitment to, treatment in, and release from state psychiatric or developmental disabilities centers and, on the whole, created restrictions on civil commitment and treatment and established rights to treatment or release.

   Some also became precedents for application of the doctrine of the least restrictive alternative to the education of students with disabilities, as in *PARC v. Commonwealth,* 334 F. Supp. 1257, 343 F. Supp. 279 (E.D. Pa., 1971, 1972), *Mills v. D.C. Board of Education,* 348 F. Supp. 866 (D.D.C., 1972), and *Maryland Association for Retarded Children v. Maryland,* Equity No. 100/182/77676 (Cir. Ct. Baltimore Co., 1974).

   In 1992, in *Heller v. Doe,* 509 U.S. 312 (1992), a case involving Tennessee's civil commitment laws, the U.S. Supreme Court ruled that a state is not required to use the least restrictive means for involuntarily committing persons who have mental retardation as long as the state's choice of commitment procedures and standards is rationally related to its purpose of providing treatment for the committed person or of assuring that the committed person does not pose a danger to others. The case is problematic for the doctrine of the least restrictive alternative because it signals a retreat from application of the doctrine and, thus, the early disability-law cases rest on shaky grounds. As of Fall, 1999, the Court has not relied on the *Heller* language in subsequent cases involving persons with disabilities.

2. D. Chambers, "Alternatives to Civil Commitment of the Mentally Ill: Practical Guides and Constitutional Imperatives," 70 *Michigan Law Review* 1108 (1972). See also H. R. Turnbull, editor, *The Least Restrictive Alternative: Principles and Practices* (Washington, DC, American Association on Mental Retardation, 1981).

3. See, e.g., *Dean Milk v. City of Madison,* 340 (U.S. 349, 1951), and *Toomer v. Witsell,* 334 (U.S. 385, 1948).

4. See, e.g., *Dunn v. Blumstein,* 405 (U.S. 330, 1972) (voting rights), *U.S. v. Robel,* 389 U.S. 258 (1967), and *NAACP v. Button,* 371 U.S. 415 (1963) (freedom of association), *Griswold v. Connecticut,* 381 (U.S. 479, 1965) (right of privacy), *Abtheker v. Sec'y. of State,* 378 U.S. 500 (1964) (right to travel), and *Talley v. California,* 362 (U.S. 60, 1960) (right to free speech).

Reference ~

Turnbull, H. R. et al. (1983). "A Policy Analysis of "Least Restrictive" Education of Handicapped Children." *Rutgers Law Journal* 14(3), 489–540.

Cases ~

A.W. v. Northwest R-1 Sch. Dist., 813 F.2d 158 (8th Cir. 1987), cert. denied, 484 U.S. 847 (1987).

Barnett v. Fairfax County School. Bd., 721 F. Supp. 757 (E.D. Va. 1989), aff'd, 927 F.2d 847 (4th Cir. 1991), cert. denied, 502 U.S. 859 (1991).

Bd. of Educ. v. Holland, 4 F.3d 1398 (9th Cir. 1994).

Board of Education v. Rowley, 458 U.S. 176 (1982).

Chris D. v. Montgomery County Bd. of Educ., 16 EHLR 1182 (M.D. Ala. 1990).

Daniel R.R. v. State Bd. of Educ., 874 F.2d 1036 (5th Cir. 1989).

DeWalt v. Burkholder, EHLR 551:550 (E.D. Va. 1980).

Flour Bluff Indep. Sch. Dist. v. Katherine M., 91 F.3d 689 (5th Cir. 1996), cert. denied, 117 S.Ct. 948 (U.S. 1997).

Gillette v. Fairland Bd. of Educ., 725 F. Supp. 343 (S.D. Ohio 1989), appeal dismissed, 895 F.2d 1413 (6th Cir. 1990), rev'd, 932 F.2d 551 (6th Cir. 1991).

Greer v. Rome City Sch. Dist., 762 F. Supp. 936 (N.D. Ga. 1990), aff'd, 950 F.2d 688 (11th Cir. 1991), withdrawn & reinstated in part, 967 F.2d 470 (11th Cir. 1992).

Harmon v, Mead School Dist. No. 354, 17 EHLR 1029 (E.D. Wash 1991).

Hendricks v. Gilhool, 709 F. Supp. 1362 (E.D. Pa. 1989).

Hulme v. Dellmuth, 17 EHLR 940 (E.D. Pa. 1991).

Liscio v. Woodland Hills Sch. Dist., 734 F. Supp. 689 (W.D. Pa. 1989), aff'd, 90 F.2d 1561, 1563 (3d Cir. 1990).

Murray v. Montrose County Sch. Dist. RE-1J, 51 F.3d 921 (10th Cir. 1995), cert. denied, 116 S.Ct. 278 (U.S. 1995).

Oberti v. Bd. of Educ. of the Borough of Clementon Sch. Dist. 995 F.2d 1204 (3rd Cir. 1993).

Pennsylvania Ass'n for Retarded Children (PARC) v. Pennsylvania, 334 F. Supp. 1257 (E.D. Pa. 1971); 343 F. Supp. 279 (E.D. Pa. 1972).

Roncker v. Walter, 700 F.2d 1058 (6th Cir. 1983), cert. denied, 464 U.S. 864 (1983).

Wall v. Mattituck-Cutchogue Sch. Dist., 945 F. Supp. 501 (E.D.N.Y. 1996).

Wyatt v. Stickney, 344 F. Supp. 373 (M.D. Ala. 1972), aff'd in part, rev'd in part sub nom.

Wyatt v. Alderholt, 503 F.2d 1305 (5th Cir. 1974).

7
Procedural Due Process

The legal expression of fairness is *procedural due process*, the right of a citizen to protest before a government takes action with respect to him or her. In the case of the child with a disability, that means having the right to protest actions of the state education agency (SEA) or the local education agency (LEA). For those who pioneered the right-to-education doctrine, the procedures for implementing the right were as crucial as the right itself. Procedural due process is a means of challenging the multitude of discriminatory practices that the schools had followed habitually. It is a way of enforcing the first four principles of IDEA. Without due process, the children would have found that their right to be included in an educational program and to be treated nondiscriminatorily (to receive a free appropriate education) would have a hollow ring.

Procedural due process also is a constitutional requisite under the requirements of the Fifth and Fourteenth Amendments that no person shall be deprived of life, liberty, or property without due process of law. In terms of the education of children with disabilities, this means that no child with a disability can be deprived of an education without the opportunity of exercising the right to protest what happens to him or her.

The success of the right-to-education movement reaffirmed a belief held widely by lawyers—namely, that fair procedures tend to produce acceptable, correct, and fair results. Due process takes many forms under IDEA.

Individuals with Disabilities Education Act ~

Each SEA and LEA must give assurances to the U.S. Department of Education that it has adopted appropriate due-process procedures [20 U.S.C. § 1412 (a)(6) (applicable to the SEA); 20 U.S.C. § 1413 (a)(l) (applicable to the LEA); and 20 U.S.C. §

1415 (applicable to both)]. Except where Part C (birth to age three) has a special provision regarding due-process rights, all of IDEA's due process rights apply to all students—those in Part C programs and those in Part B programs. The special Part C provisions are set out below.

Consent

Parental consent must be obtained for preplacement evaluation and for the child's initial placement in a special education program [20 U.S.C. § 1414 (a)(1)(C); 34 C.F.R. § 300.505]. In addition, LEAs must obtain parental consent for reevaluations of students with disabilities. An LEA may proceed to *reevaluate* a student without parental consent only if it can show that it has tried and failed to obtain such consent [20 U.S.C. § 1414 (c)(3); 34 C.F.R. § 300.505 (c)].

In the context of evaluation and in all other contexts, consent means that

1. The parents have been informed fully in their native language, or in another suitable manner of communication, of all information relevant to the activity (e.g., evaluation) for which consent was sought [34 C.F.R. § 300.500(b)(1)(i)].
2. The parents understand and agree in writing that the activity may be carried out [34 C.F.R. § 300.500 (b)(1)(ii)].
3. The consent describes the activity and lists the records (if any) that will be released, and to whom [34 C.F.R. § 300.500 (b)(1)(ii)].
4. The parents understand that they give their consent voluntarily and may revoke it at any time [34 C.F.R. § 300.500 (b)(1)(iii)] (Note that such revocation is not retroactive).

If parents refuse to consent when consent is required, the agency may initiate mediation or a due-process hearing, as long as that is not inconsistent with state law. Should a hearing officer rule in favor of the agency, the parents' refusal will be overruled and the agency may evaluate or place the child, notifying the parents of its actions so that they may appeal [34 C.F.R. §§ 300.505 (b), 300.506, 300.507-300.509, 300.510].

Part C (birth to age three) has its own rules about consent. Early intervention service providers must obtain written parental consent before (a) conducting the initial evaluation and assessment of the child and (b) initiating the provision of early intervention services for the first time. If the parents do not give consent, the providers must make reasonable efforts to ensure that the parents (a) are fully aware of the nature of the evaluation and assessment or the services that would be available, and (b) understand that the child will not be able to receive the evaluation and assessment or services unless consent is given. Also, if the parents do not give consent, the provider may initiate a due-process hearing or other procedures to override the parents' refusal [34 C.F.R. § 303.404].

Surrogate Parents

20 U.S.C. § 1415 (b)(2) and 34 C.F.R. § 300.515 require the SEA to ensure that the child's rights are protected if his or her parents are unknown or unavailable or if the

child is a ward of the state. (The child's rights are not the SEA's responsibility when the parents are simply uncooperative or unresponsive.) The SEA may comply with this requirement by assigning a surrogate parent. There are other ways, but 20 U.S.C. § 1415 (b)(2) and 34 C.F.R. § 300.515 mention only this one.

If the SEA adopts the surrogate parents' option, it must devise methods for determining whether a child needs a surrogate and then for assigning one. The regulations give no guidance as to the methods. Nevertheless, they do set out the criteria for selecting a surrogate. Primarily, there should be no conflict of interest, and the individual should have the skill to represent the child. Thus, a superintendent or other employee of an institution in which a child resides may not serve as a surrogate. The regulations also make clear that a person paid by a public agency solely for the purpose of being a surrogate does not thereby become an agency employee. The surrogate may represent the child in matters affecting his or her identification, evaluation, and placement, and right to a free appropriate public education [34 C.F.R. § 300.515].

Notice Generally

An SEA or LEA must give prior written notice to parents, guardians, or surrogates whenever it proposes to initiate or change, or refuses to initiate or change, a child's identification, evaluation, or placement of the student, or the provision of a free appropriate public education [20 U.S.C. § 1415 (b)(3)]. The prior written notice must contain

1. a description of the action the agency proposes to take or refuses to take,
2. an explanation of why the agency reached that decision,
3. a description of any other options the agency considered and why those options were rejected,
4. a description of each evaluation procedure, test, record, or report that the agency used as a basis for its decision,
5. a description of any other factors relevant to the agency's decision,
6. a statement that the parents have certain procedural safeguards (i.e., due-process protections) and, if the notice is not an initial referral for evaluation, the means by which they can obtain a copy of a description of the procedural safeguards, and
7. the sources the parents may contact to obtain assistance in understanding Part B (student and parent rights) [20 U.S.C. § 1415 (c)].

34 C.F.R. § 300.503 (c) requires that the notice be

1. written in language understandable to the general public, and
2. provided in the parent's native language or parent's other mode of communication, unless it clearly is not feasible to do so.

If the parents' native language or other mode of communication is not a written language, the SEA or LEA must take steps to ensure that

1. the notice is translated orally or by other means to the parent in his or her native language or other mode of communication,
2. the parent understands the content of the notice, and
3. there is written evidence that the requirements (of oral translation and parent understanding) have been met.

Notice of Procedural Safeguards

IDEA requires specifically that parents be given a copy of the procedural safeguards that are available to them on at least three occasions:

1. upon the initial referral of the student for evaluation;
2. upon each notification of an IEP meeting or reevaluation; and
3. upon registration of a complaint regarding the identification, evaluation, educational placement, or free appropriate public education of a child [20 U.S.C. § 1415 (d)(1)].

The notice of procedural safeguards must be written in an easily understandable manner and, unless it clearly is not feasible to do so, in the parents' native language [20 U.S.C. § 1415 (d)(2)]. The notice must contain a full explanation of the procedural safeguards available under the IDEA and its regulations, including information regarding

1. independent educational evaluations,
2. prior written notice,
3. parental consent,
4. access to educational records,
5. the opportunity to present complaints,
6. the child's placement during the pendency of due-process proceedings,
7. procedures for students who are subject to placement in an interim alternative educational setting,
8. requirements for unilateral placement by parents of children in private schools at public expense,
9. mediation,
10. due-process hearings, including the requirements for disclosure of evaluation results and recommendations,
11. state-level appeals (if applicable in the state),
12. civil actions, and
13. attorney fees [20 U.S.C. § 1415(d)(2)].

Actual Notice

Quite properly, the courts that have had to rule on "notice" requirements have insisted that SEAs or LEAs meet not only the letter of the law but also its spirit—an approach that is quite proper because, without notice that actually informs the parents of their rights, the parents may not know what their rights are or how to assert them.

Thus, for example, an LEA that omits the notice concerning parents' rights to a due-process hearing violates IDEA (*Farrell v. Carol Stream Sch. Dist. No. 25*, 1996). Likewise, if a student transfers into one LEA from another, the receiving LEA must give the parents the requisite notice, even if the receiving state decides not to classify the student into special education (though the sending school had so classified him) (*Salley v. St. Tammany Parish Sch. Bd.*, 1995). Thus, failing to give notice is an error.

What if the LEA gives the notice but the parent misunderstands it? In that case, the LEA has complied; the burden rests on the parent to make sure that he or she understands an already clear and understandable notice (*Tennessee Department of Mental Health and Mental Retardation v. Paul B.*, 1996).

Sometimes, however, the LEA's notice is so deliberately misleading or vague that even a parent who reads it carefully might be misled by it. In such a case, the LEA has failed to comply, and parents will not be held to have waived their rights to any benefits that the notice should have described more adequately, such as extended school-year enrollment (*Reusch v. Fountain*, 1994).

The simplest way for an LEA to comply with the notice requirement is to follow it word for word. Anything less creates a risk of violation. In addition, an LEA that must give notice to parents who are not literate in English or in any other language, cannot read because they themselves have a disability, or use a language that is not written (as is the case for some American Indians) has the obligation of making sure that the parents actually receive an understandable notice. This is a requirement of due process generally and of the "reasonable accommodations" provisions of the Americans with Disabilities Act as it applies to a parent who has a disability.

Access to Records and Confidentiality

As explained in detail in the next chapter, parents, families (in the case of Part C, birth to age three), and usually the student (upon reaching the age of majority), have rights to read and copy the school records related to the student and to the LEA and SEA as a whole, and to prohibit, with exceptions, the disclosure of those records to others [20 U.S.C. §§ 1415 (b)(1), 1412 (a)(8), 1417 (c); 34 C.F.R. §§ 300.560-300.577]. Clearly, access to records and confidentiality of records are two different, but related, ways to hold the schools accountable.

If families do not know what the schools are doing, they hardly can be effective in holding the schools accountable. Access lets them know what the schools are doing. Moreover, the confidentiality rules protect students' privacy interests, especially as a great deal of information about them will appear in the school records.

Evaluation

The parents are entitled to an independent (nonagency) educational evaluation of their child [20 U.S.C. § 1415 (b)(1); 34 C.F.R. § 300.502]. 34 C.F.R. § 300.500 (2) defines evaluation as "procedures used in accordance with [34 C.F.R. §§ 300.530-300.536] to determine whether a child has a disability and the nature and extent of the special education and related services that the child needs." The term *evaluation* refers to procedures used selectively with an individual child and does not include basic tests administered to, or procedures used with, all children in a school, grade, or class.

34 C.F.R. § 300.502 (a)(3)(i) defines who may make an independent evaluation—namely, a qualified examiner not employed by the public agency responsible for educating the child. A qualified person is one who has met SEA– approved or SEA-recognized certification, licensing, registration, or other comparable requirements in the area in which he or she provides special education or related services [34 C.F.R. § 300.23]. 34 C.F.R. § 300.502 (a)(2) also provides that public agencies, upon request, must inform parents about where they may have independent educational evaluations made.

Under some circumstances, the independent evaluation must be made at public expense. The public agency either pays for the full cost of the evaluation or ensures that the evaluation is otherwise provided without cost to the parent. Parents have the right to an independent evaluation at public expense if the hearing officer requests one for use in a due-process hearing or if the parents disagree with the evaluation made by the public agency. But if, in a due process hearing that it initiates, the agency can prove that its evaluation was appropriate, the agency will not be required to pay for the independent evaluation (though the parents may obtain one at their own expense). When parents obtain an independent evaluation at their own expense and it meets agency criteria, the agency must take it into consideration as a basis for providing the child an appropriate education, or as evidence in a due-process hearing, or both [34 C.F.R. § 300.502 (b), (c), (d)].

Complaints and Due Process Hearings

Right to Hearing

The right to a due-process hearing is not limited to parents, families, and surrogates. Under 34 C.F.R. § 300.507, an SEA or LEA also may initiate a due-process hearing on its proposal or refusal to initiate or change the identification, evaluation, or placement of a child with a disability, or the provision of free appropriate public education to the child.

An SEA or LEA must give the parents, guardians, or surrogates an opportunity to present and resolve complaints relating to any matter concerning the child's identification, evaluation, or placement, or the provision of a free appropriate public education [20 U.S.C. § 1415 (b)(6)]. If the parents (or guardians) file a complaint with an agency, they are entitled to an opportunity for an impartial hearing. The agency must inform the parents about any low-cost or free legal aid in the geographical area [34 C.F.R. § 300.507 (a)(3)].

Timing

Unless the parties agree to an extension, the hearing must be held and a final decision reached within 45 days after the hearing is requested, and a copy of the decision must be mailed to the parties. (The hearing officer may extend this deadline.)

The time and place of a hearing involving oral argument must be reasonably convenient to the parents and child [34 C.F.R. §§ 300.511 (a), (d)].

Mediation

20 U.S.C. § 1415 (e) of IDEA makes clear that parents must be offered an opportunity to resolve disputes concerning their child's education through mediation (see also 34 C.F.R. § 300.506). Each public agency shall establish and implement procedures to ensure that mediation is available, including maintenance of a list of qualified mediators who have knowledge relevant to IDEA-related issues [34 C.F.R. § 300.506 (a), (b)(2)]. If a student's parents decline an agency's offer for mediation, the LEA or SEA may require, before proceeding to a due-process hearing, that they meet (at a time and location convenient to the parents) with a disinterested third party who will explain the benefits and encourage the use of mediation [20 U.S.C. § 1415 (e)(2)(b); 34 C.F.R. § 300.506 (d)].

The statute also makes it clear, however, that the parties must enter into mediation voluntarily and the mediation provisions may not be used to deny or delay a parent's rights to procedural due process or any other rights under Part B [20 U.S.C. § 1415 (e)(2)(A)(ii); 34 C.F.R. § 300.506 (b)(1)(ii)]. Thus, even if a parent does not participate in the "pre-mediation" meeting described above, they may not be denied their rights to a due-process hearing [34 C.F.R. § 300.506 (d)(2)].

If the parents do engage in mediation, the state bears the financial responsibility for the mediation, each mediation session must be scheduled in a timely manner (so as to not delay the right to an impartial hearing), and these sessions must be held in a location convenient to both the parents and the LEA. If the parents and LEA reach an agreement during mediation, the agreement must be written (and is called a mediation agreement). The content of the proceedings must be kept confidential. Thus, any statements the parties make during the mediation process cannot be used as evidence in subsequent hearings or trials [20 U.S.C. § 1415 (e); 34 C.F.R. § 300.506 (b)(3), (4), (5), (6)]. Furthermore, the mediator must be impartial, having no personal or professional conflict of interest [34 C.F.R. § 300.506 (c)].

Impartial Hearing Officers

Each agency must keep a list of impartial hearing officers and their qualifications [34 C.F.R. § 300.508 (c)]. The hearing officer may not be an employee of the agency involved in educating or otherwise providing services to the child, and must not otherwise have any personal or professional interest that might conflict with objectivity in the hearing [34 C.F.R. § 300.308 (a)]. A person who otherwise qualifies to conduct a hearing is not considered to be an employee of the agency solely because the agency pays him or her to serve as a hearing officer [34 C.F.R. § 300.308 (b)].

Courts are meticulous about assuring that hearing officers are impartial. They have disqualified a state superintendent of education (*Robert M. v. Benton*, 1980), because he was an employee of the state agency responsible for special education. On the other hand, they have permitted members of the state board of education to serve (*Vermont Association for Children with Learning Disabilities v. Kaagan*, 1982,

1983). Likewise, they have not disqualified employees of the state education agency from being hearing officers at the SEA level (*Smith v. Cumberland School Committee*, 1979).

The rationale behind these cases was well expressed in a later case: For a conflict of interest to disqualify the hearing officer, the SEA or LEA must do more than pay the officer's fee for conducting the hearing; it must have not only other but also substantial control over their decision-making authority and judgment (*Jacky W. v. N.Y.C. Bd. of Ed.*, 1994). Thus, even though college professors generally are not disqualified (*Silvio v. Commonwealth*, 1982), those who help formulate state special education policy have been found not to be disinterested and have been disqualified because the policy they make directly affects the children whose rights they adjudicate (*Mayson v. Teague*, 1984); (*Kotowicz v. Mississippi State Bd. of Ed.*, 1986).

Rights at Hearing

At the initial hearing and on appeal, each party has the right to [20 U.S.C. § 1415 (f),(h)]:

1. be accompanied and advised by an attorney and by individuals with special knowledge or training with respect to the problems of children with disabilities,
2. present evidence and confront, examine, cross-examine, and compel the attendance of witnesses,
3. exclude any evidence offered by any party unless it was disclosed at least 5 business days before the hearing,
4. receive a written or (at the option of the parents) an electronic verbatim record of the hearing,
5. receive written or (at the option of the parents) electronic findings of fact and decisions [34 C.F.R. § 300.509 (a)].

At least 5 business days prior to a hearing, each party shall disclose to all other parties all evaluations completed by that date and recommendations based on those evaluations that are intended to be used at the hearing. If either party fails to meet this requirement and attempts to introduce such an evaluation or recommendation without the other party's consent, the hearing officer may bar the introduction of that evidence [34 C.F.R. § 300.509 (b)].

Parents involved in hearings must be given the right [34 C.F.R. § 300.509 (c)]:

1. to have the child present, and
2. to have the hearing open to the public.

The hearing officer's decision must be sent to the state special education advisory panel established under Section 1415(h)(4) and 34 C.F.R. § 300.650. These findings and decisions also must be made available to the public [34 C.F.R. § 300.509 (d)].

Right to Free Transcript

An indigent parent representing herself in an IDEA action against an LEA is entitled to both an electronic tape-recorded record of the due-process hearing and a written transcript of the same hearing, but the right to the written transcript exists under federal law relating to indigents who represent themselves *(in forma pauperis),* not under IDEA (*Militello v. Bd. of Educ. of City of Union City,* 1992) (see also "Rights at Hearing," above).

Right to Appeal

Unless a party appeals, the initial hearing officer's decision is final [20 U.S.C. § 1415 (i)(1)(A); 34 C.F.R. § 300.510 (a)]. If the hearing is conducted by an LEA, an aggrieved party may appeal to the SEA, which is required to conduct an impartial review of the hearing (which includes examining the hearing record, ensuring that hearing procedures were consistent with due process, seeking additional evidence as necessary, and affording the parties opportunity for oral or written argument as needed), to reach an independent decision, and to send a copy of the decision to the parties within 30 days [34 C.F.R. § 300.511 (b)]. If the reviewing official determines that oral argument will be held, the time and place of a review involving oral argument must be reasonably convenient to the parents and the child [34 C.F.R. § 300.511 (d)]. Findings and decisions on appeal must be transmitted to the state advisory panel and made available to the public, as is required after the initial hearing [34 C.F.R. § 300.510 (c)].

Persons who are aggrieved by the findings and decision in the initial hearing (who do not have a right to an appeal as described above), or who are aggrieved by the findings and decision on appeal, may file a civil action in either a state court or federal district court. The court, whether state or federal, is to receive the records of the administrative proceedings, hear additional evidence at the request of any party, and, on the basis of the preponderance of the evidence, grant appropriate relief [20 U.S.C. §§ 1415 (i)(2)(A) and (B); 34 C.F.R. § 300.512].

Standard of Review in Courts

As the Supreme Court in *Rowley* made clear, when a court hears an appeal, the review includes a *de novo* (from anew or new) review of the administrative record and of the legal issues presented (*Polk v. Central Susquehanna Intermediate Unit 16,* 1988). Not only may a court review the record before it, but it also may admit new evidence and must do so if a party requests it (*Carroll v. Metropolitan Governments of Nashville and Davidson Co.,* 1992; *Lenn v. Portland Sch. Comm.,* 1993). These elements have been codified as described above.

Then the court must make its decision on the basis of the entire record before it—the administrative record and the new evidence; and it must give due weight to the administrative record and the hearing officer's decision. It must follow that decision unless it is clearly wrong and unless the newly admitted evidence is contradictory and more persuasive (*Roncker v. Walter,* 1983; *Doe v. Smith,* 1989; *School Board of Prince William County v. Malone,* 1985; *Burke County Bd. of Educ. v. Denton,*

1990; *Gillette v. Fairland Board of Education*, 1989; *Matta v. Indian Hill Exempted Village Schools*, 1990).

When, as usual, the review involves mixed questions of fact and law, a court may be tempted to decide on its own exactly what constitutes a free appropriate public education in the least restrictive setting. That, however, would not be proper. A court's role is not to second-guess state and local policy decisions and methods, because making policy and deciding about the methods for educating children properly belong to state and local school officials (*Daniel R.R. v. State Bd. of Educ.*, 1989).

Rather, a court's narrow task is to determine whether those officials have complied with IDEA. Have they followed its process (the *Rowley* standard, also called the process definition), and have they thereby assured that the student will receive some educational benefit (the *Rowley* standard, also called the benefit standard) (*Salley v. St. Tammany Parish Sch. Bd.*, 1995)? And only if a trial court's findings of fact are clearly wrong may a court of appeals find other facts (*Christopher M. v. Corpus Christi Indep. Sch. Dist.*, 1991).

Stay-Put Rule

During the pendency of any administrative or judicial proceeding (relating to the identification, evaluation, or educational placement of a child with a disability or the provision of FAPE thereto), the child remains in his or her current educational placement unless the SEA or LEA and the parents or guardians agree otherwise, or unless the child has been removed for weapon or drug violations or for dangerousness (see Chapter 3). If applying for initial admission to school, the child will be placed in the public school program (with parental consent) until all hearings (including appeals) have been completed [20 U.S.C. § 1415 (j); 34 C.F.R. §§ 300.514, 300.524 (c), 300.526].

In a stay-put case, *Corbett v. Regional Center for the East Bay, Inc.* (1988), a federal district court ruled that the LEA, not the parent, has the burden of overcoming the presumption that the child will remain in the present placement. The burden is overcome, the court said, if the child's present placement is "substantially likely to cause injury to himself or herself, or to others." This decision allocates the burden of proof to the school to justify the change in placement—that is, to create an exception to the stay-put rule. That result follows the settled law that, where the stay-put rule is at issue, the burden is with the schools, as announced in *Doe v. Brookline School Committee* (1983).

Part C Procedural Safeguards

Under Part C (birth to age three), states must adopt procedures for resolving individual complaints. The procedures must provide for an impartial decision-maker (hearing officer) to resolve disputes (see 34 C.F.R. § 303.421) and require that service providers implement such decisions unless they are reversed on appeal. Part C mandates that the state must, at a minimum, provide for

1. the timely administrative resolution of parents' complaints, including appeal to courts,

2. the right to confidentiality of personally identifiable information, including the right of parents to written notice of and written consent to the exchange of such information among agencies consistent with state and federal law,

3. the right of parents to determine whether they, their infant or toddler, or other family members will accept or decline any early intervention service without jeopardizing other early intervention services,

4. the opportunity for parents to examine records relating to assessment, screening, eligibility determinations, and development and implementation of the IFSP,

5. the appointment of surrogates for parents who are not available,

6. written prior notice to parents whenever the agency or service provider proposes to initiate or change, or refuses to initiate or change, the identification, evaluation, or placement of the infant or toddler with a disability, or the provision of appropriate early intervention services to the infant or toddler,

7. provision of the aforementioned notice to the parents in their native language unless it clearly is not feasible to do so, and

8. the right of parents to use mediation in accordance with 20 U.S.C. § 1415 (e), except that references in that section to an SEA shall be considered a reference to the state's lead agency responsible for carrying out Part C, and any reference to an LEA shall be considered a reference to the local service provider or the state's lead agency. Further, references to FAPE are to be considered to be a reference to the provision of appropriate early intervention services to infants or toddlers with disabilities [20 U.S.C. § 1439 (a) (1)-(8)].

As in Part B, a state must offer mediation as an intervening step before implementing due-process procedures, but it may not require parents to use mediation. If parents refuse to use mediation, they may be required to meet with a disinterested third party to learn about the benefits of mediation before proceeding to a due-process hearing, though they cannot be required to participate in mediation proceedings [20 U.S.C. §§ 1415(e); 34 C.F.R. § 300.506].

Any party aggrieved by an administrative decision on a complaint under Part C has the right to bring a civil action in state or federal district court. The court must receive the records of the administrative proceedings, hear any additional evidence (at a party's request), and grant appropriate relief based upon a preponderance of the evidence [20 U.S.C. § 1439 (a)(1)].

All hearings must be in places and at times convenient to the parents, and all disputes must be resolved within 30 days after the lead agency receives a complaint [34 C.F.R. § 303.423]. Any parents involved in administrative proceedings have the rights to be accompanied and advised by counsel or other people with special knowledge or training in early intervention; to present evidence and confront, cross-examine, and compel the attendance of witnesses; to prohibit the use of evidence not disclosed to them at least 5 days before the proceeding; to obtain a written or electronic verbatim transcript; and to obtain written findings of fact and decisions [34 C.F.R. § 303.422].

As in the case of Part B, the infant/toddler also is protected by a specific stay-put rule under Part C [20 U.S.C. § 1439 (b); 34 C.F.R. § 303.425]. If a complaint is pending at any administrative level or on appeal to a federal or state court, then, unless the state agency and parents or guardians agree otherwise, the infant/toddler is entitled to continue to receive the appropriate early intervention services currently being provided, or, if applying for initial services, is entitled to receive those services that are not in dispute.

These rules under Part C deal only with complaints about individual children. Part C's regulations, however, also require the state lead agency to establish procedures to resolve complaints about how the state itself—so-called systemic complaints—implements Part C and its site plan [34 C.F.R. § 303.501].

Section 504

The relevant Section 504 regulation [34 C.F.R. § 104.36] provides that an SEA or LEA may satisfy Section 504 due-process requirements by complying with the procedural safeguards of IDEA Section 1415. The alternative, and minimum, requirement for the SEA and LEA is to furnish notice, to make the child's records accessible, to guarantee an impartial hearing, to afford the right to counsel, and to assure an impartial review.

Case Law ⌒

Lawyers love procedures. They have a continuing *affaire d'amour* with procedures for many reasons. Two are especially relevant here.

1. Lawyers believe (and with good justification) that fair procedures will provide fair results. This fundamental premise undergirds IDEA, which is rife with procedural requirements (e.g., nondiscriminatory evaluation, IEPs, procedural due process).
2. Lawyers often use procedural requirements successfully to establish or to circumvent their clients' substantive rights. Out of these two reasons have grown a plethora of judicial decisions, none of which is likely to be changed by the 1997 amendments.

Exhaustion of Remedies

A highly vexatious issue is whether parents or an LEA must exhaust their administrative remedies under IDEA before they may file a lawsuit in federal or state courts. To exhaust one's administrative remedies simply means that one first must go through all of the local (LEA-level) and state (SEA-level) due-process hearings before one may file a lawsuit in state or federal court.

Purpose of Exhaustion Rule

The purpose of the exhaustion-of-remedies rule is manifold (*Association for Retarded Citizens of Alabama, Inc. v. Teague*, 1987; *Crocker v. Tennessee Secondary*

School Athletic Ass'n., 1989; *Association for Community Living v. Romer*, 1993; and *Prins v. Independent School District No. 761*, 1995):

1. It permits the LEA to exercise discretion and apply the agency's expertise to students' education.
2. It allows full development of technical issues and factual records before a court hears the case.
3. It prevents deliberate disregard and circumvention of agency procedures that Congress has clearly established.
4. It avoids unnecessary judicial decision, and thereby economizes judicial resources, by giving the LEA the first opportunity to correct any errors it may have made.
5. It ensures accuracy in the findings of fact, because the administrative hearings (the due-process hearings) can be scheduled more rapidly than a court trial, given the backlog of cases in state and federal courts, and thus the administrative hearings will occur when the evidence, especially witnesses' memories, are fresh and more reliable.
6. It ensures efficiency in the administration of IDEA, because many conflicts can be solved at the administrative level and thus not have to wait on court hearings, rapid resolution being desirable because justice delayed often is justice denied.

For these reasons, 20 U.S.C. §§ 1415 (l) and 34 C.F.R. § 300.512 (d) requires parties—parents and schools alike—to exhaust their administrative remedies before filing their cases in any court. Predictably, because the rule is set out clearly within IDEA and because the reasons for the rule are sound, the courts have enforced this rule (*Sessions v. Livingston Parish*, 1980; *Davis v. Maine Endwell Central School District*, 1982; *Hope v. Cortines*, 1995; *Farrell v. Carol Stream School*, 1996).

Futility Exception

Such a simple rule as the exhaustion rule should not, it would seem, create so many difficulties. Yet that is exactly what the rule has done. One of the more problematic issues is the longstanding exception to the exhaustion rule commonly called the futility exception.

Because the exhaustion rule can create hardships, the courts, using their equitable powers, have excused parties from exhausting their administrative remedies when doing so would be futile for them—that is, when exhausting the remedies would contribute little or nothing to resolving the disputes between the parties (*Christopher T. v. San Francisco U.S.D.*, 1982; *Monahan v. Nebraska*, 1980; *Howard S. v. Friendswood I.S.D.*, 1978; *Association for Retarded Citizens in Colorado v. Frazier*, 1981; *Miener v. Missouri*, 1980). The question, then, is what constitutes futility with respect to IDEA's exhaustion rule?

A related question—whether the party seeking to avoid the exhaustion rule has the burden of proving that exhaustion would be futile—has been answered. The party wanting to avoid the rule has the burden of proving that exhaustion would be futile (*Stauffer v. William Penn Sch. Dist.*, 1993).

Courts have invoked the futility exceptions and excused exhaustion in several types of cases, including those in which:

1. The LEA, as a respondent/defendant, waives the exhaustion rule where a portion of a case already has been adjudicated at the administrative level, as in *North v. D.C. Bd. of Ed.* (1979), in which the parties were bound by the prior order of the same court (see also *Jose P. v. Ambach* (1982)).

2. More than one parent (complainant/plaintiff) files a class action lawsuit (one brought on one's own behalf and on behalf of other parents similarly aggrieved), alleges that an LEA has failed in the past to carry out its IDEA obligations, and another court has so found (*United Cerebral Palsy of NYC v. Bd. of Ed. of City of N.Y.*, 1983).

3. Facts are undisputed that an LEA is not complying with IDEA (the student is excluded totally from any IDEA benefits and from school itself) and that the LEA will take no action at all to provide an appropriate education to the student, *Harris v. Campbell* (1979).

4. An SEA has failed, and continues to refuse, to appoint surrogate parents for residents of a state institution for people with mental retardation, thereby making it impossible for the residents (who are IDEA-entitled) to use their administrative remedies (*Garrity v. Gallen*, 1981; *Ruth Anne M. v. Alvin I.S.D.*, 1982).

5. A student challenges the SEA's own regulations, alleging that they are inconsistent with IDEA and therefore invalid, and, at the same time, challenges the state education commissioner's performance of his or her duties, alleging that, as a result of the improper regulations and malfeasance in the performance of duty, the student has been expelled from school contrary to IDEA, as in *J.G. v. Bd. of Educ.* (1982, 1983), a suit designed to correct alleged systemwide violation of IDEA's procedures.

6. A student seeks a remedy that cannot be provided, in any way, under IDEA— for example, damages from an LEA because of its alleged failure to comply with IDEA (see Chapter 9 for the cases on damages under IDEA and other laws) (*Loughran v. Flanders*, 1979; *Quackenbush v. Johnson City School District*, 1983; *Kerr Center Parents Association v. Charles*, 1983; *J.G. v. Bd. of Educ.*, 1987).

7. A student seeks a remedy that cannot be provided under IDEA—namely, a systemwide remedy (cutoff of federal funds to an SEA or LEA) that is available under Section 504 (*New Mexico Association for Retarded Citizens v. New Mexico*, 1982; *United Cerebral Palsy of NYC v. Bd. of Ed. of City of N.Y.*, 1982).

8. A student will experience severe harm, not of his or her own making, as a result of having to exhaust his or her remedies (*Phipps v. New Hanover County Bd. of Educ.*, 1982; *Vander Malle v. Ambach*, 1982; *J. G. v. Bd. of Educ.*, 1987;

Crocker v. Tennessee Secondary School Athletic Ass'n., 1989). But if a student is dangerous to others and the LEA uses the *Honig* safety valve to suspend the student temporarily (for up to 10 days) or to seek a court order enjoining a dangerous student from attending school temporarily (see Chapter 3, explaining that under *Honig* the Supreme Court allowed an LEA to take all necessary steps to safeguard other students in the extreme likelihood of danger to them from the expelled student), the LEA itself need not exhaust the IDEA administrative remedies [64 Fed. Reg. 12,621—Discussion on 34 C.F.R. § 300.521] (*Honig v. Doe,* 1988; *School Board of Hillsborough County v. Student 2649325TS,* 1995).

9. An SEA or LEA absolutely denies the student access to an administrative remedy, refusing to appoint a hearing officer or to attend a due-process hearing (*Ezratty v. Commonwealth of Puerto Rico,* 1981; *Kerr Center Parents Association v. Charles,* 1983; *Quackenbush v. Johnson City School Dist.,* 1983; *Mrs. W. v. Tirozzi,* 1987; *Christopher W. v. Portsmouth School Committee,* 1989).

What does not constitute futility?

1. The fact that the administrative process is protracted does not constitute futility (*Cluff v. Johnson City School Dist.,* 1982; *Kresse v. Johnson City School Dist.,* 1982).

2. The fact that a case involves many students and requires a finding of fact and conclusion of law regarding each of them (as to their IDEA rights) does not constitute futility (*Riley v. Ambach,* 1981; *Phipps v. New Hanover County Bd. of Ed.,* 1982; *Calhoun v. Illinois State Bd.,* 1982).

Section 504, ADA, IDEA, and Exhaustion

As explained in Chapter 2, students with disabilities have rights under IDEA (the right to a free appropriate public education) and under Section 504 and ADA as well (a right not to be discriminated against solely on account of their disability). Often, students will be covered by IDEA on the one hand and by Section 504 and ADA on the other; they will be entitled to be included in special education and receive its benefits (an IDEA right), as well as to be free of discrimination on account of disability.

One aspect of being free from discrimination includes receiving, under Section 504, an appropriate education [34 C.F.R. § 104.33], procedural safeguards regarding classification and placement [34 C.F.R. § 104.36], and an opportunity to protest noncompliance [34 C.F.R. § 104.36]. Likewise, one aspect of being free from discrimination includes receiving, under ADA, an appropriate education comparable to that available under IDEA ([28 C.F.R. § 35.103]; *Urban v. Jefferson County School Dist.,* 1994; *Prins v. Independent School District No. 761,* 1995). In a very real sense, then, IDEA-type protection—the right to an appropriate education and to procedural safeguards—also exists under Section 504 and ADA.

Other students, however, will not be classified into special education: Some students have disabilities, but the disabilities do not render them incapable of benefiting from general education (for example, a student who is HIV-positive but has not yet experienced any loss of function). IDEA provides no rights and no remedies for these students. Instead, they must rely on Section 504 and ADA, and even then they can make only two claims.

1. They can claim that they were subjected to discrimination solely because of their disability. For example, they can claim that, like the students with HIV who had to sue to be enrolled in school, they were excluded totally from participating in school solely because of their disability.

2. They can claim that, even after they were enrolled (allowed to participate), they still experienced discrimination because the LEA refused to make a reasonable accommodation to their disability. They can claim that, for example, the LEA refused to adjust curricular requirements (e.g., that all assignments be typed— a difficult task for a person who has no use of his or her hands and who dictates his or her assignments) or extracurricular requirements (e.g., that students not exceed a certain age to be allowed to participate in high school sports).

As just pointed out above, these students' 504 and ADA rights are coextensive with their IDEA rights. A significant difference, however, can be pointed out between IDEA on the one hand and Section 504 and ADA on the other: Exhaustion is not required under either Section 504 or ADA (*Prins v. Indep. Sch. Dist. No. 761*, 1995; *Jeremy H. v. Mount Lebanon Sch. Dist.,* 1996). That fact alone will tempt a student to claim under Section 504 or ADA even though his or her basic claim is a violation of IDEA.

If a student is entitled to IDEA as well as Section 504 and ADA protection, must the student exhaust the IDEA administrative remedies? Yes. Simply joining the Section 504 or ADA claim with an IDEA claim does not excuse exhaustion of IDEA remedies (*Smith v. Ambach*, 1981; *Shannon v. Ambach*, 1981). Where claims overlap (i.e., claims under IDEA and under Section 504 and ADA), the IDEA exhaustion rule must be complied with [20 U.S.C. § 1415 (l); 34 C.F.R. § 300.512 (d); *Prins v. Indep. Sch. Dist. No. 761,* 1995 and *Jeremy H. v. Mount Lebanon Sch. Dist.,* 1996].

Moreover, some students may assert that they are entitled to a remedy that is not available under IDEA but is available under Section 504 or ADA, or both (for example, damages) and that they therefore are excused from exhausting their IDEA remedies. For example, they may seek compensatory damages from an LEA. In such a case, where damages are not available under IDEA but are available under Section 504, they need not exhaust their IDEA remedies (*Boxall v. Sequoia Union High School Dist.*, 1979). Or they may seek physical access to an LEA facility (a 504/ADA right but not an IDEA right) (*Sullivan v. Vallejo City Unified School Dist.*, 1990); here, too, they are excused from any IDEA exhaustion requirements.

Students who assert a Section 504 or an ADA remedy that also is available under IDEA, however, may be tempted to rely on Section 504 and ADA. This is because Section 504 and ADA do not require exhaustion, a 504 violation is apt to be identical to an ADA violation and thus will be joined with the ADA violation, and, by relying on both Section 504 and ADA, the student can avoid the IDEA exhaustion remedy.

These cases make overlapping claims, though they frame the claims as Section 504 and ADA but not as IDEA violations. Even if they file their claim as only an ADA or only an ADA-plus-504 claim, but essentially they are claiming a violation of IDEA—that is, their underlying grievance "sounds" in IDEA and is inextricably linked to that statute—they must exhaust their IDEA remedies and may not go directly to federal court on the Section 504 and ADA claims (*Prins v. Indep. Sch. Dist. No. 761*, 1995; *Hope v. Cortines*, 1995; *Jeremy H. v. Mount Lebanon Sch. Dist.*, 1996).

The crucial issue in such a case is whether the students seek relief that also is available under IDEA, so that exhaustion is required under IDEA [20 U.S.C. § 1415 (l)]. If so—for example, the student has not been classified into special education but seeks the functional equivalent of an IEP (available under IDEA but not under Section 504) and the student also seeks a court order requiring the LEA to provide in-service training to its faculty concerning attention deficit/hyperactivity disorder and instruction of students with that disabling condition—the student must exhaust the IDEA remedies (*Hope v. Cortines*, 1995; *Mrs. W. v. Tirozzi*, 1987 *v. Indep. Sch. Dist. No. 761*, 1995; *Prins*; *Jeremy H. v. Mount Lebanon Sch. Dist.*, 1996).

The reasons why this is so are manifold:

1. IDEA, Section 1415 (due process hearings), particularly § 1415 (l), contains no exceptions; the language is clear that the exhaustion rule applies to Section 504 and ADA cases.
2. The enforcement provisions of ADA incorporate the enforcement provisions of Section 504 [42 U.S.C. § 12133; 28 C.F.R. § 35.103]; because Section 504 claims that are linked inextricably to IDEA or the provision of special education require the parties to exhaust their administrative remedies [20 U.S.C. § 1415 (l)], it follows that ADA-based claims related to the education of students with disabilities must be pursued through the administrative (due process) hearing first, before being brought to court (*Hope v. Cortines*, 1995; *Jeremy H. v. Mount Lebanon Sch. Dist.*, 1996).

Post-Hearing Claims

It having been clearly settled that an IDEA claimant must exhaust the IDEA administrative remedies and may not avoid them (except in cases of futility) even when claiming under Section 504 and ADA when those claims are fundamentally IDEA claims, it would seem that there would be no further issues to clarify. That is not the case, however.

What if a student, who already has concluded a due-process hearing on one or more grievances finds that he or she has yet another, later-occurring grievance against the same LEA? Must the student exhaust the administrative remedies as to the later-discovered grievance, or may the student consolidate that grievance with the other grievances in the appeal to a court? To require the student to exhaust his or her administrative remedies on the later-discovered grievance would be consistent with IDEA and the purposes and principles of exhaustion, but it also would prevent the student from having a hearing on all of the claims, those being appealed and those just discovered—hardly an efficient process for the student and the LEA. The answer—in the only case yet decided on that point—is that the student must exhaust his IDEA remedies as to the later-discovered claims (*Jeremy H. v. Mt. Lebanon Sch. Dist.*, 1996).

The fact that two different administrative procedures apply to aggrieved students with disabilities has created some confusion, too. The most commonly used procedures are those under IDEA, discussed in this chapter. But the U.S. Department of Education, which administers IDEA, has promulgated other regulations providing for adjudication of student-school grievances. These are the so-called EDGAR regulations (Education Department General Administrative Regulations).

Must a student exhaust the EDGAR procedures (which are similar to the IDEA ones) as well as the IDEA procedures? The short answer is "no." The EDGAR regulations predated the IDEA regulations and are optional, not mandatory (*Jeremy H. v. Mount Lebanon School District*, 1996).

Burden of Proof

When one party brings a lawsuit against another, the law typically requires the party bringing the suit to prove his or her claim. Another way of stating this is to say that the burden of proof falls on the party bringing the suit. Because IDEA does not assign the burden of proof to any potential party, the courts have relied on this general proposition, or on state law, to determine which party has the burden of proof. Generally, the courts have held that the party bringing the case has the burden of proof.

Thus, if a parent disagrees with the curriculum portion of an IEP as proposed by the student's school district or with a proposed placement within the continuum or within a district school but not a private school, the parent has the burden of showing, by a preponderance of the evidence, that the district is incorrect in its decision and would violate IDEA if it carried out its decision (*Bales v. Clark*, 1981; *Fitz v. Intermediate Unit #29*, 1979; *Savka v. Commonwealth, Dept. of Ed.*, 1979; *Salley v. St. Tammany Parish School Board*, 1995). Moreover, the burden of overturning a decision of a state due-process hearing officer falls on the party appealing the decision, and that party must show that the decision was not supported by substantial evidence, was arbitrary or capricious, or is clearly erroneous under law (*Levy v. Commonwealth, Dept. of Ed.*, 1979).

When a Hearing Is Not Available

General Rule

Although IDEA grants a due-process hearing as a matter of right to any party in matters involving child identification, classification, or services, limitations are placed on the right to obtain a hearing. The courts are unwilling to grant a hearing in every instance of an educational dispute. They are especially loath to grant a due-process hearing if the party (typically, a parent) seeking the hearing is trying to prevent an SEA or LEA from carrying out administrative, organizational, or fiscal decisions that affect more than one child.

For example, parents of a child in a private school do not have the right to use the due-process hearing to challenge a state-level decision to terminate the school's state-provided funding (*Windward School v. State*, 1978). Likewise, neither the parents of students in a private school nor the school itself may go to due-process to challenge a district's decision to terminate a contract with a private school (*Dima v. Macchiarola*, 1981); to challenge an SEA or LEA decision to reduce the tuition-reimbursement that it has paid a private school (*Fallis v. Ambach*, 1983; *Language Dev. Program, Inc. v. Ambach*, 1983; *Tilton v. Jefferson County Bd. of Educ.*, 1983); or to freeze the rates it pays to reimburse a private school for educating students it places there (*Behavior Research Institute v. Secretary of Administration*, 1991).

Similarly, when an LEA decides to close a school—called "experimental" because it uses innovative techniques to integrate students with and without disabilities—the parents of the students in that school may not use IDEA due process to prevent the school's closure, as long as the students are transferred to another school where they will receive substantially the same kind of educational benefits (*Concerned Parents and Citizens for Continuing Education at Malcolm X (PS 79) v. New York City Bd. of Educ.*, 1980; *Tilton v. Jefferson County Bd. of Educ.*, 1983). If, however, a closure decision would deprive students entirely of an appropriate education, at least one court has been willing to prevent the closure   not through due-process hearings but instead by other types of lawsuits (*Kerr Center Parents' Ass'n. v. Charles*, 1983).

Notwithstanding these decisions, any parent who alleges that any change of placement, even one resulting from administrative, organizational, or fiscal decisions about the education of a group of students, may go to due process to challenge the change as it affects the one child; access to due process is still open if the systemwide change causes a change in the particular special education program or services for an individual child (*Brown v. Dist. of Columbia Board of Educ.*, 1978; *Concerned Parents and Citizens for Continuing Education at Malcolm X (PS 79) v. New York City Bd. of Educ.*, 1980).

Reasons for the Rule

The reasons for the courts' reluctance to allow parents to use the due-process hearing remedy in cases involving administrative, organizational, or fiscal decisions are fairly well grounded:

1. Although Congress intended a hearing to be available when placement changes (the child is moved from one type of program, such as a residential one, to another, such as an integrated one; or from one type of setting, such as a resource room, to another, such as a fully integrated program), the due process route is not needed unless the change in placement or program substantially affects the student's rights to an appropriate education.
2. Allowing a due-process hearing in all changes of placement or program, even those that are not likely to affect the student's rights to an educational benefit,

would open up the floodgates for many insubstantial claims. The administrative and judicial hearing process could become clogged with essentially frivolous cases.

3. Allowing a due-process hearing in all changes of placement and program would involve the courts in oversight of school-district decisions that are based on administrative grounds. To function effectively and efficiently, school authorities have to redraw school boundaries, open or close schools, move students from one building to another, and so on. If every such administrative decision can be challenged, the courts will become super-ordinary school boards and the administrative efficacy of the schools will be impaired.

4. Allowing a due-process hearing in all such changes may put the courts in the position of having the opportunity to substitute their educational or administrative policy decisions for those of the elected or appointed school boards and their professional staff. As has been argued throughout this book, courts are reluctant to take on that kind of authority, preferring to defer to the experts in those matters.

5. IDEA reference to placement—challengeable in a due-process hearing—is limited to basic decisions regarding evaluation and appropriate education. A broad interpretation might impair an LEA's ability to implement even minor changes.

Statute of Limitations

In general law, a lawsuit or administrative action (such as a due-process hearing) must be begun within a certain period of time. This rule ensures that disputes are heard when evidence is relatively fresh—when the witnesses are only recently removed from the time during which the facts arose. The rule also prompts parties to resolve their disputes sooner or later so they may get on with their lives without the inevitable uncertainty and burdens that come with a lawsuit.

The means by which the rule for prompt litigation is enforced is called the statute of limitations. It is a law (usually a statute enacted by a legislature) that limits the period of time beyond which a lawsuit may be filed. Because IDEA contains no statute of limitation, the courts have been compelled to create one.

In most cases, they have borrowed the statute of limitations that applies to administrative actions (a due-process hearing) as enacted by the state legislature in which the hearing is heard (*Mayson v. Teague*, 1984; *Kotowicz v. Mississippi State Bd. of Ed.*, 1986; *Manchester City Sch. Dist. v. Jason N.*, 1991; *Dell v. Bd. of Educ.*, 1994; *Livingston School Dist. Nos. 4 & 1 v. Keenan*, 1996; and *Farrell v. Carol Stream Sch. Dist. No. 25*, 1996).

At least one court, however, has rejected the state administrative procedures act limitation of 30 days and allowed a year for filing the case. The reasoning was that the longer timeframe is analogous to other federal and state education law and will permit the parties enough time to prepare for and argue the merits of a case (*York County Sch. Bd. v. Nicely*, 1991).

Where a lawyer represents his client (student with disabilities) competently in all respects except that the student files the case after the statute of limitations has barred him or her from doing so, a court will not overlook that mistake and will bar the student from proceeding against the school district. This teaches the lesson that lawyers and students must be careful about statutes of limitations and suggests that the student should sue the lawyer for malpractice (*I.D. v. Westmoreland Sch. Dist.*, 1992).

The statute of limitations is harsh and unforgiving: Either the party requests the hearing or trial within the period allowed or the party is barred from doing so. This rule, of course, can create problems for parents who do not know about it or have some bona fide reason for not complying. In a few such cases, the courts have been forgiving and found ways around the statute.

For example, if a state changes its period of limitations for IDEA actions (reducing the time for filing the complaint) but the parents are not informed of the change by the LEA or otherwise, and thus would be barred from going forward because the newer and shorter period of limitations would apply, at least one court has exercised its equitable powers to let them rely on the older and longer statute of limitations (*Hebert v. Manchester N.H. School Dist.*, 1993).

Open Hearings

To protect the privacy of parents and students where sensitive matters are involved in due-process hearings (such as a student's mental health), a parent may require a due-process hearing to be closed to the public, especially to newspapers or other media (*Webster Groves Sch. Dist. v. Pulitzer Publ. Co.*, 1990).

Involuntary Dismissal

If a parent refuses to participate in any part of an administrative or judicial hearing (for example, the parent refuses to participate in pretrial discovery proceedings), the court may dismiss the parent's complaint against the parent's objection (involuntary dismissal) (*Nathaniel L. v. Exeter Sch. Dist.*, 1990).

Parental Waiver of Rights and Estoppel

Just as a court may dismiss a parent's complaint through the process known as involuntary dismissal, so, too, may a parent forfeit IDEA rights by "waiving" them. The doctrine of waiver basically means that a party who has certain rights foregoes them voluntarily; the party surrenders them and therefore is "estopped" (barred) from insisting that schools must follow them. Waiver has occurred when

1. parents have failed to request a due-process hearing and then later in court sought relief that would have been available at such a hearing (*Gillette v. Fairland Bd. of Ed.*, 1989).
2. parents knew of but did not insist on exercising their child's IDEA rights (the child had been in special education in one state, though the family now lived in another and did not want the child classified into special education in the

state of the new residence) (*Salley v. St. Tammany Parish Board of Education*, 1995).

3. parents received the requisite notice of their child's IEP meetings, did not participate in those meetings, and, 5 years after they could have participated, claimed their child was entitled to compensatory education, based on the fact that the IEP meetings from 5 years ago did not comply with IDEA (*Buser v. Corpus Christi Indep. School*, 1995).

Mootness

Some parents render their disputes with a school district moot—a term meaning that the dispute no longer is alive, viable, and in contention. For example, if a parent complains that the LEA did not follow IDEA's process exactly, but that parent participates in developing an IEP and agrees to the IEP, the parent creates a "moot" complaint about due process (*I.D. v. New Hampshire Dept. of Educ.*, 1994). Likewise, if a student dies while the parents and LEA are involved in a due-process hearing or in a court trial, the issues concerning the student's rights (classification, program, and placement) are moot; because the issues dividing the parents and schools are moot, the parent also may not recover attorney fees from the school district (*Randolph Union High School District No. 2 v. Byard*, 1995). Chapter 9 will explain the parents' rights to attorney fees in greater detail.

Minors and Age of Majority

The general rule of law is that a person under age 18 (in some states, age 21) is a "minor" and is presumed incapable of exercising any legal rights on his or her behalf. Minors' rights are exercised on their behalf by their parents; that is why, for the most part, IDEA refers to the students' parents as the ones who can invoke IDEA rights.

When, however, the student attains the age of majority, the student becomes competent to exercise, on his or her own behalf, all IDEA rights, unless the student has been adjudicated to be mentally incompetent (under state law). In that case, the student's parent or other legal guardian, appointed by the court that found the student to be incompetent, exercises the student's rights [20 U.S.C. § 1415 (m)(1); 34 C.F.R. § 300.517 (a)]. If a student reaches the age of 18 and has not been deemed incompetent but is unable to give "informed consent" and the parents do not have guardianship rights, the IDEA authorizes schools to establish procedures to appoint the student's parents or other appropriate individuals to represent the student's educational interests [20 U.S.C. § 1415 (m)(2); 34 C.F.R. § 300.517 (b)].

Conclusion ⌣

The reality of due process in IDEA is fairly stark, and problems remain. The largest one seems to be the cost of due process. Cost consists of three elements: (a) the actual financial cost of the hearings—preparing for them, hiring attorneys and expert witnesses, paying for the documents required for evidence, and pursuing an appeal;

(b) the emotional or psychic cost—the enormous energy and stress involved in a hearing and its appeal; and (c) the cost that consists of time spent, and perhaps lost, when the child may (or may not) be receiving an appropriate education.

A good measure of the actual costs involved in due process is the dramatic increase in the number of due-process hearings since IDEA was enacted and IDEA made due process available. Another measure of the actual cost is the increased use of mediation as a way of preventing due process. Mediation involves the use of less formal, less adversarial, more negotiated-settlement meetings for resolving disputes. It is increasingly evident that the psychic costs—the exacerbation of ill will that parents and educators already feel about each other—are the more serious ones, from the viewpoint of the parents and the educators alike who are involved in due process. That is not to minimize the huge financial costs, which are increasingly affordable by only the middle and upper classes and by schools.

Moreover, there is evidence that due process hearings do not satisfactorily resolve the disputes between parents and school systems. There is a perception on the part of some parents that schools have the "home-court advantage" in due process and that parent-initiated due process will not be particularly helpful even if the parents gain the legal victory they seek. That is why many parents, especially those whose income level is upper-middle class and upper-class, can afford to withdraw their children from public education if they fail, in a due process hearing, to obtain the private school placement or other expensive service they sought for their child.

For all of its problems, however, due process remains an important—indeed, an indispensable—element of IDEA and the right to education. Like many other aspects of the legal process, it requires extraordinary amounts of energy, time, and money. The fault lies mainly with the system of dispute resolution in our society. The necessity of due process, however, is beyond dispute.

Cases ∼

Association for Community Living v. Romer, 992 F.2d 1040 (10th Cir. 1993).

Association for Retarded Citizens of Alabama, Inc. v. Teague, 830 F.2d 158 (11th Cir. 1987).

Association for Retarded Citizens in Colorado v. Frazier, 517 F. Supp. 105 (D. Colo. 1981).

Bales v. Clarke, 523 F. Supp. 1366 (E.D.Va. 1981).

Behavior Research Institute v. Secretary of Administration, 577 N.E.2d 297 (Mass. 1991).

Board of Education v. Rowley, 458 U.S. 176 (1982).

Boxall v. Sequoia Union High School Dist., 464 F. Supp. 1104 (N.D.Cal. 1979).

Brown v. D.C. Bd. of Educ., 551 IDELR 101 (D.D.C. 1978).

Burke County Bd. of Educ. v. Denton, 895 F.2d 973 (4th Cir. 1990).

Buser v. Corpus Christi Indep. School, 56 F.3d 1387 (5th Cir. 1995), cert. denied, 116 S. Ct. 305 (1995).

Calhoun v. Illinois State Bd., 550 F. Supp. 796 (N.D.Ill. 1982).

Carroll v. Metropolitan Government of Nashville and Davidson County, No.91-5749, 1992 U.S. App. Lexis 538 (6th Cir. 1992).

Christopher M. v. Corpus Christi Indep. Sch. Dist., 933 F.2d 1285 (5th Cir. 1991).

Christopher T. v. San Francisco U.S.D., 553 F. Supp. 1107 (N.D.Cal. 1982).

Christopher W. v. Portsmouth School Committee, 877 F.2d 1089 (1st Cir. 1989).

Cluff v. Johnson City School Dist., 553 IDELR 598 (N.D.N.Y. 1982).

Concerned Parents and Citizens for Continuing Education at Malcolm X (PS 79) v. New York City Board of Education, 629 F.2d 751 (2nd Cir. 1980), cert. denied, 449 U.S. 1078 (1981).

Corbett v. Regional Center for East Bay, Inc., 676 F. Supp. 964 (N.D.Cal. 1988), clarification of other issue, 699 F. Supp. 230 (N.D.Cal. 1988).

Crocker v. Tennessee Secondary School Athletic Ass'n, 873 F.2d 933 (6th Cir. 1989), aff'd, 908 F.2d 972 (6th Cir. 1990).

Daniel R.R. v. State Bd. of Educ., 874 F.2d 1036 (5th Cir. 1989).

Davis v. Maine Endwell Central School District, 542 F. Supp. 1257 (N.D.N.Y. 1982).

Dell v. Bd. of Educ., 32 F.3d 1053 (7th Cir. 1994).

Dima v. Macchiarola, 513 F. Supp. 565 (E.D.N.Y. 1981).

Doe v. Brookline School Committee, 722 F.2d 910 (1st Cir. 1983).

Doe v. Smith, 879 F.2d 1340 (6th Cir. 1989), cert. denied, *Doe v. Sumner County Bd. of Educ.*, 493 U.S. 1025 (1990).

Ezratty v. Commonwealth of Puerto Rico, 648 F.2d 770 (1st Cir. 1981).

Fallis v. Ambach, 710 F.2d 49 (2nd Cir. 1983).

Farrell v. Carol Stream Sch. Dist. No. 25, No. 96 C 1489, 1996 U. S. Dist. Lexis 9062 (N.D.Ill. 1996).

Fitz v. Intermediate Unit #29, 403 A.2d 138 (Pa. Com. Ct. 1979).

Garrity v. Gallen, 522 F. Supp. 171 (D.N.H. 1981).

Gillette v. Fairland Bd. of Educ., 725 F. Supp. 343 (S.D.Ohio 1989), further proceedings, 932 F.2d 551 (6th Cir. 1991).

Harris v. Campbell, 472 F. Supp. 51 (E.D.Va. 1979).

Hebert v. Manchester Sch. Dist., 833 F. Supp. 80 (D.N.H. 1993).

Honig v. Doe, 484 U.S. 305 (1988).

Hope v. Cortines, 872 F. Supp. 14 (E.D.N.Y. 1995), aff'd, 69 F.3d 687 (2d Cir. 1995).

Howard S. v. Friendswood I.S.D., 454 F. Supp. 634 (S.D.Tex. 1978).

I.D. v. Westmoreland School Dist., 788 F. Supp. 634 (D.N.H. 1992).

I.D. v. New Hampshire Dept. of Educ., 878 F. Supp. 318 (D.N.H. 1994).

J.G. v. Bd. of Educ., EHLR 554:265 (W.D.N.Y. 1982), EHLR 555:190 (W.D.N.Y. 1983), 648 F. Supp. 1452 (W.D.N.Y. 1986), aff'd in part, modified in part, 830 F.2d 444 (2nd Cir. 1987).

Jacky W. v. N.Y.C. Bd. of Educ., 848 F. Supp. 358 (E.D.N.Y. 1994).

Jeremy H. v. Mt. Lebanon Sch. Dist., 95 F.3d 272 (3rd Cir. 1996).

Jose P. v. Ambach, 669 F.2d 865 (2nd Cir. 1982).

Kerr Center Parents Association v. Charles, 572 F. Supp. 448 (D.Ore. 1983), aff'd in part, rev'd in part, 897 F.2d 1463 (9th Cir. 1990).

Kotowicz v. Mississippi State Bd. of Ed., 630 F. Supp. 925 (S.D.Mass. 1986).

Kresse v. Johnson City School Dist., 553 IDELR 601 (N.D.N.Y. 1982).

Language Dev. Program, Inc. v. Ambach, 466 N.Y.S.2d 734 (N.Y. App. Div. 1983).

Lenn v. Portland Sch. Comm., 998 F.2d 1083 (1st Cir. 1993).

Levy v. Commonwealth, Dept. of Ed., 399 A.2d 159 (Pa. 1979).

Livingston School Dist. Nos. 4 & 1 v. Keenan, 82 F.3d 912 (9th Cir. 1996).

Loughran v. Flanders, 470 F. Supp. 110 (D.Conn. 1979).

Manchester City Sch. Dist. v. Jason N., 18 IDELR 384 (D.N.H. 1991).

Matta v. Indian Hill Exempted Village Schools, 731 F. Supp. 253 (S.D.Ohio 1990).

Mayson v. Teague, 749 F.2d 652 (11th Cir. 1984).

Miener v. Missouri, 498 F. Supp. 944 (E.D.Mo. 1980), aff'd in part, rev'd in part, 673 F.2d 969 (8th Cir. 1982), cert. denied, 459 U.S. 909, 916, on remand, *Miener v. Special Sch. Dist.*, 580 F. Supp. 562 (E.D. Mo. 1984), aff'd in part, rev'd in part, 800 F.2d 749 (8th Cir. 1986).

Militello v. Bd. of Educ., 803 F. Supp. 974 (D.N.J. 1992).

Monahan v. Nebraska, 491 F. Supp. 1074 (D.Neb. 1980), aff'd in part, vacated in part, 645 F.2d 592 (9th Cir. 1981).

Mrs. W. v. Tirozzi, 832 F.2d 748 (2nd Cir. 1987).

Nathaniel L. v. Exeter Sch. Dist., 16 IDELR 1073 (D.N.H. 1990).

New Mexico Association for Retarded Citizens v. New Mexico, 495 F. Supp. 391 (D.N.M. 1980), rev'd, 678 F.2d 847 (10th Cir. 1982).

North v. D.C. Bd. of Ed., 471 F. Supp. 136 (D.D.C. 1979).

Phipps v. New Hanover County Bd. of Ed., 551 F. Supp. 732 (E.D.N.C. 1982).

Polk v. Central Susquehanna Intermediate Unit 16, 853 F.2d 171 (3rd Cir. 1988), cert. denied, 488 U.S. 1030 (1989).

Prins v. Indep. Sch. Dist. No. 761, 23 IDELR 544 (D.Minn. 1995).

Quackenbush v. Johnson City School District, 716 F.2d 141 (2nd Cir. 1983), cert. denied, 465 U.S. 1071 (1984).

Randolph Union High School District No. 2 v. Byard, 897 F. Supp. 174 (D.Vt. 1995), aff'd, 24 IDELR 928 (D.Vt. 1996).

Reusch v. Fountain, 872 F. Supp. 1421 (D.Md. 1994).

Riley v. Ambach, 508 F. Supp. 1222 (E.D.N.Y. 1980), rev'd, 668 F.2d 635 (2d Cir. 1981).

Robert M. v. Benton, 634 F.2d 1139 (8th Cir. 1980), further proceedings, 671 F.2d 1104 (8th Cir. 1982).

Roncker v. Walter, 700 F.2d 1058 (6th Cir. 1983), cert. denied, 464 U.S. 864 (1983).

(Ruth Anne) M. v. Alvin I.S.D., 532 F. Supp. 460 (S.D.Tex. 1982).

Salley v. St. Tammany Parish Sch. Bd., 57 F.3d 458 (5th Cir. 1995).

Savka v. Commonwealth, Dept. of Ed., 403 A.2d 142 (Pa.Comm. Ct. 1979).

School Board of Prince William County v. Malone, 762 F.2d 1210 (4th Cir. 1985), further proceedings, 662 F. Supp. 999 (E.D. Va. 1987).

School Board of Hillsborough County v. Student 26493257S, 23 IDELR 93 (M.D.Fla. 1995).

Sessions v. Livingston Parish Sch. Bd., 501 F. Supp. 251 (M.D.La. 1980).

Shannon v. Ambach, 553 IDELR 198 (E.D.N.Y. 1981).

Silvio v. Commonwealth, Dept. of Ed., 439 A.2d 893 (Pa. Comm. Ct. 1982), aff'd, 456 A.2d 1366 (Pa. 1983).

Smith v. Ambach, EHLR 552:490 (N.D.N.Y. 1981).

Smith v. Cumberland School Committee, EHLR 551:639 (R.I. 1979), further proceedings on other issues, 703 F.2d 4 (1st Cir. 1983), aff'd sub nom., *Smith v. Robinson*, 468 U.S. 992 (1984).

Stauffer v. William Penn Sch. Dist., 829 F. Supp. 742 (E.D.Pa. 1993).

Sullivan v. Vallejo City Unified School Dist., 731 F. Supp. 947 (E.D.Cal. 1990).

Tennessee Dept. of Mental Health & Mental Retardation v. Paul B., 88 F.3d 1466 (6th Cir. 1996).

Tilton v. Jefferson County Bd. of Educ., 705 F.2d 800 (6th Cir. 1983); cert. denied 465 U.S. 1006 (1984).

United Cerebral Palsy of NYC v. Bd. of Ed. of City of N.Y., 669 F.2d 865 (2d Cir. 1982), further proceedings, 557 F. Supp. 1230 (E.D.N.Y. 1983).

Urban v. Jefferson County School Dist., 870 F. Supp 1558 (D.Colo. 1994); aff'd 89 F.3d 720 (10th Cir. 1996).

Vander Malle v. Ambach, 673 F.2d 49 (2nd Cir. 1982), further proceedings, 667 F. Supp. 1015 (S.D.N.Y. 1987).

Vermont Association for Children with Learning Disabilities v. Kaagan, EHLR 554:349 (1982), EHLR 554:447 (1983).

Webster Groves Sch. Dist. v. Pulitzer Pub. Co., 898 F.2d 1371 (8th Cir. 1990).

Windward School v. State, EHLR 551:219 (S.D.N.Y. 1978), aff'd EHLR 551:224 (2nd Cir. 1979).

York County Sch. Bd. v. Nicely, 408 S.E.2d 545 (Va.Ct. App. 1991).

8

Parent Participation and Shared Decision-Making

Shared decision-making in the schools and in other public agencies is called participatory democracy. It refers to the legal right or political opportunity of those affected by a public agency's decisions to participate in making those decisions. Although it is a longstanding tenet of U.S. government, it has not always been in good standing. Too often it has been given little more than lip service. As this chapter shows, however, IDEA makes inroads against unilateral decision-making in the schools.

Although the legal foundations for parents' participating in their children's education are not well articulated, they nevertheless exist and can be identified and explained. At the core of these principles is the common-law doctrine that parents have a duty to support their children and a corollary right to their children's services and earnings for as long as the children have the legal status of minors. Under common law, and even by today's statutes, these rights and interests mean that parents may control their children in various ways.

For example, parents have the right to consent (on the minor's behalf) to their child's medical treatment. Further, compulsory school-attendance laws usually make the parents criminally liable if they do not require their child to attend the public schools. Also, state statutes make parents criminally liable for failing to support their minor children. The reason for these and similar laws is that a minor is presumed incapable, because of age, of acting on his or her own behalf except in limited ways, as granted by statute or, as recognized recently under the constitutional "privacy interest," by the courts (for example, the rights to abortion, contraception, and treatment for substance abuse). Parents, then, have rights that they can exercise on behalf of their child, and in many instances the parents exercise the child's right to have an education.

Individuals with Disabilities Education Act ∽

IDEA declares that the Act is intended to ensure protection of the children's rights and those of their parents or guardians [20 U.S.C. § 1400 (d)(1)(B)]. It carries out its policy of shared decision-making in the following ways (in addition to those mentioned already in conjunction with enrollment/zero reject, evaluation, individualized education programs, least restrictive placement, and procedural due process).

Participation and Partnerships

One of the primary purposes of the 1997 amendments to IDEA was to expand the opportunities for partnerships between parents and agency staff (34 C.F.R. 300 Appendix A, p.34.300-60A). The term "parents" under IDEA includes natural or adoptive parents, legal guardians, or surrogate parents [20 U.S.C. § 1401 (19)]. Even though the public agency has the ultimate responsibility to decide when the team as a whole cannot agree, they still must consider parents' concerns and the information parents have provided in making any decisions [34 C.F.R. 300.343(c)(iii) and 300.346(a)(1) and (b)].

In offering full educational opportunities to all children with disabilities, LEAs must provide for the participation and consultation of the children's parents or guardians. Parents accordingly have a right to provide information, express concerns, participate in discussions, and join with the other participants in making decisions about the education of their child (34 C.F.R. 300 Appendix A, p.34.300-60A).

Notice and Hearings

IDEA also requires SEAs to establish procedures for making the state policies and procedures available to the public and to the parents [34 C.F.R. § 300.284]; for having public hearings [34 C.F.R. § 300.280] and for giving adequate notice of those hearings; and for allowing the general public to comment on proposed policies, programs, and procedures required by the IDEA before they are adopted [20 U.S.C. § 1412(a)(20) and 34 C.F.R. § 300.282].

Under 300.282, SEAs also must give public notice of policy hearings, provide an opportunity for public participation and public comment,to review public comments before adopting policies and procedures, and publish and make the policies and procedures generally available [34 C.F.R. §§ 300.280-300.284].

Advisory Panels

SEAs must create an advisory panel whose members are to be appointed by the Governor or any other authorized official. The panel should be representative of the state's population and be composed of individuals involved in or concerned with the education of children with disabilities, including

1. parents of children with disabilities,
2. individuals with disabilities,
3. teachers of children with disabilities,
4. representatives of institutions of higher education that prepare special education and related services personnel,
5. state and local education officials,
6. administrators of programs for children with disabilities,
7. representatives of other state agencies involved in the financing or delivery of related services,
8. representatives of private schools or public charter schools,
9. at least one representative of a vocational, community, or business organization concerned with the provision of transition services, and
10. representatives from the state juvenile and adults corrections agencies [20 U.S.C. § 1412 (a)(21)(B) and 34 C.F.R. § 300.651].

A majority of the membership on state advisory panels for special education must be individuals with disabilities or parents of children with disabilities [20 U.S.C. § 1412 (a)(21)(C)].

The state advisory panel is to advise the SEAs on the development of corrective action plans to address findings identified in federal monitoring reports, the development of policies relating to the coordination of services for students with disabilities and on the unmet needs of students with disabilities. The panel also may make public comment on any state rules or regulations to be issued by the SEA and assist the state in developing and reporting whatever data and evaluations the U.S. Secretary of Education might require [20 U.S.C. § 1412 (a)(21)(D)].

Access to System Records

IDEA requires that certain information about school programs for children with disabilities and about the children themselves be treated as public information, available to all, including parents of the children with disabilities. An LEA must give assurances that its application for federal funds and all documents related to the application are available to parents, or guardians, and other members of the general public. This includes information that is necessary for an SEA to perform its evaluation duties and information relating to the educational achievement of children with disabilities in programs financed under the Act [20 U.S.C. § 1413 (a)(7)]. Likewise, before submitting any amendments to its policies and procedures, an SEA must give to parents, or guardians, and other members of the general public adequate notice of such amendments, hold public hearings, and provide opportunities for the public to comment [20 U.S.C. § 1412 (a)(20)].

Protection of Student Records

IDEA also provides for the confidentiality of student records and access to those records by parents or guardians [20 U.S.C. § 1412 (a)(8) and § 1417 (c)]. The SEAs and LEAs both are subject to the Family Educational Rights and Privacy Act (FERPA), codified at 20 U.S.C. § 1232g, with regulations at 34 C.F.R. Part 99.

General Rule Under Family Educational Rights and Privacy Act (FERPA)

FERPA requires recipients of federal education grants to give parents, or guardians, and in some cases, pupils, access to their own public school records. Parents must be given an opportunity for a hearing to challenge the content of the records, and certain parts of the records cannot be released without parental consent. The IDEA confidentiality regulations [34 C.F.R. §§ 300.560-300.576] conform to FERPA. Thus, the general rule—as it affects students with disabilities—is twofold: access to system and individual-student records by a limited number of people, and confidentiality of individual-student records (privacy).

To assure access and still preserve confidentiality of student records, the regulations implementing FERPA clarify the meaning of various terms, and thus the extent to which confidentiality is assured.

Under FERPA regulations and for the purposes of IDEA only, the following definitions apply [34 C.F.R. § 99.3]:

1. "Education records" is defined by inclusion and exclusion.
   a. Included in the term are those records that are
      i. related directly to a student and
      ii. maintained by an LEA or party acting on its behalf.
   b. Excluded from the term, and therefore not assured confidentiality, are the following records:
      i. Records of instructional, supervisory, and administrative and educational personnel ancillary to those persons that are kept in the sole possession of the maker of the record and are not accessible or revealed to any other person except a temporary substitute for the maker of the record—that is, an educator's "private" notes about a student
      ii. Records of a law enforcement unit of an LEA, but only if the education records the LEA maintains are not disclosed to that unit and only if the law-enforcement records are (a) maintained separately from education records, (b) maintained solely for law-enforcement purposes, and (c) disclosed only to law-enforcement officials of the same jurisdiction as LEA (that is, the LEA's city or county or other jurisdiction's law-enforcement agency)
2. "Parent" refers to a natural parent, guardian, or individual acting as a parent in the absence of a natural parent or guardian.
3. "Student" refers to an individual who is, or has been, in attendance at an education agency (an LEA or a state-operated school or program) and regarding whom the agency maintains education records.

4. "Eligible student" refers to a student who has reached 18 years of age.

5. "Personally identifiable information" includes, without limitation, the student's name, the name of the student's parent or other family member, the address of the student or student's family, any personal identifier (such as the student's Social Security number or an agency's assigned student number).

6. "Directory information" is information contained in a student's education record that generally would not be considered harmful or an invasion of privacy if disclosed, and includes, without limitation, name, address, telephone listing, date and place of birth, major field of study, participation in officially recognized activities and sports, weight and height of athletic teams, dates of attendance, degrees and awards received, and the most recent previous educational institution attended.

7. "Disclosure" means permitted access to, or the release, transfer, or other communication of, education records or the personally identifiable information contained in those records to any party, by any means, including oral, written, or electronic means.

Additional Protections

Besides FERPA protection, parents (including surrogate parents and guardians) have additional rights under IDEA. Thus, an SEA must notify parents (in the parents' native language) that personally identifiable information is on file [34 C.F.R. § 300.561]. Further, it must explain the type of information it plans to collect and how it plans to collect and use the information. For example, an SEA might collect information on the number of children with a certain disabling condition, or it might seek data for a description of the educational achievement of a group of children with disabilities [§ 300.561].

In addition, parents must be provided with a summary of policies and procedures to be used by a "participating agency" (any agency or institution that collects, maintains, and uses or provides information) for storing information, releasing it to third parties, or destroying it, as well as the agency's plan for protecting personally identifiable information. An SEA must announce publicly, through the newspapers or some other appropriate media, any child identification and evaluation activities it plans [34 C.F.R. § 300.561].

Thus, the SEA has the responsibility for developing policies for access to system records and protection of student records, to be followed by all participating agencies. Representatives from LEAs may wish to request an opportunity to participate in the SEA's development of these policies.

Parents and their representatives have the right to inspect personally identifiable information in their child's records within 45 days, maximum, after requesting to inspect the records. If the record includes information on more than one child, parents are entitled to see, or to be informed about, only the portion relating to their child [34 C.F.R. § 300.564]. The agency may presume that the parent has access rights unless it is advised otherwise in cases of guardianship, separation, or divorce.

Parents may request an explanation or interpretation of the information and must be provided with copies if failure to provide copies would result in their being unable to inspect or review the information [34 C.F.R. § 300.562]. A fee for copies may be charged, unless the fee would prevent a parent from having access to the record [34 C.F.R. § 300.566]. Upon request, parents also must be provided with a list of the types and locations of information the agency has collected and used [34 C.F.R. § 300.565]. The school must keep a record of access [34 C.F.R. § 300.563].

After reading the records and having them interpreted appropriately, parents may request that the participating agency amend the information. The agency must consider the request and give an affirmative or negative response within a reasonable time. If the agency disagrees with the request, it must inform the parents of their right to a hearing to protest this decision [34 C.F.R. §§ 300.567-300.570]. Thus, parents not only have rights of access to student records but they also have rights to informally or formally challenge the contents of student records. This underscores the necessity for educators to recognize the importance of their responsibilities in maintaining accurate student records and developing skills in documenting educational progress.

The regulations safeguarding the confidentiality of student information set forth clear implementation guidelines for public schools. First, one official must be appointed at each participating agency to assume overall responsibility for ensuring that personally identifiable information remains confidential [34 C.F.R. § 300.572(b)]. This person might be the director of special education, the director of special services, or some other administrator who has concomitant responsibility for implementing IDEA and Section 504. All persons who participate in the collection or use of confidential information must receive training related to the state's policies and procedures on confidentiality of personally identifiable information [34 C.F.R. § 300.572(c)]. The participating agency also must maintain an updated roster of persons (and their positions) the agency employs who have access to personally identifiable information. This list is to be available for public inspection [34 C.F.R. § 300.572(d)].

Before releasing personally identifiable information to anyone other than the agency officials authorized to collect and use this information, public agencies must obtain parental consent, unless otherwise authorized to do so under the Family Educational Rights and Privacy Act. When a parent refuses to give consent [34 C.F.R. § 300.571], the SEA must establish policies and procedures to be followed.

Public agencies must notify parents when personally identifiable information that had been collected and maintained is no longer needed for educational services. Upon the parent's request, the information must be destroyed. Permanent information that can be kept without regard to time limitations includes a student's name, address, phone number, grades, attendance record, classes attended, grade level completed, and year completed [34 C.F.R. § 300.573].

Public agency officials should advise parents that their child's records may be needed for purposes such as securing Social Security benefits or qualifying for certain income-tax deductions. In addition, the safeguards for maintaining confidentiality of records should be explained fully to parents before they make a decision about having the records destroyed.

In their annual program plans, SEAs are required to specify policies and procedures to assure the rights of children as well as the rights of their parents. Consideration should be given to the child's age and the type or severity of disability [34 C.F.R. § 300.574]. Also, the regulations mandate adherence to the Family Educational Rights and Privacy Act requirement that parental rights pertaining to educational records be transferred to the student at age 18 [34 C.F.R. § 300.574(b)]. This requirement has major implications for schools serving students with disabilities in the 18-to-21 age range.

Case Law on Access to Records

So far, few cases have been decided involving access to the records of students in special education. Because the issues in these cases are so varied, no trends can be discerned.

In *Belanger v. Nashua Sch. Dist. (1994)* the court held that a parent has the right to read and copy the child's juvenile court records that were in the LEA's possession. The bases for the decision were two:

1. The school's attorney maintained the records on behalf of the district and in his capacity as its lawyer, thereby indicating that the records had some bearing on the student's education.
2. The records themselves contained information directly relevant to the student's education, and indeed the student's involvement with a juvenile justice system affected his school placement directly.

The point of the case is straightforward: When an agent of the district maintains records and when the district uses them for making decisions about free appropriate education, the records, even though they normally would not be accessible to the parents (as juvenile court records were not, in New Hampshire), will become accessible to them.

Criminal court proceedings were involved in still another FERPA-related case. In *State of Connecticut v. Bruno (1996)*, a defendant in a murder trial sought access to the records of two students who were witnesses against him, alleging that he needed to know about their educational and psychiatric history to prove that they were mentally incapable of giving credible testimony. A trial court found that the defendant failed to show that the students' records would help him attack their credibility and, therefore, denied him access. If, however, he had been able to show that he needed access to the records to impeach their testimony, possibly a court would have granted access.

Finally, the disclosure of districtwide records can become risky, as illustrated by *Maynard v. Greater Hoyt School Dist. No. 61-4 (1995)*. There, a rural South Dakota school district entered into an agreement with a neighboring school district in Iowa to educate its special education students. The Iowa LEA decided that one student, J.M., required out-of-state placement in a private residential program, and, upon placing the student there, it also paid the student's tuition and related fees and then billed the South Dakota district for reimbursement.

The South Dakota district reimbursed the Iowa district but raised the local property tax immediately to meet that cost. In this case, it raised the tax so substantially that taxpayers noticed and began to investigate the sudden and dramatic increase in their taxes, coming to believe that it was caused solely by the placement of the well known student (well known in a very small community).

Upon looking into the matter, a reporter for the local South Dakota newspaper sought access to the district's financial records and, without learning the name of the student who was "contracted out" to the Iowa district, concluded that the out-of-state placement was the sole reason for the tax increase.

Upon publication of the story and conclusion, the taxpayers turned on the students' parents, blaming them for the increase in taxes. Aghast that the newspaper had published the story and conclusion, the parents sued the newspaper, claiming, among other things, that the local school district had violated their and their child's privacy rights (under FERPA) by allowing the reporter to have access to the district's records.

The court ruled against the parents, holding that FERPA had not been violated because (a) the district disclosed only districtwide records, not personally identifiable information, and (b) in making those records public, the district also was complying with a state law requiring the financial records of each district to be compiled, reported to the state education agency, and made accessible to the public.

Thus, when an LEA complies with state law regarding public records and does so without directly revealing the identity of any student, it apparently does not violate FERPA. The key, it seems, is that the particular records of a particular student are not revealed; the fact that costs can be attributed to one or more students does not necessarily mean that the identity of those students can be ascertained. In such a small school district as the South Dakota one, however, identity is difficult to conceal; it can be inferred because the number of students in special education is small and because the out-of-state or other high expense incurred on behalf of one student is traceable by access to districtwide, but not personal, records.

Related Services and Benefits to Parents ∼

As pointed out in Chapter 5, IDEA defines an appropriate education as special education and the related services and other support services that are necessary for the student to benefit from special education. Related services commonly are targeted to students only, but they can benefit the students' family as well. That is because of a simple fact: Whatever benefits the student also benefits the student's family.

In addition to this "family systems" approach, families or parents are entitled to a much more direct benefit from related services. This is so because the following related services, by their very definitions in the regulations, are available to the students' parents or family members:

1. Training and technical assistance related to "assistive technology services" [34 C.F.R. § 300.6(e)]
2. Counseling and guidance for parents related to hearing loss, as part of the related service of "audiology" [34 C.F.R. § 300.24 (b)(1)(v)]
3. "Parent counseling and training" [34 C.F.R. § 300.24 (a)]
4. Psychological counseling for parents, as part of the related service of "psychological services" [34 C.F.R. § 300.24 (b)(9)(v)]
5. Group and individual counseling with the student's family, as part of the related service of "social work services in school" [34 C.F.R. § 300.24 (b)(13)(ii)]
6. Counseling and guidance of parents, as part of the related service of "speech pathology" [34 C.F.R. § 300.24 (b)(14)(v)].

These services do not depend on the student's age; the parents or family of any student in special education (birth through 21) may receive these services, but only if the services are regarded as "necessary" to help the student benefit from special education and are included in the student's IEP.

Age-limited services, however, also can directly benefit the student's family or parents. Foremost among these, of course, are those set out in Part C (birth to age three—infants and toddlers), as long as they are incorporated into the individualized family service plan (IFSP) (see Chapter 5 for a full discussion of Part C).

Part C ❧

Other Part C rules apply to parent participation. The law establishes a State Interagency Coordinating Council and requires that 20 percent of the Council's membership be parents of infants or toddlers with disabilities [20 U.S.C. § 1441 (b)(1)(A)].

In addition, all of the parent rights available under Part B relating to access to and confidentiality of information apply to Part C programs. Parents and other members of the public may have access to information about state and local early intervention programs. Generally, parents and other members of the public may obtain all information concerning the programs that the state or local agency runs. (This is different from the rights of parents to have access to their child's education records. That type of access does not belong to the public.)

Parents have the right to consent or object to the release of personally identifying information about their children [20 U.S.C. § 1439 (a)(2)]. This protects family privacy. In addition to the right to assure confidentiality, parents have the right of access to their own children's educational records [20 U.S.C. § 1439 (a)(4)]. This assures the basis for a long-term and constructive relationship.

The state also must publish its proposed plan, give notice of when hearings will be held, allow for public opportunity to comment on the plan, hold public hearings, and review and comment on the public comments [20 U.S.C. § 1437 (a)(7)]. It also must establish a public-awareness program, comprehensive child-find system, and a central directory of information [20 U.S.C. § 1435 (a)(5)-(7)].

Parent Responsibilities ⌐∿

Although IDEA's main focus is on how LEAs and SEAs interact with parents and students, the statute also contains a few provisions addressing the responsibilities of parents. If the parents of a student with a disability wish to file a complaint regarding their child's education, they (or their attorney, if they have one) must include in the complaint

1. the student's name, residential address, and the school the student is attending
2. a description of the nature of the student's problem relating to the proposed initiation or change in the student's identification, evaluation, placement, or free appropriate public education, including the facts relating to the problem
3. a proposed resolution to the problem to the extent known and available to the parents at the time [20 U.S.C. § 1415 (b)(7)].

SEAs must develop a model form to assist parents in filing complaints that contain this information [20 U.S.C. § 1415 (b)(8)].

Including this information in a complaint is important, especially for complaints filed by attorneys representing parents. If an attorney fails to include the above information in a complaint filed on behalf of a student's parents and the parents eventually prevail in court, the court may reduce the amount of attorney fees awarded to the parents [20 U.S.C. § 1415 (i)(F)(iv)].

Significance of ADA
and IDEA for Families ⌐∿

Chapters 3 and 5 covered the significance of IDEA, Section 504, and ADA for the student. And these three laws, especially IDEA and ADA, clearly have implications for families as well. Not all of the implications are positive. For example, excluding the insurance industry from ADA's coverage is highly problematic. Insurance is a major fringe benefit in many jobs and is essential in ensuring access to affordable and appropriate health care. The frankly political compromise—exclude the insurance industry or lose the votes necessary to pass ADA—may be addressed on two levels: in the state legislatures as they regulate the sale of insurance in their respective states, or in Congress as part of health-care legislation. For families, then, the goal has to be to complement ADA with comprehensive health-care legislation.

The power of public opinion also is problematic politically. For many years now, incrementalism in law reform has been the pattern. It is not only effective (after all, ADA is a product of the Civil Rights Act of 1964 and the Rehabilitation Act antidiscrimination provisions of 1975) but also politically adept (to lose the sympathetic imagination of the dominant majority without disabilities would be politically disastrous). For families, then, the future requires the skillful courting of public opinion.

Legally, families still must be involved in the regulation-making phases. They need to ensure effective advocacy to enforce the laws and create factual defenses (chock-full of economic rationale) to match the "reasonable accommodations/undue burden" defenses.

Despite these problematic aspects of IDEA and ADA interface, the two laws indisputably can confer great benefits for families. On a personal and immediate level and as pointed out in the previous chapters, individual families face the future with optimism and more arrows in their quivers than ever before. IDEA now creates a new equal-access doctrine: Students with disabilities have access to the same and different resources of the education system, for the same and different purposes as children without disabilities.

There is a major boon, expressed in the provisions related to individualized transition plans and IDEA's orientation from a process-oriented law to an outcome-oriented law. It is a boon because it teaches families that appropriate education is assured principally by a community-based, community-referenced curriculum that helps a student develop the skills needed to participate in those sectors of society now affected by ADA. It also is a boon because, even though Congress refuses to amend the least-restrictive-education provisions of IDEA, Congress did, through the transition provisions, send the signal that it intends the curriculum to be delivered in integrated settings.

ADA expands the equal-access doctrine from education to other domains of the person's and family's life. Individuals with disabilities now are entitled to access to the same resources as other individuals, for the same purposes. The same resources are opportunities in employment, transportation, public accommodations, state/local government services, and telecommunications. And the access is for the same purposes: to participate in the mainstream [Senator Harkin, 136 Cong. Rec. S. 9684, 9689; President Bush, statement, July 26, 1990] and to have "equality of opportunity, full participation, independent living, and economic self-sufficiency" [42 U.S.C. § 2(a)(8)].

The parallels between IDEA and ADA reinforce the new access, all-domains doctrine that IDEA and ADA create. IDEA's "zero reject" principle, with its tenet of "educability" and purpose of inclusion, has become ADA's "zero-reject" principle for all of life, with tenets of "employability" and "ability" and thus of inclusion. IDEA's "appropriate education" principle has become ADA's "reasonable accommodation" rule. IDEA's "least restrictive environment" principle has become ADA's ban against physical and attitudinal barriers in adult life—its promise of inclusion and "full participation." IDEA's due-process principle has been incorporated into ADA's enforcement provisions. And IDEA's "parent participation" principle has become ADA's participation rule: that the person with a disability (and thus the person's family, under the family-systems approach) will participate in deciding whether, how, and how much to exercise the new equality of opportunity that ADA creates.

But more than mere legal parallelism, more than a continuation of the promises of education, is involved. Just as IDEA began to shape the views and values of families and students, so too does ADA affect them. ADA (together with IDEA) gives families reasons for great expectations, for realizing the positive contributions their members can make, for being able to act on their choices and play from their strengths, and for attaining full citizenship.

Also beyond argument is that IDEA and ADA together create a contract of lifetime support and access for individuals with disabilities and their families. IDEA's rights to free appropriate public education are the basis for ADA's rights to nondiscrimination and participation. IDEA's Part C rights to early intervention become, in due course, Part B rights to early childhood education and then, also in due course, to appropriate education and transition services.

Simultaneously, ADA's rights to nondiscrimination and participation are available to the infant/toddler, preschooler, and student as well. The social contract envisioned by Rousseau and the Enlightenment philosophers has, at last, been realized (at least as a matter of the formal law, if not yet fully as a matter of reality) for individuals with disabilities.

Accordingly, as rights to education and participation are enforced, and as individuals with disabilities, their families, and the majority without disabilities see each other in new ways (as educable/employable/able and entitled to and benefiting from education and participation), the "norms" of society change. The "norm" in the schools has become one of inclusion of students with disabilities and the participation of their families. As ADA is implemented, the norm in the world outside school mirrors that school norm.

The consequence is that the "forms" of society change, too. The physical, attitudinal, economic, and other barriers that excluded students with disabilities from education have been disappearing steadily, and they have begun to disappear in the rest of the United States as well.

What can be said in summary of ADA, IDEA, and families?

1. These two laws affect families, not just their members with disabilities.
2. These laws change the laws, the slogans, and the results by which families can live.
3. These laws extend the Supreme Court's decision in *Brown v. Bd. of Educ.* (1954). That decision, like these laws, had a singular, albeit vital, purpose: to ensure by law that the rights of citizenship apply to all alike, not just to a few.
4. These two laws reflect the "social construct" or "transactional" nature of disability: Impairment or disability may be an unchangeable trait of the person, but "handicap" is that which the world creates by failing to accommodate to that difference. These laws affect the individual and enable the person and the family to overcome the effects of disability. And they equally affect the world in which the person and family live and require it to adapt and accommodate.
5. The underlying motives of federal law at last have been confirmed and applied to all sectors of American life. These motives are altruism (a concern to help those with disabilities), rebalancing power (eliminating the disadvantage that

individuals with disabilities have experienced), anti-institutionalization (ensuring participation in the mainstream and barring segregation in institutions), and equal opportunity (creating a level playing field on which all may participate).

In the last analysis, families of individuals with disabilities, while still facing macro-level and individual-level obstacles, have a different life before them. Not since 1975, when Congress enacted IDEA as PL 94–142 and the antidiscrimination provisions of the Rehabilitation Act [§ 504], has there been such a confluence of opportunity: the opportunity to apply and benefit from new laws that have complementary purposes and provisions; to adopt and live by new creeds and slogans; and to establish, through laws and creeds, new norms and forms.

Case Law on Parent Participation ~

Perhaps reflecting the fact that family nowadays includes more than just parents, incorporating brothers, sisters, grandparents, other blood or by-marriage relatives, and even "extended family" who are not related by blood or marriage, the term "parent" includes more than simply the natural (biological) parent of a child with a disability. Thus, permanent foster parents, appointed by the state welfare agency to be the student's "parents," are entitled to exercise all of the rights the LEA gives to natural parents, and the foster parents, not the state agency, are entitled to make decisions about enforcing rights under IDEA. Likewise, the state may not appoint surrogate parents for the student who has permanent foster parents (*Criswell v. State Dept. of Educ.*, 1986).

Even when a surrogate parent has been appointed for the student, the natural parents may sue an LEA to enforce their rights under IDEA. This is true even if the child has attained the age of majority. The reason for this result is that the appointment of a surrogate is for the purpose of enforcing the child's rights. The appointment does not displace the natural parents' own rights. Moreover, even after the child reaches the age of majority, the natural, adoptive, or foster parents retain the right to enforce their rights, if not their child's, under IDEA (*John H. v. McDonald*, 1986).

When a child's natural parents have separated or divorced, the general practice has been for the LEA to deal only with the parent to whom the child's custody has been awarded. This has proven to be sound practice and probably should not be modified except in one situation: the situation in which the noncustodial parent is responsible for the child's educational expenses. In that case, the LEA must seek to involve the noncustodial parent in all parent-rights matters and must accede to that parent's wishes to be involved as fully as the custodial parent, such as in IEP development (*Doe v. Anrig, 1983*).

A natural parent can lose the rights of participation by his or her own action. Thus, when a parent, to obtain the child's admission to a state psychiatric institution, arranges for the county department of human services to be appointed as the child's conservator (guardian) and for a lawyer to be appointed as the guardian *ad litem* (a guardian for the purpose of a lawsuit only), and when the same parent fails to obtain a court appointment as the child's next of friend (a legal term designating the continuing parent-child relationship), the parent loses his or her right to sue on the child's behalf (*Susan R.M. v. Northwest I.S.D., 1987*).

Sometimes parents who live in one school district try to get another school district to pay for their child's education. These parents have "gone shopping" for the best education they can find, wherever they could find it. They try to shift their responsibility from the school district where they reside, but they generally fail in their efforts. Almost uniformly, the courts have held that the residence of a student's parents is also the residence of the student. This is the customary rule: A student resides where the parents reside. Sometimes parents have separated or divorced, and the issue arises as to whether the school district of one parent is responsible or whether the school district of the other parent—where the separated or divorced parents live in different districts—is responsible. The school district where the parent who has custody of a child (pursuant to a valid divorce decree and agreement) lives is the school district that is responsible for the student's special education costs, not the district where the noncustodial parent lives (*George H. and Irene L. Walker Home for Children v. Town of Franklin,* 1993).

Sometimes parent participation actually can disrupt the legal process and jeopardize a child's rights under IDEA. That was the situation when a parent was so abusive of the legal process that he willingly disobeyed court orders in a case that he brought on his own behalf and on his child's behalf. To secure the judicial process and punish him, the court fined him $500 for contempt of court and dismissed the lawsuit that he filed on his own behalf. Recognizing, however, that his child, the student, should not be penalized because of the father's misconduct, the court did not dismiss the child's case (*Mylo v. Baltimore County Board of Education,* 1991).

It is settled law that parents have a right to tape-record an IEP conference when they have a hearing or physical disability that prevents them from participating fully in the conference and the recording does not violate any rights to privacy of teachers or the LEA, because IDEA and its regulations seek to ensure full participation of parents in the IEP process (*E.H. v. Tirozzi,* 1990; and *V. W. and R.W. v. Favolise,* 1990).

Conclusion ∼

Clearly, IDEA recognizes a new role for families and parents—that of education decision-makers. This is not, however, a perfectly realized role, in part because the roles that families and parents have been expected to play have not evolved fully, and in part because parents still defer to educators and educators expect parents to do just that. What, then, have been those roles? As Turnbull and Turnbull (1997) point out, the basic roles are

1. parents or families as the source or causes of their children's disabilities

2. parents and families as members of family-centered, family-directed organizations that exist to satisfy families' needs
3. parents and families as developers of services for their children, including education, recreation, residential, and vocational services
4. parents and families as the relatively passive recipients of professionals' decisions, as the second (and less active) party in the principle of deference to expert opinion
5. parents and families as the follow-through educators of their children, as auxiliary teachers who are expected to carry out school-planned education and other interventions
6. parents and families as political advocates, as the primary constituency behind laws such as IDEA and others that create rights or entitlements or protection from discrimination
7. parents and families as education decision-makers, as partners with educators in developing "I-plans" and helping to carry them out—this being the current role envisioned by IDEA.

An emerging eighth role builds on the "partner/education decision-maker" role and extends it significantly. As Turnbull and Turnbull (1997) note, the newest role is as collaborators. This role involves more than just the parents; it opens up opportunities for the parents and for all other members of the family, as well as friends of the student, to be involved. This role recognizes that families are systems; whatever happens to one member affects all others.

The new role does more than change the beneficiaries from "just" parents to all family members (and selected friends). It also recognizes that families are affected by, and also affect, service delivery systems, including schools.

Turnbull and Turnbull refer to these systems as the "contexts" in which families operate. Accordingly, they refer to collaboration as "the dynamic process of connecting families' resources (that is, motivation and knowledge/skills) to an empowering context to make decisions collectively" (Turnbull & Turnbull, 1997). In their role as collaborators, families are expected to be (if they want to be) "equal and full partners with educators and school systems"—so the collaboration between families and educators "will affect the student and school system operations as well."

The interaction—the dynamic interplay—between families, educators, the family system, and the school system will require families and educators to "grapple with the difficult task of providing a free appropriate education to each student" (Turnbull & Turnbull, 1997). As they confront this daunting task jointly, they will find that sometimes the families' views will prevail, and at other times the educators' views will prevail.

Nonetheless, collaboration will create two classes of beneficiaries (Turnbull & Turnbull, 1997).

1. Students will benefit because the "multiple perspectives" of the collaborators will be brought to bear to improve the outcomes of special education.

2. The collaborators themselves will benefit, because every collaborator will have made available to him or her the motivation and knowledge/skills of every other collaborator.

What is IDEA's contribution to the parent/family roles? It is to reduce the early roles—sources or causes of disability, organization members, service developers, recipients of professionals' decisions, teachers, and advocates. Simultaneously, it is to increase the more recent role of parents/families as decision-makers, and, in time, to extend that role so families will be collaborators with educators. Just how that is done is beyond the scope of this book but is well set out in the Turnbull and Turnbull (1997) text on the special partnership and empowerment of families and educators.

Reference

Turnbull, A. P., & Turnbull, H. R. (1997). *Families, professionals, and exceptionality: A special partnership.* Columbus: Merrill/Prentice Hall.

Cases

Belanger v. Nashua Sch. Dist., 856 F. Supp. 40 (D.N.H. 1994).
Brown v. Bd. of Educ., 347 U.S. 483 (1954).
Criswell v. State Dept. of Ed., EHLR 558:156 (M.D.Tenn. 1986).
Doe v. Anrig, 561 F. Supp. 121 (D. Mass. 1983), aff'd 728 F.2d 30 (1st Cir. 1984), aff'd sub nom., *School Committee of Burlington v. Department of Education*, 471 U.S. 359 (1985).
E. H. v. Tirozzi, 735 F. Supp. 53 (D.Conn. 1990).
George H. & Irene L. Walker Home for Children v. Town of Franklin, 621 N.E.2d 376 (Mass. 1993).
John H. v. McDonald, EHLR 558:336 (D.N.H. 1986).
Maynard v. Greater Hoyt School Dist. No. 61-4, 876 F. Supp. 1104 (D.S.D. 1995).
Mylo v. Baltimore County Board of Education, No. 91-2563, 1991 U.S. App. Lexis 27029 (4th Cir. 1991), cert. denied, 507 U.S. 934 (1993).
State of Connecticut v. Bruno, 673 A.2d 1117 (Conn. 1996).
Susan R.M. v. Northwest I.S.D.,818 F.2d 455 (5th Cir. 1987).
V. W. and R. W. v. Favolise, 131 F.R.D. 654 (D. Conn. 1990).

Part
3

Enforcing
The Law

9
Compliance Through the Courts

Litigation has been a major—and indeed was the original—source for establishing the educational rights of children with disabilities. Were it not for the early landmark decisions (especially *PARC* and *Mills*), it is doubtful whether Congress would have enacted IDEA.

Court orders, however, are not self-executing. Although they demand compliance by the parties involved, they cannot assure or guarantee it, and they are truly effective only if the school authorities are willing or able to carry them out. When, as sometimes happens, these authorities are neither willing nor able to do so, students and their parents are compelled to return to court and seek additional relief. The alternative types of relief that they usually seek, and that they sought after winning the right to an education in court but before persuading Congress to enact IDEA, are described in the sections that follow.

Compliance: Pre-IDEA Techniques

Contempt Citations

When a court issues an order, the party subject to the order is obliged to comply with it. If the party does not comply, the other party in the lawsuit must find a way to enforce the order; otherwise, noncompliance renders the court order meaningless. Moreover, the court itself has an interest in having its order obeyed; otherwise, its orders will be easily flouted and its legal power undercut.

A traditional way for a party to secure compliance and for the court itself to assure that its orders are obeyed is for the court to hold the noncomplying party in contempt of court. The term *"contempt"* refers to the refusal to comply. For a party to disobey the court's order is contemptuous. The contempt order itself, usually issued after a hearing at which the noncomplying party has the right to offer explanations for noncompliance, almost always restates the original order, directs the party to comply within a specified time (gives the noncomplying party an opportunity to cure the default), and, depending on the validity of the party's reasons for not complying earlier, either orders the noncomplying party to pay a fine to the court or to be imprisoned for a specified time.

In some of the earliest right-to-education cases, compliance was not forthcoming. This forced courts to hold noncomplying school authorities in contempt and to reissue their original or modified orders. This was the situation in *Mills v. D.C. Bd of Educ.* (1972). In *Mills*, the court found the District of Columbia's school superintendent, board of education, and department of human resources out of compliance but refused to impose any penalties because the District's governing body eventually and at the last moment made funds available to implement the court order.

Similarly, in *Rainey v. Tennessee* (1976), the court found the SEA in contempt for not implementing a consent order, refused to accept the excuse that the agency lacked funds to carry out the consent order, and ordered the agency to file implementation plans for that and subsequent years. (A consent order or decree is one that all parties and the court agree should be entered as the court's judgment.)

Not only is lack of funds generally not an excuse, but neither is an agency's repeated failure to exercise its good faith efforts to carry out a court order. In *Allen v. School Committee of Boston* (1987), for example, the court held the LEA in contempt of court and levied a fine based on the daily value of services that the LEA's students would have received if the district had complied with state special education law, multiplied by the number of students for whom services had been withheld. Moreover, the court gave each student's family the right to decide which compensatory service they wanted (up to the value of the per-day per-student fine). (See also *ASPIRA of New York v. Bd. of Educ.* (1976), in which the court held the New York City Board of Education in contempt for failing to implement a consent decree.)

To fail to comply precisely with every aspect of a court's order does not necessarily subject an agency to a contempt citation. If an agency substantially complies and does so in good faith, it may escape a contempt citation (*United States v. Oregon*, 1991).

Court-Appointed Masters

The initial effect of a contempt proceeding in both *Mills* and *Rainey* was to hold the individual defendants and the school systems potentially liable to the court by imposing a fine. A contempt citation itself does not assure that court orders will be carried out; it only holds out the threat of punishment to those who fail to carry them out. Thus, it is of limited value for accomplishing the education of the students. Something more may be needed.

In *Mills*, the court attached to the contempt order a separate order appointing a special master. A master is an agent of the court, appointed to accomplish certain court-assigned tasks to ensure that the defendants carry out the court's orders. In

Mills, the court assigned extensive duties to the master, similar in scope and type to those the school superintendent and the school board normally would have. A master in effect becomes both the superintendent and the school board, assuring that the court's order is carried out, reporting to the court regularly on the ways in which the order is being carried out, and making recommendations to the court for other appropriate orders. Typically, the school board must pay the master for performing these duties.

Other Judicial Remedies

Contempt citations and masters are not the only judicial remedies. Indeed, courts have extensive power to enforce their decrees. For example, a court may order an LEA to file with the court regularly its plans for implementing a court decree or state statute, retain jurisdiction over a case in order to monitor the school's implementation of the court's order, and set dates by which certain of the orders must be carried out.

Financial Reallocation and Withholding of Funds

One of the earliest defenses in right-to-education suits is the defendants' contention that they do not have sufficient funds to provide an appropriate education to all children with disabilities. In *Mills*, the court made short shrift of this argument, stating (in now well-known dicta) that absence of funds is no defense of failure to provide constitutional rights (equal educational opportunities) to the students, and that the burden of inadequate funds may not fall more heavily on students with disabilities than on nondisabled ones. In *MARC v. Maryland* (1974), a Maryland trial court also gave little heed to the defense claims of financial difficulty when it ordered the defendants to request additional funds from the state legislature.

To say that defendants must be equitable in the use of funds or that an LEA should request more from its funding sources is one thing, but to step into the budget process is altogether another. Throughout the right-to-education cases, the courts have been extremely reluctant to interfere in any way with the financing of public education.

The *Mills* court hesitated to appoint a master because it recognized that compensation to the master would drain off funds that otherwise would be available to educate children with disabilities. When it finally did appoint a master, it ordered only that he must review the school board's budget process.

Further evidence of judicial reluctance to interfere with the traditional legislative function of taxation and appropriation is shown in *Rainey*. In response to the defendant's claim that it could not comply with the consent decree because it had insufficient funds, the trial court ordered the LEA to submit an implementation plan by March 1977 and to put it into effect by July. Voicing a threat that it had the power to enforce, the court said, "From and after that date, the defendants shall be enjoined from expending money for the operation of a public school system in this state unless the plan to be submitted is incorporated into the operation of the department of education and fully pursued to implement the consent decree."

The appeals court reversed this part of the order, holding that the trial court's remedy was excessive and would cause more damage than it would yield benefits. Nonetheless, a court can enjoin (prevent) schools from making various expenditure decisions, and it also can order them to take affirmative steps that have serious fiscal impact.

The authority for a court to affect the budget of school authorities lies in the traditional "equity" power of a court. Fundamentally, a court may take whatever action it deems proper to require a defendant school authority to comply with its order, especially if the order implements a federal constitutional right of a student or group of students.

For example, the U.S. Supreme Court, reviewing the order of a federal district court in a case involving the racial desegregation of the Kansas City, Missouri, public schools, approved the court's use of its equity power to require the state and local school authorities to reallocate already-raised funds, to expend those funds in certain ways, to apportion among themselves the costs of desegregation, and to seek voter approval for new school bonds and levies (*Missouri v. Jenkins*, 1995). The Court, however, did not allow the trial court to actually impose the taxes the court believed were necessary to carry out its desegregation orders, and, in a later decision in that case, held that the trial court exceeded its equity powers in ordering across-the-board salary increases for district teachers, finding that order to be unrelated to the state and local district's operation of an unconstitutionally segregated school system (*Missouri v. Jenkins*, 1995).

In both cases, the Supreme Court was conscious of two fundamental issues: federalism and separation of powers. Federalism was a concern in *Jenkins*, as in all right-to-education cases decided by federal courts, because state-local authorities share powers and responsibilities in a federal system. When a federal agency (here, a court) takes on some of those powers (oversight of a state-local school system), the power between the state-local and federal governments is shifted toward the federal (see Chapters 1 and 3 for a discussion of the federalism issue).

The doctrine of separation of powers is a concern in all right-to-education cases because the role of the courts is to adjudicate disputes, applying the existing law; it is not to take on the function of a legislature (deciding what programs should be authorized and what funds should be appropriated to operate those programs) or an executive agency (actually carrying out the education laws and operating school systems).

In an era when courts are increasingly conservative (that is, concerned with rebalancing the federal-state/local relationship so it disfavors the federal government and favors more the state/local governments), the 1995 decision in *Jenkins* not surprisingly stands as a warning to all courts: Do not go too far in becoming a school authority, especially if you are a federal court.

Federal Abstention, Mootness, Dormancy, and Voluntary Dismissals

Not every case reaches the stage at which judicial remedies become necessary. Indeed, several avenues out of litigation and enforcement of court orders are possible. One way out is through use of the doctrine of federal abstention. When a right-to-education suit is filed in a federal court (on the grounds that the defendants are violating the equal protection and due process guarantees of the Fifth and Fourteenth Amendments), this doctrine permits the court to rule that the case, although involving federal claims, should be tried first in state courts because it also involves state issues that may dispose of the case and make it unnecessary for the federal constitutional issues to be tried. In their discretion, federal courts may refuse to hear right-to-education cases on this ground, and to remit the plaintiffs to state courts. Defendants favor the abstention doctrine because it enables them to try their cases in forums traditionally less hostile to school systems and less inclined to find constitutional violations.

If a court does not employ the doctrine of abstention, it may avoid the issues on the ground of mootness. Typically, a case is moot (and thus need not be tried) if state legislation or state agency regulations provide a sufficient answer to the claims the plaintiffs raise in their lawsuit. If the student no longer has any quarrel with the school (for example, the student has graduated, withdrawn from school, moved to another state school district, or died), no controversy exists. Finally, it is permissible for plaintiffs to dismiss their cases voluntarily on their own motion, but this is done rarely.

Damages and Educational Malpractice ⌒

A traditional legal remedy for any wrong is the "pocketbook" remedy of damages—the assessment of monies against a wrongdoer to reimburse the wronged party for any loss and, in some cases, to punish the wrongdoer for egregious acts of harm. The first kind of monetary damage award is called "compensatory" damages because it reimburses or compensates the wronged party. The second is called "punitive" damages because it punishes, and arguably deters others from engaging in similar acts. Both ultimately transfer money from the wrongdoer (a state or local education agency) to the aggrieved person (a student and parent).

Elements of a Tort

Education malpractice cases belong to the type of cases called "tort" cases. The word *tort* means a "wrong." A student or family who sues an education agency for educational malpractice must prove four facts in order to recover.

1. The plaintiff must prove that the education agency owes a duty to the student. In cases involving special education, the duty arises from IDEA and its six principles (zero reject, nondiscriminatory evaluation, appropriate education, least restrictive environment, procedural due process, and parent/student participation).
2. The plaintiff must show that the education agency breached its duty by failing to do what it should have done under IDEA, by doing what it should have done but doing it negligently, or by contravening IDEA. Merely breaching an

alleged duty is not always sufficient to justify an award of damages to a student or family or to some other client of a professional. That is so because it is well-settled law that in situations where professionals, such as educators, have a duty to others (students, families, clients, or patients), they are entitled to exercise their professional judgment when complying with that duty, and indeed courts defer to a professional's judgment and are loath to second-guess professionals.

Thus, the breach of duty also must entail failure to adhere to professional standards. As the U.S. Supreme Court said in a case involving injury to a resident of a state institution for persons with mental retardation,

> [T]he decision, if made by a professional, is presumptively valid; liability may be imposed only when the decision by the professional is such a substantial departure from accepted professional judgment, practice or standards as to demonstrate that the person responsible actually did not base the decision on such a judgment. (*Youngberg v. Romeo*, 1982)

3. The plaintiff must prove that the education agency's breach of duty was the direct cause of harm or injury to the student or family. The breach and the harm suffered must have a causal connection.
4. The student or family actually must suffer some measurable harm as a result of the agency's breach of duty. An LEA's breach may not always cause harm; for example, a school district may violate a procedural safeguard within the nondiscriminatory evaluation, due process, or parent participation principles but still actually not cause the student to be denied an appropriate education. "No harm, no foul" is the rule in that case—a "harmless error" case. If an LEA's breach of duty does cause a denial of appropriate education and least restrictive placement, a student or family may recover compensatory damages to reimburse them for the harm they suffered.

To recover in an education malpractice suit, the students or families must meet these four standards and also must overcome the doctrine of "presumptive validity" of professional decisions (*Youngberg v. Romeo*, 1982).

Education Malpractice Cases: Establishing Duty and Breach

Despite the majority rule that "education malpractice" is not a cause of action that the courts generally recognize, and although students who seek damages for torts committed by educators generally have been unsuccessful, a minority trend is developing. This recent trend is multifaceted, as the following discussion reveals.

Mandatory Functions

A general rule of law is that a person may hold a public official liable for not doing a job the official must do. This rule of law creates liability for the official who fails to carry out a mandatory function of his or her public office. It recognizes that the proper role of the public official is to obey certain duties created by a law-making body (such as Congress, a state legislature, a local governing body, or a school board) and that, if the official refuses to carry out those mandatory duties and an individual is thereby damaged, the individual should be able to sue and recover compensation for the damages.

Another general rule of law, however, is that a person may not hold a public official liable for exercising his or her authorized discretion. For example, if a school administrator decides to assign a teacher to a certain subject or class or to schedule school activities at a certain time, the administrator is exercising discretion about how to conduct the functions of the job. The administrator should have the freedom to exercise this discretion and not be held liable for doing so within the scope of the authority that comes with the job.

This distinction between mandatory and discretionary functions has entered into the education malpractice case law, with differing results. In *Tinkham v. Groveport Madison Local Sch. Dist.* (1991), a state court in Ohio held that a taxicab company is liable to a special-education student who was sexually molested by a driver (the liability attaches under state tort law affecting common carriers). But the court did not impose liability on the school district because, under state law, it was exercising a discretionary function, not a mandatory one, when it contracted with the taxicab company to transport the student.

The alternative to the district's entering into that contract would have been to provide transportation by its own personnel, as a regular school district function, to carry out federal and state special education law. By entering into the contract, it exercised discretion about transportation.

The term "discretionary function" refers to decisions that involve the exercise of judgment, discretion, and decision-making capacity (such as whether to run its own transportation system or to contract with a private taxicab company to do so). In contrast, if the school district was exercising a "mandatory function" and had no opportunity to make any kind of judgment but simply had to carry out law under a statutory mandate, the district could be liable. Thus, the usual distinction between "discretionary" and "mandatory" functions made the school district immune from liability.

This "discretionary function" defense also was successful in *Bencic v. City of Malden* (1992). *Bencic* involved a student who was not classified under IDEA. Instead, the student was regarded as "disabled" under Sec. 504 but received no behavior modification services from the LEA. The student attacked and injured another student. The court ruled that to provide a student with an IEP or similar program related to aggressive behavior was within a district's discretion under Section 504. When there is no IEP and no program for behavioral management, the district is not liable to another student when the special education student attacks and injures another student. Therefore, the court held that LEA was not liable to the injured student.

A similar defense is available to a school principal, school nurse, and special education director who were sued when a school aide catheterized a student improperly. The Alabama Supreme Court held that these three individuals are protected from liability for training and supervising a classroom aide improperly. Immunity attends their "discretionary function" because supervision and training require constant decision-making and the exercise of judgment on their part; the more a person has to exercise judgment, the more the person is engaged in a discretionary function and is immune. The court held, however, that the aide is not immune and may be held liable for improper catheterization (*Nance v. Matthews*, 1993; see also *L.S.B. v. Howard*, 1995), in which the court granted immunity in a case alleging failure to supervise a student who was sexually assaulted by other students on school property, the degree of supervision necessary to prevent an assault being a matter for the exercise of school officials' discretion.

Just the opposite result from these cases was reached in *Kansas State Bank & Trust Company v. Specialized Transp. Services, Inc.* (1991). In that case, the Kansas Supreme Court held that the bus company and the LEA that contracted with it to transport special education students were both liable for the driver's sexual molestation of a student. Again, the issue was whether the school district had exercised a "discretionary function" in contracting with the company.

The court held that the LEA was executing a mandatory function because the district has a statutory duty to supervise the bus driver (imposed under state regulations governing common carriers such as the bus company) and to oversee whether the driver was carrying out his duties properly. (There had been several reports that he was sexually abusing the special education students whom he transported, and these reports should have resulted in charges brought against him for child abuse and neglect or for failure to perform his duties properly.)

The court reasoned that when a legal duty is imposed, there is no discretion. The district simply has no choice but to comply with the duty. By failing to comply with the legal duties to supervise and to follow up reports of abuse, the district subjected itself to liability. The distinction between the Ohio and the Kansas cases lies in the fact that the Ohio court found no legal duty and thus determined that the district was executing a discretionary function; the Kansas court found that district had a mandatory legal duty to provide transportation. These cases encourage students to sue and to attempt to prove that a school district committed a violation while executing a mandatory function.

In light of the Supreme Court's 1999 decision in *Davis v. Monroe* and its 1992 decision in *Franklin v. Gwinett* (both discussed below), the "no immunity" results in the cases noted above may be in jeopardy. The *Davis* case held that a school district may be liable for student-on-student sexual harassment, and the *Franklin* case held that a school district may be liable for teacher-on-teacher sexual harassment. Undoubtedly, students will try to extend these holdings to cover injury that is not sexual in nature but that violates a federal statute (under *Davis* and *Franklin*, the statute was T. IX of the Education Amendments of 1972 prohibiting sex discrimination in education) such as IDEA, Sec. 504, or ADA. See "Failure to supervise student-on-student actions" below, for further discussion.

Foreseeability and Special Relationship

In tort law, one person may be held liable if he or she reasonably can foresee that his or her action may injure a second person and the first person does in fact act in a way that is the proximate cause of injury to the second person. The underlying basis for this rule is that one should be held liable for reasonably foreseeable injurious consequences.

This rule has come into the education malpractice forum through a rather circuitous route. Its origins lie in *Tarasoff v. Regents of Univ. of California* (1976). In that case, a student at the University of California told his treating psychologist, who was a university employee, that, because he was upset about losing his former girlfriend to another man, he intended to kill her. The psychologist telephoned the campus police, who temporarily took the patient into custody but released him later when he appeared to be rational, but the psychologist did not warn the former girlfriend. When the patient killed his former girlfriend, the woman's family sued the university, alleging that the therapist had a duty to warn others about the intentions of a patient if those intentions could be carried out and would be dangerous if carried out.

In a highly controversial opinion, the California Supreme Court held that, because a therapist and a patient have a special relationship, the therapist, if he or she determines or should determine, pursuant to the standards of the profession, that his or her patient presents a serious danger of violence to another, must use reasonable care to protect the intended victim of the danger. If the therapist does not exercise reasonable care to protect the third party (intended victim), the therapist (and the employer) may be held liable to the victim for damages.

Taking the *Tarasoff* case as its lead and relying on its "special relationship/duty to warn" rationale, at least one court has imposed liability on school districts and their employees in cases involving students, whether they have or have not been classified into special education. Thus, Maryland's highest court has interpreted state law to mean that a school counselor has a legal duty to try to prevent a student's suicide when the counselor has notice of the student's suicidal intent (*Eisel v. Bd. of Educ. of Montgomery County*, 1991). *Eisel* rests on these bases:

1. There is a special relationship between the student and a counselor.
2. The special relationship consists of two components—a counselor's special duty to exercise care to protect a pupil from harm and the counselor's therapeutic relationship to the student.
3. General tort law imposes a duty to act to prevent harm when the harm is reasonably foreseeable and certain.
4. The state's education statutes impose an obligation on schools to prevent youth suicide.
5. There is a close connection between the counselor's conduct in not informing the student's parents or otherwise acting to prevent the suicide and the suicide itself.
6. The sum of these five factors results in liability against the counselor.

In *Eisel*, the student was not enrolled in special education. For that reason, the case is all the more important because some special education students may be more at risk than other students, being less competent than other students to protect themselves against harm.

Custody

A special form of the "special relationship creates duty" rule has manifested itself in cases that involve state custody over an individual. Although it is a general rule of law that the Due Process Clause creates no affirmative duty on the part of a state to provide services, even those as basic and necessary as law enforcement, it is equally well recognized that an exception to this rule exists when a state takes a person into custody and physically has the person in the care or supervision of its employees. In such situations, the state is responsible for assuring the safety and general well-being of that person. For example, a state that confines a prisoner is responsible for his safety and well-being (*Estelle v. Gamble*, 1976). Likewise, a state that holds a person with a mental disability in custody must assure not only safety and well-being but also treatment that may lead to the person's release from custody (*Youngberg v. Romeo*, 1982).

In these situations the key is that the state physically has custody over the person; when a person is imprisoned or committed to a mental-treatment facility, physical custody is beyond question, as is the duty of safety and well-being. The person's claim is that the Eighth Amendment to the Constitution, protecting against "cruel and unusual punishment," creates an affirmative duty on the state to provide for the safety and well-being of that person.

Extending this affirmative duty of protection from harm to persons who are under the state's supervision and jurisdiction but are not physically in the state's custody, however, has met with serious obstacles. The leading case is *DeShaney v. Winnebago County Dep't of Social Services* (1989). In *DeShaney*, the county department of social services had investigated alleged abuse and neglect of a minor child, Joshua DeShaney, by his biological father. After having obtained a court order allowing it to hold Joshua in temporary custody for 3 days so it could investigate the allegations, the department concluded that Joshua (who had been hospitalized and treated for injury that occurred while in his father's custody) should be returned to his father, but it recommended various interventions so the father would be able to care for his son more effectively. When Joshua returned to his father, he once again was the victim of such severe paternal abuse that he was permanently and seriously impaired, mentally and physically.

Joshua and his mother sued the county, alleging that he is entitled to recover damages under Section 1983 because the county deprived Joshua of his constitutional right to liberty (under the Fourteenth Amendment's Due Process Clause) by failing to intervene to protect him against a risk of violence, of which they knew or should have known, at his father's hands.

The Supreme Court disagreed. First, the Court stated that the Due Process Clause does not create any affirmative rights to services from the state; it exists as a shield, as a negative force, to protect individuals against actions by the state. Second, the

Court emphasized that the state's obligation to ensure an individual's safety and well-being derives only from the state's physical custody of that person.

In Joshua DeShaney's case, however, the state did not have him in its physical custody. Although the state may have been aware of the dangers Joshua faced in his father's custody, it played no part in creating those dangers, nor did it do anything that would increase their likelihood. Despite having had Joshua in custody, the state, by returning him to his father's custody, placed him in no worse position than he would have been in if it had not acted in the first place.

The Court held that "the state does not become the permanent guarantor of an individual's safety by having once offered him shelter." This is so even when there has been or may yet be a "special relationship" between the state and the injured party—a relationship that, under some circumstances, creates a duty on the state to safeguard those under its custody and jurisdiction, as is so when the state places a child into foster care.

Although the *DeShaney* case found that the State had no duty to protect under the facts, it created two exceptions to the general rule that the State has no affirmative duty to act to prevent harm to others and therefore is not liable for such injuries: (1) the special relationship of custody doctrine, and (2) the "State-created danger" theory.

Several attempts have been made to extend the custody exception created in *DeShaney* to situations in which students are enrolled in residential schools and therefore in the "physical custody" of the school. The courts have unanimously refused to extend the exception to any situation in which the "custody" is not entirely involuntary. Arguments that the necessity of the services provided by such schools (i.e., a school for the blind) make them as effectively involuntary as incarceration or civil commitment have not persuaded the courts. State-operated special schools do not, therefore, have any generalized affirmative duty under the custody exception to protect their students (*Walton v. Alexander*, 1995; *Stevens v. Umstead*, 1996).

An even bolder line of cases attempted to apply the custody exception to non-residential schools, relying on the "truancy laws." Under these laws, a parent may be held liable to the state if he or she deliberately flouts the truancy laws and fails to assure the child's attendance in school. Sometimes these laws also make the student liable for not attending school. Students who have been injured by school staff have argued that these laws create the kind of "state custody" that imprisonment (*Estelle v. Gamble*) and involuntary commitment (*Youngberg v. Romeo*) create: Compulsory school attendance creates a situation of mandatory involvement of the person (student) with the state.

Not surprisingly, most courts have refused, on the facts before them, to hold that the compulsory-attendance laws create a "special relationship" that gives rise to an affirmative duty on the part of the school to protect its students (*Dorothy J. v. Little Rock Sch. Dist.*, 1993; *Maldonado v. Josey*, 1992; *J.O. v. Alton Community Unif. Sch. Dist.*, 1990; *Black v. Indiana Area Sch. Dist.*, 1993; *Stoneking v. Bradford Area Sch. Dist.*, 1989). Other courts, while recognizing a custodial relationship, dismissed such claims on the ground that the school district did not manifest deliberate indifference sufficient to breach the custodial duty (*D.R. v. Middle Bucks Area Voc. Tech. Sch.*, 1992; *Tilson v. School Dist. of Philadelphia*, 1990).

The most recent case along that line (*Doe v. Hillsboro Independent Sch. Dist.*, 1997) held that the school district was not liable for the rape of a 14-year-old female student by a school custodian. In answering the custody claim, the court joined every other circuit that has considered the issue of custody in school settings and held that compulsory school attendance does not create the custody envisioned by *DeShaney*. The court rebuffed the argument that the restrictions imposed by attendance laws are analogous to the restraints of prisons and mental institutions. It noted that, though attendance is not always voluntary, the children are not physically restrained from leaving (citing *Ingraham v. Wright*, 1977). It further stated that custody in schools is only intermittent, and the home and parents remain the primary source for satisfaction of the basic needs of the child. Whether *Doe v. Hillsboro* does or does not provide the last nail in the coffin for the custody-in-school line of cases, there seems to be little evidence that any future courts will premise school liability on the custody exception of *DeShaney*.

State-Created Danger

The state-created danger theory has spawned several lines of cases distinguished by the type of facts on which liability is premised. Although the original source for this theory of liability was the *DeShaney* case, the theory has grown beyond the boundaries originally formed in that case. The state-created danger rule now encompasses mandatory function-based liability cases (discussed previously), where the action of carrying out the mandatory function (or failure to carry out the mandatory function) is a direct cause of the harm, and cases in which the school district's failure to supervise those within or under its control, despite notice of wrongdoing, caused the harm.

Failure to Supervise Employees of School District

The approach the courts take in many cases turns on the intentional infliction of harm or bad faith of the state's employees (teachers and other staff). These factors come into play in cases involving students who experience sexual, physical, and verbal abuse from a teacher (*C.M. v. Southeast Delco Sch. Dist.*, 1993; *K.L. v. Southeast Delco Sch. Dist.*, 1993). In these cases, the courts allowed the students to sue because the student alleged that a continuing, widespread, and persistent pattern of conduct had violated the students' right to privacy and right of freedom from invasion of one's physical integrity; that the school district had been deliberately indifferent to, or had tacitly authorized, the teacher's conduct, even after being notified about it; and that the deliberate indifference or tacit authorization contributed directly to the students' injury.

Indeed, in *Franklin v. Gwinnett County Public School* (1992) the Supreme Court held that, under T. IX of the Education Amendments of 1972 (prohibiting discrimination in federally assisted programs of education, on the basis of sex), a school district may be held liable where one of its employees sexually harasses a student.

This decision supports the line of cases that hold districts liable because of the acts of their employees in so adversely treating a student that the student is denied access to the school program.

The deliberate indifference factor reflects the general rule that the school district can be held liable only for its own actions. Even where an employee of the school acts intentionally to harm a student, the school district will not be held liable (although the individual teacher will be) unless it failed to act to prevent the harm after notification created a duty to act. Courts have refused to adopt "respondent superior" or general rules of agency liability in the context of school districts (*Bd. of County Comm'rs v. Brown*, 1997). The school district's own "act" of deliberate indifference must in some way contribute by allowing or promoting a pattern of unconstitutional conduct by its employee.

Larson v. Miller (1996) held that, to prove a "pattern of unconstitutional conduct" in a case where the student, suing for damages under Section 1983 and alleging that the school district had failed to supervise the bus driver who had been the subject of one prior complaint about sexual abuse of special education students, the student must show

1. the existence of a continuing, widespread, persistent pattern of unconstitutional misconduct by the district's employees;
2. deliberate indifference to, or tacit authorization of, that conduct on the part of the district's policy-making officials, after notice to the officials of the misconduct; and
3. injury to the student through acts undertaken pursuant to the district's custom, that is, that the custom was the moving force behind the constitutional violation.

Moreover, the student cannot recover damages where he or she alleges that the district failed to train or screen its employees unless he or she can prove "deliberate indifference" to the students' rights (*Thelma D. v. Bd. of Educ.*, 1991; *Larson v. Miller*, 1996). This result is consistent with the law, as established by the Supreme Court, relating to liability of a municipality for acts of its employees, in cases where the plaintiff (student or other injured party) alleges that the municipality is liable because of its failure to provide sufficient training to, or screening of, its employees and that such a failure is the cause of the plaintiff's injury.

In a 1997 case, *Bd. of County Comm'rs v. Brown*, the Supreme Court seemed to raise this standard even higher. The issue there was whether a county's failure to carefully review the employment history of a deputy sheriff who injured a woman whom he arrested could be the basis for holding the county liable to the woman. In concluding that the failure-to-screen could not be the basis for the woman's recovery, the Court reviewed its precedents and their implications for this case.

The Court had held in an earlier case, *Canton v. Harris* (1989), that the plaintiff must prove that the municipal action was taken with "deliberate indifference" to its known or obvious consequences; it is not enough for a plaintiff to prove that the municipality acted with simple or even "heightened" negligence. In *Canton*, the

Court concluded that "inadequate training" can be the basis of Section 1983 liability in "limited circumstances." One of those is the instance of an inadequate training "program," namely, a program that applies over time to more than one employee. The "lack of proper training, rather than a one-time negligent administration of the program or factors peculiar to the officer (employee) involved in a particular incident, is the 'moving force' behind the plaintiff's injury" *(Canton).*

In the failure-to-train cases, the Court has limited municipal liability by establishing a two-part test, involving the likelihood of recurrence on one hand, and predictability on the other.

The likelihood that the situation (involving one employee's negligence) will recur and the predictability that an officer lacking specific tools to handle that situation will violate citizens' rights could justify a finding that policy-makers' decision not to train the officer reflected "deliberate indifference" to the obvious consequences of the policy-makers' choice—namely, a violation of a specific constitutional or statutory right. The high degree of predictability also may support a finding of causation—that the municipality's indifference led directly to the very consequence that was so predictable *(Bd. of County Comm'rs v. Brown).*

The "deliberate indifference" standard is "stringent" and "requires proof that a municipal actor disregarded a known or obvious consequence of his or her action. Unlike the risk from a particular glaring omission in a training program, the risk from a single instance of inadequate screening of an applicant's background is not 'obvious' in the abstract" *(Bd. of County Comm'rs v. Brown).* The municipality will not be liable unless there is proof that the particular employee was "highly likely to inflict the particular injury suffered by the plaintiff" *(Bd. of County Comm'rs v. Brown).*

The "connection" between the failure to screen and the action that caused the injury "must be strong" *(Bd. of County Comm'rs v. Brown).* Finding that the county's failure to completely screen the deputy sheriff was not connected strongly to the injury and reflected neither a policy nor a practice, the Court ruled in the county's favor and dismissed the woman's lawsuit.

In *Bd. of County Comm'rs v. Brown,* the Supreme Court seems to have substantially raised the standard that a student must meet to recover from a school district for its failure to carefully screen (before hiring) or its failure to offer a training program. This new standard may make it all the more difficult for "deliberate indifference" cases to become "winners" for students, even when those cases are not brought under Section 1983.

Failure to Supervise and Student-on-Student Actions; The Davis Case

When the student was injured by people who are not employed by the school district, even while the student is in school, on school grounds, and under the supervision of the school and its employees, courts have, in the past, been even more reluctant than in teacher conduct cases to hold a school district liable.

For example, *D.R. v. Middle Bucks Area Voc. Tech. Sch.* (1992) involved two female students, one of whom had a physical disability, who were assaulted physically and sexually by several male students. The students sued the school district to recover damages for violation of their constitutional rights (they said they have constitutional rights to be protected from abuse during the school day). The court not only refused to apply the custodial exception to create liability, but also found that the school did not create or exacerbate the danger posed by male students and that the victims' injuries did not result from any policy, custom, or practice established by state officials. The school, therefore, had not violated any duty toward the students.

In yet another line of cases, plaintiffs have attempted to base liability on the theory that the school district had a duty to supervise the student who caused the harm. In these cases the student who has a disability injures another person. Is the district liable?

IDEA takes into account that placing a student with disabilities into a general education setting may not be appropriate if the student may jeopardize other students (the "danger to others" exception to the rebuttable presumption in favor of least restrictive placement; see Chapter 6). Therefore, if a district follows this presumption and has no reason to believe the special education student will be aggressive to nondisabled students, the school district does not violate constitutional due-process rights (life, liberty, property) of a nondisabled student who is attacked by the student with disabilities (*Cohen v. Sch. Dist. of Philadelphia*, 1992)).

Likewise, in *Rankins v. Aytch* (1991), the court held that under state law, parents and teachers of a student with severe emotional disabilities, who had been acting out and aggressive at the time the teachers placed her forcibly on the school bus, are not liable to the bus driver whom the student attacked because they did not have reasonable grounds to think the student would attack the driver.

Despite an attitude of general reluctance, courts have not been unanimous in their refusal to find liability in school supervision of student-on-student conduct cases. In *Doe v. Escambia County Sch. Bd.* (1992), the court held the LEA liable for violating state statutory law and common law when it failed to provide adequate supervision of a special education student who was taken from the school grounds and raped by several male students.

The Supreme Court recently held in *Davis v. Monroe County Bd. of Ed.* that, in some situations, the school district could be liable for student-on-student sexual harassment under Title IX. This holding could have a broad and lasting effect on the liability of school districts for student-on-student discriminatory or tortious actions.

Such liability will, under the *Davis* decision, stem from statutory guarantees of equal access to the resources and benefits provided by the school. In the area of disability, this means that any application of *Davis* most likely will rest on the relevant requirements of the ADA, Section 504, or IDEA as compared to those analyzed under Title IX.

Comparison of Title IX and ADA, § 504, and IDEA for the Purpose of the Davis Case

Hurdles for liability to attach include the following:

1. **There must be a private right of action (for damages).**

In *Davis*, the court relied on a previous holding (in *Cannon v. University of Chicago*) that there was an implied private cause of action (right to sue) for damages under Title IX. The *Cannon* decision was based primarily on the legislative history indicating that the congressional intent was to allow a private cause of action.

ADA expressly creates a private cause of actions for damages. IDEA does not expressly create a private right of action but sometimes can be coupled with other statutory claims that enable the student to include a damages claim (discussed in detail *supra*). Almost all of the decisions in the federal Courts of Appeals have upheld a private damages claim under Section 504, following the same reasoning employed in *Cannon*, but the Supreme Court has not specifically authorized such an action. Nevertheless, a private cause of action seems to exist under Section 504, on the basis of the Court of Appeals decisions and the Supreme Court decision in *Lane v. Pena* (1996), which implied the validity of such claims (the dissent would have specifically authorized private damage claims).

2. There must be notice of potential liability.

In *Davis*, the court noted that because Title IX was enacted pursuant to Congress's authority under Article I of the Constitution (the Spending Clause), private damages actions are available only where the recipient of federal funds had adequate notice that it could be held liable for the conduct at issue. Congress must "speak with a clear voice" so the state is aware of the liabilities it accepts by accepting the federal funds. There is no express notice of liability for student-on-student sexual harassment in Title IX. Nevertheless, the court found that there was notice based on four factors:

a. *Franklin v. Gwinnett County Public Schools* held that notice is unnecessary when liability is premised on intentional violation of the statute.
b. The common law gives notice of liability for student-on-student torts.
c. School attorneys and administrators were being advised by the funding agency (U.S. Department of Education) that student-on-student sexual harassment could trigger district liability.
d. The language of the statute defines the scope of prohibited conduct based on the degree of control over the actor (harassing student) and the environment in which the actions occur (not on the identity of the actor).

The Office of Civil Rights (OCR) also adopted policy guidelines providing that student-on-student harassment falls within the scope of Title IX protections, but the Court did not include this factor in its calculus because these guidelines were promulgated after the litigation began.

This issue of whether a state is aware of its liabilities pursuant to a receipt of federal funds under the Spending Clause is irrelevant with respect to ADA claims because the ADA was established pursuant to the Commerce Clause and the Fourteenth Amendment (42 U.S.C. § 12202). Therefore, damages seem to be available under ADA for a state or local official's discrimination or for student-on-student discrimination.

Likewise, damages seem to be available under Sec. 504 for student-on-student discrimination. This is so because Sec. 504, like Title IX, applies to federally assisted programs and, like Title IX, is an anti-discrimination statute. The only difference between the Section 504 and Title IX is the trait of the protected persons: In the case of Section 504, the trait is disability, whereas in the case of Title IX, it is sex.

3. **There must be discriminatory actions.**

Possibly the greatest hurdle to recovery under the *Davis* ruling is the requirement that the discriminatory behavior be "so severe, pervasive, and objectively offensive that it denies its victims the equal access to education that Title IX is designed to protect." Insults, banter, teasing, shoving, pushing, and other discriminatory conduct must be so serious as to have a prohibited overall effect on the injured student's access to educational programs or activities. The Court noted that children regularly interact in a manner that would be unacceptable among adults. For a child's conduct to rise to the level of discriminatory effect, thus, is a very high standard.

The Court gave the simple example of when the threshold level is reached by contemplating a situation where one student physically prevents another's access to school resources. The Court did not rule on the level of nonphysical activity that would meet this standard but merely emphasized that it must undermine or detract from the victim's educational experience so much that the victim is effectively denied equal access to an institution's resources and opportunities. The basic test is really the same, whether the actor is a teacher or a peer of the victim, but the relationship between the teacher and the student is such that it is much more likely that the misconduct will breach the guarantee of equal access to educational benefits provided by the statute.

When determining whether the conduct rises to the level of actionable harassment, other factors may be considered including, but not limited to, the ages of the students involved on both sides, the number of students involved, and the location of the incidents. Courts should look at "the entire constellation of surrounding circumstances, expectations, and relationships."

ADA, Section 504, and IDEA all require that individuals with disabilities be allowed to access resources and opportunities in a nondiscriminatory fashion to the maximum extent possible. Only when denial of access can be inferred by the extent of the conduct will any of the statutes (such as Title IX) create a valid basis for recovery. The same basis for violation exists in these statutes as exists in Title IX, and the courts doubtless will apply the same high standard of discriminatory conduct when examining liability in relation to peer discrimination against individuals with disabilities.

The *Davis* decision seems to have three results. First, it may create a higher degree of monitoring of student behavior than obtained before the case was decided. If the monitoring is of students without disabilities in inclusive settings (in the "general curriculum"), there may be greater access to the general curriculum by students with disabilities. This would be the case because LEAs will assure (through monitoring) that the behavior of nondisabled students does not deny disabled students access to the general curriculum.

Second, the potential for liability may, on the contrary, limit access to the general curriculum by students with disabilities. This would be the case if an LEA determines that some students with disabilities are so harassing that their behavior denies access to the benefits of an education to students (with or without a disability). In this case, the harassing students would be denied the access to the general curriculum. The limited access also would obtain if the students with disabilities would be more subject to harassment in the general curriculum than they would be in the separate special education curriculum. Thus, the case may have a chilling effect on inclusion.

Third, the case may prompt LEAs to join parents of harassing students in a case where the LEA is sued for student-on-student harassment, and that prospect—that the LEA and the parents of the offending student would be joint defendants against an injured (harassed) student with a disability—may create yet another flashpoint in the political backlash against inclusion.

4. There must be school district misconduct.

In *Davis,* the Court reasserted the principle that a recipient of federal funds is liable only for its own misconduct under Title IX in the absence of any statutory justification for the expansion of its duty. The Court identified the relevant statutory section as saying, "The recipient itself must exclude [persons] from participation in, . . . deny [persons] the benefits of, or . . . subject [persons] to discrimination under its programs or activities in order to be liable under Title IX."

The Court then stated that a funding recipient (school district) is liable for its own misconduct when the district itself intentionally acted in violation of Title IX by remaining deliberately indifferent to acts of harassment of which it had actual knowledge. The Court did not impute the actions of the harassing student to the school district. Instead, the school district's misconduct in *Davis* is created by two factors: (1) knowledge of the harassment, and (2) "intentional" inaction resulting from "deliberate" indifference. The school district is held liable for accepting, with knowledge, a situation, within its province and power to change, that severely violates the provisions of Title IX. It should be noted that these levels of intent are generally implied by the Court where the school district has knowledge of severe, pervasive, and objectively offensive discriminatory harassment.

The only real hurdle these factors create is that the school must have knowledge of the wrongful activities. The Court does not discuss at length the requisite level of knowledge (how many complaints). It can, however, be inferred by the Court's attempts to stress the narrowness of the holding that only knowledge that communicates the severe, pervasive, and objectively offensive nature of the acts will meet the standard.

A similar standard seems analogous when pursuing a cause of action under ADA (its discrimination definition uses language parallel to that used in Title IX), but under Section 504 the standard arguably may be lower. This is so because Section 504 (20 U.S.C. Sec. 794 (2)) explicitly provides that Title VI remedies are available to any person aggrieved by any act or failure to act by any recipient of federal funds. Section 504 already makes school districts liable for failing to act to prevent discriminatory conduct in its students and its wording does not, as in the *Davis* court, mention "intentional" indifference. Section 504, then, could impose liability based on mere negligent indifference, although no court has considered this question in light of the *Davis* decision.

Scope of the Ruling in *Davis*. The *Davis* case and the above discussion center on liability created by a statutory violation of a student's rights. Though the *Davis* case applies to this situation explicitly, it also might be applied to a situation where the rights violated extend directly from the constitution or the common law. The difficulty involved in extending the *Davis* decision lies in the cases holding that schools have no general common law or constitutional duty to protect their students. If a common law or constitutional basis for liability is found by the courts or explicitly created by Congress or a state legislature, the test for liability outlined in *Davis* probably would be applied.

Individuals with Disabilities Education Act ⌒

It is axiomatic that, for every right, there is a corresponding duty; and for every wrong, there should be (and usually is) a remedy. Under IDEA, students and their parents have a vast array of rights. Correspondingly, state and local education agencies and their staffs owe the students and parents the duty of satisfying those rights.

As pointed out in Chapters 3 through 8, students' and parents' rights derive from IDEA's six principles, as do the agencies' and professionals' duties. The principles, as applied to these rights and duties, are as follows.

1. The right to attend school—the principle of zero reject (Chapter 3)—means that agencies and professionals may not expel or suspend students for certain behaviors or without following certain procedures; they may not exclude students on the basis that they are incapable of learning; and they may not limit their access to school on the basis of their having contagious diseases. A student's remedy for violating any of these or other zero-reject rights includes a court order that the schools readmit the students. Essentially, the remedy is a "start-over" remedy: The schools must restart the process of including the student in school.

2. The right to a fair appraisal of their strengths and needs—the principle of nondiscriminatory evaluation (Chapter 4)—means that agencies and professionals must obtain an accurate, nonbiased portrait of each student. A student's remedy for a violation of that right is, again, a "start-over" remedy: The schools must conduct a correct evaluation. In addition, the student's remedy

includes the right to secure an independent evaluation and to have the schools consider it as part of their evaluation process; in some instances, the school must pay for that evaluation.

3. The right to a beneficial experience in school—the principle of free appropriate public education (Chapter 5)—means that schools must individualize each student's education, provide needed related services, engage in a fair process for determining what is appropriate for each student, and ensure that the students' education indeed confers a benefit. The remedy includes the "start-over" remedy; schools will have to develop and deliver a legally sufficient (fair process, plus benefit) individualized program. In addition, schools may be obliged to reimburse the student's parent(s) for tuition or other necessary costs they have paid to secure an appropriate education in a private setting; to provide compensatory education; or to furnish an extended school year (12-month education).

4. The right to be included in the general education curriculum and other activities—the principle of the least restrictive environment (Chapter 6)—means that the schools must include the student in the general education program and may not remove a student from it unless the student cannot benefit from being in that program, even after the provision of supplementary aids and services and necessary related services. The remedy includes a "start-over" one: The school must complete again the process of evaluation and individualization, especially the provision of support services, so the student may be included in the general education program. In addition, the remedy includes placement in an appropriate program, even if it is at great cost to the school (such as in a private or public out-of-state program).

5. The right to be treated fairly—the principle of procedural due process (Chapter 7)—means the schools must provide certain kinds of information (notice and access to records) to students, special protection when natural parents are unavailable (surrogate parents), and access to a fair-hearing process. The remedies include the "start-over" one, but, as this chapter points out below, a host of others, too.

6. The right to be included in the decision-making process—the principle of parent and student participation (Chapter 8)—means the schools must structure the statewide and local decision-making process in such a way that parents and students have opportunities to meaningfully affect the education they are receiving. The remedy includes a "start-over" one.

As pointed out in the next chapter, students and parents have a variety of other, essentially administrative remedies. The U.S. Department of Education may withhold federal funds from a state that does not comply with IDEA; the state education agency may withhold funds from a noncomplying local education agency; and the state agency may have to provide services directly to students when a local agency does not or cannot.

In addition to the process-based "start-over" remedy and the substantive remedies mentioned above, students and their parents may exercise clearly and explicitly stated remedies. IDEA is unequivocal in granting other remedies. IDEA provides that none of its provisions, including the remedies it explicitly grants, may be construed to restrict or limit the rights, procedures, and remedies available under the federal Constitution, the Americans with Disabilities Act, Title V of the Rehabilitation Act of 1973, particularly the Section 794 antidiscrimination provisions (also known as Section 504 in the original public law) and the Section 795 attorney-fee-recovery provisions (also known as Section 505), or other federal laws protecting the rights of children with disabilities [20 U.S.C. § 1415(l)].

This is an extraordinarily important provision because it means that a student may sue an SEA or an LEA under IDEA, the ADA, the Rehabilitation Act, Section 1983 of the Civil Rights Act, and any other federal law. As the discussion in the rest of this chapter highlights, the students who have sued under IDEA and these other laws have found that, in many cases, it has helped them tremendously to be able to resort to these other laws to enforce their rights to equal educational opportunities and to FAPE.

Only one condition is placed on students' rights to sue under those other laws: The student first must "exhaust" IDEA's administrative remedies (essentially, the local and state-level due process hearings) before being entitled to sue under those other laws if the student seeks relief under them that is available also under IDEA [20 U.S.C. § 1415(l)]. If the student can get relief under IDEA, the student must seek it via local and state-level due process. If the relief is not granted or seems insufficient, then and only then may the student sue under the other laws. Students and parents also have been ingenious in trying to secure other remedies, although these are not so unambiguously provided by IDEA or by other laws. Set out below are descriptions of both the clear and the tenuous remedies for enforcing IDEA.

Damages Under IDEA and Other Federal Statutes ⌁

Refusing to Award Damages

Shortly after Congress enacted IDEA, students and parents began to seek monetary damages for its violations—almost invariably without success. These plaintiffs learned that state law (not IDEA) generally does not allow them to recover damages, as no "educational malpractice" has been committed, and thus they have no recovery for what an education agency may do or not do to a student. (For an early case that reviews all previous education malpractice cases and discusses the reasons they have failed, see *Hunter v. Board of Education of Montgomery Co.*, 1982).

These families also learned a second lesson: IDEA does not allow them to recover damages. For example, courts have refused to hold LEAs liable for

1. failing to implement a student's IEP (*Loughran v. Flanders*, 1979).
2. placing a student into special education programs erroneously (*Powell v. Defore*, 1983).
3. failing to provide an educational benefit (*Miener v. Missouri*, 1980; *Silano v. Tirozzi*, 1987; *Valerie B. v. Conway Sch. Dist.*, 1991).
4. failing to identify a student as having a learning disability and thereby being qualified for special education (*Johnson v. Clark*, 1987; *Hall v. Knott County Bd. of Educ.*, 1991).
5. failing to exclude from special education a student who does not have a disability and should not have been placed into special education (*Agostine v. School Dist. of Philadelphia*, 1987).

Reasons for Refusing to Award Damages

These and other courts have refused to award damages for alleged violations of IDEA for many reasons.

1. Because Congress in IDEA has not expressly granted a right to sue agencies for IDEA violations, courts are highly reluctant to imply a damages remedy in IDEA. Indeed, as the Supreme Court noted in *Smith v. Robinson* (1984), IDEA creates other remedies. Because IDEA is both comprehensive in identifying those remedies and makes clear that those identified remedies are the exclusive remedies, it is contrary to IDEA's express language and congressional intent to create any other remedies, including (in *Smith v. Robinson*) attorney fees.

   This reasoning, as applied to attorney fees, was extended to damages. Because *Smith* was overturned by Congress' enactment of the Handicapped Children's Protection Act (discussed under "Attorney Fees," above and immediately below), it is arguable that *Smith* and its rationale (remedies will be enforced only if Congress clearly expresses them) are still valid with regard to damages. The general rationale in *Smith*—that Congress must expressly grant the student the right to recover monetary damages—certainly persists and still dissuades some courts from awarding damages.
2. Some courts refuse to award damage awards because they believe that malpractice suits will usurp IDEA's explicit remedies, which are largely procedural in nature but which include other substantive remedies.
3. Malpractice suits are inherently inconsistent with IDEA's fundamental purpose, which is to ensure to students and families their rights under the federal and state constitutions and laws by assisting the states financially (*Davis v. Maine Endwell Cent. Sch. Dist.*, 1982). Because IDEA helps state and local education agencies provide services, the proper remedy for an IDEA violation is not money but, rather, compensatory services (*White v. California*, 1987).
4. Malpractice lawsuits are apt to discourage implementation of IDEA by educators who, because of the threat of lawsuits, will be more concerned about their

liability than about the education of students (*Davis v. Maine Endwell Cent. Sch. Dist.*, 1982). It simply is not good practice for schools to practice "defensive education" when they should be innovators on behalf of students with disabilities.

5. To create a right to sue for damages for "educational malpractice" involves the courts in a determination of what constitutes "good" or "bad" practice. Given that, under *Youngberg v. Romeo* (1982), the Supreme Court made clear that courts must defer to professionals' decisions, there is no particular reason why courts should second-guess professionals.

   As the Maryland Court of Appeals observed in *Hunter v. Bd. of Educ.* (1982), "the absence of a workable rule of care against which the [professionals'] conduct may be measured" deters courts from entering the educational malpractice arena. The *Hunter* case also raised the point that courts find difficulty in measuring who or what caused a damage and how much compensation should be awarded for the damage. This reasoning surfaces and resurfaces in IDEA cases (*Anderson v. Thompson*, 1981; *Rich v. Kentucky Country Day, Inc.*, 1990).

6. Courts fear that if they become involved in determining the damages that education agencies owe to students or families, they also will become involved in the daily governance of schools; assessing damages would, as the Maryland court said in *Hunter*, "impose an extreme burden" on the "already strained resources of the public school system" and invariably require the courts to determine which elements of the school system should have to bear the burden of paying damages.

7. The courts also are concerned that schools simply are unable to afford damages and would have to redirect their resources from educating students to paying off lawsuits (*Miener v. Missouri*, 1980).

8. Further, courts fear that, if they allow educational malpractice cases to go forward, they will open their own doors to countless lawsuits, each of which will sap the courts' resources (*Hunter v. Bd. of Educ.*, 1982). Conserving judicial resources for other kinds of dispute resolution is a factor that weighs against malpractice cases.

9. Students without disabilities generally do not have the right to sue for educational malpractice; the principles of equality, then, push to the conclusion that students with disabilities should not have that right either.

10. Finally, public policy outweighs an individual's right to sue for damages. Taxpayers who support the schools should not have to pay for both the education and the damages that arise when the education is not provided properly.

In summary, the case law and the reasons underlying the courts' decisions create nearly insurmountable obstacles for students and families who seek the pocketbook remedy.

Reasons for Deciding to Award Damages

Despite the overwhelming body of case law and many valid reasons why educational malpractice should not be recognized, students and families have been somewhat successful in holding education agencies liable for damages. They have been successful, to some extent, because there are valid policy reasons to award damages.

1. Compensatory damages are available traditionally whenever any person or agency (such as a state or a local education agency) violates a duty (such as the IDEA duty to provide a free appropriate public education to a student). The "private enforcement model" (a private person brings a lawsuit for damages to enforce a right owed him or her by another person) is a longstanding and effective way to recover for harm suffered. Because IDEA creates relatively new rights, identifiable rights, there is every reason why, like other rights-creating and duty-imposing laws, its violation should be compensated by money damages.

2. If compensatory damages are awarded under IDEA, education agencies will be far more inclined to comply with IDEA. Damages are powerful incentives for schools to comply. When schools have to worry about paying damages, proclivity toward compliance is created.

3. Even though Congress intended IDEA to be a vehicle for distributing federal aid to the states, it also intended IDEA to be the means for implementing the federal constitution's guarantee of equal protection—i.e., equal educational opportunity. In other laws enacted to carry out the constitution, Congress has provided that persons who are denied their rights under those laws may recover damages. Similarly, students and families should be able to recover under IDEA.

4. Congress has not explicitly forbidden students and their families to secure damages for violations of IDEA. From the moment it was enacted, IDEA has allowed courts to "grant such relief as [they deem] appropriate" [20 U.S.C. § 1415 (i)(2)(B)(iii)], and the Supreme Court has interpreted "appropriate" to mean "appropriate in light of the purposes of the Act" (*Burlington Sch. Comm. v. Dep't. of Educ.*, 1985). For the reasons stated above, awarding damages for a violation of IDEA is appropriate.

In light of these reasons, and in consideration of the fact that schools sometimes have acted in wholly unconscionable ways, some courts do award damages or recovery that seem very much like damages, and others at least hold open the prospect that they would award damages.

Tuition Reimbursement as Damages

As discussed in Chapter 5, IDEA generally does not provide for parents to be reimbursed for private-school tuition in cases in which they place their child in a private school without the consent of or referral by the LEA and the LEA made a free appropriate public education available to the child [20 U.S.C. § 1412 (a)(10)(C)(i)]. An exception to this rule exists, however, if the hearing officer or court finds that the LEA did not make a free appropriate public education available to the student in a timely manner prior to the student's enrollment in the private school [20 U.S.C. § 1412 (a)(10)(C)(ii)].

Two early decisions (*Greg B. v. Bd. of Educ.*, 1982; and *Matthews v. Ambach*, 1982) allowed parents to recover the cost of tuition they paid to have their children educated in private schools when the public schools were unable or unwilling to provide a free appropriate public education. In these cases, however, the damages were easily identifiable as the amount of tuition paid. Moreover, they were not "malpractice" cases in the sense that the school was negligent in performing a duty; instead, the school simply did not perform the duty at all.

As pointed out in Chapter 5, the Supreme Court, in *Burlington School Committee v. Department of Education* (1985), held that parents have a right under IDEA to recover the tuition they paid for private education when the public system was unable or unwilling to provide an appropriate education to their children. Because *Burlington* dealt with tuition reimbursement and justified the award on grounds tied so tightly to IDEA's purposes and provisions, to regard the tuition-reimbursement cases that preceded *Burlington* as "damages/malpractice" cases seems unwarranted.

"Bad Faith" Dealing by Schools

One of the earliest "malpractice" cases, *Anderson v. Thompson* (1981), created an opening for students and their families to receive damages. In that case, the federal court of appeals held that, as a general rule, damages are not available under IDEA but that, as an exception, they may be available in two unusual circumstances. One exception exists where the school is guilty of "bad faith" in dealing with the student or family.

The "bad faith" doctrine explains the decision in *Helbig v. City of New York* (1995). In *Helbig*, a state court refused to dismiss a student's suit before trial and ruled that a student may assert a damages claim and recover if he can prove that he was injured by the LEA's actions. The student claimed that he was the victim of a fraud when his school's principal raised the student's score on citywide tests and thereby made him ineligible to be admitted to the special education program for students with specific learning disabilities. Inasmuch as the court had ruled previously that students do not have a right to sue for educational malpractice, its decision that the student may sue for fraud puts the case outside the "malpractice" area and into a different kind of "tort" area—the area of fraud, which itself involves an element of bad faith or evil intention.

A somewhat similar explanation underlies the court's decision in *Allen v. School Committee* (discussed above under "Contempt of Court"). There, the LEA had contracted with a private company for busing children to special education programs. When the private company's drivers went on strike, the students were unable to attend school for 12 days.

The court awarded damages to the students for the time they missed, reasoning that the school district could have decided not to have a private company provide transportation and thereby could have retained control over transportation. In "abdicating" its responsibilities by entering into the private-company contract, the district was held liable for the drivers' action. Because the daily cost of educating each student was $20, the award of that daily cost times the number of days missed was a proper remedy under the theory of a compensatory fine. The difference between compensatory damages and a compensatory fine is not great in their effect; the students still obtain compensation. In theory, the difference is that the "damages" are for malpractice whereas the fine is for contempt of court. The court itself had held the school district in contempt previously for failing to comply with its duties to educate children with disabilities.

Preventing Harm to Student: Parent Payment of Services

Anderson v. Thompson created still another exception to the general rule of "no damages." That exception arises when a parent takes action to secure services that ultimately are found to be necessary to protect the child's physical health and that the school should have provided under IDEA. In that situation, the student's interest in avoiding jeopardy to his or her physical health justifies the parent in seeking those services and then being reimbursed for their cost.

Note that the court was careful to state that the parent's claim is simply for reimbursement of costs the school should have assumed; this is the extent of the "damages" and, in a real sense, is not an award of damages but, rather, a reimbursement of expenses, just as a parent's recovery of tuition is a reimbursement of expenses. IDEA now makes clear that parents are excused from giving notice of their intent to seek tuition reimbursement if that requirement likely would result in physical or serious emotional harm to their child [20 U.S.C. § 1412 (10)(C)(iv)(II)].

Despite these few cases and the reasons for awarding damages, courts have been most reluctant to do so (often criticizing the reasoning in *Anderson*), forcing one to conclude that the general rule is that damages are not recoverable for violation of IDEA. Nonetheless, students and their families are not lacking in remedies, as we point out in the following discussion.

Coupled Claims Under IDEA, Section 504, ADA, and Section 1983 ⌒

Congress Overrules *Smith*

In overruling *Smith v. Robinson*, which (as noted above) held that IDEA does not authorize courts to award attorney fees, Congress, in the 1986 Handicapped Children's Protection Act, opened up a broad avenue across which students can bring their malpractice claims. The key section in IDEA is § 1415(l). Section 1415(l) provides that nothing in IDEA shall be construed to restrict or limit the rights, procedures, and remedies available under the Constitution, Section 504 of the Rehabilitation Act, or other federal statutes protecting the rights of children and youth with disabilities. The student, however, first must exhaust IDEA's local and state-level due-process hearing rights.

For the purposes of "malpractice/damages," the § 1415 (l) provision is unquestionably significant. Students and their families now are suing education agencies for IDEA violations and claiming that § 1415(l) allows them to combine their IDEA claim with claims under the other federal civil rights acts and, pursuant to those acts, recover damages. Students and families thus are

(a) coupling IDEA with claims brought under Section 504 (antidiscrimination), ADA (antidiscrimination), and Section 1983 of the Civil Rights Act (enforcement of the federal constitution and federal statutes) and

(b) claiming that, because Section 504, ADA, and Section 1983 allow courts to award damages, the courts must award damages to students and families for IDEA violations as well.

Majority View:
Identical Facts, Coupled Claims, No Damages

In deciding whether a student in a coupled lawsuit may recover damages, most courts consider whether a student's claim under Section 504, ADA, and Section 1983 is factually the same as the student's IDEA claim. If there is no factual distinction between the IDEA claim and the other claims, the majority of the courts have held that the student may not recover damages.

The leading case is *Barnett v. Fairfax County Sch. Bd.* (1989), in which the court held that the student may not base a damage claim under Section 1983 "solely upon the same violation" of IDEA and Section 504; to allow the student to "merely" re-allege a violation of IDEA and convert it also into a violation of Section 1983 would allow the student to "circumvent the comprehensive scheme" of IDEA remedies (see also *Burke County Bd. of Educ. v. Denton*, 1990; *Valerie J. v. Derry Coop. Sch. Dist.*, 1991; *Hall v. Knott County Bd. of Educ.*, 1991; *Doe v. Maher*, 1986; *Edward B. v. Paul*, 1987; *Chuhran v. Walled Lake Consol. Sch.*, 1995; *Glenn III v. Charlotte Mecklenburg Sch. Bd. of Ed.*, 1995; *Ft. Zumwalt Sch. Dist. v. Missouri State Bd. of Educ.*, 1994; *Heidemann v. Rother*, 1996; *Hoekstra v. Indep. Sch. Dist. No. 283*, 1996).

What explains this result? Several factors are at work, some of which are familiar reasons for denying recovery in the "malpractice" cases.

1. Despite the express language of § 1415(l) and its extensive congressional history, courts are not persuaded that § 1415(l) actually allows students to avail themselves of any and all other remedies, especially damages allowable under Section 504, ADA, or Section 1983. When courts determine that a student's factual allegations concerning an IDEA violation are exactly the same as the student's factual allegations of a violation of Section 504, ADA, or Section 1983, they favor IDEA and its traditionally restricted remedies over Section 504, ADA, and Section 1983. Although they do not make it explicit, courts seem to conclude that education disputes should be settled under the education

statute. This is, after all, the approach that underlies the Supreme Court's decision in *Smith v. Robinson,* as noted above.

2. Courts interpret IDEA's purpose as to assist the states in implementing the substantive and procedural rights of students with disabilities (*Ft. Zumwalt Sch. Dist. v. Missouri State Bd. of Ed.*, 1994). Accordingly, they hold that an appropriate remedy is education or the tuition spent to secure an education (the *Burlington* approach); an appropriate remedy is not damages.

   These courts, however, ignore the fact that IDEA also was enacted to implement the federal constitution's equal-protection guarantees, which normally would permit an aggrieved student to sue under Section 1983 and recover damages for an IDEA violation because Section 1983 allows a person to recover damages if someone, acting under color of law (i.e., in an official capacity), deprives him or her of rights guaranteed by the Constitution.

3. Moreover, the reasons for denying damages for "educational malpractice" simply seem to be too ingrained and persuasive (*Barnett v. Fairfax County Sch. Bd.*, 1989).

4. Because IDEA creates a comprehensive and exclusive remedy and does not specifically include damages among those remedies (*Smith v. Robinson*), the right to damages does not exist (*Barnett v. Fairfax County Sch. Bd.*, 1989; *Ft. Zumwalt Sch. Dist. v. Missouri State Bd. of Ed.*, 1994).

5. Furthermore, courts that allow students to recover damages from a school district expose the district's limited budget to unpredictable financial liability, to the detriment of all students and their teachers (*Barnett v. Fairfax County Sch. Bd.*, 1989; *Anderson v. Thompson*, 1981).

6. Some courts have held that Section 504 does not create tort liability for education malpractice unless the student can prove that the school district acted in bad faith (*Barnett v. Fairfax County Sch. Bd.*, 1989), citing *Monahan v. Nebraska* (1982), and *Timms v. Metro School District* (1983).

Minority View: "Coupling" Allowed

Not surprisingly, a minority of courts disagree with the majority view that "coupled" claims must present different violations under each statute. These courts, representing the federal courts of appeals in the Second Circuit (*Mrs. W. v. Tirozzi*, 1987), the Third Circuit (*W.B. v. Matula*, 1995; *Susan N. v. Wilson Sch. Dist.*, 1995), the Fifth Circuit (*Jonathon G. v. Caddo Parish Sch. Bd.*, 1994; *Whitehead v. Sch. Bd.*, 1996), and the Eighth Circuit (*Rodgers v. Magnet Cove Pub. Schs.*, 1994), hold that the student may sue under IDEA as well as under Section 504, ADA, or Section 1983 simultaneously and for the same factual violation.

Violations

In the earliest case, *Mrs. W. v. Tirozzi*, the LEA allegedly violated three provisions of IDEA:

1. Failure to conduct the mandatory 3-year nondiscriminatory evaluation

2. Failure to implement IDEA in a state-operated school for persons with disabilities
3. Failure to comply with IDEA's procedural due process provisions.

In this case, the court relied on the express language of Section 1415(l) and its legislative history to hold that damages are available in a combined IDEA/504/1983 case.

The two bases for the decision in *Mrs. W. v. Tirozzi* set the precedent for subsequent cases. For example, the clear language of § 1415(l) (section 1415(f) at the time) and its legislative history were the grounds on which the Third Circuit has allowed a coupled claim to go forward (*W.B. v. Matula*; *Susan N. v. Wilson Sch. Dist.*). In *Matula*, however, the Supreme Court's decision in a sex discrimination case, *Franklin v. Gwinnett County Pub. Sch.* (1992), was an additional reason to allow the student to join an IDEA claim with a 504 and 1983 claim.

Reasons for Allowing Coupling

The courts that allow coupling must have substantial reasons for doing so—reasons that outweigh the many reasons that counsel against awarding damages in coupled cases. Why do they reach this result?

Express Language Courts read § 1415(l) quite literally and without reference to any of the very real concerns about educational malpractice or other policy considerations. Section 1415(l) says that nothing in IDEA shall be construed to restrict or limit a student's rights under the federal constitution, Section 504, or other federal statutes protecting the rights of children and youth with disabilities. To the courts in the minority, "nothing" means just that: "Nothing"—not fears about educational malpractice, not the other reasons given by the majority of the courts—may prevent a student from suing under IDEA, Section 504, ADA, and Section 1983.

Congressional History Not only is the express language of § 1415(l) persuasive to these courts, but so, too, is the Congressional history behind Section 1415(l) (S. Rep. No. 112, 99th Cong., 2d Sess., p. 2, 1986; and H. Conf. Rep. No. 687, 99th Cong., 2d Sess., p. 7, 1986). That history reveals clearly Congress' strong and unequivocal intent to allow coupling and damages.

Supreme Court Sex Discrimination Precedent Moreover, these courts seem to be correct under the Supreme Court's decision in *Franklin v. Gwinnett County Pub. Sch.* (1992). *Franklin* involved a member of a high-school faculty who sexually harassed a student. The student sued the district under Title IX, which prohibits discrimination based on sex and allows an aggrieved person to recover damages. The Supreme Court restated the general rule that, "Absent clear direction to the contrary by Congress, the federal courts have the power to award any appropriate relief in a cognizable cause of action brought pursuant to a federal statute." Stated alternatively, the Court held that Congress must explicitly prohibit a person from recovering damages; otherwise, damages may well be "appropriate relief"—the same term the Court used in *Burlington*, where it interpreted IDEA as authorizing courts to award tuition reimbursement.

Inasmuch as Section 504 allows damages, and inasmuch as § 1415(l) of IDEA provides that a student may not be restricted or limited in pursuing his or her rights, procedures, and remedies under the Constitution, Section 504, or any other federal statutes protecting his or her rights, some courts have relied on *Franklin v. Gwinnett County Pub. Sch.* and allowed a student to combine an IDEA claim with a Section 504 claim and recover damages.

To summarize: The courts that allow damages under coupled cases are in the minority, and it is fair to conclude at this time (Oct., 1999) that, until the Supreme Court resolves the conflict, the student's ability to recover damages under IDEA, via Section 504, ADA, or Section 1983, will depend on whether the student has an "over-and-above" claim and whether he or she is in a jurisdiction disfavoring or favoring the damage claim.

Violations "Over and Above" IDEA

But what if the factual allegations of the coupled claim are not the same and the student can prove that he or she experienced one violation under IDEA but a factually different violation under Section 504, ADA, or Section 1983? *Barnett* recognized this possibility and the propriety of allowing such coupled claims to proceed (see also *Valerie J. v. Derry Coop. Sch. Dist.*, 1991; *Beede v. Town of Washington Sch. Dist.*, 1992). In the situation where the violation of Section 504, ADA, or Section 1983 is "over and above" the IDEA violation, the student may sue under IDEA and the other federal statutes and recover damages (but first must exhaust IDEA administrative remedies/procedures) [20 U.S.C. § 1415 (l)].

In *Begay v. Hodel* (1990), for example, a student was denied both her IDEA rights (the school district failed to notify her about her due-process rights and later refused to convene a due-process hearing at her request) and her Section 504 rights (to a barrier-free school). In addition, she experienced physical damage as a result of having to commute to an accessible school that was not in her school district. Thus, the student experienced two IDEA violations, a single Section 504 violation, and physical injury as a result of the Section 504 violation. Under these circumstances, she was entitled to bring a lawsuit based on IDEA, Section 504, and Section 1983.

Fortunately for students, *Begay v. Hodel* is not the only case allowing an "over and above" claim and damages.

- In *Howell v. Waterford Public Schools* (1990), the LEA denied the student a sufficient amount of physical therapy, thereby violating IDEA's related services provision and Section 504's equal access requirement.
- In *Sullivan v. Vallejo City Unified Sch. Dist.* (1990), the LEA prohibited the student from using a "service dog" and thereby violated the student's IDEA appropriate-education provision and Section 504's equal-access requirement.
- In *Kathryn G. v. Bd. of Educ. of Mt. Vernon* (1992), the court allowed a student to sue under IDEA, Section 504, and Section 1983 for failing, over a

4-year period, to diagnose a student as having a learning disability when the LEA should have known that the student had that disability.

- In *Ali v. Wayne-Westland Sch. Dist.* (1992), a court allowed a student to sue for damages under Section 504 and Section 1983 when he was injured in a chemistry lab experiment and proved that the LEA should have recognized (but did not recognize) that he had a learning disability. Here, the failure to diagnose the learning disability violated both IDEA and Section 504, but the injury from the explosion was grounded in Section 504.

In summary, although the majority of courts will not allow a student to sue under both IDEA and Section 504, ADA, or Section 1983 if the factual allegations are the same, the majority view also is that, if the violations are different from and "over and above" the IDEA claim, the student may recover damages.

Section 504 Claims

Section 504 prohibits a recipient of federal funds from discriminating against an otherwise qualified person with a disability solely on the basis of the person's disability. Under Section 504, students who have disabilities are entitled to attend school, receive a nondiscriminatory evaluation, receive an education that makes reasonable accommodations to their disabilities, be placed into the least restrictive education environments and programs, and sue education agencies that violate these rights [34 C.F.R. § 104.31-104.39].

Courts have had no difficulty in using Section 504 to benefit students with disabilities who are not classified into special education under IDEA (*Thomas v. Davidson Academy*, 1994; *Glenn III v. Charlotte Mecklenburg School Bd. of Educ.*, 1995; *Alexander S. v. Boyd*, 1995). Nor have most courts been reluctant to hold that Section 504 allows an aggrieved person, including a student and family, to (a) secure an injunction (court order) commanding the schools to comply with Section 504's reasonable accommodations and other commands, and (b) recover monetary damages for the school's failure to do so (*Jonathon G. v. Caddo Parrish School Bd.*, 1994; *J.B. v. Indep. Sch. Dist.*, 1995).

ADA Claims

Similarly, ADA prohibits state and local governments, including school districts, from discriminating against an otherwise qualified individual with a disability and requires them to make reasonable accommodations in their programs, including education and schools, to benefit students with disabilities. ADA also allows courts to award damages to persons whose rights under ADA have been violated.

To recover under Title III of the ADA, the student must prove that he or she has a disability (or has a history or is regarded as having a disability) and that, solely because of the disability, the school district or its employees discriminated against him or her. Discrimination under ADA includes, among other things, harassing a person because of the person's disability (*Haysman v. Food Lion*, 1995).

In *Gaither v. Barron* (1996), a student who is deaf sued a teacher for violating his ADA rights, alleging harassment because the teacher "head-butted" the student when the student, who could not hear the teacher, failed to obey the teacher's instructions to turn toward the front of the class and stop helping a student seated behind him. Was the head-butting based on the student's deafness or on the student's conduct? The court held that it was based on the conduct, not the disability, "even though the situation was arguably aggravated by the (student's) disability."

Not only does ADA bar harassment, but it also bars "discriminatory retaliation" by an agency or individual who takes action adverse to a person with a disability solely because the person has exercised his or her rights under ADA [42 U.S.C. § 12203]. If a student can prove that school officials retaliated against him because his parents attempted to secure his IDEA rights, the student may sue those officials in their individual capacities for retaliation (*Gupta v. Montgomery County Public Schs.*, 1996).

Section 1983 of the Civil Rights Act of 1871

A student's "coupling" or "joinder" of IDEA with Section 504 and ADA is made all the easier because of Section 1983 of the Civil Rights Act of 1871. Section 1983 has been the subject of a great deal of recent litigation, some of it involving school districts and their employees. Therefore, a review of the statute and the courts' interpretation, however brief, is appropriate.

Section 1983 provides that an individual whose rights under the federal constitution or a federal statute have been violated by any other person who has acted under color of state law may recover damages that compensate for the harm they have suffered and also get an injunction that orders the defendants to cease their harmful activity. The statute is the primary means whereby private citizens enforce their federal rights against state and local governments and their employees. It has been used in cases involving discrimination or other deprivation of the rights of members of racial minority groups, prisoners, persons confined in state hospitals or treatment centers, and, of course, students.

To be successful in a Section 1983 lawsuit, a student must prove certain facts. That is to say, he or she must prove that the "elements" of Section 1983 exist.

Action Under Color of State Law

The student must prove that the person who deprived him of one or more of his federal rights acted "under color of law." That phrase means that the person took action pursuant to powers granted to him or her by virtue of the state's laws; his or her action must be possible only because of the authority of the state's laws (*Monroe v. Pape*, 1961, applicable to police officers; and *Wood v. Strickland*, 1975, applicable to school officials). The action taken, however, must be within the scope of the authority granted. An LEA, for instance, cannot be held liable when a teacher, acting outside the scope of her employment, improperly punishes a student with disabilities (*Tall v. Bd. of Sch. Commissioners of Baltimore City*, 1998).

The student also may sue a private citizen or a private corporation that acts in concert with the public official. In such a case, the private citizen or corporation is regarded as the ally of the public officer and acts just as much under the color of law as the public officer. The student, however, must prove that the private person or corporation is linked closely to the public official or to a public decision. The connection must be so close that it amounts to a "symbiotic relationship" between the private defendant and the public officer or public decision (*Burton v. Wilmington Parking Authority*, 1961). What constitutes such a close, symbiotic relationship? The Supreme Court gave this direction:

> A State normally can be held responsible for a private decision only when it has "exercised coercive power or has provided such significant encouragement, either overt or covert, that the choice (by the private citizen) must in law be deemed to be that of the state." (*Blum v. Yaretsky*, 1982)

Deprivation of Rights

The student also must prove that he or she is entitled to certain rights, privileges, or immunities under the federal constitution or under any federal statute and that he or she has been deprived of one or more of those rights, privileges, or immunities by the color-of-law actor (*Maine v. Thiboutot*, 1980; *Wood v. Strickland*, 1975). Proof of a violation under IDEA, Sec. 504, or ADA is, therefore, required.

Section 1983 as a Vehicle for Enforcing IDEA

What if a student prevails in a due-process hearing (at the local or state level), the school district does not appeal, and yet the school district refuses to implement the hearing-officer decision? How can the student enforce the favorable judgment?

The answer is that the student may sue the school district under Section 1983. In *Hoekstra v. Indep. Sch. Dist. No. 283* (1996) and in *Jeremy H. v. Mount Lebanon Sch. Dist.* (1996), the courts reiterated the well-established rule (*Suter v. Artist M.*, 1992; *Howe v. Ellenbecker*, 1993) that a person may sue under Section 1983 when Congress intends a statute to benefit persons like the aggrieved person through the imposition of mandatory and direct obligations on the state and when no other comprehensive enforcement mechanism exists under which the person may secure relief.

In the case of IDEA, the students clearly are the persons whom IDEA intends to benefit: They either have or should be classified as having a disability. Likewise, IDEA explicitly imposes mandatory and direct obligations on a state that accepts IDEA funding; the state has a clear and binding obligation to comply.

Finally, the fundamental federal enforcement scheme is for the U.S. Department of Education to withhold federal funds from the state; that, however, is not a remedy available to an individual student who has prevailed at a due-process hearing and who nevertheless encounters a district that refuses to comply with the hearing officer's order. In such a situation, no comprehensive IDEA remedy is available to the student (*Robinson v. Pinderhughes*, 1987; *Reid v. Bd. of Educ.*, 1991; *Grace B. v. Lexington Sch. Comm.*, 1991; *Blazejewski v. Bd. of Educ.*, 1985).

Accordingly, the only way a student can enforce the hearing officer's decision is to sue under Section 1983. As noted above, the student may secure an injunction requiring the state or local school district to comply with the hearing officer's decision (or to be in contempt of court if it does not comply), and, in some jurisdictions and under some circumstances, the student also may be able to secure money damages if he or she suffers an injury as a direct result of the district's failure to comply with the hearing officer's decision or a court order that enforces it.

Section 1983 as a Vehicle for Enforcing FERPA

If a student may enforce IDEA hearing-officer decisions via a Section 1983 lawsuit, clearly a student also may recover damages if a school district violates his or her rights under the Federal Education Rights and Privacy Act (FERPA, 20 U.S.C. § 1232g). As pointed out in Chapter 8, one of the participation rights of students and their families is the right to keep their personally identifiable school records confidential. Another right is to have access to those records for accountability purposes. These rights arise not only under IDEA (§ 1415) but also under FERPA.

For example, in *Sean R. v. Bd. of Educ.*, (1992), a student recovered damages from a school district for breach of privacy when the district disclosed the student's school records without the student's or parents' consent. Under FERPA, which protects the privacy of school records, the student has a reasonable expectation of privacy. Because IDEA incorporates FERPA, a violation of FERPA is a violation of IDEA. But, because IDEA has no remedy for violating the confidentiality provision, the other law must have one. FERPA does not provide one; thus, Section 1983 should and, under this court's decision, does provide the remedy.

Likewise, a student may rely on Section 1983 to sue a school district that uses confidential juvenile court records concerning that student when making decisions about that student's placement in special education (*Belanger v. Nashua Sch. Dist.*, 1994). Because the school district's attorney possessed the student's court records and the district relied on them for special education placement, the student's rights under FERPA were violated and he could sue to have access to the records.

The decisive factors in a FERPA-1983 suit are, of course, whether the records are personally identifiable and are used for education decision-making. Those two factors entered into the decision in *Maynard v. Greater Hoyt Sch. Dist. No. 61-4* (1995). In *Maynard*, a reporter for a local newspaper in a small rural town in South Dakota investigated why the town's school property taxes had increased so dramatically from one year to the next. In the course of the investigation, the reporter found one, and only one, reason: The school district had contracted with a neighboring district (across the state line, in Minnesota) to educate a student with autism, and the Minnesota district had paid for the student to be educated in an expensive private school in the East.

When the local newspaper reported that fact, the student's parents, now regarded quite hostilely by their fellow townspeople, sued the district for a violation of FERPA's confidentiality rules. They were unsuccessful, because (a) the district never revealed to the reporter the name of the student, and (b) state law required the district to disclose a complete fiscal report to the state education agency.

The court determined that the district was caught in a state-law obligation and had not violated FERPA. Therefore, the court held that the school district was not liable for damages under Section 1983.

Judicial and/or Monetary Remedies

If students receive a verdict in their favor, they also may receive either or both of two remedies.

1. An injunction (court order), enjoining a defendant from repeating the wrongful act.
2. Money, called damages.

Two kinds of damages are available under Section 1983.

1. *Compensatory damages* restore the student to the position he or she was in before his or her rights were violated; they compensate the student for the value of any injury incurred. Compensatory damages may be levied against a state if it is subject to suit, against a municipality, against a person acting under color of law in his or her official or individual capacity, and against a private citizen or corporation.
2. *Punitive damages* provide the student with retribution against the wrongdoer; and they also deter others from committing similar wrongs. Punitive damages, however, will be awarded only if the wrongdoer acted with an evil motive or in reckless or callous disregard for the rights of the student (*Smith v. Wade*, 1983). Accordingly, punitive damages are assessable against a public official and a private citizen or corporation.

Because a state (if it is subject to suit) and a municipality, however, cannot be said to have acted with such motive or disregard (after all, it cannot form the requisite animus and evil intent, and it cannot act in such a negligent way, not being capable of having the state of mind that is so callous), the state and municipality are free from punitive damages. Moreover, they are free from those damages because the injured party has been compensated and because assessing the "windfall" of punitive damages against them is unfair to the taxpayers (*Newport v. Fact Concerts, Inc.*, 1981).

In short, students and their families have three other bases for suing and seeking damages—Section 504, ADA, and Section 1983—and they couple these statutes with IDEA to try to get damages. As a result, courts must decide whether those coupled claims allow students and families to recover for what are essentially IDEA violations. If the students and families may recover damages, the cases prohibiting damages under IDEA are meaningless; if they may not, students and families must find other ways, over and above IDEA, to recover damages.

Restrictions on Recovery Under Section 504, ADA, and Section 1983

The student's right to recover damages under these statutes is limited. In one of the earliest cases awarding damages, *Monahan v. State of Nebraska* (1982), the Eighth Circuit Court of Appeals interpreted Section 504 to require either "bad faith or gross misjudgment" in the education of children with disabilities. The court stated that as long as educators have exercised "professional judgment, in such a way as not to depart grossly from accepted standards among educational professionals, we cannot believe that Congress intended to create liability under Section 504."

Bad Faith and Gross Misjudgments The standard of "bad faith" or "gross misjudgment" adheres to the Supreme Court's standard in *Youngberg v. Romeo* (1982), which held that professional judgment is presumed to be valid unless a professional in fact did not exercise any judgment at all. Not only has that standard been followed in *Monahan*, but it also was applied in *John G. v. Bd. of Educ.* (1995). In *John G.*, the student proved that the district failed to comply with IDEA's nondiscriminatory evaluation provisions because it was concerned about holding down the cost of special education by using the evaluation process to screen out students who otherwise would be screened into special education. Under those facts, bad faith existed and damages were allowed.

This bad-faith standard was directly at issue in *Heidemann v. Rother* (1996). *Heidemann* involved a teacher who subjected a student to a procedure known as "body wrapping." Under that procedure, a person is wrapped into a blanket, the effect being to physically restrain the person's arms, hands, and legs. The teacher applied this procedure to a 9-year old, nonverbal student with severe mental retardation, visual impairment, epilepsy, and learning disability.

The teacher defended her behavior by saying that she used the procedure upon the recommendation of a licensed physical therapist and to provide "security and comfort" and "warmth and stability" and to induce a "calming effect" in the student. The court had no difficulty holding that there was no violation of the student's rights to be free from physical restraint (the federal constitutional right to "liberty" that was involved in the *Romeo* case) and thus the student could not recover damages under Section 1983.

In this case, the professional—a licensed physical therapist—prescribed the body wrapping; the student's teacher, who did the wrapping, was following the therapist's orders. Neither the physical therapist nor the teacher and employer school district had any reason to believe that the prescribed wrapping was a substantial departure from professional norms, and indeed the wrapping was not such a departure. Thus, the facts presented no indication of bad faith or gross misconduct on the school district's part; the school district attempted to comply with the student's educational program and no intentional violation of the student's rights could be inferred.

The "gross misjudgment" standard came into play, albeit under somewhat different terminology, in *Todd v. Elkins Sch. Dist. No. 10* (1998). There, a school district allowed a student to push another, who was confined to a wheelchair, over a rough and uneven playing field. After the student fell from his unbuckled chair and broke his leg, his parents sued the school district claiming that the school acted with "thoughtless indifference and an intentional disregard" for their son's safety. Though the Eighth Circuit agreed that thoughtless indifference and an intentional disregard for safety could indicate gross misjudgment, it ruled that the school district's decisions were not such substantial departures from accepted professional judgment to create liability.

Intentional Harm   *Jonathan G. v. Caddo Parish School Board* (1994) illustrates the intention-to-harm rule. There, the court, while conceding that the Fifth Circuit Court of Appeals (which has jurisdiction in Louisiana), had not adopted the *Monahan* "bad faith/gross misjudgment" standard, acknowledged nevertheless that the *Monahan* language is "useful in assessing whether the school district engaged in an intentional refusal of services sufficient to allow an award of damages." In *Jonathan G.* the LEA expelled a student in violation of IDEA, there being a clear causal connection between the student's behavior and disability, and then violated the "process" definition of an appropriate education.

Nonetheless, the court refused to award damages, finding that the LEA had not acted intentionally, that the student was not the victim of intentional discrimination, and that the LEA did not have an official policy of discriminating against the student and others like him. The court did not find that the LEA discriminated intentionally, and thus it disallowed damages under Section 504.

Moreover, the court interpreted Section 1983 to require proof that the LEA discriminated against the student as a result of its official policy (citing *Monell v. New York Dep't. of Social Services*, 1978), which the facts failed to show. There seems to be no doubt that intent must be proved before a court will allow a student to recover under Section 504 (*Whitehead v. Sch. Bd.*, 1996; *Thompson v. Bd. of Special Sch. Dist. No. 1*, 1996).

In summary, a minority of courts have allowed a student to combine an IDEA claim with a Section 504 or Section 1983 claim and to recover, but they have imposed three limitations:

1. The student must prove "bad faith" or gross misjudgment to recover under Section 504 or ADA.
2. The student must prove intentional discrimination to recover under Section 504 or ADA.
3. The student must prove that the LEA has adopted an official policy of discrimination to recover under Section 1983.

Parents' Lack of Good Faith

The "coupled" cases seem to have yet another limitation. Just as an LEA's acting in good faith (though technically violating IDEA) and not acting intentionally are defenses to a student's damage claim, so some courts allow an LEA to assert the parents' lack of good faith as a defense. For example, in *Marvin H. v. Austin* (1993), the parents failed to utilize state administrative procedures, as outlined in the statute, and the court declined to award damages against the LEA.

The same court in another case took note of the parents' refusal to allow their child to be placed appropriately and refused to award damages (*Jackson v. Franklin County Sch. Bd.*, 1985). Likewise, in *Hudson v. Wilson* (1987), the parents refused to allow their child to be tested to determine whether special education was necessary, and a court reduced the extent of their tuition reimbursement.

Conclusion

The issue of damages is one of the most complex in special education. It also is the one most likely to remain unsettled for some time to come. To reach any firm conclusions about liability and damages, then, is premature. The most one can conclude is that, on balance, the courts disfavor awarding damages.

Sovereign Immunity ~

State and Municipal Liability

The student normally may not sue a state itself. This is so because the state is a sovereign government and normally is immune from suit; the Eleventh Amendment to the federal constitution establishes the doctrine of sovereign immunity (*Will v. Michigan Dep't. of State Police*, 1989; *Dellmuth v. Muth*, 1989). The defense of sovereign immunity grants "absolute immunity:" The state simply may not be sued. That is the general rule but, of course, there are exceptions to the doctrine of sovereign immunity and the defense of absolute immunity.

As discussed more fully in Chapter 2, federal legislation can remove state immunity from suit in two ways. First, a state may waive its immunity and agree to be sued (*Quern v. Jordan*, 1979). Typically, a state waives its immunity so it can receive federal funds and participate in a federal-state program. If, however, a state is to waive its immunity to secure federal funds, Congress must express expressly and unequivocally its intention that a state will waive its immunity as a condition of its receiving federal aid; the state must know exactly and precisely the terms on which Congress grants the federal aid (*Pennhurst State School and Hospital v. Halderman*, 1984; *Edelman v. Jordan*, 1974).

Second, Congress simply may abrogate or overrule the state's sovereign immunity in order to enforce the Fourteenth Amendment (guaranteeing due process and equal protection of the laws to persons in a state) (*Fitzpatrick v. Bitzer*, 1976). As in the situation of a grant of federal funds conditioned on the state's waiver of immunity, Congress must make perfectly clear that it is abrogating the state's immunity and that it has authority to do so under the Fourteenth Amendment.

Because the Supreme Court had ruled in *Dellmuth v. Muth* (1989) that IDEA did not abrogate a state's immunity, Congress, responding to that decision, amended IDEA in 1990 to provide that a state shall not be immune under the Eleventh Amendment from suit in federal court for a violation of IDEA [20 U.S.C. § 1404].

As discussed in Chapter 2, more recent Supreme Court decisions, while not changing the test for abrogation of sovereign immunity on its face, have significantly increased the evidentiary requirements to prove Congressional intent and authority to so act. Nevertheless, the waivers and abrogation of immunity in ADA, Section 504, and IDEA probably meet these new standards already.

Municipal Corporations/Local Governments: No Immunity from Liability

Students may sue a municipality or other subdivision of a state (*Monell v. Dep't. of Social Services,* 1978). Unlike a state, a municipality (such as an LEA) may not claim absolute immunity from lawsuits because it is not itself a sovereign government. The municipality will be liable to the student if the student can prove that its actions or those of its employees (a) are based on official policies made by the municipalities' policy-making officials; (b) reflect deliberate indifference to the student's rights; or (c) are part of the municipality's custom or practice. The Supreme Court has limited a municipality's liability (and that of a local education agency) to a situation where the plaintiff (student) can prove that "deliberate action attributable to the municipality itself is the 'moving force' behind the plaintiff's deprivation of federal rights" (*Monell*).

To recover against a municipality or school district, the plaintiff (student) must demonstrate that, "through its deliberate conduct, the municipality was the 'moving force'," meaning that the "municipal action was taken with the requisite degree of culpability (wrong-doing)" and that the action was a "direct causal link between the municipal action and the deprivation of federal rights" (*Bd. of County Comm'rs v. Brown*, 1997). To establish culpability, the plaintiff "must establish the state of mind required to prove the underlying violation." The plaintiff must prove that the municipality's "legislative body or authorized decision-maker has intentionally deprived a plaintiff of a federally protected right" (*Bd. of County Comm'rs v. Brown*).

Moreover, to prove that the municipality had a policy that was the "moving force," the plaintiff (student) must prove that the deprivation of his rights resulted from the "decisions of (a municipality's or school district's) duly constituted legislative body (such as a school board) or of those officials whose acts may fairly be said to be those of the municipality" (*Monell*). Also, any act of the municipality that is performed pursuant to a "custom" that itself has not been approved formally by a municipality must reflect a "relevant practice (that) is so widespread as to have the force of law" (*Monell*). In summary, the plaintiff must prove both fault and causation.

State and Municipal Employees: Limited Immunity from Liability

Because a state itself normally is immune from suit, so are its officials and employees, when they are acting in their official capacities. The concept of sovereign immunity (expressed in the Eleventh Amendment) would be violated if the state's officials were liable for acts taken to carry out the state's business. This is so with respect to their acts that require them to exercise discretion and judgment.

Thus, state legislators are immune from suit for exercising their judgments about what laws to support or not, and state judges and prosecutors also are immune for exercising their judgments about how to interpret and apply the law or whether to prosecute a person for an alleged criminal violation (*Tenney v. Brandhove*, 1951; *Supreme Court v. Consumers Union of United States*, 1980).

Likewise, municipal officials are immune when they, too, exercise their discretion and judgment about how to conduct the municipality's official business (*Lake Country Estates, Inc. v. Tahoe Regional Planning Agency*, 1979). The rationale for granting immunity to state and municipal officials when they act in their official capacities is straightforward: They should not be deterred from exercising their best judgment by fear of a lawsuit. The public's business demands them to exercise their best judgment, and public needs must prevail over a private citizen's.

Although state and municipal officials are immune when they exercise their discretion and judgment, they are not immune when they are obliged to carry out duties over which they exercise no discretion and about which they may not exercise discretion. These are the so-called mandatory functions of government, as distinguished from the "discretionary" functions. In the case of mandatory functions, the officials have no choice but to act according to the law's command. If they do not carry out the law's command and thereby cause someone to be harmed, they may be sued for damages or they may be enjoined (required by a court's order or injunction) to perform the duty that the law commands (*Edelman v. Jordan*, 1974; *Harlow v. Fitzgerald*, 1982; *Will v. Michigan Dep't. of State Police*, 1989).

As noted above, a student faces obstacles in wanting to sue a state or municipal official in his "official capacity." That fact, however, does not prevent a student from suing the official in his or her "individual capacity." In that situation, the student is suing the person as an individual who, acting under color of law, deprives the student of one of his or her federal rights, privileges, or immunities. The student is not suing the defendant who was acting on behalf of the state or a municipality; instead, he or she is suing the defendant who, as an individual (not an agent of the state or municipality) deprived the student of a right. If the student can prove that the person deprived him of such rights, the student may recover damages from the defendant personally (*Hafer v. Melo*, 1991).

Let's consider this rule in light of the general immunity rule: A state is immune, but a municipality is not. Here's the rule: A state is immune from liability; it has absolute immunity unless it waives the immunity or unless Congress abrogates it. But state officials, sued in their individual capacity, or municipal officials, sued in their official or individual capacities, are not immune. How do they defend against the student's suit?

When an official is sued in his or her individual or official capacity, he or she may defend by a claim of "qualified immunity." Under this defense, the official may not be held liable if he can prove that he did not violate clearly established federal law and the student's rights under that law (*Wood v. Strickland*, 1975; *Harlow v. Fitzgerald*, 1982). His defense is that he acted "in good faith" and should not be held liable; he has "qualified" to be immune. The "good-faith" defense is available to school officials who allegedly have violated a student's IDEA rights (*Christopher P. v. Marcus*, 1990; *W.B. v. Matula*, 1995).

To be successful with a qualified immunity, good-faith defense, the defendant must prove that the law he or she allegedly violated was not clear at the time he or she acted. As the Supreme Court stated in *Harlow v. Fitzgerald*, a government official is immune if his conduct does not violate "clearly established statutory or constitutional rights of which a reasonable person would have known."

"Clearly established" means that the "contours of the right must be sufficiently clear that a reasonable official would understand that what he is doing violates that right" (*Anderson v. Creighton*, 1987). If the law and the student's rights are not clearly established, the official will not be held liable because he cannot reasonably be expected to anticipate some future legal development or doctrine (*Harlow v. Fitzgerald*).

If the official raises a "qualified immunity" defense, the student must prove that the official acted "in bad faith." The essence of bad faith is that an official acts with deliberate indifference to the consequences of his or her action. For example, a prison official who fails to provide necessary medical attention to prisoners acts in "bad faith" (*Estelle v. Gamble*, 1976).

If the student sues a municipality (school district) and its officials, the municipality itself may not raise a defense of qualified immunity. It either did or did not have a policy or custom of violating a student's federal rights; that is all the student has to prove. Moreover, the municipality may not shield itself behind the qualified immunity/good faith defense that its employees may use (*Owens v. Independence*, 1980). Finally, a private citizen or private corporation is not entitled to the good faith/qualified immunity defense (*Wyatt v. Cole*, 1992).

Attorney Fees ~

As explained in Chapter 7, a parent has various procedural due-process rights, including the right to an attorney at any due-process hearing, trial, or appeal before any state or federal court. Although parents usually have the right to represent themselves (but see *Collinsgru v. Palmyra Bd. of Ed.*, 1998), IDEA's complexities and the process of going to a hearing and trial often mean that the parents should hire an attorney to represent their and the student's interest.

Recognizing that many parents do not have the financial resources to mount a time-consuming and expensive lawsuit against the state or local education agency and that few resources are available for parents who cannot pay an attorney, Congress amended IDEA in 1986 and overturned the Supreme Court's decision in *Smith v. Robinson* (1984), which had disallowed attorney fees under IDEA. In the 1986 amendments, also known as the Handicapped Children's Protection Act (HCPA), and in the 1997 amendments to IDEA, Congress has made it clear that courts may award attorney fees for violations of IDEA.

General Rule

IDEA provides that a court may award reasonable attorney fees to the parents of a student if the parent is the prevailing party in any action or proceeding brought under IDEA [20 U.S.C. § 1415 (i)(3)(B)]. Fees are to be based on the current rates in the party's community for the kind and quality of services rendered. No bonus or multiplier (e.g., three times the actual fee) is allowable [20 U.S.C. § 1415 (i)(3)(C)].

Exceptions

The IDEA provides two exceptions to the right to recover attorney fees.

1. No fees may be awarded after an LEA makes a written offer of settlement if

    a. the offer is timely (according to the Federal Rules of Civil Procedure or within 10 days before an administrative procedure—due process hearing—begins);

    b. the offer is not accepted within 10 days after it is a made; and

    c. the court or administrative-hearing officer finds that the relief finally obtained is not more favorable to the parents than the offer of settlement [20 U.S.C. § 1415 (i)(3)(D)(i)] (fees may be awarded, however, if the parents prevail and if they are substantially justified in rejecting the settlement offer) [20 U.S.C. § 1415 (i)(3)(E)].

2. Attorney fees cannot be recovered for legal services provided at IEP meetings unless those meetings are convened as a result of administrative proceedings, court orders, or for mediation [20 U.S.C. § 1415(i)(3)(D)(ii)].

Limitations and Reductions

The court may reduce attorney fees if (a) the parent or guardian unreasonably protracts the final resolution of the controversy; (b) the amount of the fees unreasonably exceeds the prevailing rate in the community; (c) the time spent and legal services rendered were excessive in light of the nature of the action or proceeding; or (d) the attorney representing the parent did not provide the LEA with the appropriate information (such as the child's name, address, school, a description of the child's problem, and a proposed resolution to the problem) in the due-process complaint [20 U.S.C. §§ 1415 (i)(3)(E) and (b)(7)].

None of these limitations applies if the court finds that the LEA itself unreasonably protracted final resolution of the controversy or if the LEA has violated the procedural safeguards, particularly those relating to due-process hearings [20 U.S.C. § 1415 (i)(3)(G)]. Thus, if an LEA effectively denies the parents or guardian an opportunity for due-process hearings, it may not complain later if the court awards attorney fees incurred because no opportunities for due-process hearings were available and the matter had to be taken directly to court.

Prevailing Party Status

The "prevailing party" rule states that parents must succeed on a significant issue in the litigation and that this success must achieve some benefit for the student or *them*

(Texas State Teachers' Ass'n. v. Garland Indep. Sch. District, 1989; *and Kattan v. District of Columbia*, 1993; or must cause major legislative changes as a result of the suit, *Holmes v. Sobol*, 1991; *Grinsted v. Houston County Sch. Dist.*, 1993). The key is whether the parents' action in bringing the litigation caused the school or state to take some action to satisfy the parents' demand and whether the parents' action altered the status *quo (Harris v. McCarthy*, 1986; *Borgna v. Binghampton City School District*, 1991; *Joiner v. District of Columbia*, 1990).

Even if the parents obtained a slight change in the defendant's behavior or the student's evaluation, program, placement, or provision of free appropriate public education, a court may award fees (*Howey v. Tippecanoe School Corp.*, 1990). In 1996, however, a federal court of appeals backed away from the "slight change" approach, holding in *Monticello School Dist. No. 25 v. George L.* that parents who succeeded in obtaining interim reimbursement for a private placement and IEP modifications were not entitled to attorney fees, as this relief was minimal in light of the more prominent LRE issue on which the parents did not prevail. Similarly, a New Jersey District Court refused to grant attorney fees where the parents prevailed in enforcing the stay-put provision of §1415(j) (*J.C. v. Mendham Township Bd. of Ed.*, 1998).

Note that parents may recover attorney fees even if they do not prevail in an administrative hearing, if they prevail in court later (*Moore v. District of Columbia*, 1990). And they may recover fees even when a court enters a consent order (a judgment that the parties and the court agree should be entered) (*Barbara R. v. Tirozzi*, 1987)).

Protracting, Not Giving Notice, and Settling

If parents protract the litigation unreasonably (*Johnson v. Bismarck Pub. Sch. Dist.*, 1992), fail to reserve the attorney fees as part of a settlement with an *LEA (Fischer v. Rochester Community Schools*, 1991; *Abu-Sahyun v. Palo Alto Unified Sch. Dist.*, 1988), or simply fail to prevail (*Wheeler v. Towanda School Dist.*, 1992), the courts will not award attorney fees. Parents must be careful to claim the attorney fees and put the state or LEA on notice that they intend to claim them when they file their administrative hearing and lawsuit (*Rapid City School Dist. No. 51-4 v. Vahle*, 1990; *Witty v. Dukakis*, 1993). Parents may recover the fees in a settlement agreement, even if the agreement is silent about fees, as long as they previously put the defendant on notice that they would seek to recover the fees (*Barlow/Gresham Union High Sch. Dist. No. 2 v. Mitchell*, 1989).

Once parents and the school district reach a settlement, however, the parents may recover the attorney fees only for work performed before the settlement was reached (*Ramirez v. City of Manchester*, 1992; *Moore v. District of Columbia*, 1990). Clearly, parents may bring an independent lawsuit to recover fees that are due (*Ramirez* and *Moore*).

Basis for Fee

Generally, courts have interpreted IDEA's attorney fees provisions broadly, awarding fees for work done in a due-process hearing (*Unified School District No. 259 v.*

Newton, 1987; *Burpee v. Manchester School Dist.*, 1987; *Michael F. v. Cambridge Sch. Dist.*, 1987; and *School Board v. Malone*, 1987; but see *Rollison v. Biggs*, 1987), at trial and appeal *(Bd. of Educ. of East Windsor Regional School Dist. v. Diamond*, 1986), in mediation *(Masotti v. Tustin Unified School Dist.*, 1992), to secure a temporary restraining order *(Capiello v. D.C. Bd. of Educ.*, 1991; but see also *Christopher P. v. Marcus*, 1990), to monitor a school district to secure the district's adherence to the court's orders *(Mason v. Kaagan*, 1992), and before a case becomes moot *(S-1 v. State Bd. of Educ. of North Carolina*, 1993).

The attorney-fees provision does not extend to the complaint resolution procedures authorized in C.F.R. §§ 300.660-662. In a case of first impression, the Third Circuit Court in *Megan C.* held in a split decision that 20 U.S.C. § 1415(b) created a mandatory and exhaustive list of the procedures required for an impartial due-process hearing within the meaning of § 1415(b) *(Megan C. v. Independent Sch. Dist. No. 625*, 1999). The court held that a complaint initiated under the CRP provisions of §§ 300.660-662 was not an "action or proceeding" brought under § 1415 for the purpose of recovery of attorney fees.

Only attorneys, not "lay advocates," may be paid under IDEA, which speaks only about attorney fees and not about any other kind of fees *(Arons v. New Jersey State Bd. of Educ.*, 1988). In addition, the courts are split on whether an attorney who represents his or her own child can collect fees, with *Rappaport v. Vance* (1993) disallowing recovery but *Miller v. West Lafayette Community School Corp.* (1996) allowing it. Some courts avoid this conflict by holding that, if the law concerning self-representation and attorney fee recovery is unsettled at the time the attorney/parent represents his or her child, awarding of attorney fees is permissible *(Kattan v. District of Columbia*, 1993).

Usually, only the parents are awarded attorney fees, but in a somewhat unusual case *(Kreher IV v. Orleans Parish Sch. Bd.*, 1996), the court held that the school board was entitled to receive attorney fees for filing a motion to enforce a valid settlement agreement entered into by the school board and a parent. The parent failed to comply with the original agreement and unilaterally attached a paragraph to the agreement guaranteeing that her son would be admitted to a school of her choice and remain there until graduation. The dispositive factor in this case was the evidence of the parent's illegal action shrouded in bad faith.

Finally, an attorney may not bill for both his or her work and that of law clerks, as this is considered duplicative billing *(Hall v. Detroit Pub. Sch.*, 1993). But "attorney fees" includes the fees of expert witnesses *(Aranow v. D.C. Bd. of Educ.*, 1992).

Amount of Fee

How successful parents are does not determine whether they are entitled to recover the attorney fees, but it does affect the amount of the fee. The most important factors in determining the amount of the fee are the attorney's compliance with the duty to give notice to the LEA [20 U.S.C. § 1415 (i)], the attorney's time and labor, the customary fee for similar services, the amount of money (or its equivalent) involved in the case, the results the attorney obtained, and the attorney's ability and experience. Typically, a court multiplies the hours the lawyer spent times the lawyer's reasonable hourly rate (*Hannigan v. Bd. of Educ. of Brunswick Cent. Sch. Dist.*, 1997). When an out-of-state attorney tries a case, the prevailing rate for that attorney is the rate in that attorney's jurisdiction, not the rate in the jurisdiction where the case is tried (*Mr. and Mrs. W. v. Malito*, 1993).

In addition, a court may consider any special circumstances that may make the award of counsel fees unjust. For example, if a school district denies services to a student pursuant to state regulations, a court may consider this when determining the fee award. Thus, the court in *Independent Sch. Dist. v. Digre* (1990) required the parents to seek fees from the state and not from the LEA, because the state regulations forbade the school district from holding a public hearing.

LEAs have argued that fees should be proportional to the relief the parents or guardian obtained—the less the relief, the lower the fee. The court in *Rollison v. Biggs* (1987) rejected this argument, reasoning that the awarding of fees in a civil-rights case is determined according to the public benefit the litigation created. In addition, *Rollison* held that fees may be increased because of the SEA's or LEA's delay in complying with payment (see also *Moore v. District of Columbia Board of Education*, 1987).

More recently, however, the Third Circuit stated that district courts should consider "the relationship between the degree of success and the amount of the award" (*Pennsylvania Envtl. Defense Fund v. Canon-McMillan Sch. Dist.*, 1998). The district court in *David P.* employed this approach to reduce the amount claimed for attorney fees by 50% to reflect the parent's partial success (*David P. v. Lower Merion Sch. Dist.*, 1998).

Attorney-Client Privilege

When a state allows "lay advocates" to represent parents and students in IDEA administrative hearings, communications between the parents and the lay advocate are privileged, just as they would be if they were communications between a parent and a licensed lawyer representing the parent or student (*Woods v. New Jersey Dept. of Educ.*, 1993).

Statute of Limitations

IDEA does not provide a statute of limitations for claims arising under the Act, nor does it provide a statute of limitations for a claim for attorney fees as a result of an IDEA violation. Thus, federal courts must borrow statutes of limitations from applicable state law. The court in *J.B. v. Essex-Calendonia Supervisory Union* (1996) held that the parents' claim for attorney fees was timely under a state's 6-year catch-all statute of limitations. The court reasoned that the parents' claim for attorney fees is analogous to an economic claim resulting from a deprivation of rights and thus falls under the catch-all statute as opposed to a claim arising under a personal injury statute, which applies a shorter statute of limitations.

Cases ⌇

Abu-Sahyun v. Palo Alto Unified School Dist., EHLR 558:275 (N.D.Cal. 1987), 843 F.2d 1250 (9th Cir. 1988).

Agostine v. School Dist. of Philadelphia, 527 A.2d 193 (Comm.Ct.Pa. 1987).

Alexander S. v. Boyd, 876 F. Supp. 773 (D.S.C. 1995).

Ali v. Wayne-Westland School Dist., 19 IDELR 511 (E.D.Mich. 1992).

Allen v. School Committee of Boston, 508 N.E.2d 605 (Mass. 1987).

Allison v. Dept. of Corrections, 94 F.3d 494 (8th Cir. 1996).

Anderson v. Creighton, 483 U.S. 635 (1987).

Anderson v. Thompson, 658 F.2d 1205 (7th Cir. 1981).

Aranow v. Dist. of Columbia Bd. of Educ., 780 F. Supp. 46 (D.D.C. 1992), modified, 791 F. Supp. 318 (D.D.C. 1992).

Arons v. New Jersey State Bd. of Educ., 842 F.2d 58 (3rd Cir. 1988), cert. denied, 488 U.S. 942 (1988).

ASPIRA of New York v. Bd. of Educ., 423 F. Supp. 647 (S.D.N.Y. 1976).

B.M. v. Montana, 556 EHLR 195 (D.Mont. 1984).

Barbara R. v. Tirozzi, 665 F. Supp. 141 (D.Conn. 1987).

Barlow/Gresham Union High Sch. Dist. No. 2 v. Mitchell, 16 EHLR 157 (D.Or. 1989).

Barnett v. Fairfax County Sch. Bd., 721 F. Supp. 757 (E.D.Va. 1989), aff'd, 927 F.2d 146 (4th Cir. 1991), cert. denied, 502 U.S. 859 (1991).

Bd. of County Comm'rs v. Brown, 117 S.Ct. 1382 (U.S. 1997).

Bd. of Educ. of East Windsor Regional Sch. Dist. v. Diamond, 808 F.2d 987 (3rd Cir. 1986).

Beede v. Town of Washington Sch. Dist., 18 IDELR 1295 (D.Vt. 1992).

Begay v. Hodel, 730 F. Supp. 1001 (D.Ariz. 1990).

Belanger v. Nashua Sch. Dist., 856 F. Supp. 40 (D.N.H. 1994).

Bencic v. City of Malden, 587 N.E.2d 795 (Mass. App. Ct. 1992).

Bivens v. Six Unknown Named Agents of Federal Bureau of Narcotics, 403 U.S. 388 (1971).

Black v. Indiana Area Sch. Dist., 985 F.2d 707 (3rd Cir. 1993).

Blazejewski v. Bd. of Educ., 599 F. Supp. 975 (W.D.N.Y. 1985).

Blum v. Yaretsky, 457 U.S. 991 (1982).

Borgna v. Binghampton City Sch. Dist., 17 IDELR 677 (N.D.N.Y. 1991), 18 IDELR 121 (N.D.N.Y. 1991).

Burke County Bd. of Educ. v. Denton, 895 F.2d 973 (4th Cir. 1990).

Burlington Sch. Comm. v. Dep't of Educ., 471 U.S. 359 (1985).

Burpee v. Manchester School Dist., 661 F. Supp. 731 (D.N.H. 1987).

Burton v. Wilmington Parking Authority, 365 U.S. 715 (1961).

Bush v. Lucas, 462 U.S. 367 (1983).

C.M. v. Southeast Delco Sch. Dist., 19 IDELR 1084 (E.D.Pa 1993).

Canton v. Harris, 489 U.S. 378 (1989).

Capiello v. D.C. Bd. of Educ., 779 F. Supp. 1 (D.D.C. 1991).

Carter v. Orleans Parish Public Schools, 725 F.2d 261 (5th Cir. 1984).

Christopher P. v. Marcus, 915 F.2d 794 (2nd Cir. 1990), cert. denied, 498 U.S. 1123 (1991).

Chuhran v. Walled Lake Consol. Sch., 839 F. Supp. 465 (E.D.Mich. 1993), aff'd, No. 93-2621, 1995 U.S. App. Lexis 6348 (6th Cir. 1995).

Cohen v. Sch. Dist. of Philadelphia, 18 IDELR 911 (E.D.Pa. 1992).

Collinsgru v. Palmyra Bd. of Ed., 29 IDELR 377 (Conn. Sup. Ct. 1998)

D.R. v. Middle Bucks Area Voc. Tech. Sch., 972 F.2d 1364 (3rd Cir. 1992), cert. denied, 506 U.S. 1079 (1993).

David P. v. Lower Merion Sch. Dist., 29 IDELR 23, 27 (E.D.Penn. 1998).

Davis v. Maine Endwell Central Sch. Dist., 542 F. Supp. 1257 (N.D.N.Y. 1982).

Davis v. Monroe County Board of Education, 119 S.Ct. 1661 (1999).

Dellmuth v. Muth, 491 U.S. 223 (1989).

DeRosa v. City of New York, EHLR 559:108 (App. Div. 2d N.Y. 1987).

DeShaney v. Winnebago County Dep't. of Social Services, 489 U.S. 189 (1989).

Doe v. Alfred, 906 F. Supp. 1092 (S.D.W.Va. 1995), appeal dismissed, 17 F.3d 1141 (3rd Cir. 1996), dismissed, No. 96-1047, 1996 U.S. App. Lexis 4864 (3d Cir. 1996).

Doe v. Escambia County Sch. Bd., 599 So.2d 226 (Fla. Dist. Ct. App. 1992).

Doe v. Hillsboro Independent School Dist., 81 F.3d 1395, 1401 (5th Cir. 1996).

Doe v. Maher, 795 F.2d 787 (9th Cir. 1986).

Doe v. Withers, 20 IDELR 422 (W.Va. Cir. Ct. 1993).

Dorothy J. v. Little Rock Sch. Dist., 794 F. Supp. 1405 (E.D.Ark. 1992), aff'd, 7 F.3d 729 (8th Cir. 1993).

Edelman v. Jordan, 415 U.S. 651 (1974).

Edward B. v. Paul, 814 F.2d 52 (1st Cir. 1987).

Eisel v. Bd. of Educ. of Montgomery County, 597 A.2d 447 (Md. 1991).

Estelle v. Gamble, 429 U.S. 97 (1976).

Estes v. Chicago Bd. of Ed., 28 IDELR 971 (N.D.Ill. 1998).

Fischer v. Rochester Community Schools, 780 F. Supp. 1142 (E.D. Mich. 1991).

Fitzpatrick v. Bitzer, 427 U.S. 445 (1976).

Fontenot v. Louisiana Bd. of Elementary and Secondary Educ., 805 F.2d 1222 (5th Cir. 1986), aff'd, 835 F.2d 117 (5th Cir. 1988).

Franklin v. Gwinnett County Pub. Sch., 503 U.S. 60 (1992).

Ft. Zumwalt Sch. Dist. v. Missouri State Bd. of Educ., 865 F. Supp. 604 (E.D.Mo. 1994), further proceedings, 923 F. Supp. 1216 (E.D.Mo. 1996), aff'd in part, rev'd in part sub nom., *Ft. Zumwalt Sch. Dist. v. Clines*, No. 96-2503/2504, 1997 U.S. App. Lexis 17214 (8th Cir. 1997).

Gaither v. Barron, 924 F. Supp. 134 (M.D.Ala. 1996).

Glenn III v. Charlotte Mecklenburg Sch. Bd. of Educ., 903 F. Supp. 918 (W.D.N.C. 1995).

Grace B. v. Lexington Sch. Comm., 762 F. Supp. 416 (D.Mass. 1991).

Greg B. v. Bd. of Educ., 535 F. Supp. 1333 (E.D.N.Y. 1982).

Grinsted v. Houston County Sch. Dist., 826 F. Supp. 482 (M.D.Ga. 1993).

Grooms v. Marlboro, 414 S.E.2d 802 (S.C. Ct. App. 1992).

Gupta v. Montgomery County Public Schs., 25 IDELR 115 (D.Md. 1996).

Hafer v. Melo, 502 U.S. 21 (1991).

Haley v. McManus, 593 So.2d 1339 (La. Ct. App. 1991).

Hall v. Detroit Public Sch., 823 F. Supp. 1377 (E.D.Mich. 1993).

Hall v. Knott County Bd. of Educ., 941 F.2d 402 (6th Cir. 1991), cert. denied, 502 U.S. 1077 (1992).

Hannigan v. Bd. of Educ. of Brunswick Cent. Sch. Dist., No. 95-CV-1435, 1997 U.S. Dist. Lexis 291 (N.D.N.Y. 1997).

Harlow v. Fitzgerald, 457 U.S. 800 (1982).

Harris v. McCarthy, 790 F.2d 753 (9th Cir. 1986).

Haysman v. Food Lion, 893 F. Supp. 1092 (S.D.Ga. 1995).

Heidemann v. Rother, 84 F.3d 1021 (8th Cir. 1996).

Helbig v. City of New York, 622 N.Y.S.2d 316 (N.Y. App. 1995).

Hendrickson v. Spartanburg County Sch. Dist. No. 5, 413 S.E.2d 871 (S.C. Ct. App. 1992).

Heslop v. Bd. of Educ. Newfield Cent. Sch. Dist., 594 N.Y.S.2d 871 (N.Y. App. Div. 1993).

Hoekstra v. Indep. Sch. Dist. No. 283, 103 F.3d 624 (8th Cir. 1996); cert. denied 117 S.Ct. 1852 (U.S. 1997).

Holmes v. Sobol, 18 IDELR 53 (W.D.N.Y. 1991).

Howe v. Ellenbecker, 8 F.3d 1258 (8th Cir. 1993), cert. denied, 511 U.S. 1005 (1994).

Howell v. Waterford Public Schools, 731 F. Supp. 1314 (E.D.Mich. 1990).

Howey v. Tippecanoe School Corp., 734 F. Supp. 1485 (N.D.Ind. 1990).

Hudson v. Wilson, 828 F.2d 1059 (4th Cir. 1987).

Hunter v. Bd. of Educ., 439 A.2d 582 (Md. Ct. App. 1982).

Hunter v. Carbondale Area Sch. Dist., 829 F. Supp. 714 (M.D.Pa. 1993).

Hunter v. Bd. of Educ. of Montgomery County, 555 EHLR 559 (Md. Ct. App. 1982).

Independent Sch. Dist. v. Digre, 893 F.2d 987 (8th Cir. 1990).

Ingraham v. Wright, 430 U.S. 651 (1977).

J.B. v. Essex-Calendonia Supervisory Union, 943 F. Supp. 387 (D.Vt. 1996).

J.B. v. Indep. Sch. Dist., 21 IDELR 1157 (D.Minn. 1995).

J.C. v. Mendham Township Bd. of Ed., 29 IDELR 603 (N.J. Dist. 1998).

J.O. v. Alton Community Unif. Sch. Dist., 909 F.2d 267 (7th Cir. 1990).

Jackson v. Franklin County Sch. Bd., 606 F. Supp. 152 (S.D.Miss. 1985), aff'd, 765 F.2d 535 (5th Cir. 1985).

Joiner v. Dist. of Columbia, 16 EHLR 424, 87-3445 (D.D.C. 1990).

Jeremy H. v. Mount Lebanon Sch. Dist., 95 F.3d 272 (3rd Cir. 1996).

John G. v. Bd. of Educ., 891 F. Supp. 122 (S.D.N.Y. 1995).

Johnson v. Bismarck Pub. Sch. Dist., 949 F.2d 1000 (8th Cir. 1991).

Johnson v. Clark, 418 N.W.2d 466 (Ct. App. Mich. 1987).

Jonathon G. v. Caddo Parish Sch. Bd., 875 F. Supp. 352 (W.D.La. 1994).

Jose P. v. Ambach, 551 EHLR 245 & 412 (E.D.N.Y. 1979), aff'd, 669 F.2d 865 (2nd Cir. 1982), further proceedings, 557 F. Supp. 1230 (E.D.N.Y. 1983).

K.L. v. Southeast Delco Sch. Dist., 828 F Supp. 1192 (E.D.Pa. 1993).

Kansas State Bank & Trust Corp. v. Specialized Transp. Services, Inc., 819 P.2d 587 (Kan. 1991).

Kathryn G. v. Bd. of Educ. of Mt. Vernon, 18 IDELR 1026 (S.D.N.Y. 1992).

Kattan v. District of Columbia, 18 IDELR 296 (D.D.C. 1991), aff'd, 995 F.2d 274 (D.C. Cir. 1993), cert. denied, 511 U.S. 1018 (1994).

Kreher IV v. Orleans Parish School Bd., No. 95-1076, 1996 U.S. Dist. Lexis 1105 & 18578, (E.D.La. 1996).

L.S.B. v. Howard, 23 IDELR 695 (Ala. 1995).

Lake Country Estates Inc. v. Tahoe Regional Planning Agency, 440 U.S. 391 (1979).

Larson v. Miller, 76 F.3d 1446 (8th Cir. 1996).

Lane v. Pena, 518 U.S. 187 (1986).

Loughran v. Flanders, 470 F. Supp. 110 (D.Conn. 1979).

Maine v. Thiboutot, 448 U.S. 1 (1980).

Maldonado v. Josey, 975 F.2d 727 (10th Cir. 1992), cert. denied, 507 U.S. 914 (1993).

Manecke v. School Board, 762 F.2d 912 (11th Cir. 1983), cert. denied, 474 U.S. 1062 (1986).

Marvin H. v. Austin Indep. Sch. Dist., 714 F.2d 1348 (5th Cir. 1983).

Maryland Ass'n for Retarded Children (MARC) v. Maryland, Equity No. 100/182/77676 (Cir. Ct. Baltimore Co. 1974).

Mason v. Kaagan, 18 IDELR 732, (D.Vt. 1992).

Masotti v. Tustin Unified Sch. Dist., 806 F. Supp. 221 (C.D.Cal. 1992).

Matthews v. Ambach, 552 F. Supp. 1273 (N.D.N.Y. 1982).

Maynard v. Greater Hoyt Sch. Dist. No. 61-4, 876 F. Supp. 1104 (D.S.D. 1995).

Megan C. v. Independent Sch. Dist. No. 625, 30 IDELR 132 (D. Minn. 1999).

Michael F. v. Cambridge Sch. Dist., EHLR 558:269 (D. Mass. 1987).

Miener v. Missouri, 498 F. Supp. 944 (E.D. Mo. 1980), aff'd in part, rev'd in part, 673 F.2d 969 (8th Cir. 1982), cert. denied, 459 U.S. 909, 916 (1982), on remand, *Miener v. Special School Dist.*, 580 F. Supp. 562 (E.D. Mo. 1984), aff'd in part, rev'd in part, 800 F.2d 749 (8th Cir. 1986).

Miller v. West Lafayette Community School Corp., 665 N.E.2d 905 (Ind. 1996).

Mills v. D.C. Bd. of Educ., 348 F. Supp. 866 (D.D.C. 1972), contempt proceedings, EHLR 551:643 (D.D.C. 1980).

Missouri v. Jenkins, 515 U.S. 70 (1995).

Monahan v. Nebraska, 491 F. Supp. 1074 (D. Neb. 1980), aff'd in part, vacated in part, 645 F.2d 592 (8th Cir. 1981), aff'd in part, vacated in part, 687 F.2d 1164 (8th Cir. 1982), cert. denied, 460 U.S. 1012 (1983), modified sub nom., *Rose v. Nebraska*, 748 F.2d 1258 (8th Cir. 1984), cert. denied, 474 U.S. 817 (1985).

Monell v. New York Dep't. of Social Services, 436 U.S. 658 (1978).

Monroe v. Pape, 365 U.S. 167 (1961).

Monticello Sch. Dist. No. 25 v. Illinois State Bd. of Educ., 910 F. Supp. 446 (C.D.Ill. 1995), aff'd sub nom., *Monticello Sch. Dist. No. 25 v. George L.*, 102 F.3d 895 (7th Cir. 1996).

Moore v. Dist. of Columbia, 674 F. Supp. 901 (D.D.C. 1987), rev'd, 886 F.2d 335 (D.C.Cir. 1989), vacated, 907 F.2d 165 (D.C. Cir. 1990), cert. denied, 498 U.S. 998 (1990).

Mr. and Mrs. W. v. Malito, 19 IDELR 901 (C.D.Ill. 1993).

Mrs. W. v. Tirozzi, 832 F.2d 748 (2nd Cir. 1987).

Nance v. Matthews, 622 So. 2d 297 (Ala. 1993).

Newport v. Fact Concerts, Inc., 453 U.S. 247 (1981).

Norris v. Bd. of Educ. of Greenwood Community School Corp., 797 F. Supp. 1452 (S.D.Ind. 1992).

Owens v. Independence, 445 U.S. 622 (1980).

Pandazides v. Virginia Bd. of Educ., 13 F.3d 823 (4th Cir. 1994).

Passman v. Davis, 442 U.S. 228 (1979).

Pennhurst State School and Hospital v. Halderman, 446 F. Supp. 1295 (E.D. Pa. 1977), aff'd in part, rev'd in part, 612 F.2d 84 (3rd Cir. 1979), rev'd, 451 U.S.1 (1981), on remand, 673 F.2d 647 (3rd Cir. 1982), rev'd, 465 U.S. 89 (1984).

Pennsylvania Envtl. Defense Fund v. Canon-McMillan Sch. Dist., 152 F.3d 228, 232 (3rd Cir. 1998).

Planells v. San Francisco Unified Sch. Dist., 19 IDELR 477 (9th Cir. 1992).

Pottgen v. Missouri State High Sch. Activities Ass'n., 40 F.3d 926 (8th Cir. 1994), award of atty fee rev'd, 103 F.3d 720 (8th Cir. 1997).

Powell v. Defore, 699 F.2d 1078 (11th Cir. 1983).

Quackenbush v. Johnson City Sch. Dist., 716 F.2d 141 (2nd Cir. 1983), cert. denied, 465 U.S. 1071 (1984).

Quern v. Jordan, 440 U.S. 332 (1979).

Rainey v. Tennessee, No. A-3100 (Chavez Ct. Davidson County Tenn. 1976), order filed Jan. 21, 1976).

Ramirez v. City of Manchester, 16 EHLR 937, 89-217-D (D.N.H. 1992).

Rankins v. Aytch, 591 So.2d 387 (La. Ct. App. 1991).

Rapid City School Dist. No. 51-4 v. Vahle, 733 F. Supp. 1364 (D.S.D. 1990), aff'd, 922 F.2d 476 (8th Cir. 1990).

Rappaport v. Vance, 812 F. Supp. 609 (D.Md. 1993), appeal dismissed, 14 F.3d 596 (4th Cir. 1994), dismissed, No. 93-1916; 1994 U.S. App. Lexis 80 (4th Cir. 1994).

Reid v. Bd. of Educ., Lincolnshire-PrairieView Sch. Dist 103, 765 F. Supp. 965 (N.D.Ill. 1991).

Rich v. Kentucky Country Day, Inc., 793 S.W.2d 832 (Ky. Ct. App. 1990).

Richardson v. McKnight, 117 S.Ct. 2100 (U.S. 1997).

Robbins v. Maine School Administrative Dist. No. 56, 807 F. Supp. 11 (D.Me. 1992).

Robinson v. Pinderhughes, 810 F.2d 1270 (4th Cir. 1987).

Rodgers v. Magnet Cove Pub. Schs., 34 F.3d 642 (8th Cir. 1994).

Rollison v. Biggs, 656 F. Supp. 1204 (D.Del. 1987), reh'g denied, 660 F. Supp. 875 (D.Del. 1987).

Rose v. Nebraska, 748 F.2d 1258 (8th Cir. 1984), cert. denied, 474 U.S. 817 (1985).

S-1 v. State Bd. of Educ. of North Carolina, 6 F.3d 160 (4th Cir. 1993), reh'g, 21 F.3d 49 (4th Cir. 1994).

Sargi v. Kent City Bd. of Educ., 70 F.3d 907 (6th Cir. 1995).

School Board v. Malone, 762 F.2d 1210 (4th Cir. 1985), further proceedings, 662 F. Supp. 999 (E.D.Va. 1987).

Schweiker v. Chilicky, 487 U.S. 412 (1988).

Sean R. v. Bd. of Educ., 794 F. Supp. 467 (D.Conn. 1992).

Silano v. Tirozzi, 651 F. Supp. 1021 (D.Conn. 1987).

Smith v. Barton, 914 F.2d 1330 (9th Cir. 1990), cert. denied, 501 U.S. 1217 (1991).

Smith v. Robinson, 468 U.S. 992 (1984).

Smith v. Wade, 461 U.S. 30 (1983).

Spivey v. Elliott, 29 F.3d 1522 (11th Cir. 1994), withdrawn in part, reaff'd in part, 41 F.3d 1497 (11th Cir. 1995).

Squires v. Sierra Nevada Educational Foundation, 823 P.2d 256 (Nev. 1991).

Stevens v. Umstead, 921 F. Supp. 530 (C.D.Ill. 1996).

Stoneking v. Bradford Area Sch. Dist., 882 F.2d 720 (3rd Cir. 1989), cert. denied, 493 U.S. 1044 (1990).

Sullivan v. Vallejo City Unified Sch. Dist., 731 F. Supp. 947 (E.D.Cal. 1990).

Supreme Court v. Consumers Union of United States, 446 U.S. 719 (1980), on remand sub nom, *Consumers Union of United States v. American Bar Ass'n*, 505 F. Supp. 822 (E.D. Va. 1981), appeal dismissed, 451 U.S. 1012 (1981), aff'd in part, rev'd in part, 688 F.2d 218 (4th Cir. 1982), cert. denied. 462 U.S. 1137 (1983).

Susan N. v. Wilson Sch. Dist., 70 F.3d 751 (2nd Cir. 1995).

Suter v. Artist M., 503 U.S. 347 (1992).

Tall v. Board of School Comm'rs of Baltimore City, 28 IDELR 151 (Md. App. Ct. 1998).

Tarasoff v. Regents of Univ. of California, 551 P.2d 334 (Cal. 1976).

Taylor v. Honig, 19 IDELR 472 (9th Cir. 1992).

Tenney v. Brandhove, 341 U.S. 367 (1951).

Teresa Diane P. v. Alief Indep. Sch. Dist., 744 F.2d 484 (5th Cir. 1984).

Texas State Teachers Ass'n. v. Garland Indep. Sch. Dist., 837 F.2d 190 (5th Cir. 1988), rev'd, 489 U.S. 782 (1989).

Thelma D. v. Bd. of Educ., 737 F. Supp. 541 (E.D. Mo. 1990), aff'd, 934 F.2d 929 (8th Cir. 1991).

Thomas v. Davidson Academy, 846 F. Supp. 611 (M.D.Tenn. 1994).

Thompson v. Bd. of Special Sch. Dist. No. 1, 936 F. Supp. 644 (D.Minn. 1996).

Tilson v. School Dist. of Philadelphia, 932 F.2d 961 (3rd Cir. 1991).

Timms v. Metro School Dist., 722 F.2d 1310 (7th Cir. 1983).

Tinkham v. Groveport Madison Local School Dist., 18 IDELR 291 (Ohio Ct. App. 1991).

Todd v. Elkins Sch. Dist. No. 10, 28 IDELR 29 (8th Cir. 1998).

Unified School Dist. No. 259 v. Newton, 673 F. Supp. 418 (D. Kan. 1987).

United States v. Oregon, 839 F.2d 635 (9th Cir. 1988), rev'd, 782 F. Supp 502 (D. Or. 1991).

Valerie B. v. Conway Sch. Dist., 17 EHLR 806 (D.N.H. 1991).

Valerie J. v. Derry Coop. Sch. Dist., 771 F. Supp. 492 (D.N.H. 1991).

W.B. v. Matula, 67 F.3d 484 (3rd Cir. 1995).

Waechter v. Sch. Dist. No. 14-030, 773 F. Supp. 1005 (W.D.Mich. 1991).

Walton v. Alexander, 44 F.3d 1297 (5th Cir. 1995).

Wheeler v. Towanda Area School Dist., 950 F.2d 128 (3rd Cir. 1991), dismissed, No. CV 90- 1764, 1991U.S. Dist. Lexis 20139 (M.D.Pa. 1991), rehearing denied, No. 91-547, 1992 U.S. App. Lexis 46 (3d. Cir. 1992).

White v. California, 195 Cal. App. 3d 452 (Cal. Ct. App. 1987).

Whitehead v. Sch. Bd., 918 F. Supp. 1515 (M.D.Fla. 1996).

Will v. Michigan Dep't. of State Police, 491 U.S. 58 (1989).

Witty v. Dukakis, 3 F.3d 517 (1st Cir. 1993).

Wood v. Strickland, 420 U.S. 308 (1975).

Woods v. New Jersey Dept. of Educ., 19 IDELR 1092 (D.N.J. 1993).

Wyatt v. Cole, 504 U.S. 158 (1992).

Youngberg v. Romeo, 457 U.S. 307 (1982).

10

Enforcement of the Six Principles and Systems-Change for School Reform

To enforce the six principles of the law—zero reject, nondiscriminatory evaluation, individualized appropriate education, placement in the least restrictive setting, procedural due process, and parent participation—Congress provides federal funds directly to SEAs and indirectly to LEAs while requiring them to comply with IDEA, under threat of withdrawal of those funds. In short:

- Congress puts money where the students are.
- Congress requires SEAs and LEAs to be accountable to the Congress and to the intended beneficiaries of IDEA (the students, their parents, and SEA and LEA professionals).
- Congress imposes normal requirements of fiscal accountability to ensure that the federal funds are in fact used as they were intended to be used.
- Congress requires the appropriate federal and state officials and agencies to review, correct, and impose sanctions on noncomplying SEAs and LEAs.

This has been the basic approach of Congress ever since it first entered the field of special education by enacting PL 93–380 in 1973 and PL 94–142 in 1975. It is still Congress's approach under its 1997 reauthorization of IDEA by PL 105–17.

Beginning with the enactment in 1986 of the current Part C (PL 99–457) (infants/toddlers, "birth to age three"), however, Congress took a somewhat different approach to its grants-in-aid to SEAs and LEAs. The difference was that it adopted a "systems-change" approach. It still made federal funds contingent on certain state behaviors (compliance) but with a new twist. Instead of being highly prescriptive about the nature of students' rights and the means by which SEAs and LEAs would implement them, it required states to develop, within broad boundaries set by Congress, their own plans for changing their systems of early intervention.

The systems-change approach was less prescriptive and more permissive, placing greater trust in the states to know what their particular challenges are and how to solve them. Congress followed the systems-change approach in 1988 when it enacted the Technology-Related Assistance to Individuals with Disabilities Act (PL 100–407), in 1997 when it enacted Part D, and in 1999 when it enacted the Education Flexibility Partnership Act (PL 106-25). This chapter is directed, first to how Congress makes funds available to the states to carry out Parts B and C of IDEA (assistance to the states and infants/toddlers) and, second, to the national activities sponsored by Congress to improve the education of children with disabilities in Part D (discretionary programs).

Putting Money Where the Students Are ~

Federal Aid, State-Local Autonomy Reconciled

When Congress concluded in 1975 that the federal government is proper in assisting the states to provide a free appropriate education to all students with disabilities, it was both logical and practically necessary for Congress to attempt to solve the national problems of discrimination in education through existing state and local governmental mechanisms. Traditionally, public education has been a state and local concern. Thus, federalism and state and local autonomy are reconciled when federal aid is targeted to the states through SEAs, and the SEAs in turn distribute that aid to LEAs.

In 1999, Congress attempted to further reconcile the need for federal aid and local individualization of general education programs by enacting the Education Flexibility Partnership Act. Ed-Flex, as the law is commonly called, allows state and local education agencies to waive selective federal and state requirements in creating and implementing educational reforms [20 USC § 5891b(a)]. In consideration of this added flexibility, the state must agree to follow certain procedures that increase the accountability of the state education agencies to the federal government [20 USC § 5891b(a)]. In short, the state must demonstrate that its program of reform produces results that justify the waiver.

IDEA is excluded specifically from the list of federal requirements that may be waived under Ed-Flex [20 USC § 5891b(b)]. Nevertheless, Ed-Flex may have a substantial affect on individuals with disabilities who participate in state-reformed general education programs.

Direct Aid to SEAs, with Pass-Through to LEAs

Under IDEA, Congress assists SEAs and LEAs by authorizing the appropriation of funds and then by appropriating funds to distribute to the states (represented by SEAs) and then, through them, to LEAs. Thus, federal aid goes directly to the SEAs, which "pass through" most of the federal aid to LEAs. Authorization of expenditures, appropriation of funds, and pass-through requirements are the principal techniques for putting federal funds where they are most needed—namely, in the schools where the students are educated.

Federal Funding Techniques

State Applications for Federal Aid; Local Applications for Pass-Through Funds

To receive federal aid, states, through their SEAs, must apply to the U.S. Department of Education for the federal aid. Each SEA must have its application for funds approved by the Department's Office of Special Education and Rehabilitative Services. In turn, each LEA must apply to the SEA for federal aid, and its application must be approved by the SEA [20 U.S.C. §§ 1412 and 1413].

Funding Formulas

All authorizations for state and local appropriations are keyed to a formula set by IDEA. Since 1975, the formula has been based on a "head count" derived from the "child-find" provisions requiring the SEAs and LEAs to count the number of students (in each LEA and in the state as a whole) who have disabilities. For Part B (students ages 3 through 21), the formula is the number of students receiving special education and related services multiplied by 40% of the average per-pupil expenditure in all public elementary and secondary schools in the United States [20 U.S.C. § 1411 (a)(2)].

Congress also authorized expenditures for "outlying areas and freely associated states"—essentially, the territories of the United States—and for schools operated by the Bureau of Indian Affairs [20 U.S.C. § 1411 (b) and (c)]. IDEA now calls this "head-count" approach the "interim formula" because, under the 1997 amendments, it is effective for only a short while.

Beginning when the federal appropriations under IDEA reach the level of $4,924,672,200 ($4.9 billion), there will be a permanent formula for allocating funds [20 U.S.C. § 1411 (e)]. The budget for IDEA for the 1999 fiscal year did not reach this plateau, but when it does, this permanent formula will replace the interim, head-count formula and is characterized as a census-based, poverty-related formula. The following formula is based on two calculations, which are added together to determine the state's allotment:

1. the amount the state received in the year before the $4.9 billion threshold was reached plus
2. the state's proportional share of funds that exceed the previous year's appropriation, based on a census- and poverty-factor.

The census- and poverty-factor requires the Secretary of Education to allocate to each eligible state

- 85% of the funds (over and above $4.9 billion) on the basis of their relative population of children ages 3 through 21 who are of the same age as children with disabilities for whom the state ensures FAPE, and
- 15% of the funds (over and above $4.9 billion) on the basis of each state's relative populations of children who are living in poverty.

The pass-through from each SEA to its LEAs also will be based on the census-plus-poverty formula.

The formula outlined below explains how the distribution will work once the $4.9 billion is reached (Committee Report, p. 88):

1. The first part of the new formula still is based on the head-count approach. This is so because the first part establishes the ground-floor on top of which the "new" funds are built. Subject to some limitations on upward and downward adjustments of the base for inflation, a state will receive (in the year when the $4.9 billion kicks in) a guaranteed amount (the "ground-floor" amount—the same amount it received in the prior fiscal year). This guaranteed amount has the effect of a "hold-harmless" provision: The state is protected against any significant decrease in the amount of federal funds caused by the new formula. If state "X" receives $6,000,000 in the prior fiscal year, it is guaranteed to receive at least $6,000,000 in the year the new formula kicks in, plus the amount the state receives under the "second part" of the new formula.

2. The second part of the new formula, the census-plus-poverty approach, has two components: (a) the census component (the 85% component), and (b) the poverty component (the 15% component). The key to understanding the new formula is that each state gets its proportional share of the new money—its share relative or proportional to what each other state receives. 85% of the state's share (in the entire pool of new federal money) is based on the state's census data for all children ages 3–21 (if the state provides FAPE to children of these ages). 15% of the state's share (in the same entire pool of new federal money) is based on the state's poverty rate (among the same age group as described above) relative to all other states.

Purpose of Change of Formula

In changing the formula from a pure head-count to a census-plus-poverty one, Congress refused to modify the SEAs' and LEAs' obligations to implement IDEA's six principles, but it also sought to assure that SEAs and LEAs "actually use the IDEA funds for delivering services to children with disabilities" (Committee Report, p. 88).

Indeed, the new formula addresses the problem of overidentification of students with disabilities. The "old" formula had one purpose: to induce the states to count all students who have disabilities and to use the federal funds to help educate them. That purpose was based on facts as they existed in 1975—namely, the exclusion of students with disabilities from schools altogether. If students were to be included in schools, SEAs and LEAs would have to be assisted to include them. Accordingly, the more students an SEA or LEA could count, the more federal money it would receive. This approach encouraged SEAs and LEAs to locate and then educate students with disabilities (Committee Report, p. 89).

In 1997, the problem that Congress had to address was not exclusion. If anything, the problem was the reverse: the overidentification of students as having a disability when in fact they may not have a disability. As the Senate Committee noted, the challenge in 1997 was not so much how to provide students with disabilities with access to special education services but, instead, how to provide educational services appropriately to improve their educational results.

In response to the challenge of outcomes-based, results-oriented special education, an increasing number of states began to explore how to serve students with disabilities in general education, but, as they headed in that applaudable direction, they faced the prospect of reduced federal aid, as long as federal funding was tied to head-counts alone (Committee Report, p. 89).

In the case of each student classified into special education, it was unlikely that the federal fiscal incentive would be dispositive; no single group of educators would be more apt than not to classify a student into special education simply to draw down federal aid. But the fiscal incentive "reduces the scrutiny" that individual classification decisions might receive, both on a state level and on a local level (because the LEAs draw down additional state aid, not just federal aid, based on head-counts alone).

Moreover, studies have found that the fiscal incentive to overidentify students for special education is "most intense with minority children, especially African-American males" (Committee Report, p. 89). Overidentification, particularly in urban schools with high proportions of minority students, "remains a serious and growing problem" and "contributes to the referral of minority special education students to more restrictive environments" (Committee Report, p. 89). Yet, in other areas of the country, underidentification, especially of minority students, is a problem (Committee Report, p. 89).

Accordingly, the new funds (more than $4.9 billion) are tied to the total school-age population and the poverty statistics for that state. The population-based method uses objective data (the census data) and eliminates the financial incentive for "manipulating" student head counts so as to receive federal funds (Committee Report, p. 89–90). Yet, the poverty factor acknowledges "a link between poverty and certain forms of disability" (Committee Report, p. 90).

Moreover, the new formula should encourage states to address the "learning needs of more children in the regular classroom without unnecessary categorization (classification) or labeling, thereby risking the loss of Federal funds" (Committee Report, p. 90). Finally, changing the federal formula may encourage states to change the formulas on which they themselves allocate state aid to local school districts; thus, the ripple-effect of the federal formula may be powerful (Committee Report, p. 90).

State Eligibility

Under IDEA [20 U.S.C. § 1412, Committee Report, pp. 90–95], a state is eligible for federal aid (to its SEA) if it

1. agrees to provide FAPE to all eligible students,
2. establishes a goal of full educational opportunities for all students with disabilities, a timeline for meeting that goal, and procedures for child-find activities,
3. complies with IDEA's provisions regarding nondiscriminatory evaluation, IEPs, least restrictive placements, due process and parent participation safeguards, confidentiality of student records, and private-school placements,
4. agrees to provide FAPE to students who have been disciplined by being suspended or expelled from school,
5. agrees to determine if there is, in the state as a whole or in any LEA, a disproportionate number of long-term suspensions and expulsions and, if so, to undertake appropriate action and to modify policies and procedures so that the SEA and LEAs will be in compliance with IDEA,
6. meets the eligibility requirements placed on LEAs if the SEA itself provides services directly to students with disabilities,
7. establishes single-agency responsibility (the SEA is the single agency responsible for implementing IDEA),
8. permits the U.S. Secretary of Education to bypass the SEA and LEA if a state law prohibits a state from providing free appropriate public education (FAPE) to students in private schools,
9. agrees that the SEA will have general supervisory authority over all educational programs for students with disabilities (but the Governor may assign to any other public agency the duty to carry out IDEA as it applies to children with disabilities who are convicted as adults and incarcerated in adult prisons),
10. agrees to establish performance goals for students with disabilities and indicators to judge each student's progress toward achieving those goals (these performance goals and indicators are not required to be separate from, and indeed may be integrated with, the performance goals and indicators for nondisabled children, so that each SEA and LEA may be held accountable for all the results achieved by all students [20 U.S.C. § 1412 (a)(16) and Committee Report, p. 94],
11. agrees to have all students with disabilities participate in statewide and districtwide assessments of student progress (with or without accommodations for each student, as appropriate) and, by July 1, 2000, to develop and conduct alternative assessments of students who, on an individual basis, are exempted by their IEP teams from being included in the statewide or districtwide assessments,
12. agrees to report to the public on the assessment performance of students with disabilities with the same frequency and detail as it reports on the performance of students who do not have disabilities, disaggregating those reporting data

so they show performance results according to various categories (such as the type of disability, age, sex, or district of the students),

13. agrees to modify its state improvement plan (created under Part D, Subpart I) on the basis of data it derives from its assessment of student progress toward the performance goals,

14. seeks public comment before adopting policies and procedures to comply with IDEA,

15. agrees to update its application for federal funds as may be warranted because of changes in IDEA or its interpretation by the regulations of the U.S. Department of Education, a federal court, the state's own highest court, or an official Department of Education finding that a state is not in compliance with IDEA,

16. agrees to create a state-level special education advisory council that includes representatives of parents of students, the SEA and LEAs, and also representatives of private schools, charter schools, and juvenile and adult corrections agencies,

17. agrees to financial accounting requirements,

18. agrees not to commingle IDEA funds with state funds,

19. agrees not to supplant state funds with federal funds,

20. agrees to comply with the "payor of first resort" and interagency service/payment coordination provisions,

21. agrees that it will maintain its current level of expenditures (excluding federal and local funds) for special education and related services from one year to the next,

22. agrees that it will not reduce medical or other assistance to students with disabilities or alter their eligibility for Title V (maternal and child health) and Title XIX (Medicaid) benefits under the Social Security Act,

23. agrees to acquire equipment or construct new or alter existing facilities with IDEA money consistent with Americans with Disabilities Act (ADA) and the Uniform Federal Accessibility Standards [20 U.S.C. § 605], and

24. agrees to comply with the effort of the Secretary of Education as the Secretary ensures that the SEA (and LEAs) will make "positive efforts" to employ and advance in their jobs persons with disabilities [20 U.S.C. § 1406].

SEA Uses of Federal Funds

An SEA may retain 5% of the federal funds for administrative purposes. The 5% is limited based on the funds the SEA received in the 1997 fiscal year, with upward adjustments for inflation or the rate of increases in federal appropriations. In addition, the SEA may retain 20% of the federal funds for carrying out IDEA (with similar caps and adjustments after the 1997 fiscal year). The permitted SEA activities include support and direct services, administrative costs of monitoring and ensuring compliance with IDEA, establishing a mediation process, assisting LEAs in meeting personnel shortages, developing and implementing a State Program Improvement Plan, establishing and carrying out performance goals and indicators for students with disabilities, and creating a statewide system of coordinated service delivery [20 U.S.C. § 1411 (f)].

If any excess of federal appropriations above the inflation rate occurs in any year, the SEA must create a one-year fund for that excess and distribute it through grants to LEAs so they may carry out "systemic improvements" (the "systems-change" activities) or provide specific direct services to students [20 U.S.C. § 1411 (f)(4)]. In the next fiscal year, the amounts spent for those LEA activities must be distributed to the LEAs on the basis of the Part B formula for federal aid to the states; thus, there is a one-year-only "systems-change/direct aid" pool. The systems-change efforts may include direct services to students, technical assistance to LEAs and other providing agencies or entities, personnel development and training, monitoring and complaint investigation, mediation, responding to personnel shortages, complying with performance goals, and developing coordinated systems of service delivery.

LEA Eligibility

To secure the "pass-through" of federal funds from the SEA to the LEAs, each LEA must agree [20 U.S.C. § 1413] to

1. comply with IDEA's six principles,
2. submit data and reports to the SEA as required by IDEA and the SEA,
3. allow the SEA to provide services directly to students in the SEA's jurisdiction to whom it does not provide FAPE,
4. consent to submitting a joint application, on behalf of itself and another LEA, to the SEA for pass-through funds,
5. use the pass-through funds to supplement, not supplant, its local funds,
6. maintain, as a general rule, its current level of fiscal effort,
7. provide FAPE to students enrolled in charter schools it operates and fund its charter schools in the same way that other LEA-operated schools are funded,
8. upon request by the SEA, include, in each student's records, a statement of any current or previous disciplinary action taken against a student, and
9. transmit that statement, to the same extent that discipline statements concerning nondisabled students are transmitted, as part of the student's records when those records are sent to appropriate authorities (e.g., other LEAs into which a student may move or in which the student may be placed, in which case the student's IEP also must be forwarded by the "sending" LEA to the "receiving" LEA). The statement may include a description of any behavior that required disciplinary action, a description of the action taken, and any other information relevant to the safety of the student and other individuals involved with the student.

Funding Applications

To reduce the paperwork associated with implementing IDEA and making sure the SEAs and LEAs actually implement it, IDEA requires the SEA to apply only once to the Secretary of Education for IDEA funds. Indeed, if the SEA already has on file, with the Secretary of Education, policies and procedures that demonstrate that it meets the requirements for SEA eligibility, the SEA does not have to file another application unless it deems it necessary to do so. The Secretary, however, may require the SEA to modify its application so the SEA's policies, procedures, and application will be consistent with applicable interpretations or amendments of IDEA [20 U.S.C. § 1412].

Likewise, an LEA has to file with the SEA only every 3 years, instead of annually, unless the SEA requires the LEA to modify its application to be consistent with applicable interpretations or amendments of IDEA [20 U.S.C. § 1413].

Enforcement

To ensure that the SEAs comply with IDEA, the Secretary of Education may carry out a wide range of activities [20 U.S.C. §§ 1416, 1417, and 1418, Committee Report, pp. 116–117].

1. The Secretary may conduct monitoring site visits to the SEA or its LEAs.
2. The Secretary also may undertake, directly or through grantees, a host of technical assistance, research, personnel preparation, demonstration, and other activities (authorized by Part D) to assist SEAs and LEAs.
3. If the Secretary determines (after notice to the SEA and a hearing that the SEA may attend) that the SEA is not in compliance with IDEA, the Secretary may withhold Part B funds, in whole or in part, from an SEA [20 U.S.C. § 1416]. The Secretary has a great deal of discretion concerning the withholding of Part B funds. Depending on the nature and extent of an SEA's noncompliance, the Secretary may adjust the level of funding (that is, the amount of funding) and the type of funding (that is, the Secretary may withhold the "administrative" funds that an SEA otherwise would receive, thereby penalizing the SEA itself but not cutting off funds intended to benefit students themselves).
4. The Secretary may impose special conditions on how an SEA uses Part B funds.
5. The Secretary may require an SEA to submit detailed plans for achieving compliance with IDEA.
6. The Secretary may refer the matter of an SEA's noncompliance to the U.S. Department of Justice for appropriate enforcement action.

In addition, the SEA may carry out, with respect to each LEA, all of the assistance and enforcement activities the U.S. Department of Education can carry out with respect to the LEA. If the Secretary or an SEA wishes to impose any penalties under IDEA's enforcement provisions, the SEA or an LEA may seek judicial review of the proposed sanction.

IDEA provides for the U.S. Department of Education to collect data from each SEA and for each LEA to report to the SEA. Noncategorical child-find/child-count is permissive, at the SEA's discretion; but IDEA also includes data collection related to the use of interim alternative educational settings and the provision of

Part C (infant/toddler) services to children at risk for developing a developmental delay.

Before enacting any regulations to implement Parts B and C, the Secretary of Education must provide for a 90-day comment period, which gives SEAs, LEAs, and the special and general education communities the opportunity to file any complaints they may have regarding the proposed regulations. In addition, the Secretary (under a 1997-added provision) may not issue regulations, rules, or policy letters without first complying with the Federal Administrative Procedures Act (which limits the rule-making processes of executive agencies by essentially requiring the agencies' proposed rules to be reviewed and approved by Congress), disseminating a list of relevent correspondence to interested entities and, if it raises an issue of general interest or national importance, disseminating them widely to the special and general education constituents, SEAs, LEAs, and to parent and advocacy organizations [20 U.S.C. § 1406(d) and (e)].

In conclusion, through the SEA and LEA eligibility requirements, IDEA assures that the federal funds will be used to directly benefit students with disabilities, that there will be regular fiscal and other reporting between the LEAs and the SEA on the one hand and the SEA and the U.S. Department of Education on the other, and that enforcement will occur through monitoring, technical assistance, and the punitive mechanism of withholding funds.

Systemic Improvement, Systems-Change, and School Reform

Another, equally important, aspect of IDEA as it was reauthorized in 1997 deals with improving the services that SEAs and LEAs deliver to students. The "student capacity-building" inherent in Parts B and C (ages 3–21 and ages birth to three, respectively) is matched by a "system capacity-building" that is the purpose of Part D, especially Subpart 1. Before describing the system capacity-building that Subpart 1 makes possible, however, we should see how it is connected to other Part D provisions.

General Approach to System Capacity-Building

Overall, Part D creates a unified system for improving the ways in which IDEA is implemented. It does this by linking to each other those entities that implement IDEA and requiring the Secretary of Education, as the Secretary awards grants authorized by Part D, to require those entities to work collaboratively.

The entities are the SEAs, LEAs, institutions of higher education (IHEs), Parent Training and Information Centers (PTIs) that exist in each state (some states have more than one PTI), the "community parent resource centers" that serve parents of diverse racial/cultural/linguistic backgrounds, the national technical assistance center that serves the PTIs and community parent resource centers, the Regional Resource Centers, and the various entities that develop, demonstrate and use technology (including video description and captioning services) to make education accessible to students, parents, and professionals who have disabilities [20 U.S.C. §§ 1451, 1452].

The Secretary of Education is expected to fund activities of these entities in ways that create a "refocused national program" to assist states and local communities "to maintain and improve their capacity to reach and serve" infants/toddlers and students with disabilities (Committee Report, p. 119). This refocused program is to be based on a "comprehensive plan" developed by the Secretary to "guide the distribution of funds under Subpart 2" which is titled Coordinated Research, Personnel Preparation, Technical Assistance, Support, and Dissemination of Information) (Committee Report, p. 38). Thus, for example, the State Program Improvement Grants (SPIGs) authorized under Subpart 1 must be used largely for personnel training. Likewise, personnel preparation grants awarded to IHEs under Subpart 2 are expected to be connected to SEA- and LEA-identified personnel needs for preservice and inservice education.

Likewise, the Secretary is expected to fund Regional Resource Centers, clearinghouses, and other programs, authorized by Subpart 2, to help SEAs and LEAs improve their service-delivery capacities. And the Secretary is authorized to fund "systemic technical assistance" to help states implement SPIGs (Committee Report, p. 120).

State Program Improvement Grants (SPIGs)

As noted above, Subpart 1 of Part D authorizes new State Program Improvement Grants (SPIGs) [20 U.S.C. §§ 1451 through 1456]. The Secretary will award these grants on a competitive basis. Each state that receives one must demonstrate how it will engage in systemic reform, with an emphasis on personnel preparation, to improve results for students with disabilities. Although the grantee will be the SEA, the SEA will not receive a grant unless it prepares its plan in cooperation with its "contractual partners." These partners must include LEAs, parents of students with and without disabilities, individuals with disabilities, the Governor, other state and local agencies, organizations, and institutions (governmental and nongovernmental, including IHEs, that represent educators, parents, and other providers). The state plan must identify the state's needs for improving educational results, assessing students with disabilities and their performance, training a sufficiently large cadre of well prepared personnel to deliver FAPE, and evaluating the effectiveness of the state's system of special education and related services.

Because personnel preparation is such a critical need, 75% of each SPIG must be used for personnel training, but in ways identified by the states, not the federal government. The personnel preparation should include not just special education teachers and related services providers but also, and especially, regular education teachers in the early grades, so that fewer students will be referred inappropriately to special education, and so that the educational results of students served by both special and general educators will be improved (Committee Report, pp. 118–120).

Several features of Subpart D are notable:

1. Subparts 1 and 2 forcefully connect personal preparation and state improvement efforts.

2. They do so to improve student results, thereby emphasizing that special education and IDEA now are outcome-oriented, not just process-oriented.

3. Subparts 1 and 2 also connect personnel preparation and state improvement efforts to advance the doctrine of the least restrictive environment. That is why general educators must be involved in the SPIG personnel preparation and IHE personnel training/research efforts.

    Similarly, Part C (infants/toddlers) recognizes the serious personnel shortages in the area of early intervention, and it therefore allows paraprofessionals and assistants who have been trained in accordance with state law or SEA policy to help provide early intervention, but it also requires each state to require the retraining or initial hiring of personnel who meet the state's highest standards for licensure or certification to work in early intervention programs [20 U.S.C. §§ 1435 (a)(8) and (9)].

    Likewise, Part B (students ages 3 through 21) requires each SEA, as a condition of receipt of IDEA funds, to have in effect a Comprehensive System of Personnel Development (CSPD). This system must ensure an adequate supply of qualified personnel, procedures for disseminating significant research-based knowledge to them, and procedures for assuring that they will use promising practices, materials, and technology [20 U.S.C. § 1412(a)(14)].

    The SEA must coordinate its CSPD with its SPIG, to provide a single and comprehensive system of personnel development and improvement of the pre-service and inservice levels. Likewise, the SEA must train and supervise paraprofessionals and make good-faith efforts to recruit and hire appropriately and adequately trained educators and related services personnel [20 U.S.C. §§ 1412 (a)(14) and (15)].

4. Subpart 2 funds the longstanding PTIs to improve the capacity of parents to participate in IDEA and improve the educational results for their children.

5. Subpart 2 also targets traditionally underserved/unserved populations through the "community parent resource centers." These populations include students whose parents are from diverse racial, cultural, or linguistic backgrounds and those who are isolated by geographic, social, language, cultural, or racial factors. This initiative is consistent with Congress's concern about the persistent problem of overclassification and misclassification of minority students and with IDEA's increased emphasis on robust and nondiscriminatory evaluations that involve parents as members of the evaluation and IEP teams.

6. Finally, Subpart D carries out Congress's findings of fact concerning implementation of IDEA—namely, that the law and student results can be improved by strengthening parents' roles coordinating service delivery, converting special education from a place into a service, strengthening the LRE presumption, improving personnel preparation, and advancing effective teaching while

reducing paperwork [20 U.S.C. § 1400 (c)(5)]. Subpart D also advances IDEA's purposes of emphasizing student outcomes, assisting states in implementing the law, and implementing systems-change in general and special education alike [20 U.S.C. § 1400 (d)].

Local Systems-Change and Flexible Funds

In these times of fiscal conservatism, when taxpayers seem reluctant to support special education and other disability laws and a backlash against the disability rights movement is apparent, one of the major criticisms of IDEA has been that its "supplement, not supplant" requirement imposes an unduly heavy financial burden on LEAs. This requirement basically mandates that IDEA funds be used in LEAs to supplement, not supplant, their expenditures for special education. The 1997 amendments to IDEA now gives some relief to LEAs.

When appropriations under Part B exceed $4.1 billion in any fiscal year, an LEA may treat as local funds (funds derived from the local tax base and, thus, able to be used in any way that local tax support for schools is used) up to 20% of the Part B funds that exceed the amount it received in the previous fiscal year [20 U.S.C. § 1413(a)(2)(C)]. By being able to use up to 20% of the "excess" funds to reduce its maintenance of effort, an LEA escapes, to that extent, the fiscal burden of IDEA, and the opponents of special education have less to complain about when they criticize the costs of implementing the IDEA.

The 1997 IDEA amendments respond to another criticism of IDEA: that it imposes such restrictions on LEAs' use of federal funds that it impairs their ability to deliver services and limits the educational outcomes that students with disabilities achieve. To address this criticism, IDEA now allows LEAs to use Part B funds for special education and related services that are provided in general classes or other education-related settings (in accordance with a student's IEP), even if these have incidental benefits to nondisabled students [20 U.S.C. § 1413 (a)(4)(A)].

Moreover, an LEA, with SEA approval, may use Part B funds to design, implement, and evaluate a school-based improvement plan, as long as that local plan is consistent with the SPIG (State Program Improvement Plan) and the improvement plan is designed to improve the educational and transitional results for all students— those with and those without disabilities [20 U.S.C. § 1413 (g)]. This type of flexibility allows an LEA to use IDEA money consistently with other federal funds it may receive for school improvement under the Elementary and Secondary Education Act, Title I, a school-reform law. The LEA systems-change activities should be directed at improving direct services, carrying out school improvement strategies, adopting promising practices, and increasing cooperative problem-solving, mediation, or other alternative dispute resolution activities with parents.

Conclusion ⌒

A maxim that applies is, "Rights run with revenues." The more the revenues, the more rights there are apt to be. The converse is equally maximimatic: "No revenues means few rights." When appropriations are negligible, it is hard to find the means, the fiscal and programmatic wherewithal, to create new rights or to implement existing ones.

In IDEA's history, both maxims have been shown to be true. When Congress enacted IDEA's predecessors (the Elementary and Secondary Education Act of 1968 and PL 93–380 in 1973), the widespread sense throughout the country was that human service programs were affordable and necessary. This sense prevailed even at a time when the nation was engaged in an economically expensive and otherwise costly war—the conflict in Vietnam. And it continued to prevail, as far as children with disabilities were concerned, at a time when the "war on poverty" had reached or (some would say) even toppled over its zenith.

When viewed in the context of (a) the rehabilitation of Vietnam veterans, (b) the establishment of a right against disability-based discrimination for veterans and other persons with disabilities (through Section 504 of the Rehabilitation Act), and (c) the war on poverty (which was well known at that time to correlate with disability and social/ethnic/racial disadvantages), disability rights truly can be said to have run with and been established at a time of relatively free spending; they ran full-throttle with revenues. And they did so when a rights-entitlements ideology was dominant in public policy.

In 1997, the throttle is not nearly as wide open. The liberality with which money is thrown at school or other social problems approaches the "faint memory" stage. The lack of liberality is manifest in two ways.

1. The late 1990s are a time of fiscal retrenchment, characterized by balanced-budget fervor and, among some, a nearly fanatical mission to slash entitlements and retrench rights.
2. A cost-benefit consciousness justice is alive and well, and as applicable to federal aid to education as it has ever been. Ever since Congress enacted the Goals 2000 school-reform legislation in 1994, the emphasis in federal education policy has been to improve schools in the United States, not just their programs for students who do not have disabilities but also their programs for students with disabilities.

When Congress reauthorized IDEA in 1997, it predictably reflected fiscal retrenchment in the sense that federal funds now are highly targeted, and the target is improving educational outcomes by refining and strengthening the law itself. Thus:

1. The funding formula that allocates federal funds to the SEAs and from the SEAs to the LEAs removes the incentive to classify students into special education by using a census-based allotment (as to 85% of a state's allotment of the "new" federal funds, those over the $4.9 billion watershed). It does, however, retain a poverty-social justice factor as to 15% of those funds.
2. IDEA increases SEAs' and LEAs' range of discretion; it enacts the "incidental benefit rule;" it specifies the type of activities that SEAs and LEAs must consider as they engage in school program improvement efforts; it requires those

efforts to be carried out in sync with other school reform efforts; it links the SEA and LEA activities to research, personnel preparation, technical assistance, support, and dissemination activities; and it seeks thereby to develop the capacities of educational agencies to be effective.

Just as important as IDEA's strategies are its declared purposes. What was once a highly process-based law (see Chapter 2 for a description of the process) is now both process-based and outcome/result-oriented. Those results—the measures of the effectiveness of special education—are far more generic and integrative than ever before. The principle of equal access (equal access to the same and different resources for the same outcomes—see Chapter 3) evidences just how results-oriented IDEA is.

IDEA barely survived a right-wing assault during the 1995-96 session of the 104th Congress. In 1997, IDEA again was in danger of not being reauthorized. The consequences for students if it had been repealed, watered down, or underfunded are frightening. In any of those three cases, the absence of rights and revenues would have been disastrous to students with disabilities.

But that did not happen. IDEA, as reauthorized in 1997, creates a seamless web of rights, connected to outcomes and fueled by targeted and highly purposeful revenues.

If rights indeed run with revenues, IDEA/97 does more than restate the original, 1975 rights; it extends them. There is much more to nondiscriminatory evaluation, appropriate education, least restrictive placements, and parent participation than before PL 105–17 was signed on June 4, 1997.

Moreover, IDEA imposes on schools, and thereby creates for students with disabilities and their families and teachers, an expectation that rights to education are but a prelude to rights of full citizenship, full participation, in the United States. On the whole, one must be well satisfied that, in the reauthorized IDEA, students' rights run with revenues in extraordinarily positive ways.

Reference ~

Committee Report, House of Representatives Committee on Education and the Workforce, on H.R. 5 (IDEA Amendments of 1997) (Passed as P.L. 105-17), H.R. Rep. No. 95, 105th Cong., 1st Sess. (1997).

Appendix **A**

Brown v. Board of Education

(excerpts from the Supreme Court's unanimous opinion, with only Footnote 11 included)

OLIVER BROWN, et al., Appellants,

v.

BOARD OF EDUCATION OF TOPEKA, Shawnee County,
Kansas, et al. (No. 1.)

Mr. Chief Justice Warren delivered the opinion of the Court.

These cases come to us from the States of Kansas, South Carolina, Virginia, and Delaware. They are premised on different facts and different local conditions, but a common legal question justifies their consideration together in this consolidated opinion.[1]

In each of the cases, minors of the Negro race, through their legal representatives, seek the aid of the courts in obtaining admission to the public schools of their community on a nonsegregated basis. In each instance, they had been denied admission to schools attended by white children under laws requiring or permitting segregation according to race. This segregation was alleged to deprive the plaintiffs of the equal protection of the laws under the Fourteenth Amendment....

The plaintiffs contend that segregated public schools are not "equal" and cannot be made "equal," and that hence they are deprived of the equal protection of the laws....

The most avid proponents of the post-War Amendments undoubtedly intended them to remove all legal distinction among "all persons born or naturalized in the United States." Their opponents, just as certainly, were antagonistic to both the letter and the spirit of the Amendments and wished them to have the most limited effect. What others in Congress and the state legislatures had in mind cannot be determined with any degree of certainty.

An additional reason for the inconclusive nature of the Amendment's history, with respect to segregated schools, is the status of public education at that time.[4] In the South, the movement toward free common schools, supported by general taxation, had not yet taken hold. Education of white children was largely in the hands of private groups. Education of Negroes was almost nonexistent, and practically all of the race were illiterate. In fact, any education of Negroes was forbidden by law in some states. Today, in contrast, many Negroes have achieved outstanding success in the arts and sciences as well as in the business and professional world. It is true that public school education at the time of the Amendment had advanced further in the North, but the effect of the Amendment on Northern States was generally ignored in the congressional debates. Even in the North, the conditions of public education did not approximate those existing today. The curriculum was usually rudimentary; ungraded schools were common in rural areas; the school term was but three months a year in many states; and compulsory school attendance was virtually unknown. As a consequence, it is not surprising that there should be so little in the history of the Fourteenth Amendment relating to its intended effect on public education.

In the first cases in this Court construing the Fourteenth Amendment, decided shortly after its adoption, the Court interpreted it as proscribing all state-imposed discriminations against the Negro race.[5] The doctrine of "separate but equal" did not make its appearance in this Court until 1896 in the case of Plessy v. Ferguson,... involving not education but transportation.[6]... In more recent cases, all on the graduate school level, inequality was found in that specific benefits enjoyed by white students were denied to Negro students of the same educational qualifications.... In none of these cases was it necessary to reexamine the doctrine to grant relief to the Negro plaintiff. And in Sweatt v. Painter..., the Court expressly reserved decision on the question whether Plessy V. Ferguson should be held inapplicable to public education.

In the instant cases, that question is directly present. Here, unlike Sweatt v. Painter, there are findings below that the Negro and white schools involved have been equalized, or are being equalized, with respect to buildings, curricula, qualifications and salaries of teachers, and other "tangible" factors.[9] Our decision, therefore, cannot turn on merely a comparison of these tangible factors in the Negro and white schools involved in each of the cases. We must look instead to the effect of segregation itself on public education.

In approaching this problem, we cannot turn the clock back to 1868 when the Amendment was adopted, or even to 1896 when Plessy v. Ferguson was written. We must consider public education in the light of its full development and its present place in American life throughout the Nation. Only in this way can it be determined if segregation in public schools deprives these plaintiffs of the equal protection of the laws.

Today, education is perhaps the most important function of state and local governments. Compulsory school attendance laws and the great expenditures for education both demonstrate our recognition of the importance of education to our democratic society. It is required in the performance of our most basic public responsibilities, even service in the armed forces. It is the very foundation of good citizenship. Today it is a principal instrument in awakening the child to cultural values, in preparing him for later professional training, and in helping him to adjust normally to his environment. In these days, it is doubtful that any child may reasonably be expected to succeed in life if he is denied the opportunity of an education. Such an opportunity, where the state has undertaken to provide it, is a right which must be made available to all in equal terms.

We come then to the question presented: Does segregation of children in public schools solely on the basis of race, even though the physical facilities and other "tangible" factors may be equal, deprive the children of the minority group of equal education opportunities? We believe that it does.

In Sweatt v. Painter..., in finding that a segregated law school for Negroes could not provide them equal educational opportunities, this Court relied in large part on "those qualities which are incapable of objective measurement but which make for greatness in a law school." In McLaurin v. Oklahoma State Regents,....the Court, in requiring that a Negro admitted to a white graduate school be treated like all other students, again resorted to intangible considerations: "...his ability to study, to engage in discussions and exchange views with other students, and, in general, to learn his profession." Such considerations apply with added force to children in grade and high schools. To separate them from others of similar age and qualifications solely because of their race generates a feeling of inferiority as to their status in the community that may affect their hearts and minds in a way unlikely ever to be undone. The effect of this separation on their educational opportunities was well stated by a finding in the Kansas case by a court which nevertheless felt compelled to rule against the Negro plaintiffs:

"Segregation of white and colored children in public schools has a detrimental effect upon the colored children. The impact is greater when it has the sanction of the law; for the policy of separating the races is usually interpreted as denoting the inferiority of the Negro group. A sense of inferiority affects the motivation of a child to learn. Segregation with the sanction of the law, therefore, has a tendency to [retard] the educational and mental development of Negro children and to deprive them of some of the benefits they would receive in a racial[ly] integrated school system."[10]

Whatever may have been the extent of psychological knowledge at the time of Plessy v. Ferguson, this finding is amply supported by modern authority.[11] Any language in Plessy v. Ferguson contrary to this finding is rejected.

We conclude that in the field of public education the doctrine of "separate but equal" has no place. Separate educational facilities are inherently unequal. Therefore, we hold that the plaintiffs and others similarly situated for whom the actions have been brought are, by reason of the segregation complained of, deprived of the equal protection of the laws guaranteed by the Fourteenth Amendment. This disposition makes unnecessary any discussion whether such segregation also violates the Due Process Clause of the Fourteenth Amendment.[12]...

Notes 〜

11. K.B. Clark, Effect of Prejudice and Discrimination on Personality Development (Midcentury White House Conference on Children and Youth, 1950); Witmer and Kotinsky, Personality in the Making (1952), ch VI; Deutscher and Chein, The Psychological Effects of Enforced Segregation: A Survey of Social Science Opinion, 26 J Psychol 259 (1948); Chein, What are the Psychological Effects of Segregation Under Conditions of Equal Facilities?, 3 Int J Opinion and Attitude Res 229 (1949); Brameld, Educational Costs, in Discrimination and National Welfare (MacIver, ed., 1949), 44–48; Frazier, The Negro in the United States (1949), 674–681. And see generally, Myrdal, An American Dilemma (1944).

Appendix **B**

Southeastern Community College v. Davis

SOUTHEASTERN COMMUNITY COLLEGE

v.

FRANCIS B. DAVIS.

Mr. Justice Powell delivered the opinion of the Court.

This case presents a matter of first impression for this Court: Whether § 504 of the Rehabilitation Act of 1973, which prohibits discrimination against an "otherwise qualified handicapped individual" in federally funded programs "solely by reason of his handicap," forbids professional schools from imposing physical qualifications for admission to their clinical training programs.

I

Respondent, who suffers from a serious hearing disability, seeks to be trained as a registered nurse. During the 1973–1974 academic year she was enrolled in the College Parallel program of Southeastern Community College, a state institution that receives federal funds. Respondent hoped to progress to Southeastern's Associate Degree Nursing program, completion of which would make her eligible for state certification as a registered nurse. In the course of her application to the nursing program, she was interviewed by a member of the nursing faculty. It became apparent that respondent had difficulty understanding questions asked, and on inquiry she acknowledged a history of hearing problems and dependence on a hearing aid. She was advised to consult an audiologist.

On the basis of an examination at Duke University Medical Center, respondent was diagnosed as having a "bilateral, sensori-neural loss." App. 127a. A change in her hearing aid was recommended, as a result of which it was expected that she would be able to detect sounds "almost as well as a person would who has normal hearing." App. 127a 128a. But this improvement would not mean that she could discriminate among sounds sufficiently to understand normal spoken speech. Her lipreading skills would remain necessary for effective communication: "While wearing the hearing aid, she is well aware of gross sounds occurring in the listening environment. However, she can only be responsible for speech spoken to her, when the talker gets her attention and allows her to look directly at the talker." App. 128a.

Southeastern next consulted Mary McRee, Executive Director of the North Carolina Board of Nursing. On the basis of the audiologist's report, McRee recommended that respondent not be admitted to the nursing program. In McRee's view, respondent's hearing disability made it unsafe for her to practice as a nurse.[1] In addition, it would be impossible for respondent to participate safely in the normal clinical training program, and those modifications that would be necessary to enable safe participation would prevent her from realizing the benefits of the program: "To adjust patient learning experiences in keeping with [respondent's] hearing limitations could, in fact, be the same as denying her full learning to meet the objectives of your nursing programs." App. 132a–133a.

After respondent was notified that she was not qualified for nursing study because of her hearing disability, she requested reconsideration of the decision. The entire nursing staff of Southeastern was assembled, and McRee again was consulted. McRee repeated her conclusion that on the basis of the available evidence, respondent "has hearing limitations which could interfere with her safely caring for patients." App. 139a. Upon further deliberation, the staff voted to deny respondent admission.

Respondent then filed suit in the United States District Court for the Eastern District of North Carolina, alleging both a violation of § 504 of the Rehabilitation Act of 1973, 87 Stat. 394, as amended. 29 U.S.C. § 794[2] and a denial of equal protection and due process. After a bench trial, the District Court entered judgment in favor of Southeastern. 424 F Supp. 1341 (1976). It confirmed the findings of the audiologist that even with a hearing aid respondent cannot understand speech directed to her except through lipreading, and further found that,

> "[1] in many situations such as an operation room, intensive care unit, or post-natal care unit, all doctors and nurses wear surgical masks which would make lip-reading impossible. Additionally, in many situations a Registered Nurse would be required to instantly follow the physician's instructions concerning procurement of various types of instruments and drugs where the physician would be unable to get the nurse's attention by other than vocal means." *Id.,* at 1342.

Accordingly, the Court concluded that:

'[Respondent's] handicap actually prevents her from safely performing in both her training program and her proposed profession. The trial testimony indicated numerous situations where [respondent's] particular disability would render her unable to function properly. Of particular concern to the court in this case is the potential danger to future patients in such situations." *Id.,* at 1345.

Based on these findings, the District Court concluded that respondent was not an "otherwise qualified handicapped individual" protected against discrimination by § 504. In its view, "[o]therwise qualified, can only be read to mean otherwise able to function sufficiently in the position sought in spite of the handicap, if proper training and facilities are suitable and available." *Ibid.* Because respondent's disability would prevent her from functioning "sufficiently" in Southeastern's nursing program, the Court held that the decision to exclude her was not discriminatory within the meaning of § 504.[3]

On appeal, the Court of appeals for the Fourth Circuit reversed. 574 F 2d 1158 (1978). It did not dispute the District Court's findings of fact, but held that the Court had misconstrued § 504. In light of administrative regulations that had been promulgated while the appeal was pending, see 42 Fed. Reg. 22676 (May 4, 1977),[4] the appellate court believed that § 504 required Southeastern to "reconsider plaintiffs application for admission to the nursing program without regard to her hearing ability." *Id.,* at 1160. It concluded that the District Court had erred in taking respondent's handicap into account in determining whether she was "otherwise qualified" for the program, rather than confining its inquiry to her "academic and technical qualifications." *Id.,* at 1161. The Court of appeals also suggested that § 504 required "affirmative conduct" on the part of Southeastern to modify its program to accommodate the disabilities of applicants, "even when such modifications become expensive." *Id.,* at 1162.

Because of the importance of this issue to the many institutions covered by § 504, we granted certiorari. 439 U.S._____ (1979). We now reverse.[5]

II ⁓

This is the first case in which this Court has been called upon to interpret § 504. It is elementary that "[t]he starting point in every case involving the construction of a statute is the language itself." *Blue Chip Stamps v. Manor Drug Stores,* 421 U.S. 723, 756 (1975) (Powell, J., concurring); see *Greyhound Corp. v. Mt. Hood Stages, Inc.,* 437 U.S. 322, 330 (1978); *Santa Fe Industries, Inc. v. Green,* 430 U.S. 462, 472 (1977). Section 504 by its terms does not compel educational institutions to disregard the disabilities of handicapped individuals or to make substantial modifications in their programs to allow disabled persons to participate. Instead, it requires only that an "otherwise qualified handicapped individual" not be excluded from participation in a federally funded program "solely by reason of his handicap," indicating only that mere possession of a handicap is not a permissible ground for assuming an inability to function in a particular context.[6]

The court below, however, believed that the "otherwise qualified" persons protected by § 504 include those who would be able to meet the requirements of a particular program in every respect except as to limitations imposed by their handicap. See 574 F 2d. at 1160. Taken literally, this holding would prevent an institution from taking into account any limitation resulting from the handicap, however disabling. It assumes, in effect, that a person need not meet legitimate physical requirements in order to be "otherwise qualified." We think the understanding of the District Court is closer to the plain meaning of the statutory language. An otherwise qualified person is one who is able to meet all of a program's requirements in spite of his handicap.

The regulations promulgated by the Department of Health, Education, and Welfare (HEW) to interpret § 504 reinforce, rather than contradict, this conclusion. According to these regulations, a "[q]ualified handicapped person" is, "[w]ith respect to postsecondary and vocational education services, a handicapped person who meets the academic and technical standards requisite to admission or participation in the [school's] education program or activity...." 45 CFR § 84.3 (k)(3) (1978). An explanatory note states:

> "The term 'technical standards' refers to all nonacademic admissions criteria that are essential to participation in the program in question." 45 CFR pt. 84, App. A, at p. 405 (emphasis supplied).

A further note emphasizes that legitimate physical qualifications may be essential to participation in particular programs.[7] We think it clear, therefore, that HEW interprets the "other" qualifications which a handicapped person may be required to meet as including necessary physical qualifications.

III ～

The remaining question is whether the physical qualifications Southeastern demanded of respondent might not be necessary for participation in its nursing program. It is not open to dispute that, as Southeastern's Associate Degree Nursing program currently is constituted, the ability to understand speech without reliance on lipreading is necessary for patient safety during the clinical phase of the program. As the District Court found, this ability also is indispensable for many of the functions that a registered nurse performs.

Respondent contends nevertheless that § 504, properly interpreted, compels Southeastern to undertake affirmative action that would dispense with the need for effective oral communication. First, it is suggested that respondent can be given individual supervision by faculty members whenever she attends patients directly. Moreover, certain required courses might be dispensed with altogether for respondent. It is not necessary, she argues, that Southeastern train her to undertake all the tasks a registered nurse is licensed to perform. Rather, it is sufficient to make § 504 applicable if respondent might be able to perform satisfactorily some of the duties of a registered nurse or to hold some of the positions available to a registered nurse.[8]

Respondent finds support for this argument in portions of the HEW regulations discussed above. In particular, a provision applicable to postsecondary educational programs requires covered institutions to make "modifications" in their programs to accommodate handicapped persons, and to provide "auxiliary aids" such as sign-language interpreters.[9] Respondent argues that this regulation imposes an obligation to ensure full participation in covered programs by handicapped individuals and, in particular, requires Southeastern to make the kind of adjustments that would be necessary to permit her safe participation in the nursing program.

We note first that on the present record it appears unlikely respondent could benefit from any affirmative action that the regulation reasonably could be interpreted as requiring. Section 84.44 (d)(2), for example, explicitly excludes "devices or services of a personal nature" from the kinds of auxiliary aids a school must provide a handicapped individual. Yet the only evidence in the record indicates that nothing less than close, individual attention by a nursing instructor would be sufficient to ensure patient safety if respondent took part in the clinical phase of the nursing program. See 424 F Supp., at 1346. Furthermore, it also is reasonably clear that § 84.44 (a) does not encompass the kind of curricular changes that would be necessary to accommodate respondent in the nursing program. In light of respondent's inability to function in clinical courses without close supervision, Southeastern with prudence could allow her to take only academic classes. Whatever benefits respondent might realize from such a course of study, she would not receive even a rough equivalent of the training a nursing program normally gives. Such a fundamental alteration in the nature of a program is far more than the "modification" the regulation requires.

Moreover, an interpretation of the regulations that required the extensive modifications necessary to include respondent in the nursing program would raise grave doubts about their validity. If these regulations were to require substantial adjustments in existing programs beyond those necessary to eliminate discrimination against otherwise qualified individuals, they would do more than clarify the meaning of § 504. Instead, they would constitute an unauthorized extension of the obligations imposed by that statute.

The language and structure of the Rehabilitation Act of 1973 reflect a recognition by Congress of the distinction between the evenhanded treatment of qualified handicapped persons and affirmative efforts to overcome the disabilities caused by handicaps. Section 501 (b), governing the employment of handicapped individuals by the Federal Government, requires each federal agency to submit "an affirmative action program plan for the hiring, placement, and advancement of handicapped individuals...." These plans "shall include a description of the extent to which and methods whereby the special needs of handicapped employees are being met." Similarly, § 503 (a), governing hiring by federal contractors, requires employers to "take affirmative action to employ and advance in employment qualified handicapped individuals...." The President is required to promulgate regulations to enforce this section.

Under § 501 (c) of the Act, by contrast, state agencies such as Southeastern are only "encourage[d]...to adopt such policies and procedures." Section 504 does not refer at all to affirmative action, and except as it applies to federal employers it does not provide for implementation by administrative action. A comparison of these provisions demonstrates that Congress understood accommodation of the needs of handicapped individuals may require affirmative action and knew how to provide for it in those instances where it wished to do so.[10]

Although an agency's interpretation of the statute under which it operates is entitled to some deference, "this deference is constrained by our obligation to honor the clear meaning of a statute, as revealed by its language, purpose and history." *International Brotherhood of Teamsters v. Daniel,* 439 U.S. ____, ____ n. 20 (1979). Here neither the language, purpose, nor history of § 504 reveals an intent to impose an affirmative action obligation on all recipients of federal funds." Accordingly, we hold that even if HEW has attempted to create such an obligation itself, it lacks the authority to do so.

IV 〜

We do not suggest that the line between a lawful refusal to extend affirmative action and illegal discrimination against handicapped persons always will be clear. It is possible to envision situations where an insistence on continuing past requirements and practices might arbitrarily deprive genuinely qualified handicapped persons of the opportunity to participate in a covered program. Technological advances can be expected to enhance opportunities to rehabilitate the handicapped or otherwise to qualify them for some useful employment. Such advances also may enable attainment of these goals without imposing undue financial and administrative burdens upon a State. Thus situations may arise where a refusal to modify an existing program might become unreasonable and discriminatory. Identification of those instances where a refusal to accommodate the needs of a disabled person amounts to discrimination against the handicapped continues to be an important responsibility of HEW.

In this case, however, it is clear that Southeastern's unwillingness to make major adjustments in its nursing program does not constitute such discrimination. The uncontroverted testimony of several members of Southeastern's staff and faculty established that the purpose of its program was to train persons who could serve the nursing profession in all customary ways. See, *e.g.,* App. 35a, 52a, 53a, 7 la, 74a. This type of purpose, far from reflecting any animus against handicapped individuals, is shared by many if not most of the institutions that train persons to render professional service. It is undisputed that respondent could not participate in Southeastern's nursing program unless the standards were substantially lowered. Section 504 imposes no requirement upon an educational institution to lower or to effect substantial modifications of standards to accommodate a handicapped person.[12]

One may admire respondent's desire and determination to overcome her handicap and there well may be various other types of service for which she can qualify. In this case, however, we hold that there was no violation of § 504 when Southeastern concluded that respondent did not qualify for admission to its program. Nothing in the language or history of § 504 reflects an intention to limit the freedom of an educational institution to require reasonable physical qualifications for admission to a clinical training program. Nor has there been any showing in this case that any action short of a substantial change in Southeastern's program would render unreasonable the qualifications it imposed.

V ~

Accordingly, we reverse the judgment of the court below, and remand for proceedings consistent with this opinion.

So ordered.

Notes ~

1. McRee also wrote that respondent's hearing disability could preclude her practicing safely in "any setting" allowed by a "a license as L[icensed] P[ractical] N[urse]." App. 132a. Respondent contends that inasmuch as she already was licensed as a practical nurse, McRee's opinion was inherently incredible. But the record indicates that respondent had "not worked as a practical nurse except to do a little bit of night duty," App. 32a, and had not done that for several years before applying to Southeastern. Accordingly, it is at least possible to infer that respondent in fact could not work safely as a practical nurse in spite of her license to do so. In any event, we note the finding of the District Court that "a Licensed Practical Nurse, unlike a Licensed Registered Nurse, operates under constant supervision and is not allowed to perform medical tasks which require a great degree of technical sophistication." 424 F Supp., 1341, 1342–1343 (EDNC 1976).
2. The statute provides in full: "No otherwise qualified handicapped individual in the United States, as defined in section 706 (6) of this title, shall, solely by reason of his handicap, be excluded from the participation in, or be denied the benefits of, or be subjected to discrimination under any program or activity receiving Federal financial assistance *or under any program or activity conducted by any Executive agency or by the United States Postal Service. The head of each such agency shall promulgate such regulations as may be necessary to carry out the amendments to this section made by the Rehabilitation, Comprehensive Services, and Developmental Disabilities Act of 1978. Copies of any proposed regulation shall be submitted to appropriate authorizing committees of the Congress, and such regulation may take effect no earlier than the thirtieth day after the date on which such regulation is so submitted to such committees."* The italicized portion of the section was added by § 119 of the Rehabilitation, Comprehensive Services, and Developmental Disabilities Act of 1978, 92 Stat. 2982. Respondent asserts no claim under this portion of the statute.
3. The District Court also dismissed respondent's constitutional claims. The Court of appeals affirmed that portion of the order, and respondent has not sought review of this ruling.
4. Relying on the plain language of the Act, the Department of Health, Education, and Welfare (HEW) at first did not promulgate any regulations to implement § 504. In a subsequent suit against HEW, however, the United States District Court for the District of Columbia held that Congress had intended regulations to be issued and ordered HEW to do so. *Cherry v.*

Mathews, 419 F Supp. 922 (1976). The ensuing regulations currently are embodied in 45 CFR pt. 84.

5. In addition to challenging the construction of § 504 by the Court of appeals, Southeastern also contends that respondent cannot seek judicial relief for violations of that statute in view of the absence of any express private right of action. Respondent asserts that whether or not § 504 provides a private action, she may maintain her suit under 42 U.S.C. § 1983. In light of our disposition of this case on the merits, it is unnecessary to address these issues and we express no views on them. See *Norton v. Mathews,* 427 U.S. 524, 529–531 (1976); *Moor v. County of Alameda,* 411 U.S. 693, 715 (1973): *United States v. Augenblick,* 393 U.S. 348, 351–352 (1969).

6. The Act defines "handicapped individual" as follows: "The term 'handicapped individual' means any individual who (A) has a physical or mental disability which for such individual constitutes or results in a substantial handicap to employment and (B) can reasonably be expected to benefit in terms of employability from vocational rehabilitation services provided pursuant to subchapters I and III of this chapter. For the purposes of subchapters IV and V of this chapter, such term means any persons who (A) has a physical or mental impairment which substantially limits one or more of such person's major life activities, (B) has a record of such an impairment, or (C) is regarded as having such an impairment." Section 7 of the Rehabilitation Act of 1973, 87 Star. 359, as amended, 88 Stat. 1619, 89 Stat. 2, 29 U.S.C. § 706 (6). This definition comports with our understanding of § 504. A person who has a record of or is regarded as having an impairment may at present have no actual incapacity at all. Such a person would be exactly the kind of individual who could be "otherwise qualified" to participate in covered programs. And a person who suffers from a limiting physical or mental impairment still may possess other abilities that permit him to meet the requirements of various programs. Thus it is clear that Congress included among the class of "handicapped" persons covered by § 504 a range of individuals who could be "otherwise qualified." See S. Rep. No. 1297, 93d Cong., 2d Sess., 38–39 (1974).

7. The note states: "Paragraph (k) of § 84.3 defines the term 'qualified handicapped person.' Throughout the regulation, this term is used instead of the statutory term 'otherwise qualified handicapped person.' The Department believes that the omission of the word 'otherwise' is necessary in order to comport with the intent of the statute because, read literally, 'otherwise' qualified handicapped persons include persons who are qualified except for their handicap, rather than in spite of their handicap. Under such a literal reading, a blind person possessing all the qualifications for driving a bus except sight could be said to be 'otherwise qualified' for the job of driving. Clearly, such a result was not intended by Congress. In all other respects, the terms 'qualified' and 'otherwise qualified' are intended to be interchangeable." 45CFR pt. 84, App. A, at p. 405.

8. The court below adopted a portion of this argument: "[Respondent's] ability to read lips aids her in overcoming her hearing disability; however, it was argued that in certain situations such as in an operating room environment where surgical masks are used this ability would be unavailing to her. "Be that as it may, in the medical community, there does appear to be a number of settings in which the plaintiff could perform satisfactorily as an RN, such as in industry or perhaps a physician's office. Certainly [respondent] could be viewed as possessing extraordinary insight into the medical and emotional needs of those with hearing disabilities. "I [respondent] meets all the other criteria for admission in the pursuit of her RN career, under the relevant North Carolina statues, N.C. Gen. Star. §§ 90–158, *et seq.,* it should not be foreclosed to her simply because she may not be able to function effectively in all the roles which registered nurses may choose for their careers." 574 F 2d 1158, 1161 n. 6 (CA4 1978).

9. This regulation provides in full: "(a) *Academic requirements.* A recipient [of federal funds] to which this subpart applied shall make such modifications to its academic requirements as are necessary to ensure that such requirements do not discriminate or have the effect of discriminating, on the basis of handicap, against a qualified handicapped applicant or student. Academic requirements that the recipient can demonstrate are essential to the program of

instruction being pursued by such student or to any directly related licensing requirement will not be regarded as discriminatory within the meaning of this section. Modifications may include changes in the length of time permitted for the completion of degree requirements, substitution of specific courses required for the completion of degree requirements, and adaptations of the manner in which specific courses are conducted. "(d) *Auxiliary aids.* (1) A recipient to which this subpart applied shall take such steps as are necessary to ensure that no handicapped student is denied the benefits of, excluded from participation in, or otherwise subjected to discrimination under the education program or activity operated by the recipient because of the absence of educational auxiliary aids for students with impaired sensory, manual, or speaking skills. "(2) Auxiliary aids may include taped texts, interpreters or other effective methods of making orally delivered materials available to students with hearing impairments, readers in libraries for students with visual impairments, classroom equipment adapted for use by students with manual impairments, and other similar services and actions. Recipients need not provide attendants, individually prescribed devices, readers for personal use or study, or other devices or services of a personal nature." 45 CFR § 84.44.

10. § 115(a) of the Rehabilitation Act of 1978 added to the 1973 Act a section authorizing grants to state units for the purpose of providing "such information and technical assistance (including support personnel such as interpreters for the deaf) as may be necessary to assist those entities in complying with this Act, particularly the requirements of § 504." 92 Stat. 2971, codified at 29 U.S.C. § 775. This provision recognizes that on occasion the elimination of discrimination might involve some costs; it does not imply that the refusal to undertake substantial changes in a program by itself constitutes discrimination. Whatever effect the availability of these funds might have on ascertaining the existence of discrimination in some future case, no such funds were available to Southeastern at the time respondent sought admission to its nursing program.

11. The Government, in a brief *amicus curiae* in support of respondent, cites a report of the Senate Committee on Labor and Public Welfare on the 1974 amendments to the 1973 Act and several statements by individual Members of Congress during debate on the 1978 amendments, some of which indicate a belief that § 504 requires affirmative action. See Brief for the Government as *Amicus Curiae* 44–50. But these isolated statements by individual Members of Congress or its committees, all made after the enactment of the statute under consideration, cannot substitute for a clear expression of legislative intent at the time of enactment. *Quern v. Mandley,* 436 U.S. 725, 736 n. 10 (1978); *Los Angeles Dept. of Water & Power v. Manhart,* 435 U.S. 702, 714 (1978). Nor do these comments, none of which represents the will of Congress as a whole, constitute subsequent "legislation" such as this Court might weigh in construing the meaning of an earlier enactment. Cf. *Red Lion Broadcasting Co. v. FCC,* 395 U.S. 367, 380 381(1969). The Government also argues that various amendments to the 1973 Act contained in the Rehabilitation Act of 1978 further reflect Congress' approval of the affirmative action obligation created by HEWs regulations. But the amendment most directly on point undercuts this position. In amending § 504, Congress both extended that section's prohibition of discrimination to "any program or activity conducted by an Executive agency or by the United Postal Service" and authorized administrative regulations to implement only *this amendment.* See n. 2, *supra.* The fact that no other regulations were mentioned supports an inference that no others were approved. Finally, we note that the assertion by HEW of the authority to promulgate any regulations under § 504 has been neither consistent nor long-standing. For the first three years after the section was enacted, HEW maintained the position that Congress had not intended any regulations to be issued. It altered its stand only after having been enjoined to do so. See n. 4, *supra.* This fact substantially diminishes the deference to be given to HEW's present interpretation of the statute. See *General Electric Co. v. Gilbert,* 429 U.S. 125, 143 (1976).

12. Respondent contends that it is unclear whether North Carolina law requires a registered nurse to be capable of performing all functions open to that profession in order to obtain a license to practice, although McRee, the Executive Director of the state Board of nursing, had

informed Southeastern that the law did so require. See App. 138a–139a. Respondent further argues that even if she is not capable of meeting North Carolina's present licensing requirements, she still might succeed in obtaining a license in another jurisdiction. Respondent's argument misses the point. Southeastern's program, structured to train persons who will be able to perform all normal roles of a registered nurse, represents a legitimate academic policy and is accepted by the State. In effect it seeks to ensure that no graduate will pose a danger to the public in any professional role he or she might be cast. Even if the licensing requirements of North Carolina or some other State are less demanding, nothing in the Act requires an educational institution to lower its standards.

Appendix C

Board v. Rowley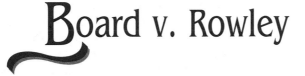

(excerpts from Court's majority opinion only; concurring and dissenting opinions are omitted, as are some footnotes from the majority opinion)

BOARD OF EDUCATION OF THE HENDRICK HUDSON CENTRAL
SCHOOL DISTRICT BD. OF ED., WESTCHESTER COUNTY, ET AL.,
PETITIONERS
v.
AMY ROWLEY, BY HER PARENTS AND NATURAL GUARDIANS,
CLIFFORD AND NANCY ROWLEY, ETC.

Justice Rehnquist delivered the opinion of the court.

I

The Education for All Handicapped Children Act of 1975 (Act), 20 U.S. C. § 1401 *et seq.,* provides federal money to assist state and local agencies in educating handicapped children, and conditions such funding upon a State's compliance with extensive goals and procedures. The Act represents an ambitious federal effort to promote the education of handicapped children, and was passed in response to Congress' perception that a majority of handicapped children in the United States "were either totally excluded from schools or [were] sitting idly in regular classrooms awaiting the time when they were old enough to 'drop out.'" H.R. Rep. No. 94-332, p. 2 (1975). The Act's evolution and major provisions shed light on the questions of statutory interpretation which is at the heart of this case.

Congress first addressed the problem of educating the handicapped in 1966 when it amended the Elementary and Secondary Education Act of 1965 to establish a grant program "for the purpose of assisting the States in the initiation, expansion, and improvement of programs and projects ... for the education of handicapped children." Pub. L. No. 89-750, § 161, 80 Stat. 1204 (1966). That program was repealed in 1970 by the Education for the Handicapped Act, Pub. L. No. 91-230, 84 Stat. 175, Part B of which established a grant program similar in purpose to the repealed legislation. Neither the 1966 nor the 1970 legislation contained specific guidelines for state use of the grant money; both were aimed primarily at stimulating the States to develop educational resources and to train personnel for educating the handicapped.[1]

Dissatisfied with the progress being made under these earlier enactments, and spurred by two district court decisions holding that handicapped children should be given access to a public education,[2] Congress in 1974 greatly increased federal funding for education of the handicapped and for the first time required recipient States to adopt "a goal of providing full educational opportunities to all handicapped children." Pub. L. 93-380, 88 Stat. 579, 583 (1974) (the 1974 statute). The 1974 statute was recognized as an interim measure only, adopted "in order to give the Congress an additional year in which to study what if any additional Federal assistance [was] required to enable the States to meet the needs of handicapped children." H. R. Rep. No. 94-332, *supra,* p. 4. The ensuing year of study produced the Education for All Handicapped Children Act of 1975.

In order to qualify for federal financial assistance under the Act, a State must demonstrate that it "has in effect a policy that assures all handicapped children the right to a free appropriate public education." 20 U.S.C. § 1412(1). That policy must be reflected in a state plan submitted to and approved by the Commissioner of Education,[3] § 1413, which describes in detail the goals, programs, and timetables under which the State intends to educate handicapped children within its borders. §§ 1412, 1413. States receiving money under the Act must provide education to the handicapped by priority, first "to handicapped children who are not receiving an education" and second "to handicapped children...with the most severe handicaps who are receiving an inadequate education," § 1412(3), and "to the maximum extent appropriate" must educate handicapped children "with children who are not handicapped." § 1412(5).[4] The Act broadly defines "handicapped children" to include "mentally retarded, hard of hearing, deaf, speech impaired, visually handicapped, seriously emotionally disturbed, orthopedically impaired, [and] other health impaired children, [and] children with specific learning disabilities." § 1401(1).[5]

The "free appropriate public education" required by the Act is tailored to the unique needs of the handicapped child by means of an "individualized educational program" (IEP). § 1401(18). The IEP, which is prepared at a meeting between a qualified representative of the local educational agency, the child's teacher, the child's parents or guardian, and, where appropriate, the child, consists of a written document containing

"(A) a statement of the present levels of educational performance of the child, (B) a statement of annual goals, including short-term instructional objectives, (C) a statement of the specific educational services to be provided to such child, and the extent to which such child will be able to participate in regular educational programs, (D) the projected date for initiation and anticipated duration of such service, and (E) appropriate objective criteria and evaluation procedures and schedules for determining, on at least an annual basis, whether instructional objectives are being achieved." § 1401(19).

Local or regional educational agencies must review, and where appropriate revise, each child's IEP at least annually. § 1404(a)(5). See also §§ 1413(a)(11), 1414(a)(5).

In addition to the state plan and the IEP already described, the Act imposes extensive procedural requirements upon States receiving federal funds under its provisions. Parents or guardians of handicapped children must be notified of any proposed change in the "identification, evaluation, or educational placement of the children of the provision of a free appropriate public education to the child," and must be permitted to bring a complaint about "any matter relating to" such evaluation and education. § 1415(b)(1)(D) and (E).[6] Complaints brought by parents or guardians must be resolved at "an impartial due process hearing," and appeal to the State educational agency must be provided if the initial hearing is held at the local or regional level. § 1415(b)(2) and (c).[7] Thereafter, "[a]ny party aggrieved by the findings and decisions" of the state administrative hearing has "the right to bring a civil action with respect to the complaint ... in any State court of competent jurisdiction or in a district court of the United States without regard to the amount in controversy." § 1415(e)(2).

Thus, although the Act leaves to the States the primary responsibility for developing and executing educational programs for handicapped children, it imposes significant requirements to be followed in the discharge of that responsibility...

II ~

This case arose in connection with the education of Amy Rowley, a deaf student at the Furnace Woods School in the Hendrick Hudson Central School District, Peekskill, New York. Amy has minimal residual hearing and is an excellent lipreader. During the year before she began attending Furnace Woods, a meeting between her parents and school administrators resulted in a decision to place her in a regular kindergarten class in order to determine what supplemental services would be necessary to her education. Several members of the school administration prepared for Amy's arrival by attending a course in sign-language interpretation, and a teletype machine was installed in the principal's office to facilitate communication with her parents who are also deaf. At the end of the trail period it was determined that Amy should remain in the kindergarten class, but that she should be provided with an FM hearing aid which would amplify words spoken into a wireless receiver by the teacher or fellow students during certain classroom activities. Amy successfully completed her kindergarten year.

As required by the Act, and IEP was prepared for Amy during the fall of her first-grade year. The IEP provided that Amy should be educated in a regular classroom at Furnace Woods, should continue to use the FM hearing aid, and should receive instruction from a tutor for the deaf for one hour each day and from a speech therapist for three hours each week. The Rowleys agreed with the IEP but insisted that Amy also be provided a qualified sign-language interpreter in all of her academic classes. Such an interpreter had been placed in Amy's kindergarten class for a two-week experimental period, but the interpreter had reported that Amy did not need his services at that time. The school administrators likewise concluded that Amy did not need such an interpreter in her first-grade classroom. They reached this conclusion after consulting the school district's Committee on the Handicapped, which had received expert evidence from Amy's parents on the importance of a sign-language interpreter, received testimony from Amy's teacher and other persons familiar with her academic and social progress, and visited a class for the deaf.

When their request for an interpreter was denied, the Rowleys demanded and received a hearing before an independent examiner. After receiving evidence from both sides, the examiner agreed with the administrators' determination that an interpreter was not necessary because "Amy was achieving educationally, academically, and socially" without such assistance. App. to Pet. for Cert. F-22. The examiner's decision was affirmed on appeal by the New York Commissioner of Education on the basis of substantial evidence in the record.... Pursuant to the Act's provision for judicial review, the Rowleys then brought an action in the United States District Court for the Southern District of New York, claiming that the administrators' denial of the sign-language interpreter constituted a denial of the "free appropriate public education" guaranteed by the Act.

The District Court found that Amy "is a remarkably well-adjusted child" who interacts and communicates well with her classmates and has "developed an extraordinary rapport" with her teachers. 483 E Supp. 528, 53 1. It also found that "she performs better than the average child in her class and is advancing easily from grade to grade," *id.,* at 534, but "that she understands considerably less of what goes on in class than she would if she were not deaf " and thus "is not learning as much, or performing as well academically, as she would without her handicap " *id.,* at 532. This disparity between Amy's achievement and her potential led the court to decide that she was not receiving a "free appropriate public education," which the court defined as "an opportunity to achieve [her] full potential commensurate with the opportunity provided to other children." *Id.,* at 534. According to the District Court, such a standard "requires that the potential of the handicapped child be measured and compared to his or her performance, and that the remaining differential or 'shortfall' be compared to the shortfall experienced by nonhandicapped children." *Ibid.* The District Court's definition arose from its assumption that the responsibility for "giv[ing] content to the requirement of an 'appropriate education'" had "been left entirely to the federal courts and the hearing officer." *Id.,* at 533.[8]

A divided panel of the United States Court of Appeals for the Second Circuit affirmed. The Court of Appeals "agree[d] with the [D]istrict (C]ourt's conclusions of law," and held that its "findings of fact [were] not clearly erroneous." 632 E 2d 945, 947 (1980).

We granted certiorari to review the lower courts' interpretation of the Act. 454 U.S.—1981. Such review requires us to consider two questions: What is meant by the Act's requirement of a "free appropriate public education?" And what is the role of state and federal courts in exercising the review granted by § 1415 of the Act? We consider these questions separately.[9]

III 〜

A

This is the first case in which this Court has been called upon to interpret any provision of the Act. As noted previously, the District Court and the Court of Appeals concluded that "[t]he Act itself does not define 'appropriate education,'" 483 E Supp., at 533, but leaves "to the courts and the hearing officers" the responsibility of "giv[ing] content to the requirement of an appropriate education." *Ibid.* See also 632 E 2d, at 947. Petitioners contend that the definition of the phrase "free appropriate public education" used by the courts below overlooks the definition of that phrase actually found in the Act. Respondents agree that the Act defines "free appropriate public education," but contend that the statutory definition is not "functional" and thus "offers judges no guidance in their consideration of controversies involving the 'identification, evaluation, or educational placement of the child or the provision of a free appropriate public education.'" Brief for Respondents 28. The United States, appearing as *amicus curiae* on behalf of the respondents, states that "[a]lthough the Act includes definitions of 'free appropriate public education' and other related terms, the statutory definitions do not adequately explain what is meant by 'appropriate.'" Brief for United States as *Amicus Curiae* 13.

We are loath to conclude that Congress failed to offer any assistance in defining the meaning of the principal substantive phrase used in the Act. It is beyond dispute that, contrary to the conclusions of the courts below, the Act does expressly define "free appropriate public education":

> "The term 'free appropriate public education' means *special education* and *related services* which (A) have been provided at public expense, under public supervision and direction, and without charge, (B) meet the standards of the State educational agency, (C) include an appropriate preschool, elementary, or secondary school education in the State involved, and (D) are provided in conformity with the individualized education program required under section 1414(a)(5) of this title." § 1401(18) (emphasis added).

"Special education'" as referred to in this definition, means "specially designed instruction, at no cost to parents or guardians, to meet the unique needs of a handicapped child, including classroom instruction, instruction in physical education, home instruction, and instruction in hospitals and institutions." § 1401(16). "Related services" are defined as "transportation, and such developmental, corrective, and

other supportive services...as may be required to assist a handicapped child to benefit from special education." § 1401(17).[10]

Like many statutory definitions, this one tends toward the cryptic rather than
the comprehensive, but that is scarcely a reason for abandoning the quest for legislative intent. Whether or not the definition is a "functional" one, as respondents
contend it is not, it is the principal tool which Congress has given us for parsing the
critical phrase of the Act. We think more must be made of it than either respondents
or the United States seems willing to admit.

According to the definitions contained in the Act, a "free appropriate public
education" consists of educational instruction specially designed to meet the unique
needs of the handicapped child, support by such services as are necessary to permit
the child "to benefit" from the instruction. Almost as a checklist for adequacy under
the Act, the definition also requires that such instruction and services by provided at
public expense and under public supervision, meet the State's educational standards,
approximate the grade levels used in the State's regular education, and comport with
the child's IEP. Thus, if personalized instruction is being provided with sufficient
supportive services to permit the child to benefit from the instruction, and the other
items on the definitional checklist are satisfied, the child is receiving a "free appropriate public education" as defined by the Act.

Other portions of the statute also shed light upon congressional intent. Congress found that of the roughly eight million handicapped children in the United
States at the time of enactment, one million were "excluded entirely from the public
school system" and more than half were receiving an inappropriate education. Note
to § 1401. In addition, as mentioned in Part 1, the Act requires States to extend educational services first to those children who are receiving no education and second
to those children who are receiving and "inadequate education." § 1412(3). When
these express statutory findings and priorities are read together with the Act's extensive procedural requirements and its definition of "free appropriate public education," the face of the statute evinces a congressional intent to bring previously
excluded handicapped children into the public education systems of the States and
to require the States to adopt *procedures* which would result in individualized consideration of and instruction for each child.

Noticeably absent from the language of the statute is any substantive standard
prescribing the level of education to be accorded handicapped children. Certainly the
language of the statute contains no requirement like the one imposed by the lower
courts—that States maximize the potential of handicapped children "commensurate
with the opportunity provided to other children." 483 E Supp., at 534. That standard
was expounded by the District Court without reference to the statutory definitions or
even to the legislative history of the Act. Although we find the statutory definition
of "free appropriate public education" to be helpful in our interpretation of the Act,
there remains the question of whether the legislative history indicates a congressional intent that such education meet some additional substantive standard. For an
answer, we turn to that history."

B

(i). As suggested in Part 1, federal support for education of the handicapped is a fairly recent development. Before passage of the Act some States had passed laws to improve the educational services afforded handicapped children," but many of these children were excluded completely from any form of public education or were left to fend for themselves in classrooms designed for education of their nonhandicapped peers. The House Report begins by emphasizing this exclusion and misplacement, noting that millions of handicapped children "were either totally excluded from schools or [were] sitting idly in regular classrooms awaiting the time when they were old enough to 'drop out.'" H. R. Rep. No. 94-332, supra, at 2. See also S. Rep. No. 94-168, p. 8 (1975). One of the Act's two principal sponsors in the Senate urged its passage in similar terms:

> "While much progress has been made in the last few years, we can take no solace in that progress until all handicapped children are, in fact, receiving an education. The most recent statistics provided by the Bureau of Education for the Handicapped estimate that...1.75 million handicapped children do not receive any educational services, and 2.5 million handicapped children are not receiving an appropriate education." 121 Cong. Rec. 19486 (1975) (remarks of Sen. Williams).

This concern, stressed repeatedly throughout the legislative history,[13] confirms the impression conveyed by the language of the statute: By passing the Act, Congress sought primarily to make public education available to handicapped children. But in seeking to provide such access to public education, Congress did not impose upon the States any greater substantive educational standard than would be necessary to make such access meaningful. Indeed, Congress expressly "recognize[d] that in many instances the process of providing special education and related services to handicapped children is not guaranteed to produce any particular outcome." S. Rep. No. 94-168, *supra,* at 11. Thus, the intent of the Act was more to open the door of public education to handicapped children on appropriate terms than to guarantee any particular level of education once inside.

Both the House and the Senate reports attribute the impetus for the Act and its predecessors to two federal court judgments rendered in 1971 and 1972. As the Senate Report states, passage of the Act "followed a series of landmark court cases establishing in law the right to education for all handicapped children

Mills and *PARC* both held that handicapped children must be given *access* to an adequate, publicly supported education. Neither case purports to require any particular substantive level of education.[15] Rather, like the language of the Act, the cases set forth extensive procedures to be followed in formulating personalized educational programs for handicapped children. See 348 E Supp., at 878–883; 334 E Supp., at 1258–1267." The fact that both *PARC* and *Mills* are discussed at length in the legislative reports" suggests that the principles which they established are the principles which, to a significant extent, guided the drafters of the Act. Indeed, immediately after discussing these cases the Senate Report describes the 1974 statute as having "incorporated the major principles of the right to education cases."

S. Rep. No. 94-168, *supra,* at 8. Those principles in turn became the bases of the Act, which itself was designed to effectuate the purposes of the 1974 statute. H. R. Rep. No. 94-332, *supra,* at 5.[18]

That the Act imposes no clear obligation upon recipient States beyond the requirement that handicapped children receive some form of specialized education is perhaps best demonstrated by the fact that Congress, in explaining the need for the Act, equated an "appropriate education" to the receipt of some specialized educational services....

It is evident from the legislative history that the characterization of handicapped children as "served" referred to children who were receiving some form of specialized educational services from the States, and that the characterization of children as "unserved" referred to those who were receiving no specialized educational services.... By characterizing the 3.9 million handicapped children who were "served" as children who were "receiving an appropriate education," the Senate and House reports unmistakably disclose Congress' perception of the type of education required by the Act: an "appropriate education" is provided when personalized educational services are provided.[21]

(ii). Respondents contend that "the goal of the Act is to provide each handicapped child with an equal educational opportunity." Brief for Respondents 35. We think, however, that the requirement that a State provide specialized educational services to handicapped children generates no additional requirement that the services so provided be sufficient to maximize each child's potential "commensurate with the opportunity provided other children." Respondents and the United States correctly note that Congress sought "to provide assistance to the States in carrying out their responsibilities under ... the Constitution of the United States to provide equal protection of the laws." S. Rep. No. 94-168, *supra,* at 13.[22] But we do not think that such statements imply a congressional intent to achieve strict equality of opportunity or services.

The educational opportunities provided by our public school systems undoubtedly differ from student to student, depending upon a myriad of factors that might affect a particular student's ability to assimilate information presented in the classroom. The requirement that States provide "equal" educational opportunities would thus seem to present an entirely unworkable standard requiring impossible measurements and comparisons. Similarly, furnishing handicapped children with only such services as are available to nonhandicapped children would in all probability fall short of the statutory requirement of "free appropriate public education"; to require, on the other hand, the furnishing of every special service necessary to maximize each handicapped child's potential is, we think, further than Congress intended to go. Thus to speak in terms of "equal" services in one instance gives less than what is required by the Act and in another instance more. The theme of the Act is "free appropriate public education," a phrase which is too complex to be captured by the word "equal" whether one is speaking of opportunities or services.

The legislative conception of the requirements of equal protection was undoubtedly informed by the two district court decisions referred to above. But cases such as *Mills* and *PARC* held simply that handicapped children may not be excluded entirely from public education.... The right of access to free public education enunciated by these cases is significantly different from any notion of absolute equality of opportunity regardless of capacity. To the extent that Congress might have looked further than these cases which are mentioned in the legislative history, at the time of enactment of the Act this Court had held at least twice that the Equal Protection Clause of the Fourteenth Amendment does not require States to expend equal financial resources on the education of each child. *San Antonio School District v. Rodriguez,* 411 U.S. 1 (1975); *McInnis v. Shapiro,* 293 E Supp. 327 (ND Ill. 1968), *aff'd sub nom, McInnis v. Ogilvie,* 394 U.S. 322 (1969).

In explaining the need for federal legislation, the House Report noted that "no congressional legislation has required a precise guarantee for handicapped children, i.e., a basic floor of opportunity that would bring into compliance all school districts with the constitutional right of equal protection with respect to handicapped children." H. R. Rep. No. 94-332, *supra,* at 14. Assuming that the Act was designed to fill the need identified in the House Report-neither the Act nor its history persuasively demonstrates that Congress thought that equal protection required anything more than equal access. Therefore, Congress' desire to provide specialized educational services, even in furtherance of "equality," cannot be read as imposing any particular substantive educational standard upon the States.

The District Court and the Court of Appeals thus erred when they held that the Act requires New York to maximize the potential of each handicapped child commensurate with the opportunity provided nonhandicapped children. Desirable though that goal might be, it is not the standard that Congress imposed upon States which receive funding under the Act. Rather, Congress sought primarily to identify and evaluate handicapped children, and to provide them with access to a free public education.

(iii). Implicit in the congressional purpose of providing access to a "free appropriate public education" is the requirement that the education to which access is provided be sufficient to confer some educational benefit upon the handicapped child. It would do little good for Congress to spend millions of dollars in providing access to a public education only to have the handicapped child receive no benefit from that education. The statutory definition of "free appropriate public education," in addition to requiring that States provide each child with "specially designed instruction," expressly requires the provision of "such...supportive services...as may be required to assist a handicapped child *to benefit* from special education." § 1401(17) (emphasis added). We therefore conclude that the "basic floor of opportunity" provided by the Act consists of access to specialized instruction and related services which are individually designed to provide educational benefit to the handicapped child.[23]

The determination of when handicapped children are receiving sufficient educational benefits to satisfy the requirements of the Act presents a more difficult problem. The Act requires participating States to educate a wide spectrum of hand-icapped children, from the marginally hearing-impaired to the profoundly retarded and palsied. It is clear that the benefits obtainable by children at one end of the spectrum will differ dramatically from those obtainable by children at the other end, with infinite variations in between. One child may have little difficulty competing successfully in an academic setting with nonhandicapped children while another child may encounter great difficulty in acquiring even the most basic of self-maintenance skills. We do not attempt today to establish any one test for determining the adequacy of educational benefits conferred upon all children covered by the Act. Because in this case we are presented with a handicapped child who is receiving substantial specialized instruction and related services, and who is performing above average in the regular classrooms of a public school system, we confine our analysis to that situation.

The Act requires participating States to educate handicapped children with nonhandicapped children whenever possible." When that "mainstreaming" preference of the Act has been met and a child is being educated in the regular classrooms of a public school system, the system itself monitors the educational progress of the child. Regular examinations are administered, grades are awarded, and yearly advancement to higher grade levels is permitted for those children who attain an adequate knowledge of the course material. The grading and advancement system thus constitutes an important factor in determining educational benefit. Children who graduate from our public school systems are considered by our society to have been "educated" at least to the grade level they have completed, and access to an "education" for handicapped children is precisely what Congress sought to provide in the Act.[25]

C

When the language of the Act and its legislative history are considered together, the requirements imposed by Congress become tolerably clear. Insofar as a State is required to provide a handicapped child with a "free appropriate public education," we hold that it satisfies this requirement by providing personalized instruction with sufficient support services to permit the child to benefit educationally from that instruction. Such instruction and services must be provided at public expense, must meet the State's educational standards, must approximate the grade levels used in the State's regular education, and must comport with the child's IEP. In addition, the IEP, and therefore the personalized instruction, should be formulated in accordance with the requirements of the Act and, if the child is being educated in the regular classrooms of the public education system, should be reasonably calculated to enable the child to achieve passing marks and advance from grade to grade.[26]

D

In assuring that the requirements of the Act have been met, courts must be careful to avoid imposing their view of preferable educational methods upon the States.[29] The primary responsibility for formulating the education to be accorded a handicapped child, and for choosing the educational method most suitable to the child's needs, was left by the Act to state and local educational agencies in cooperation with the parents or guardian of the child. The Act expressly charges States with the responsibility of "acquiring and disseminating to teachers and administrators of programs for handicapped children significant information derived from educational research, demonstration, and similar projects and [of] adopting, where appropriate, promising educational practices and materials." Section 1413(a)(3). In the face of such a clear statutory directive, it seems highly unlikely that Congress intended courts to overturn a State's choice of appropriate educational theories in a proceeding conducted pursuant to § 1415(c)(2).[30]

We previously have cautioned that courts lack the "specialized knowledge and experience" necessary to resolve "persistent and difficult questions of educational policy." *San Antonio School District v. Rodriguez,* 411 U.S. 1, 42 (1973). We think that Congress shared that view when it passed the Act. As already demonstrated, Congress' intention was not that the Act displace the primacy of States in the field of education, but that States receive funds to assist them in extending their educational systems to the handicapped. Therefore, once a court determines that the requirements of the Act have been met, questions of methodology are for resolution by the States.

V

Entrusting a child's education to state and local agencies does not leave the child without protection. Congress sought to protect individual children by providing for parental involvement in the development of State plans and policies, *supra,* at 4-5 and n. 6, and in the formulation of the child's individual educational program. As the Senate Report states:

> "The Committee recognizes that in many instances the process of providing special education and related services to handicapped children is not guaranteed to produce any particular outcome. By changing the language [of the provision relating to individualized educational programs] to emphasize the process of parent and child involvement and to provide a written record of reasonable expectations, the Committee intends to clarify that such individualized planning conferences are a way to provide parent involvement and protection to assure that appropriate services are provided to a handicapped child." S. Rep. No. 94-168, *supra,* at 11-12. See also S. Conf. Rep. No. 94-445, p. 30 (1975); 45 CFR § 121a.345 (1980).

As this very case demonstrates, parents and guardians will not lack ardor in seeking to ensure that handicapped children receive all of the benefits to which they are entitled by the Act.[31]

Notes

4. Despite this preference for "mainstreaming" handicapped children-educating them with non-handicapped children—Congress recognized that regular classrooms simply would not be a

suitable setting for the education of many handicapped children. The Act expressly acknowledges that "the nature or severity of the handicap [may be] such that education in regular classes with the use of supplementary aids and services cannot be achieved satisfactorily." § 1412(5). The Act thus provides for the education of some handicapped children in separate classes or institutional settings. See *ibid.;* § 1413(a)(4).

6. The requirements that parents be permitted to file complaints regarding their child's education, and be present when the child's IEP is formulated, represent only two examples of Congress' effort to maximize parental involvement in the education of each handicapped child....

15. The only substantive standard which can be implied from these cases comports with the standard implicit in the Act. *PARC* states that each child must receive "access to a free public program of education and training *appropriate to his learning capacities,*" 334 F. Supp., at 1258, and that further state action is required when it appears that "the needs of the mentally retarded child are not being *adequately* served," *id.,* at 1266. (Emphasis added.) *Mills* also speaks in terms of "adequate" educational services, 348 E Supp., at 878, and sets a realistic standard of providing some educational services to each child when every need cannot be met.

21. In seeking to read more into the Act than its language or legislative history will permit, the United States focuses upon the word "appropriate," arguing that "the statutory definitions do not adequately explain what [it means]." Brief for the United States as *Amicus Curiae* 13. Whatever Congress meant by an "appropriate" education, it is clear that it did not mean a potential-maximizing education.

The term as used in reference to educating the handicapped appears to have originated in the *PARC* decision, where the District Court required that handicapped children be provided with "education and training appropriate to [their] learning capacities." 334 F. Supp., at 1258. The word appears again in the *Mills* decision, the District Court at one point referring to the need for "an appropriate educational program," 348 F. Supp., at 879, and at another point speaking of a "suitable publicly-supported education," *id.,* at 878. Both cases also refer to the need for an "adequate" education. See 334 F. Supp., at 1266; 348 F. Supp., at 878.

The use of "appropriate" in the language of the Act, although by no means definitive, suggests that Congress used the word as much to describe the settings in which handicapped children should be educated as to prescribe the substantive content or supportive services of their education. For example, § 1412(5) requires that handicapped children be educated in classrooms with nonhandicapped children "to the maximum extent appropriate." Similarly, § 1401(19) provides that, "whenever appropriate," handicapped children should attend and participate in the meeting at which their IEP is drafted. In addition, the definition of the "free appropriate public education" itself states that instruction given handicapped children should be at an "appropriate preschool, elementary, or secondary school" level. § 1401(18)(C). The Act's use of the word "appropriate" thus seems to reflect Congress' recognition that some settings simply are not suitable environments for the participation of some handicapped children. At the very least, these statutory uses of the word refute the contention that Congress used "appropriate" as a term of art which concisely expresses the standard found by the lower courts.

23. This view is supported by the congressional intention, frequently expressed in the legislative history, that handicapped children be enabled to achieve a reasonable degree of self sufficiency. After referring to statistics showing that many handicapped children were excluded from public education, the Senate Report states: "The long range implications of these statistics are that public agencies and taxpayers will spend billions of dollars over the lifetimes of these individuals to maintain such persons as dependents and in a minimally acceptable lifestyle. With proper education services, many would be able to become productive citizens, contributing to society instead of being forced to remain burdens. Others, through such services, would increase their independence, thus reducing their dependence on society." S. Rep. No. 94-168, *supra,* at 9. See also H. R. Rep. No. 94-332, *supra,* at 11. Similarly, one of the principal Senate sponsors of the Act stated that "providing appropriate educational services now means that many of these individuals will be able to become a contributing part of our

society, and they will not have to depend on subsistence payments from public funds." 121 Cong. Rec. 19492 (1975) (remarks of Sen. Williams). See also 121 Cong. Rec. 25541 (1975) (remarks of Rep. Harkin); 121 Cong. Rec. 37024-37025 (1975) (remarks of Rep. Brademas); 121 Cong. Rec. 37027 (1975) (remarks of Rep. Gude); 121 Cong. Rec. 37410 (1975) (remarks of Sen. Randolph); 121 Cong. Rec. 37416 (1975) (remarks of Sen. Williams).

The desire to provide handicapped children with an attainable degree of personal independence obviously anticipated that state educational programs would confer educational benefits upon such children. But at the same time, the goal of achieving some degree of self sufficiency in most cases is a good deal more modest than the potential-maximizing goal adopted by the lower courts.

Despite its frequent mention, we cannot conclude, as did the dissent in the Court of Appeals, that self sufficiency was itself the substantive standard which Congress imposed upon the States. Because many mildly handicapped children will achieve self sufficiency without state assistance while personal independence for the severely handicapped may be an unreachable goal, "self sufficiency" as a substantive standard is at once an inadequate protection and an overly demanding requirement. We thus view these references in the legislative history as evidence of Congress' intention that the services provided handicapped children be educationally beneficial, whatever the nature or severity of their handicap.

25. We do not hold today that every handicapped child who is advancing from grade to grade in a regular public school system is automatically receiving a "free appropriate public education." In this case, however, we find Amy's academic progress, when considered with the special services and professional consideration accorded by the Furnace Woods school administrators, to be dispositive.

29. In this case, for example, both the state hearing officer and the District Court were presented with evidence as to the best method for educating the deaf, a question long debated among scholars. See Large, Special Problems of the Deaf Under the Education for All Handicapped Children Act of 1975, 58 Washington UL.Q. 213, 229 (1980). The District Court accepted the testimony of respondents' experts that there was "a trend supported by studies showing the greater degree of success of students brought up in deaf households using [the method of communication used by the Rowleys]." 483 E Supp., at 535.

30. It is clear that Congress was aware of the States' traditional role in the formulation and execution of educational policy. "Historically, the States have had the primary responsibility for the education of children at the elementary and secondary level." 121 Cong. Rec. 19498 (1975) (remarks of Sen. Dole). See also *Epperson v. Arkansas,* 393 U.S. 97, 104 (1968) ("[b]y and large, public education in our Nation is committed to the control of state and local authorities").

31. In addition to providing for extensive parental involvement in the formulation of state and local policies, as well as the preparation of individual educational programs, the Act ensures that States will receive the advice of experts in the field of educating handicapped children. As a condition for receiving federal funds under the Act, States must create "an advisory panel, appointed by the Governor or any other official authorized under State law to make such appointments, composed of individuals involved in or concerned with the education of handicapped children, including handicapped individuals, teachers, parents or guardians of handicapped children, State and local education officials, and administrators of programs for handicapped children, which (A) advises the State educational agency of unmet needs within the State in the education of handicapped children, [and] (B) comments publicly on any rules or regulations proposed for issuance by the State regarding the education of handicapped children." § 1413(a)(12).

Glossary

affirmed (aff'd.) a word that indicates in a citation to a case that a higher court has agreed with the result, and usually the reasoning, of a lower court and approved the judgment of the lower court. Sometimes a higher court can affirm part of a lower court's judgment and reverse part of it, depending on the nature of the judgment.

amicus curiae a Latin term indicating an individual or organization that is neither plaintiff nor defendant in a civil case but, because of special expertise or interest, is allowed by a court to become involved in the case as a "friend of the court." The involvement usually consists of submitting a brief (written presentation) containing supporting legal arguments and special facts to the court.

appeal the process whereby a court of appeals reviews the record of proceedings and judgment of a lower court to determine if errors of law or fact were made which might lead to a reversal or modification of the lower court's decision. If substantial errors are not found, the lower court's decision will be affirmed. If they are, its decision will be reversed or modified.

C.F.R. an abbreviation for *Code of Federal Regulations,* a publication of the U.S. government that contains the regulations of the executive agencies of government (e.g., U.S. Department of Education) implementing laws (statutes) passed by Congress (e.g., PL 97–142).

cert. den. an abbreviation that indicates in a citation to a case that a higher court (usually, the Supreme Court) has declined to order a lower court to send the case to it for review. By contrast, *cert. granted* means the higher court has ordered a lower court to send a case to it for review.

certiorari (cert.) a Latin term that indicates in a citation to a case that an order from an appeals court (usually, the Supreme Court) to a lower court has been entered, either requiring or declining to require the lower court to send up a case for review. The right-to-education cases decided by the U.S. Supreme Court usually go to that court on a petition (request) for *certiorari* by one of the parties (and the Court sometimes grants the request and orders the lower court to send the case to it for review).

civil case a lawsuit brought by one or more individuals to seek redress of some legal injury (or aspect of an injury) for which there are civil (non-criminal) remedies. In right-to-education cases, these remedies are based on the federal or state constitutions, federal or state statutes, or federal or state agency regulations, or a combination of federal and state constitutions, statutes and regulations. Right-to-education cases are always civil suits.

class action a civil case brought on behalf of the plaintiffs who are named in the suit, as well as on behalf of all other persons similarly situated, to vindicate their legally protected interests. *Mills v. D. C Board of Education* was brought on behalf of 12-year-old Peter Mills and six other school-age children who were named in the complaint, as well as all other exceptional children in the District. By contrast, *Board v. Rowley* was not a class action lawsuit because it was brought on behalf of only one person, who sued to protect only her rights, not the rights of other people.

competing equities a term describing a situation in which two or more people or groups of people have rights or privileges that cannot be fully satisfied without infringing on the rights or privileges of each other. For example, children with disabilities have some rights to be integrated with nondisabled children, but nondisabled children also have rights to an education that is not disrupted by children with disabilities (see chapter 6). In such a case, the competing equities of both children must be weighed against each other and a decision made by a court or other policy maker as to which claims prevail. Another way of thinking about competing equities is to ask: Whose rights or privileges are to be reduced for the benefit of other people?

complaint a legal document submitted to the court by plaintiffs, in which they inform the court and the defendants that they are bringing a lawsuit and set out the underlying reasons for which they sue and the relief they want.

concur a term that indicates in a citation to a case that one court agrees with the judgment of another and follows the precedent of that court's decision.

consent agreement an out-of-court agreement reached by the parties to a suit, which is formally approved by the court. In *Pennsylvania Association for Retarded Children v. Pennsylvania,* a court entered an order that it adopted pursuant to a consent agreement between plaintiffs and defendants.

constitutional right a legal right based on provisions of the U.S. Constitution or a state constitution. Equal protection and the due process of law are the federal constitutional rights most relevant to the right to education. The Fourteenth Amendment applies to state (and therefore, local) governments and guarantees the rights of due process and equal protection. (See chapters 2 through 8.)

damages money awarded by a court to someone who has been injured (the plaintiff), which must be paid by the one who is responsible for the injury (the defendant).

de facto a Latin term that means, literally, "by reason of the fact." Integration by race and disability now is required by law (*de jure* integration), but may not actually occur in some schools or among some students (*de facto* segregation).

defendant the person against whom a lawsuit is brought for redress of a violation of one or more of a plaintiffs legally protected interests.

defense a reason cited by a defendant why a lawsuit against him or her is without merit or why he or she is not responsible for the injury or violation of rights as alleged by the plaintiff.

de jure a Latin term that means, literally, "by law." Segregation of the schools by race or disability was required by laws of some states; thus, *de jure* segregation was enforced. Present law requires *de jure* integration.

dicta a Latin term describing language in a judicial opinion that is not essential to the disposition of the case or to the court's reasoning and that is regarded as gratuitous. *Dicta* are persuasive but not binding on other courts, whereas the court's holding and reasoning are.

discovery the process by which one party to a civil suit can find out about matters relevant to the case, including information about what evidence the other side has, what witnesses will be called, and so on. Discovery devices for obtaining information include depositions and interrogatories to obtain testimony, requests for documents or other tangibles, and requests for physical or mental examinations.

due process of law a right to have any law applied by the federal or state government reasonably and with sufficient safeguards, such as hearings and notice, to ensure that an individual is dealt with fairly. Due process is guaranteed under the Fifth and Fourteenth Amendments to the federal Constitution.

EHLR an abbreviation for the works of a commercial publisher that report the opinions and judgments of many of the special education cases decided by state and federal courts in reports cited as *Education for the Handicapped Law Reporter (EHLR).* In this book, the citation is stated in this way: *EHLR* 552:104-indicating that the report begins at section 552 of *EHLR* and at page 104. The case name precedes the *EHLR* citation, and the abbreviation of the court and date of judgment are set out in parentheses after the page reference.

Eighth Amendment the Eighth Amendment to the federal Constitution guarantees that the federal government will not impose a cruel and unusual punishment upon conviction of a crime. The amendment does not forbid the use of corporal punishment on students. It is not a factor in right-to-education cases.

en banc a Latin term referring to a situation in which a court consisting of more than one member (such as the federal appeals courts) hears a case with all of its members present at the hearing and participating in the decision. Usually, federal courts of appeals are divided into panels (or groups) of judges; a panel hears a case and normally makes the judgment of the court by itself, without participation of the other members of the court. Sometimes, however, a case is so difficult or important that all members of the court hear the case and decide the outcome. The court then sits *en banc*—all together.

equal protection of law a right not to be discriminated against for any unjustifiable reason, such as because of race or handicap. Equal protection is guaranteed under the Fourteenth Amendment. (See chapters 2 and 3.)

et seq. a Latin term that means "and following" (et means "and"; *seq.* is an abbreviation for *sequens,* which means "following"). The phrase always follows a noun (e.g., Vol. 20, United States Code, Sections 1401 *et seq.*—hence, "and the following sections").

ex rel. a Latin term that indicates a lawsuit is brought on behalf of one person by another (e.g., the attorney general of a state may sue on behalf of an individual; thus, the case is captioned *"State of Kansas, ex rel. Jane Doe, an incompetent, v. Superintendent, State Hospital"*). The lawsuit normally is one in which the state attorney general seeks to vindicate a legal position that is favorable to the state and its citizens on behalf of a person not able to bring a lawsuit directly.

expert witness a person called to testify because he or she has a recognized competence in an area. For example, experts in the *PARC* right-to-education case had doctoral degrees in the field of special education, were authors of numerous professional publications pertaining to exceptional children, and were consultants to advisory committees on education.

F.2d an abbreviation, in a citation to a lawsuit's reported judgment and order, that indicates that the case was decided by a federal court of appeals and is reported in a certain volume of the reports of the federal courts of appeals (shown as "Cir." for Circuit Court(s) of Appeal(s)). The volume of the reports precedes the *F 2d (Federal Report, 2d Series)* designation; the page at which the report begins follows the F 2d designation; and the identity of the court and the date of the judgment are set out in parentheses after the page number. Thus, *Smuck v. Hobson,* 408 R 2d 175 (D.C. Cir. 1969), shows that the appellate judgment (in the case involving school classification practices of the District of Columbia Board of Education) is reported at volume 408 of the *Federal Reports, 2d Series,* beginning at page 175, and is a decision of the federal court of appeals (D.C. Circuit Court of Appeals) for the District of Columbia in 1969.

F. Supp. an abbreviation, in a citation to a lawsuit's reported judgment and order, that indicates that the case was decided by a federal trail court (a "district" court) and is reported in a certain volume of the reports of the federal trail courts. The volume of the reports precedes the *F. Supp. (Federal Supplement)* designation; the page at which the report begins follows the *F. Supp.* designation; and the identity of the court and the date of the judgment are set out in parentheses after the page. Thus, in *PARC v. Commonwealth of Pennsylvania,* 343 F Supp. 279 (E.D. Pa. 1972), the case is reported at volume 343 of the *Federal Supplement,* beginning at page 279, and is a decision of the federal district court for the Eastern District (section) of Pennsylvania in 1972.

Fed. Reg. an abbreviation for *Federal Register,* a daily publication of Congress that contains the text of new laws and regulations and comments by members of Congress on matters of public policy.

Fifth Amendment the amendment to the federal Constitution that guarantees that the rights of life, liberty, and property will not be taken from a citizen by the federal government without due process of law. Due process guarantees apply to state and local governments under the Fourteenth Amendment.

First Amendment the amendment to the federal Constitution that guarantees free speech, assembly, worship, and petition for redress of grievances.

Fourteenth Amendment the amendment to the federal Constitution that applies to the states (not the federal government, which is bound by the first 10 amendments) and guarantees the rights of due process and equal protection to the citizens of each state.

in re a Latin term in a captioned title of a case that indicates "in the matter of" and always is followed by the name of a party to a lawsuit (e.g., In Re: John Doe, a minor-here, the caption/title to the lawsuit reads "in the matter of John Doe, a minor/child").

infra a Latin word in a citation to a case that indicates that the same case is referred to in a later part of the same article, chapter, book, judicial opinion, or other writing (e.g., the court may refer to the *Rowley* case, *infra,* meaning later, or, literally, within, its opinion).

injunctive relief a remedy granted by the court forbidding or requiring some action by the defendant. Injunctive relief includes temporary restraining orders and preliminary and final injunctions. The difference among these types of relief is that they are issued for varying lengths of time, at various stages of the litigation process, and on the basis of varying degrees of proof

judgment an order by a court after a verdict has been reached. The judgment declares the relief to be granted.

on remand a reference in a citation to a case that indicates that a lower court has entered a judgment, for at least a second time, when it received the case from a higher court with a judgment and order to act in a particular way (e.g., the court's initial judgment is appealed, the appeals court enters a judgment to reverse in part and affirm in part and directs the lower court to change its original order, and the lower court then does so when the case is "on remand" to it from the higher court).

parens patriae a Latin term that means, literally, "father of the country," and that refers nowadays to the doctrine that a state may act in a paternalistic way on behalf of its citizens, especially those who are children or who are mentally disabled and therefore less effective than other people in protecting themselves. The *parens patriae* doctrine justifies compulsory education, which is regarded as beneficial to children and the state alike but, because of its benefit to children, can be required for their own good.

per curiam a Latin term in a citation to a case that refers to the judgment of a court entered "by the court" (rather than by a judge who writes the opinion for the court). *Per curiam* cases normally do not have opinions of the judges, only the court's disposition of the case (e.g., affirmed, petition denied, etc.).

P.L. an abbreviation for "Public Law," referring to a statute passed by Congress as a public law. Every public law has a number that follows the P.L. designation thus, P.L. 94–142 refers to Public Law 142 of the 94th Congress.

plaintiff a person who brings a suit to redress a violation of one or more of his or her legal rights.

precedent a decision by a judge or court that serves as a rule of guide to support other judges in deciding future cases involving similar or analogous legal questions. In the early right-to-education cases, courts cited some famous education decisions as precedents, including *Brown v. Board of Education,* outlawing segregated schools, and *Hobson v. Hansen,* outlawing the track system in the District of Columbia. Just as *PARC* and *Mills* were cited as precedent by other courts for finding a constitutional right to education, so *Rowley* is now cited on various legal issues (see chapter 5).

private action a case brought on behalf of one or more individuals to vindicate violation of their own legally protected interests. As distinguished from a class action, where the relief applies to all persons similarly situated or within the class represented by the plaintiffs (e.g., *PARC*), any relief granted in private action applies only to those plaintiffs actually before the court (e.g., *Rowley*).

procedural right a right that relates to the process of enforcing substantive rights or to obtaining relief, such as the right to a hearing, the right to present evidence in one's defense, and the right to counsel.

quid pro quo a Latin term that literally means "something for something" and indicates an exchange of money and/or goods (e.g., a school district provides inservice training in exchange for—as a *quid pro quo* for—state aid to defray expenses).

relief a remedy for some legal wrong. Relief is requested by a plaintiff to be granted by a court, against a defendant.

reversed (rev'd.) a word that indicates in a citation to a case that a higher court has over-turned the result, and usually the reasoning, of a lower court and entered (or ordered the lower court to enter) a different judgment. Sometimes a higher court can reverse part of a lower court's judgment and affirm part of it, depending on the nature of the judgment.

settlement an out-of-court agreement among parties to a suit, which resolves some or all of the issues involved in a case.

statutory right a right based on a statute or law passed by a unit of federal, state, or local governments (see chapter 1).

sub nom. a Latin abbreviation in a citation to a case that indicates the case was decided by another court under a different name (*sub* meaning "under," and *nom.* being an abbreviation for the Latin word *nomine,* meaning "name").

substantive right a right such as the right to an education, usually granted by statutes and constitutions.

supra a Latin word in a citation to a case that indicates that the same case has been referred to in an earlier part of the same article, chapter, book, judicial opinion, or other writing. It means the opposite of *infra.*

U.S. an abbreviation, in a citation to a decision of the U.S. Supreme Court, that indicates that a judgment of that Court is reported at a certain volume of the *United States Reports,* which contain only the judgments and other orders of the US. Supreme Court. The volume number precedes the *U.S.* designation, the page number follows it, and the date of judgment is set out in parentheses after the page reference.

U.S.C. (also U.S.C.A.) an abbreviation for *United States Code,* and official publication of the United States government (or *United States Code Annotated,* a commercial publication) that contains the codified acts of Congress.

U.S.L.W. a commercial publication that reports the judgments of various courts in *United States Law Week.* The volume of *USLW* precedes the USLW designation, and the page of the report follows it, with the identity of the court and date of judgment set out in parentheses after the page number.

vacated an abbreviation that indicates in a citation to a case that a higher court has set aside the judgment of a lower court.

verdict a decision by a judge or jury in favor of one side or the other in a case.

Table of Cases

(Ruth Anne) M. v. Alvin I.S.D., 532 F. Supp. 460 (S.D.Tex. 1982).

A.W. v. Northwest R-1 Sch. Dist., 813 F.2d 158 (8th Cir. 1987), cert. denied, 484 U.S. 847 (1987).

Abu-Sahyun v. Palo Alto Unified School Dist., EHLR 558:275 (N.D.Cal. 1987), 843 F.2d 1250 (9th Cir. 1988).

Addington v. Texas, 441 U.S. 418 (1979).

Agostine v. School Dist. of Philadelphia, 527 A.2d 193 (Comm.Ct.Pa. 1987).

Agostini v. Felton, 138 L.Ed.2d 391 (U.S. 1997).

Albertsons, Inc. v. Kirkingburg, No. 98–591 (U.S. Supreme Court, June 22, 1999), 143 F.3d 1228 (9th Cir. 1998).

Alden v. Maine, No. 98-436 (U.S. Supreme Court, June 23, 1999), 715 A.2d 172 (Me. 1998).

Alexander S. v. Boyd, 876 F. Supp. 773 (D.S.C. 1995).

Ali v. Wayne-Westland School Dist., 19 IDELR 511 (E.D.Mich. 1992).

Allen v. School Committee of Boston, 508 N.E.2d 605 (Mass. 1987).

Allison v. Dept. of Corrections, 94 F.3d 494 (8th Cir. 1996).

Amann v. Stow School System, 982 F.2d 644 (1st Cir. 1992).

Anderson v. Creighton, 483 U.S. 635 (1987).

Anderson v. Thompson, 658 F.2d 1205 (7th Cir. 1981).

Angevine v. Jenkins, 752 F.Supp. 24 (D.D.C. 1990), rev'd sub nom., *Angevine v. Smith*, 959 F.2d 292 (D.C. Cir. 1992).

Aranow v. Dist. of Columbia Bd. of Educ., 780 F. Supp. 46 (D.D.C. 1992), modified, 791 F. Supp. 318 (D.D.C. 1992).

Armstrong v. Kline, 476 F. Supp. 583 (E.D. Pa. 1979), aff'd in part sub. nom, *Battle v. Commonwealth of Pennsylvania*, 629 F.2d 269 (3rd Cir. 1980), further proceedings, 513 F.Supp. 425 (E.D.Pa. 1980).

Arons v. New Jersey State Bd. of Educ., 842 F.2d 58 (3rd Cir. 1988), cert. denied, 488 U.S. 942 (1988).

Ashland Sch. Dist. v. New Hampshire Div. for Children, Youth & Families, 681 A.2d 71 (N.H. 1996).

ASPIRA of New York v. Bd. of Educ., 423 F. Supp. 647 (S.D.N.Y. 1976).

Association for Community Living v. Romer, 992 F.2d 1040 (10th Cir. 1993).

Association for Retarded Citizens in Colorado v. Frazier, 517 F. Supp. 105 (D. Colo. 1981).

Association for Retarded Citizens of Alabama, Inc. v. Teague, 830 F.2d 158 (11th Cir. 1987).

B.M. v. Montana, 556 EHLR 195 (D.Mont. 1984).

Babb v. Knox County School System, 965 F.2d 104 (6th Cir. 1992), cert. denied, 506 U.S. 941 (1992).

Bales v. Clarke, 523 F. Supp. 1366 (E.D.Va. 1981).

Barbara R. v. Tirozzi, 665 F. Supp. 141 (D.Conn. 1987).

Barlow/Gresham Union High Sch. Dist. No. 2 v. Mitchell, 16 EHLR 157 (D.Or. 1989).

Barnett v. Fairfax County Sch. Bd., 721 F. Supp. 757 (E.D.Va. 1989), aff'd, 927 F.2d 146 (4th Cir. 1991), cert. denied, 502 U.S. 859 (1991).

Barnett v. Fairfax County School. Bd., 721 F. Supp. 757 (E.D. Va. 1989), aff'd, 927 F.2d 847 (4th Cir. 1991), cert. denied, 502 U.S. 859 (1991).

Bd. of County Comm'rs v. Brown, 117 S.Ct. 1382 (U.S. 1997).

Bd. of Ed. of East Windsor Regional Sch. Dist. v. Diamond, 808 F.2d 987 (3rd Cir. 1986).

Bd. of Educ. of Cabell v. Dienelt, 843 F.2d 813 (4th Cir. 1988).

Bd. of Educ. of City of Plainfield v. Cooperman, 523 A.2d 655 (N.J. 1987).

Bd. of Educ. of Community Consolidated Sch. Dist. No. 21 v. Illinois State Board of Education, 938 F.2d 712 (7th Cir. 1991), cert. denied, 502 U.S. 1066 (1992).

Bd. of Educ. of Kiryas Joel Village School Dist. v. Grumet, 618 N.E.2d 94 (N.Y. 1993), aff'd, 512 U.S. 687 (1994).

Bd. of Educ. v. Holland, 4 F.3d 1398 (9th Cir. 1994).

Bd. of Educ. v. Rowley, 458 U.S. 176 (1982).

Beede v. Town of Washington Sch. Dist., 18 IDELR 1295 (D.Vt. 1992).

Begay v. Hodel, 730 F. Supp. 1001 (D.Ariz. 1990).

Behavior Research Institute v. Secretary of Administration, 577 N.E.2d 297 (Mass. 1991).

Belanger v. Nashua Sch. Dist., 856 F. Supp. 40 (D.N.H. 1994).

Bencic v. City of Malden, 587 N.E.2d 795 (Mass. App. Ct. 1992).

Bevin H. v. Wright, 666 F. Supp. 71 (W.D.Pa 1987).

Bivens v. Six Unknown Named Agents of Federal Bureau of Narcotics, 403 U.S. 388 (1971).

Black v. Indiana Area Sch. Dist., 985 F.2d 707 (3rd Cir. 1993).

Blazejewski v. Bd. of Educ., 599 F. Supp. 975 (W.D.N.Y. 1985).

Blum v. Yaretsky, 457 U.S. 991 (1982).

Board of Education v. Rowley, 458 U.S. 176 (1982).

Bonadonna v. Cooperman, 619 F.Supp. 401 (D.N.J. 1985).

Borgna v. Binghampton City Sch. Dist., 17 IDELR 677 (N.D.N.Y. 1991), 18 IDELR 121 (N.D.N.Y. 1991).

Borgna v. Binghampton City School Dist., 18 IDELR 121 (N.D.N.Y. 1991).

Bowen v. Massachusetts, 487 U.S. 879 (1988).

Boxall v. Sequoia Union High School Dist., 464 F. Supp. 1104 (N.D.Cal. 1979).

Bragdon v. Abbott, 118 S.Ct. 2196, 524 U.S. 624 (1998).

Briere v. Fair Haven, 948 F. Supp. 1242 (D.Vt. 1996).

Brown v. Board of Education, 347 U.S. 483 (1954).

Brown v. D.C. Bd. of Educ., 551 IDELR 101 (D.D.C. 1978).

Brown v. Wilson County School Board, 747 F. Supp. 436 (M.D. Tenn. 1990).

Burke County Bd. of Educ. v. Denton, 895 F.2d 973 (4th Cir. 1990).

Burlington Sch. Comm. v. Dep't of Educ., 471 U.S. 359 (1985).

Burpee v. Manchester School Dist., 661 F. Supp. 731 (D.N.H. 1987).

Burton v. Wilmington Parking Authority, 365 U.S. 715 (1961).

Buser v. Corpus Christi Indep. School, 56 F.3d 1387 (5th Cir. 1995), cert. denied, 116 S. Ct. 305 (1995).

Bush v. Lucas, 462 U.S. 367 (1983).

C.A. v. Christina Sch. Dist., 20 IDELR 967 (D. Del. 1993).

C.M. v. Southeast Delco Sch. Dist., 19 IDELR 1084 (E.D.Pa 1993).

Calhoun v. Illinois State Bd., 550 F. Supp. 796 (N.D.Ill. 1982).

Canton v. Harris, 489 U.S. 378 (1989).

Capiello v. D.C. Bd. of Educ., 779 F. Supp. 1 (D.D.C. 1991).

Capistrano Unified Sch. Dist. v. Wartenberg, 59 F.3d 884 (9th Cir. 1995).

Carlisle Area Sch. Dist. v. Scott P., 62 F.3d 520 (3rd Cir. 1995), cert. denied, 116 S.Ct. 1419 (U.S. 1996).

Carroll v. Metropolitan Government of Nashville and Davidson County, No.91-5749, 1992 U.S. App. Lexis 538 (6th Cir. 1992).

Carter v. Orleans Parish Public Schools, 725 F.2d 261 (5th Cir. 1984).

Catlin v. Sobol, 881 F. Supp. 789 (N.D.N.Y. 1995), rev'd, 93 F.3d 1112 (2nd Cir. 1996).

Cedar Rapids Community Sch. Dist. v. Garrett F., 106 F.3d 822 (8th Cir. 1997).

Cefalu v. East Baton Rouge Parish Sch. Bd., 907 F. Supp. 966 (M.D.La. 1995); vacated 103 F.3d 393 (5th Cir. 1997).

Chris D. v. Montgomery County Bd. of Educ., 16 EHLR 1182 (M.D. Ala. 1990).

Christen G. v. Lower Merion Sch. Dist., 919 F. Supp. 793 (E.D.Pa. 1996).

Christopher M. v. Corpus Christi Indep. Sch. Dist., 933 F.2d 1285 (5th Cir. 1991).

Christopher P. v. Marcus, 915 F.2d 794 (2nd Cir. 1990), cert. denied, 498 U.S. 1123 (1991).

Christopher T. v. San Francisco U.S.D., 553 F. Supp. 1107 (N.D.Cal. 1982).

Christopher W. v. Portsmouth School Committee, 877 F.2d 1089 (1st Cir. 1989).

Chuhran v. Walled Lake Consol. Sch., 839 F. Supp. 465 (E.D.Mich. 1993), aff'd, No. 93-2621, 1995 U.S. App. Lexis 6348 (6th Cir. 1995).

Cleburne v. Cleburne Living Center, Inc., 473 U.S. 432 (1985).

Clovis Unified School Dist. v. California Office of Admin. Hearings, 903 F.2d 635 (9th Cir. 1990).

Cluff v. Johnson City School Dist., 553 IDELR 598 (N.D.N.Y. 1982).

Cohen v. Sch. Dist. of Philadelphia, 18 IDELR 911 (E.D.Pa. 1992).

Colin K. v. Schmidt, 715 F.2d 1 (1st Cir. 1983).

College Savings Bank v. Florida Prepaid Postsecondary Education Expense Board, No. 98–149 (U.S. Supreme Court, June 23, 1999), 131 F.3d 353 (3d Cir. 1997).

Collinsgru v. Palmyra Bd. of Ed., 29 IDELR 377 (Conn. Sup. Ct. 1998)

Concerned Parents and Citizens for Continuing Education at Malcolm X (PS 79) v. New York City Board of Education, 629 F.2d 751 (2nd Cir. 1980), cert. denied, 449 U.S. 1078 (1981).

Connelly v. Gibbs, 445 N.E.2d 477 (Ill. App.Ct. 1983).

Corbett v. Regional Center for East Bay, Inc., 676 F. Supp. 964 (N.D.Cal. 1988), clarification of other issue, 699 F. Supp. 230 (N.D.Cal. 1988).

County of San Diego v. California Special Education Hearing Office, 93 F.3d 1458 (9th Cir. 1996).

Criswell v. State Dept. of Ed., EHLR 558:156 (M.D.Tenn. 1986).

Crocker v. Tennessee Secondary School Athletic Ass'n, 873 F.2d 933 (6th Cir. 1989), aff'd, 908 F.2d 972 (6th Cir. 1990).

D.R. v. Middle Bucks Area Voc. Tech. Sch., 972 F.2d 1364 (3rd Cir. 1992), cert. denied, 506 U.S. 1079 (1993).

Daniel R.R. v. State Bd. of Educ., 874 F.2d 1036 (5th Cir. 1989).

Darlene L. v. Illinois State Bd. of Educ., 568 F. Supp. 1340 (N.D.Ill. 1983).

David B. v. Patla, 24 IDELR 952 (N.D.Ill. 1996).

David D. v. Dartmouth School Committee, 615 F. Supp. 639 (D.Mass. 1984), aff'd, 775 F.2d 411 (1st Cir. 1985), cert. denied, 475 U.S. 1140 (1986).

David P. v. Lower Merion Sch. Dist., 29 IDELR 23, 27 (E.D.Penn. 1998).

Davis v. Maine Endwell Central School District, 542 F. Supp. 1257 (N.D.N.Y. 1982).

Davis v. Monroe County Board of Education, 119 S.Ct. 1661 (1999).

Day v. Radnor Township School Dist., 20 IDELR 1237 (E.D. Pa. 1994).

Dell v. Bd. of Educ., 32 F.3d 1053 (7th Cir. 1994).

Dellmuth v. Muth, 491 U.S. 223 (1989).

DeRosa v. City of New York, EHLR 559:108 (App. Div. 2d N.Y. 1987).

DeShaney v. Winnebago County Dep't. of Social Services, 489 U.S. 189 (1989).

Detsel v. Bd. of Educ. of the Auburn Enlarged City School Dist., 820 F.2d 587 (2nd Cir. 1987), cert. denied, 484 U.S. 981 (1987).

Detsel v. Sullivan, 895 F.2d 58 (2nd Cir. 1990).

DeWalt v. Burkholder, EHLR 551:550 (E.D. Va. 1980).

Diana v. State Bd. of Ed., No. C-70-37 (N.D. Cal. 1973).

Dima v. Macchiarola, 513 F. Supp. 565 (E.D.N.Y. 1981).

Dist. 27 Community School Bd. v. Bd. of Educ. of New York City, 502 N.Y.S.2d 325 (Sup. Ct. NY 1986).

Doe v. Alfred, 906 F. Supp. 1092 (S.D.W.Va. 1995), appeal dismissed, 17 F.3d 1141 (3rd Cir. 1996), dismissed, No. 96-1047, 1996 U.S. App. Lexis 4864 (3d Cir. 1996).

Doe v. Anrig, 561 F. Supp. 121 (D. Mass. 1983), aff'd 728 F.2d 30 (1st Cir. 1984), aff'd sub nom., *School Committee of Burlington v. Department of Education,* 471 U.S. 359 (1985).

Doe v. Bd. of Ed. of Tullahoma City Schools, IDELR 18/1089 (E.D.Tenn. 1992), aff'd, 9 F.3d 455 (6th Cir. 1993), cert. denied, 511 U.S. 1108 (1994).

Doe v. Belleville Public Schools Dist. No. 118, 672 F. Supp. 342 (S.D. Ill. 1987).

Doe v. Brookline School Committee, 722 F.2d 910 (1st Cir. 1983).

Doe v. Defendant I, 898 F.2d 1186 (6th Cir. 1990).

Doe v. Escambia County Sch. Bd., 599 So.2d 226 (Fla. Dist. Ct. App. 1992).

Doe v. Hillsboro Independent School Dist., 81 F.3d 1395, 1401 (5th Cir. 1996).

Doe v. Maher, 795 F.2d 787 (9th Cir. 1986).

Doe v. Rockingham County School Bd., 658 F. Supp. 403 (W.D.Va. 1987).

Doe v. Smith, 879 F.2d 1340 (6th Cir. 1989), cert. denied, *Doe v. Sumner County Bd. of Educ.*, 493 U.S. 1025 (1990).

Doe v. Withers, 20 IDELR 422 (W.Va. Cir. Ct. 1993).

Dorothy J. v. Little Rock Sch. Dist., 794 F. Supp. 1405 (E.D.Ark. 1992), aff'd, 7 F.3d 729 (8th Cir. 1993).

E. H. v. Tirozzi, 735 F. Supp. 53 (D.Conn. 1990).

Edelman v. Jordan, 415 U.S. 651 (1974).

Edward B. v. Paul, 814 F.2d 52 (1st Cir. 1987).

Eisel v. Bd. of Educ. of Montgomery County, 597 A.2d 447 (Md. 1991).

Espino v. Besteiro, 520 F. Supp. 905 (S.D. Tex. 1981), rev'd, 708 F.2d 1002 (5th Cir. 1983).

Estelle v. Gamble, 429 U.S. 97 (1976).

Estes v. Chicago Bd. of Ed., 28 IDELR 971 (N.D.Ill. 1998).

Evans v. Bd. of Ed. of the Rhinebeck Central Sch. Dist., 930 F. Supp. 83 (S.D.N.Y. 1996).

Evans v. District No. 17, 841 F.2d. 824 (8th Cir. 1988).

Evans v. Tuttle, 613 N.E.2d 854 (Ind. Ct. App. 1993).

Ezratty v. Commonwealth of Puerto Rico, 648 F.2d 770 (1st Cir. 1981).

Fairfield Bd. of Educ. v. Connecticut State Dept. of Educ., 466 A.2d 343 (Super. Ct. 1983), aff'd, 503 A.2d 1147 (1986).

Fallis v. Ambach, 710 F.2d 49 (2nd Cir. 1983).

Farrell v. Carol Stream Sch. Dist. No. 25, No. 96 C 1489, 1996 U. S. Dist. Lexis 9062 (N.D.Ill. 1996).

Felter v. Cape Girardeau School Dist., 830 F. Supp. 1279 (E.D.Mo. 1993).

Field v. Haddonfield Bd. of Educ., 769 F. Supp. 1313 (D.N.J. 1991).

Fischer v. Rochester Community Schools, 780 F. Supp. 1142 (E.D. Mich. 1991).

Fitz v. Intermediate Unit #29, 403 A.2d 138 (Pa. Com. Ct. 1979).

Fitzpatrick v. Bitzer, 427 U.S. 445 (1976).

Florence County Sch. Dist. Four v. Carter, 510 U.S. 7 (1993).

Florida Prepaid Postsecondary Eduation Expense Board v. College Savings Bank, No. 98–531 (U.S. Supreme Court, June 23, 1999), 148 F.3d 1343 (Fed. Cir. 1998).

Flour Bluff Indep. Sch. Dist. v. Katherine M., 91 F.3d 689 (5th Cir. 1996), cert. denied, 117 S.Ct. 948 (U.S. 1997).

Fontenot v. Louisiana Bd. of Elementary and Secondary Educ., 805 F.2d 1222 (5th Cir. 1986), aff'd, 835 F.2d 117 (5th Cir. 1988).

Franklin v. Gwinnett County Pub. Sch., 503 U.S. 60 (1992).

Ft. Zumwalt Sch. Dist. v. Missouri State Bd of Ed., 865 F. Supp. 604 (E.D. Mo. 1994), further proceedings, 923 F. Supp. 1216 (E.D.Mo. 1996), aff'd in part, rev'd in part sub nom., *Ft. Zumwalt Sch. Dist. v. Clynes*, Nos. 96-2503/2504, 1997 U.S. App. Lexis 17214 (8th Cir. 1997).

Fulginiti v. Roxbury Township Public Schools, 921 F. Supp. 1320 (D.N.J. 1996), aff'd, 166 F.3d 468 (3rd Cir. 1997).

Gaither v. Barron, 924 F. Supp. 134 (M.D.Ala. 1996).

Garcia v. California, 24 IDELR 547 (E.D.Cal. (1996).

Garland Independent School District v. Wilks, 657 F. Supp. 1163 (N.D. Tex. 1987).

Garrity v. Gallen, 522 F. Supp. 171 (D.N.H. 1981).

Geis v. Bd. of Educ., 589 F. Supp. 269 (D.N.J. 1984), aff'd, 774 F.2d 575 (3rd Cir. 1985).

George H. & Irene L. Walker Home for Children v. Town of Franklin, 621 N.E.2d 376 (Mass. 1993).

Georgia State Conference of Branches of NAACP v. Georgia, 775 F.2d 1403 (11th Cir. 1985).

Gillette v. Fairland Bd. of Educ., 725 F. Supp. 343 (S.D. Ohio 1989), appeal dismissed, 895 F.2d 1413 (6th Cir. 1990), rev'd, 932 F.2d 551 (6th Cir. 1991).

Gillette v. Fairland Bd. of Educ., 725 F. Supp. 343 (S.D.Ohio 1989), further proceedings, 932 F.2d 551 (6th Cir. 1991).

Glenn III v. Charlotte Mecklenburg Sch. Bd. of Educ., 903 F. Supp. 918 (W.D.N.C. 1995).

Goodall v. Stafford County School Bd., 930 F.2d 363 (4th Cir. 1991), cert. denied, 502 U.S. 864 (1991), appeal granted, 60 F.3d 168 (4th Cir. 1995); cert. denied, 133 L.Ed2d 661 (U.S. 1996).

Goss v. Lopez, 419 U.S. 565 (1975).

Grace B. v. Lexington Sch. Comm., 762 F. Supp. 416 (D.Mass. 1991).

Granite Sch. Dist. v. Shannon M., 787 F. Supp. 1020 (D.Utah 1992).

Green v. Johnson, 513 F. Supp. 965 (D.Mass. 1981).

Greenbush School Committee v. Mr. & Mrs. K., 25 IDELR 200 (D.Me. 1996).

Greer v. Rome City Sch. Dist., 762 F. Supp. 936 (N.D. Ga. 1990), aff'd, 950 F.2d 688 (11th Cir. 1991), withdrawn & reinstated in part, 967 F.2d 470 (11th Cir. 1992).

Greg B. v. Bd. of Educ., 535 F. Supp. 1333 (E.D.N.Y. 1982).

Grinsted v. Houston County Sch. Dist., 826 F. Supp. 482 (M.D.Ga. 1993).

Grooms v. Marlboro, 414 S.E.2d 802 (S.C. Ct. App. 1992).

Grube v. Bethlehem Area School Dist., 550 F. Supp. 418 (E.D.Pa. 1982).

Guadalupe Org., Inc. v. Tempe Elementary Sch. Dist. No. 3, 587 F. 2d 535 (10th Cir. 1979)

Gupta v. Montgomery County Public Schs., 25 IDELR 115 (D.Md. 1996).

Hacienda La Puente Unified School Dist. v. Honig, 976 F.2d 487 (9th Cir. 1992).

Hafer v. Melo, 502 U.S. 21 (1991).

Haley v. McManus, 593 So.2d 1339 (La. Ct. App. 1991).

Hall v. Detroit Public Sch., 823 F. Supp. 1377 (E.D.Mich. 1993).

Hall v. Knott County Bd. of Educ., 941 F.2d 402 (6th Cir. 1991), cert. denied, 502 U.S. 1077 (1992).

Hall v. Shawnee Mission School Dist., 856 F. Supp. 1521 (D. Kan. 1994).

Hall v. Vance County Bd. of Ed., 774 F.2d 629 (4th Cir. 1985).

Hannigan v. Bd. of Educ. of Brunswick Cent. Sch. Dist., No. 95-CV-1435, 1997 U.S. Dist. Lexis 291 (N.D.N.Y. 1997).

Harlow v. Fitzgerald, 457 U.S. 800 (1982).

Harmon v. Mead School Dist. No. 354, 17 EHLR 1029 (E.D. Wash 1991).

Harris v. Campbell, 472 F. Supp. 51 (E.D.Va. 1979).

Harris v. D.C Bd. of Ed., IDELR 19/105 (D.D.C. 1992)

Harris v. McCarthy, 790 F.2d 753 (9th Cir. 1986).

Haysman v. Food Lion, 893 F. Supp. 1092 (S.D.Ga. 1995).

Hebert v. Manchester Sch. Dist., 833 F. Supp. 80 (D.N.H. 1993).

Heidemann v. Rother, 84 F.3d 1021 (8th Cir. 1996).

Helbig v. City of New York, 622 N.Y.S.2d 316 (N.Y. App. 1995).

Helms v. Indep. School Dist. No. 3 of Broken Arrow, 750 F.2d 820 (10th Cir. 1984), cert. denied, 471 U.S. 1018 (1985).

Hendricks v. Gilhool, 709 F. Supp. 1362 (E.D. Pa. 1989).

Hendrickson v. Spartanburg County Sch. Dist. No. 5, 413 S.E.2d 871 (S.C. Ct. App. 1992).

Heslop v. Bd. of Educ. Newfield Cent. Sch. Dist., 594 N.Y.S.2d 871 (N.Y. App. Div. 1993).

Hobson v. Hansen, 269 F. Supp. 401 (D.D. C 1967), cert. dismissed, 393 U.S. 801 (1968), aff'd in part, rev'd in part sub nom., *Smuck v. Hobson,* 408 F.2d 175 (D.D.C. 1969).

Hoekstra v. Indep. Sch. Dist. No. 283, 103 F.3d 624 (8th Cir. 1996); cert. denied 117 S.Ct. 1852 (U.S. 1997).

Hoffman v. East Troy Community Sch. Dist. 26 IDELR 1074 (E.D. Wisc. 1999).

Holmes v. Sobol, 18 IDELR 53 (W.D.N.Y. 1991).

Honig v. Doe, 484 U.S. 305 (1988).

Hope v. Cortines, 872 F. Supp. 14 (E.D.N.Y. 1995), aff'd, 69 F.3d 687 (2d Cir. 1995).

Howard S. v. Friendswood I.S.D., 454 F. Supp. 634 (S.D.Tex. 1978).

Howe v. Ellenbecker, 8 F.3d 1258 (8th Cir. 1993), cert. denied, 511 U.S. 1005 (1994).

Howell v. Waterford Public Schools, 731 F. Supp. 1314 (E.D.Mich. 1990).

Howey v. Tippecanoe School Corp., 734 F. Supp. 1485 (N.D.Ind. 1990).

Hudson v. Wilson, 828 F.2d 1059 (4th Cir. 1987).

Hulme v. Dellmuth, 17 EHLR 940 (E.D. Pa. 1991).

Hunter v. Bd. of Educ. of Montgomery County, 555 EHLR 559 (Md. Ct. App. 1982).

Hunter v. Bd. of Educ., 439 A.2d 582 (Md. Ct. App. 1982).

Hunter v. Carbondale Area Sch. Dist., 829 F. Supp. 714 (M.D.Pa. 1993).

I.D. v. New Hampshire Dept. of Educ., 878 F. Supp. 318 (D.N.H. 1994).

I.D. v. Westmoreland School Dist., 788 F. Supp. 634 (D.N.H. 1992).

In re Phillip B., 156 Cal. Reptr. 48 (1979).

Independent Sch. Dist. v. Digre, 893 F.2d 987 (8th Cir. 1990).

Ingraham v. Wright, 430 U.S. 651 (1977).

Irving Indep. School Dist. v. Tatro, 703 F.2d 823 (5th Cir. 1983), aff'd in part, rev'd in part, 468 U.S. 883 (1984).

J.B. v. Essex-Calendonia Supervisory Union, 943 F. Supp. 387 (D.Vt. 1996).

J.B. v. Indep. School Dist., 21 IDELR 1157 (D.Minn. 1995).

J.C. v. Mendham Township Bd. of Ed., 29 IDELR 603 (N.J. Dist. 1998).

J.G. v. Bd. of Educ., EHLR 554:265 (W.D.N.Y. 1982), EHLR 555:190 (W.D.N.Y. 1983), 648 F. Supp. 1452 (W.D.N.Y. 1986), aff'd in part, modified in part, 830 F.2d 444 (2nd Cir. 1987).

J.O. v. Alton Community Unif. Sch. Dist., 909 F.2d 267 (7th Cir. 1990).

Jackson v. Franklin County Sch. Bd., 606 F. Supp. 152 (S.D.Miss. 1985), aff'd, 765 F.2d 535 (5th Cir. 1985).

Jacky W. v. N.Y.C. Bd. of Educ., 848 F. Supp. 358 (E.D.N.Y. 1994).

Jeanette H. v. Pennsbury School District, No. 91-CV-3273, 1992 U.S. Dist. Lexis 7283 (E.D.Pa. 1992).

Jefferson County Bd. of Educ. v. Breen, 694 F. Supp. 1539 (N.D. Ala. 1987).

Jenkins v. Florida, 931 F.2d 1469 (11th Cir. 1991).

Jeremy H. v. Mount Lebanon Sch. Dist., 95 F.3d 272 (3rd Cir. 1996).

John G. v. Bd. of Educ., 891 F. Supp. 122 (S.D.N.Y. 1995).

John H. v. McDonald, EHLR 558:336 (D.N.H. 1986).

Johnson v. Bismarck Pub. Sch. Dist., 949 F.2d 1000 (8th Cir. 1991).

Johnson v. Clark, 418 N.W.2d 466 (Ct. App. Mich. 1987).

Johnson v. Ind. Sch. Dist. No. 4, 921 F.2d 1022 (10th Cir. 1990), cert. denied, 500 U.S. 905 (1991).

Johnson v. Westmoreland County School Bd., 19 IDELR 787 (E.D. Va. 1993).

Joiner v. Dist. of Columbia, 16 EHLR 424, 87-3445 (D.D.C. 1990).

Jonathon G. v. Caddo Parish Sch. Bd., 875 F. Supp. 352 (W.D.La. 1994).

Jose P. v. Ambach, 551 EHLR 245 & 412 (E.D.N.Y. 1979), aff'd, 669 F.2d 865 (2nd Cir. 1982), further proceedings, 557 F. Supp. 1230 (E.D.N.Y. 1983).

Jose P. v. Ambach, 669 F.2d 865 (2nd Cir. 1982).

K.L. v. Southeast Delco Sch. Dist., 828 F Supp. 1192 (E.D.Pa. 1993).

K.R. v. Anderson Community Sch. Corp., 81 F.3d 673 (7th Cir. 1996), vacated, 138 L.Ed.2d 1007 (U.S. 1997).

Kaelin v. Grubbs, 682 F.2d 595 (6th Cir. 1982).

Kansas State Bank & Trust Corp. v. Specialized Transp. Services, Inc., 819 P.2d 587 (Kan. 1991).

Kathryn G. v. Bd. of Educ. of Mt. Vernon, 18 IDELR 1026 (S.D.N.Y. 1992).

Kattan v. District of Columbia, 18 IDELR 296 (D.D.C. 1991), aff'd, 995 F.2d 274 (D.C. Cir. 1993), cert. denied, 511 U.S. 1018 (1994).

Kerr Center Parents Association v. Charles, 572 F. Supp. 448 (D.Ore. 1983), aff'd in part, rev'd in part, 897 F.2d 1463 (9th Cir. 1990).

Kotowicz v. Mississippi State Bd. of Ed., 630 F. Supp. 925 (S.D.Mass. 1986).

Kreher IV v. Orleans Parish School Bd., No. 95-1076, 1996 U.S. Dist. Lexis 1105 & 18578, (E.D.La. 1996).

Kresse v. Johnson City School Dist., 553 IDELR 601 (N.D.N.Y. 1982).

L.S.B. v. Howard, 23 IDELR 695 (Ala. 1995).

Lachman v. Illinois State Bd. of Educ., 852 F.2d 290 (7th Cir. 1988), cert. denied, 488 U.S. 925 (1988).

Lake Country Estates Inc. v. Tahoe Regional Planning Agency, 440 U.S. 391 (1979).

Lane v. Pena, 518 U.S. 187 (1986).

Language Dev. Program, Inc. v. Ambach, 466 N.Y.S.2d 734 (N.Y. App. Div. 1983).

Larry P. v. Riles, 343 F. Supp. 1306 (N.D. Cal. 1972), 502 F. 2d 963 (9th Cir. 1974), No. C-71-2270 RF P (N.D. Cal., October 16, 1979), 793 F.2d. 969 (9th Cir. 1984).

Larson v. Miller, 76 F.3d 1446 (8th Cir. 1996).

Lau v. Nichols, 483 F. 2d 791 (9th Cir. 1973)

LeBanks v. Spears, 417 F. Supp. 169 (E.D. La. 1976)

Lemon v. Kurtzman, 411 U.S. 192 (1973).

Lenn v. Portland School Committee, 998 F.2d 1083 (1st Cir. 1993).

Leo P. v. Board of Education, EHLR 553:644 (N.D.Ill. 1982).

Lester H. v. Gilhool, 916 F.2d 865 (3d Cir. 1990), cert. denied, 499 U.S. 923 (1991).

Levine v. New Jersey, 522 EHLR 163 (N.J.Sup. Ct. 1980).

Levy v. Commonwealth, Dept. of Ed., 399 A.2d 159 (Pa. 1979).

Liscio v. Woodland Hills Sch. Dist., 734 F. Supp. 689 (W.D. Pa. 1989), aff'd, 90 F.2d 1561, 1563 (3d Cir. 1990).

Livingston School Dist. Nos. 4 & 1 v. Keenan, 82 F.3d 912 (9th Cir. 1996).

Loughran v. Flanders, 470 F. Supp. 110 (D.Conn. 1979).

Lunceford v. District of Columbia Bd. of Ed., 745 F.2d 1577 (D.C. Cir. 1984).

M. C. v. Central Regional School Dist., 22 IDELR 1036 (D.N.J. 1995).

M.P. by D.P. v. Grossmont Union High School Dist., 858 F. Supp. 1044 (S.D.Cal. 1994).

Maine v. Thiboutot, 448 U.S. 1 (1980).

Maldonado v. Josey, 975 F.2d 727 (10th Cir. 1992), cert. denied, 507 U.S. 914 (1993).

Manchester City Sch. Dist. v. Jason N., 18 IDELR 384 (D.N.H. 1991).

Manecke v. School Board, 762 F.2d 912 (11th Cir. 1983), cert. denied, 474 U.S. 1062 (1986).

Marbury v. Madison, 5 U.S. 137 (1803).

Martinez v. School Bd. of Hillsborough County, 675 F. Supp. 1574 (M.D.Fla. 1987), vacated, 861 F.2d 1502 (11th Cir. 1988).

Marvin H. v. Austin Indep. Sch. Dist., 714 F.2d 1348 (5th Cir. 1983).

Maryland Ass'n for Retarded Children (MARC) v. Maryland, Equity No. 100/182/77676 (Cir. Ct. Baltimore Co. 1974).

Mason v. Kaagan, 18 IDELR 732, (D.Vt. 1992).

Masotti v. Tustin Unified Sch. Dist., 806 F. Supp. 221 (C.D.Cal. 1992).

Mather v. Hartford School Dist., 928 F. Supp. 437 (D. Vt. 1996).

Matta v. Indian Hill Exempted Village Schools, 731 F. Supp. 253 (S.D.Ohio 1990).

Matthews v. Ambach, 552 F. Supp. 1273 (N.D.N.Y. 1982).

Mattie T. v. Holiday, 522 F. Supp. 72 (N.D. Miss. 1979).

Maynard v. Greater Hoyt School Dist. No. 61-4, 876 F. Supp. 1104 (D.S.D. 1995).

Mayson v. Teague, 749 F.2d 652 (11th Cir. 1984).

McKenzie v. Jefferson, 566 F. Supp. 404 (D.D.C. 1983).

McManus v. Wilmette School Dist. 39 Bd. of Ed., IDELR 19/485, 1992 U.S. Dist. Lexis 18167 (N.D. Ill. 1992).

McMillan v. Cheatham County Schools, 25 IDELR 398 (M.D.Tenn. 1997).

Megan C. v. Independent Sch. Dist. No. 625, 30 IDELR 132 (D. Minn. 1999).

Metropolitan Nashville & Davidson County Sch. System v. Guest, 900 F. Supp. 905 (M.D.Tenn. 1995).

Michael F. v. Cambridge Sch. Dist., EHLR 558:269 (D. Mass. 1987).

Miener v. Missouri, 498 F. Supp. 944 (E.D. Mo. 1980), aff'd in part, rev'd in part, 673 F.2d 969 (8th Cir. 1982), cert. denied, 459 U.S. 909, 916 (1982), on remand, *Miener v. Special School District*, 580 F. Supp. 562 (E.D. Mo. 1984), aff'd in part, rev'd in part, 800 F.2d 749 (8th Cir. 1986).

Militello v. Bd. of Educ., 803 F. Supp. 974 (D.N.J. 1992).

Miller v. West Lafayette Community School Corp., 665 N.E.2d 905 (Ind. 1996).

Mills v. District of Columbia Bd. of Ed., 348 F. Supp. 866 (D.D.C. 1972); contempt proceedings, EHLR 551:643 (D.D.C. 1980).

Missouri v. Jenkins, 515 U.S. 70 (1995).

Monahan v. Nebraska, 491 F. Supp. 1074 (D. Neb. 1980), aff'd in part, vacated in part, 645 F.2d 592 (8th Cir. 1981), aff'd in part, vacated in part, 687 F.2d 1164 (8th Cir. 1982), cert. denied, 460 U.S. 1012 (1983), modified sub nom., *Rose v. Nebraska*, 748 F.2d 1258 (8th Cir. 1984), cert. denied, 474 U.S. 817 (1985).

Monahan v. Nebraska, 491 F. Supp. 1074 (D.Neb. 1980), aff'd in part, vacated in part, 645 F.2d 592 (9th Cir. 1981).

Monell v. New York Dep't. of Social Services, 436 U.S. 658 (1978).

Monroe v. Pape, 365 U.S. 167 (1961).

Monticello Sch. Dist. No. 25 v. Illinois State Bd. of Educ., 910 F. Supp. 446 (C.D.Ill. 1995), aff'd sub nom., *Monticello Sch. Dist. No. 25 v. George L.*, 102 F.3d 895 (7th Cir. 1996).

Moore v. Dist. of Columbia, 674 F. Supp. 901 (D.D.C. 1987), rev'd, 886 F.2d 335 (D.C.Cir. 1989), vacated, 907 F.2d 165 (D.C. Cir. 1990), cert. denied, 498 U.S. 998 (1990).

Morgan v. Chris L., No. 94-6561, 1997 U.S. App. Lexis 1041 (6th Cir. 1997), cert. denied, 138 L.Ed.2d 207 (U.S. 1997).

Mr. and Mrs. W. v. Malito, 19 IDELR 901 (C.D.Ill. 1993).

Mrs. B. v. Milford Bd. of Educ., 103 F.3d 1114 (2nd Cir. 1997).

Mrs. C. v. Wheaton, 916 F.2d 69 (2nd Cir. 1990).

Mrs. W. v. Tirozzi, 832 F.2d 748 (2nd Cir. 1987).

Murphy v. Timberlane Regional Sch. Dist., 22 F.3d 1186 (1st Cir. 1994), cert. denied, 513 U.S. 987 (1994).

Murphy v. United Parcel Service, Inc., No. 97–1992 (U.S. Supreme Court, June 22, 1999), 141 F.3d 1185 (10th Cir. 1998).

Murphysboro Community Unit School Dist. v. Illinois State Bd. of Educ., 41 F.3d 1162 (7th Cir. 1994).

Murray v. Montrose County Sch. Dist. RE-1J, 51 F.3d 921 (10th Cir. 1995), cert. denied, 116 S.Ct. 278 (U.S. 1995).

Myles S. v. Montgomery County Bd. of Ed., 824 F. Supp. 1549 (M.D.Ala. 1993).

Mylo v. Baltimore County Board of Education, No. 91-2563, 1991 U.S. App. Lexis 27029 (4th Cir. 1991), cert. denied, 507 U.S. 934 (1993).

Nance v. Matthews, 622 So. 2d 297 (Ala. 1993).

Natchez-Adams School Dist. v. Searing, 918 F. Supp. 1028 (S.D.Miss. 1996).

Nathaniel L. v. Exeter Sch. Dist., 16 IDELR 1073 (D.N.H. 1990).

Neely v. Rutherford County School, 851 F. Supp. 888 (M.D. Tenn. 1995), rev'd, 68 F.3d 965 (6th Cir. 1995), cert. denied, 116 S.Ct. 1418 (U.S. 1996).

New Hampshire Dept. of Educ. v. City of Manchester, 23 IDELR 1057 (D.N.H. 1996).

New Mexico Association for Retarded Citizens v. New Mexico, 495 F. Supp. 391 (D.N.M. 1980), rev'd, 678 F.2d 847 (10th Cir. 1982).

Newport v. Fact Concerts, Inc., 453 U.S. 247 (1981).

Norris v. Bd. of Educ. of Greenwood Community School Corp., 797 F. Supp. 1452 (S.D.Ind. 1992).

North v. D.C. Bd. of Ed., 471 F. Supp. 136 (D.D.C. 1979).

O'Connor v. Donaldson, 422 U.S. 563 (1975).

Oberti v. Bd. of Educ. of the Borough of Clementon Sch. Dist. 995 F.2d 1204 (3rd Cir. 1993).

Ojai Unified Sch. Dist. v. Jackson, 4 F.3d 1467 (9th Cir. 1993), cert. denied, 513 U.S. 825 (1994).

Olmstead v. L.C., No. 98–536 (U.S. Supreme Court, June 22, 1999), 138 F.3d 893 (11th Cir. 1998).

Owens v. Independence, 445 U.S. 622 (1980).

P.F. ex rel. B.F. v. New Jersey Div. of Developmental Disabilities, 656 A.2d 1 (N.J. 1995).

Pace v. Dryden Central School Dist., 574 N.Y.S.2d 142 (Sup. Ct. 1991).

Pandazides v. Virginia Bd. of Educ., 13 F.3d 823 (4th Cir. 1994).

Papacoda v. Connecticut, 528 F. Supp. 68 (D.Conn. 1981).

Parents of Student W. v. Puyallup, 31 F.3d 1489 (9th Cir. 1994).

Parents v. Coker, 676 F. Supp. 1072 (E.D. Okla. 1987).

Parham v. J.R., 442 U.S. 584 (1979).

Parks v. Pavkovic, 536 F. Supp. 296 (N.D. Ill. 1982), further proceedings, 557 F. Supp. 1280 (N.D. Ill. 1983), aff'd in part, rev'd in part, 753 F.2d 1397 (7th Cir. 1985), cert. denied, 473 U.S. 906 (1985).

Parks v. Pavkovic, 753 F.2d 1397 (7th Cir. 1985).

PASE v. Hannon, 506 F.Supp. 831 (N.D. Ill. 1980).

Passman v. Davis, 442 U.S. 228 (1979).

Pennhurst State School and Hospital v. Halderman, 446 F. Supp. 1295 (E.D. Pa. 1977), aff'd in part, rev'd in part, 612 F.2d 84 (3rd Cir. 1979), rev'd, 451 U.S.1 (1981), on remand, 673 F.2d 647 (3rd Cir. 1982), rev'd, 465 U.S. 89 (1984).

Pennhurst State School and Hospital v. Halderman, 465 U.S. 89 (1984).

Pennsylvania Ass'n for Retarded Children (PARC) v. Pennsylvania, 334 F. Supp. 1257 (E.D.Pa 1971); 343 F. Supp 279 (E.D.Pa 1972).

Pennsylvania Department of Corrections v. Yeskey, 524 U.S. 206, 118 S.Ct. 1952 (1998).

Pennsylvania Dept. of Corrections v. Yeskey, 524 U.S. 206 (1998).

Pennsylvania Envtl. Defense Fund v. Canon-McMillan Sch. Dist., 152 F.3d 228, 232 (3rd Cir. 1998).

Petersen v. Hastings Public Schools, 831 F. Supp. 742 (D.Neb. 1993), aff'd, 31 F.3d 705 (8th Cir. 1994).

Petties v. District of Columbia, 897 F. Supp. 626 (D.D.C. 1995).

Phipps v. New Hanover County Bd. of Ed., 551 F. Supp. 732 (E.D.N.C. 1982).

Planells v. San Francisco Unified Sch. Dist., 19 IDELR 477 (9th Cir. 1992).

Plyler v. Doe, 457 U.S. 202 (1982).

Polk v. Central Sasquehanna Intermediate Unit 16, 853 F.2d 171 (3rd Cir. 1988), cert. denied, 488 U.S. 1030 (1989).

Pottgen v. Missouri State High Sch. Activities Ass'n., 40 F.3d 926 (8th Cir. 1994), award of atty fee rev'd, 103 F.3d 720 (8th Cir. 1997).

Pottgen v. Missouri State High School Activities Ass'n., 40 F.3d 926 (8th Cir. 1994).

Powell v. Defore, 699 F.2d 1078 (11th Cir. 1983).

Prince William County School Bd. v. Wills, 16 EHLR 1109 (1989).

Prins v. Indep. Sch. Dist. No. 761, 23 IDELR 544 (D.Minn. 1995).

Printz v. United States, 138 L.Ed.2d 914 (U.S. 1997).

Pullen v. Cuomo, 18 IDELR 132 (N.D.N.Y. 1991)

Quackenbush v. Johnson City School District, 716 F.2d 141 (2nd Cir. 1983), cert denied, 465 U.S. 1071 (1984).

Quern v. Jordan, 440 U.S. 332 (1979).

Rainey v. Tennessee, No. A-3100 (Chavez Ct. Davidson County Tenn. 1976), order filed Jan. 21, 1976).

Ramirez v. City of Manchester, 16 EHLR 937, 89-217-D (D.N.H. 1992).

Randolph Union High School District No. 2 v. Byard, 897 F. Supp. 174 (D.Vt. 1995), aff'd, 24 IDELR 928 (D.Vt. 1996).

Rankins v. Aytch, 591 So.2d 387 (La. Ct. App. 1991).

Rapid City School Dist. No. 51-4 v. Vahle, 733 F. Supp. 1364 (D.S.D. 1990), aff'd, 922 F.2d 476 (8th Cir. 1990).

Rappaport v. Vance, 812 F. Supp. 609 (D.Md. 1993), appeal dismissed, 14 F.3d 596 (4th Cir. 1994), dismissed, No. 93-1916; 1994 U.S. App. Lexis 80 (4th Cir. 1994).

Raymond S. v. Ramirez, 918 F.Supp. 1280 (N.D. Iowa 1995).

Rebecca S. v. Clarke County School Dist., 22 IDELR 884 (M.D. Ga. 1995).

Reid v. Bd. of Educ., Lincolnshire-PrairieView Sch. Dist 103, 765 F. Supp. 965 (N.D.Ill. 1991).

Rettig v. Kent City School Dist., 94 F.R.D. 12 (N.D. Ohio 1980).

Reusch v. Fountain, 872 F. Supp. 1421 (D.Md. 1994).

Rhodes v. Ohio High School Athletic Ass'n., 939 F. Supp. 584 (N.D.Ohio 1996).

Rich v. Kentucky Country Day, Inc., 793 S.W.2d 832 (Ky. Ct. App. 1990).

Richardson v. McKnight, 117 S.Ct. 2100 (U.S. 1997).

Riley v. Ambach, 508 F. Supp. 1222 (E.D.N.Y. 1980), rev'd, 668 F.2d 635 (2d Cir. 1981).

River Forest School Dist. #90 v. Laurel D., No. 95 C 5503, 1996 U.S. Dist. Lexis 4988 (N.D.Ill. 1996).

Robbins v. Maine School Administrative Dist. No. 56, 807 F. Supp. 11 (D.Me. 1992).

Robert M. v. Benton, 634 F.2d 1139 (8th Cir. 1980), further proceedings, 671 F.2d 1104 (8th Cir. 1982).

Robinson v. Pinderhughes, 810 F.2d 1270 (4th Cir. 1987).

Rodgers v. Magnet Cove Pub. Schs., 34 F.3d 642 (8th Cir. 1994).

Rodiriecus L. v. Waukegan School Dist. #60, 90 F.3d 249 (7th Cir. 1996).

Rollison v. Biggs, 656 F. Supp. 1204 (D.Del. 1987), reh'g denied, 660 F. Supp. 875 (D.Del. 1987).

Roncker v. Walter, 700 F.2d 1058 (6th Cir. 1983), cert. denied, 464 U.S. 864 (1983).

Rose v. Chester County Intermediate Unit, No. 95-239, 1996 U.S. Dist. Lexis 6105 (E.D.Pa. 1996), aff'd, 114 F.3d 1173 (3rd Cir. 1997).

Rose v. Nebraska, 748 F.2d 1258 (8th Cir. 1984), cert. denied, 474 U.S. 817 (1985).

Russell v. Jefferson Sch. Dist., 609 F. Supp. 605 (N.D.Cal. 1985).

Russman v. Sobol, 85 F.3d 1050 (2nd Cir. 1996), vacated, 138 L.Ed.2d 1008 (U.S. 1997).

S-1 v. State Bd. of Educ. of North Carolina, 6 F.3d 160 (4th Cir. 1993), reh'g, 21 F.3d 49 (4th Cir. 1994).

S-1 v. Turlington, 635 F.2d 342 (5th Cir. 1981); cert. denied, 454 U.S. 1030 (1981).

Salley v. St. Tammany Parish Sch. Bd., 57 F.3d 458 (5th Cir. 1995).

San Jose Unified School Dist., 29 IDELR 813 (Cal. 1998).

Sandison v. Michigan High School Athletic Ass'n Inc., 863 F. Supp. 483 (E.D.Mich. 1994), rev'd in part, appeal dismissed in part, 64 F.3d 1026 (6th Cir. 1995).

Sanger v. Montgomery County Bd. of Ed., 916 F. Supp. 518 (D.Md. 1996).

Sargi v. Kent City Bd. of Educ., 70 F.3d 907 (6th Cir. 1995).

Savka v. Commonwealth, Dept. of Ed., 403 A.2d 142 (Pa.Comm. Ct. 1979).

School Bd. of Nassau County v. Arline, 480 U.S. 273 (1987).

School Bd. of Nassau County v. Arline, 480 U.S. 273, 107 S.Ct. 1123 (1987).

School Board of Hillsborough County v. Student 26493257S, 23 IDELR 93 (M.D.Fla. 1995).

School Board of Prince William County v. Malone, 762 F.2d 1210 (4th Cir. 1985), further proceedings, 662 F. Supp. 999 (E.D. Va. 1987).

School Board v. Malone, 762 F.2d 1210 (4th Cir. 1985), further proceedings, 662 F. Supp. 999 (E.D.Va. 1987).

School Committee of the Town of Burlington v. Dept. of Educ. of Massachusetts, 736 F.2d 773 (1st Cir. 1984), aff'd, 471 U.S. 359 (1985).

Schweiker v. Chilicky, 487 U.S. 412 (1988).

Scituate School Committee v. Robert B., 620 F. Supp. 1224 (D.R.I. 1985), aff'd 795 F.2d 77 (1st Cir. 1986).

Seals v. Loftis, 614 F. Supp. 302 (E.D.Tenn. 1985).

Sean R. v. Bd. of Educ., 794 F. Supp. 467 (D.Conn. 1992).

Seminole Tribe of Florida v. Florida, 517 U.S. 44 (1996).

Sessions v. Livingston Parish Sch. Bd., 501 F. Supp. 251 (M.D.La. 1980).

Shannon v. Ambach, 553 IDELR 198 (E.D.N.Y. 1981).

Silano v. Tirozzi, 651 F. Supp. 1021 (D.Conn. 1987).

Silvio v. Commonwealth, Dept. of Ed., 439 A.2d 893 (Pa. Comm. Ct. 1982), aff'd, 456 A.2d 1366 (Pa. 1983).

Sioux Falls School Dist. v. Koupal, 526 N.W.2d 248 (S.D. 1994), cert. denied, 115 S.Ct. 2580 (U.S. 1995).

Smith v. Ambach, EHLR 552:490 (N.D.N.Y. 1981).

Smith v. Barton, 914 F.2d 1330 (9th Cir. 1990), cert. denied, 501 U.S. 1217 (1991).

Smith v. Cumberland School Committee, EHLR 551:639 (R.I. 1979), further proceedings on other issues, 703 F.2d 4 (1st Cir. 1983), aff'd sub nom., *Smith v. Robinson*, 468 U.S. 992 (1984).

Smith v. Robinson, 468 U.S. 992 (1984).

Smith v. Wade, 461 U.S. 30 (1983).

Sonya C. v. Arizona School for Deaf and Blind, 743 F. Supp. 700 (D.Ariz. 1990).

Southeastern Community College v. Davis, 442 U.S. 397 (1979).

Spivey v. Elliott, 29 F.3d 1522 (11th Cir. 1994), withdrawn in part, reaff'd in part, 41 F.3d 1497 (11th Cir. 1995).

Squires v. Sierra Nevada Educational Foundation, 823 P.2d 256 (Nev. 1991).

Stafford County School Bd. v. Farley, 16 EHLR 1119 (Va. Cir. Ct. 1990).

State of Connecticut v. Bruno, 673 A.2d 1117 (Conn. 1996).

Stauffer v. William Penn Sch. Dist., 829 F. Supp. 742 (E.D.Pa. 1993).

Steldt v. School Bd. of the Riverdale School Dist., 885 F. Supp. 1192 (W.D.Wis. 1995).

Stevens v. Umstead, 921 F. Supp. 530 (C.D.Ill. 1996).

Still v. Debuono, 101 F.3d 888 (2nd Cir. 1996).

Stoneking v. Bradford Area Sch. Dist., 882 F.2d 720 (3rd Cir. 1989), cert. denied, 493 U.S. 1044 (1990).

Sullivan v. Vallejo City Unified School Dist., 731 F. Supp. 947 (E.D.Cal. 1990).

Supreme Court v. Consumers Union of United States, 446 U.S. 719 (1980), on remand sub nom, *Consumers Union of United States v. American Bar Ass'n*, 505 F. Supp. 822 (E.D. Va. 1981), appeal dismissed, 451 U.S. 1012 (1981), aff'd in part, rev'd in part, 688 F.2d 218 (4th Cir. 1982), cert. denied. 462 U.S. 1137 (1983).

Susan N. v. Wilson Sch. Dist., 70 F.3d 751 (2nd Cir. 1995).

Susan R.M. v. Northwest I.S.D.,818 F.2d 455 (5th Cir. 1987).

Suter v. Artist M., 503 U.S. 347 (1992).

Sutton v. United Air Lines, Inc., No. 97–1943 (U.S. Supreme Court, June 22, 1999), 130 F.3d 893 (10th Cir. 1997).

Tall v. Board of School Comm'rs of Baltimore City, 28 IDELR 151 (Md. App. Ct. 1998).

Tarasoff v. Regents of Univ. of California, 551 P.2d 334 (Cal. 1976).

Taylor v. Honig, 19 IDELR 472 (9th Cir. 1992).

Teague Indep. School Dist. v. Todd L., 999 F.2d 127 (5th Cir. 1993).

Tennessee Dept. of Mental Health & Mental Retardation v. Paul B., 88 F.3d 1466 (6th Cir. 1996).

Tenney v. Brandhove, 341 U.S. 367 (1951).

Teresa Diane P. v. Alief Indep. Sch. Dist., 744 F.2d 484 (5th Cir. 1984).

Texas City Indep.School Dist. v. Jorstad, 752 F. Supp. 231 (S.D.Tex. 1990).

Texas State Teachers Ass'n. v. Garland Indep. Sch. Dist., 837 F.2d 190 (5th Cir. 1988), rev'd, 489 U.S. 782 (1989).

Thelma D. v. Bd. of Educ., 737 F. Supp. 541 (E.D. Mo. 1990), aff'd, 934 F.2d 929 (8th Cir. 1991).

Thomas v. Atascadero Unified School Dist., 662 F. Supp. 376 (C.D.Cal. 1986).

Thomas v. Cincinnati Bd. of Educ., 918 F.2d 618 (6th Cir. 1990).

Thomas v. Davidson Academy, 846 F. Supp. 611 (M.D. Tenn. 1994).

Thompson v. Bd. of Special Sch. Dist. No. 1, 936 F. Supp. 644 (D.Minn. 1996).

Thornrock v. Boise Indep. School Dist., 767 P.2d 1241 (Idaho 1988), cert. denied, 490 U.S. 1068 (1989).

Tilson v. School Dist. of Philadelphia, 932 F.2d 961 (3rd Cir. 1991).

Tilton v. Jefferson County Bd. of Educ., 705 F.2d 800 (6th Cir. 1983); cert. denied 465 U.S. 1006 (1984).

Timms v. Metro School Dist., 722 F.2d 1310 (7th Cir. 1983).

Timothy W. v. Rochester School Dist., 559 EHLR 480 (D.N.H. 1988), 875 F.2d 954 (1st Cir. 1989), cert. denied, 493 U.S. 983 (1989).

Tinkham v. Groveport Madison Local School Dist., 18 IDELR 291 (Ohio Ct. App. 1991).

Todd v. Elkins Sch. Dist. No. 10, 28 IDELR 29 (8th Cir. 1998).

Township High School Dist. Bd. of Educ. v. Kurtz-Imig, 16 EHLR 17 (N.D.Ill. 1989).

Unified School Dist. No. 259 v. Newton, 673 F. Supp. 418 (D. Kan. 1987).

Union School Dist. v. Smith, 15 F.3d 1519 (9th Cir. 1994), cert. denied, 513 U.S. 965 (1994).

United Cerebral Palsy of NYC v. Bd. of Ed. of City of N.Y., 669 F.2d 865 (2d Cir. 1982), further proceedings, 557 F. Supp. 1230 (E.D.N.Y. 1983).

United States v. Lopez, 514 U.S. 549 (1995).

United States v. Oregon, 839 F.2d 635 (9th Cir. 1988), rev'd, 782 F. Supp 502 (D. Or. 1991).

Urban v. Jefferson County School Dist R-1, 870 F. Supp. 1558 (D.Co. 1994), aff'd, 89 F.3d 720 (10th Cir. 1996).

V. W. and R. W. v. Favolise, 131 F.R.D. 654 (D. Conn. 1990).

Valerie B. v. Conway Sch. Dist., 17 EHLR 806 (D.N.H. 1991).

Valerie J. v. Derry Coop. Sch. Dist., 771 F. Supp. 492 (D.N.H. 1991).

Vander Malle v. Ambach, 673 F.2d 49 (2nd Cir. 1982), further proceedings, 667 F. Supp. 1015 (S.D.N.Y. 1987).

Vermont Association for Children with Learning Disabilities v. Kaagan, EHLR 554:349 (1982), EHLR 554:447 (1983).

Virginia Dept. of Educ. v. Riley, 23 F.3d 80 (4th Cir. 1994), appeal, 86 F.3d 1337 (4th Cir. 1996), on reh'g, 106 F.3d 559 (4th Cir. 1997).

W.B. v. Matula, 67 F.3d 484 (3rd Cir. 1995).

Waechter v. Sch. Dist. No. 14-030, 773 F. Supp. 1005 (W.D.Mich. 1991).

Walker v. San Francisco Unified School Dist., 46 F.3d 1449 (9th Cir. 1995).

Wall v. Mattituck-Cutchogue Sch. Dist., 945 F. Supp. 501 (E.D.N.Y. 1996).

Walton v. Alexander, 44 F.3d 1297 (5th Cir. 1995).

Webster Groves Sch. Dist. v. Pulitzer Pub. Co., 898 F.2d 1371 (8th Cir. 1990).

Wheeler v. Towanda Area School Dist., 950 F.2d 128 (3rd Cir. 1991), dismissed, No. CV 90- 1764, 1991U.S. Dist. Lexis 20139 (M.D.Pa. 1991), rehearing denied, No. 91-547, 1992 U.S. App. Lexis 46 (3d. Cir. 1992).

White v. California, 195 Cal. App. 3d 452 (Cal. Ct. App. 1987).

Whitehead v. Sch. Bd., 918 F. Supp. 1515 (M.D.Fla. 1996).

Will v. Michigan Dep't. of State Police, 491 U.S. 58 (1989).

Wilson v. McDonald, EHLR 558: 364 (E.D.Ky. 1987).

Windward School v. State, EHLR 551:219 (S.D.N.Y. 1978), aff'd EHLR 551:224 (2nd Cir. 1979).

Wise v. Ohio Dept. of Educ., 80 F.3d 177 (6th Cir. 1996).

Witty v. Dukakis, 3 F.3d 517 (1st Cir. 1993).

Wood v. Strickland, 420 U.S. 308 (1975).

Woods v. New Jersey Dept. of Educ., 19 IDELR 1092 (D.N.J. 1993).

Wyatt v. Alderholt, 503 F.2d 1305 (5th Cir. 1974).

Wyatt v. Cole, 504 U.S. 158 (1992).

Wyatt v. Stickney, 325 F. Supp. 781 (M.D. Ala. 1971), 344 F. Supp. 373 (M.D. Ala. 1972). This case has a long history and is ongoing. The most recent filing in the case is *Wyatt by & Through Rawlins v. Rogers*, U.S. Dist. LEXIS 7429 (M.D. Ala. 1998).

Wyatt v. Stickney, 344 F. Supp. 373 (M.D. Ala. 1972), aff'd in part, rev'd in part sub nom.

York County Sch. Bd. v. Nicely, 408 S.E.2d 545 (Va.Ct. App. 1991).

Youngberg v. Romeo, 457 U.S. 307 (1982).

Zobrest v. Catalina Foothills School Dist., 963 F.2d 1190 (9th Cir. 1992), rev'd, 509 U.S. 1 (1993).

Hearing Officer Decisions ⌒

Academy School Dist., No. 20, 21 IDELR 965 (1994).

Bay County School Dist., 20 IDELR 920 (1995).

Beaumont Indep. School Dist., 21 IDELR 261 (1994).

Bryan County School Dist., 20 IDELR 930 (1993).

In re J.W., 23 IDELR 459 (1995).

Kershaw School Dist., 20 IDELR 445 (1993).

Lakeland Sch. Corp., 29 IDELR 1133 (1999).

Limestone County (AL) Sch. Dist., 27 IDELR 231 (1997).

Modesto City School, 21 IDELR 685 (1995).

Oakland Unified School Dist., 20 IDELR 1338 (1993).

Oconee County Sch. Sys., 27 IDELR 629 (1997).

Philadelphia School Dist., 21 IDELR 318 (1994).

Snowline Joint Unified School Dist., 21 IDELR 491 (1994).

Walpole Public School, 22 IDELR 1075 (1995).

Case Index

A

Abu-Sahyun v. Palo Alto Unified School Dist., 365
Addington v. Texas, 128
Agostine v. School Dist. of Philadelphia, 344
Agostini v. Felton, 71, 73, 131
Albertsons, Inc. v. Kirkingburg, 44-45
Alden v. Maine, 49-51
Alexander S. v. Boyd, 79, 353
Ali v. Wayne-Westland School Dist., 353
Allen v. School Committee of Boston, 324, 347
Amman v. Stow School System, 241
Anderson v. Creighton, 363
Anderson v. Thompson, 345, 347, 348, 350
Angevine v. Jenkins, 219
Aranow v. Dist. of Columbia Bd. of Educ., 366
Armstrong v. Kline, 220, 236
Arons v. New Jersey State Bd. of Educ., 366
Ashland Sch. Dist. v. New Hampshire Div. for Children, Youth & Families, 79
ASPIRA of New York v. Bd. of Educ., 324
Association for Community Living v. Romer, 291
Association for Retarded Citizens of Alabama, Inc., v. Teague, 290
Association for Retarded Citizens in Colorado v. Frazier, 291
A.W. V. Northwest R-1 Sch. Dist., 264

B

Bales v. Clarke, 296
Barlow/Gresham Union High Sch. Dist. No. 2 v. Mitchell, 365
Barnett v. Fairfax County School Bd., 271, 349, 350
Bd. of County Comm'rs v. Brown, 335, 336, 361
Bd. of Ed. of East Windsor Regional Sch. Dist. v. Diamond, 218
Bd. of Educ. of Caball v. Dicnclt, 224
Bd. of Educ. of City of Plainfield v. Cooperman, 116
Bd. of Educ of Community Consolidated Sch. Dist. No. 21 v. Illinois State Board of Education, 219
Bd. of Educ. of East Windsor Regional Sch. Dist. v. Diamond, 366
Bd. of Educ. v. Holland, 261, 268-269, 275
Bd. of Educ. of Kiryas Joel Village School Dist. v. Grumet, 71
Bd. of Educ. v. Rowley, 111, 112, 174-175, 201, 204, 205, 212, 216, 217, 218, 219, 220, 226, 230, 232, 233, 236, 239, 273, 403-415 (Appendix C)

Beede v. Town of Washington Sch. Dist., 352
Begay v. Hodel, 352
Behavior Research Institute v. Secretary of Administration, 297
Belanger v. Nashua Sch. Dist., 311, 356
Bencic v. City of Malden, 329
Bevin H. v. Wright, 208, 214
Black v. Indiana Area Sch. Dist., 333
Blazejewski v. Bd. of Educ., 355
Bonadonna v. Cooperman, 223, 229
Borgna v. Binghampton City School Dist., 81, 365
Bowen v. Massachusetts, 75
Bragdon v. Abbott, 47, 116
Briere v. Fair Haven, 224
Brown v. Board of Education, 7, 9-11, 24, 118, 122, 124, 125, 129, 237, 299, 316, 389-392 (Appendix A)
Burke County Bd. of Educ. v. Denton, 225, 287, 349
Burlington Sch. Comm. v. Dep't. of Educ., 347, 350, 352
Burpee v. Mancheser School Dist., 366
Burton v. Wilmington Parking Authority, 355
Buser v. Corpus Christi Indep. School, 300

C

C.A. v. Christina Sch. Dist., 103

Calhoun v. Illinois State Bd., 293
Cannon v. University of Chicago, 338
Canton v. Harris, 335-336
Capistrano Unified Sch. Dist. v. Wartenberg, 227
Capiello v. D.C. Bd. of Educ., 366
Carlisle Area Sch. Dist. v. Scott P., 234
Carroll v. Metropolitan Government of Nashville and Davidson County, 287
Catlin v. Sobol, 121
Cedar Rapids Community Sch. Dist. v. Garrett F., 206-207, 208, 212, 239, 211, 212, 214
Cefalu v. East Baton Rouge Parish Sch. Bd., 72-73
Chris D. v. Montgomery County Bd. of Educ., 270
Christen G. v. Lower Merion Sch. Dist., 224
Christopher M. v. Corpus Christi Indep. Sch. Dist., 288
Christopher P. v. Marcus, 363
Christopher T. v. San Francisco U.S.D., 291
Christopher W. v. Portsmouth School Committee, 293
Chuhran v. Walled Lake Consol. Sch., 349
Cleburne v. Cleburne Living Center, Inc. 118
Cliff v. Johnson City School Dist., 293
Clovis Unified School Dist. v. California Office of Admin. Hearings, 229
C.M. v. Southeast Delco Sch. Dist., 334
Cohen v. Sch. Dist. of Philadelphia, 337
College Savings Bank v. Florida Prepaid Postsecondary Education Expense Board, 49-51
Collinsgru v. Palmyra Bd. of Ed., 363
Concerned Parents and Citizens for Continuing Education at Malcolm X (PS 79) v. New York City Board of Education, 297
Connelly v. Gibbs, 120
Corbett v. Regional Center for East Bay, Inc., 288

County of San Diego v. California Special Education Hearing Office, 218
Criswell v. State Dept. of Ed., 317
Crocker v. Tennessee Secondary School Athletic Ass'n, 290, 293

D

Daniel R.R. v. State Bd. of Educ., 260, 265-268, 275, 288
Darlene L. v. Illinois State Bd. of Ed., 211
David B. v. Partla, 78
David D. v. Dartmouth School Committee, 217
Davis v. Maine Endwell Central School District, 291, 344-345
Davis v. Monroe County Board of Education, 330, 337-341
Day v. Radnor Township School Dist., 224
Dell v. Bd. of Educ., 298
Dellmuth v. Muth, 360
DeShaney v. Winnebago, 332, 333, 334
Detsel v. Bd. of Educ. of the Auburn Enlarged City School Dist., 206-207
Detsel v. Sullivan, 206-207, 208, 212, 239
DeWalt v. Burkholder, 273
Diana v. State Bd. of Ed., 136, 137
Dima v. Macchiarola, 297
Dist. 27 Community School Bd. v. Bd of Educ. of New York City, 117
Doe v. Anrig, 317
Doe v. Bd. of Ed. of Tullahoma City Schools, 217, 230
Doe v. Belleville Public Schools Dist. No. 118, 117
Doe v. Brookline School Committee, 288
Doe v. Defendant, 225
Doe v. Escambia County Sch. Bd., 337
Doe v. Hillsboro Independent School Dist., 334
Doe v. Smith, 287
Doe v. Rockingham County School Bd., 74
Dorothy J. v. Little Rock Sch. Dist., 333
D.R. v. Middle Bucks Area Voc. Tech. Sch., 334, 336-337

E

Edelman v. Jordan, 360, 362
Edward B. v. Paul, 349
E.H. v. Tirozzi, 318
Eisel v. Bd. of Educ. of Montgomery County, 331-332
Espino v. Bestiero, 215
Estelle v. Gamble, 332, 333, 363
Evans v. Bd. of Ed. of the Rhinebeck Central Sch. Dist., 224
Evans v. District No. 17, 229
Evans v. Tuttle, 64
Ezratty v. Commonwealth of Puerto Rico, 293

F

Fairfield Bd. of Educ. v. Connecticut State Dept. of Educ., 120
Fallis v. Ambach, 297
Farrell v. Carol Stream Sch. Dist. No. 25, 283, 288, 291
Felter v. Cape Girardeau School Dist., 71
Field v. Haddonfield Bd. of Educ., 211
Fischer v. Rochester Community Schools, 365
Fitz v. Intermediate Unit #29, 296
Fitzpatrick v. Bitzer, 360
Florence County Ach. Dist. Four v. Carter, 226-227
Florida Prepaid Postsecondary Education Expense Board v. College Savings Bank, 49-51
Flour Bluff Indep. Sch. Dist. v. Katherine M., 272
Franklin v. Gwinnett County Pub. Sch., 330, 334, 338, 351-352
Ft. Zumwalt Sch. Dist v. Missouri State Bd. of Ed., 218, 349-350
Fulginiti v. Roxbury Township Public Schools, 208

G

Gaither v. Barron, 354
Garcia v. California, 232
Garland Independent School District, 229
Garrity v. Gallen, 292
Geis v. Bd. of Educ., 236

George H. & Irene L. Walker
 Home or Children v. Town of
 Franklin, 318
Georgia State Conference of
 Branches of NAACP v.
 Georgia, 158, 159
Gillette v. Fairland Bd. of Educ,
 270, 288, 299
Glenn III v. Charlotte
 Mecklenburg Schl. Bd. of
 Educ., 349, 353
Goss v. Lopez, 82, 95
Grace B. v. Lexington Sch.
 Comm., 355
Granite Sch. Dist. v. Shannon M.,
 208
Green v. Johnson, 79
Greer v. Rome City Sch. Dist.,
 267
Greensbush School Committee v.
 Mr. & Mrs. K., 218
Greg B. v. Bd. of Educ., 347
Grinsted v. Houston County Sch.
 Dist., 365
Grube v. Bethlehem Area School
 Dist., 119
Guadalupe Org., Inc. v. Tempe
 Elementary Sch. Dist. No. 3,
 136, 137
Gupa v. Montgomery County
 Public Schs., 354

H

Hacienda La Puente Unified
 School Dist. v. Honig, 107,
 108
Hafer v. Melo, 362
Hall v. Detroit Public Sch., 366
Hall v. Knott County Bd. of
 Educ., 344, 349
Hall v. Shawnee Mission School
 Dist., 231
Hall v. Vance County Bd. of Ed.,
 217
Hannigan v. Bd. of Educ. of
 Brunswick Cent. Sch. Dist., 367
Harlow v. Fitzgerald, 362, 363
Harmon v. Mead School Dist.,
 267
Harris v. Campbell, 292, 365
Harris v. D.C. Bd. of Ed., 233
Harris v. McCarthy, 365
Haysman v. Food Lion, 353
Hebert v. Manchester Sch. Dist.,
 299

Heidemann v. Rother, 349, 358
Helbig v. City of New York, 347
Helms v. Indep. School Dist. No.
 3 of Broken Arrow, 64
Hendricks v. Gilhool, 270
Hobson v. Hansen, 136, 138
Hoekstra v. Indep. Sch. Dist. No.
 283, pp. 349, 355
Hoffman v. East Troy Community
 Sch. Dist., 139
Holmes v. Sobol, 365
Honig v. Doe, 73-74, 80-82, 91,
 92, 123, 145, 220, 272, 273,
 293
Hope v. Cortines, 291
Howard S. v. Friendswood I.S.D.,
 291
Howe v. Ellenbecker, 355
Howell v. Waterford Public
 Schools, 352
Howey v. Tippecanoe School
 Corp., 365
Hudson v. Wilson, 360
Hulme v. Dellmuth, 270
Hunter v. Carbondale Area Sch.
 Dist., 343

I

I.D. v. New Hampshire Dept. of
 Educ., 300
I.D. v. Westmoreland School
 Dist., 291
Independent Sch. Dist. v. Digre,
 367
Ingraham v. Wright, 334
In re Phillip B., 164
Irving Indep. School Dist. v.
 Tatro, 205-206, 208, 209, 211,
 212, 214, 238-239

J

Jackson v. Franklin County Sch.
 Bd., 360
J.B. v. Essex-Calendonia
 Supervisory Union, 367
J.B. v. Indep. School Dist., 108
J.C. v. Mendham Township Bd. of
 Ed., 365
Jeanette H. v. Pennsbury School
 District, 234
Jacky W. v. N.Y.C. Bd. of Educ.,
 286, 292
Jeremy H. v. Mt. Lebanon Sch.
 Dist., 294, 296, 355
J.G. v. Bd. of Educ., 286, 292

J.O. v. Alton Community Unif.
 Sch. Dist., 333
John G. v. Bd. of Educ., 358
John H. v. McDonald, 317
Johnson v. Bismarck Pub. Sch.
 Dist., 365
Johnson v. Clark, 344
Johnson v. Ind. School Dist. No.
 4, 231
Johnson v. Westmoreland County
 School Bd., 231
Joiner v. Dist. of Columbia, 365
Jonathon G. v. Caddo Parish Sch.
 Bd., 350, 353, 359
Jose P. v. Ambach, 292

K

Kaelin v. Gruggs, 107
Kansas State Bank & Trust Corp.
 v. Specialized Transp. Services,
 Inc., 330
Kathryn G. v. Bd. of Educ. of
 Mt. Vernon, 352-353
Kattan v. District of Columbia,
 365
Kerr Center Parents Association v.
 Charles, 292, 293, 297
K.L. v. Southest Delco Sch. Dist.,
 334
Kotowicz v. Mississippi State Bd.
 of Ed., 286, 298
K.R. v. Anderson Community
 Sch. Corp., 72
Kreher IV v. Orleans Parish
 School Bd., 366
Kresse v. Johnson City School
 Dist., 293

L

Lachman v. Illinois State Bd. of
 Educ., 220
Lake County Estates Inc. v. Tahoe
 Regional Planning Agency, 362
Lane v. Pena, 338
Language Dev. Program, Inc. v.
 Ambach, , 297
Larry P. v. Riles, 136, 137,
 153-155, 158, 159, 168
Larson v. Miller, 335
Lau v. Nichols, 137
LeBanks v. Spears, 136, 137
Lemon v. Kurtzman, 70
Lenn v. Portland School
 Committee, 230, 287
Leo P. v. Board of Education, 229

Lester H. v. Gilhool, 234
Levine v. New Jersey, 110, 111
Levy v. Commonwealth, Dept. of
   Ed., 296
Liscio v. Woodland Hills Sch.
   Dist., 270
Livingston School Dist., Nos. 4 &
   1 v. Keenan, 298
Loughran v. Flanders, 292, 344
L.S.B. v. Howard, 330
Lunceford v. District of Columbia
   Bd. of Ed., 107

M

Maine v. Thiboutot, 355
Maldonado v. Josey, 333
Manchester City Sch. Dist. v.
   Jason, 298
Marbury v. Madison, 4
Marvin H. v. Austin Indep. Sch.
   Dist., 359-360
Maryland Ass'n for Retarded
   Children (MARC) v. Maryland
   Equity, 325
Martinez v. School Bd. of
   Hillsborough County, 116
Mason v. Kaagan, 366
Masotti v. Tustin Unified Schl.
   Dist., 366
Mather v. Hartford School Dist. 230
Matta v. Indian Hill Exempted
   Village Schools, 287
Matthews v. Ambach, 347
Mattie T. v. Holiday, 135
Maynard v. Greater Hoyt School
   Dist. No. 61-4, 311-312
Maynard v. Greater Hoyt Sch.
   Dist. No. 61-4, 356
Mayson v. Teague, 286, 298
M.C. v. Central Regional School
   Dist., 233, 235
McKenzie v. Jefferson, 211
McManus v. Wilmette School
   Dist., 233
McMillan v. Cheatham County
   School, 225
Megan C. v. Independent Sch.
   Dist. No 625, 366
Metropolitan Nashville &
   Davidson County Sch. System
   v. Guest, 223
Michael F. v. Cambridge Sch.
   Dist., 366
Miener v. Missouri, 234, 291,
   344, 345

Miller v. West Lafayette
   Community School Corp., 366
Mills v. District of Columbia Bd.
   of Ed., 16, 112, 122, 124, 173,
   174, 323, 324-325
Missouri v. Jenkins, 326
Mititello v. Bd. of Educ., 287
Monahan v. Nebraska, 350, 358,
   359
Monell v. New York Dep't. of
   Social Services, 359, 361
Monroe v. Pape, 354
Monticello Sch. Dist. No. 25 v.
   Illinois State Bd. of Educ., 365
Moore v. Dist. of Columbia, 365
Morgan v. Chris L., 107
M.P. by D.P. v. Grossmont Union
   High School Dist., 108
Mr. and Mrs. W. v. Malito, 367
Mrs. B. v. Milford Bd. of
   Education, 210, 212
Mrs. C. v. Wheaton, 233, 235
Mrs. W. v. Tirozzi, 293, 350-351
Murray v. Montrose County Sch.
   Dist., 271
Murphy v. Timberland Regional
   Sch. Dist., 234, 235
Murphy v. United Parcel Service,
   Inc., 44
Murphysboro Community Unit
   School Dist. v. Illinois State
   Bd. of Educ., 227-228
Myles S. v. Montgomery County
   Bd. of Ed., 224
Mylo v. Baltimore County Board
   of Education, 318

N

Nance v. Matthews, 330
Natchez-Adams School Dist v.
   Seaering, 71
Neely v. Rutherford County
   School, 207-208
New Hampshire Dept. of Educ. v. ·
   City of Manchester, 79
New Mexico Association for
   Retarded Citizens v. New
   Mexico, 292
Newport v. Fact Concerts, Inc., 357
North v. D.C. Bd. of Ed., 292

O

Oberti v. Bd. of Educ. of the
   Borough of Clementon Sch.
   Dist., 268

O'Connor v. Donaldson, 118
Ojai Unified Sch. Dist. v. Jackson,
   229
Olmstead v. L.C., 23, 24-25, 29,
   31, 57
Owens v. Independence, 363

P

Pace v. Dryden Central School
   Dist., 119
Papacoda v. Connecticut, 210, 212
Parents v. Coker, 117
Parents of Student W. v. Puyallup,
   234, 235
Parham v. J.R., 23, 128
Parks v. Pavkovic, 229
PASE v. Hannon, 153, 155-158,
   159, 168, 220
Pennhurst State School and
   Hospital v. Halderman, 22, 49,
   360
Pennsylvania Ass'n for Retarded
   Children (PARC) v.
   Pennsylvania, 110, 112, 122,
   124, 173, 174, 323
Pennsylvania Department of
   Corrections v. Yeskey, 46, 49,
   51, 79, 111
Pennsylvania Envtl. Defense Fund
   v. Canon-McMillan Sch. Dist,
   367
Peterson v. Hastings Public
   Schools, 230
Petties v. District of Columbia, 77
P.F. ex rel. B.F. v. New Jersey Div.
   of Developmental Disabilities,
   219
Phipps v. New Hanover County
   Bd. of Ed., 292, 293
Polk v. Central Susquehanna Inter-
   mediate Unit 16, pp. 217, 287
Plyler v. Doe, 118
Pottgen v. Missouri State High
   School Activities Ass'n, 120
Powell v. Defore, 344
Prince William County School
   Bd. v. Wills, 81
Prins v. Indep. Sch. Dist. No. 761,
   291, 293, 294
Printz v. United States, 105
Pullen v. Cuomo, 207

Q

Quackenbush v. Johnson City
   School District, 229, 292, 293

R

Rainey v. Tennessee, 324, 325
Ramirez v. City of Manchester, 365
Randolph Union High School District No. 2 v. Byard, 300
Rapid City School Dist. No. 51-4, 365
Rappaport v. Vance, 366
Rebecca S. v. Clarke County School Dist. 232
Reid v. Bd. of Educ., 355
Reusch v. Fountain, 236, 283
Rettig v. Kent City School Dist., 145
Rhodes v. Ohio High School Athletic Ass'n, 120
Rich v. Kentucky Country Day, Inc., 345
Riley v. Ambach, 293
Robert M. v. Benton, 285
Robinson v. Pinderhughes, 355
Rodgers v. Magnet Cove Pub. Schs., 350
Rodiriecus L. v. Waukegan School Dist, 108
Rollison v. Biggs, 366, 367
Roncker v. Walter, 262-265, 268, 275, 287
Rose v. Chester County Intermediate Unit, 224
Russell v. Jefferson Sch. Dist., 223, 228
Russman v. Sobol, 71
Ruth Anne M. v. Alvin I.S.D., 292

S

S-1 v. State Bd. of Educ., 366
S-1 v. Turlington, 107
Salley v. St. Tamany Parish Sch. Bd., 223, 283, 288, 296, 300
Sandison v. Michigan High School Athletic Ass'n Inc., 119
Sanger v. Montgomery County Bd. of Ed., 232
San Jose Unified School Dist., 139
Savka v. Commonwealth Dept. of Ed., 296
School Board of Hillsborough County v. Student, 287, 293
School Board v. Malone, 366
School Bd. of Nassau County v. Arline, 43, 114, 220

School Committee of the Town of Burlington v. Dept. of Educ. of Massachusetts, 220, 221, 227, 229, 232, 233
Scituate School Committee v. Robert B., 229
Sean R. v. Bd. of Educ., 356
Seminole Tribe of Florida v. Florida, 50, 51
Sessions v. Ligingston Parish Sch. Bd., 291
Shannon v. Ambach, 294
Silano v. Tirozzi, 344
Silvio v. Commonwealth, 286
Sioux Falls School Dist., v. Koupal, 214
Smith v. Ambach, 294
Smith v. Cumberland School Committee, 286, 292
Smith v. Robinson, 344, 348, 350, 363
Smith v. Wade, 357
Sonya C. v. Arizona School for Deaf and Blind, 121
Southeastern Community College v. Davis, 42-43, 393-402 (Appendix B)
Stevens v. Umstead, 333
Stafford County School Bd. v. Farley, 81
State of Connecticut v. Bruno, 311
Steldt v. School Bd. of the Riverdale School Dist. 108
Still v. Debuono, 228
Stoneking v. Bradford Area Sch. Dist., 333
Stouffer v. William Penn Sch. Dist., 286, 292
Sullivan v. Vallejo City Unified School Dist., 215, 294, 352
Supreme Court v. Consumers Union of United States, 362
Susan N. v. Wilson Sch. Dist., 350, 351
Susan R.M. v. Northwest, 318
Suter v. Artist M., 355
Sutton v. United Air Lines, Inc., 44

T

Tall v. Board of School Comm'rs of Baltimore City, 354
Tarasoff v. Regents of Univ. of California, 331
Taylor v. Honig, 212

Teague Indep. School Dist. v. Todd L., 231
Tennessee Dept. of Mental Health & Mental Retardation, 283
Tenney v. Brandhove, 362
Texas City Indep. School Dist. v. Jorstad, 81
Texas State Teachers Ass'n. v. Garland Indep. Sch. Dist., 365
Thelma D. v. Bd. of Educ., 335
Thomas v. Atascadero Unified School Dist., 117
Thomas v. Cincinnati Bd. of Educ., 217
Thomas v. Davidson Academy, 353
Thompson v. Bd. of Special Sch. Dist. No. 1, 359
Thornrock v. Boise Indep. School Dist., 218
Tilson v. School Dist, of Philadelphia, 334
Tilton v. Jefferson County School Dist., 293
Timms v. Metro School Dist., 350
Timothy W. v. Rochester School Dist., 110-113
Tinkham v. Groveport Madison Local School Dist., 329
Todd v. Elkins Sch. Dist. No. 10, 358
Township High School Dist. Bd. of Educ. v. Kurtz-Imig, 81

U

Unified School Dist. No. 259 v. Newton, 365-366
Union School Dist. v. Smith, 227
United Cerebral Palsy of NYC v. Bd. of Ed. of City of N.Y., 292
United States v. Lopez, 105
United States v. Oregon, 324
Urban v. Jefferson County School Dist. R-1, 225, 293

V

Valerie B. v. Conway Sch. Dist., 344
Valerie J. v. Derry Coop. Sch. Dist., 349, 352
Vander Malle v. Ambach, 210, 212, 292
Vermont Association for Children with Learning Disabilities v. Kaagan, 285

Virginia Dept. of Educ., 107
V.W. and R.W. v. Favolise, 318

W

Walczak v. Florida Union Free
School District, 212
Walker v. San Francisco Unified
School Dist., 71
Wall v. Mattituck-Cutchogue Sch.
Dist., 271
Walpole Public School, 103
Walton v. Alexander, 333
W.B. v. Matula, 350, 351, 363

Wheeler v. Towanda Area School
Dist., 365
White v. California, 344
Whitehead v. Sch. Bd., 350, 359
Will v. Michigan Dep't. of State
Police, 360, 362
Wilson v. McDonald, 74
Windward School v. State, 297
Wise v. Ohio Dept. of Educ., 120
Witty v. Dukakis, 365
Wood v. Strickland, 354, 355, 362
Woods v. New Jersey Dept. of
Educ., 367

Wyatt v. Cole, 363
Wyatt v. Stickney, 22, 23, 244

Y

York County Sch. Bd. v. Nicely,
298
Youngberg v. Romeo, 328, 332,
333, 345, 358

Z

Zobrest v. Catalina Foothills
School Dist., 70, 71, 72, 73,
131

Hearing Officer Decisions Index ∿

Academy School Dist., 103
Bay County School Dist., 102
Beaumont Indep. School Dist., 104
Bryan County School Dist., 104
In re J.W., 102
Kershaw School Dist., 104
Lakeland Sch. Corp., 103
Limestone County (AL) Sch. Dist., 103
Modesto City School, 103
Oakland Unified School Dist., 102
Oconee County Sch. Sys., 104
Philadelphia School Dist., 104
Snowline Joint Unified School Dist., 103
Walpole Public School, 103

Name Index

B
Blatt, B., 56, 163, 166
Braddock, David, 52

C
Committee Report, House of Representatives Committee on Education and The Workforce, 33, 34, 35, 86, 92, 125, 126, 142, 180, 181, 182, 183, 376, 377, 378, 381, 383

D
Doris, J., 160, 161, 166

E
Erickson, K., 165

G
Gleidman, J., 161, 166

K
Kaplan, F., 163

L
Levy, Robert M., 52, 164

M
Mercer, J., 52, 164
Morse, S., 162

R
Roth, W., 161, 166
Rubenstein, Leonard S., 52

S
Sailor, W., 184
Sarason, S., 160, 161, 166
Silverstein, Robert, 52
Sorgen, M., 162
Stone, A., 164

T
Trilling, L., 165
Turnbull, A. P., 54, 162, 179, 184, 318, 319, 320
Turnbull, H. R., 54, 162, 179, 184, 261, 318, 319, 320

W
Wald, P., 163
Wickham, D., 184
Wilcox, B., 184

Subject Index

A
Ability grouping, cases involving, 158-160
Abstention, doctrine of, 327
Abuse, from teacher, 334. *See also* Child abuse
Accountability, 58
    of agencies, for student performance, 378
    fiscal, 373
    and IEPs, 202, 203
    provision of IDEA amendments, 148
    of schools, 283
    of SEAs to federal government, 374
Accreditation requirement, state, 227
Administrative hearings/remedies, 291-292, 294, 295, 352, 367

Advisory panels, 306-307
Advocacy, 315
    under Developmental Disabilities Act, 150
    by parents/families, 319
African-American
    and *PASE*, 155-157
    second-class status of, 122
    students in special education, 33, 153, 159
    testing of, 136, 153-154
"Aging out."
    See Transition
AIDS
    categories of, 115
    Section 504 and, 114-115
Air conditioning, 215
Alcohol use in school, 106
    hearing officer rulings on, 103-104

Alternative dispute resolution, 49
Altruism, 25-26, 56, 58, 163, 165-166, 316
American Association on Mental Retardation, 163, 169
American Indian students in special education, 33
American Psychiatric Association, 163
Americans with Disabilities Act, 23, 379
    and AIDS, 116
    as antidiscrimination law, 43, 123, 254, 293, 294, 353
    and confidentiality, 54
    and coupled claims, 349, 352, 359
    courts' interpretation of, 45
    and *Davis*, 337-341
    and due process, 295

and employment
    discrimination, 44-46, 131
and exclusion, 110
and imprisoned students, 79
integration principle of, 30,
    256
and participation in sports,
    119-120
and placement, 28
and public services, 31, 46-47,
    48
purpose of, 25, 33, 53, 56-57
"reasonable accommodations"
    provision of, 52, 283
recreation programs of, 253
remedies under, 343
and state immunity, 49
and telecommunications, 48
and transportation, 47
Animals, specially trained, 215,
    352
Annual goals of IEP, 144, 181,
    183, 193, 249
Antidiscrimination. *See also*
    Section 504
    ADA and, 43, 45
    IDEA and, 52, 343
    laws, 10, 52, 317
    Section 504 and, 40
Applied behavioral analysis
    (ABA) therapy, 228
Appropriate education, 53, 54, 56,
    58, 83, 125, 135, 148, 151,
    174, 216, 231, 239, 244,
    245, 258, 292, 293, 373,
    387
    ADA and, 256
    definition of, 173-174, 312
    and extended school year,
        236
    family involvement in, 315
    IEP and, 175, 179
    LRE and, 257-259, 261, 275
    provisions of, 204
    and Roncker, 262-265
    Rowley and, 174-175,
        216-217, 223
    and tuition reimbursement,
        224
        cases involving, 226-229,
        231-232, 273, 352
ARC, The, 21
Architectural barriers, 77
Asian-American students, 33
Assessment(s)

behavioral, 84, 89, 93
bias-free, 149
classroom-based, 141, 144
family, 146
functional, 126-127, 186,
    251
and IEP, 182
IFSP's multidisciplinary, 134
improper, 124
individualized, 145
parent consent to, 280
parent right to request, 142
of progress, 378
tools and strategies, 249
Assistive devices/technology, 45,
    66, 123, 124, 184
    under Part B, 198-199
    under Part C, 195-196, 197,
        198
    as related service, 313
Association, freedom of, 257.
    See also Right(s}
Attendance, compulsory, 305,
    333, 334
Attention deficit hyperactivity
    disorder (ADHD), 295
    classified as disability, 169-
        170
    and *Hall v. Shawnee Mission
        School Dist.*, 231-232
    and impeding behaviors, 189
    Section 504 and, 254
    and weapons hearing, 104
Attorney-client privilege, 367
Attorney fees, 348
    amount of, 366-367
    under ADA, 48
    exceptions in right to recover,
        364
    under IDEA, 282, 343-344,
        364, 365, 366
    and *Smith v. Robinson*, 363
Audiology services
    under Part B., 194
    under Part C, 196
Autism, 169, 170, 189, 214
    ABA therapy with, 228
    court cases involving, 227,
        232, 356
Autonomy
    local, 374
    right of, 28
    state, 63, 64
Aversive interventions, 126-127,
    191

B

"Bad faith," 347, 350, 358, 363,
    366
Barriers, 315, 316
    architectural, 77
Behavior(al)
    adaptive, 152, 154, 186, 197
    addressed by IEP, 184
    assessment, 93
    consequences, 186
    discriminatory, 339
    impeding, 186-187, 188,
        189-190
    injurious, 91-93, 94, 95, 99
    interventions, 110
    management, 84, 184, 191,
        329
"Behavioral incapacity" defense,
    86
Behavioral intervention plan
    (BIP), 93-94, 97, 98, 99
Behavioral supports, 126-127
Benefit
    educational, 219, 227, 230,
        232, 234, 264, 342
    test, 226, 262
Bilingual instruction, 137
Birth defects, as policy issue, 129
Black race, discrimination against,
    24. *See also* African-
    American
"Brady bill," 105
Breach of duty, 328
"Bright-line" rule, 206, 208, 209,
    217
Brown v. Board of Education,
    389-392 (Appendix A)
    as affecting ADA and IDEA,
        316
    equal-protection clause of, 10,
        122
    as landmark case, 7. 9-11, 24
Burden of proof, 296
Bureau of Indian Affairs, 375

C

Categorical approach to
    identification, 35, 38, 42
Catheterization (*Tatro* case), 205
Census-plus-poverty approach to
    federal funding, 376, 386
Charter schools, 67, 73, 380
Child abuse, neglect, delinquency,
    77, 129, 330, 332

Child census, 76-77
Child find, 69, 129, 139, 238, 314, 375, 378, 381
Church/state separation, 130, 131
Civil rights, 52-53, 56
  Act
    (1871), 354
    (1964), 153, 158, 314, 343, 349, 354
  activism, 10
  ADA and, 44
  and disabilities, 52-53, 122
  and dual accommodations, 52
  movement, 122
Classification, 137, 139, 160, 163, 167, 293
  court cases dealing with, 158
  by extent of disability, 262
  IDEA and, 138-139, 149, 168
  and LRE, 151
  of minority students, 158-159
  by professionals, 162-163, 167
  motives for, 165-167, 377
  reasons for, 138
Closed captioning, 48
Collaboration, 57, 319-320
"Color of law," 350, 354-355, 357, 362
Commerce clause, 105, 338
Communication skills training, visual, 198
Community-based
  curriculum, 315
  instruction, 201
  services, 254
Community settings/placements, 25, 26, 28, 29, 128, 129
  ADA and, 31, 46, 57
  costs of, 212
  Part B and, 198
  Part C and, 65
Compensatory damages, 294, 327, 328, 345, 346
Compensatory education, 232-233, 235, 342
  defenses, 234
  and deprivation, 233-234
  under IDEA, 342
  legal standard of, 233
Competing equities, 29
Competing
  equities, 272-273, 275
  interests of students and faculty, 81

Compliance, 323
  and federal funding, 342, 379
Comprehensive System of Personnel Development (CSPD), 204, 384
Compulsory school attendance, 305, 333, 334
Confidentiality, 283
  under FERPA, 356
  of hearings and mediation, 285, 289
  under Part B and Part C., 313
  of student records, 308, 310-311, 378
  under IDEA, 54
Conflict of interests, 27
Conflict management, 84
Consent, right to, 28, 55
  informed, 200, 300
  parent, 142-143, 145, 150, 280, 282, 305, 313
  Part C and, 280
  substitute, 150
Constitution
  federal, 3, 4
  state, 4
Contagious disease
  LRE and, 273, 275
  and Section 504 requirements, 254
  and zero-reject, 113, 341
Contempt of court, 321, 323-324, 348
Cost as a defense in *Roncker*, 264-265, 276
Cost-benefit approach, 264, 386
"Counseling services," 331
  under Part B, 194
  as related service, 313
Coupled (court) cases, 349-354, 359
Court(s)
  appellate (appeals), 6
  -appointed masters, 324-325
  circuit, 6
  contempt of, 321-324
  district, 6
  federal, 6-7
  state, 7
  trial, 6
Cultural
  background and testing, 137, 138
  bias in testing, 140, 145, 153, 154, 156, 158

diversity in schools, 128
  responsiveness in special education, 57-58
Curriculum, regular/general, 249, 250, 262, 339-340, 341
Custody, state cases, 332-334, 337

D

Daily living skills, 200, 201, 225
Damages, 327-328, 338, 351, 360
  compensatory, 327, 328, 345, 348, 357
  monetary, 343-344
  punitive, 327, 357
  reasons to award, 346
  restrictions on recovering, 358
  tuition reimbursement as, 346-347, 348
Danger, state-created, 334-337
"Dangerousness" provision, 89, 91, 92, 93, 99, 107, 128, 288, 293
  and AIDS, 117, 118
Darwinism, social, 20
Decision making
  executive, 30
  by families, 54, 318, 319, 320
  under IDEA, 342
  individualized, 27, 244
  legislative, 30
  majoritarian, 30
  participatory, 150
  shared, 305, 306
Decision Tree, 100-101
"Defective" newborns, 129, 161
Deinstitutionalization, 22, 23, 24, 31, 58, 128
Deliberate indifference, 335, 336, 361, 363
Democracy, direct, 4
Deprivation, "gross," 233-234
Desegregation, 243
  Brown and, 9, 12, 122, 237
  cases, 158-159, 326
Developmental delays, 35, 64-65
  Part C and, 254, 382
  model, 53
  and *Still* case, 228
Developmental Disabilities Assistance and Bill of Rights Act, 17, 22, 37-38, 55, 204
  P & A system of, 150
  purposes of, 37-38, 53, 123

Diagnostic and Statistical Manual, 163
Direct services
  by LEA, 74
  by SEA, 73-74
Disability(ies) (children with), 24, 316. *See also* Student(s)
  Brown and, 122
  categories of, 141, 144
  and discipline, 83
  and educability, 112-113
  as defined by IDEA, 96, 169
  law, 52-53, 122
  and LRE, 257
  and participation in sports, 119
  policy, 52, 57
  prevalence and incidence of, 169
  residence of, 120
  right to education and, 9, 31, 34
  as defined by Section 504, 40
  severe, 67, 75
  as social construct, 161
  stigma of, 136
  and suspension/expulsion, 107
  as term, 20
Discipline, 380. *See also* Expulsion
  under IDEA, 79, 92, 108, 272
  impeding behaviors and, 189
  and LRE, 251, 274, 275
  change in placement as, 93, 96, 98
  by schools, 82, 89-90, 108, 109, 125
  short-term, 87, 88
Discretionary functions, 329-339
Discrimination
  ADA and, 25, 43, 48, 151, 294
  and contagious diseases, 114, 118
  because of disability, 293
  educational, 44-46, 48
  employment, 44-46
  because of HIV, 41
  history of, in education, 279, 374
  against newborns with birth defects, 129
  racial, 51, 15, 154
  Section 504 and, 40, 151, 294, 359
  sex, 330, 351
  in sports participation, 119-120

  student-on-student, 338-339
  under Title IX, 340
  in transportation, 47
Diversity
  in schools, 128
  in U.S. society, 137
Documentation, under IDEA, 168
Dominance theory, 160
Down syndrome (*Daniel R.* case), 265-268
Dropout rates of students with disabilities, 33
Drugs in schools, 90-91, 95-103
  and discipline, 251, 272
  exception to stay-put rule, 90, 95, 106, 288
  and removals to IAES, 99, 107
Dual
  accommodations, 52, 239, 249, 259
  diagnosis, 170-171, 208-209
  racial system of education, 136
  system of law, 160, 167
  system of education, 122, 262
Due process, 27, 58, 204, 315, 327, 332, 343, 378
  and AIDS, 118
  Brown and, 10
  and classification, 165
  cost of, 300-301
  and discipline, 82
  and evaluation, 139, 144, 149
  hearing, 143, 229, 280, 282, 284, 296-297, 298, 349, 364, 365-366
  in IEPs, 202
  and institutions, 128
  parents' rights to, 283
  and placement, 84, 97, 99, 297
  procedural, 36, 69, 244, 245, 342, 351, 363, 373
  and residency, 121
  safeguards, 149
  substantive, 244-245
"Dumping," 26
Duty
  to act, 335
  breach of, 328
  to provide FAPE, 346
  to give notice to LEA, 366
  and rights, 341
  to provide safety, 332, 337
  statutory, 330
  to warn, 331

E

Early intervention, 19, 57, 64-65, 129-130, 145, 175, 176, 178, 198, 289-290, 313, 316, 374
  under Part C., 195-198, 254, 280
  education, 147
  personnel shortages in, 384
  and *Still* case, 228
Economic Opportunities Act of 1972, 17
EDGAR regulations, 296
Educability, 20-21, 110-113, 273, 315
  and *Timothy W. v. Rochester*, 239
Educable mentally retarded (handicapped), 137, 153, 157
Education(al)
  benefit, 219, 220, 223, 225, 226, 229, 230, 232, 234, 288
  compensatory, 232-233, 235, 342
  general/regular, 246, 248, 253, 255, 257, 266-267, 268-269, 342
  holistic, 218-219
  inclusive, 163
  individualized, 173
  malpractice, 327-328, 329, 331
  new functions of, 238
  outcome-oriented, 202
  reforms, 374
  right to, 10, 12, 31, 110, 122, 124, 126, 128, 147, 258, 316
    court cases, 323, 324, 325, 326, 327
  separate but equal, 11
  traditional roles of, 237
  vocational, 182
Education Flexibility Partnership Act (Ed-Flex), 374
Education for All Handicapped Children Act, 16, 17
  original purposes of, 31-32
  principles of, 16
Education of the Handicapped Act (EHA), 16.
  See also Individuals with Disabilities Education Act.

Eighth Amendment, 332
Elementary and Secondary
    Education Act of 1965
    (PL 89-750), 15, 17, 385,
    386
Eleventh Amendment, 49, 360,
    361
Eligibility
    for Part C, 65, 289
    for funds under idea, 378-379,
        382
    for special education, 34, 38
        under IDEA amendments,
        63, 130, 141, 142, 149
    for special education of
        juvenile offenders, 78
    standards under IDEA, 150-
        151
    stay-put, 88
Emotional disturbance/disability
    category, 208, 210
    and *Chris D.* case, 270-271
    severe, 218, 223, 231, 232,
        234, 236, 337
Employment, 195, 200
    ADA and, 44
    discrimination, 44-46, 48
    integrated, 200, 202
    as priority of IDEA, 123, 131
    supported, 38, 56, 67, 123,
        201
Enforcement of IDEA, 381-382
Entitlements, 31, 36, 59, 386
    and accommodations, 52
    IDEA as, 31, 52, 259, 319
    under Section 504, 40-44
    under Social Security Act, 39
    to special education, 113, 235
Environmental alterations (PBIS),
    185-186, 187
Equal access (for students with
    disabilities), 123-124, 257,
    315, 337, 339, 352
Equal educational opportunity, 44,
    51, 52, 53, 122-123, 127,
    217, 317
    ADA and, 256, 315
    IDEA and, 217, 343
Equality, 52-53, 56, 122, 129,
    130, 345
    new definitions of, 122, 123
Equal protection, 58, 63, 129,
    153, 327, 360
    and AIDS, 118
    Brown and, 10, 11, 124

clause of Fourteenth
    Amendment, 158
    as Constitutional principle,
        245
    IDEA and, 32, 83, 110, 346,
        350
    PL 93-380 and, 16
    and residency, 121
Establishment clause, 70, 71, 72
Evaluation, educational, 135, 204,
    See also Nondiscriminatory
        evaluation
    definition of, 283-284
    and IEP, 180, 202
    improper, 138
    independent, 342
    parent consent to and
        participation in, 142-143,
        280, 283
    under Part C, 145
    and placement, 145, 283-284
    reasons for, 138
    and reevaluation, 143-145
    standards, 140-141
    team, 139-140, 141, 142, 144,
        147, 148, 181
    vocational, 200, 201
Exclusion, 17, 63, 122, 124, 135,
    224, 239, 273
    functional, 17, 174
    HIV and, 41, 118
    learning disabilities and, 146-
        147
    of minority students, 141
    and participation in sports,
        119
    PL 93-380 and, 16
    state law basis for, 110
    of students with disabilities,
        245, 377
Executive branch of government,
    29, 30
Exhaustion of remedies rule, 290-
    291, 292, 293-294
    futility exception to, 292-293
Expert
    judgment, 219
    witnesses, 366
Expulsion, 79-80, 106, 229, 257,
    273, 274, 275, 341, 378
    and weapons, 105
Extended school year (ESY), 199,
    236-237, 283, 342
Extracurricular activities, 255,
    256, 271, 275, 294

F

Failure-to-train/supervise cases,
    334-336
    Davis, 336-337
Family(ies)
    ADA and, 314-317
    and advocacy, 315
    IDEA and, 130-131, 312, 314-
        317
    involvement with IFSP, 175-
        176, 179
    Part C and 66, 175
    integrity and unity, 57
    as leading the rights
        revolution, 21
    make-up of, 317
    roles of, 318-319
    support services, 129
Family Educational Rights and
    Privacy Act (FERPA), 109,
    308-311
    and *Maynard* case, 356-357
"Feasibility" standard/test, of
    Roncker, 262, 264, 266,
    268, 275
Federal aid, 252, 374. *See also*
    Funding
Federal Administrative Procedures
    Act, 382
Federal Controlled Substances
    Act, 90-91
Federal system/federalism, 3, 4,
    30, 31, 49, 50, 374
    abstention, doctrine of, 327
    and education, 12, 327
    funding under Rehabilitation
        Act, 39
    and Gun-Free Schools Act,
        104-105
    and *Jenkins*, 326
    oversight, 124
    principle of, 4, 29
Fifth Amendment, 279, 327
First Amendment, 54
    establishment clause of, and
        placement in religious
        school, 70
    and freedom of association, 257
First/last pay provisions, 214
Foggarty, James, 21
Foreseeability, 330-332
"Four-corners" cases, 231-232
Fourteenth amendment, 10, 22,
    50-51, 54, 338, 360

Brown and, 12
and AIDS, 118
due process clause of, 279,
    332
equal protection clause of,
    153-158, 327
and PL 93-380, 16
Fraud, as a tort, 347
Free appropriate public education,
    31, 36, 107, 238, 342, 378.
    See also Appropriate
    education
and discipline, 88-90
family participation in, 319
juvenile offenders and, 78-79
and LRE, 288
personnel development and,
    77
and placement, 69, 87, 106, 178
and zero reject, 63, 64, 73
Functional
analysis, 210
approach to eligibility, 38, 39
assessments, 126-127
behavioral assessment (FBA),
    93, 97, 99, 186, 188, 189,
    190
vocational evaluation, 200,
    201
"Fundamental alteration" defense,
    28-29
Funding/federal funds
applications for, 380-381
under ADA, 43
by Department of Education,
    251-252
for disabilities, 21
formula, 386
under IDEA, 36, 64, 355, 373,
    375, 379
lack of, as no defense, 325
and pass-through funds, 375
for placement in private
    schools, 68
under Rehabilitation Act, 39
and school district
    misconduct, 340
for severe disabilities, 75
waiving, 360
Futility exceptions to exhaustion
    rule, 291-293

G

"Gene pool" argument, 154, 155
General education. *See* Education

Genetic argument in *Larry P.,* 153
Gifted and talented, 127
Goals
annual (of IEP), 144, 181,
    183, 193, 249
performance, 378, 379, 380
2000, 386
"Good faith" defense, 359, 362-
    363
Government(s)
mandatory functions of, 362
parallel, 3
Grade-to-grade advancement, 218
Gross misjudgment cases, 358-
    359
Guardian *ad litem,* 318
Gun-Free Schools Act, 104-105

H

"Handicapped," 20
Handicapped Children's
    Protection Act, 344, 348,
    363
Harassment, 340, 351, 354. *See
    also* Abuse; Child abuse
Harkin, Sen. Tom, 21, 51
Harm, freedom from, 55
in court cases, 328, 331-332,
    334, 348
intentional, 335, 359
"likelihood of," 222, 223
Harmful effects. *See* Competing
    equities
Harmless error rule, 225-226, 328
"Head count" funding technique,
    375-376, 377
Head Start, 17
Health Care Financing Agency,
    75, 207
"Health services" under Part C.,
    196
Hearing(s)
due-process, 86, 92-93, 95,
    224, 280, 284, 290, 294,
    296, 364, 366
evidentiary, 82
Hearing officer, 109, 280, 287
and change in placement or
    removal, 69, 89, 91-92, 93,
    94, 95, 99, 347
decisions on manifestation
    determination, 102-104
enforcement decisions of, 356
impartial, 285-286
overturning ruling of, 296

and reimbursement, 223
request for evaluation, 284
Higher Education Amendments of
    1972, 17
Hispanic/Latino students
in special education, 33, 137
separation of, 160
HIV
Bragdon v. Abbott case
    involving, 47
under Section 504, 41, 114-
    115, 294
"Hold harmless" provision in
    funding, 376
Holistic education, 218-219
Honig
decision on discipline, 82-84
decision on expulsion, 80-82
stay-put rule and, 86-87
and suspension, 87
Humphrey. Hubert, 21

I

IDEA amendments (1997), 148-
    149, 385
and application for funding,
    381
and appropriate education, 174
and attorney fees, 363
and classification, 170
and discipline, 272-273
and federal funds, 130, 131
and functional assessments,
    126
and manifestation
    determination, 102, 103
and mental retardation, 169
and minority students, 159
procedural safeguards of, 107-
    108
and tuition reimbursement,
    220, 229
and weapons, 104
Identification, early, 66, 194
Immunity, 355
absolute, 360, 362
in court cases, 329-330
general, 362
from liability, 361-363
limited, 361-363
qualified, 362, 363
sovereign, 49-51, 360-361
waiving, 360
Inclusion, 186, 239, 247-248, 249
ADA and, 31, 44, 56-57

and AIDS, 116
IDEA and, 128, 246, 276
LRE and, 257
partial, 248
PBIS and, 188
Roncker and, 262
Immigration, history of, 160
Impairment. *See also*
    Disability(ies).
    under Section 504, 41
"Incidental benefit" provision,
    252
Inclusion, 315, 316. *See also*
    Integration
Independence, as a goal of IDEA,
    53, 186, 188, 195, 246
Independent living, 200, 202, 254,
    256, 315
Individualization, 173-174, 236,
    374
    under IDEA, 342, 373
    as policy of, IFSPs, IEPs, and
        transition plans, 203
    and *Rowley* standard, 226
Individualized education program
    (IEP), 55, 56, 68, 127,
    141, 174, 175, 224, 236
    accountability of, 202, 203
    annual goals of, 144, 148, 183,
        193, 202
    and assistive technology, 198-
        199
    and assessment/evaluation, 97,
        141, 148, 192
    benefit standard of, 226
    and compensatory damages,
        346
    components of, 181-183
    conferences/meetings, 193,
        282, 318
    court cases involving, 344
    and discipline, disruptive
        behavior, 83-84, 189-190
    emphasis on extracurricular
        activities, 255, 256, 271
    and equal opportunity, 217
    evaluating, 202
    exhaustion of remedies rule
        of, 291-292
    IDEA and, 174-175, 248, 290,
        378
    inadequate, 233
    for juvenile offenders, 78, 79
    and manifestation
        determination, 84-86

parent participation in, 180,
    203, 221-222
and PBIS, 192
and placement, 87, 89, 90, 93-
    94, 95, 96, 98, 99, 106,
    180, 181, 182, 183
    in private schools, 192
rationale for, 202-204
"special factors" and, 188
team, 139-140, 142, 149, 179,
    180, 248, 249, 250, 253,
    259
Individualized family service(s)
    plan (IFSP), 55, 58, 65,
    66, 174, 175, 198, 289,
    313
    components of, 176-177
    evaluation of, 178
    impact of, 178-179
    team, 175-176
    and transition services, 201
Individualized transition plan, 53,
    315
Individualized Disabilities
    Education Act (IDEA), 12,
    30, 109, 153, 244, 387
    and access to records, 309
    accountability, 204
    ages covered in, 63-64
    and AIDS, 117
    and applying for funds, 380-
        381
    and appropriate education, 312
    and budgets/financing, 124,
        130, 251
    bypass provision of, 73
    child's rights under, 318
    compliance with, 381-382
    and contagious diseases, 11
    and cost-shifting, 214
    and coupled claims, 348-349,
        352
    and *Davis*, 339-341
    definition of "parents," 308
    position on "dangerousness,"
        91
    definition of "controlled
        substances," 90
    definition of specific learning
        disability, 146
    discipline under, 82, 96, 108
    and discrimination, 48, 293-
        294
    and eligibility, 34
    enforcement of, 355

exclusionary role of, 141, 292-
    293
as entitlement, 31
funding under, 252, 355, 375,
    379
and equal protection, 83
and evaluation, 137, 139, 167,
    168
and IEPS, 224
and impeding behavior, 191
implementation of, under Part
    B, 382 -383, 384
and juvenile offenders, 78-79
and manifestation
    determination review, 84,
    103
open-doors intent of, 216
and parent participation, 142.
    292-293
placements under, 26, 87, 270
procedural safeguards of, 81,
    290
as pro-family, 130, 320
purposes/goals of, 32, 53, 63,
    246, 258, 350
and residency, 121
rights under, 341-342, 363
and *Roncker*, 262
and *Rowley*, 111, 174
six principles of, 36-37, 327,
    373, 380
and state sovereignty, 51, 64,
    363
stay-put provision of, 80
tort cases, 327-328
transition amendments, 202
and tuition reimbursement,
    220
waiving rights to, 299
Individualized transition plan, 53,
    315
Infants/toddlers law (PL 99-457),
    238, 289. *See also* Part C
Injurious behavior, 91-93, 94, 95,
    99
Institutionalization, 18, 24, 28, 56,
    163, 166, 167
Instruction
    community-based, 201
    skill (PBIS), 186
Insurance, private
    medical, under ADA, 314
    for students with disabilities,
        76
Integration, 58, 127, 128

and ADA, 30, 31, 57
LRE and, 258, 268
as purpose of Developmental
    Disabilities Act, 38
as rebuttable presumption,
    254, 256, 263
of students with disabilities,
    23, 239
Intelligence
    and *PASE*, 155
    tests, 137, 152, 153, 168
Interagency
    agreements, 216, 237, 238
    and financial
        responsibility, 75, 379
    responsibilities in transition
        services, 182, 200, 201
Intergovernmental coordination,
    215
Interim alternative educational
    setting (IAES), 381
    because of injurious behavior
        or disciplinary problems,
        85, 87, 89, 90, 91, 92, 94,
        95-96, 99, 103, 104, 105,
        106, 107, 251
    placement into, 282
Intermediate educational units
    (IEUs), 67
Interpreter, for deaf, 122-123, 180
    in *Peterson v. Hastings Public
        Schools*, 230
    in *Rowley*, 174-175, 216
    in *Zobrest*, 70
Interstate Commerce Clause and
    Gun Free Schools Act, 105
Intervention(s). *See also* Early
    intervention(s)
    aversive, 126-127
    behavioral, in IEP, 184
    medical
        under Part C, 254
        with newborns, 129
    under IDEA, 148
IQ tests, 136, 137, 138, 152, 157,
    158, 159, 168

J

Job coach(ing), 39, 67
Judiciary/judicial branch
    functions of, 6, 29
    remedies, 326
Juvenile offenders with
    disabilities, 78

incarcerated, 78
and LRE, 253

K

Kennedy, John F., 21
Kennedy, Rose Fitzgerald, 21

L

Labeling, 136, 152, 253, 377
Laches (parental delay), 235
Law(s)
    antidiscrimination, 10
    constitutional, 5
    case, 6
    color of, 350, 354-355, 357,
        362
    disability, 52-53
    role of, 12
    "spirit of," 282
    state, 10
    tort, 327-328, 330
Lawsuit, civil, 10
Learning
    environments, 198
    styles, 219
Learning disabilities, 163
    classification,169
    court cases involving, 146,
        347, 352-353
    definition of, 146-148
    IDEA and, 147
    and impeding behaviors, 189
    and weapons hearings, 104
Least restrictive environment
    (LRE), 23, 36, 56, 57, 58,
        128, 143, 152, 202, 240,
        245, 273
    and AIDS, 117, 118
    constitutional basis for, 243-
        245
    costs of, 264
    courts' interpretation of, 261
    determining, 259
    and discipline, 251
    in employment, 201, 202
    goals of, 258
    under IDEA, 59, 151, 175,
        204, 276, 315, 342, 373,
        378, 387
    and incarcerated juveniles,
        253
    for juvenile offenders, 78,
        109
    under Part B, 199
    and Part D, 384

placement considerations, 255,
    266-267
principle, 231, 243-244
as rebuttable presumption,
    244, 256, 258-259, 265,
    272, 337
related services in, 215
Roncker and, 262-263, 264
under Section 504, 353
Legal Services Corporation, 150
Legislature/legislative branch, 5,
    6, 29, 30
Liability
    of counselor, 331-332
    potential, and *Davis*, 338
    of public officials/agencies,
        328-329, 334-335, 337,
        346
    state and municipal, 360-361,
        362
Liberty, right to, 55, 244
Limited English
    population, 33, 137
    proficiency, 140, 141, 151,
        184, 249
Local education agency (LEA),
    12, 73, 239
    and breach of duty, 328
    acting on "dangerousness," 91
    and charter schools, 67, 73
    and child's residency, 120
    and compliance cases, 324
    and costs of education, 221
    court cases involving, 359-360
    and gun laws, 105
    dealing with parent, 317
    and denial of tuition
        reimbursement, 230
    eligibility for pass-through
        federal funds, 380
    and evaluation for special
        education, 143, 145
    funding to, 125, 130, 177,
        251, 373, 375
    and IDEA, 31, 32, 36, 64, 96,
        225
    and IEP, 226
    and IEPS, 192, 193, 201, 202,
        217
    and medical services, 205
    and mental health services,
        208
    and nursing services, 207
    and personnel development,
        77

and placement, 85-86, 87, 89, 91, 92, 93, 99, 107, 212, 224, 226
power to discipline, 83, 90-91
and private school placement, 67-69, 70, 72, 229, 346
and procedural due process 279
reporting of student crime, 109
responsibility for costs, 208, 342
responsibility for juvenile offenders, 79
and sports participation, 120
and suspension/expulsion, 80, 81, 82, 107
and transportation, 96
and written notice to parents, 283
and zero-reject, 74

M

Mainstreaming, 58, 263. *See also* Inclusion
"Major life activities," 41, 116, 196, 254
Malpractice, educational, 327, 328-330, 331, 344-345, 348
coupled claims, 349-350
Mandatory functions/duties, 328-330, 334
Manifestation rule (*Honig*), 82-84, 89, 93, 94, 97, 99, 125, 274
and alcohol and drug use, 103
and nondangerous behavior, 102-103
and sexual misconduct, 103
team to determine, 84-86
and weapons, 103, 104-106
Mediation
and attorney fees, 366
as due process requirement, 97, 143, 149, 285, 289
under IDEA, 285, 379, 380, 385
procedural safeguards and, 282
Medical model
Clovis and, 211
of mental retardation, 163, 166
"Medical services," 205, 208, 214
CIC as, 205-206

under Part B, 194
under Part C., 196
Medicare/Medicaid, 15, 22, 39, 75, 128, 207, 238
Medicare/Medicaid Catastrophic Coverage, 75, 207
Mental health services, 208-209, 211-212, 214
financial responsibility for, 210-211
"Mental incapacity" defense, 86
Mental retardation/disabilities, 20-21, 170, 292
under ADA, 30
classification of, as reflection of social policy, 160-161
continuum of services or, 26-27
court cases involving, 233, 268, 328, 358
defining, 169
and exclusion, 18, 19, 25
and extended school year, 236
under IDEA, 34
and impeding behaviors, 189
institutions, 22, 128
and *Larry P.*, 153, 154
medical model and, 163
and *PASE*, 156
Mills, and equal protection, 16
Minority children
classification of, 137, 158-159
evaluation and, 135
under IDEA, 125
overrepresentation/ ' overidentification of, 33-34, 57
under Section 1983 of Civil Rights Act (1871), 354
in special education programs, 18, 153, 154, 158-159, 377
unequal status of, 122
Minors' rights, 300
Misclassification, 18, 136, 138, 151
Mobility training, 198
Mootness, 327, 366
Municipality, liability of, 360-363

N

National Centers for Disease Control and Prevention, and AIDS, 115
Negligence, state, 335-336

Noncategorical approach, under Developmental Disabilities Act, 37
Nondiscrimination. *See also* Nondiscriminatory evaluation
ADA and, 44, 316
IEP team and, 44
and PBIS, 192
Nondiscriminatory evaluation, 36, 138, 248, 274, 378, 384, 387
and appropriate education, 204
and *Burlington,* 229
court cases on, 160, 167, 353, 358
effects of, 168
and HIV/AIDS, 115
IEP as, 202
learning disabilities and, 146
and least restrictive alternative/environment, 151, 253
and manifestation determination, 99, 106, 108
and mental retardation, 169
Part C and, 145
as principle of IDEA, 174-175, 341-342, 373
and Rowley standard, 226
team, 139
tuition reimbursement, 222, 223
Normalization doctrine, 58-59
Notice, 281, 289
actual, 282-283
of procedural safeguards, 281, 282, 289
"Nursing services," 196-197, 206-208

O

Occupational therapy, 71, 72, 194, 197
Office of Civil Rights (OCR), 338
Office of Special Education and Rehabilitative Services, 375
"Official capacity," 362
"Open doors" intent of IDEA, 216
"Orientation and mobility services" under Part B, 194

"Other health impaired," and
AIDS, 117
"Otherwise qualified," 42, 43, 353
and sports participation, 119,
120
"Over and above" claims, 352-
354, 357
Overidentification/overclassificati
on, avoiding, 252, 376,
377

P

Paraprofessionals, 77
Parallel governments, 3
PARC, and equal protection, 16
Parent(al)
access to school records, 308,
310
and attorney fees, 363-364
involvement in child's
education, 34, 37, 58, 84,
306, 315, 342, 373, 378,
384, 385
as collaborators, 319
consent to/involvement in
placement, 68-69, 84, 85,
87, 93, 97, 121, 131,
221-222, 226, 227
custodial, 317
participation in IEP, 180, 183, 203
on IFSP team, 175, 179
involvement in evaluation,
142, 144, 148, 284
and "notice and cure"
conditions, 221
responsibilities under IDEA,
314
right to due process, 299-300
rights to reimbursement, 229
and technological assistance,
198
vigilance, 235
waiver of due process, 299-
300
"Parent counseling and training"
under Part B., 194
Parent Training and Information
Centers (PTIs), 382
Parlow State School and
Hospital, 27
Part B, 64, 175, 281, 382
and due process, 285, 289
funding, 177, 381, 385
funding formula, 375, 380
and IEP, 179

requirements, 246-247
and SPIGS, 384
Part C – Infants and Toddlers, 64,
130, 145, 316, 373-374,
382
and consent, 280
due process rights under, 280
and IFSP, 175-179
LRE requirements, 254
parent participation under, 313
procedural safeguards, 288-290
purpose of, 254
services available under, 195-
198, 313, 382
Part D, 374, 379, 381, 385
provisions, 382-383
and SPIGs, 384
Participatory democracy, 203, 305
Pass-through funds, 375-376, 380
Patent and Plant Variety
Protection Remedy
Clarification Act, 50
Pennhurst State School and
Hospital, 22
Personnel
development/preparation,
77, 204, 214, 380
CSPDs, 253
under SPIGs, 383-385
Physical education, under Part B,
199
"Physical therapy"
under Part B., 194
under Part C., 197
PL 94-142, 137, 317, 373. *See
also* Education for All
Handicapped Children Act
"Place of Service" test, 212-213
Placement(s). *See also* Evaluation;
Private schools/Residential
placement
appropriate, 138, 212
and *Burlington*, 227
change in, 145, 297
as discipline, 97, 99
"educational" vs.
"therapeutic," 213
elective, 68
homebound, 57, 231
in IAES, 92, 107
IEP and, 94, 98, 106, 180, 226
improper, 124, 138, 154
integrated, 261
LEA and 86, 96, 107, 202,
212, 219, 220

least restrictive, 143, 202, 204,
247, 274
nonelective, 69
parent involvement in and
rights, 68-69, 84, 108, 142,
180, 227
requirement of, 97-98
responsibility for, 81, 210
school personnel and, 95
and stay-put rule, 86-87, 88,
89
Pluralism, in schools, 128
"Portability" test/standard of
Roncker, 262-264, 268, 275
Positive behavioral interventions
and supports (PBIS), 184-
188, 189, 190, 191-192,
251
and nondiscriminatory
evaluation, 191-193
Poverty factor in funding, 376
Powers, separation of, 29-30, 326
Presumption, rebuttable
in favor of PBIS, 188
in *Honig*, 81
LRE as, 244, 256, 258-259,
265, 272
Preschool, transition to, 177
President's Committee on Mental
Retardation, 21
Presumptive validity, 328
"Prevailing party" rule, 364-365
Private school placement, 67-68,
77, 130, 131, 192
funding, 238, 378
and tuition reimbursement,
220-221, 224, 227, 229,
230, 342, 346-347, 365
Privacy, right to, 54, 129, 283,
299, 305, 313, 318
court cases involving 334, 356
Procedural
due process, 36, 118, 224,
244, 342, 351, 373
errors/deprivation of rights,
225, 226, 233
requirements of IDEA, 290
safeguards, 37, 58, 93, 223,
293
IDEA's, 81, 108, 139, 290,
364
Process definition, 223-225, 226,
288, 359
Productivity, 186, 188
IDEA and, 56, 246

Professional
    judgment, 27, 328, 358, 359
    standards, 328
Proximity to placement, 255
"Psychological services," 209-210
    under Part B, 194
    under Part C, 197
    as related service, 313
Psychotherapy, 209-210, 211
Public
    accommodations under ADA,
        47, 48, 120
    notice, 306
Public agencies, 54
    and evaluation, 284
    private placement by, 68
    responsibility for costs, 76, 378
Public education.
    See also Education
    Brown and, 10
Public policy
    Brown and, 11, 12
    and right to sue, 345
    values, 257-259
Public services, under ADA,
    46-47, 48
Punitive damages, 327

R

Racial
    bias/discrimination in testing,
        153-154, 157, 158
    discrimination (as addressed
        by Section 1983), 354
    imbalance in special
        education, 137, 153
    minorities and ability
        grouping, 158-159
"Reasonable accommodations,"
    42, 52, 131, 294, 315, 353
Reasonable care, 331
Rebuttable presumption
    in favor of PBIS, 188
    in *Honig,* 81
    LRE as, 244, 256, 258-259,
        265, 272, 337
Records, 380
    access to, 149, 204, 282, 283,
        287, 290, 307, 356
    protecting students', 308-312
"Recreation" under Part B, 195
Reevaluation for special
    education, 143-145
Regional Resource Centers, 382-
    383

Rehabilitation Act, 17, 33, 38-39,
    53, 56, 67, 153, 204, 314,
    317. *See also* Section 504
    and claims under IDEA, 348
    and residency, 121
    services, 55
    and supported employment, 123
"Rehabilitation counseling
    services," 195
Related services, 36, 58, 238
    barriers to, 215
    cost of, 208
    court cases involving, 312-313,
        342, 352
    and *Detsel,* 239
    evaluation and, 141, 144, 152
    for discipline problems, 84
    under IDEA, 149, 173, 209,
        229, 312-313, 342
    IEP and, 181, 182, 184, 193
    medical, 214
    under Part B., 194-195, 199
    under Part C, 195
    personnel, 77, 204
    psychotherapy as, 210, 211
    in religious schools, 70
    and suspension/expulsion, 107
    and *Tatro,* 206
    and transition services, 200
    and zero-reject, 74, 75
Relaxation techniques, 186
Remedial
    classes in parochial schools,
        71
    reading, 147
Remedies
    administrative, 291-292, 294,
        295, 343
    for complaints filed with
        EEOC, 48
    exhaustion of, 290-291
    under IDEA, 343, 350
    judicial, 326
    "start-over," 341-342
Removal. *See* Placement
Residency requirements, 120-121,
    318
Residential
    facilities, 67, 213
    placement
        court cases concerning,
            209, 211, 212, 223, 224,
            230, 232
        and LRE, 255
        under Part B, 199

Right(s)
    to appeal hearing officer's
        decision, 287
    of association, 257, 258, 270,
        271, 275
    to consent, 28, 55
    deprivation of, 355, 362, 367
    to due-process hearings, 284,
        287
    to education, 10, 12, 31, 122,
        124, 126, 128, 243, 245,
        258, 265, 279, 293
    court cases, 323, 324, 325,
        326, 327
    to free appropriate public
        education, 316
    parents', under Part C, 313
    of parents to student's records,
        310, 313
    to privacy, 54, 129, 283, 299,
        305, 313, 318, 334
    to sue, 344-345, 362
    to treatment, 22, 23
    to written notice, 289
Rowley standard, 230
    benefit test of, 226-229
    and process definition, 223-
        225

S

Safety
    in schools, 80, 104-105, 106,
        125
    in custody case, 332-333
School(s). *See also* Education
    charter, 67, 73, 380
    discipline, 82
    and due-process hearing, 297
    and IEP, 192
    neighborhood, 271-272
    nurse, on IEP team, 181
        and *Detsel,* 207
    personnel authority of, 95, 99
    private, 67-68, 77, 130, 131,
        220-221, 277
    religious, 70-73
    safety, 80, 104-105, 106, 125
    segregated, 263
    special, for students with
        disabilities, 15, 333
"School-day test," 211-212
"School health services" under
    Part B, 195
Section 504 of Rehabilitation Act,
    40, 43, 63, 292, 294

compared to ADA, 45-46
and AIDS, 115-116
and *Arline* case, 114-116
and *Benic* case, 329, 358
and classification, 151-152
coupled claims, 349, 352, 353, 359
and *Davis* case, 42, 337-341
definition of "individuals with disabilities," 44
and employment, 131
and exclusion, 110
and discrimination, 52, 158, 293, 343, 353
and *Larry P.*, 153
and participation in sports, 119
purpose of, 53
remedies under, 348
and Vietnam veterans, 386
Section 1415 (*Mrs. W. v. Tirozzi*), 351
Section 1983, 335-336, 349, 350, 352
damages available under, 357
and discrimination, 354
and privacy, 356
as a vehicle for enforcing FERPA, 356-357
Segregation, 160
of people with disabilities, 23, 24, 31, 56, 165, 239
racial, 11
Separation of powers, 29-30, 326
Service(s)
continuum of, 256, 257, 259, 267, 296
coordination, 57
delivery, 54, 59
and disciplinary action, 83
duty to provide, 332
individualized and appropriate, 55
plan, 69
reimbursable, 75
"Service benefit standard," 210, 211
"Service coordination services," under Part C, 197
Settlement agreements, 365, 366
Sex(ual)
abuse, 335. See also Child abuse
discrimination, 330, 351
harassment, 340, 351
misconduct and manifestation determination, 103

Signing system for hard of hearing/deaf, 230
Skill instruction (PBIS), 186, 187
Skills, functional, 197
Social
Darwinism, 20
policy, 160
Social Security Act, 39
applied to persons with disabilities, 15
funding of state institutions under, 21
Title XIX of, 22, 26, 379
Social Security Disability Insurance (SSDI), 39
"Social work services"
under Part B, 195
under Part C., 197-198
as related service, 313
Socioeconomic argument in *Larry P.*, 153, 154, 157
Special
accommodations, 123
schools for children with disabilities, 15
Sovereign immunity, state, 49-51, 360-361
Sovereignty, and gun laws, 105
Special education, 18, 54, 160
ADA and, 45, 47
admission to, 86-87
as appropriate education, 173-174, 312
barriers to, 127
benefits for those with severe disabilities, 67
categories of, 34-35
classification into, 138, 158-159
consent to, 55, 280
in correctional facilities, 138
costs, 64, 318
and *Daniel R.* case, 266-268
definition of, 35
effectiveness of, 130, 387
eligibility for, 34, 142
and employment, 56
entitlement to, 113, 235
erroneous placement in, 344
evaluation for, 138
and exclusion, 141-142
expelled/suspended students, 106, 107
expenditures or, 385
federal aid for, 16, 17, 252

funding for, 379
homebound, 118
hospital-based, 118
under IDEA, 31, 52, 113, 123, 149, 246, 293, 384
IEP as part of, 181-182, 193
incentives/disincentives or placement in, 170, 253
laws, 16, 17
LRE and, 257
minority overrepresentation in, 18, 33, 57, 153, 155
outcomes of, 202
parent participation in, 141
Part B and, 246-247
placement, 19, 108, 136, 138, 158-159, 356
in private placements, 67-68
purposes of, 110
in religious schools, 70
role of, 47, 48
SEA and, 14
services, 377
tort cases, 327-328
zero-reject in, 131
Special education teacher, 87, 99, 140
on IEP team, 179
"Special instruction," under Part C, 198
"Special relationship," 331, 333
"Speech pathology"
under Part B, 195
under Part C, 198
Speech therapy/pathology, 72
as related service, 313
"Standards" standard, 213
Sports
age requirement to participate in, 119-120
participation in, 119-120
Stanford Binet test, and PASE, 156, 157
State
-created danger, 334-337
custody of child, 77
immunity under ADA, 49-51
and right to education, 10
policy making under ADA, 30, 31
prison system, 49
sovereign immunity, 49-51, 63-64
sovereignty, 105
statutes on residency, 121

State education agency (SEA), 12, 238
   budgets of, 124-125, 130, 251
   and compliance, 324, 342
   data compilation on suspension/expulsion, 109-110
   direct services by, 73-74
   and gun laws, 105
   and IDEA, 31, 32, 36, 64, 67, 121, 373
   and parents, 314
   and personnel development, 77, 204
   and placement, 69
   and procedural due process, 279
   and student records, 307, 309
   and surrogate parents, 150, 281
   and transition services, 200
   uses of federal aid to, 375, 379-380
State Interagency Coordinating Council, 313
State Program Improvement Grants (SPIGs), 383-384, 385
State Program Improvement Plan, 379, 383-385
Statute(s), 5
   catch-all, 367
   of limitations, 298-299, 367
   state, and residency, 121
Stay-put provision, 86, 125, 288
   and attorney fees, 365
   and *Corbett*, case, 288
   as due process requirement, 97
   exceptions to, 90-93
   and expulsion/suspension, 80, 87-88, 107, 108
   and LRE, 251
   versus safety, 105
Stigma of disability, 257-258
Student(s). *See also* Disabilities
   IEP focus on strengths of, 183-184
   incarcerated, 378
   participation in special education delivery, 37, 342
   problem-solving, 186
   rights to sue, 343, 361, 362, 363
   standard, 213
Suicide cases, 331

Supplementary aids and services, 36, 199, 253, 266, 268, 269, 274, 342
Supplementary Security Income (SSI), 15, 39
Supported employment, 38, 56, 67, 123
Surrogate parents, 280-281, 289, 292, 317
Suspension, 74, 229, 341
   and dangerousness provision, 293
   under IDEA, 378
   of students with disabilities, 81, 87, 88
   and weapons, 105
Systems change (PBIS), 185, 187, 374

T

TDDs, 48
TEACCH method, 214
Teacher(s)
   regular education, on IEP team, 179-180, 181
   of special education, 18, 87, 99, 140, 179, 307
   training, 214
Team. *See also* Individualized education program (IEP)
   interdisciplinary, 224, 226
Technology Related Assistance for Individuals with Disabilities Act, 123, 199, 238, 374
Text(ing)
   bias in, 153
   discrimination, 138
   inappropriate, 136
   intelligence/IQ, 136, 137, 138, 152, 153, 155, 157, 158, 159, 168
   standardized, 138, 140, 145, 153, 155, 168
   validity of, 140
Therapeutic recreation, 253
Title V, eligibility for, 379
Title VI remedies, 341
Title IX, 330, 334, 337
   and *Davis*, 337-340
   and *Franklin*, 351-352
Title XIX, 379. *See also* Medicare/Medicaid
Torts, 331
   elements of, 327-328, 330

student-on-student, 338
Trademark Remedy Clarification Act, 50
"Trainable mentally handicapped," 117, 218, 262
Transactional phenomenon, 161
Transition
   under IDEA, 66, 129
   IEP and, 182, 199-201
   individualization in, 203
   from school to work, 53
   services, 36, 57, 200-201, 202, 225, 250-251, 316
   of toddler to preschool, 177
Transportation
   under ADA, 315
   court cases, 329, 330, 347-348
   discrimination in, 47, 48, 123
   under Part C, 66
   and private schools, 71, 72
   if suspended, 96
"Transportation and related costs"
   under Part B, 195
   under Part C, 198
Treatment of "defective" newborns, 129
Truancy laws, 333
Tuition reimbursement
   amount of, 221
   court cases on, 223, 225, 226-229, 237, 275, 297, 365
   as damages, 346-347, 348, 360
   denial of, 230-231
   general rule of, 221
   limitations of, 221
   notice to LEA, 221-222
   provisions of IDEA, 220-221, 342

U

"Unclean hands," 235
Uniform Federal Accessibility Standards, 379
United States Constitution, 3, 10
   rights under, 350
   source of, 4
Unreasonableness provision, and tuition reimbursement, 222-223
U.S. Department of Education/Secretary of Education, 36, 296